The **Rough Guide** to

# Florence and the best of Tuscany

written and researched by

**Jonathan Buckley and Tim Jepson**

NEW YORK • LONDON • DELHI

www.roughguides.com

# Contents



**Colour section 1**

Introduction .............................. 4
When to go ............................... 9
Things not to miss ................... 11

**Basics 17**

Getting there ........................... 19
Getting around ......................... 22
Accommodation ....................... 24
Food and drink ........................ 27
The media ............................... 30
Festivals .................................. 31
Travelling with children ............ 33
Travel essentials ...................... 34

**Florence 39**

Arriving in Florence ............. 41
1 Piazza del Duomo and around ................................ 46
2 Piazza della Signoria and around ................................ 62
3 West of the centre: from Via dei Calzaiuoli to the Cascine..... 88
4 North of the centre: the San Lorenzo, San Marco and Annunziata districts........... 106
5 East of the centre: Santa Croce to Campo di Marte ... 133
6 Oltrarno ............................ 145
7 Fiesole ............................. 164

**Listings 167**

8 Accommodation ................ 169
9 Eating and drinking ........... 183
10 Nightlife and cultural events ............................... 197
11 Shopping ......................... 204
12 Directory .......................... 210

**Tuscany 211**

13 Prato and Pistoia .............. 213
14 Pisa and Lucca ................. 227
15 Chianti .............................. 250
16 Siena ................................ 257
17 Sienese hill-towns ............. 297
18 San Gimignano and Volterra ............................. 316
19 Arezzo and Cortona .......... 327

**Contexts 343**

History .................................. 345
A directory of artists and architects ...................... 359
Books .................................... 371

**Language 377**

Pronunciation ......................... 379
Italian words and phrases ...... 379
Italian menu reader ................ 383

**Travel store 389**

**Small print & Index 391**

**Florence as capital of Italy** colour section following p.144

**Tuscan food and wine** colour section following p.272

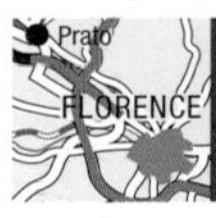


**Colour maps** following p.400

◀◀ Frieze on Ospedale del Ceppo, Pistoia ◀ Hercules Slaying the Centaur, Florence

## Introduction to

# Florence and the best of Tuscany

**Since the early nineteenth century, Florence (Firenze in Italian) has been celebrated as the epitome of everything that is beautiful in Italy: Stendhal staggered around the city's medieval streets in a stupor of delight, the Brownings sighed over its charms and E.M. Forster's *A Room with a View* portrayed it as the great antidote to the bloodless sterility of Anglo-Saxon life. The whole region of Tuscany has been equally lauded, not just for its innumerable art-filled towns and villages but also for its terrain – the classic landscapes of cypress-topped hills, vineyards, villas and poppy-dappled fields.**

For most visitors, first impressions tend to confirm the myth. The stupendous dome of Florence's cathedral is visible over the rooftops from afar, and in Siena the first view of the Campo, the city's central piazza, is one of the most memorable of any in the region. Pisa's Leaning Tower, so familiar from photographs, is even more remarkable at first hand, and while wending through Chianti's wooded hills, or the magnificent uplands south of Siena, it's hard to imagine pastoral countryside more beautiful.

Of course, the wonders of Florence and Tuscany are nowadays accessible to millions, which means that in high season the sheer number of tourists at the major sights is overwhelming – the Uffizi, for instance, is all but impossible to get into unless you've pre-booked your tickets a few days in advance. And yet such is the wealth of monuments and artistic treasures here, it's impossible not to find the experience an enriching one. Tuscany was the powerhouse of what has come to be known as the Renaissance, and

▲ Landscape of Le Crete Senesi

Florence – the region's dominant political and cultural centre – is the supreme monument to European civilization's major evolutionary shift into modernity.

The development of this new sensibility can be plotted stage by stage in the vast picture collection of the **Uffizi**, and charted in the sculpture of the **Bargello**, the **Museo dell'Opera del Duomo** and the guild church of **Orsanmichele**. Equally revelatory are the fabulously decorated chapels of **Santa Croce** and **Santa Maria Novella**, forerunners of such astonishing creations as Masaccio's frescoes at **Santa Maria del Carmine**, Fra' Angelico's serene paintings at **San Marco** and Andrea del Sarto's work at **Santissima**

## Fact file

**Tuscany** (Toscana) has a **population** of around 3.6 million, with some 370,000 (including 60,000 students) in **Florence**, its capital. In recent years the population of Florence has been steadily declining (it was 450,000 in 1981).

Though many factories closed in the 1970s and 1980s, the province of Florence is still the third largest **industrial centre** in Italy. Textiles, metalwork, glass, ceramics, pharmaceuticals and chemical production remain major industries in the province, while in Florence itself many long-established crafts continue to thrive, notably jewellery and gold-working, perfumery, leatherwork and the manufacture of handmade paper.

**Siena** is the capital of its province (*provincia*) but is a far more modest metropolis than Florence. Its current population of around 54,000 is relatively stable (about a third of its medieval peak) and is bolstered by a student population of some 20,000.

Light industry such as food-processing and furniture-making dots the city's immediate hinterland, but business in Siena itself and the region's main historic towns revolves around service industries and – inevitably – tourism. A few towns have local specialities: **Arezzo**, for example, is one of Europe's largest jewellery-making centres (goldware in particular) and **Lucca** has a tradition of silk and lingerie production. In rural areas, notably **Chianti** and around Montalcino and Montepulciano, wine is big business.

▲ The Ponte Vecchio, Florence

**Annunziata**, to name just a few. During the fifteenth century, the likes of Brunelleschi and Alberti began to transform the cityscape of Florence, raising buildings that were to provide generations of architects with examples to follow. The Renaissance emphasis on harmony and rational design is expressed with unrivalled eloquence in Brunelleschi's interiors of **San Lorenzo**, **Santo Spirito** and the **Cappella dei Pazzi**, and in Alberti's work at Santa Maria Novella and the Palazzo Rucellai. The bizarre architecture of San Lorenzo's **Sagrestia Nuova** and the marble statuary of the **Accademia** – home of the David – display the full genius of **Michelangelo**, the dominant creative figure of sixteenth-century Italy. Every quarter of Florence can boast a church or collection worth an extended call, and the enormous **Palazzo Pitti** constitutes a museum district on its own: half a dozen museums are gathered here, one of them - the Galleria Palatina - an art gallery that any city would envy.

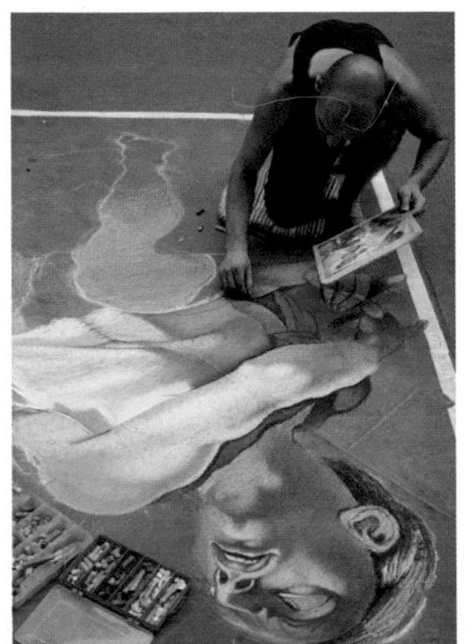
▲ Street artist, Florence

So there are sights enough to fill a month, but to enjoy a visit fully it's best to ration yourself to a couple each day and spend the rest of your time strolling and involving yourself in the life of the city. Though Florence might seem sedate on the surface, the city has some excellent **restaurants**, **clubs** and **café-bars** amid the tourist joints, as well as the biggest and liveliest **markets** in Tuscany and plenty of high-quality **shops**. And there's no shortage of special events – from the high-art festivities of the **Maggio Musicale** to the licensed bedlam of the **Calcio Storico**, a series of costumed football matches held in the last week of June.

Few regions in Europe are as rich in food, wine, festivals, landscapes and artistic allure as Tuscany, a place where many villages have sights of which capital cities would be proud. The main draw after Florence is **Siena**, a majestic ensemble of well-preserved medieval buildings set on three ridges, affording a succession of beautiful vistas over terracotta rooftops to the bucolic Tuscan countryside beyond. In its great scallop-shaped piazza, **Il Campo**, Siena has the loveliest of all Italian public squares and in its zebra-striped **Duomo**, a religious focus to match. The finest of the city's paintings – many of which are collected in the Palazzo's **Museo Civico** and the separate **Pinacoteca Nazionale** – are in the Gothic tradition. Siena is also a place of immediate charm: airy, easy-going, largely pedestrianized and refreshingly quiet away from the main sights. The city hosts the undisputed giant of Italian festivals, the **Palio**, an exciting and chaotic bareback horse race around the Campo, held on July 2 and August 16.

After Siena, most visitors flock to **San Gimignano**, renowned for its crop of medieval towers and a skyline as evocative as any in Europe. More so than any other destination in Tuscany, however, this is a place where day-trippers run riot, and to get the best from what is at heart

▼ Torre del Mangia, Siena

still a delightful village, you should aim to spend the night. This is less true of **Pisa**, where the famous tower and the equally compelling ensemble of surrounding sights – the Baptistery, Duomo and Camposanto – are easily seen in a couple of hours. Perhaps aim to stay instead in nearby **Lucca**, a likeable and relatively unsung town still enclosed within its walls and with enough to occupy you for at least a couple of days. Ultimately, though, Lucca is one of those towns where it's enough simply to walk (or cycle) the streets to uncover its charm.

▼ Camposanto, Pisa

Closer to Florence, the thriving towns of **Prato** and **Pistoia** each warrant a day-trip, and it would be feasible to visit **Arezzo** – to the southeast – as an excursion from the capital too. Like Pisa, Arezzo suffered bomb damage in World War II – and has similarly bland modern quarters as a result, but it, too, has managed to preserve a tight historic core, which has one great sight: Piero della Francesca's fresco cycle of *The Legend of the True Cross*. Nearby **Cortona** is a classic Tuscan hill-town and there are others within easy reach of Siena, notably lofty **Volterra**, and a cluster of small towns and

▶ Festival in Pistoia

## Popes and Saints

Siena may have produced the most famous Tuscan saint – St Catherine, the joint patron saint of Italy – but Florence's contribution to the religious life of the nation is by no means negligible, even if none of the godlier Florentines has achieved a degree of fame to equal that of the supremely secular Niccolò Machiavelli, for example.

The city's first Christian martyr, Minias (see p.160), was beheaded here in the third century AD, and immediately offered incontrovertible proof of his holiness by carrying his severed head up the hill to the spot where the church dedicated to him – San Miniato – now stands. Around 345 AD the boy who would grow up to become the very first bishop of Florence was baptized in the church of San Lorenzo; canonized as St Zenobius, he's commemorated by a column that stands close to the Baptistery. Frescoes in Santa Trìnita (see p.94) record the life of St Giovanni Gualberto, founder of this church and of the Vallombrosan order of Benedictines, while in the monastery of San Marco (and in paintings all over the city) you'll find images of the implacably zealous St Peter Martyr. The only Renaissance artist to have been beatified, Fra' Angelico (see p.121) was a Dominican friar at San Marco, which was later to be the base of the firebrand preacher Girolamo Savonarola (see p.124), the city's de facto ruler for a while in the 1490s. From the ranks of the Pazzi family – one of Florence's pre-eminent clans – came St Maria Maddalena dei Pazzi (see p.142), who was famed for her wild religious visions and excesses of self-punishment; and the most eminent of all Florentine families, the Medici, raised two popes: Leo X, who was the second son of Lorenzo il Magnifico, and Clement VII, the illegitimate son of Giuliano de' Medici, Lorenzo's brother. Neither of these pontiffs, it has to be admitted, could be ranked alongside Siena's Aeneas Sylvius Piccolomini (see p.275), an eminent scholar, poet, humanist and patron of the arts who, in 1458, became Pope Pius II.

villages: **Pienza**, **Montalcino** – famed for its wine – and **Montepulciano**, which lie close to the sublime monasteries of **Sant'Antimo** and **Monte Oliveto Maggiore**.

# When to go

Florence and the rest of Tuscany are often stiflingly hot in midsummer – Florence especially so, as the hills that ring the city form a natural roasting pan. The combination of heat and countless tour groups can take a lot of the pleasure out of a visit between early June and the end of August – the latter month, moreover, is when the great majority of Italians take their holidays, which means that many restaurants and bars

▲ Young Florentines by the Ponte Trinita

are closed. This is less true in rural areas like Chianti, but towns like Siena and San Gimignano are as busy as Florence in high summer. If possible, you should go shortly **before Easter** or **between September and mid-October**, when the weather should be fine and you'll be able to savour the sights at your leisure. The period of maximum tranquillity is from November to March, a season that can be quite wet and misty (and sharply cold, when the *tramontana* wind comes whistling off the Apennines) but is equally likely to give you days of magical clarity.

If you do have to go in the summer months, make sure that you've reserved your accommodation long before your trip: Siena and Lucca don't have a profusion of hotels, and although Florence has scores of them it's by no means rare for every single bed in the city to be taken. The table below shows average daytime temperatures and average monthly rainfall.

| | January | April | July | October |
|---|---|---|---|---|
| **Florence** | | | | |
| °C | 6 | 13 | 25 | 16 |
| °F | 42 | 55 | 77 | 60 |
| mm | 62 | 70 | 23 | 96 |
| inches | 2.5 | 3 | 1 | 4 |

# things not to miss



*It's not possible to see everything that Florence and Tuscany have to offer in one trip – and we don't suggest you try. What follows is a selective taste of the region's highlights: great places to visit, outstanding buildings, glorious art works and tranquil scenery. They're arranged in five colour-coded categories, which you can browse through to find the very best things to see and experience. All entries have a page reference to take you straight into the Guide, where you can find out more.*

**01 Florence's Piazza del Duomo** Page **46** • The marble-clad Duomo, Baptistery and Campanile make the Piazza del Duomo one of Italy's most impressive public spaces.

**02 The Bargello** Page **83** • An astounding collection of Renaissance sculpture is the principal attraction at Florence's former prison.

**03 The Palazzo Vecchio** Page **67** • The craggy Palazzo Vecchio was for centuries the nerve-centre of the Florentine state.

**04 Santa Maria Novella** Page **98** • Remarkable frescoes make the Florentine church of Santa Maria Novella an unforgettable experience.

**05 The Uffizi** Page **71** • The galleries of the Uffizi are packed with masterpieces by Botticelli and almost every other front-rank Italian Renaissance painter.

**06 Shopping** Page **209** • Funky bags at Sol Gabriel – if you want to take home an item handmade in Italy, Florence's shops offer plenty of choice.

**07 San Lorenzo** Page **106** • The ancient church of San Lorenzo was both the parish church and the mausoleum of the Medici.

**08 San Miniato al Monte** Page **159** • Visible all over Florence, San Miniato is as perfect inside as out.

**09 Palazzo Pitti** Page **148** • Palazzo Pitti, the largest private building in Florence, contains one of Italy's richest art collections and has the city's finest garden.

**10 Santa Croce** Page **134** • With paintings by Giotto and a wonderful chapel by Brunelleschi, the church of Santa Croce is another essential stop on the Florentine art-circuit.

**11 Wine bars** Page **193** • Florence's wine bars are terrific places not just for a quick glass but for a delicious snack too.

**12 Santa Maria del Carmine** Page **154** • If one single spot can be said to mark the emergence of Renaissance art, it's the Brancacci chapel in Santa Maria del Carmine.

**13 Pienza** Page **304** • Designed as an utopian Renaissance city in the fifteenth century, Pienza overlooks vast tracts of classic Tuscan countryside.

**15 San Gimignano** Page **317** • The tower-houses are what have made San Gimignano famous, but it has some superb paintings too – notably the frescoes of Benozzo Gozzoli.

**14 Siena** Page **257** • Viewed from the top of the Torre del Mangia, Siena offers an astounding townscape of medieval churches, *palazzi* and terracotta roofs.

**16 Lucca** Page **239** • From the thirteenth-century facade of San Michele in Foro the archangel Michael gazes over the centre of the graceful small city of Lucca.

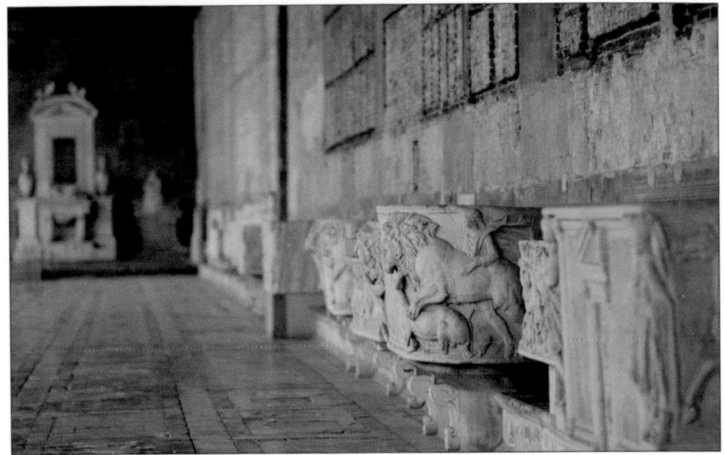

**17 Pisa** Page **227** • The Leaning Tower is the sight that everyone knows in Pisa, but the adjacent Camposanto – perhaps the most beautiful cemetery in the world – is just as impressive.

**18 Sant'Antimo** Page **302** • Splendid and serene, Sant'Antimo is one of several working abbeys set in the hilly terrain to the south of Siena.

**19 Wine tasting in the Sienese hill-towns** Page **297** • The vineyards around Montalcino produce Italy's premier heavyweight red, the luscious Brunello di Montalcino.

**20 Arezzo** Page **327** • Piero della Francesca's frescoes are the must-see attraction in the historic centre of the well-heeled city of Arezzo.

# Basics

# Basics

Getting there .... 19

Getting around .... 22

Accommodation .... 24

Food and drink .... 27

The media .... 30

Festivals .... 31

Travelling with children .... 33

Travel essentials .... 34

# Getting there



**Most visitors to Tuscany fly to Pisa airport, an easy train or bus journey from the centre of Florence. The smaller Florence Perétola (Amerigo Vespucci) airport, located on the edge of the city, is served by a small number of international flights. Bologna's Marconi airport is also within easy reach.**

**From the UK and Ireland**, competitive prices for charter or scheduled flights outweigh the inconvenience of the long rail or bus journey. Most flights **from North America and Australasia** come into Rome (or, less conveniently, Milan), from where you can move on by plane or overland. From down under, you may find it cheaper to fly to London and get a budget flight from there.

Airfares depend on the **season**, with the highest being around Easter, from June to August, and from Christmas to New Year; fares drop during the "shoulder" seasons – September to October and April to May – and you'll get the best prices during the November to March low season (excluding Christmas and New Year). Note also that it is generally more expensive to fly at weekends; price ranges quoted below assume midweek travel. You can often cut costs by going through a **discount flight agent** who may also offer special student and youth fares and a range of other travel-related services such as travel insurance, rail passes, car rentals, tours and the like. Some agents specialize in **charter flights**, which may be cheaper than anything available on a scheduled flight, but departure dates are fixed and withdrawal penalties are high. You may find it cheaper to pick up a **package deal**, which takes care of flights and accommodation for an all-in price.

## Flights from the UK and Ireland

The biggest **budget airlines** serving Pisa from the UK are Ryanair, flying from London Stansted, Bournemouth, East Midlands, Liverpool, Edinburgh and Glasgow, and easyJet, flying from Gatwick, Luton and Bristol. In summer Jet2 flies from Manchester, Leeds, Newcastle and Bradford, and Thomsonfly flies from Gatwick, Coventry, Leeds and Manchester. If you book well in advance you can sometimes find tickets for as little as £25 return for midweek off-peak flights, though these rock-bottom prices tend to apply only to early-morning or late-evening flights. For more reasonable flight times from these airlines, you're looking at something in the region of £100–150 return in summer, as long as you make your reservation well in advance: prices can rise so much for last-minute bookings (ie within two weeks of departure date) that they become as expensive as their full-service rivals. You may also find **charter flight** bargains in high season: it's worth checking with a specialist agent or scouring the classified section of the weekend newspapers for last-minute deals.

Of the **full-service airlines** in the UK British Airways serves Pisa several times daily out of London Gatwick and Manchester, and Alitalia flies via Milan or Rome. A return flight with Alitalia or BA from London to Pisa in low season can cost around £100, with prices from £150 to around £300 in high season. Again, it pays to book as far in advance as possible, and to keep your eyes open for special offers, which have become more numerous in the wake of the competition from the no-frills outfits. Meridiana is currently the only airline with nonstop flights from Gatwick to Florence Perétola; their tickets tend to be more expensive than anyone else's – from £150 off-peak and £200 in summer.

There are also regular British Airways flights to **Bologna** Marconi from London Gatwick. This is generally a cheaper option than flying to Pisa, and because Bologna is a less popular destination you can often find seats when the Pisa flights are sold out. Bologna airport is a shuttle-bus ride from Bologna main train station, from where Florence is an hour's rail journey away. (Forlì airport, the point of arrival for Ryanair flights to Bologna, is a good deal more distant and will add an extra hour to your journey.)

**From Dublin**, Aer Lingus has two flights a week to Bologna (Marconi), and daily services to Rome Fiumicino; Alitalia has regular flights to Bologna and Rome as well, but you have to change in Paris. You can find high-season return deals for around €200 if you book early (special offers may be even lower), but prices in high season can rise to more than €500. In high season Ryanair flies from Dublin to Pisa daily for around €150; otherwise you could pick up a Ryanair flight from Dublin or Shannon to Stansted and catch a Pisa plane from there.

There are no direct flights from Northern Ireland; the cheapest option from Belfast is to buy an easyJet ticket to London and an onward flight to Pisa.

## Flights from the US and Canada

The only **direct service** between North America and Tuscany is offered by Delta, which flies from New York JFK to Pisa five times a week. Otherwise, there are plenty of flights **from the USA and Canada** to Rome or Milan Malpensa, from where you can pick up an onward train to Pisa or Florence. Alitalia and Delta have daily flights to Milan from New York, Miami, Chicago and Boston, and to Rome from New York. Other options to Rome include American Airlines from Chicago, and Alitalia and Air Canada from Toronto (usually with a connection in Europe en route). Many European carriers also fly from major US and Canadian cities (via their capitals) to Rome, Milan and Pisa. The cheapest **return fares** to Rome from New York, travelling midweek in low season, are around US$750, rising to US$1500 during the summer.

## Flights from Australia and New Zealand

There are no direct flights to Italy **from Australia or New Zealand**, but plenty of airlines fly to Rome via Asian hubs. Return fares from Sydney with the major airlines (Alitalia, Qantas, Japan, Singapore or Malaysian) start at around A$2000 in low season, rising to upwards of A$3500 in high season. From New Zealand you can expect to pay from around NZ$2200 in low season to NZ$3500 in high season.

### Fly less – stay longer! Travel and Climate Change

Climate change is perhaps the single biggest issue facing our planet. It is caused by a build-up in the atmosphere of carbon dioxide and other greenhouse gases, which are emitted by many sources – including planes. Already, **flights** account for three to four percent of human-induced global warming: that figure may sound small, but it is rising year on year and threatens to counteract the progress made by reducing greenhouse emissions in other areas.

Rough Guides regard travel as a **global benefit**, and feel strongly that the advantages to developing economies are important, as are the opportunities for greater contact and awareness among peoples. But we also believe in travelling responsibly, which includes giving thought to how often we fly and what we can do to redress any harm that our trips may create.

We can travel less or simply reduce the amount we travel by air (taking fewer trips and staying longer, or taking the train if there is one); we can avoid night flights (which are more damaging); and we can make the trips we do take "climate neutral" via a carbon offset scheme. **Offset schemes** run by climatecare.org, carbonneutral .com and others allow you to "neutralize" the greenhouse gases that you are responsible for releasing. Their websites have simple calculators that let you work out the impact of any flight – as does our own. Once that's done, you can pay to fund projects that will reduce future emissions by an equivalent amount. Please take the time to visit our website and make your trip climate neutral, or get a copy of the *Rough Guide to Climate Change* for more detail on the subject.

**www.roughguides.com/climatechange**

## By train from the UK

Travelling **by train** to Italy won't save any money, but the beauty of train travel is that you can break up your journey en route. The choice of train routes and fares is hugely complex, but the most direct route is to take the Eurostar from London to Paris, then pick up the "Palatino" overnight service from Paris to Florence, via Milan (ⓦwww.artesia.eu), or take the high-speed TGV from Paris to Milan, and change there for Florence; total journey time is around 14–18hr. One-way tickets can go for a little over £100 in low season, though peak prices can go as high as £250. If you're planning to include Italy as part of a longer European trip you could invest in a **rail pass**: the InterRail passes offer a month's unlimited rail travel throughout Europe but you have to buy it before leaving home.

### Train information and tickets

**European Rail** ⓦwww.europeanrail.com. Independent specialist in European rail travel.
**Eurostar** ⓦwww.eurostar.com.
**Rail Europe** ⓦwww.raileurope.co.uk. First stop for information on everything to do with international train travel, including purchase of tickets and passes.
**The Man in Seat 61** ⓦwww.seat61.com. This excellent website is packed with tips on European train travel.
**Trainseurope** ⓦwww.trainseurope.co.uk. Another good agency for European rail tickets.

## Airlines, agents and operators

### Online booking

ⓦ**www.expedia.co.uk (UK)**, ⓦ**www.expedia.com (US)**, ⓦ**www.expedia.ca** (Canada)
ⓦ**www.lastminute.com** (UK)
ⓦ**www.opodo.co.uk** (UK)
ⓦ**www.orbitz.com** (US)
ⓦ**www.skyscanner.net** (UK)
ⓦ**www.travelocity.co.uk** (UK), ⓦ**www.travelocity.com** (US), ⓦ**www.travelocity.ca** (Canada), ⓦ**www.travelocity.co.nz** (New Zealand)
ⓦ**www.travelonline.co.za** (South Africa)
ⓦ**www.zuji.com.au** (Australia)

### Airlines

**Aer Lingus** ⓦwww.aerlingus.com
**Air Canada** ⓦwww.aircanada.com
**Alitalia** ⓦwww.alitalia.com
**American Airlines** ⓦwww.aa.com
**British Airways** ⓦwww.ba.com
**Delta** ⓦwww.delta.com
**easyJet** ⓦwww.easyjet.com
**Jet2** ⓦwww.jet2.com
**Meridiana** ⓦwww.meridiana.it
**Ryanair** ⓦwww.ryanair.com
**Thomsonfly** ⓦwww.thomsonfly.com

### Agents and operators

**Abercrombie & Kent** US ⓦwww.abercrombiekent.com. Deluxe village-to-village hiking and biking tours, as well as rail journeys.
**CIT** Australia ⓦwww.cittravel.com.au. Italian specialists, with packages to Florence and elsewhere.
**Citalia** UK ⓦwww.citalia.com. Long-established company offering city-break packages in mid-range three-star and smarter four-star hotels.
**Flight Centre** AUS ⓦwww.flightcentre.com.au, ⓦwww.flightcentre.co.nz. Specializes in discount airfares and holiday packages.
**Italiatours** UK ⓦwww.italiatours.co.uk, US ⓦwww.italiatours.com. Package deals, city breaks and specialist Italian-cuisine tours. Also offers tailor-made itineraries and can book local events and tours.
**Kirker Holidays** UK ⓦwww.kirkerholidays.com. Independent operator renowned for excellent city- and short-break deals to Tuscany.
**Martin Randall** UK ⓦwww.martinrandall.com. One of the best operators in the sector: imaginative art, music and cultural tours ranging from three to twelve nights, including Piero della Francesca, Florence & Siena and Florence Revisited (lesser-known sights and private palaces).
**North South Travel** UK ⓦwww.northsouthtravel.co.uk. Friendly, competitive travel agency, offering discounted fares worldwide. Profits are used to support projects in the developing world, especially the promotion of sustainable tourism.
**STA Travel** UK ⓦwww.statravel.co.uk, US ⓦwww.statravel.com, Australia ⓦwww.statravel.com.au, ⓦwww.statravel.co.nz. Worldwide specialists in low-cost flights and tours for students and under-26s, though other customers welcome. Also offers student IDs, travel insurance, car rental, rail passes and more.
**Sunvil Holidays** UK ⓦwww.sunvil.co.uk. City breaks and hotel and villa packages, but especially strong on tailor-made fly-drive packages in three- to five-star hotels.
**Trailfinders** Australia ⓦwww.trailfinders.com.au. One of the best informed and most efficient agents for independent travellers.

# Getting around

**There are good rail and bus connections between the major towns of Tuscany, but if you want to explore the more rural areas a car is a major advantage – away from the main routes, public transport services tend to be slow and sporadic.**

## By car

Travelling **by car** in Italy is relatively painless. The roads are generally good, the motorway *(autostrada)* network comprehensive and Italian drivers rather less erratic than their reputation suggests. The major motorways are **toll-roads**, on which you take a ticket as you join and pay as you exit. **Speed limits** are 50kph in built-up areas, 90kph on minor roads outside built-up areas, 110kph on main roads (dual carriageways), and 130kph on nearly all motorways (a few stretches have a 150kph limit). Note that in wet weather limits of 80kph hour apply on minor roads, 90kph on main roads and 110kph on motorways. If you **break down**, dial ⓣ116 at the nearest phone and tell the operator (who will sometimes speak English) where you are, the type of car and your number plate; the Automobile Club d'Italia (ACI) will send someone out to fix your car – at a price, so you might consider getting cover with a motoring organization in your home country before you leave.

Bringing your own vehicle, you need a valid full driving licence (with paper counterpart if you have a photocard licence) and an international driving permit if you are a non-EU licence-holder. It's compulsory to carry your car documents and passport while you're driving: you may be required to present them if stopped by the police – not an uncommon occurrence.

**Car rental** is pricey, with a Fiat Punto (a standard "subcompact" model) costing more than €300 per week with unlimited mileage. There are plenty of companies at Pisa airport and in the major cities, but it works out cheapest to book before leaving. Most firms will only rent to drivers over 21 who have held a licence for a year.

### Car rental agencies

**Avis** ⓦwww.avis.com
**Budget** ⓦwww.budget.com
**Europcar** ⓦwww.europcar.com
**Hertz** ⓦwww.hertz.com
**Holiday Autos** ⓦwww.holidayautos.com
**National** ⓦwww.nationalcar.com
**Sixt** ⓦwww.sixt.com
**Thrifty** ⓦwww.thrifty.com

## By train

The **train** service offered by Trenitalia (ⓦwww.trenitalia.it) is reasonably comprehensive and fairly efficient. There are various categories of train, the quickest of which are the **Eurocity** services (EC), which connect major cities across Europe, perhaps stopping at only two or three places in each country. **Eurostar** trains (ES) are express trains that connect the larger Italian cities; seat reservations are compulsory on these services, and are automatically allocated when you buy your ticket. **Intercity** (IC) and Intercity Plus trains connect a larger number of towns and cities, and are slower and cheaper than the Eurostars; reservations are optional, but are a good idea for long journeys. The workhorses of the system are the **Regionali** (R) trains, which serve the smaller towns within a region as well as the major ones; these trains are inexpensive and quite slow, as are the Diretti (D) and Interregionali (IR) that cover somewhat longer distances than the standard Regionali.

At train stations, separate posters display departures (*partenze* – usually yellow) and arrivals (*arrivi* – usually white); be careful not to confuse the two. Pay attention to the **timetable notes**, which may specify the dates between which some services run (*"si effetua dal ... al ..."*) or whether a service is seasonal (*periodico*). The term *giornaliero* means the service runs daily, *feriale* from Monday to Saturday, *festivi* on Sundays and holidays only.

### Train services in Tuscany

**Florence** is the hub of the Tuscan rail network. Two lines run westwards from the city, one of them passing through **Prato**, **Pistoia**, Montecatini and **Lucca** on its way to the coast at Viareggio, the other going through Empoli and **Pisa** before reaching the sea at Livorno. From Lucca, a picturesque line runs through the Garfagnana to Aulla, providing access to the Lunigiana region and connections to La Spezia and Milan. To the east, a line rises through the Mugello district and then loops out of Tuscany towards Faenza, roughly parallel to the route through the mountains to Bologna.

South of Florence, mainline trains follow the River Arno to **Arezzo**, then south past **Cortona** to Chiusi, Orvieto and Rome. From Arezzo, a private line branches up into the Casentino region. Trains also run directly from Florence to **Siena** – sometimes with a change at Empoli – although the direct bus journey is quicker and easier. From Siena, train routes continue southeast to Chiusi, and southwest to Grosseto.

### Tickets and fares

**Fares** are calculated by the kilometre: a return fare (*andata e ritorno*) is exactly twice that of a single (*andata*). A ticket (*un biglietto*) can be bought from a station ticket office (*la biglietteria*), ticket machines at the station, some travel agents and sometimes from station news kiosks or bars (for short trips). All tickets must be **validated** just before travel: once validated, tickets for journeys up to 200km are valid for six hours, over 200km for 24 hours. Children aged 4–12 pay half-price; under-4s travel free.

## By bus

If you're limited to public transport and want to get to know Tuscany thoroughly, sooner or later you'll have to use regional **buses** (*autobus* or *pullman*). Unlike the state-owned train network, there are dozens of different bus companies, all of which are under joint public and private ownership. Some of the companies operate solely on local routes, others run nationwide between major cities; almost everywhere has some kind of bus service, but schedules can be sketchy, and are drastically reduced – sometimes nonexistent – at weekends. Bear in mind also that in rural areas schedules are often designed with the working and/or school day in mind, meaning a frighteningly early start if you want to catch the sole bus out of town and perhaps no buses at all during school holidays.

In larger towns, the **bus terminal** (*autostazione*), where you can buy tickets and pick up timetables, is usually very close to the train station; in smaller towns and villages, most buses pull in at the central piazza, which may have a newsstand selling bus tickets (if not, you can buy tickets on the bus).

**City buses** are always cheap, usually in the region of €1 for a ticket that's valid either for a single journey or for any number of journeys within a set period (typically 40–60min). You must always buy a ticket before getting on the bus, from local *tabacchi* or the kiosks at bus terminals and stops; and you must validate them in the machine inside the bus. In most cities there are regular ticket checks, with hefty spot-fines for offenders.

## By bike or motorbike

**Cycling** is seen in Italy as a sport rather than a way of getting around: on a Sunday you'll see plenty of people out for a spin on their Campagnolo-equipped machines, but you'll not come across many luggage-laden tourers. Only in major towns will you find a

### Ticket machines

All stations have small yellow machines at the end of the platforms or in ticket halls in which you must **stamp your ticket** immediately before getting on the train; however, don't stamp the return portion of your ticket until you embark on the return journey. If you don't validate your ticket, you become liable for an on-the-spot fine.

shop stocking spares for non-racing bikes, so make sure you take a supply of inner tubes, spokes and any other bits you think might be handy. It's possible to rent bikes in major towns, but **mopeds** and **scooters** are easier to hire: expect to pay around €60–70 a day. Crash helmets are compulsory.



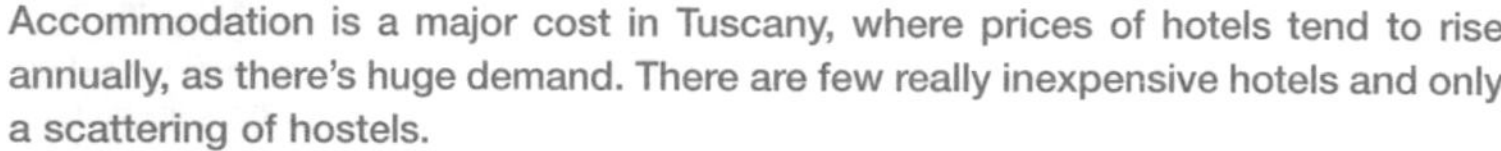

# Accommodation

**Accommodation is a major cost in Tuscany, where prices of hotels tend to rise annually, as there's huge demand. There are few really inexpensive hotels and only a scattering of hostels.**

Accommodation in Italy is strictly regulated. All hotels are **star-rated** from one to five; prices are officially registered for each room and must be posted at the hotel reception and in individual rooms (usually on the back of the door). Ask to see a variety of rooms if the first you're shown is too expensive or not up to scratch; there may be cheaper rooms available, perhaps without a private bathroom. Most tourist offices carry full **lists of hotels** and other accommodation such as bed and breakfasts and agriturismo options. They may be able to help you find a room at short notice, but few have dedicated accommodation services.

In high season it is essential to **book rooms in advance;** for Florence and Siena, it's advisable to book in advance at any time of year. Always establish the full price of your room – including breakfast and other extras (tax and service charges are usually included) – before you accept it. It's often a good idea to call or email a day or so before arrival to **confirm your room booking**. If you're going to be arriving late in the evening, it's even worth another call that morning to reconfirm.

## Hotels

Hotels in Italy are known by a variety of names. Most are simply tagged **hotel** or **albergo**. Others may be called a **locanda**, a name traditionally associated with the cheapest sort of inn, but now sometimes rather self-consciously applied to smart new hotels. A **pensione** was also traditionally a cheap place to stay, though the name now lacks any official status: anywhere still describing itself as a *pensione* is probably a hotel in the one-star class.

The star system is the best way to get an idea of what you can expect from a hotel, though it's essential to realize the system is based on an often eccentric set of criteria relating to facilities (say, the presence of a restaurant or an in-room TV) rather than notions of comfort, character or location. A three-star, for example, must have a phone in every room: if it hasn't, it remains a two-star, no matter how magnificent the rest of the hotel.

**One-star** hotels in tourist towns in high season tend to start at about €50 for a

### Accommodation price codes

Throughout this guide, all accommodation prices have been graded with the codes below, indicating the least you can expect to pay for a double room in high season.

1 €60 and below
2 €61–100
3 €101–150
4 €151–200
5 €201–250
6 €251–300
7 €301–400
8 over €400

double room without private bath; **two-star** hotels cost upwards of €80 for an en-suite double; **three-star** places are rarely cheaper than €100. **Four-star** hotels are a marked step up: everything has more polish, and in rural four-stars you'll probably get a swimming pool; €150–200 is the typical range here (though some establishments are much pricier), while for a deluxe **five-star** (rare outside the major centres) you should expect to pay more than €250 a night. Prices in Florence and Siena are much higher than anywhere else in the region: you can pay around €100 for an en-suite one-star room in peak season, while €500 per night is far from rare in the five-stars.

In the more popular cities, especially Florence, it's not unusual for hotels to impose a **minimum stay** of three nights in summer. Note also that single rooms nearly always cost far more than half the price of a double, although kindlier hoteliers – if they have no singles available – may offer you a double room at the single rate.

## Self-catering and agriturismo

High hotel prices in much of Tuscany make **self-catering** an attractive proposition. Many package companies offer self-catering as an alternative to hotel accommodation, but better selections of apartments are provided by specialist agents such as those listed below, all of which have a good reputation.

Travelling with a group of people, or even just in a pair, it's worth considering renting a **villa** or **farmhouse** for a week or two. These are not too expensive if you can split costs, are of a consistently high standard, and often enjoy marvellous locations. Alternatively, you could investigate **agriturismo**, a scheme whereby farmers rent out converted barns and farm buildings. Usually these comprise a self-contained flat or building, though a few places just rent rooms on a bed-and-breakfast basis. This market has boomed over the last few years, and while some rooms are still annexed to working farms or vineyards, many are smart self-contained rural vacation properties. Attractions may include home-grown food, swimming pools and a range of activities from walking and riding to archery and mountain biking. Many



agriturismi have a minimum-stay requirement of one week in busy periods.

Tourist offices keep lists of local properties, or you can search one of the growing number of agriturismo websites – there are hundreds of properties at Ⓦwww.agriturismo.com, Ⓦwww.agriturismo.net, Ⓦwww.agriitalia.it and Ⓦwww.agriturist.it.

### Property rental companies

**Bridgewater's** Ⓦwww.bridgewater-travel.co.uk. A company with over 25 years' experience of apartments in Florence and Siena, and of agriturismo in the surrounding countryside.

**Carefree Italy** Ⓦwww.carefree-italy.com. Farmhouses and villas, often in shared complexes; also has a range of small hotels and city apartments.

**Cottages to Castles** Ⓦwww.cottagestocastles.com. Over a hundred Tuscan cottages, villas and apartments.

**Cuendet** Ⓦwww.italianlife.co.uk. Large database of hundreds of properties in Tuscany.

**Holiday Rentals** Ⓦwww.holiday-rentals.co.uk. This site puts you directly in touch with the owners of scores of Tuscan properties.

**IST Italian Breaks** ⓦwww.italianbreaks.com. A good range of villas and apartments.
**Owners' Syndicate** ⓦwww.ownerssyndicate.com. Leading operator, with more than 150 properties in Tuscany.
**Traditional Tuscany** ⓦwww.traditionaltuscany.co.uk. Offers B&B in Florentine palaces and on working farms and vineyards, plus a selection of villas and converted farms.
**Tuscan Holidays** ⓦwww.tuscanholidays.co.uk. A small company with around 130 carefully selected properties in Tuscany, many with pools.
**Veronica Tomasso Cotgrove** ⓦwww.vtcitaly.com. Carefully chosen villas and apartments, including some huge properties.

## Bed and breakfast

Legal restrictions used to make it very difficult for Italian home-owners to offer bed and breakfast accommodation, but in 2000 the law was relaxed, and now there are hundreds of B&Bs in Tuscany, with the greatest concentration – unsurprisingly – in Florence. Prices at the lower end of the scale are comparable to one-star hotels, but one unexpected consequence of the change in the law has been the emergence of upscale B&B options in castles, palaces and large private homes. Tourist offices or local *comune* and other websites often carry lists of B&Bs, and ⓦwww.bed-and-breakfast.it is another useful resource. In addition to registered B&Bs you'll also find **"rooms for rent"** (*affitacamere*) advertised in some towns. These differ from B&Bs in that breakfast is not always offered, and they are not subject to the same regulations as official B&Bs; nearly all *affitacamere* are priced in the one-star range.

## Hostels and student accommodation

Most hostels belong to the **Hostelling International (HI)** network (ⓦwww.iyhf.org), and strictly speaking you need to be an HI member to stay at them. Many, however, allow you to join on the spot, or simply charge you a small supplement. Whether or not you're an HI member, you'll need to **book ahead** in the summer months. The most efficient way to book at main city hostels is using HI's own International Booking Network (ⓦwww.hostelbooking.com); for more out-of-the-way locations, you should contact the hostel direct.



## Religious organizations

Religious organizations all over Tuscany offer cheap accommodation in lodgings annexed to **convents** or **monasteries**, or in pilgrim hostels. Most offer rooms with and without bathroom; only a few have dorm rooms with bunks. Some accept women only, others families only or single travellers of either sex. Most have a curfew, but few, contrary to expectations, pay much heed to your coming and going. Virtually none offers meals.

## Camping

There are surprisingly few campsites in rural Tuscany, but camping is popular along the coast, where the sites are mostly on the upmarket side. Prices in high season tend to start from around €10 per person, plus €15 per pitch, though some of the smaller sites may be a little cheaper. If you're camping extensively, it's worth checking Italy's very informative camping website, ⓦwww.camping.it, for details of each site and booking facilities.

# Food and drink

The traditional dishes of Tuscany are Italy's most influential cuisine: the ingredients and culinary techniques of the region have made their mark not just on the menus of the rest of Italy but also abroad. And wine has always been central to the area's economy and way of life, familiar names such as Chianti and Brunello representing just a portion of the enormous output from Tuscan vineyards. For a detailed menu reader, see p.383, and for more on specialities of the region and wine, see the *Tuscan food and drink* colour section.

## Breakfast and snacks

Most Italians start their day in a bar, **breakfast** (*prima colazione*) consisting of a coffee and the ubiquitous *cornetto* or *brioche* – a jam-, custard- or chocolate-filled croissant, which you usually take yourself from the counter. Unfilled croissants can be hard to find; ask for *un cornetto vuoto* or *normale*.

At other times of the day, **sandwiches** (panini) can be pretty substantial. Specialized sandwich bars (*paninoteche*) can be found in many larger towns; grocers' shops (*alimentari*), who'll make sandwiches to order, are another standard source. Bars may also offer *tramezzini*, ready-made sliced white bread with mixed fillings – tasty and slightly cheaper than the average panino. Toasted sandwiches (*toast*) are common too: in a *paninoteca* you can get whatever you want toasted; in ordinary bars it's more likely to be a variation on cheese or ham with tomato.

There are a number of options for **take-away food**. It's possible to find slices of pizza (*pizza a taglio* or *pizza rustica*) pretty much everywhere – buy it by weight (an *etto* is 100g) – while you can get pasta, chips and even hot meals in a **tavola calda**, a sort of snack bar that's at its best in the morning when everything is fresh.

Other sources of quick snacks are **markets**, some of which sell takeaway food from stalls, including *focacce*, oven-baked pastries topped with cheese or tomato or filled with spinach, fried offal or meat; and *arancini* or *suppli*, deep-fried balls of rice filled with meat (*rosso*) or butter and cheese (*bianco*).

### Pizza

All across Italy, **pizza** comes thin and flat, not deep-pan, and the choice of toppings is fairly limited. Most are cooked in the traditional way, in wood-fired ovens (*forno a legna*): they arrive blasted and bubbling on the surface, and with a distinctive charcoal taste. **Pizzerie** range from a stand-up counter selling slices (*a taglio*) to a fully fledged sit-down restaurant.

### Ice cream

Italian **ice cream** (*gelato*) is justifiably famous: a cone (*un cono*) or better-value "cup" (*una coppa*) are indispensable accessories to the evening *passeggiata*. Most bars have a fairly good selection, but for real choice go to a **gelateria**, where the range is a tribute to the Italian imagination and flair for display. You'll sometimes have to go by appearance rather than attempting to decipher their exotic names, many of which don't mean much even to Italians; often the basics – chocolate, strawberry, vanilla – are best. There's no problem locating the finest *gelateria* in town: it's the one that draws the crowds. The procedure is to ask for a *cono* or *coppa*, indicating the size you want.

## Restaurants

Traditionally, Tuscan **restaurant** meals (lunch is *pranzo*, dinner is *cena*) are long affairs, starting with an antipasto, followed by a risotto or a pasta dish, leading on to a fish or meat course, cheese, and finished with fresh fruit and coffee. Even everyday meals are a miniaturized version of this. Modern minimalism has made inroads into the more expensive restaurants, but the staple fare at the majority of places is exactly what it might have been a century ago.

Restaurants are most commonly called either **trattorie** or **ristoranti**. Traditionally, a trattoria is a cheaper and more basic purveyor of home-style cooking (*cucina casalinga*), while a *ristorante* is more upmarket, with aproned waiters and tablecloths. These days, however, there's a fine line between the two, as it's become rather chic for an expensive restaurant to call itself a trattoria. It's in the rural areas that you're most likely to come across an old-style trattoria, the sort of place where there's no written menu (the waiter will simply reel off a list of what's available) and no bottled wine (it comes straight from the vats of the local farm). A true *ristorante* will always have a written menu and a reasonable choice of wines, though even in smart places it's standard to choose the ordinary house wine. In Florence, you may well find restaurants unwilling to serve anything less than a full meal: no lunchtime restraint of a pasta and salad allowed.

Increasingly, too, you'll come across **osterie**. These used to be old-fashioned places specializing in home cooking, though recently they have had quite a vogue and the *osteria* tag more often signifies a youngish ownership and clientele, and adventurous foods. Other types of restaurant include **spaghetterie** and **birrerie**, bar-restaurants which serve basic pasta dishes, or beer and snacks.

### The menu and the bill

The cheapest – though not the most rewarding way – to eat in bigger city restaurants is to opt for a set price **menù turistico**. This will usually give you a first course (pasta or soup), main course, dessert (usually a piece of fruit), half a litre of water and a quarter litre of wine per person. Beware the increasingly common *prezzo fisso* menu, which excludes cover, service, dessert and beverages.

Working your way through an Italian menu (*la lista*, or sometimes *il menù*) is pretty straightforward. **Antipasto** (literally "before the meal") is a course generally consisting of various cold cuts of meat, seafood and cold vegetable dishes. *Prosciutto* is a common antipasto dish, ham either cooked (*cotto*) or just cured and hung (*crudo*), served alone or with melon, figs or mozzarella cheese. Also very common are *crostini*, canapés of minced chicken liver and other toppings.

The next course, **il primo**, consists of soup or a risotto, polenta or pasta dish. This is followed by **il secondo** – the meat or fish course, usually served alone, except for perhaps a wedge of lemon or tomato. Watch out when ordering fish or Florence's famous *bistecca alla fiorentina,* which will usually be served by weight: 250g is usually plenty for one person, or ask to have a look at the fish before it's cooked. Anything marked *S.Q.* or *hg* means you are paying by weight: *hg* stands for a hectogram (*etto* in Italian) – 100g, or around 4oz. Vegetables (**il contorno**) and salads (**insalata**) are ordered and served separately, and often there won't be much choice, if any: most common are beans (*fagioli*), potatoes (*patate*), and salads either green (*verde*) or mixed (*mista*).

For afters, you nearly always get a choice of fresh fruit (*frutta*) and a selection of desserts (**dolci**) often focused on ice cream or usually dull home-made flans (*torta della casa*).

In many trattorie, the bill/check (**il conto**) amounts to no more than an illegible scrap of paper, and if you want to be sure you're not being ripped off, ask to have a receipt (*ricevuta*), something all bars and restaurants are legally bound to provide anyway. Bear in mind that almost everywhere you'll pay a **cover charge** (*pane e coperto* or just *coperto*) of €1–1.50 a head. As well as the *coperto*, **service** (*servizio*) will often be added, generally about ten percent; if it isn't, you should perhaps **tip** about the same amount.

## Drinking

**Drinking** is essentially an accompaniment to food: there's little emphasis on drinking for its own sake. Locals sitting around in bars or cafés – whatever their age – will spend hours chatting over one drink. And even in bars, most people you see sipping one of the delicious Italian grappas or brandies will take just one, then be on their way. The snag is that, since Italians drink so little, prices can be high.

**Bars** are often very functional, brightly lit places, with a chrome counter, a Gaggia coffee machine and a picture of the local football team on the wall. There are no set licensing hours and children are always allowed in. People come to bars for ordinary drinking – a coffee in the morning, a quick beer, or a cup of tea – but don't generally idle away the day or evening in them. It's nearly always cheapest to drink **standing** at the counter (there's often nowhere to sit anyway), in which case you often pay first at the cash desk (*la cassa*), present your receipt (*scontrino*) to the barman and give your order; sometimes you simply order your drink and pay as you leave. There's always a list of prices (*listino prezzi*) behind the bar. If there's waiter service, you can **sit** where you like, though bear in mind that to do this means your drink will cost perhaps twice as much, especially if you **sit outside** on the terrace. These different prices for the same drinks are shown on the price list as *bar*, *tavola* and *terrazza*.

## Coffee, tea and soft drinks

One of the most distinctive smells in an Italian street is that of fresh **coffee**, usually wafting out of a bar. The basic choice is either small and black (espresso, or just *caffè*), or white and frothy (cappuccino). If you want a longer *espresso* ask for a *caffè lungo* or *americano*; a double espresso is *una doppia*, while a short, extra-strong espresso is a *ristretto*. A coffee topped with unfrothed milk is a *caffè latte*; with a drop of milk it's *caffè macchiato*; with a shot of alcohol it's *caffè corretto*. Although most places let you help yourself to sugar, a few add it routinely; if you don't want it, you can make sure by asking for *caffè senza zucchero*. Many places also now sell decaffeinated coffee (ask for the brand-name Hag, even when it isn't). In summer you might want to have your coffee cold (*caffè freddo*); for a real treat, ask for *caffè granita*, cold coffee with crushed ice, usually topped with cream. Hot **tea** (*tè caldo*) comes with lemon (*con limone*) as standard, unless you ask for milk (*con latte*); in summer you can drink it cold (*tè freddo*). **Milk** itself is drunk hot as often as cold, or you can get it with a dash of coffee (*latte macchiato*) and sometimes as a milkshake (*frappé*).

There are numerous **soft drinks** (*analcoliche*). A *spremuta* is a fruit juice, usually orange (*... d'arancia*), lemon (*... di limone*) or grapefruit (*... di pompelmo*), fresh-squeezed at the bar, with optional added sugar. A *succo di frutta* is a bottled fruit juice, widely drunk at breakfast. Home-grown Italian cola, Chinotto, is less sweet than Coke – good with a slice of lemon. An excellent thirst-quencher is Lemon Soda (the brand name), a widely available bitter-lemon drink.

**Tap water** (*acqua normale* or *acqua dal rubinetto*) is quite drinkable, and free in bars. **Mineral water** (*acqua minerale*) is a more common choice, either still (*senza gas*, *liscia*, *non gassata* or *naturale*) or sparkling (*con gas, gassata* or *frizzante*).

## Beer and spirits

**Beer** (*birra*) is nearly always a lager-type brew that comes in bottles or on tap (*alla spina*) – standard measures are a third of a litre (*piccola*) and two-thirds of a litre (*media*). Commonest and cheapest are the Italian brands Peroni, Moretti and Dreher, all of which are very drinkable; to order these, either state the brand name or ask for *birra nazionale* – otherwise you may be given a more expensive imported beer. You may also come across darker beers (*birra scura* or *birra rossa*), which have a sweeter, maltier taste and resemble stout or bitter.

All the usual **spirits** are on sale and known mostly by their generic names. There are also Italian brands of the main varieties: the best local brandies are Stock and Vecchia Romagna. The home-grown Italian firewater is **grappa**, originally from Bassano di Grappa in the Veneto but now produced just about everywhere. Grappas are made from the leftovers of the winemaking process (skins, stalks and the like) and drunk as *digestivi* after a meal. The best Tuscan varieties are from Montalcino (Brunello) and Montepulciano.

You'll also find **fortified wines** like Martini, Cinzano and Campari. For the real thing, order *un Campari bitter*; ask for a "Campari-soda" and you'll get a ready-mixed version from a little bottle. Lemon Soda and Campari bitter makes a delicious and dangerously drinkable combination. The non-alcoholic Crodino, easily recognizable by its lurid orange colour, is also a popular *aperitivo*. You might also try Cynar, an artichoke-based sherry-type liquid often drunk as an aperitif.

There's a daunting selection of **liqueurs**. Amaro is a bitter after-dinner drink, and probably the most popular way among Italians to round off a meal. The top brands, in rising order of bitterness, are Montenegro, Ramazotti, Averna and Fernet Branca. Strega is another drink you'll see in every bar – the yellow stuff in elongated bottles: it's as sweet as it looks but not unpleasant. Also popular, though considered slightly naff in Italy, is *limoncello*, a bitter-sweet lemon spirit that's becoming increasingly trendy abroad.

### Wine

Pursuit of **wine** is as good a reason as any for a visit to Tuscany. The province constitutes the heartland of Italian wine production, with sales of Chianti accounting for much of the country's wine exports, and the towns of Montalcino and Montepulciano producing two of the very finest Italian vintages (Brunello and Vino Nobile respectively). The area around Bólgheri, in the Maremma, produces many of the so-called Super Tuscan wines, including two of the country's most celebrated and expensive vintages, Sassicaia and Ornellaia.

The snobbery associated with "serious" wine drinking remains for the most part mercifully absent. Light reds, such as those made from the *dolcetto* grape, are refrigerated in hot weather, while some full-bodied whites are drunk at or near room temperature. Wine is also very inexpensive: in some bars you can get a glass of good local *vino* for less than €1 or so, and table wine in restaurants – often decanted from the barrel – rarely costs more than about €6 per bottle.

# The media

**Local and national newspapers form an essential accompaniment to Tuscan bar culture: in small towns, folk are drawn to a bar for a read, not a drink. Television also plays a central role in Italian life: many households have the TV switched on from morning to night, regardless of the poor quality of Italy's numerous local and national channels.**

## Newspapers

Tuscany's major **newspaper** is the Florence-based *La Nazione*. This is technically a national paper but its sales are concentrated in the central provinces of Italy. It produces local editions, with supplements, including informative entertainments listings, for virtually every major Tuscan town. Of the other nationals, the centre-left *La Repubblica* and right-slanted *Corriere della Sera* are the two most widely read and available. *L'Unità*, which has evolved from the newspaper of the former Italian communist party, has experienced hard times, even in the party's Tuscan strongholds, but now seems to have regained some lost ground. The most avidly read papers of all are the pink *Gazzetta dello Sport* and *Corriere dello Sport*; essential reading for the serious Italian sports fan, they devote as much attention to players' ankle problems as most papers would give to the resignation of a government. News **magazines** are also widely read in Italy, from *L'Espresso* and *Panorama* to the lighter offerings of *Gente* and *Oggi*. **English and US newspapers** can be found for two or three times the normal price in all the larger towns and resorts, usually on the day of issue in bigger cities like Florence and Siena.

## TV and radio

Italy's three main national **TV** channels are RAI 1, 2 and 3. Silvio Berlusconi's Fininvest runs three additional nationwide channels: Canale 5, TG4 and Italia 1. Although all six are blatantly pro-Berlusconi, the degree of sycophancy displayed on the TG4 news has reached such ludicrous heights (newscaster Emilio Fede is variously overcome by tears of joy or despair, depending on the fortunes of Berlusconi) that many Italians now tune in solely for a giggle. The other main channel is Telemontecarlo, currently reaching seventy percent of the country. Although the stories of Italian TV's stripping housewives are overplayed, the output is generally unchallenging (and sexist) across the board, with the accent on quiz shows, soaps and plenty of American imports. The RAI channels carry less advertising and try to mix the dross with above-average documentaries and news coverage. Numerous other channels concentrate on sport; if you want to see the weekend's Italian League football action, settle into a bar from 5pm on a Sunday.

The situation in **radio** is even more anarchic, with FM so crowded that you continually pick up new stations whether you want to or not. There are some good small-scale stations if you search hard enough, but on the whole the RAI stations are the most professional. The **BBC World Service** (Ⓦwww.bbc.co.uk) is in English on 648kHz medium wave most of the day; they also broadcast continuously online, as do Voice of America (Ⓦwww.voa.gov) and Radio Canada (Ⓦwww.rcinet.ca).

# Festivals

Tuscany has a plethora of **local festivals**, with saints' days being the most common excuse for some kind of binge. All cities, small towns and villages have their home-produced saint, whose mortal remains or image are generally paraded through the streets amid much noise and spectacle. There are plenty of other occasions for a **festa** – either to commemorate a local miracle or historic event, or to show off the local products or artistic talent. Many happen at Easter, in May or September, or around Ferragosto (Aug 15); local dates are detailed below. See individual chapters for further information on the major festivals.

Tickets for major cultural festivals – such as the Maggio Musicale in Florence – can be difficult to obtain. If you have no luck with a festival's box office, it may be worth trying **Liaisons Abroad** (Ⓦwww.liaisonsabroad.com), an agency for tickets to major Italian opera and musical events, timed museum tickets, Siena's Palio, Serie A football matches, and more.

### Religious and traditional festivals

Many local **religious processions** have strong pagan roots, marking important dates on the calendar subsequently adopted and sanctified by the Church. **Good Friday** is also a popular time for processions, with images of Christ on the cross paraded through towns accompanied by white-robed, hooded figures singing penitential hymns. The separate motivations to make some money, have a good time and pay your spiritual dues all merge in the celebrations for a town's **saint's day**, where it's not unusual to find a left-wing mayor and local bishop officiating side by side.

In Tuscany, however, the best traditional festivals are of a more secular nature. Top honours go to the Palio horse races in **Siena**, which see jockeys careering around the central square in a fiercely contested spectacle. Other towns put on medieval-origin contests, too, though they are somewhat phoney, having

## Festival calendar

### Easter

**Florence** Scioppio del Carro (Easter Sun). Fireworks in Piazza del Duomo.

### April

**Lucca** Sacred music festival (April–June).

**Florence** Maggio Musicale music festival (April–June).

### June

**Pisa** Luminara torchlit procession precedes Regatta di San Ranieri boat race (June 16 & 17).

**Pisa** Gioco del Ponte (3rd Sun). Costumed mock battle.

**Florence** Festa di San Giovanni marked by fireworks and the Gioco di Calcio Storico football game (week beginning June 24).

**Fiesole** Estate Fiesolana (mid-June to Aug). Music, cinema, ballet and theatre.

**San Gimignano** Summer festival of music and film (late June to Oct).

### July

**Siena** Palio horse races (July 2), preceded by trial races on June 29 and 30, and July 1.

**Siena** Settimana Musicale (mid-July).

**Lucca** Festa di San Paolino (3rd Sun). Torchlit parade and crossbow contest.

**Pistoia** Giostro dell'Orso (July 25) – jousting.

### August

**Montepulciano** Food and wine festival (2nd Sun).

**Lucca** Luminaria di Santa Croce (Aug 14). Torchlit processions.

**Montepulciano** Il Bruscello (Aug 14–16). Folkloric song festival.

**Cortona** Festa della Bistecca (Aug 15). Excessive consumption of local beef.

**Florence** Festa del Grillo (Aug 15). Fair in the Cascine park.

**Siena** Palio horse races (Aug 16), preceded by trial races on August 14 and 15.

**Arezzo** International choral festival (last two weeks).

**Montepulciano** Bravio delle Botti (last Sun). Barrel race through the town.

### September

**Arezzo** Giostro del Saracino (1st Sun). Jousting by knights in armour.

**Florence** Festa delle Rificolone (Sept 7). Torchlit procession.

**Prato** Festa degli Omaggi (Sept 8). Costumed procession.

**Sansepolcro** Return crossbow matches against Gubbio (2nd Sun).

**Greve** Chianti Classico wine festival (2nd Sun).

**Lucca** Festa della Santa Croce (Sept 14). Procession of sacred image.

### December

**Siena** Festa di Santa Lucia (Dec 13). Pottery fair.

**Prato** Display of Holy Girdle (Dec 25 & 26).

been revived recently for commercial ends. Among the most enjoyable are the Gioco di Calcio Storico, a rough-and-tumble football game played between the four quarters of **Florence** in June, and the crossbow competitions between teams from **Sansepolcro** and the Umbrian town of **Gubbio**, held during May and September.

## Food, wine and arts festivals

**Food**- and **wine**-inspired festivals are more low-key affairs than the religious and traditional events, but no less enjoyable for that. They generally celebrate the edible speciality of the region to the accompaniment of dancing, music from a local brass band and noisy fireworks at the end of the evening. At Easter and through the summer and autumn there are literally hundreds of such events, most of them catering to locals rather than tourists; for details, ask at tourist offices or check the local newspapers (where you'll find them listed as *sagre*).

The ancient inter-town rivalries across Tuscany – encapsulated neatly by the term *campanilismo*, implying that the only things that matter are those that take place within the sound of your village's church bells – find a highly positive expression in the willingness of local councils to put money into promoting their own **arts festivals**. For the size of the towns involved, the events are often almost ludicrously rich, celebrating the work of a native composer or artist by inviting major international names to perform or direct. Many festivals are given an added enjoyment by their location: in summer, open-air performances are often staged in restored ancient amphitheatres, churches or town squares.

# Travelling with children

**Kids are adored in Italy and will be made a fuss of in the street, and are welcomed and catered for in bars and restaurants. Two recent laws have improved the situation for parents even further: the ban on smoking in restaurants and bars has made them far more family-friendly, while the law on disabled access make it far easier to take a pushchair (*passeggino*) into museums and churches.**

The only hazards in summer are the heat and sun; sunblock can be bought in any pharmacy, and bonnets or straw hats in most markets. The rhythms of the summer climate tend to modify the way you approach the day, and you'll soon find it quite natural to use siesta-time to recover flagging energy, and to carry on past normal bedtimes at night. In high summer, it's not unusual to see Italian children out at midnight, and not looking much the worse for it. You can buy **baby** equipment – nappies, creams and foods – in pharmacies.

It has to be said, however, that Florence is not the most child-friendly of cities. There are sights that might well excite – climbing to the top of the dome of the Duomo, for example, or visiting the waxworks of La Specola – but with younger children you might find that their patience begins to wear thin quite quickly: it's easy for them to get the feeling that Florence is just one damned church or museum after another. Florence has very few green spaces, with just one central playground of any size, at Piazza Torquato Tasso, near the Carmine in Oltrarno. The main park, the Cascine, is some way out of the centre of town. Smaller Tuscan towns, however, should be a lot more fun: for one thing, places such as Lucca or Montepulciano are considerably more relaxed and less traffic-choked, and for another you can quite easily find accommodation near to town that has that most welcome of facilities – a swimming pool. It's also easier, if you're based in a smaller centre, to strike out into the countryside for a spot of rural recreation. As for accommodation, nearly all hotels will gladly put a cot or an extra bed in your room, usually for a surcharge of 10–25 percent.

See the website ⓦwww.travelforkids.com for more information on child-friendly sights and activities in Italy.

# Travel essentials

## Costs

Delicious picnic **meals** can be put together for under €6.50/£5/$10, and a pizza or plate of pasta in a cheap pizzeria or trattoria will come to around €7.50/£6/$12 on average. However, in most restaurants in Florence and Siena you'll be lucky to get away with paying €35 a head for a three-course meal with house wine. In almost every restaurant you'll pay a **cover charge** (*coperto*) of €1–3 a head on top of the cost of your food and drink. As well as the *coperto*, **service** (*servizio*) will often be added, generally about ten percent; if it isn't, you should **tip** this amount, and if it is included it's usual to leave a few extra euros – but no more than five percent or so. **Public transport** is good value: the train journey from Florence to Siena (100km) costs around €9/£7/$14 for a second-class return. **Accommodation** in Florence and Siena is expensive (see p.24).

Overall, an average minimum **daily budget** for a couple staying in one-star hotels and eating one modest-priced meal out a day would be in the region of €75/£60/$120 per person. In view of the disproportionate cost of single hotel rooms, a person travelling alone can expect this figure to increase by about twenty-five percent – though not, of course, if staying in a hostel.

**Youth/student ID cards** soon pay for themselves in savings, principally on entertainment and admission to larger museums and attractions. Full-time students are eligible for the International Student ID Card (**ISIC**); anybody aged 26 or less qualifies for the **International Youth Travel Card**; and teachers qualify for the **International Teacher Card** – all of which carry the same benefits. Check Ⓦwww.isiccard.com for details of outlets selling the cards. Reductions and discounts for under-18s and over-65s are also usually available for major attractions and state museums.

## Crime and personal safety

In Florence and Siena, the only trouble you're likely to come across are gangs of **scippatori** ("snatchers"), often kids, who operate in crowded streets or markets, train stations and packed tourist sights. As well as handbags, *scippatori* grab wallets, tear off any visible jewellery and, if they're really adroit, unstrap watches. You can **minimize the risk** of this happening by being discreet: wear money in a belt or pouch; don't put anything down on café or restaurant tables; don't flash anything of value; keep a firm hand on your camera; and carry shoulder bags slung across your body. Never leave anything valuable in your car and park in car parks or well-lit, well-used streets.

Italy's reputation for **sexual harassment** of women is based largely on experiences in the south of the country. However, even in the "civilized" north, travelling on your own, or with another woman, you can expect to attract occasional unwelcome attention. There are few things you can do to ward it off. Indifference is often the most effective policy, as is looking as confident as possible, walking with a purposeful stride and maintaining a directed gaze.

In Italy there are several different branches of the **police**, ostensibly to prevent any single branch seizing power. You're not likely to have much contact with the Guardia di Finanza, who investigate smuggling, tax evasion and other finance-related felonies. Drivers may well come up against the **Polizia Urbana**, or town police, who are mainly concerned with traffic

### Emergency phone numbers

**Police** (*Carabinieri*) Ⓣ112
**Any emergency service** (*Soccorso Pubblico di Emergenza*) Ⓣ113
**Fire service** (*Vigili del Fuoco*) Ⓣ115
**Roadside assistance** (*Soccorso Stradale*) Ⓣ116

and parking offences, and also the **Polizia Stradale**, who patrol motorways.

If you're unlucky, you may have dealings with the **Carabinieri**, dressed in military-style uniforms and white shoulder belts (they're part of the army), who deal with general crime, public order and drugs control. These are the ones Italians are most rude about, but a lot of this stems from the north–south divide: eighty percent of the Carabinieri are from southern Italy, and joining the police is one way to escape the poverty trap.

The **Polizia Statale**, the other general crime-fighting branch, enjoy a fierce rivalry with the Carabinieri, and are the ones to whom thefts should be reported at their base, the **Questura** (police station). They'll issue you with a *denuncia*, an impressively stamped report form which you'll need for any insurance claims after you get home. The Questura is also where you should to go to obtain a visa extension or a *permesso di soggiorno* (permit to stay).

## Electricity

The supply is 220V, though anything requiring 240V will work. Most plugs are two round pins: UK equipment will need an adaptor, US equipment a 220 to 110 transformer as well.

## Entry requirements

All EU citizens can enter Italy, and stay as long as they like, simply on production of a valid passport. Citizens of the United States, Canada, Australia and New Zealand need only a valid passport, but are limited to stays of ninety days. All other nationals should consult the relevant embassies about visa requirements. Legally, you're required to **register with the police** within three days of entering Italy, though if you're staying at a hotel this will be done for you. Some policemen are more punctilious about this than ever, though others would be astonished by any attempt to register yourself while on holiday.

### Italian embassies and consulates abroad

**Australia** Embassy: 12 Grey St, Deakin, Canberra, ACT 2600 ⓣ02/6273 3333, ⓦwww.ambcanberra.esterl.it.au. Consulates in Melbourne ⓣ03/9867 5744 and Sydney ⓣ02/9392 7900.
**Canada** Embassy: 275 Slater St, Ottawa, ON K1P 5H9 ⓣ613/232-2401, ⓦwww.ambottawa.esteri.it. Consulates in Montréal ⓣ514/849-8351 and Toronto ⓣ416/977-1566.
**Ireland** Embassy: 63–65 Northumberland Rd, Dublin 4 ⓣ01/660 1744, ⓦwww.ambdublino.esteri.it.
**New Zealand** Embassy: 34–38 Grant Rd, PO Box 463, Thorndon, Wellington ⓣ04/473 5339, ⓦwww.ambwellington.esteri.it.
**UK** Embassy: 14 Three King's Yard, London W1Y 2EH ⓣ020/7312 2200, ⓦwww.amblondra.esteri.it. Consulates in Edinburgh ⓣ0131/226 3695 and Manchester ⓣ0161/236 9024.
**USA** Embassy: 3000 Whitehaven St NW, Washington DC 20008 ⓣ202/612-4400, ⓦwww.ambwashingtondc.esteri.it. Consulates in Chicago ⓣ312/467-1550, New York ⓣ212/737-9100 and San Francisco ⓣ415/292-9210.

### Embassies and consulates in Italy

**Australia** Embassy: Via Alessandria 215, 00198 Roma ⓣ06.852.721, ⓦwww.australian-embassy.it.
**Canada** Embassy: Via G B de Rossi 27, 00161 Roma ⓣ06.445.981, ⓦwww.canada.it.
**Ireland** Embassy: Piazza di Campitelli 3, 00186 Roma ⓣ06.697.9121.
**New Zealand** Embassy: Via Zara 28, 00198 Roma ⓣ06.441.7171.
**UK** Embassy: Via XX Settembre 80a, 00187 Roma ⓣ06.4220.0001, ⓦwww.britain.it. Consulate in Florence: Lungarno Corsini 2 ⓣ055.284.133.
**US** Embassy: Via V Veneto 119/a, 00187 Roma ⓣ06.46.741, ⓦwww.usembassy.it. Consulate in Florence: Lungarno Vespucci 38 ⓣ055.266.951, ⓦwww.florence.usconsulate.gov.

## Gay and lesbian travellers

Attitudes to gays and lesbians in Tuscany are on the whole tolerant, and Florence has a particularly thriving gay scene, but public displays of affection that extend much beyond hand-holding might raise a few eyebrows, especially outside the bigger towns. The national gay organization ARCI-Gay (ⓦwww.arcigay.it) has branches in most big towns; ⓦwww.gay.it has a wealth of information. The age of consent in Italy is 18.

## Health

If you're arriving in Italy from elsewhere in Europe, North America or Australasia, you don't need any jabs. Citizens of all EU countries are entitled to emergency medical care under the same terms as the residents of the country. As proof of entitlement, British citizens will need a **European Health Insurance Card (EHIC)**, which is free of charge and valid for five years – application forms are issued at UK post offices, or you can apply online at Ⓦwww.dh.gov.uk. Note, however, that the EHIC won't cover the full cost of major treatment, and the high medical charges make travel insurance essential. You normally have to pay the full cost of emergency treatment upfront, and claim it back when you get home (minus a small excess); make very sure you hang onto full doctors' reports, signed prescription details and all receipts.

Italian **pharmacists** (*farmacie*) are well qualified to give advice on minor ailments and to dispense prescriptions; there's generally one open all night in the bigger towns and cities. They work on a rota system, and the address of the one currently open is posted on any farmacia door. If you require a **doctor** (*médico*), ask for help in the first instance at your hotel or the local tourist office. Alternatively look in the Yellow Pages (*Pagine Gialle*): larger towns will have English-speaking doctors. Follow a similar procedure if you have dental problems. Again, keep all receipts for later insurance claims.

If you are taken **seriously ill** or are involved in an **accident**, go to the *Pronto Soccorso* (Casualty/A&E) section of the nearest hospital; in a real emergency, phone Ⓣ113 and ask for *ospedale* or *ambulanza*. Major train stations and airports often have first-aid facilities with qualified doctors on hand.

**Mosquitoes** (*zanzare*) can be a nuisance between June and September; most supermarkets and pharmacies sell sprays, mosquito coils and after-bite cream.

## Insurance

Even though EU health care privileges apply in Italy, you'd do well to take out an insurance policy before travelling to cover against theft, loss, illness or injury. Before paying for a new policy, however, it's worth checking whether you're already covered: some all-risks home insurance policies may cover your possessions when overseas, and many private medical schemes include cover when abroad. In Canada, provincial health plans usually provide partial cover for medical mishaps overseas, while holders of official student/teacher/youth cards in Canada and the US are entitled to meagre accident coverage and hospital in-patient benefits. Students will often find that their student health coverage extends during the vacations and for one term beyond the date of last enrolment.

After checking the possibilities above, you might want to contact a specialist **travel insurance** company, or consider Rough Guides' own travel insurance deal (see box, below). A typical travel insurance policy usually provides cover for the loss of baggage, tickets and – up to a certain limit – cash or cheques, as well as cancellation or curtailment of your journey. Most exclude so-called dangerous sports unless an extra premium is paid: in Italy this can mean scuba-diving, windsurfing, trekking or skiing. If you do take medical coverage, ascertain whether benefits will be paid as treatment proceeds or only after you return home, and whether there is a 24-hour medical emergency number. When securing baggage cover, make sure that the per-article limit will cover your most valuable

### Rough Guides travel insurance

Rough Guides has teamed up with Columbus Direct to offer you tailor-made **travel insurance**. Products include a low-cost **backpacker** option for long stays; a **short break** option for city getaways; a typical **holiday package** option; and others. There are also annual **multi-trip** policies for those who travel regularly. Different sports and activities (trekking, skiing, etc) can usually be included.

See our website (Ⓦwww.roughguides.com/website/shop) for eligibility and purchasing options. Alternatively, UK residents can call Ⓣ0870/033 9988; Australians Ⓣ1300/669 999 and New Zealanders Ⓣ0800/559 911. All other nationalities should call Ⓣ+44 870/890 2843.

possession. If you need to make a claim, you should keep receipts for medicines and medical treatment, and in the event you have anything stolen, you must obtain an official statement from the police.

## Internet

Internet points are now widespread in the larger towns of Tuscany, though many of them are short-lived ventures, occupying business premises on a short lease. The company with the widest network is Internet Train, whose franchises are listed at ⓦwww.internettrain.it. Reckon on paying around €5 for an hour online. It's increasingly common for hotels and even hostels to provide internet access, usually free of charge; in Florence, Siena and a few of Tuscany's more sizeable towns, you'll also come across cafés and bars offering free wi-fi.

## Mail

Opening hours of main **post offices** are usually Monday to Saturday 8.30am to 7.30pm, although smaller offices are open mornings only (Mon–Fri 8.30am–1.00pm, Sat 8.30am–noon). You can also buy **stamps** (*francobolli*) in *tabacchi*, and in some gift shops. The Italian postal system is one of the slowest in Europe so if your letter is urgent make sure you send it *posta prioritaria*, which has varying rates according to weight and destination. Letters can be sent **poste restante** (general delivery) to any Italian post office by addressing them "*Fermo Posta*" followed by the name of the town; your surname should be double-underlined for easier identification, when picking items up take your passport, and – in case of difficulty – make sure they also check under your middle names and initials.

## Maps

The **maps** in this guide should be fine for most purposes, and nearly all tourist offices hand out free maps as well. More detailed maps are produced by a multitude of companies, notably Italy's leading street-plan publisher LAC (Litografia Artistica Cartografica), and the TCI (Touring Club Italiano). Combining the cities on one sheet, the *Rough Guide Map: Florence and Siena* has the additional benefit of being printed on waterproof, crease-resistant paper, as is Rough Guides' 1:200,000 Tuscany map, which has all the information you'll need for driving around the area.

## Money

The Italian currency is the **euro** (€), which is composed of 100 cents. You'll usually get the best rate of exchange (*cambio*) from a **bank**. Banking hours vary slightly, but generally are Monday to Friday 8.30am–1.30pm and 3–4.30pm, with some major branches staying open continuously 8.30am–4.30pm and opening for a couple of hours on Saturday morning. American Express and Travelex offices are open longer hours and in the larger towns you'll find an **exchange bureau** at the train station that stays open late. As a rule, though, the kiosks offer pretty bad rates.

Although it's a good idea to have some cash when you first arrive, **credit and debit cards** can be used either in an ATM (*bancomat*) or over the counter. MasterCard, Visa and American Express are accepted in most larger city stores, hotels and restaurants, but cash still reigns supreme in much of Italy, so check first before embarking on a big meal out. ATMs are found in even small towns, and most accept all major cards. Remember that all cash advances on a credit card are treated as loans, with interest accruing daily.

## Opening hours and public holidays

Most shops in Tuscany are open daily from 8 or 9am until around 1pm, and again from about 3pm until 7 or 8pm; in Florence, though, it's become increasingly common for shops to

### Public holidays

**Jan 1**
**Jan 6** Epiphany
**March/April** Good Friday, Easter Monday
**April 25** Liberation Day
**May 1** Labour Day
**June 2** Day of the Republic
**Aug 15** Ferragosto; Assumption
**Nov 1** Ognissanti; All Saints
**Nov 4** National Unity Day
**Dec 8** Immaculate Conception
**Dec 25**
**Dec 26**

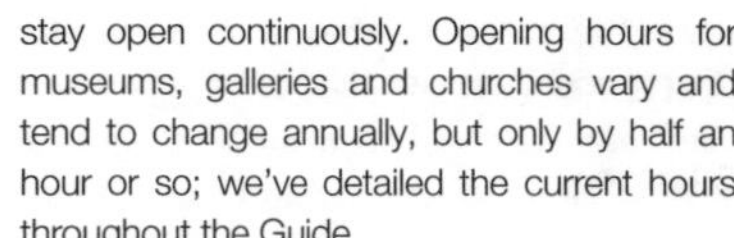

stay open continuously. Opening hours for museums, galleries and churches vary and tend to change annually, but only by half an hour or so; we've detailed the current hours throughout the Guide.

Whenever you visit, you may well find your travel plans disrupted by **national holidays** and local saints' days. Local religious holidays don't generally close down shops and businesses, but they do mean that accommodation space may be tight. However everything, except some bars and restaurants, closes on Italy's official national holidays.

## Phones

**Public phone** tariffs are among the most expensive in Europe. For national calls, the off-peak period runs Monday to Friday 6.30pm to 8am, then Saturday 1pm until Monday 8am. Area codes are now an integral part of the number and must always be dialled, regardless of where you're calling from. Numbers beginning ⓣ800 are free, an English-speaking operator is on ⓣ170 and international directory enquiries is ⓣ176.

To use your **mobile phone**, check with your provider whether it will work in Italy and what the charges will be. Technology in Italy is GSM (ⓦwww.gsmworld.com). Unless you have a triband phone, it's unlikely that a US mobile will work elsewhere.

## Time

Italy is on Central European Time (CET): 1hr ahead of London, 6 hours ahead of New York and 8 hours behind Sydney.

## Tourist information

Before you leave home, you might want to contact the Italian State Tourist Office (ENIT) for a selection of maps and accommodation listings – though you can usually pick up far fuller information from tourist offices in Italy. Details of every town's tourist offices are given in the Guide, along with individual town websites. The following are general websites on Tuscany and Italy.

ⓦ**www.enit.it** Italian State Tourist Board.
ⓦ**www.meteo.it** Italian weather forecast.
ⓦ**www.museionline.it** Links to museums and exhibition sites.
ⓦ**www.paginegialle.it** Italian *Yellow* Pages.
ⓦ**www.terraditoscana.com** Well-designed, informative site covering every aspect of Tuscany from walking and sleeping to wild flowers and local cuisine.
ⓦ**www.turismo.toscana.it** Official website of the Tuscan tourist board.
ⓦ**www.zoomata.com** New ezine with loads of information about Italy today.

## Travellers with disabilities

As part of the European *Turismo per Tutti* (Tourism for All) project – administered in Italy by the national disabled support organization CO.IN – museum, transport and accommodation facilities have improved remarkably in recent years. However, stairs and steps continue to present the most obvious difficulties (restaurants often have their bathrooms downstairs, for instance), while other problems can arise from cars being parked thoughtlessly, and from the sheer distances of car parks from old-town centres. Public transport is becoming more attuned to the needs of disabled travellers, but town bus services are still more of a challenge than the trains. Another thing to bear in mind – especially in Florence – is that budget hotels often occupy the upper floors of town houses, and may not have elevator access; always check the hotel website before booking.

### Calling home from abroad

Note that the initial zero is omitted from the area code when dialling the UK, Ireland, Australia and New Zealand from abroad.
**US and Canada** international access code + 1 + area code.
**Australia** international access code + 61 + city code.
**New Zealand** international access code + 64 + city code.
**UK** international access code + 44 + city code.
**Republic of Ireland** international access code + 353 + city code.
**South Africa** international access code + 27 + city code.

# Florence

# The City

Arriving in Florence: Practicalities ........................................... 41

1 Piazza del Duomo and around.......................................... 46

2 Piazza della Signoria and around ..................................... 62

3 West of the centre: from Via dei Calzaiuoli to the Cascine ........................................................... 88

4 North of the centre: the San Lorenzo, San Marco and Annunziata districts.......................................................... 106

5 East of the centre: Santa Croce to Campo di Marte...... 133

6 Oltrarno ........................................................................ 145

7 Fiesole.......................................................................... 164

# Arriving in Florence: Practicalities

Florence is an easy city to find your way around: most of the main sights lie north of the Arno, the river which bisects the city from west to east, but a handful are scattered in the district to the south, an area known as the Oltrarno. In both cases distances between sights are easily manageable on foot, with very few exceptions.

North of the river the city hinges around two main piazzas, **Piazza del Duomo** and **Piazza della Signoria**, and their connecting street, Via dei Calzaiuoli. Here you'll find some of the big set-piece sights – the Duomo, Baptistery and Uffizi gallery – as well as attractions such as the Palazzo Vecchio and the Museo dell'Opera del Duomo (the cathedral museum).

Immediately to the east of these pivotal squares there's the magnificent **Bargello** sculpture gallery, and beyond that lies an appealing district which is focused on the great church of **Santa Croce**. To the north of the centre you'll find the **San Lorenzo** quarter, visited primarily for its markets, its church, and the Michelangelo sculptures in the Cappelle Medicee. Further north, the **San Marco** area has two key sights: the Museo di San Marco, a monastery filled with paintings by Fra' Angelico, and the Accademia, home to Michelangelo's *David*. On the western flank of the city centre, the streets around the medieval church of **Orsanmichele** hide some low-key attractions among clusters of designer shops. Further north and west of here, towards the train station, the principal attraction is the remarkable church of **Santa Maria Novella**.

South of the river, in the **Oltrarno**, the city has a different feel: somewhat quieter on the whole, and a touch more pleasant to explore for its own sake. The central area, just across the Ponte Vecchio, centres on the huge **Palazzo Pitti**, with its major picture gallery and the lovely Bóboli gardens behind. To the west are two important churches and their equally well-known squares: **Santo Spirito**'s piazza is the hub of a lively and increasingly gentrified neighbourhood, while **Santa Maria del Carmine** is home to the Cappella Brancacci and its famous fresco cycle. The chief sight of eastern Oltrarno is the exquisite hilltop church of **San Miniato al Monte**, one of Florence's principal landmarks.

## Arrival

Unless you're driving into the city, your point of arrival will be **Santa Maria Novella station**, which is located within a few minutes' walk of the heart of the historic centre: bus connections as well as train services terminate here.

### By air

If you're flying to **Pisa** – the routine approach – it's an effortless hour or so's journey by train from the airport into Florence. Flying to Florence's own ever-expanding airport at **Perétola**, it's about twenty minutes by shuttle bus or taxi to the city centre. An alternative arrival point is **Bologna** (Marconi airport), though this takes longer and involves both bus and train transfers.

#### Pisa airport

Most scheduled and charter flights fly to Pisa's **Galileo Galilei** airport (Ⓣ050.849.300, Ⓦwww.pisa-airport.com), 95km west of Florence. For details of connections between Pisa airport and Florence, see p.229.

#### Perétola airport

A small but increasing number of international air services use Florence's **Perétola** (or Amerigo Vespucci) airport (Ⓣ055.306.1300, Ⓦwww.aeroporto.firenze.it), 5km northwest of the city centre. There's a tiny arrivals hall with an exchange machine, half a dozen car-rental desks, a lost-baggage counter and a small tourist office (daily 8.30am–8.30pm; Ⓣ055.315.874). The SITA and ATAF bus companies operate a joint service called **Volainbus** (Ⓦwww.ataf.net), which provides half-hourly shuttles into the city from immediately outside the arrivals area. The first bus into the city is at 6am (last 11.30pm), the first out to the airport at 5.30am (last 11pm). Tickets (€4.50) can be bought on board or from machines at the airport and bus station, and the journey takes thirty minutes. Most buses arrive at and depart from the main SITA bus terminal on Via Santa Caterina da Siena, off Piazza della Stazione, a few steps west of Santa Maria Novella train station; after 9pm, however, the buses depart from outside **Bar Cristallo** in Largo Alinari, off the eastern side of Piazza della Stazione. A **taxi** from Perétola into central Florence should cost about €20 and will take around twenty minutes.

### Bologna airport

Bologna's **Marconi** airport (Ⓦwww.bologna-airport.it) – about the same distance from Florence as Pisa – is an alternative gateway. Aerobus shuttles depart every twenty minutes (7.30am–11.45pm) from outside the airport's Terminal A to Bologna's main train station (about 25min), from where regular trains run to Florence's Santa Maria Novella station in about an hour. Note, however, that Ryanair services to Bologna in fact fly to Forlì airport, which is more than 60km southeast of Bologna, and very inconvenient for Florence.

## By train and bus

Nearly all **trains** arrive at Florence's main central station **Santa Maria Novella**, called "**Firenze SMN**" on the timetables. It's located just north of the church and square of Santa Maria Novella, a couple of blocks west of the Duomo. (A few trains – mostly in the small hours of the morning – use Campo di Marte station, over in the east of the city, from where there are regular buses into the centre.) At SMN station you'll find left-luggage facilities (see p.210) and a 24-hour pharmacy. While in and around the station, you should keep a close eye on your bags at all times: it's a prime hunting ground for thieves and **pickpockets**. Also avoid the concourse's various taxi and hotel touts, however friendly they may appear.

A few **bus** services from outside Florence pull in at the bus bays on the east side of the train station. The majority, however, use the station in Via Santa Caterina da Siena, a very short distance west of the station's entrance.

## By car

Only residents are allowed to **park** on the streets in the centre, so you have to leave your car in one of the city's main car parks. North of the Arno, the car parks nearest the centre are underneath the train station, just off Piazza della Libertà, and at Piazza Annigoni, near Santa Croce; south of the river the best option is Piazza della Calza, at the southwest tip of the Bóboli gardens. The lowest tariff you'll find is around €1 per hour; a more typical rate is €1.50, or around €15 for 24 hours.

If you want to leave your car for a prolonged period, try Piazzale Michelangelo, the nearest substantial **free parking** area to the centre. It's about twenty minutes' walk to the Piazza della Signoria from here, or a short ride into the centre of town on buses #12 or #13. Watch out for a **scam** in which bogus car-park attendants direct you into a parking space, thus implying there's a charge: there isn't.

> Note that there is a double **address** system in Florence, one for businesses and one for all other properties – that, at least, is the theory behind it, though in fact the distinction is far from rigorous. Business addresses are followed by the letter **r** (for *rosso*) and are marked on the building with a red number on a white plate, sometimes with an r after the numeral, but not always. There's no connection between the two series: no. 20 might be a long way from no. 20r. Properties are numbered according to their relation to the river: if the street is parallel to the Arno, numbers start from the east and proceed west; if the street is perpendicular to the river, the numbering starts from the end nearer the water.

# Information

For information about Florence's sights and events, the main **tourist office** is at Via Cavour 1r, five minutes' walk north of the Duomo (Mon–Sat 8.30am–6.30pm, Sun 8.30am–1pm; Ⓣ055.290.832 or 055.290.833, Ⓦwww.firenzeturismo.it). Smaller and less busy offices are to be found just off Piazza Santa Croce at Borgo Santa Croce 29r (April–Oct Mon–Sat 9am–7pm, Sun 9am–2pm; Nov–March Mon–Sat 9am–5pm, Sun 9am–2pm; Ⓣ055.234.0444), and close to the train station, at Piazza della Stazione 4, at the back of Santa Maria Novella church (Mon–Sat 8.30am–7pm, Sun 8.30am–2pm; ⓣ055.212.245). All three provide an adequate **map** and various leaflets, including a sheet with updated opening hours and entrance charges. The office at Via Cavour also handles information on the whole of Florence province, while the office at the station can book accommodation for a fee.

One of the best sources of information on events is **Firenze Spettacolo** (ⓦwww.firenzespettacolo.it; €1.80), a monthly, partly bilingual listings magazine available from bookshops and larger newsstands. Also useful is **The Florentine** (ⓦwww.theflorentine.net) a bi-weekly English-language paper, available at the tourist office, most bookshops and various other spots (the website lists all of the places it can be picked up).

## City transport

Within the historic centre, walking is generally the most efficient way of getting around, and the imposition of the **zona a traffico limitato** (ZTL) – which limits traffic in the centre to residents' cars, delivery vehicles and public transport – has reduced the once unbearable pollution and noise, though many of the central streets are nonetheless so busy that you'll find it hard to believe that any restrictions are in operation.

### Buses

Pending completion of the Tramvia, if you want to cross town in a hurry, or visit some of the peripheral sights, your best option is to use one of the frequent and speedy orange **ATAF buses**.

**Tickets** are valid for unlimited use within seventy minutes (€1.20), 24 hours (€5) or 72 hours (€12). A **Biglietto Multiplo** gives four seventy-minute tickets for €4.50; better value is the ATAF electronic card ticket called the **Carta Agile**, which comes in two versions – the €10 one is equivalent to ten seventy-minute tickets, whereas the €20 card is equivalent to 21. Each Carta Agile can be used by more than one passenger at a time, and is valid for one year. Tickets can be bought from the main ATAF information office in the bays to the east of Santa Maria Novella train station (daily 7am–8pm; ⓦwww.ataf.net); from any shops and stalls displaying

### The Tramvia

A few years ago, in an attempt to solve the perpetual problem of traffic management in central Florence, the authorities planned to construct something called the **MicroMetro**, a neat little loop which would have operated in one direction only, following a tight circuit from the train station, past the Duomo and Santa Croce, then over into Oltrarno before returning to the station. This project was eventually shelved, partly because of the difficulties of digging tunnels deep enough to get under the Arno, and has now been replaced by a highly controversial tram network called **Tramvia**. This is intended to consist of three lines: one connecting Santa Maria Novella with Scandicci, to the southwest of the city; the second running from Perétola to Piazza della Libertà, via the station; and the last going from Careggi, to the north of the city centre, all the way to Bagno a Ripoli, in the southeast.

Objectors argued from the start that the streets in the centre of Florence are simply too narrow to accommodate tramlines, and their arguments gained force when it was revealed that to squeeze the trains past Piazza della Signoria it would be necessary to knock a lump out of the Palazzo Vecchio. That aspect of the masterplan was ditched, and construction of the Tramvia is now going ahead, but – leaving aside the question as to whether Florence is suited to such a system – there are various other tricky local issues to be solved, such as how to run a line past the Duomo without disfiguring this unique urban landscape with a web of overhead cables. At the time of publication, just one line – #1, from Santa Maria Novella to Scandicci – was anywhere near completion. It seems a fair bet that it'll be quite some time before the system is operational.

the ATAF sign; and from automatic machines all over Florence. Once you're on board, you must stamp your ticket in the machine to begin its period of validity; the Carta Agile is validated electronically by the same machine. There's a hefty on-the-spot **fine** for any passenger without a validated ticket.

Most of the routes that are useful to tourists stop by the station, notably #7 (for Fiesole), and #12/#13: #13 goes clockwise through Piazzale Michelangelo, San Miniato and Porta Romana (all on the south side of the river), while #12 goes anticlockwise round the same route. In addition to these, small **electric buses** run along four very convenient central city routes. Bus #A runs from the station right through the historic centre, passing close by the Duomo and Signoria, then heading east just north of Santa Croce; #B follows the north bank of the Arno; while #C descends from Piazza San Marco, heading south past Santa Croce and across the Ponte delle Grazie on its way to Via Bardi. These three buses follow similar routes on their return journeys. Bus #D leaves the station and crosses the river at Ponte Vespucci; from here it becomes a handy Oltrarno bus, running right along the south bank of the river and, on the return journey, jinking up past Palazzo Pitti, Santo Spirito and the Carmine church on its way back to the Ponte Vespucci.

## Taxis

Taxis are white with yellow trim. You can't flag down a cab in the street – you have to phone for one (ⓣ055.4242, 055.4798, 055.4799 or

## Florence museum admission

All of Florence's state-run museums belong to an association called **Firenze Musei** (ⓦwww.firenzemusei.it), which sets aside a daily quota of tickets that can be reserved in advance. The Uffizi, the Accademia and the Bargello belong to this group, as do the Palazzo Pitti museums (including the Bóboli gardens), the Medici chapels in San Lorenzo, the archeological museum and the San Marco museum.

You can **reserve tickets** (booking fee of €4 for Uffizi and Accademia, €3 for the rest) by phoning ⓣ055.294.883 (Mon–Fri 8.30am–6.30pm, Sat 8.30am–12.30pm), or through the Firenze Musei website, or at the Firenze Musei booth at Orsanmichele (Mon–Sat 10am–5.30pm), or at the museums themselves, in the case of the Uffizi and Pitti. If you use the phone, an English-speaking operator will allocate you a ticket for a specific hour, to be collected at the museum, again at a specific time, shortly before entry. That's the theory, but in reality the line tends to be engaged for long periods at a stretch, so persèverance is nearly always required. Generally, the under-publicized Orsanmichele booth – which is set into the wall of the church on the Via Calzaiuoli side – is the easiest option. Pre-booking is very strongly recommended at any time of year for the Uffizi (see p.71 for more) and the Accademia, whose allocation of reservable tickets is often sold out many days ahead.

If you're in Florence for an extended stay, and intend to visit a lot of museums, it may well be worth investing in an **Amici degli Uffizi** card. Costing €60 (€40 for those under 26), it's valid for a year and gives you unlimited access (with no queuing), not just to the Uffizi but to all of Florence's state museums. The card can be obtained at the Amici degli Uffizi desk at the Uffizi (Tues–Sun 10am–5pm), but they issue a very limited number each day, so you may find that you'll have to wait several days to receive your card. Better to order it through the website: ⓦwww.amicidegliuffizi.it.

Note that on-the-door admission to all state-run museums is free for EU citizens under 18 and over 65, on presentation of a passport; 18–25s get a fifty percent discount, as do teachers, on proof of identity. Nearly all of Florence's major museums are routinely **closed on Monday**, though some are open for a couple of Mondays each month. In the majority of cases, museum ticket offices close thirty minutes before the museum itself. At the Palazzo Vecchio and Museo Stibbert, however, it's one hour before, while at the Uffizi, Bargello, Museo dell'Opera del Duomo, the dome of the Duomo, the Campanile and Pitti museums it's 45 minutes.

055.4390) or go to a taxi rank, of which there are plenty in the centre of town. Key locations include the station, Piazza della Repubblica, Piazza del Duomo, Piazza Santa Maria Novella, Piazza San Marco, Piazza Santa Croce and Piazza Santa Trìnita. If you call for a cab, you'll be given the car's code name – usually a town, city or country – and its number, both of which are emblazoned on the vehicle, together with the phone number of the company. Italians tend not to order cabs far in advance: simply call up a few minutes beforehand.

All rides are **metered**; at the start of the journey the meter should be set at €3.20, or €5.10 if it's a Sunday or public holiday, or €6.40 between 10pm and 6am. Supplements are payable for journeys outside the city limits (to Fiesole, for example), for each piece of luggage placed in the boot (€1), and for phoning for a cab (€1.90). The charge per kilometre is €1.

# Piazza del Duomo and around

From the train station, first-time visitors inevitably gravitate towards **Piazza del Duomo**, beckoned by the pinnacle of Brunelleschi's dome, which lords it over the cityscape with an authority unmatched by any architectural creation in any other Italian city. Yet even though the magnitude of the **Duomo** is apparent from a distance, the close-up sight of the church and the adjacent **Baptistery** still comes as a jolt, their colourful patterned exteriors making a startling contrast with the dun-toned buildings around. Each of these great buildings is as remarkable inside as out, and an ascent of the cathedral's **dome** will give you astounding views over the city to the hazy Tuscan hills beyond.

After exploring the cathedral, you can escape the crowds by climbing the **Campanile**, the Duomo's belltower, or visit the **Museo dell'Opera del Duomo**, a repository for works of art removed over the centuries from the Duomo, Baptistery and Campanile. With pieces by Donatello, Michelangelo and many others, it's one of the city's two great sculpture collections, the other being the Bargello. On a considerably smaller scale, the **Loggia del Bigallo** contains a tiny museum relating to one of the city's oldest philanthropic institutions, while the **Museo di Firenze com'era** – a short distance east of the piazza – is devoted to the evolution of the Florentine cityscape. If you're in need of a break after this architectural and artistic overload, you can recharge your batteries at one of the cafés on nearby **Piazza della Repubblica**, a square that was planned as a showcase for the capital city of the newly united Italy.

# The Duomo

Some time in the seventh century the seat of the Bishop of Florence was transferred from San Lorenzo to Santa Reparata, a sixth-century church that stood on the site of the present-day **Duomo**, or **Santa Maria del Fiore** (Mon–Fri 10am–5pm, Thurs closes 3.30pm, Sat 10am–4.45pm, Sun 1.30–4.45pm; on first Sat of month closes 3.30pm; free). Later generations modified this older church until 1294, when Florence's rulers were stung into action by the magnificence of newly commissioned cathedrals in Pisa and Siena. Their own cathedral, they lamented, was too "crudely built and too small for such a city".

A suitably immodest plan to remedy this shortcoming was ordered from Arnolfo di Cambio, who drafted a scheme to create the largest church in the Roman Catholic world and "surpass anything of its kind produced by the Greeks and Romans in the times of their greatest power". Progress on the project faltered after Arnolfo's death in 1302, but by 1380 Francesco Talenti and a string of other architects had brought the nave to completion. By 1418 the tribunes (apses) and the dome's supporting drum were also completed. Only the dome itself – no small matter – remained unfinished (see box, p.52).

## The exterior

Parts of the Duomo's **exterior** date back to Arnolfo's era, but most of the overblown and pernickety main **facade** is a nineteenth-century simulacrum of a Gothic front. The original facade, which was never more than quarter-finished, was pulled down in 1587 on the orders of Ferdinand I. A competition to produce a new facade proved fruitless, and for three centuries the cathedral remained faceless. After Florence became capital of Italy in 1865, however, no fewer than 92 plans were submitted. The winning entry, by the otherwise obscure Emilio de Fabris, was completed in 1887. To its credit, the new frontage at least retained the original colour scheme and materials, with marble quarried from three different sources: white from Carrara, red from the Maremma and green from Prato.

The cathedral's south side is the oldest part of the exterior but the most attractive adornment is the **Porta della Mandorla** (number 32 on our plan), on the other side. This takes its name from the almond-shaped frame (or *mandorla*) that contains the grime-streaked relief of *The Assumption of the Virgin* (1414–21), sculpted by

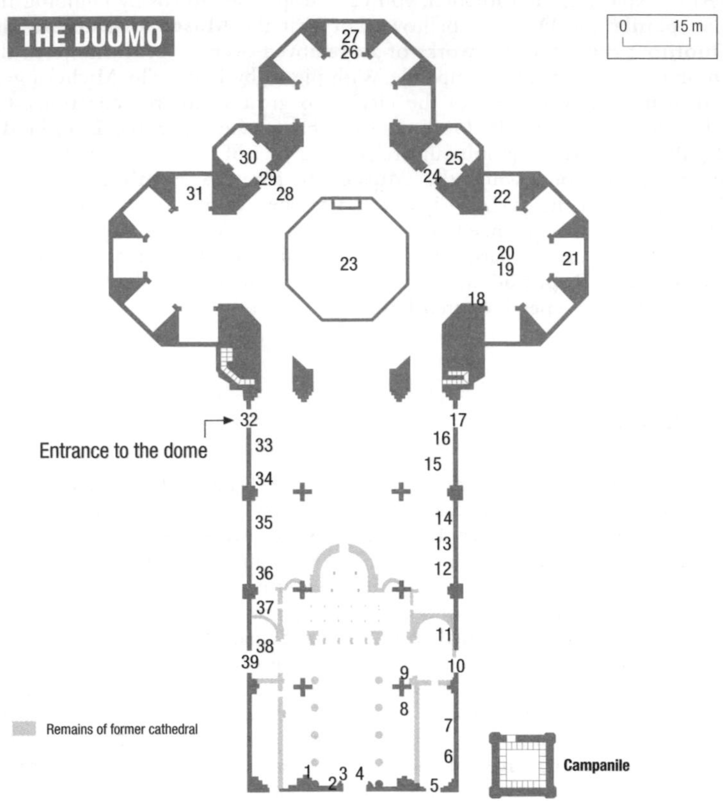


1 Stained glass: St Stephen (left), Assumption (centre) and St Lawrence (right), Lorenzo Ghiberti
2 Tomb of Antonio d'Orso, bishop of Florence (1323), Tino da Camaino
3 Mosaic: *Coronation of the Virgin* (1300), attributed to Gaddo Gaddi
4 Clock (1443) – decoration, Paolo Uccello
5 Stained glass: *St Lawrence and Angels*, Lorenzo Ghiberti
6 Tondo: *Bust of Brunelleschi* (1447), Andrea Cavalcanti
7 Bust: *Giotto at Work* (1490), Benedetto da Maiano
8 Gothic water stoup (1380), attributed to Urbano da Cortona
9 Entrance and steps to Santa Reparata
10 Porta del Campanile
11 Painting: *St Bartholomew Enthroned* (1408), Rossello di Jacopo Franchi
12 Painted sepulchral monument: Fra Luigi Marsili (1439), Bicci di Lorenzo
13 Statue: *Isaiah* (1427), Bernardo Ciuffagni
14 Painted sepulchral monument: Archbishop Pietro Corsino of Florence (1422), Bicci di Lorenzo
15 Stained glass: *Six Saints* (1395), Agnolo Gaddi
16 Bust: Marsilio Ficino (1521), philosopher friend of Cosimo de' Medici/ holding a copy of Plato's works
17 Porta dei Canoncini: sculpture (1395–99), Lorenzo d'Ambrogio
18 Eight statues of the Apostles (1547–72) against the pillars of the octagon
19 Tribune: each tribune has five chapels; each chapel has two levels of stained glass, most by Lorenzo Ghiberti
20 Frescoes below windows of west and east tribunes: *Saints* (1440), attributed to Bicci di Lorenzo
21 Altar, attributed to Michelozzo
22 Fresco fragment: *Madonna del Popolo* (13th century), attributed to Giotto
23 Dome fresco cycle: *The Last Judgement* (1572–79), Giorgio Vasari and Federico Zuccari
24 Enamelled terracotta (above door): *Ascension* (1450), Luca della Robbia
25 Sagrestia Vecchia (Old Sacristy)
26 Bronze reliquary (1432–42) of St Zenobius (below altar), Lorenzo Ghiberti
27 Candle-holders: *Two Angels* (1450), Luca della Robbia
28 Enamelled terracotta: *Resurrection* (1444), Luca della Robbia
29 Bronze doors (1446–67), Luca della Robbia and Michelozzo
30 Sagrestia Nuova (New Sacristy): intarsia (1436–45), Benedetto and Giuliano da Maiano
31 Former site of Michelangelo's Pietà, currently in the Museo dell'Opera
32 Porta della Mandorla: sculpture, Nanni di Banco and Donatello
33 Painting: *Dante explaining the Divine Comedy* (1465), Domenico di Michelino
34 Fresco: *SS Cosmas and Damian* (1429), Bicci di Lorenzo; two windows by Agnolo Gaddi
35 Statue (in recess) designed for old cathedral facade: *King David* (1434), Bernardo Ciuffagni
36 Equestrian portrait: *Sir John Hawkwood* (1436), Paolo Uccello
37 Equestrian portrait: *Niccolò da Tolentino* (1456), Andrea del Castagno
38 Bust: *Antonio Squarcialupi* (former cathedral organist, 1490), Benedetto da Maiano
39 *The Prophet Joshua* (1415), Nanni di Bartolo; the head is by Donatello

Nanni di Banco; the lunette features a mosaic of the *Annunciation* (1491) to a design by Ghirlandaio. The two heads in profile either side of the gable might be early works by Donatello.

## The interior

The Duomo's **interior** – a vast, uncluttered enclosure of bare masonry – is the converse of its exterior. The fourth-largest church in Europe, it once held a congregation of ten thousand to hear Savonarola preach, and the ambience is still more that of a public assembly hall than of a devotional building. Its apparently barren walls, however, hold a far greater accumulation of treasures than at first appears.

The most conspicuous decorations are a pair of memorials to *condottieri* (mercenary commanders). Paolo Uccello's monument to **Sir John Hawkwood** (36), created in 1436, is often cited as the epitome of Florentine mean-spiritedness; according to local folklore – unsupported by any evidence – the mercenary captain of Florence's army was promised a proper equestrian statue as his memorial, then was posthumously fobbed off with this trompe l'oeil version. Perhaps the slight was deserved. Before being employed by Florence, Hawkwood and his White Company had marauded their way through Tuscany, holding entire cities to ransom under threat of ransack. The monument features a strange shift of perspective, with the pedestal depicted from a different angle from what's on it; it's known that Uccello was ordered to repaint the horse and rider, presumably because he'd shown them from the same point of view as the base, which must have displayed the horse's belly and not much else. Look back at the entrance wall and you'll see another Uccello contribution to the interior – a **clock** (4) adorned with the four Evangelists. It uses the old *hora italica*, common in Italy until the eighteenth century, when the 24th hour of the day ended at sunset.

Andrea del Castagno's monument to **Niccolò da Tolentino** (37), created twenty years later than the Hawkwood fresco, is clearly derived from it, but has an aggressive edge that's typical of this artist. Just beyond the horsemen, Domenico di Michelino's 1465 work *Dante Explaining the Divine Comedy* (34) gives Brunelleschi's dome – then only nearing completion – a place scarcely less prominent than the mountain of Purgatory. Dante stands outside the walls, a symbol of his exile from Florence.

Judged by mere size, the major work of art in the Duomo is the 1572–79 fresco of **The Last Judgement** (23), which fills much of the interior of the dome. At the time of its execution, however, a substantial body of opinion thought Vasari's and Zuccari's combined effort did nothing but deface Brunelleschi's masterpiece, and quite a few people today are of the same opinion.

Barriers usually prevent you from going any further than Michelino's painting, but if you're lucky you'll be able to get a peep into the **Sagrestia Nuova** (30), where the lavish panelling is inlaid with beautiful intarsia work (1436–45) by Benedetto and Giuliano Maiano, notably a delicate trompe l'oeil *Annunciation* in the centre of the wall facing the door. The relief of the *Resurrection* (1442) above the entrance is by Luca della Robbia, his first important commission in the glazed terracotta for which he became famous. The stunning **sacristy door** (1445–69), created in conjunction with Michelozzo, was his only work in bronze. It was in this sacristy that Lorenzo de' Medici took refuge in 1478 after his brother Giuliano had been mortally stabbed on the altar steps by the Pazzi conspirators (see box, pp.50–51): the bulk of della Robbia's recently installed doors protected him from his would-be assassins. Small portraits on the handles commemorate the brothers.

## The Pazzi Conspiracy

The **Pazzi Conspiracy**, perhaps the most compelling of all Florentine acts of treachery, had its roots in the election in 1472 of **Sixtus IV**, a pope who distributed money and favours with a largesse remarkable even by papal standards. Six of his supposed nephews were made cardinals, one of them, the uncouth **Girolamo Riario**, coming in for particularly preferential treatment, probably because he was Sixtus's illegitimate son. Sixtus's plan was that Riario should take over the town of Imola as a base for papal expansion, and accordingly he approached Lorenzo de' Medici for the necessary loan. Aware that Imola was too close to Milan and Bologna to be allowed to fall into papal hands, Lorenzo rebuffed the pope, despite the importance of the Vatican account with the Medici bank, and the family's role as agents for the papacy's alum mines in Tuscany. (Alum was a vital part of the dyeing industry, and therefore essential to Florence's textile trade.) Enraged by the snub, and by Lorenzo's refusal to recognize **Francesco Salviati** as archbishop of Pisa (Sixtus had ignored an agreement by which appointments within the Florentine domain could only be made by mutual agreement), Sixtus turned to the Pazzi, the Medici's leading Florentine rivals as bankers in Rome.

Three co-conspirators met in Rome in the early months of 1477: Riario, now in possession of Imola but eager for greater spoils; Salviati, incandescent at Lorenzo's veto and desperate to become archbishop of Florence; and **Francesco de' Pazzi**, head of the Pazzi's Rome operation and determined to usurp Medici power in Florence. Any plot, however, required military muscle, and the man chosen to provide it, a plain-speaking mercenary called **Montesecco**, proved intensely wary of the whole enterprise: "Beware of what you do," he counselled, "Florence is a big affair." In the end he made his cooperation conditional on papal blessing, a benediction that was readily obtained. "I do not wish the death of anyone on any account," was Sixtus's mealy-mouthed observation, "since it does not accord with our office to consent to such a thing" – yet he knew full well Lorenzo's death was essential if the plot was to succeed. "Go, and do what you wish," he added, "provided there be no killing." **Jacopo de' Pazzi**, the Pazzi's wizened godfather, was also won over by Sixtus's disingenuous support, despite being on good terms with the Medici

Across the way, in a section that's invariably closed off to visitors, della Robbia's *Ascension* (1450) can be seen above the door of the **Sagrestia Vecchia** (25); it was once accompanied by Donatello's *cantoria*, or choir-loft, now in the Museo dell'Opera. Luca della Robbia's equally fine *cantoria* (in the same museum) occupied a matching position above the Sagrestia Nuova.

### Santa Reparata

In the 1960s, remnants of the Duomo's predecessor, **Santa Reparata** (9), were uncovered underneath the west end of the nave, where a flight of steps leads down into the excavation. The remains (admission €3) are extensive, as the nave of the Duomo was built on the same alignment several feet above that of the old church, which was thus not fully demolished. Subsequent excavations have revealed a complicated jigsaw of Roman, Paleochristian and Romanesque remains, plus fragments of mosaics and fourteenth-century frescoes. The explanatory diagrams tend to intensify the confusion: to make sense of it all, you'll have to keep referring to the colour-coded model in the farthest recess of the crypt. In 1972, further digging revealed **Brunelleschi's tomb**, an unassuming marble slab so simple that it had lain forgotten under the south aisle. The tombstone's present position is hardly any more glorious (it can be seen, without paying, through a grille to the left at the foot of the steps), but the

After numerous false starts, it was decided to **murder** Lorenzo and Giuliano whilst they attended Mass in the cathedral. The date set was Sunday, April 26, 1478. Montesecco, however, now refused "to add sacrilege to murder", so Lorenzo's murder was delegated to two embittered priests, Maffei and Bagnone, whereas Giuliano was to be dispatched by Francesco de' Pazzi and **Bernardo Baroncelli**, a violent Pazzi sidekick deeply in debt to the family. Salviati, meanwhile, accompanied by an armed troop, was to seize control of the Palazzo della Signoria.

It all went horribly wrong. Giuliano was killed in a crazed frenzy, his skull shattered and his body rent with nineteen stab wounds, but Lorenzo managed to escape, fleeing wounded to the Duomo's new sacristy, where he and his supporters barricaded themselves behind its heavy bronze doors. Across the city, Salviati was separated from his troops, thanks to newly installed secret doors and locks in the Palazzo della Signoria, and arrested by the *Gonfaloniere*, Cesare Petrucci.

Apprised of the plot, a furious mob dispensed summary justice to several of the conspirators: Salviati's troops were massacred, whilst Salviati and Francesco de' Pazzi were hanged from a window of the Palazzo della Signoria. Of the latter execution, Poliziano, the eminent humanist, noted that "as the archbishop rolled and struggled at the end of his rope, his eyes goggling in his head, he fixed his teeth into Francesco de' Pazzi's naked body". Maffei and Bagnone, the bungling priests, were castrated and hanged. Baroncelli escaped to Constantinople but was extradited and executed. Montesecco was tortured, but given a soldier's execution in the Bargello. Jacopo de' Pazzi's end was the most sordid. Having escaped Florence, he was recaptured, tortured, stripped naked and hanged alongside the decomposing body of Salviati. He was then buried in Santa Croce, but exhumed by the mob, who blamed heavy rains on his evil spirit. His corpse was dragged through the streets, tipped in a ditch, and finally propped up outside the Pazzi palace, where his rotting head was used as door knocker. Eventually the putrefying body was thrown in the Arno, fished out, flogged and hanged again by a gang of children and finally cast back into the river.

architect does at least have the honour of being one of the very few Florentines to be buried in the Duomo itself.

## The dome

Climbing the **dome** (Mon–Fri 8.30am–7pm, Sat 8.30am–5.40pm; €6) is an amazing experience, both for the views from the top and for the insights it offers into Brunelleschi's engineering genius. Be prepared to queue at the Porta della Mandorla entrance, on the north side of the church; also be ready for the 463 lung-busting steps, and claustrophobics should note that the climb involves some confined spaces.

After an initial ascent, you emerge onto a narrow gallery that runs around the interior of the dome, with a dizzying view down onto the maze-patterned pavement of the nave. It's also the best vantage point from which to inspect the seven **stained-glass roundels**, designed by Uccello, Ghiberti, Castagno and Donatello, below Vasari's *Last Judgement* fresco. Beyond the gallery, you enter the more cramped confines of the dome itself. As you clamber up between the inner and outer shells, you can observe many ingenious features of Brunelleschi's construction: the ribs and arches, the herringbone brickwork, the wooden struts that support the outer shell – even the hooks and holes left for future generations of repairers. From the base of the white marble lantern that crowns the dome, the views across the city are breathtaking.



## Brunelleschi's dome

Since Arnolfo di Cambio's model of the Duomo collapsed under its own weight some time in the fourteenth century, nobody has been sure quite how the architect intended to crown his achievement. What is known is that in 1367, half a century after Arnolfo's death, the master mason Neri di Fioravanti proposed the construction of a magnificent **cupola** (dome) that was to span nearly 43m, broader than the dome of Rome's Pantheon, and rise from a base some 55m above the floor of the nave – taller than the highest vaulting of any Gothic cathedral. Just as radical was Fioravanti's decision to dispense with flying buttresses, regarded as ugly vestiges of the Gothic barbarism of enemy states such as France and Milan.

There was just one problem: nobody had worked out how to build the thing. Medieval arches were usually built on wooden "centring", a network of timbers that held the stone in place until the mortar was set. In the case of the Duomo, the weight of the stone would have been too great for the timber (the entire dome is thought to weigh some 33,000 tonnes) and the space to be spanned was too great for the measuring cords that would be needed to guide the masons – any cord strung across the church would sag and stretch too much for accuracy. A committee of the masons' guild was set up to solve the dilemma. One idea was to build the dome from pumice. Another, according to Giorgio Vasari, was to support the dome on a vast mound of earth that would be seeded with thousands of coins; when the dome was finished, the mound would be cleared by inviting Florence's citizens to excavate the money.

After years of bickering, the project was thrown open to competition in 1418. A goldsmith and clockmaker called **Filippo Brunelleschi** presented the winning scheme, defeating Ghiberti in the process – revenge of sorts for Ghiberti's triumph seventeen years earlier in the competition to design the Baptistery doors. Doom-mongers, Ghiberti among them, criticized Brunelleschi at every turn, eventually forcing the authorities to employ both rivals. An exasperated Brunelleschi feigned illness and resigned. Ghiberti, left to his own devices, found himself baffled, and in 1423 Brunelleschi was invited back to become the dome's sole "inventor and chief director".

The key to Brunelleschi's success lay in the construction of the dome as two masonry shells, each built as a stack of ever-diminishing rings. Secured with hidden stone beams and enormous iron chains, these concentric circles formed a lattice that was filled with lightweight bricks laid in a herringbone pattern that prevented the higher sections from falling inward. Brunelleschi's relentless inventiveness extended to a new hoist with a reverse gear, a new type of crane and even a boat for transporting marble that was so ungainly it was nicknamed *Il Badalone* (The Monster).

The dome's completion was marked by the **consecration** of the cathedral on March 25, 1436 – Annunciation Day, and the Florentine New Year – in a ceremony conducted by the pope. Even then, the topmost piece, the lantern, remained unfinished, with many people convinced the dome could support no further weight. But once again Brunelleschi won the day, beginning work on the dome's final stage in 1446, just a few months before his death. The whole thing was finally completed in the late 1460s, when the cross and gilded ball, both cast by Verrocchio, were hoisted into place.

This is still the largest masonry dome in the world. Only the gallery around the base remains incomplete – abandoned with just one face finished after Michelangelo compared it to "cages for crickets". This criticism aside, Michelangelo was awestruck: gazing on the cupola he is supposed to have said: *Come te non voglio, meglio di te non posso* ("Similar to you I will not, better than you I cannot").

## The Campanile

The **Campanile** (daily 8.30am–7.30pm; €6) – the cathedral's belltower – was begun in 1334 by Giotto during his period as official city architect and *capo maestro* (head of works) in charge of the Duomo. By the time of his death three years later, the base, the first of five eventual levels, had been completed. Andrea Pisano, fresh from creating the Baptistery's south doors, continued construction of the second storey (1337–42), probably in accordance with Giotto's plans. Work was rounded off by Francesco Talenti, who rectified deficiencies in Giotto's original calculations in the process: the base's original walls teetered on the brink of collapse until he doubled their thickness. When completed, the belltower reached 84.7m, well over the limit set by the city in 1324 for civic towers, the building of which had long been a means of expressing aristocratic or mercantile power.

The lower parts of the tower are adorned with **sculptures and reliefs** which mirror mankind's progress from original sin to a state of divine grace, a progress facilitated by manual labour, the arts and the sacraments, and guided by the influence of the planets and the cardinal and theological virtues. (These are copies – you can get a close look at the age-blackened originals in the Museo dell'Opera del Duomo.) On the first storey there are two rows of bas-reliefs: the lower register, in hexagonal frames – some designed by Giotto, but all executed by Pisano and pupils – illustrates the *Creation and The Arts and Industries*, while in the diamond-shaped panels of the upper register are allegories of the *Seven Planets* (then believed to influence human lives), *Seven Sacraments* (which sanctify human existence) and *Seven Virtues* (which shape human behaviour). A century or so later Luca della Robbia added the *Five Liberal Arts* (Grammar, Philosophy, Music, Arithmetic and Astrology) – which shape the human spirit – on the north face. Further works in the second-storey niches by Pisano were eventually replaced by Donatello and Nanni di Bartolo's figures of the *Prophets*, *Sibyls*, *Patriarchs* and *Kings* (1415–36).

The parapet at the top of the tower is a less lofty but in many ways more satisfying viewpoint than the cathedral dome, if only because the view takes in the Duomo itself. Be warned, though, that there are 414 steps to the summit – and no lift. George Eliot made the ascent in 1861, finding it "a very sublime getting upstairs indeed", her "muscles much astonished at the unusual exercise".

# The Baptistery

Florence's **Baptistery** (Mon–Sat noon–7pm, Sun & first Sat of month 8.30am–2pm; €3) stands immediately west of the Duomo, whose geometrically patterned marble cladding mirrors that of the smaller, older building. Generally thought to date from the sixth or seventh century, the Baptistery is the oldest building in Florence, first documented in 897 AD, when it was recorded as the city's cathedral before Santa Reparata. Though its origins lie buried in the Dark Ages, no building better illustrates the special relationship between Florence and the Roman world.

The Florentines were always conscious of their **Roman** ancestry, and for centuries believed that the Baptistery was a converted Roman temple to Mars, originally built to celebrate the defeat of Fiesole and the city's foundation. This belief was bolstered by the interior's ancient granite columns, probably taken from the city's old Roman Capitol. Further proof was apparently provided by traces of an ancient pavement mosaic, now thought to belong to an old Roman bakery. But if the building itself is not Roman, its exterior marble cladding – applied in a Romanesque reworking between about 1059 and 1128 – is clearly classical in inspiration, while its most famous embellishments, the gilded **bronze doors**, mark the emergence of a more scholarly interest in the art of the ancient world.

## The south doors

Responsibility for the Baptistery's improvement and upkeep lay with the *Arte di Calimala*, the wool merchants' guild – the most powerful guild in the city. It was they who initiated the building's eleventh-century revamp, and they who in the 1320s turned their attention to the exterior, and in particular to the question of a suitably majestic entrance. In this they were stung into action by arch-rival Pisa, whose cathedral was not only famous for its bronze portals, but whose craftsmen had recently completed some celebrated bronze doors for the great cathedral at Monreale in Sicily.

The arrival of **Andrea Pisano** in Florence in 1330 offered the chance of similar glories. Within three months the Pisan sculptor had created wax models for what would become the Baptistery's **south doors**. (They were originally placed in the east portal, but were displaced when Ghiberti's "Gates of Paradise" were finished.) Over the next eight years the models were cast in bronze, probably with the assistance of Venetian bell-makers, then Italy's most accomplished bronzesmiths. Twenty of the doors' 28 panels, installed in 1339, form a narrative on the life of St John the Baptist, patron saint of Florence and the Baptistery's dedicatee; the lowest eight reliefs depict Humility and the Cardinal and Theological Virtues. The bronze frame (1452–62) is the work of Vittorio Ghiberti, son of the more famous Lorenzo. The figures above the portal – the Baptist, Salome and executioner – are copies of late sixteenth-century additions; the originals are in the Museo dell'Opera del Duomo.

## The north doors

Some sixty years of financial and political turmoil, and the ravages of the Black Death, prevented further work on the Baptistery's other entrances until 1401. That year a competition was held to design a new set of doors, with each of the six main entrants asked to create a panel showing the Sacrifice of Isaac. The doors were to be a votive offering, a gift to God to celebrate the passing of another plague epidemic.

The judges found themselves equally impressed by the work of two young goldsmiths, Brunelleschi and **Lorenzo Ghiberti** (both winning entries are displayed in the Bargello). Unable to choose between the pair, it appears that the judges suggested that the two work in tandem. Brunelleschi replied that if he couldn't do the job alone he wasn't interested – whereupon Ghiberti was handed the contract. Barely 20 years old, Ghiberti was to devote much of the next quarter-century years to this one project, albeit in the company of distinguished assistants such as Masolino, Donatello and Paolo Uccello. His fame rests almost entirely on the extraordinary result.

His **north doors** (1403–24) show a new naturalism and classicized sense of composition, copying Pisano's 28-panel arrangement while transcending its traditional Gothic approach: the upper twenty panels depict scenes from the New Testament, while the eight lower panels describe the four Evangelists and Four Doctors of the Church.

▲ Baptistery, the east doors

## The east doors

The north doors, while extraordinary, are as nothing to the sublime **east doors** (1425–52), ordered from Ghiberti as soon as the first set was finished. The artist would spend some 27 years on the new project, work which he pursued, in his own words, "with the greatest diligence and greatest love". These doors have long been known as the "Gates of Paradise", supposedly because Michelangelo once remarked that they were so beautiful they deserved to be the portals of heaven. However, it's more likely that the name came about because these doors face the

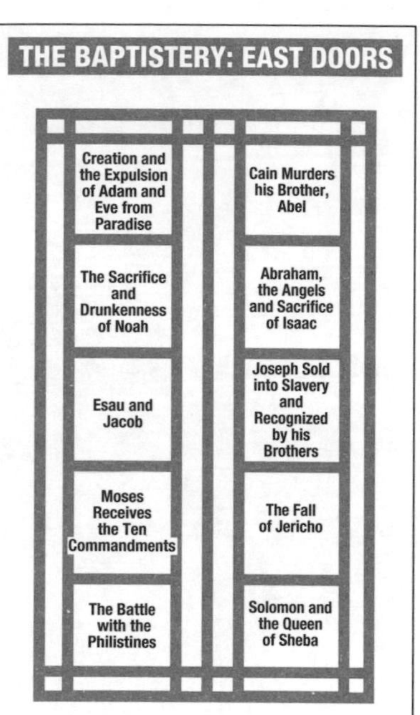


cathedral – the space between a cathedral and its baptistery was known as the *Paradiso*, because the sacrament of baptism put its recipient on the threshold of paradise.

The doors have just ten panels, a departure from both previous sets of doors, while their enclosing squares abandon the Gothic diamond or quatrefoil frame. Unprecedented in the subtlety of their casting, the **Old Testament scenes** – the Creation, the Ten Commandments, the Sacrifice of Isaac, and so on – are a primer of early Renaissance art, using rigorous perspective, gesture and sophisticated groupings to intensify the drama of each scene. The sculptor has also included an understandably self-satisfied self-portrait in the frame of the left-hand door: his is the fourth head from the top of the right-hand band – the bald chap with the smirk. The other 23 medallions portray Ghiberti's artistic contemporaries, while the 24 statuettes depict the Prophets and Sibyls. The golden doors now in place are reproductions; the original panels have been restored and exhibited, to great effect, in the Museo dell'Opera del Duomo.

The pair of pitted **marble columns** to the side of the east doors were presented by the city of Pisa in the twelfth century, and would have been slotted into the walls had they not turned out to be too weak to bear any substantial weight. The story goes that when the Pisans set off to attack Mallorca in 1117 they were so fearful of a raid by the city of Lucca in their absence that they begged the Florentines to watch over their city. In gratitude, on their return they made Florence a gift of the two pillars, part of the booty seized during the Mallorcan raid. However, the columns were deemed to have magic powers too valuable to be left to the Florentines – their polished surfaces were supposed to foretell acts of treason – and the Pisans allegedly weakened them deliberately by baking them in embers.

Another marble column, just north of the Baptistery, is decorated with bronze branches and leaves to commemorate a miracle of January 429 AD, brought about by the body of St Zenobius, Florence's first bishop; as the corpse was being carried from San Lorenzo into Santa Reparata it brushed against a barren elm here, which thereupon sprang into leaf.

## The interior

The Baptistery interior is stunning, with its black-and-white marble cladding and ancient columns below a blazing **mosaic ceiling**. Mosaics were never a Florentine speciality and this is the only large-scale one in the city; the impetus for it came partly from a desire to match the great mosaics in Venice, and partly from the interest surrounding mosaic restoration then taking place in the early Christian basilicas of Rome and Ravenna.

The earliest mosaics (1225), constructed with the aid of Venetian craftsmen, lie above the square apse, and depict the Virgin and John the Baptist. Above them, a wheel of prophets encircles the Lamb of God. The main vault (begun in the mid-thirteenth century) is dominated by a vast figure of Christ in Judgement, flanked by depictions of Paradise and Hell. Just to the left of the monstrous, man-eating Lucifer, the poet Virgil (in a white cloak) can be seen leading Dante (in black) through the Inferno. The figures were a later insertion, added after the poet's death during something of a frenzy of recognition. The other five sections of the octagonal ceiling depict biblical scenes, beginning above the north doors with the Creation, and proceeding through the stories of Joseph and John the Baptist towards the Crucifixion and Resurrection, seen above the south doors.

The interior's semi-abstract **mosaic pavement** also dates from the thirteenth century. The empty octagon at its centre marks the spot once occupied by the huge font in which every child born in the city during the previous twelve months would be baptized on March 25 (New Year's Day in the old Florentine calendar). When a child was born, a coloured bean was dropped into an urn in the Baptistery: black for a boy, white for a girl – a system that allowed the birth rate to be calculated.

To the right of the altar lies the **tomb of Baldassare Cossa**, the schismatic Pope John XXIII, who was deposed in 1415 and died in Florence in 1419. At the time of his death he was a guest of his financial adviser and close friend, Giovanni di Bicci de' Medici, the man who established the Medici at the political forefront in Florence. It was through Pope John that Giovanni became chief banker to the Papal Curia, a deal that laid the foundations of the Medici fortune: for years over half the Medici's profits would come from just two Rome-based banks. That Pope John achieved a resting place here was certainly not due to his piety. At his deposition he was accused of heresy, murder and the seduction of more than two hundred women in Bologna during his sojourn in the city as a papal legate. His monument, draped by an illusionistic marble canopy, is the work of Donatello and his pupil Michelozzo.

# The Museo dell'Opera del Duomo

In 1296 a body called the Opera del Duomo, literally the "Work of the Duomo", was created to oversee the maintenance of the Duomo. Since the early fifteenth century its home has been the building behind the east end of the cathedral at Piazza del Duomo 9, which now also houses the **Museo dell'Opera del Duomo** (Mon–Sat 9am–7.30pm, Sun 9am–1.40pm; €6), a repository of the most precious and fragile works of art from the Duomo, Baptistery and Campanile. As an overview of the sculpture of Florence the museum is second only to the Bargello. (Incidentally, you can see the stonemasons of the present-day Opera at work in their studio at Via dello Studio 23a, on the south side of the Duomo.)

## The ground floor

Beyond the ticket office, rooms devoted to sculpture from the Baptistery (mostly works by Tino da Camaino) and the Duomo's lateral doors precede the museum's **courtyard**, the site on which much of Michelangelo's *David* was sculpted. Now glazed over, the courtyard is home to all eight of Ghiberti's panels from the "Doors of Paradise", finally brought together following restoration, and now sharing the space with the graceful *Baptism of Christ* (1502–25), by Andrea Sansovino and assistants.

The largest room on this floor is a large hall devoted to the original sculptures of the cathedral's west front, foremost among which are works by the cathedral's first architect, **Arnolfo di Cambio** (and his workshop), including an eerily glass-eyed *Madonna and Child*; all were rescued from Arnolfo's quarter-finished cathedral facade, which was pulled down by Ferdinand I in 1587. Equally striking is the sculptor's vase-carrying figure of *St Reparata*, one of Florence's patron saints, a work long thought to be of Greek or Roman origin. Along the entrance wall are four seated figures of the Evangelists, also wrenched from the facade: Nanni di Banco's *St Luke* and **Donatello**'s *St John* are particularly fine. Also noteworthy is the ramrod-straight statue of the pugnacious Boniface VIII, whose insistence that "God has set popes over kings and kingdoms" brought him into conflict with Philip IV of France, a clash that led, in 1303, to the pope's imprisonment by Philip's allies; thereafter, no pope was to repeat Boniface's claim for the secular supremacy of the papacy. In Dante's *Divina Commedia* – partly written during Boniface's pontificate – it's revealed to the poet that the pope is destined for hell for his corruption.

The room off the far end of the hall features a sequence of **marble reliefs** (1547–72), by Bacio Bandinelli and Giovanni Bandini, part of an unfinished sequence of three hundred panels proposed for the choir of the cathedral. Also here is a collection of paintings from a series of altars in the cathedral, all torn from their original home in 1838 as they were considered an affront to the purity of the building. One of the most eye-catching is Giovanni di Biondo's triptych portraying episodes from the *Martyrdom of St Sebastian*: the smaller predella panels depict some of the more hair-raising events in the saint's life, notably a violent cudgelling and the panel in which he is tipped head-first into a well.

The adjoining modern **octagonal chapel** features an assembly of reliquaries that contain, among other saintly remains, the jaw of Saint Jerome and an index finger of John the Baptist. From here a vaulted gallery leads to the museum's main stairs – note the marker on the right-hand wall indicating the water level in the building after the 1966 flood. It's easy to miss the room off to the right of the **Lapidarium** (a collection of modest works in stone), which contains items removed from the cathedral's Porta della Mandorla, including a lovely terracotta *Creation of Eve* (1410) attributed to Donatello.

## The upper floor

Up the stairs on the mezzanine level stands **Michelangelo**'s anguished **Pietà** (1550–53), moved from the cathedral as recently as 1981 while restoration of the dome was in progress, but probably fated to stay here forever. This is one of the sculptor's last works, carved when he was almost 80, and was intended for his own tomb; Vasari records that the face of Nicodemus is a self-portrait. Dissatisfied with the quality of the marble, Michelangelo mutilated the group by hammering off the left leg and arm of Christ; his pupil Tiberio Calcagni restored the arm, then finished off the figure of Mary Magdalene, turning her into a blank-faced supporting player.

Although he's represented on the lower floor, it's upstairs that **Donatello**, the greatest of Michelangelo's precursors, really comes to the fore. The first room at the top of the stairs features his magnificent **Cantoria**, or choir-loft (1433–39), with its playground of boisterous *putti*. Facing it is another splendid *cantoria* (1431–38), the earliest known major commission of the young **Luca della Robbia** (the originals are underneath, with casts replacing them in the *cantoria* itself); the earnest musicians embody the text from Psalm 150, which is inscribed on the frame: "Praise him with the sound of the trumpet; praise him with the psaltery and harp." Both lofts were removed from their position above the cathedral's sacristies in 1688 on the occasion of the marriage of Violante Beatrice of Bavaria to Ferdinand de' Medici, a ceremony that gave the cathedral authorities the excuse to decorate the cathedral in a more fitting "modern" style.

Around the room are arrayed the life-size figures that Donatello carved for the Campanile, perhaps the most powerful of which is the prophet Habbakuk (1427–35), the intensity of whose anguished gaze is said to have prompted the sculptor to seize it and yell "Speak, speak!" Donatello was apparently also responsible for the statue's nickname *Lo Zuccone* (The Pumpkin), after its bald head. Keeping company with Donatello's work are four Prophets (1348–50) and two Sybils (1342–8) attributed to Andrea Pisano, and *The Sacrifice of Isaac* (1421), a collaboration between Nanni di Bartolo and Donatello.

Donatello's angular later style is exemplified by the gaunt wooden figure of Mary Magdalene (1453–5), which confronts you on entering the room off the *cantorie* room. The *Magdalene* came from the Baptistery, as did the silver altar-front at the far end of the room, a dazzling summary of the life of St John the Baptist. Begun in 1366, the altar-front was completed in 1480, the culmination of a century of labour by, among others, Michelozzo (responsible for the central figure of *John the Baptist*), Verrocchio (the *Decapitation* to the right) and Antonio del Pollaiuolo (the *Birth of Jesus* on the left side), who was the chief creator of the silver cross atop the altar. Ranged around the walls are more reliquaries, fabrics, copes and other religious vestments, including 27 sublimely worked **needlework panels** – former vestments and altar panels from the Baptistery – produced between 1466 and 1487 by French, Flemish and Florentine artists, working to designs by Pollaiuolo. Not surprisingly, given their provenance, they portray scenes from the life of the Baptist, one of Florence's patrons and the Baptistery's dedicatee.

In the room on the other side of the *cantorie* room you'll find the **bas-reliefs** that once adorned the Campanile. Though darkened with age, their allegorical panels remain both striking and intelligible, depicting the spiritual refinement of humanity through labour, the arts and, ultimately, the virtues and sacraments. The display reproduces the reliefs' original arrangement, the key panels being the hexagonal reliefs of the lower tier, all of which – save for the last five, by Luca della Robbia (1437–39) – were the work of Andrea Pisano and his son Nino (c.1348–50), probably to designs by Giotto.

A corridor at the end of Room II leads past a mock-up of Brunelleschi's building site, complete with broken bricks, wooden scaffolding and some of the tools that were used to build the dome, many invented specifically for the purpose by the architect himself. More arresting is Brunelleschi's **death mask**, which almost – but not quite – looks out of the window at the dome just across the way.

The sequence of rooms beyond displays various proposals for completing the balcony of the drum below the cupola and the Duomo's west front, including models created by Michelangelo, Giuliano da Maiano, Antonio da Sangallo and other leading architects. The wooden model of the **cathedral lantern** is presumed to have been made by Brunelleschi as part of his winning proposal for the design of the lantern in 1436. The final room, just off the main staircase, shows plans submitted to the three competitions held in the 1860s, when Florence was briefly capital of Italy and the question of the facade standing "ignominious in faded stucco", as George Eliot put it, once more became pressing. Emilio de Fabris's winning design of 1876 is mostly remarkable for how little it differs from the other nineteenth-century Gothic pastiches.

# The Museo di Firenze com'era

The top of Via del Proconsolo, just a few yards from the Museo dell'Opera del Duomo, forms a major junction with Via dell'Oriuolo, home to the **Museo di Firenze com'era** (June–Sept Mon & Tues 9am–2pm, Sat 9am–7pm; Oct–May Mon–Wed 9am–2pm, Sat 9am–7pm; €2.70). This "Museum of Florence as it used to be" is one of the city's unsung museums, but its contents and setting – in a pleasant garden-fronted *palazzo* – are delightful. There are plans to move the museum to the Palazzo Vecchio, but the transfer does not appear to be imminent.

The story begins with a collection of models, plans and photographs of the excavation of the Piazza della Signoria that took place in the 1980s. As one would expect, a number of discoveries were made, but for want of any better ideas the piazza was simply paved over once the dig was complete. A large, somewhat speculative model of the **Roman city** stands at the far end of the room, with coloured sections showing the buildings whose locations the archeologists are sure of.

The long, vaulted main gallery stands on the other side of the entrance corridor. Maps, prints, photos and topographical paintings chart the growth of Florence from the fifteenth century to the present, and while none of the exhibits is a masterpiece, most of them are at least informative. Perhaps the most impressive item comes right at the start: a meticulous 1887 reproduction of a colossal 1472 aerial view of Florence called the *Pianta della Catena* (Chain Map), the original of which was destroyed in Berlin during World War II. It's the oldest accurate representation of the city's layout.

Almost as appealing are the twelve lunette pictures (1555) of the **Medici villas**, reproductions of which you'll see on postcards and posters across the city. They are the work of Flemish painter Justus Utens and were painted for the Medici's Villa dell'Artimino. A poignant wooden model portrays the labyrinthine jumble of the **Mercato Vecchio**, the city's ancient heart, which was demolished to make space for the Piazza della Repubblica at the end of the nineteenth century. Elsewhere, a graphic picture portrays Savonarola's execution (see p.125), and eighteenth-century Florence is celebrated in the elegiac engravings of Giuseppe Zocchi.

# The Museo del Bigallo and Piazza della Repubblica

On the other side of Piazza del Duomo, at the top of Via de' Calzaiuoli, stands the **Loggia del Bigallo**, which was built in the 1350s for the Compagnia della Misericordia, a charitable organization founded by St Peter Martyr in 1244, to give aid to the sick and to bury the dead. (The Misericordia still exists: their headquarters is just across the way, with their ambulances parked outside.) By the time the loggia was built, the Misericordia was also functioning as an orphanage – the building was commissioned as a place to display abandoned babies, in the hope that they might be recognized before being given to foster parents. For most of the fifteenth century the Misericordia was united with another orphanage, Compagnia del Bigallo (from the village in which it began), hence the loggia's name. Nowadays it houses the undervisited and overpriced **Museo del Bigallo** (daily except Tues 9.30am–5.30pm; €5), which consists of just three rooms, containing a tiny collection of religious paintings commissioned by the two companies. As you might

▲ Street band in Piazza della Repubblica

expect, the Madonna and Child is a dominant theme, and St Peter Martyr is present as well, but the two highlights are a remnant of a fresco painted on the outside of the loggia in 1386, showing the transfer of infants to their adoptive parents, and the *Madonna of the Misericordia*, painted by a follower of Bernardo Daddi in 1342, which features the oldest known panorama of Florence.

A minute's stroll south of the Bigallo museum you'll find the vacant expanse of **Piazza della Repubblica**. Impressive solely for its size, this square was planned in the late 1860s, when it was decided to demolish the central marketplace (Mercato Vecchio), the Jewish ghetto and other insalubrious tenements to give Florence a public space befitting the capital of the recently formed Italian nation. The clearance of the area had not even begun when, at the start of 1871, the capital was transferred to Rome, and it wasn't until 1885 that the Mercato Vecchio and the surrounding slums were finally removed. On the west side a vast arch bears the triumphant inscription: "The ancient city centre restored to new life from the squalor of centuries." The freestanding column is the solitary trace of the piazza's history: it used to be topped by a bell that was rung to signal the start and close of trading, and by Donatello's statue of Abundance, which long ago rotted away and had to be replaced with a replica. (For more on the piazza and the rebuilding of Florence in the late nineteenth century, see the colour insert "Florence as the Capital of Italy".)

Nowadays, Piazza della Repubblica is best known for the three large and expensive **cafés** that stand on the perimeter: the *Gilli*, the most attractive of the trio, which was founded way back in 1733 (albeit on a different site – it moved here in 1910); the *Giubbe Rosse*, once the intellectuals' café of choice (the Futurist manifesto was launched here in 1909); and the *Paszkowski*, which began business as a beer hall in the 1840s, is now a listed historic monument, and bears the suffix "Caffè Concerto", betokening the piano bar-style music that emanates from it most evenings.

2

# Piazza della Signoria and around

Whereas the Piazza del Duomo provides the focus for Florence's religious life, the **Piazza della Signoria** - site of the mighty **Palazzo Vecchio** and forecourt to the **Uffizi** - has always been the centre of its secular existence. The Palazzo Vecchio is still the headquarters of the city's councillors and bureaucrats, and the piazza in front of it is the stage for major civic events and political rallies. After work, hundreds of Florentines gather here for a gossip before taking the evening *passeggiata* back and forth between the Signoria and Piazza del Duomo, along the broad pedestrianized avenue of **Via dei Calzaiuoli.** This street is shop-lined for almost its entire length but does boast one great monument, **Orsanmichele**, a church as notable for its statuary as for the structure itself. There's one other major religious building in this area: the **Badìa Fiorentina**, the most important of several buildings in a district that has strong associations with Italy's foremost poet, Dante Alighieri. Immediately opposite the Badìa stands the forbidding bulk of the **Bargello**, once the city's prison, now home to a superb assemblage of sculpture, plus excellent collections of enamels, ivories, glassware, silverware and other *objets d'art.* To get a full idea of the achievement of the Florentine Renaissance, a visit to the Bargello is as important as a day in the Uffizi. And as a corrective to the notion that Florence's contribution to European civilization has been limited to the arts, you might want to call in at the fascinating **Museo di Storia della Scienza**, which is tucked away at the back of the Uffizi.

## Piazza della Signoria

For so important a square, **Piazza della Signoria** evolved in an oddly haphazard and piecemeal manner. Originally this portion of land belonged to the Uberti family, leading members of the city's Ghibelline faction. When the Ghibellines were defeated in 1268, the land and buildings on it were confiscated and allowed to fall into ruin, supposedly as a lasting memorial to Ghibelline treachery. In time, part of the area was paved, a further act of humiliation designed to prevent the Uberti – exiled from the city – from ever raising another building within its precincts. The alleged reluctance of the city authorities to encroach on this "tainted" land partly explains the asymmetrical shape of the square and the Palazzo Vecchio.

The piazza took on a public role in 1307, when a small area was laid out to provide a suitable setting for the Palazzo Vecchio, then known as the Palazzo dei Priori. Though efforts to enlarge it were hampered by work on the palace and Loggia della Signoria, by 1385 it was completely paved and wheeled traffic was banned from the area (as it still is). Further restructuring occurred during Cosimo I's reordering of the Uffizi around 1560 and more alterations followed in 1871, when the medieval Loggia dei Pisani was demolished, opening up much of the square's present-day westward sweep.

| RESTAURANTS | | BARS & CAFÉS | |
|---|---|---|---|
| Antico Fattore | 11 | Caffè Italiano | 6 |
| Da Ganino | 5 | Cantinetta dei Verrazzano | 1 |
| Gustavino | 7 | I Fratellini | 4 |
| **GELATERIA** | | Mayday | 2 |
| Perchè No! | 3 | Quasigratis | 10 |
| **CLUB** | | Rivoire | 9 |
| Tabasco | 8 | | |

Though it's always busy, the piazza is at its liveliest during political campaigns, when speakers address the crowds from the terrace in front of the Palazzo Vecchio. (The terrace is called the *arringhiera*, from the same root as the English word "harangue".) Tempers can get frayed at such gatherings, but things used to be a lot wilder than they are today: in 1343, for example, one inflammatory meeting ended with a man being eaten by a mob. Most famously, it was here that Savonarola held his "Bonfires of the Vanities" (see p.124) – on the very spot where, on May 23, 1498, he was to be executed for heresy. A circular plaque in the pavement near the fountain marks the place.

## The statues

Florence's political volatility is encapsulated by the Piazza della Signoria's array of **statues**, most of which were arranged in the sixteenth century to accentuate the axis of the Uffizi. From left to right as you face the Palazzo Vecchio, the line-up starts with Giambologna's equestrian statue of **Cosimo I** (1587–94). An echo of the Marcus Aurelius statue in Rome, it was designed to draw parallels between the power of Florence (and thus Cosimo) and the glory of imperial Rome. Three bas-reliefs at the base portray key events in Cosimo's career: becoming duke of Florence in 1537, the conquest of Siena in 1555, and acquiring the title Grand Duke of Tuscany from Pius V in 1569.

Next comes Ammannati's fatuous **Neptune Fountain** (1565–75), a tribute to Cosimo's prowess as a naval commander. Neptune himself is a lumpen lout of a figure, which provoked Michelangelo to coin the rhyming put-down *Ammannato, Ammannato, che bel marmo hai rovinato* ("... what a fine piece of marble you've ruined"). Ammannati doesn't seem to have been too embarrassed, though in a late phase of piety he did come to regret the lasciviousness of the figures round the base, created with the assistance of Giambologna and other junior sculptors. Florentine superstition has it that Neptune wanders the piazza when struck by the light of a full moon.

## The Florentine Republic

Dante compared Florence's constant political struggles to a sick man forever shifting his position in bed, and indeed its medieval history often appears a catalogue of incessant civic unrest. Yet between 1293 and 1534 – bar the odd ruction – the city maintained a **republican** constitution that was embodied in well-defined institutions. The nucleus of this structure was formed by the city's merchants and guilds, who covertly controlled Florence as early as the twelfth century and formalized their influence during the so-called **Primo Popolo** (1248–59), a quasi-democratic regime whose ten-year rule, claimed Dante, was the only period of civic peace in Florence's history. During the **Secondo Popolo** (1284), the leading guilds, the *Arti Maggiori*, introduced the **Ordinamenti della Giustizia** (1293), a written constitution that entrenched mercantile power still further and was to be the basis of Florence's government for the next 250 years.

The rulers of this much-vaunted republic were drawn exclusively from the ranks of guild members over the age of 30, and were chosen in a public ceremony held every two months, the short tenure being designed to prevent individuals or cliques assuming too much power. At this ceremony, the names of selected guild members were placed in eight leather bags (*borse*) kept in the sacristy of Santa Croce; the ones picked from the bags duly became the **Priori** (or *Signori*), forming a government called the **Signoria**, usually comprising nine men, most of them from the *Arti Maggiori*. Once elected, the *Priori* moved into the Palazzo della Signoria, where they were expected to stay, virtually incommunicado, for their period of office – though they were waited on hand and foot, and enjoyed the services of a professional joke-teller, the *Buffone*.

Headed by the **Gonfaloniere** (literally the "Standard-Bearer"), the *Signoria* consulted two elected councils or **Collegi** – the **Dodici Buonomini** (Twelve Citizens) and **Sedici Gonfalonieri** (Sixteen Standard Bearers) – as well as committees introduced to deal with specific crises (the Ten of War, the Eight of Security, the Six of Commerce, etc). Permanent officials included the Chancellor (a post once held by Machiavelli) and the **Podestà**, a chief magistrate brought in from a neighbouring city as an independent arbitrator, and housed in the Bargello. In times of extreme crisis, such as the Pazzi Conspiracy (see p.50), all male citizens over the age of 14 were summoned to a **Parlamento** in Piazza della Signoria by the tolling of the Palazzo Vecchio's famous bell, known as the *Vacca* (Cow), after its deep, bovine tone. When a two-thirds quorum was reached, the people were asked to approve a **Balìa**, a committee delegated to deal with the situation as it saw fit.

All this looked good on paper but in practice the set-up was far from democratic. The lowliest workers, the **Popolo Minuto**, were totally excluded, as were the **Grandi**, or nobles. And despite the *Signoria*'s apparently random selection process, political cliques had few problems ensuring that only the names of likely supporters found their way into the *borse*. If a rogue candidate slipped through the net, or things went awry, then a *Parlamento* was summoned, a *Balìa* formed, and the offending person replaced by a more pliable candidate. It was by such means that the great mercantile dynasties of Florence – the Peruzzi, the Albizzi, the Strozzi and, of course, the Medici – retained their power even when not technically in office.

After a copy of Donatello's **Marzocco** (1418–20), the original of which is in the Bargello, comes a copy of the same sculptor's **Judith and Holofernes** (1456–60), which freezes the action at the moment Judith's arm begins its scything stroke – a dramatic conception that no other sculptor of the period would have attempted. Commissioned by Cosimo de' Medici, this statue doubled as a fountain in the Palazzo Medici but was removed to the Piazza della Signoria after the expulsion of the family in 1495, to be displayed as an emblem of vanquished tyranny; a new inscription on the base reinforced the message. The original is inside the Palazzo Vecchio.

Michelangelo's **David**, at first intended for the Duomo, was also installed here as a declaration of civic solidarity by the Florentine Republic; the original is now in the Accademia. Conceived as partner piece to the *David*, Bandinelli's **Hercules and Cacus** (1534) was both a personal emblem of Cosimo I and a symbol of Florentine fortitude. Benvenuto Cellini described the musclebound Hercules as looking like "a sackful of melons", and it's a sobering thought that the marble might well have ended up as something more inspiring. In the late 1520s, when the Florentines were once again busy tearing the Medici emblem from every building on which it had been stuck, Michelangelo offered to carve a monumental figure of Samson to celebrate the Republic's latest victory over tyranny; other demands on the artist's time put paid to this project, and the stone passed to Bandinelli, who duly vented his mediocrity on it.

## The Loggia della Signoria

The square's grace note, the **Loggia della Signoria**, was begun in 1376, prompted by that year's heavy rains, which had washed out Florence's entire calendar of public ceremonies. It was completed in 1382, serving as a dais for city dignitaries, a forum for the reception of foreign emissaries, and a platform for the swearing-in of public officials. Its alternative name, the Loggia dei Lanzi, comes from Cosimo I's bodyguard of Swiss lancers, who were garrisoned nearby; its third name, the Loggia dell'Orcagna, derives from the idea that Orcagna (Andrea del Cione) may have had a hand in its original design.

Although Donatello's *Judith and Holofernes* was placed here as early as 1506, it was only in the late eighteenth century that the loggia became exclusively a showcase for sculpture. In the corner nearest the Palazzo Vecchio stands a figure that has become one of the iconic images of the Renaissance, Benvenuto Cellini's **Perseus** (1545), now back in its rightful place after a painstaking restoration. (The base is a copy, however; the original is in the Bargello.) Made for Cosimo I, the statue symbolizes the triumph of firm Grand Ducal rule over the monstrous indiscipline of all other forms of government. The traumatic process of the statue's creation is vividly described in Cellini's rip-roaring and self-serving autobiography: seeing the molten bronze beginning to solidify too quickly, he saved the day by flinging all his pewter plates into the mix. When the bronze cooled the figure was missing only three toes, which were added later.

Equally attention-seeking is Giambologna's last work, to the right, **The Rape of the Sabine** (1583), conjured from the largest single piece of sculptural marble ever seen in Florence, and the epitome of the Mannerist obsession with spiralling forms. The sculptor supposedly intended the piece merely as a study of old age, male strength and female beauty: the present name was coined later. The figures along the back wall are Roman works, traditionally believed to portray Roman empresses, while of the three central statues only one – Giambologna's **Hercules**

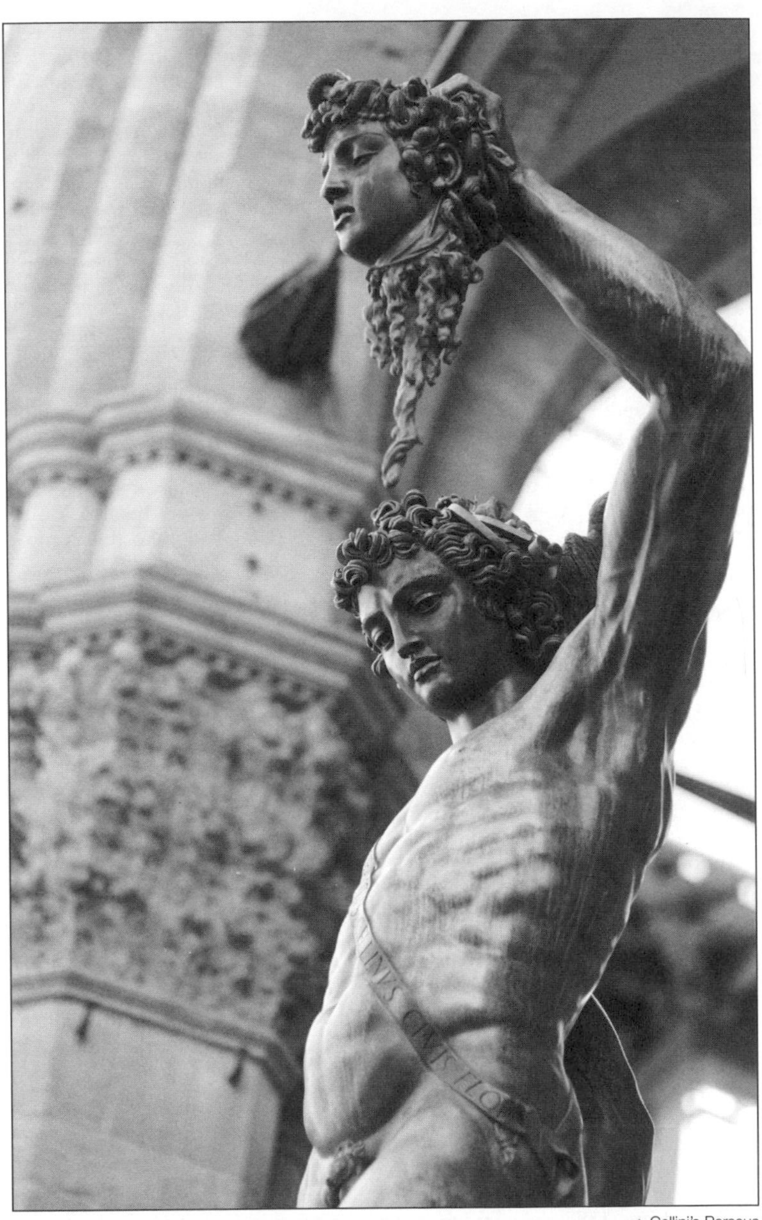

▲ Cellini's Perseus

**Slaying the Centaur** (1599) – deserves its place. The seven figures in the spandrels between the arches above depict the Virtues, all carved to designs by Agnolo Gaddi (1384–89) save the head of *Faith*, which was replaced by Donatello when the original crashed to the ground.

# The Palazzo Vecchio

Probably designed by Arnolfo di Cambio, Florence's fortress-like town hall, the **Palazzo Vecchio** (daily 9am–7pm; Thurs closes 2pm; €6), was begun as the Palazzo dei Priori in 1299 to provide premises for the *Priori* or *Signoria*, the highest tier of the city's republican government. Changes in the Florentine constitution over the years entailed alterations to the layout of the palace, the most radical coming in 1540, when Cosimo I moved his retinue here from the Palazzo Medici and grafted a huge extension onto the rear. The Medici remained in residence for only nine years before moving to the Palazzo Pitti – largely, it seems, at the insistence of Cosimo's wife, Eleonora di Toledo, who dipped into her fortune to purchase the more spacious accommodation on the south side of the river. (As well as finding the Palazzo Vecchio too cramped, she objected to the stink and din created by the lions that were kept caged at the back of the palace, and also didn't much care for the drunken nocturnal carousings of the Swiss guards who were garrisoned in the Loggia dei Lanzi.) The "old" (*vecchio*) palace, which they left to their son, Francesco, then acquired its present name. Between 1865 and 1870, during Florence's brief tenure as capital of Italy, the palace housed the country's parliament and foreign ministry.

As for the sights, much of the palace's decoration comprises a relentless eulogy to Cosimo and his relations, propaganda that's made tolerable by some of the palace's examples of Mannerist art – among the finest pieces produced by that ultra-sophisticated and self-conscious movement. There are also frescoes by Domenico Ghirlandaio and some outstanding sculptures, not least works by Michelangelo and Donatello. It's also possible to visit hidden parts of the palace on guided tours known as **Percorsi Segreti** (see p.68), as well in the course of events under the **Emozioni da Museo** programme (see p.71).

## The courtyard and first floor

Work on the palace's beautiful inner **courtyard** was begun by Michelozzo in 1453, but the decoration was largely added by court architect Vasari for Francesco de' Medici's marriage to Johanna of Austria in 1565. The bride's origin explains the presence of cities belonging to the Habsburg Empire

## Percorsi Segreti

The Palazzo Vecchio's various so-called **Percorsi Segreti** ("Secret Passageways") allow access – on guided tours only, of up to twelve people at a time – to parts of the building that are normally off-limits. Most impressive visually is the trip up through the palace and into the attic of the **Salone del Cinquecento**. From the vantage point of a balcony high above the hall, the guide describes the complex way in which Vasari created such a huge space within the medieval structure, and explains the allegorical meaning of the paintings. You are then led up into the vast attic itself, where two sets of trusses support the roof above and the ceiling below. Some of the beams are more than 20m long.

Less spectacular, but still worth it for the guide's commentary, is the route leading from the street outside up through the secret **Stairway of the Duke of Athens**. The doorway was knocked through the exterior wall of the Palazzo in 1342 as an emergency escape route for the duke, who briefly took up the reins of power here. He never actually used the staircase, but only because his fall from grace came rather sooner than he had imagined. Another *Percorso Segreto* allows you inside the **Studiolo di Francesco I**, then through one of the hidden doors and up a secret little staircase to the *studiolino* or **Tesoretto** (6), Cosimo's tiny private study, which was built ten years before the *studiolo*.

Tours cost €8 (including admission to the Palazzo Vecchio), last roughly 75 minutes, and are held every day between 10am and 5pm in Italian, French and/or English. Exactly what language the tours are conducted in depends on demand, but there's usually at least one English-language party for each *Percorso* every day. Places must be reserved in advance, either in person (in the room next to the Palazzo Vecchio ticket desk) or by phone, on ⓣ055.276.8224 or 055.276.8558.

amid the wall's painted townscapes. Vasari also designed the central fountain, though the winsome *putto* and dolphin (1476) at its crown are the work of Verrocchio (the present statues are copies; the originals are on the palace's second floor). The **monumental staircase** (marked 1 on our plan) is also Vasari's, a far more satisfying work that leads to the palace's first floor – though visitors are often directed to take a different route upstairs.

Vasari was given full rein in the huge **Salone dei Cinquecento**, which was originally built in 1495 as the meeting hall for the Consiglio Maggiore (Great Council), the ruling assembly of the penultimate republic. The chamber might have had one of Italy's most remarkable decorative schemes: Leonardo da Vinci and Michelangelo were employed to paint frescoes on opposite sides of the room, but Leonardo's work, *The Battle of Anghiari*, was abandoned (or destroyed) after his experimental technique went badly wrong, while Michelangelo's *The Battle of Cascina* was no more than a fragmentary cartoon when he was summoned to Rome by Pope Julius II in 1506. Instead the hall received six drearily bombastic murals (1563–65) – painted either by Vasari or under his direction – illustrating Florentine military triumphs over Pisa (1496–1509) and Siena (1554–55). It was assumed that Vasari obliterated whatever remained of Leonardo's fresco before beginning his work, but the recent discovery of a cavity behind *The Battle of Marciano* raises the possibility that Vasari instead contructed a false wall for his fresco, to preserve his great predecessor's painting. Investigations are proceeding.

The **ceiling**'s 39 panels, again by Vasari and his team, celebrate the *Apotheosis of Cosimo I* (centre), a scene surrounded by the crests of the city's guilds and further paeans to the prowess of Florence and the Medici. One of the *Percorsi Segreti* takes you into the attic above the roof, an extraordinary space where it's possible to see how Vasari pulled off the trick of suspending so large a ceiling without visible supports. The **sculptural** highlight is Michelangelo's *Victory* (4), almost opposite the entrance door. Carved for the tomb of Pope Julius II, the statue was donated to the Medici by the artist's nephew, then installed here by Vasari in 1565 to celebrate Cosimo's defeat of the Sienese ten years earlier. Directly opposite, on the entrance wall, is the original plaster prototype of a companion piece for the *Victory*, Giambologna's **Virtue Overcoming Vice** (2), another metaphor for Florentine military might – this time Florence's victory over Pisa. (The marble version is in the Bargello.) The remaining statues, the masterpiece of sixteenth-century artist Vincenzo de' Rossi, portray the **Labours of Hercules** (3) and are yet another example of Florentine heroic propaganda: Hercules is also one of Florence's many civic symbols.

### The Studiolo di Francesco I

From the Salone del Cinquecento, a roped-off door allows a glimpse of the most bizarre room in the building, the **Studiolo di Francesco I** (5). Created by Vasari towards the end of his career and decorated by no fewer than thirty Mannerist artists (1570–74), this windowless cell was created as a retreat for Francesco I, the introverted son of Cosimo and Eleonora. Each of the miniature bronzes and nearly all the paintings reflect Francesco's interest in the sciences and alchemy: the entrance wall pictures illustrate the theme of Earth, while the others, reading clockwise, signify Water, Air and Fire. The outstanding paintings are the two that don't fit the scheme: Bronzino's portraits of the occupant's parents, facing each other across the room. The oval paintings on the panels at the base hinted at the presence of Francesco's most treasured knick-knacks, which were once concealed in the compartments behind; the wooden structure is actually a nineteenth-century re-creation, though the paintings are original.

Much of the rest of this floor is still used by council officials, though if the seven rooms of the **Quartiere di Leone X** and **Sala dei Dugento** are open (they rarely are), don't miss the opportunity. The latter, in particular, is outstanding: Benedetto and Giuliano da Maiano, excellent sculptors both, were responsible for the design (1472–77) and for the fine wooden ceiling; the tapestries (1546–53) were created to designs by Bronzino, Pontormo and others.

## The second floor

Steps lead from the Salone to the second floor, passing an intriguing fireworks fresco (1558) showing Piazza della Signoria during the celebrations for the feast of St John the Baptist. Turn left at the top of the stairs and you enter the **Quartiere degli Elementi**, one of the floor's three distinct suites of rooms. All five salons here are slavishly devoted to a different member of the Medici clan. Persevere, though, if only to enjoy the city **views** from the Terrazza di Saturno and Verrocchio's original *Putto and Dolphin* statue on the Terrazzo di Giunone.

Return to the stairs and head straight on and you cross a gallery with views down into the Salone. Immediately afterwards come the private apartments of **Eleonora di Toledo**. The first room, the **Camera Verde** (9) has some charming wildlife on its ceiling, but the star turn is the exquisite **Cappella di Eleonora** (8), vividly decorated by Bronzino in the 1540s. It seems that the artist used a new and time-consuming technique to give these paintings the same glassy surface as his canvases, executing a first draft in fresco and then

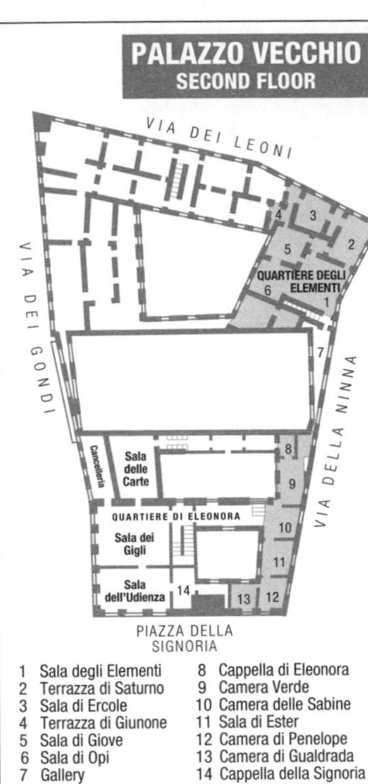


glazing it with tempera. They show scenes from the life of Moses, episodes probably intended to draw parallels with the life of Cosimo. In the *Annunciation* that flanks the *Deposition* on the back wall, Bronzino is said to have used Cosimo's and Eleonora's eldest daughter as the model for the Virgin.

Those who find all this Mannerist stuff unhealthily airless can take refuge in the more summery rooms that follow. The **Sala dell'Udienza**, originally the audience chamber of the Republic, boasts a stunning gilt-coffered ceiling by Giuliano da Maiano. The Mannerists reassert themselves with a vast fresco sequence (1545–48) by Cecchino Salviati, a cycle widely considered to be this artist's most accomplished work.

Giuliano was also responsible, with his brother Benedetto, for the intarsia work on the doors and the lovely doorway that leads into the **Sala dei Gigli**, named after the lilies (*gigli*) that adorn most of its surfaces – the lily is the emblem of St Zenobius and of the Virgin, both patron saints of Florence. The room has another splendid ceiling by the Maiano brothers, and a wall frescoed by Domenico Ghirlandaio with *SS Zenobius, Stephen and Lorenzo* (1481–85) and lunettes portraying *Six Heroes of Ancient Rome*. The undoubted highlight here, however, is Donatello's original *Judith and Holofernes* (1455–60), removed from Piazza della Signoria.

Two small rooms are attached to the Sala dei Gigli: the **Cancelleria**, once Machiavelli's office and now containing a bust and portrait of the maligned political thinker, and the lovely **Sala delle Carte**, formerly the *Guardaroba* (Wardrobe), the repository of Cosimo's state finery. Now it is decorated with 57 maps painted in 1563 by the court astronomer Fra' Ignazio Danti, depicting what was then the entire known world. One map, in the far right-hand corner, conceals a door to a hidden staircase.

A door (very often locked) leads out from the second floor onto the broad balcony of the Palazzo Vecchio's **tower**. The views are superb, if not as good as those enjoyed from the cell in the body of the tower above, which was known ironically as the *Alberghinetto* (Little Hotel); such troublemakers as Cosimo de' Medici and Savonarola were once imprisoned here. The final section of the museum, just before the exit, is something of an afterthought, with second-rate pictures once owned by the American collector Charles Loeser; it's often closed anyway.

## Emozioni da Museo

The **Emozioni da Museo** scheme organizes a range of guided tours, performances and workshops in the Palazzo Vecchio, some of them aimed at children (eg a shadow-theatre show narrated by mice, or a session in which the kids get to reconstruct a model of the building to see how it was built), some designed for all ages (eg a guided tour of the Palazzo Vecchio and its secret passageways by an actor in the role of Giorgio Vasari, or encounters with impersonators of Eleonora di Toledo and Cosimo I). The children's events are aimed more at local *ragazzi* than visitors' kids, but some are held in English (usually at weekends, but more frequently during the school holidays), and even when the actors are speaking Italian, English-speaking guides are on hand to translate. The Emozioni da Museo tours change frequently – the tourist offices and the ticket desk of the Palazzo Vecchio will have details of what's on offer. Tickets cost the same as for the *Percorsi Segreti* and the booking procedure is the same as well (see p.68).

# The Uffizi

Florence can prompt an over-eagerness to reach for superlatives; in the case of the **Galleria degli Uffizi**, the superlatives are simply the bare truth – this is the finest picture gallery in Italy. So many masterpieces are collected here that if you try to see everything in a single visit you'll only skate over the surface and exhaust yourself in the process. Though you may not want to emulate Edward Gibbon, who visited the Uffizi fourteen times on a single trip to Florence, it makes sense to limit your initial tour to the first fifteen rooms, where the Florentine Renaissance works are concentrated, and to explore the rest another time.

The gallery is housed in what were once government offices (*uffizi*) built by Vasari for Cosimo I in 1560. After Vasari's death, work on the building was continued by Buontalenti, who was asked by Francesco I to glaze the upper storey so that it could house his art collection. Each of the succeeding Medici added to the family's trove of art treasures. The accumulated collection was preserved for public inspection by the last member of the family, Anna Maria Lodovica, whose will specified that it should be left to the people of Florence and never be allowed to leave the city. In the nineteenth century a large proportion of the statuary was transferred to the Bargello, while most of the antiquities went to the Museo Archeologico, leaving the Uffizi as essentially a gallery of paintings supplemented with some classical sculptures.

## Uffizi practicalities

The Uffizi's **opening hours** are Tuesday–Sunday 8.15am–6.50pm; in high summer and at festive periods it sometimes stays open until 10pm. After the Vatican this is the busiest museum in the country, with more than 1.5 million visitors each year, so during peak season you've almost no chance of getting in without paying the €4 surcharge for booking a ticket **in advance**. For next-day tickets, there's a reservations desk that opens at 8.15am at Door 2, and has an allocation of just two hundred. For reservations further in advance, go to Door 3, or call the Firenze Musei line on ⓣ055.294.883, or reserve through the Firenze Musei website (ⓦwww.firenzemusei.it), or call at the Orsanmichele ticket office (see p.44 for more). Even if you have bought an advance ticket, get there half an hour before your allotted admission time, because the queue is often enormous and very slow-moving. If you're planning on visiting the Uffizi and the other state museums repeatedly, an **Amici degli Uffizi** card would be a wise investment – see p.44 for details.

Full **admission** costs €6.50 but EU citizens aged 18–25 pay half-price and entry is free to under-18s and over-65s; there are, however, frequent special exhibitions, during which the full price is raised to €10. You should be aware that it's very rare for the whole Uffizi to be open; a board by the entrance tells you which sections are closed. In 2004 it was announced that over the next few years the Uffizi would be doubling the number of rooms open to the public, to show some eight hundred works that have usually been kept in storage. This €60 million project got off to a rather inauspicious start, when excavations in preparation for the building of a new exit (a controversial high-rise canopy designed by Japanese architect Arata Isozaki) unearthed the remains of the medieval houses that were demolished in the 1560s to make way for the Uffizi. The new exit was promptly scrapped, but work on the exhibition spaces is now underway, which will mean that some pictures may not be on show precisely where they appear in the following account.

## Pre-Renaissance

You can take a lift up to the galleries, but if you take the staircase instead, you'll pass the entrance to the Uffizi's **prints and drawings** section. The bulk

### The Uffizi bombing

At 1am on May 27, 1993, a colossal **explosion** occurred on the west side of the Uffizi, killing five people, demolishing the headquarters of Europe's oldest agricultural academy, blasting holes through the walls of the Uffizi itself, and damaging numerous paintings inside, some of them irreparably. Initially it was supposed that a gas leak was responsible, but within hours the country's head prosecutor, after discussions with forensic experts and the anti-terrorist squad, issued a statement: "Gas does not come into it. We have found a crater one and a half metres wide. The evidence is unequivocal." Fragments of the car that had carried the estimated 100kg of TNT had been found some 30m from the rubble.

Instantly it was put about that the **Mafia** lay behind the atrocity, though it was not very clear what the Mafia had to gain from the murder of the academy's curator and her family, or from the mutilation of a few Renaissance paintings. While some were willing to believe that the Mafia may have planted the bomb, most Florentines were convinced that the orders had originated within the country's political and military establishment. Frightened by the political realignments taking place all over Italy, with the rise of northern separatists, the reformed Communist Party and other groups, the old guard were – so it seemed to many – once again trying to destabilize the country. Italians imagined a repeat of the 1970s' "Strategy of Tension", when organized criminals and right-wing politicians colluded in a sequence of terrorist attacks to ensure the public's loyalty to the supposedly threatened state. Just days before the Uffizi bombing, the Italian secret service had been implicated in the murders of Giovanni Falcone and Paolo Borsellino, the country's most powerful anti-Mafia investigators, and it seemed plain to some that the same unholy alliances had been at work in Florence.

Three Mafia bosses and eleven underlings were sentenced in June 1998 to life imprisonment for the Uffizi bombing and for two subsequent car bombings in Rome. The prosecution had argued that the Sicilian mobsters had intended to destabilize the government and damage Italy's image abroad. In the opinion of many Italians, however, the true causes of the outrage remain unrevealed. The victims are commemorated by an ancient olive tree, planted in Via de' Georgofili on the spot where the car-bomb was detonated.

of this vast collection is reserved for scholarly scrutiny but samples are often on public show.

Upstairs, all the rooms lead off the statue-lined corridor that runs round the building, which has a sequence of portraits of famous men high on the walls on both sides; commissioned by the Medici in the sixteenth century, the array inevitably includes plenty of images of Florence's first family. **Room 1**, housing an assembly of antique sculptures, many of which were used as a kind of source book by Renaissance artists, is often shut. The beginnings of the stylistic evolution of that period can be traced in the three altarpieces of the *Maestà* (Madonna Enthroned) that dominate **Room 2**: the *Madonna Rucellai*, *Maestà di Santa Trìnita* and *Madonna d'Ognissanti*, by **Duccio**, **Cimabue** and **Giotto** respectively. These great works, which dwarf everything around them, show the softening of the hieratic Byzantine style into a more tactile form of representation.

Painters from fourteenth-century Siena fill **Room 3**, with several pieces by Ambrogio and Pietro Lorenzetti and **Simone Martini**'s glorious *Annunciation*, the Virgin cowering from the angel amid a field of pure gold. Also in this room is Giottino's *San Remigio Pietà* (c.1360), notable both for its emotional intensity and for the alluring portrait of one of the donors – a very elegant young woman, dressed in what was then the height of fashion.

Beyond a room of Giotto-esque artists such as **Orcagna** and **Bernardo Daddi** comes a display of paintings that marks the summit of the precious style known as International Gothic. **Lorenzo Monaco** is represented by an *Adoration of the Magi* and his greatest masterpiece, *The Coronation of the Virgin* (1415). Equally arresting is the *Adoration of the Magi* (1423) by **Gentile da Fabriano**, a picture crammed with so much detail that there's no real distinction between what's crucial and what's peripheral, with as much attention lavished on incidentals such as a snarling leopard as on the protagonists. The right-hand panel of the predella, below, was stolen by Napoleon and replaced with a copy that, unlike the rest of the painting, is not painted directly onto gold – hence the dullness of its surface. Nearby is the *Thebaid*, a beguiling narrative that depicts monastic life in the Egyptian desert as a sort of holy fairy tale; though labelled as being by the young Fra' Angelico, it's also been attributed to the now-obscure Gherardo di Jacopo Starnina, who in his time (he died around 1410) was one of Florence's major artists, and is thought to have been the master of Masolino.

## Early Renaissance

**Room 7** reveals the sheer diversity of early Renaissance painting. **Fra' Angelico**'s *Coronation of the Virgin* takes place against a Gothic-like field of gold, but there's a very un-Gothic sensibility at work in its individualized depiction of the attendant throng. **Paolo Uccello**'s *The Battle of San Romano* once hung in Lorenzo il Magnifico's bedchamber, in company with its two companion pieces now in the Louvre and London's National Gallery. Warfare is the ostensible subject, but this is really a compendium of perspectival effects (a toppling knight, a horse and rider keeled onto their sides, the foreshortened legs of a kicking horse, a thicket of lances) rather than a fight scene with any real sense of violence. The Madonna and Child in **Masolino**'s *Madonna and Child with St Anne* is thought to have been added by his pupil Masaccio, to whom the nearby tiny *Madonna and Child* is also attributed. *The Madonna and Child with SS Francis, John the Baptist, Zenobius and Lucy* is one of only twelve extant paintings by **Domenico Veneziano**, who spent much of his life in Venice but died destitute in Florence.

Veneziano's greatest pupil, **Piero della Francesca**, is represented in **Room 8** by the paired portraits of *Federico da Montefeltro and Battista Sforza*, the duke and duchess of Urbino. These panels were painted two years after Battista's death; in the background of her portrait is the town of Gubbio, where she died giving birth to her ninth child and only son, Guidobaldo. A lot of space in Room 8 is given over to **Filippo Lippi**, whose *Madonna and Child with Two Angels* supplies one of the gallery's most popular faces: the model was Lucrezia Buti, a convent novice who became the object of one of his more enduring sexual obsessions. Lucrezia puts in another appearance in Lippi's crowded *Coronation of the Virgin*, where she's the young woman gazing out in the right foreground; Filippo himself, hand on chin, makes eye contact on the left side of the picture. Their liaison produced a son, the aptly named **Filippino** "Little Philip" **Lippi**, whose *Madonna degli Otto* – one of several works by him here – is typical of the more melancholic cast of the younger Lippi's art.

## The Pollaiuolo brothers and Botticelli

Lippi's great pupil, Botticelli, steals some of the thunder in **Room 9** – *Fortitude*, one of the series of cardinal and theological virtues, is a very early work by him. The rest of the series is by the brothers **Piero** and **Antonio del Pollaiuolo**, whose *SS Vincent, James and Eustace*, one of their best works, is chiefly the work of Antonio; he also painted the two sinewy images of Hercules, which shows evidence of the brothers' revolutionary study of anatomy. This room usually contains the *Portrait of Young Man in a Red Hat*, sometimes referred to as a self-portrait by Filippino Lippi, but believed by some to be an eighteenth-century fraud.

It's in the merged **rooms 10–14** that the greatest of **Botticelli**'s productions are gathered. A century ago most people walked past his pictures without breaking stride; nowadays – despite their elusiveness – the *Primavera* and the *Birth of Venus* stop all visitors in their tracks. The identities of the characters in the **Primavera** are not contentious: on the right Zephyrus, god of the west wind, chases the nymph Cloris, who is then transfigured into Flora, the pregnant goddess of spring; Venus stands in the centre, to the side of the three Graces, who are targeted by Cupid; on the left Mercury wards off the clouds of winter. What this all means, however, has occupied scholars for decades. Some see it as an allegory of the four seasons, but the consensus now seems to be that it shows the triumph of Venus, with the Graces as the physical embodiment of her beauty and Flora the symbol of her fruitfulness.

Botticelli's most winsome painting, the **Birth of Venus**, probably takes as its source the myth that the goddess emerged from the sea after it had been impregnated by the castration of Uranus, an allegory for the creation of beauty through the mingling of the spirit (Uranus) and the physical world. The supporting players are the nymph, Cloris, and Zephyrus, god of the west wind. Zephyrus blows the risen Venus to the shore where the goddess is clothed by Hora, daughter and attendant of Aurora, goddess of dawn. A third allegory hangs close by: *Pallas and the Centaur*, perhaps symbolizing the ambivalent triumph of reason over instinct.

Botticelli's devotional paintings are generally less perplexing. *The Adoration of the Magi* is traditionally thought to contain a gallery of Medici portraits: Cosimo il Vecchio as the first king, his sons Giovanni and Piero as the other two kings, Lorenzo the Magnificent on the far left, and his brother Giuliano as the black-haired young man in profile on the right. Only the identification of Cosimo is reasonably certain, along with that of Botticelli himself, on the right in the yellow robe. In later life, influenced by Savonarola's teaching, Botticelli confined himself to devotional pictures and moral fables, and his style became increasingly severe and didactic. The transformation is clear when comparing the easy grace of the *Madonna of the Magnificat* and the *Madonna of the Pomegranate* with the more rigidly composed *Pala di Sant'Ambrogio* or the angular *Calumny*. Even the *Annunciation* (1489), painted just as Savonarola's preaching began to grip Florence, reveals a new intensity in the expression of the angel and in the twisting body of the Virgin, whose posture embodies her ambivalent reaction to the message.

Not quite every masterpiece in this room is by Botticelli. Set away from the walls is the *Adoration of the Shepherds* by his Flemish contemporary **Hugo van der Goes**. Brought to Florence in 1483 by Tommaso Portinari, the Medici agent in Bruges, it provided the city's artists with their first large-scale demonstration of the realism of Northern European oil painting, and had a great influence on the way the medium was exploited here.

## Leonardo to the Tribuna

Works in **Room 15** trace the formative years of **Leonardo da Vinci**, whose distinctive touch appears first in the *Baptism of Christ* by his master Verrocchio. Vasari claimed that only the wistful angel in profile was by the 18-year-old apprentice, and the misty landscape in the background, but X-rays have revealed that Leonardo also worked heavily on the figure of Christ. A similar terrain of soft-focus mountains and water occupies the far distance in Leonardo's slightly later *Annunciation*, in which a diffused light falls on a scene where everything is observed with a scientist's precision: the petals of the flowers on which the angel alights, the fall of the Virgin's drapery, the carving on the lectern at which she reads. In restless contrast to the poise of the *Annunciation*, the sketch of *The Adoration of the Magi* – abandoned when Leonardo left Florence for Milan in early 1482 – presents the infant Christ as the eye of a vortex of figures.

Most of the rest of the room is given over to Raphael's teacher, **Perugino**, who is represented by a typically placid and contemplative *Madonna and Child with Saints* (1493), and *Pietà* (1494–95). It also contains an *Incarnation* by **Piero di Cosimo**, of whom more later.

**Room 18**, the octagonal **Tribuna**, now houses the most important of the Medici's collection of classical sculptures, chiefly the *Medici Venus*, a first-century BC copy of the Praxitelean *Aphrodite of Cnidos*. She was kept in the Villa Medici in Rome until Cosimo III began to fret that she was having a detrimental effect on the morals of the city's art students, and ordered her removal to Florence. The move clearly didn't affect the statue's sexual charisma, however: it became traditional for eighteenth-century visitors to Florence to caress her buttocks. Around the walls are hung some fascinating portraits by **Bronzino**: Cosimo de' Medici, Eleonora di Toledo, Bartolomeo Panciatichi and his wife Lucrezia Panciatichi, all painted like figures of porcelain. More vital is Andrea del Sarto's flirtatious *Ritratto d'Ignota* (*Portrait of an Unknown Young Woman*), and there's a deceptive naturalism to Vasari's portrait of Lorenzo the Magnificent and Pontormo's of Cosimo il Vecchio, both painted long after the death of their subjects.

## Signorelli to Mantegna

The last section of this wing throws together Renaissance paintings from outside Florence, with some notable Venetian and Flemish works. **Signorelli** and **Perugino** are the principal artists in **Room 19**, and after them comes a room largely devoted to **Cranach** and **Dürer**. Each has an *Adam and Eve* here, Dürer taking the opportunity to show off his proficiency as a painter of wildlife. Dürer's power as a portraitist is displayed in the *Portrait of the Artist's Father*, his earliest authenticated painting, and Cranach has a couple of acute pictures of Luther on display, one of them a double with his wife. Here you'll also find a bizarre *Perseus Freeing Andromeda* by **Piero di Cosimo**, the wild man of the Florentine Renaissance. Shunning civilized company, Piero did everything he could to bring his life close to a state of uncompromised nature, living in a house that was never cleaned, in the midst of a garden he refused to tend, and eating nothing but hard-boiled eggs. Where his contemporaries might seek inspiration in commentaries on Plato, he would spend hours staring at the sky, at peeling walls, at the pavement – at anything where abstract patterns might conjure fabulous scenes in his imagination.

A taste of the Uffizi's remarkable collection of Venetian painting follows, with an impenetrable *Sacred Allegory* by **Giovanni Bellini**, and three works attributed to **Giorgione**. A clutch of Northern European paintings includes some superb portraits by **Holbein** (notably *Sir Richard Southwell* and a self-portrait) and **Hans Memling**. In the following room – called the **Correggio** room, after the trio of pictures by him on show here – there's a triptych by **Mantegna** which is not in fact a real triptych, but rather a trio of exquisite small paintings shackled together. To the side of them are a couple of other pictures by Mantegna – a swarthy portrait of Carlo de' Medici and the *Madonna of the Stonecutters*, which takes its name from the minuscule figures at work in the quarry in the background.

## Michelangelo, Mannerism and Titian

Beyond the stockpile of statues in the short corridor overlooking the Arno, the main attraction in **Room 25** is **Michelangelo**'s *Doni Tondo*, the only easel painting he came close to completing. (Regarding sculpture as the noblest of the visual arts, Michelangelo dismissed all non-fresco painting as a demeaning chore.) Though the significance of the whole picture isn't fully understood, the five naked figures behind the Holy Family seem to be standing in a half-moon-shaped cistern or font, which would relate to the infant Baptist to the right, who – in the words of St Paul – prefigured the coming of Christ just as the new moon is "a shadow of things to come". In the same epistle, Paul goes on to commend the virtues of mercy, benignity, humility, modesty and patience, which are perhaps what the five youths represent. **Albertinelli**'s *Visitation* tends to get upstaged by Michelangelo, but it's a lustrous and extraordinarily touching picture.

**Room 26** contains **Andrea del Sarto**'s sultry *Madonna of the Harpies* and a number of compositions by **Raphael**, including his self-portrait, the lovely *Madonna of the Goldfinch* and *Pope Leo X with Cardinals Giulio de' Medici and Luigi de' Rossi* – as shifty a group of ecclesiastics as was ever gathered in one frame. The Michelangelo tondo's contorted gestures and virulent colours were greatly influential on the Mannerist painters of the sixteenth century, as can be gauged from *Moses Defending the Daughters of Jethro* by **Rosso Fiorentino**, one of the seminal figures of the movement, whose works hang in **Room 27**, along with major works by Bronzino and his adoptive father, Pontormo.

**Room 28** is almost entirely given over to another of the great figures of sixteenth-century art, **Titian**, with nine paintings on show. His *Flora* and *A Knight of Malta* are stunning, but most eyes tend to swivel towards the *Urbino Venus*, the most provocative of all Renaissance nudes, described by Mark Twain as "the foulest, the vilest, the obscenest picture the world possesses". **Sebastiano del Piombo**'s *Death of Adonis* was reduced to little more than postage-stamp tatters by the 1993 bomb; the restoration is little short of miraculous.

A brief diversion through the painters of the sixteenth-century Emilian school follows, centred on **Parmigianino**, whose *Madonna of the Long Neck* is one of the pivotal Mannerist creations. Parmigianino was an introverted character who abandoned painting for alchemy towards the end of his short life, and many of his works show a sort of morbid refinement, none more so than this one. The Madonna's tunic clings to every contour, an angel advances a perfectly turned leg, the infant Christ drapes himself languorously on his mother's lap – prefiguring the dead Christ of the Pietà – while in the background an emaciated figure unrolls a scroll of parchment by a colonnade so severely foreshortened that it looks like a single column.

**Rooms 31 to 34** feature a miscellany of sixteenth-century artists (look out for the El Greco) and some superb works from Venice and the Veneto, including work by **Moroni**, **Paolo Veronese**, Tintoretto and Lorenzo Lotto, and a female nude by **Bernardino Licino** that's unusual in seeming to have no mythological pretext – the subject is not Venus, but simply a naked woman.

## The seventeenth and eighteenth centuries

The Uffizi's collection of seventeenth-century art features strong work from **Van Dyck** and **Rubens**, whose *Portrait of Isabella Brandt* is perhaps his finest painting here. The most overwhelming, however, are Rubens' huge *Henry IV at the Battle of Ivry* and *The Triumphal Entry of Henry IV into Paris*, which are displayed in the majestic Neoclassical Niobe Room; Henry's marriage to Marie de' Medici is the connection with Florence.

In this section of the gallery you'll also see some superb portraits by **Rembrandt**. His sorrow-laden *Self-Portrait as an Old Man*, painted five years or so before his death, makes a poignant contrast with the self-confident self-portrait of thirty years earlier. Although there are some good pieces from Giambattista **Tiepolo** in the adjacent room of eighteenth-century paintings, portraits again command the attention, notably **Goya**'s image of Maria Theresa on horseback and **Chardin**'s demure children.

The rooms downstairs are used for temporary exhibitions and as a showcase for Italian art of the seventeenth century. Dramatic images from Salvator Rosa, Luca Giordano and Artemisia Gentileschi make quite an impression, but the presiding genius is **Caravaggio**, with his virtuosic *Medusa* (the severed head is painted on a shield), the smug little *Bacchus*, and the throat-grabbing *Sacrifice of Isaac*. Works by lesser (but still impressive) talents show the huge influence of Caravaggio's high-contrast and high-impact art.

### The Corridoio Vasariano

A door on the west corridor, between rooms 25 and 34, opens onto the **Corridoio Vasariano**, a passageway built by Vasari in 1565 to link the Palazzo Vecchio to the Palazzo Pitti, via the Uffizi. Winding its way down to the river, over the Ponte Vecchio, through the church of Santa Felìcita and into the Giardino di Bóboli, it gives a fascinating series of clandestine views of the city. As if that weren't pleasure enough, the corridor is lined with paintings, the larger portion of which comprises a gallery of **self-portraits**, featuring such greats as Andrea del Sarto, Bronzino, Bernini, Rubens, Velázquez, David, Delacroix and Ingres. However, the corridor is currently **closed for restoration**, and there are plans to move the best of the paintings into the extended Uffizi galleries. The corridor used to be open two mornings a week for small-group **guided tours**, and in all likelihood that will be the arrangement when the restoration is completed. For the latest situation, ask at the Amici degli Amici office at the Uffizi or at one of the tourist offices.

**ORSANMICHELE**

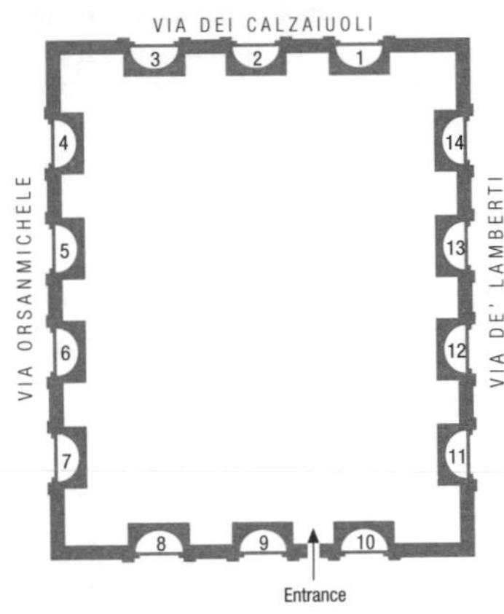


1 John the Baptist (1412–16), Lorenzo Ghiberti for the Arte di Calimala (Textiles Guild); niche, Albizzo di Piero to a design by Ghiberti
2 The Incredulity of St Thomas (1473–83), Verrocchio for the Mercatanzia (Merchants' Tribunal); niche (1423–5), Donatello and Michelozzo
3 St Luke (1610), Giambologna for the Giudici e Notai (judges and notaries); niche, Niccolò di Pietro Lamberti (1404–6)
4 St Peter (1408–13), attrib. Bernardo Ciuffagni for the Beccai (butchers)
5 St Philip (1412–15), Nanni di Banco for the Conciapelli (tanners)
6 Quattro Coronati (1409–17), Nanni di Banco for the Maestri di Pietre e Legname (masons and carpenters)
7 St George (1416–7) and relief of St George and Dragon, Donatello for the Corazzai (armourers)
8 St Matthew (1419–22), Lorenzo Ghiberti for the Cambio (bankers); tabernacle to a design by Ghiberti
9 St Stephen (1427–8), Lorenzo Ghiberti for the Arte della Lana (wool)
10 St Eligius (1417–21), Nanni di Banco for the Maniscalchi (smiths)
11 St Mark (1411–13), Donatello for the Linaiuoli (linen-drapers); niche (1411), Perfetto di Giovanni and Albizo di Piero
12 St James (1420) and bas relief of the Martyrdom of St James, attrib. Niccolò di Pietro Lamberti for the Pellicciai (furriers)
13 Madonna della Rosa (1400), attrib. Pietro di Giovanni Tedesco for the Medici e Speziali (doctors and pharmacists); Madonna Enthroned (above), Luca della Robbia (1465)
14 St John the Evangelist (1515), Baccio da Montelupo for the Setaiuoli (silk)

# Orsanmichele

Looming like a fortress over Via dei Calzaiuoli, the foursquare **Orsanmichele** (Tues–Sun 10am–5pm; free) is the oddest church in Florence – a unique hybrid of the sacred and secular, it's not even immediately apparent which of its walls is the front. Its exterior was once the most impressive outdoor **sculpture gallery** in the city, and while nowadays all of the pieces outside are replicas (most of the originals are on display in the attached museum), this church is nevertheless one of the city's great sights.

The first building here was a small oratory secreted in the orchard or vegetable garden (*orto*) of a now-vanished Benedictine monastery. A larger church stood on the site from the ninth century: San Michele ad Hortum, later San Michele in Orte – hence the compacted form of Orsanmichele. Even after a **grain market** replaced the church in the thirteenth century, the place retained its religious associations, and in 1300, the chronicler Giovanni Villani claimed "the lame walked and the possessed were liberated" after visiting a miraculous image of the Virgin painted on one of the market pillars. After a fire in 1304, the building was eventually replaced by a **loggia** designed by Francesco Talenti to serve as a trade hall for the *Arti Maggiori*, the great guilds which governed the city. Between 1367 and 1380 the loggia was walled in, after which the site was again dedicated almost exclusively to religious functions, while leaving two upper storeys for use as emergency grain stores.

As far back as 1339, plans had been made to adorn each pillar of the building with a patron statue, each assigned to a different guild. But by 1408, only a statue of *St Stephen* commissioned by the *Arte della Lana* had been finished, and the exasperated city elders set a ten-year deadline, warning that the niches would be allocated to rival guilds if commissions remained unfulfilled. The delay was to posterity's benefit, for the statues that were eventually produced spanned the emergent years of the Renaissance.

## The exterior

Beginning on the far left of Orsanmichele's Via dei Calzaiuoli flank, the first tabernacle is occupied by Ghiberti's **John the Baptist** (number 1 on our plan), the earliest life-size bronze statue of the Renaissance. It was made for the *Calimala*, the guild of wholesale cloth importers. Doubtful whether Ghiberti could cast the figure in one piece, his cautious patrons made him liable for the cost of the metal should he fail. In the event it came out intact, except for one toe, which had to be welded on later. The adjacent niche is occupied by *The Incredulity of St Thomas* (2) by Verrocchio, which replaced an earlier gilded statue by Donatello, *St Louis of Toulouse*, now in the Museo dell'Opera del Duomo.

Round the corner there are two works from Nanni di Banco: *St Philip* (5) and his masterpiece, the so-called **Quattro Coronati** (6). The original *Quattro Coronati* were four anonymous Romans who were martyred by Diocletian; known as the Four Crowned Ones simply because the crown was a badge of martyrdom, they somehow became conflated with a group of Christian stonemasons, executed by Diocletian for refusing to carve a pagan idol – the latter group (who were actually five in number), became the patron saints of the masons' guild, sponsors of this niche. Donatello's *St George* (7) occupies the next niche – the original is in the Bargello, as is the original accompanying bas-relief of *St George and the Dragon*.

On the church's west side stand *St Matthew* (8) and *St Stephen* (9); the *St Matthew*, posed and clad like a Roman orator, makes a telling comparison with the same artist's *St John*, cast just ten years before but still semi-Gothic in its sharp-edged drapery and arching lines. Earlier than either is Donatello's **St Mark** (11), made in 1411 when the artist was 25; the work is often considered one of the first statues of the Renaissance, a title based on the naturalism of St Mark's stance and the brooding intensity of his gaze. Pietro Lamberti's *St James* (12) precedes the benign **Madonna della Rosa** (13), probably by Pietro di Giovanni Tedesco. The latter was damaged in 1493 when one Signor Marrona went berserk and set about axing lumps out of every statue of the Madonna he could find. A lynch mob of Savonarola's monks caught up with him just after he'd started work on the infant Christ.

## The interior and the museum

Orsanmichele's interior centrepiece is a pavilion-sized glass and marble **tabernacle** by Orcagna, the only significant sculptural work by the artist. Decorated with lapis lazuli, coloured glass and gold, it's somewhat obscure in its iconography, though most of the imagery refers to the life of the Virgin. It frames a *Madonna delle Grazie* painted in 1347 by Bernardo Daddi as a replacement for the miraculous image destroyed by the 1304 fire. The brotherhood that administered Orsanmichele paid for the tabernacle from thanksgiving donations in the aftermath of the Black Death; so many people attributed their survival to the Madonna's intervention that the money received in 1348 alone was greater than the annual tax income of the city coffers. Other paintings can be seen on the pillars: devotional images of the guilds' patron saints, they can be regarded as the low-cost ancestors of the Orsanmichele statues.

The original lines of the bricked-up loggia are still clear and the vaulted halls of the upper granaries also survive. The lower of these halls now houses the **Museo di Orsanmichele** (Mon–Sat 10am–3pm; free), entered via the footbridge from the Palazzo dell'Arte della Lana, the building opposite the church entrance. Having been restored, nearly all of the exterior **statues** are on show here – the main exception is the most famous of all, Donatello's *St George*, which belongs to the Bargello. From time to time one-off exhibitions are held here, in which case an entrance fee is charged.



## The Badìa Fiorentina

The **Badìa Fiorentina** (Florentine Abbey) is one of the most impressive churches in the centre of the city, and is also a place of special significance for admirers of **Dante**, for this was the parish church of Beatrice Portinari, for whom he conceived a lifelong love as he observed her during Mass here. Furthermore, it was here that Boccaccio delivered his celebrated lectures on *The Divine Comedy*.

Founded in 978 by Willa, widow of the Margrave of Tuscany, in honour of her husband, the Badìa was one of the focal buildings in medieval Florence: the city's sick were treated in a hospital founded here in 1031, while the main bell marked the divisions of the working day. The hospital also owed much to Willa's son, Ugo, who further endowed his mother's foundation after a vision of the hellish torments which awaited him by "reason of his worldly life, unless he should repent". The 1280s saw the church overhauled along Cistercian Gothic lines,

### Dante Alighieri

**Dante** signed himself "Dante Alighieri, a Florentine by birth but not by character", a bitter allusion to the city he served as a politician but which later cast him into exile and was to inspire some of the most vitriolic passages in *La Divina Commedia* (The Divine Comedy).

Dante was born in 1265 into a minor and impoverished noble family. He was educated at Bologna and later at Padua, where he studied philosophy and astronomy. The defining moment in his life came in 1274 when he met the 8-year-old **Beatrice Portinari**, a girl whom Boccaccio described as possessed of "habits and language more serious and modest than her age warranted". Her features were "so delicate and so beautifully formed," he went on, "and full, besides mere beauty, of so much candid loveliness that many thought her almost an angel."

Dante – just 9 at the time of the meeting – later described his own feeling following the encounter. "Love ruled my soul," he wrote, "and began to hold such sway over me ... that it was necessary for me to do completely all his pleasure. He commanded me often that I should endeavour to see this so youthful angel, and I saw in her such noble and praiseworthy deportment that truly of her might be said these words of the poet Homer – *She appeared to be born not of mortal man but of God*."

Unhappily, Beatrice's family had decided their daughter was to marry someone else – Simone de' Bardi. The ceremony took place when she was 17; seven years later she was dead. Dante, for his part, had been promised – aged 12 – to Gemma Donati. Their wedding eventually took place in 1295, when the poet was 30.

His romantic hopes dashed, Dante settled down to a military and political career. In 1289 he fought for Florence against Arezzo and helped in a campaign against Pisa. Later he joined the Apothecaries' Guild, serving on a variety of minor civic committees. In 1300 he was dispatched to San Gimignano, where he was entrusted with the job of coaxing the town into an alliance against Pope Boniface VIII, who had designs on Tuscany. In June of the same year he sought to settle the widening breach between the **Black** (anti-imperial) and **White** (more conciliatory) factions of Florence's ruling Guelph party. The dispute had its roots in money: the Whites contained leading probably under the direction of Arnolfo di Cambio, architect of the Duomo and Palazzo Vecchio. Later Baroque additions smothered much of the old church in 1627, though the narrow **campanile** – Romanesque at its base, Gothic towards its apex – escaped unharmed. Completed in 1330, it remains a prominent feature of the Florentine skyline.

Nowadays the church belongs to the Fraternity of Jerusalem, a French monastic order founded in the 1970s. **Tourist visits** are allowed on Monday afternoons (3–6pm); at other times the church is open for prayer only. On the left, as you enter from Via Dante Alighieri, hangs **Filippino Lippi**'s superb *Apparition of the Virgin to St Bernard*, painted in 1485 for the Benedictine monastery at Campora and commissioned by Piero del Pugliese: Lippi has included a portrait of the donor at the bottom of the painting. Bernard is shown in the act of writing a homily aimed at those caught between the "rocks" of tribulation and the "chains" of sin; the presence of the four monks reinforces the message that redemption lies in the contemplative life.

Set back to the right is the church's second highlight, the **tomb monument** to Ugo, sculpted by Mino da Fiesole between 1469 and 1481. Mino was also responsible for the nearby tomb of Bernardo Giugni and an altar frontal of the *Madonna and Child with SS Leonard and Lawrence*. Giugni was a lawyer and diplomat, hence the figures of Justice and Faith accompanying his effigy.

A staircase from the choir – take the door immediately right of the high altar – leads to the upper storey of the **Chiostro degli Aranci** (Cloister of the

bankers to the imperial powers (the Cerchi, Mozzi, Davanzati and Frescobaldi), while the Blacks counted the Pazzi, Bardi and Donati amongst their number, all prominent papal bankers. Boniface, not surprisingly, sided with the Blacks, who eventually emerged triumphant.

Dante's White sympathies sealed his fate. In 1302, following trumped-up charges of corruption, he was sentenced with other Whites to two years' exile. While many of the deportees subsequently returned, Dante rejected his city of "self-made men and fast-got gain". He wandered instead between Forlì, Verona, Padua, Luni and Venice, writing much of *The Divine Comedy* as he went, before finally settling in Ravenna, where he died in 1321.

Running to more than fourteen thousand lines, **The Divine Comedy** is an extraordinarily rich and detailed allegory, recounting the poet's journey through Inferno (Hell), Purgatorio (Purgatory) and Paradiso (Paradise), accompanied initially by the Roman poet Virgil (Dante was fully aware that his work would bear comparison with the greats) and then by Beatrice. Each of these three realms of the dead is depicted in 33 *canti* (a "prologue" to the Inferno brings the total up to 100), composed in a verse scheme called terza rima, in which lines of eleven syllables follow the rhyme scheme aba, bcb, cdc, ded, etc. This may seem an inflexible framework, but Dante employs it to achieve an amazing variety of tone, encompassing everything from the desperate abuse of the damned, through the complex theological argumentation of Purgatory to the exalted lyricism of his vision of heaven. And the range of subject matter is astonishing too: *The Divine Comedy* is both a metaphysical epic in which the entire medieval view of the cosmos is encapsulated, and an incisive critique of the society in which Dante lived – one in which he doesn't shirk from naming names. Equally remarkable is that Dante wrote his poem in the Tuscan dialect, at a time when Latin would have been regarded as the only language suitable for subjects of such seriousness. Before *The Divine Comedy*, Tuscan was the vulgar language of the street; afterwards, it began to be seen as the language of all Italian people, from peasants to philosophers.

Oranges), named after the fruit trees that used to be grown here. Two of its flanks are graced with an anonymous but highly distinctive fresco cycle (1436–39) on the life of St Benedict. A later panel – showing the saint throwing himself into bushes to resist temptation – is by the young Bronzino (1526–28). The cloister itself (1432–38) is the work of Bernardo Rossellino, one of the leading lights of early Renaissance architecture.



## Casa di Dante and around

After visiting the Badìa Fiorentina, you might want to explore the city's knot of buildings with **Dante** associations – some of them admittedly spurious – that are clustered in the grid of narrow streets behind the Badìa, between Piazza del Duomo and Piazza della Signoria. Somewhat fraudulently marketed as Dante's house, the **Casa di Dante** (Tues–Sun 10am–5pm; €4) is actually a medieval pastiche dating from 1910. The museum upstairs is a homage to the poet rather than a shrine: it contains nothing directly related to his life, and in all likelihood Dante was born not on the house's site but somewhere in the street that bears his name. Numerous editions of the *Divina Commedia* are on show – including a poster printed with the whole text in minuscule type – along with copies of Botticelli's illustrations to the poem and a variety of context-setting displays.

As contentious as the Casa di Dante's claims to authenticity is the story that Dante married Gemma Donati in **Santa Margherita de' Cerchi** (Mon–Sat 10am–noon & 3–5pm, Sun 10am–noon; free), the ancient little church up the street from the Casa di Dante. Documented as early as 1032, the building does, however, contain several tombs belonging to the Portinari, Beatrice's family name; the porch also features the Donati family crest, as this was also their local parish church. These are probably the limits of the Dantesque associations, though the church is worth a look anyway, chiefly for a nice altarpiece of the *Madonna and Four Saints* by Neri di Bicci.

Over Via Dante Alighieri from the poet's house, on Piazza San Martino, lies the tiny **San Martino del Vescovo** (Mon–Thurs & Sat 10am–noon & 3–5pm, Fri 10am–noon), built on the site of a small oratory founded in 986 that served as the Alighieri's parish church. Rebuilt in 1479, it became the headquarters of the Compagnia di Buonomini, a charitable body dedicated to aiding impoverished better-class citizens for whom begging was too demeaning a prospect. (This confraternity is still in existence.) The Buonomini commissioned from Ghirlandaio's workshop a sequence of frescoes showing various altruistic acts and scenes from the life of St Martin, and the result is as absorbing a record of daily life in Renaissance Florence as the Ghirlandaio frescoes in Santa Maria Novella.

Opposite San Martino soars the thirteenth-century **Torre della Castagna**, meeting place of the city's *priori* before they decamped to the Palazzo Vecchio. This is one of the most striking remnants of Florence's medieval townscape, when more than 150 such towers rose between the river and the Duomo, many of them over two hundred feet high. Allied clans would link their towers with wooden catwalks, creating a sort of upper-class promenade above the heads of the lowlier citizens. In 1250 the government of the *Primo Popolo* ordered that the towers be reduced by two-thirds of their height; the resulting rubble was voluminous enough to extend the city walls beyond the Arno.

# The Bargello

In Renaissance Florence, sculpture assumed an importance unmatched in any other part of Italy, perhaps because this most public of arts was appropriate to a city with such a strong sense of itself as a cohesive community. On a less abstract level, Florence is surrounded by quarries, and the art of stonecutting had always been nurtured here. Whatever the reason for this pre-eminence, the Renaissance sculpture collection of the **Museo Nazionale del Bargello** (Tues–Sat 8.15am–1.50pm; second and fourth Sun of month and first, third and fifth Mon of month same hours; €4; longer hours and higher charge for special shows), at Via del Proconsolo 4, is the richest in Italy. Sculpture apart, the museum also devotes a vast amount of space to the decorative arts: superb carpets, enamels, ivories, glassware, tapestries, silverware and other *objets d'art*.

The Bargello's home, the daunting Palazzo del Bargello, was built in 1255 immediately after the overthrow of the aristocratic regime. The first of the city's public palaces, it soon became the seat of the *Podestà*, the city's chief magistrate, and the site of the main law court. Numerous malefactors were tortured, tried, sentenced and executed here, the elegant courtyard having been the site of the city's gallows and block. The building acquired its present name after 1574, when the Medici abolished the post of *Podestà*, the building becoming home to the chief of police – the *Bargello*. Torture and capital punishment were banned in 1786 (the first such abolition in Europe), but the building remained a prison until 1859.

## The ground floor

You've no time to catch your breath in the Bargello: the first room to the right of the ticket office is crammed with extraordinary objects, chief of which are the work of **Michelangelo**, in whose shadow every Florentine sculptor laboured from the sixteenth century onwards. The tipsy, soft-bellied figure of *Bacchus* (1496–97) was his first major sculpture, carved at the age of 22, a year or so before his great *Pietà* in Rome. Michelangelo's style later evolved into something less immediately virtuosic, as is shown by the delicate *Tondo Pitti* of the Madonna and Child (1503–05). The square-jawed *Bust of Brutus* (1539–40) is the artist's sole work of this kind; a powerful portrait sketch in stone, it's a coded celebration of anti-Medicean republicanism, carved soon after the murder of the nightmarish Duke Alessandro de' Medici (see p.118).

Works by Michelangelo's followers and contemporaries are ranged in the immediate vicinity; some of them would command prolonged attention in less exalted company. **Benvenuto Cellini**'s huge *Bust of Cosimo I* (1545–47), his first work in bronze, was a sort of technical trial for the casting of the *Perseus*, his most famous work. Alongside the two preparatory models for the *Perseus* in wax and bronze are displayed the original marble base and four statuettes that comprise the statue's pedestal; *Perseus* himself still stands in his intended spot, in the Loggia della Signoria.

Close by, **Giambologna**'s *Virtue Overcoming Vice* (or *Florence Defeating Pisa*; 1575) – a disingenuous pretext for a voluptuous female nude if ever there were one – takes up a lot of space, but is eclipsed by his best-known creation, the wonderful *Mercury* (1564), a nimble figure with no bad angles. Comic relief is provided by the reliably inept Bandinelli, whose coiffured *Adam and Eve* look like a grandee and his wife taking an *au naturel* stroll through their country estate. The highly erotic *Leda and the Swan* by **Ammannati** (1540–50) was inspired by a painting of the subject by Michelangelo that was later destroyed.

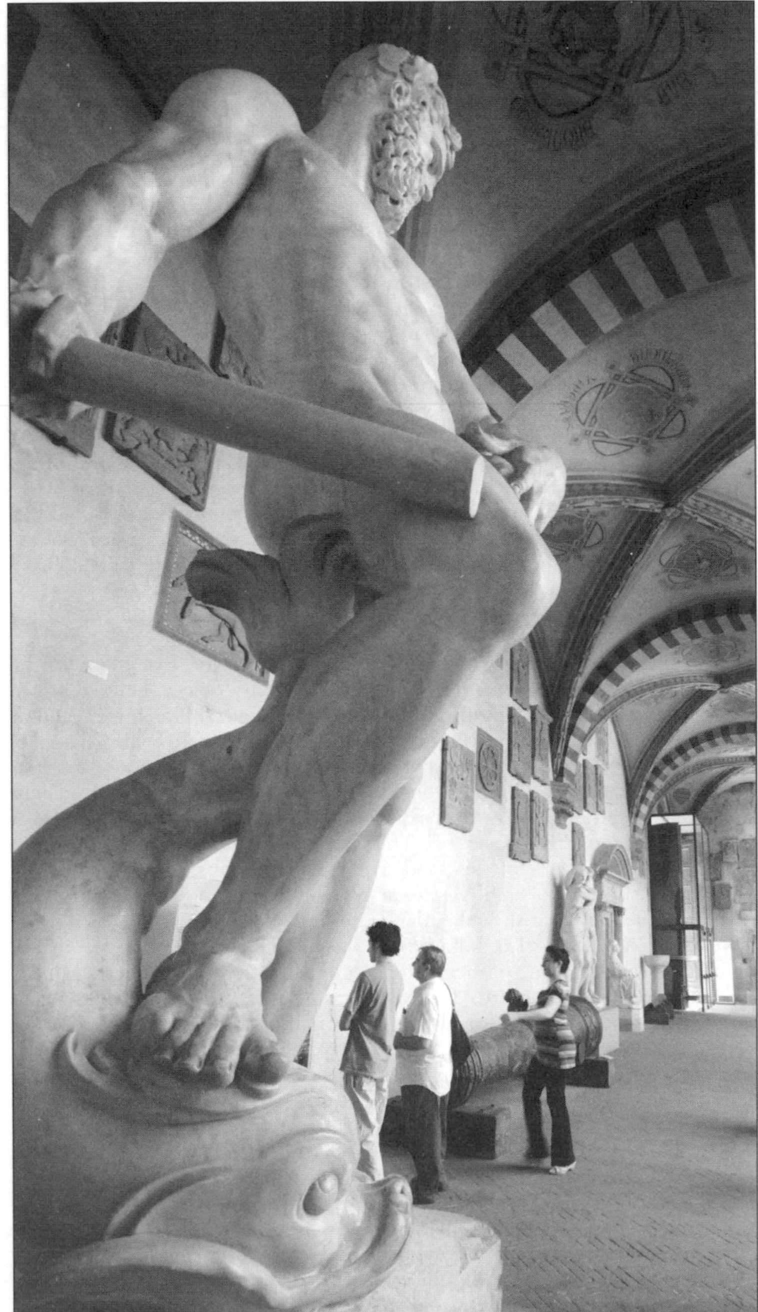

▲ Courtyard, the Bargello

Part two of the ground floor's collection lies across the Gothic **courtyard**, which is plastered with the coats of arms of the *Podestà*. Against the far wall stand six allegorical figures by Ammannati from the fountain of the Palazzo Pitti courtyard. Of the two rooms across the yard, the one to the left features largely fourteenth-century works, notably pieces by Arnolfo di Cambio and Tino da Camaino; temporary exhibitions are often held in the room to the right.

## The first floor

At the top of Giuliano da Sangallo's courtyard **staircase** (1502), the first-floor loggia has been turned into a menagerie for Giambologna's quaint bronze animals and birds, imported from the Medici villa at Castello, just outside Florence. The nearer doorway to the right opens into the tall, Gothic **Salone del Consiglio Generale**. Here again the number of masterpieces is breathtaking, and this time the presiding genius is the restlessly innovative **Donatello**.

Vestiges of the sinuous Gothic manner are evident in the drapery of his marble *David* (1408), but there's nothing antiquated in the **St George** (1416), carved for the tabernacle of the armourers' guild at Orsanmichele and installed in a replica of its original niche at the far end of the room. If any one sculpture could be said to encapsulate the humanist sensibility of fifteenth-century Florence, this is it: whereas St George was previously little more than a symbol of valour, this alert, tensed figure represents not the act of heroism but the volition behind it. The slaying of the dragon is depicted in the small, badly eroded marble panel underneath.

Also here is the sexually ambivalent bronze **David** (1430–40), the first freestanding nude figure created since classical times. Created for the courtyard of the Palazzo Medici, it might have been intended as a Neoplatonic allegory of the triumph of divine love over erotic love – the scene on Goliath's visor shows Eros enthroned on a chariot. A decade later the sculptor produced the strange prancing figure known as *Amor-Atys*, which was later mistaken for a genuine statue from classical antiquity. This was one of the highest compliments a Renaissance artist could have wished for – as is attested by the story of Michelangelo's heaping soil over one of his first works, a sleeping cupid, in order to give it the appearance of an unearthed ancient piece. Donatello was just as comfortable with portraiture as with Christian or pagan imagery, as his breathtakingly vivid terracotta *Bust of Niccolò da Uzzano* demonstrates; this may be the earliest Renaissance portrait bust. When the occasion demanded, Donatello could also produce a straightforwardly monumental piece like the nearby *Marzocco* (1418–20), Florence's heraldic lion.

Donatello's master, **Ghiberti**, is represented by his relief of *Abraham's Sacrifice*, his entry in the competition to design the Baptistery doors in 1401, easily missed on the right-hand wall; the treatment of the theme submitted by Brunelleschi, effectively the runner-up, is hung alongside. Set around the walls of the room, a sequence of glazed terracotta Madonnas constitute a perfect introduction to the sweet-natured piety of **Luca della Robbia**.

The rest of this floor is occupied by a superb collection of European and Islamic applied art, with dazzling specimens of work in enamel, glass, silver, majolica and ivory: among the ivory pieces from Byzantium and medieval France you'll find combs, boxes, chess pieces, and devotional panels featuring scores of figures crammed into a space the size of a paperback. Room 9, the **Cappella di Santa Maria Maddalena**, is decorated with frescoes discovered in 1841 when the room was converted from a prison cell; they're now thought to be by followers of Giotto rather than Giotto himself. The scenes from *Paradiso* on the altar (end) wall feature a portrait of Dante holding *The Divine Comedy* – he's the figure in maroon in the right-hand group, fifth from the left. The chapel's beautiful pulpit, lectern and stalls (1483–88) all came from San Miniato al Monte, while the impressive altar triptych is a mid-fifteenth-century work by Giovanni di Francesco.



### The second floor

Sculpture resumes upstairs, with rooms devoted to the della Robbia family, a prelude to the **Sala dei Bronzetti**, Italy's best assembly of small Renaissance bronzes. Giambologna's spiralling designs predominate, a testament to his popularity in late sixteenth-century Florence: look out for the *Hercules* (Ercole) series, showing the hero variously wrestling and clubbing his opponents into submission. An interesting contrast is provided by **Antonio del Pollaiuolo**'s earlier and much more violent *Hercules and Antaeus* (c.1478), which stands on a pillar nearby. Like Leonardo, Pollaiuolo unravelled the complexities of human musculature by dissecting corpses.

Also on this floor there's a splendid display of bronze medals, featuring specimens from the great pioneer of this form of portable art, **Pisanello**, among whose coin-sized portraits you'll see Leonello d'Este (the lord of Ferrara), Sigismondo Malatesta (the lord of Rimini) and John Paleologus III (the penultimate emperor of Byzantium). Lastly, there's a room devoted mainly to **Renaissance portrait busts**, including Mino da Fiesole's busts of Giovanni de' Medici and Piero il Gottoso (the sons of Cosimo de' Medici). Antonio del Pollaiuolo's *Young Cavalier* is probably another thinly disguised Medici portrait, while the bust labelled *Ritratto d'Ignoto* (Portrait of an Unknown Man), beside Verrocchio's *Madonna and Child*, may in fact depict the face of Macchiavelli. Also outstanding are Francesco Laurana's *Battista Sforza*, an interesting comparison with the Piero della Francesca portrait in the Uffizi, and the *Woman Holding Flowers* by Verrocchio. The centre of the room is shared by Verrocchio's *David*, clearly influenced by the Donatello figure downstairs, and a wooden crucifix (c.1471) attributed to the same artist.

## The Museo di Storia della Scienza

Down the Uffizi's east flank runs **Via dei Leoni**, named after the lions that were once housed in this street. When the ancestors of these mascots were brought to the city, in the thirteenth century, they were caged close to the Baptistery, on the site now occupied by the Loggia del Bigallo. In 1319 the lions were moved into an enclosure on Piazza della Signoria, but half a century later were evicted again, to make way for the Loggia dei Lanzi. They remained in their new quarters on Via dei Leoni until the time of Cosimo I, whose wife – Eleanor of Toledo – insisted that the malodorous and raucous beasts had to go.

At the river end, Via dei Leoni opens into Piazza dei Giudici, so called from the tribunal that used to meet in the building that now houses the city's science museum, the **Museo di Storia della Scienza** (Mon & Wed–Fri 9.30am–5pm, Tues & Sat 9.30am–1pm; Oct–May open Sat until 5pm; €4). Long after Florence had declined from its artistic apogee, the intellectual reputation of the city was maintained by its scientists, many of them directly encouraged by the ruling Medici-Lorraine dynasty. Two of the latter, Grand Duke Ferdinando II and his brother Leopoldo, both of whom studied with Galileo, founded a scientific academy at the Pitti in 1657. Called the Accademia del Cimento (Academy of Experiment), its motto was "Try and try again". The instruments made and acquired by this academy are the core of the museum, which has recently been smartened up considerably; a monumental sundial has also been installed outside, in an attempt to catch the attention of art-obsessed tourists, but this still remains a somewhat overlooked attraction.

Some of **Galileo's original instruments** are displayed on the first floor, such as the lens with which he discovered the four moons of Jupiter, which he tactfully named the Medicean planets. (An enormous lodestone given by Galileo to Ferdinando II is on display by the ticket desk.) On this floor you'll also find the museum's equivalent of a religious relic – bones from one of Galileo's fingers. Other cases are filled with beautiful Arab astrolabes, calculating machines, early telescopes, and some extraordinary meteorological equipment, including several delicate and ornate thermometers. The most imposing single exhibit on this floor is a massive armillary sphere made in 1593 for Ferdinando I, to provide a visual proof of the supposed veracity of the earth-centred Ptolemaic system.

On the floor above there are all kinds of exquisitely manufactured **scientific and mechanical equipment**, several of which were built to demonstrate the fundamental laws of physics. Dozens of clocks and timepieces are on show too, along with some spectacular old electrical machines, and a huge lens made for Cosimo III, with which Faraday and Davy managed to ignite a diamond by focusing the rays of the sun. At the end there's a **medical section** full of alarming surgical instruments and anatomical wax models for teaching obstetrics, plus the contents of a medieval pharmacy, displaying such unlikely cure-alls as Sangue del Drago (Dragon's Blood) and Confetti di Seme Santo (Confections of Blessed Semen).

3

# West of the centre: from Via dei Calzaiuoli to the Cascine

Despite the urban improvement schemes of the nineteenth century and the bombings and shellings of World War II, several of the streets immediately to the west of Piazza della Signoria retain their medieval character. An amble through streets such as Via Porta Rossa, Via delle Terme and Borgo Santi Apostoli will give you some idea of the feel of Florence in the Middle Ages, when every big house was an urban fortress. Best of these medieval redoubts is the **Palazzo Davanzati**, whose interior looks little different from the way it did six hundred years ago. Nearby, the fine church of **Santa Trìnita** is home to an outstanding fresco cycle by Domenico Ghirlandaio, while beyond the glitzy **Via de' Tornabuoni** – Florence's prime shopping street – you'll find the marvellous Alberti-designed **San Sepolcro** chapel and a museum devoted to the work of Marino Marini. The exquisite ancient church of **Santi Apostoli** shouldn't be overlooked, but the most significant sight in this quarter of the city, is the profusely frescoed **Santa Maria Novella**, where you can see masterpieces by Paolo Uccello, Giotto, Filippino Lippi, Masaccio and another superb cycle by Ghirlandaio. A few minutes' walk away, there's yet more Ghirlandaio, and work by Botticelli, in the church of **Ognissanti**. And if all this art is beginning to take its toll, you could take a break in the tree-lined avenues of the **Cascine** park, right on the western edge of the city centre.

## From the Mercato Nuovo to Santi Apostoli

One block west of the southern end of Via dei Calzaiuoli lies the **Mercato Nuovo**, or Mercato del Porcellino (mid-Feb to mid-Nov daily 9am–7pm; mid-Nov to mid-Feb Tues–Sat 9am–5pm), where there's been a market since the eleventh century, though the present loggia dates from the sixteenth. Having forked out their euros at the souvenir stalls, most people join the small group that's invariably gathered round the bronze boar known as *Il Porcellino*: you're supposed to earn yourself some good luck by getting a coin to fall from the animal's mouth through the grille below his head. This superstition has a social function, as the coins go to an organization that runs homes for abandoned children.

## Palazzo Davanzati

Perhaps the most imposing exterior in this district is to be seen on the south side of the market – the thirteenth-century **Palazzo di Parte Guelfa**, financed from the confiscated property of the Ghibelline faction and later expanded by Brunelleschi. However, for a more complete recreation of medieval Florence you should visit the fourteenth-century **Palazzo Davanzati** in Via Porta Rossa. In the nineteenth century the *palazzo* was divided into apartments, but at the beginning of the twentieth it was thoroughly restored. It exterior is now very close to its appearance in the 1580s, when a loggia replaced the battlements on the roof and the Davanzati stuck their coat of arms on the front. (The immense amount of metalwork on the exterior was used variously for tying up animals, draping wool and washing out to dry, suspending bird cages or fixing banners, carpets and other hangings on the occasion of festivities and processions.) Apart from those haute-bourgeois emendations, the building looks much as it did when first inhabited. Virtually every room is furnished and decorated in predominantly medieval style, using genuine artefacts gathered from a variety of sources.

Nowadays the *palazzo* is maintained as the **Museo della Casa Fiorentina Antica**. The building was closed in 1995 for major structural repairs, an operation that was at last drawing to a close as this guide went to press. Pending completion of the project, only a few sections of the house are open (Tues–Sat 8.15am–1.50pm; first, third and fifth Sun of month and second and fourth Mon of month same hours); there's no entrance charge, but this will change when the whole *palazzo* is once again accessible. The description that follows gives you an idea of the interior of the museum before its closure.

### The lower floors

The owners of this house were obviously well prepared for the adversities of urban living, as can be seen in the siege-resistant doors, the huge storerooms for the hoarding of provisions, and the private water supply. The courtyard's **well** was something of a luxury at a time when much of Florence was still dependent on public fountains: a complex series of ropes and pulleys allowed it to serve the entire house; similarly the palace's **toilets**, state-of-the art affairs by the standards of 1330. Such arrangements were far from common: Boccaccio describes the more basic facilities of most Florentines in the *Decameron* – two planks suspended over a small pit.

An ancient staircase – the only one of its kind to survive in the city – leads to the **first floor** and the Sala Grande or **Sala Madornale**. This room, used for family gatherings, underlines the dual nature of the house: furnished in the best style of the day, it also has four wood-covered hatches in the floor to allow the bombarding of a besieging enemy. Merchants' houses in the fourteenth century would typically have had elaborately painted walls in the main rooms, and the Palazzo Davanzati preserves some fine examples of such decor, especially in the dining room or **Sala dei Pappagalli**, where the imitation wall-hangings of the lower walls are patterned with a parrot (*pappagallo*) motif, while the upper walls depict a garden terrace.

Before the development of systems of credit, wealth had to be sunk into tangible assets such as the tapestries, ceramics, sculpture and lacework that alleviate the

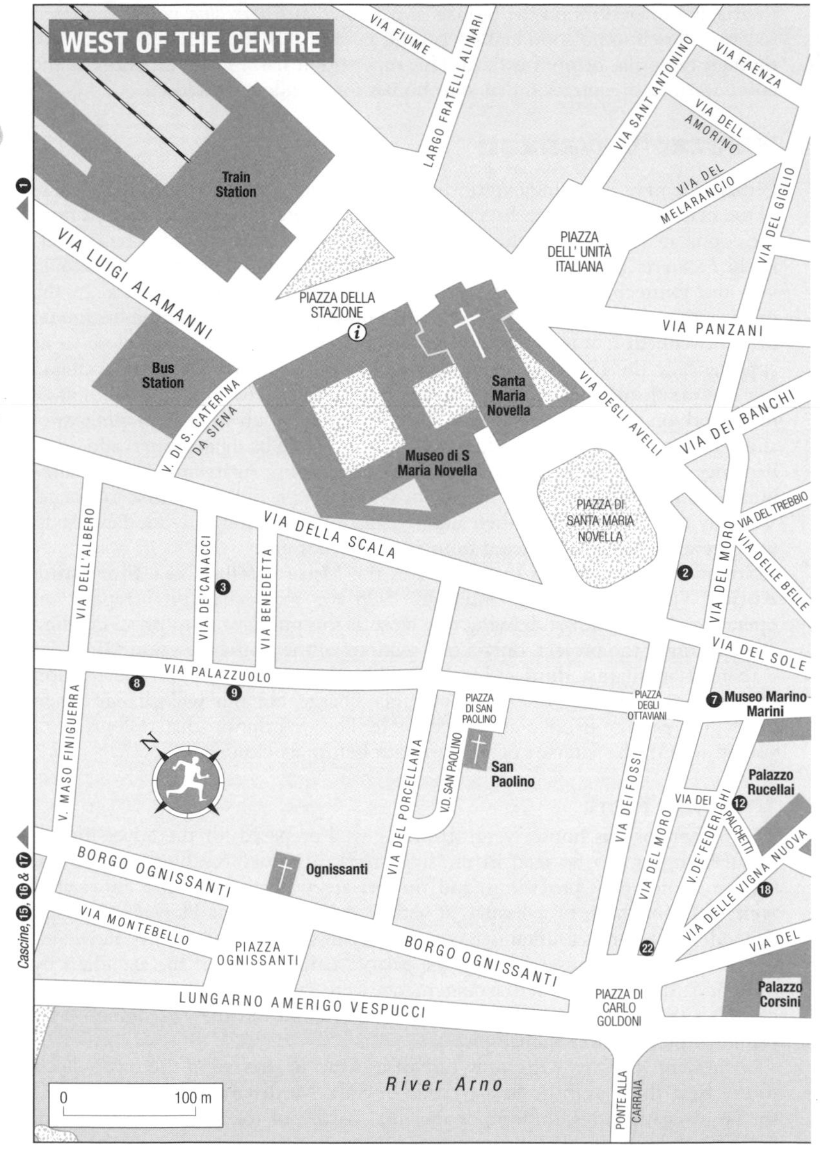


austerity of many of these rooms; any surplus cash would have been locked away in a strongbox like the extraordinary example in the **Sala Piccola**, whose locking mechanism looks like the innards of a primitive clock. There's also a fine collection of *cassoni*, the painted chests in which the wife's dowry would be stored.

Plushest of the rooms is the first-floor **bedroom**, or Sala dei Pavoni – complete with en-suite bathroom. It takes its name from the beautiful frescoed frieze of trees, peacocks (*pavoni*) and other exotic birds: the coats of arms woven into the

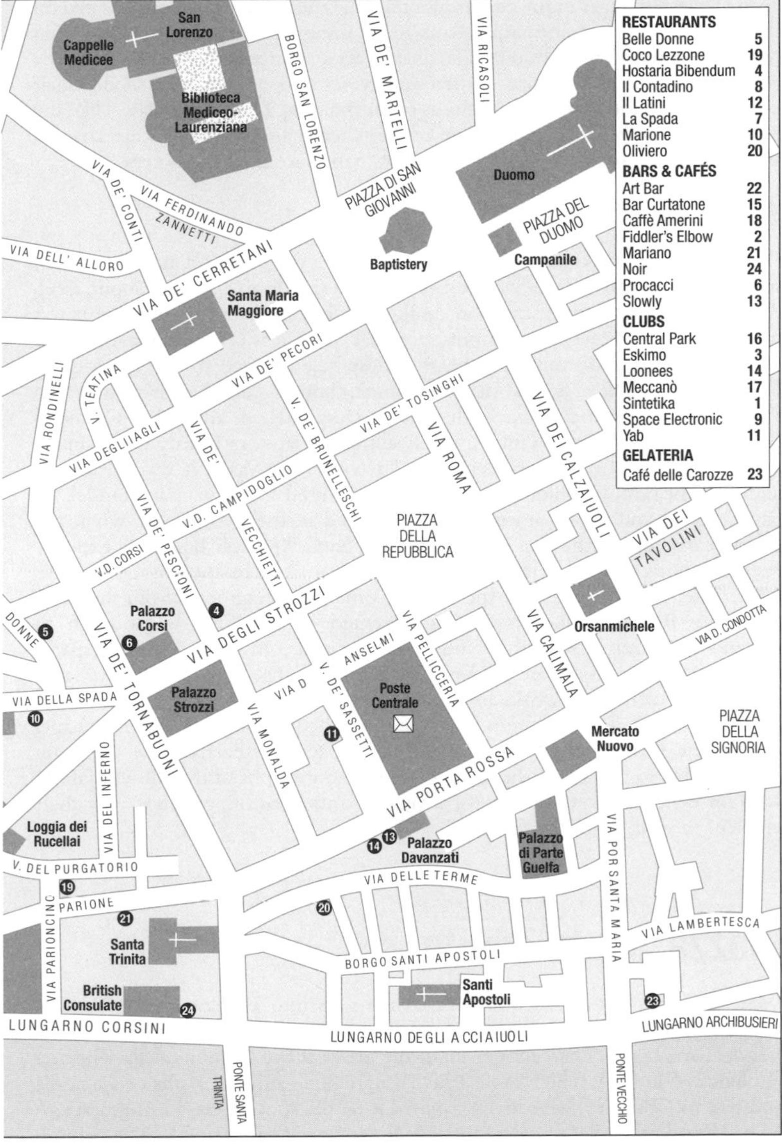


decoration are the crests of families related to the Davanzati. The rare Sicilian linen bed-cover is decorated with scenes from the story of Tristan.

## The upper floors

The arrangements of the rooms on the upper two floors, together with their beautiful furniture and decoration, mirror that of the first floor. For all the splendour of the lower rooms, the spot where the palace's occupants would have been likeliest to linger in the cooler months is the third-floor **kitchen**. Located on the uppermost floor to minimize damage if a fire broke out, it would have been the warmest room in the house. A fascinating array of utensils is on show here: the *girapolenta*, the polenta-stirrer, is extraordinary. Set into one wall is a service shaft connecting the kitchen to all the floors of the building. The leaded glass – like the toilets – was considered a marvel at a time when many windows were covered with turpentine-soaked rags stretched across frames to repel rainwater.



### Santi Apostoli

Between Via Porta Rossa and the Arno, on Piazza del Limbo stands the church of **Santi Apostoli** (Mon–Sat 10am–noon & 4–5.30pm, Sun 4–5.30pm; free). A replica of an ancient inscription on the facade records the legend that it was founded by Charlemagne – it's not quite that old, but it certainly pre-dates the end of the first millennium. It bears a close resemblance to the city's other Romanesque basilica, San Miniato al Monte, though side chapels were added to it in the fifteenth and sixteenth century. Despite these and other Counter-Reformation alterations, Santi Apostoli still has an austere beauty quite unlike any other church in the city centre, and according to Vasari it was this "small and most beautiful" building that Brunelleschi used as his primary model for San Lorenzo and Santo Spirito. Badly damaged in the 1966 flood, when the waters came up to the top of the doorway, Santi Apostoli has been expertly restored, though some of its paintings are still not fit to be shown.

The chief treasures of Santi Apostoli are some stone fragments from the Holy Sepulchre in Jerusalem, supposedly presented by Godfrey de Bouillon to Pazzino de' Pazzi as reward for his crusading zeal. On Holy Saturday sparks struck from these stones are used to light the flame that ignites the "dove" that in turn sets off the fireworks in front of the Duomo (see p.200). The copper brazier in which the holy fire is borne to the cathedral is kept in the first chapel on the left. Other notable features are the terracotta tabernacle by Giovanni della Robbia to the left of the chancel, and various tombs of the Altoviti family, who for centuries were the chief patrons of Santi Apostoli, which is why their emblem (a wolf) is on the facade.

## Piazza Santa Trìnita

West of Palazzo Davanzati, Via Porta Rossa runs into **Piazza Santa Trìnita,** which is not so much a square as a widening of the city's most expensive street, Via de' Tornabuoni. The centrepiece of the piazza is the Colonna della Giustizia (Column of Justice), which Pope Pius IV uprooted from the Baths of Caracalla and sent to Cosimo I, who in 1565 raised it on the spot where, in August 1537, he had heard of the defeat of the anti-Medici faction at Montemurlo. The column stands on the axis of the sleek **Ponte Santa Trìnita**, construction of which began in 1567 on Cosimo's orders, ten years after its predecessor was demolished in a flood – and a decade after Siena had finally become part of Florentine territory, a subjugation which the bridge was intended to commemorate. What makes this the classiest bridge in Florence is the sensuous shallow curve of its arches; ostensibly the design was conjured up by Ammannati, one of the Medici's favourite artists, but the curves so closely resemble the arc of Michelangelo's Medici tombs that it's likely the credit belongs to him.

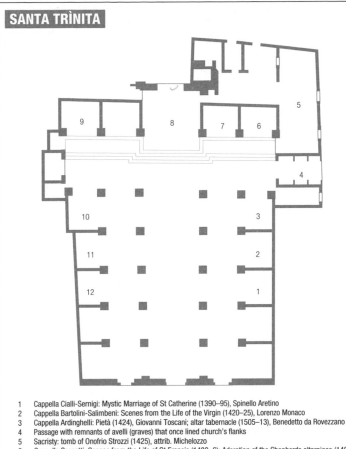

## SANTA TRÌNITA

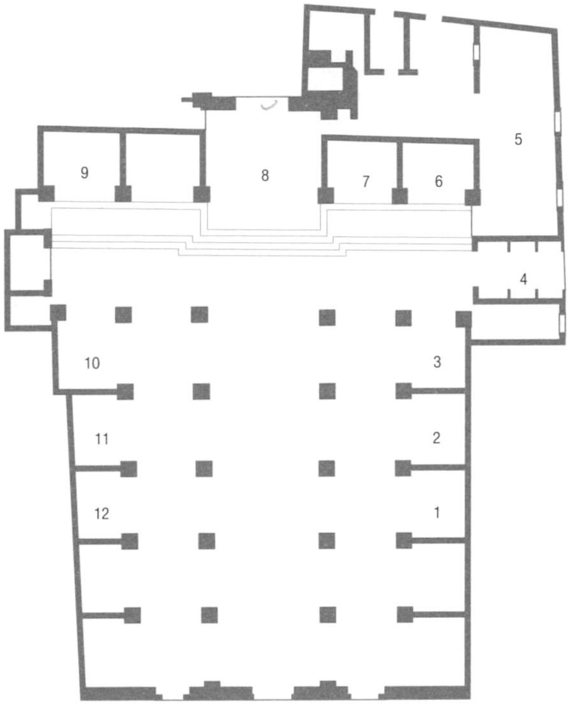


1 Cappella Cialli-Sernigi: Mystic Marriage of St Catherine (1390–95), Spinello Aretino
2 Cappella Bartolini-Salimbeni: Scenes from the Life of the Virgin (1420–25), Lorenzo Monaco
3 Cappella Ardinghelli: Pietà (1424), Giovanni Toscani; altar tabernacle (1505–13), Benedetto da Rovezzano
4 Passage with remnants of avelli (graves) that once lined church's flanks
5 Sacristy: tomb of Onofrio Strozzi (1425), attrib. Michelozzo
6 Cappella Sassetti: Scenes from the Life of St Francis (1483–6); Adoration of the Shepherds altarpiece (1485), Domenico Ghirlandaio
7 Cappella Doni: "Miraculous" crucifix removed from the church of San Miniato al Monte
8 Chancel
9 Cappella Scali: tomb of Benozzo Federighi (1454–7), Luca della Robbia (left wall)
10 Cappella Spini: wooden statue of Mary Magdalen (1455), Desiderio da Settignano and Benedetto da Maiano
11 Cappella Compagni: entrance arch – San Giovanni Gualberto Pardons his Brother's Murderer (1440), Lorenzo di Bicci; right wall – Annunciation; altar wall – San Giovanni Gualberto and Members of the Vallombrosan Order (1455), Neri di Bicci
12 Cappella Davanzati: altarpiece – Coronation of the Virgin and Twelve Saints (1430), Bicci di Lorenzo; left wall – Tomb of Giuliano Davanzati (d.1444), attrib. Bernardo Rossellino (includes third-century Roman sarcophagus)

In 1944 the Nazis blew the bridge to smithereens and a seven-year argument ensued before it was agreed to rebuild it using as much of the original material as could be dredged from the Arno. To ensure maximum authenticity in the **reconstruction**, all the new stone that was needed was quarried from the Bóboli gardens – where the stone for Ammannati's bridge had been cut – and hand tools were used to trim it, as electric blades would have given the blocks too crisp a finish. Twelve years after the war, the reconstructed bridge was opened, lacking only the head from the statue of *Spring*, which had not been found despite the incentive of a hefty reward. At last, in 1961, the missing head was fished from the riverbed; having lain in state for a few days on a scarlet cushion in the Palazzo Vecchio, it was returned to its home.

Incidentally, Ponte Santa Trìnita is perhaps Florence's best spot for observing **urban wildlife**: at dusk the bridge swarms with bats, and you'll often see polecats dabbling around on the riverbanks here; sometimes egrets can be seen wading in the shallows, though you're likelier to observe them upstream of Ponte Vecchio.

## Santa Trìnita church

The antiquity of **Santa Trìnita** (Mon–Sat 8am–noon & 4–6pm, Sun 4–6pm; free) is manifest in the Latinate pronunciation of its name: modern Italian stresses the last, not the first syllable. The church was founded in 1092 by a Florentine nobleman called **Giovanni Gualberto**, scenes from whose life are illustrated in the frescoes in the fourth chapel of the left aisle. One Good Friday, so the story goes, Gualberto left home intent on avenging the murder of his brother. On finding the murderer he decided to spare his life – it was Good Friday – and proceeded to San Miniato (see p.159), where a crucifix is said to have bowed its head to honour his act of mercy. Giovanni went on to become a Benedictine monk and found the reforming Vallombrosan order and – notwithstanding the mayhem created on Florence's streets by his militant supporters – was eventually canonized.

The church was rebuilt between about 1300 and 1330, work being interrupted by the plague of 1348. Further rebuilding took place between 1365 and 1405, while the facade – by Buontalenti – was added in 1594. The end result has a pleasantly hybrid air: the largely Gothic interior contrasts with the Mannerist exterior, which is itself at odds with the Romanesque interior facade.

Ghirlandaio's frescoes are the best-known works of art here, but you should resist the temptation to head straight for these, and work round the church, beginning at the **Cappella Cialli-Sernigi** (1), which contains a damaged fresco and detached *sinopia* depicting the *Mystical Marriage of St Catherine* (1389) by Spinello Aretino, recently discovered below the frescoes in the adjoining chapel.

The next chapel, the **Cappella Bartolini-Salimbeni** (2), is one of only a handful in the city whose decorative scheme has remained uncorrupted by subsequent additions and changes. The frescoes (1420–25) of episodes from the **Life of the Virgin** are by Lorenzo Monaco, who also painted its *Annunciation* altarpiece. The lunette and right wall of the next chapel, the **Cappella Ardinghelli** (3), features Giovanni Toscani's contemporaneous frescoes of the *Pietà* (1424–25) and an unfinished altar tabernacle by Benedetto da Rovezzano (1505–13): the latter, intended for the tomb of Giovanni Gualberto, was damaged during the 1530 siege of the city.

The sacristy, or **Cappella di Onofrio Strozzi** (5), was designed by Ghiberti between 1418 and 1423. To the left of the main altar (which once held Gentile da Fabriano's majestic *Adoration of the Magi*, now in the Uffizi) is the tomb of Onofrio Strozzi, one thought to be the work of Donatello, but now cautiously attributed to Michelozzo.

Next comes the church's highlight, the **Cappella Sassetti** (6), whose frescoes of scenes from the *Life of St Francis* (1483–86) were commissioned from **Domenico Ghirlandaio** by Francesco Sassetti, and were intended, in part, to rival the Ghirlandaio frescoes in Santa Maria Novella, commissioned by Sassetti's rival, Giovanni Tornabuoni. St Francis is shown raising a boy from the dead in Piazza Santa Trìnita: the church of Santa Trìnita is in the background (with its old facade), as is an image of the child plummeting from a window of what's now the Ferragamo HQ over the road. *St Francis Receiving the Rule* (in the lunette above the altar) sets the action in Piazza della Signoria – note the Loggia della Signoria – and features (right foreground) a portrait of Sassetti between his son, Federigo, and Lorenzo the Magnificent (Sassetti was general manager of the Medici bank). On the steps below them are the humanist Poliziano and three of his pupils, Lorenzo's sons. Ghirlandaio (hand on hip) is present as a self-portrait.

Ghirlandaio also painted the chapel's altarpiece, the *Adoration of the Shepherds* (1485), a persuasive Renaissance fusion of Classical and Christian iconography. Mary and the shepherds are painted amid Classical columns, a Roman sarcophagus (used as the manger) and a triumphal arch transplanted from the Roman forum. The figures of the donors – Sassetti and his wife, Nera Corsi – kneel to either side; they are buried in the tombs that Giuliano da Sangallo constructed under the side arches of the chapel.

Displayed in the neighbouring **Cappella Doni** (7) is the miraculous crucifix, formerly in San Miniato, that's said to have bowed its head to Gualberto. The **chancel** (8) features further early fresco fragments – similar tantalizing fragments are dotted around the church. The third of the church's major works, a powerful composition by Luca della Robbia – the **tomb of Benozzo Federighi, bishop of Fiesole** (9) – occupies the left wall of the Cappella Scali; moulded and carved for the church of San Pancrazio, it was transported here in 1896. The fine wooden

▲ Santa Trìnita

**statue of Mary Magdalene** (10), which owes much to Donatello's *Magdalene* in the Museo dell'Opera del Duomo, was begun by Desiderio da Settignano and completed, according to Vasari, by Benedetto da Maiano.



# Via de' Tornabuoni and around

The shops of **Via de' Tornabuoni** are effectively out of bounds to those who don't travel first class. Versace, Ferragamo, Prada, Pucci, Cavalli, Gucci and Armani all have big outlets here: indeed, in recent years Italian deluxe brands have come to monopolize the street (and nearby Piazza Strozzi), to the dismay of many, who see further evidence of the loss of Florentine identity in the eviction of local institutions such as the Seeber bookshop, the Farmacia Inglese and the *Giacosa* café. The last of this trio now exists in name only, as an adjunct to the huge Roberto Cavalli shop, with pictures of catwalk shows providing the decoration. A rather more discreet conversion was carried out at the former Seeber premises: it's now occupied by fashion house MaxMara, whose architects uncovered two sets of frescoes (one sixteenth-century, the other nineteenth-century) when the old paintwork was stripped away. Trumpeting the refined taste of MaxMara boss Achille Maramotti (a major collector of modern art), a company spokesperson said of the decision to leave the frescoes on show: "It may take up floor space in terms of selling, but it is more important to fill people with knowledge and beauty than sell an extra coat."

Conspicuous wealth is nothing new on Via de' Tornabuoni. Towering above everything is the vast **Palazzo Strozzi**, the most intimidating of all Florentine Renaissance palaces, with windows as big as gateways, and embossed with boulder-like lumps of stone. It was begun by the banker Filippo Strozzi, a figure so powerful that he was once described as "the first man of Italy", and whose family provided the ringleaders of the anti-Medici faction in Florence. In the 1470s he set about acquiring properties in this locality, with a view to demolishing them and raising a new house on the land; in the end, a dozen town houses were razed to make space for the mighty *palazzo*, which was built between 1489 and 1536 to a design by Giuliano da Sangallo. Not until the 1930s did the Strozzi family relinquish ownership of the building, which is now state property. The interior is open only for special exhibitions.

## The Palazzo Rucellai

Some of Florence's other plutocrats made an impression with a touch more subtlety than the Strozzi. In the 1440s Giovanni Rucellai, one of the richest businessmen in the city (and an esteemed scholar too), decided to commission a new house from Leon Battista Alberti, whose accomplishments as architect, mathematician, linguist and theorist of the arts prompted a contemporary to exclaim, "Where shall I put Battista Alberti: in what category of learned men shall I place him?" The resultant **Palazzo Rucellai**, two minutes' walk from the Strozzi house at Via della Vigna Nuova 18, was the first palace in Florence to follow the rules of classical architecture; its tiers of pilasters, incised into smooth blocks of stone, evoke the exterior wall of the Colosseum. Alberti later produced another equally elegant design for the same patron – the front of the church of Santa Maria Novella. In contrast to the feud between the Medici and the Strozzi, the Rucellai were on the closest terms with the city's *de facto* royal family: the **Loggia dei Rucellai**, across the street (now a shop), was in all likelihood built for the wedding of Giovanni's son to the granddaughter of Cosimo il Vecchio, and the frieze on the Palazzo Rucellai features the heraldic devices of the two families, the Medici emblem alongside the Rucellai sail.

## The Museo Marino Marini and the Cappella di San Sepolcro

Round the corner from the Palazzo Rucellai stands the ex-church of San Pancrazio, deconsecrated by Napoleon, then successively the offices of the state lottery, the magistrates' court, a tobacco factory and an arsenal. It is now the swish **Museo Marino Marini** (Mon & Wed–Sat 10am–5pm; €4), where the attire of the attendants might make you think you'd strayed into a well-appointed fashion house. Holding around two hundred works left to the city in Marini's will, the museum is a superb space, but it's debatable whether Marini's pieces can stand up to the reverential atmosphere imposed by the display techniques. Variations on the sculptor's trademark horse-and-rider theme make up much of the show.

Once part of the church but now entirely separate from the museum, the **Cappella Rucellai**, which was redesigned by Alberti, houses the **Cappella di San Sepolcro**, the most exquisite of his creations (June–Sept, hours vary but usually Mon–Fri 10am–noon; Oct–May Mon–Sat 10am–noon & 5–5.30pm; free). Designed as the funerary monument to Giovanni Rucellai, it takes the form of a diminutive reconstruction of Jerusalem's Church of the Holy Sepulchre. Access to the cappella is dependent upon voluntary staff, so it's prone to unscheduled periods of closure.

# Piazza Santa Maria Novella

Scurrying from the train station in search of a room, or fretting in the queues for a rail ticket, most people barely give a glance to **Santa Maria Novella train station**, but this is a building that deserves as much attention as many of the city's conventional monuments. Its principal architect, Giovanni Michelucci – who died in January 1991, just two days short of his hundredth birthday – was one of the leading figures of the Modernist movement, which in Mussolini's Italy was marginalized by the officially approved Neoclassical pomposities. Accordingly, there was some astonishment when, in 1933, Michelucci and his colleagues won the open competition to design the main rail terminal for one of the country's showpiece cities. It's a piece of impeccably rational planning, so perfectly thought-out that no major alterations were deemed necessary until very recently, when approval was given for the construction of a new terminal for the high-speed Milan–Rome rail line beneath the station, which is due to open in 2011.

On the other side of the church of Santa Maria Novella – whose back directly faces the station – lies **Piazza Santa Maria Novella**. Once the venue for the wild festivities of the Palio dei Cocchi (chariot race), which was introduced by Cosimo I in 1540 and continued as an annual event until 1858, this square has for many years had a distinctly squalid undertone. Now the area is being transformed, with the repaving of the whole piazza, the development of an upmarket hotel complex on the eastern side and the long-awaited opening of the Alinari photography museum.

## The church of Santa Maria Novella

The magnificent church of **Santa Maria Novella** (Mon–Thurs & Sat 9am–5pm, Fri & Sun 1–5pm; €2.50) is the Florentine base of the Dominican order. It is the successor of the more humble Santa Maria delle Vigne, which in 1221 was handed to the Dominicans, who then set about altering the place to their requirements. By 1360 the interior was finished, but only the Romanesque lower part of the **facade** had been completed. This state of affairs lasted until 1456, when Giovanni Rucellai asked Alberti to design a classicized upper storey that would blend with the older section while improving the proportions. The sponsor's name is picked out across the marble facade in Roman capitals (iohanes·oricellarivs …), while the Rucellai family emblem, the billowing sail of Fortune, runs as a motif through the central frieze. One other external feature is worth noting: the route into the church takes you through the cemetery, which is ringed by an arcade of *avelli*, the collective burial vaults of upper-class families.

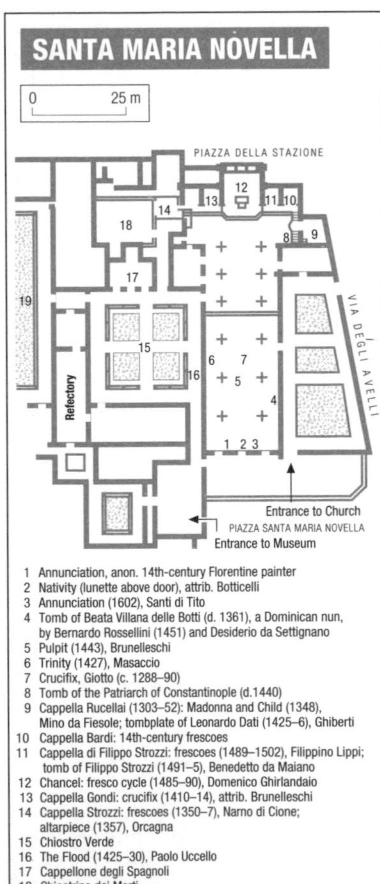


Santa Maria Novella's **interior** was designed to enable preachers to address their sermons to as large a congregation as possible. To enhance the sensation of spaciousness, its architects employed an ingenious trompe l'oeil: the distance between the columns diminishes with proximity to the altar, which makes the nave seem longer than it is. Treasures aplenty fill the interior, even though Vasari and his minions ran amok in a frenzy of "improvement" in the 1570s, ripping out the choir and bleaching over frescoes; restorers in the nineteenth century managed to reverse much of his damage.

### The nave

Entwined around the second nave pillar on the left is a **pulpit**, designed by Brunelleschi and notorious as the spot from which the Dominicans first denounced Galileo. The actual carving was completed by Buggiano, Brunelleschi's adopted son, who may well have advised Masaccio on the architectural details present in the background of his extraordinary fresco of the **Trinity** (number 6 on our plan), which was painted on the nearby wall in 1427. This was one of the earliest works in which the rules of perspective were rigorously employed, and Florentines queued to view the illusion on

▲ Santa Maria Novella

its unveiling, stunned by a painting which appeared to create three-dimensional space on a solid wall. Amazingly, the picture was concealed behind an altar in 1570 and rediscovered only in 1861. The painting's theme was suggested by the fact that the Dominicans' calendar began with the Feast of the Trinity. Surmounting a stark image of the state to which all flesh is reduced (bearing the motto: "I was that which you are / You will be that which I am"), the main scene is an illustration of the mechanics of Christian redemption: the lines of the painting lead from the picture's donors, the judge Lorenzo Lenzi and his wife, through to the Virgin and the Baptist (humanity's mystical link with the Holy Trinity), to the crucified Christ and the stern figure of God the Father at the pinnacle.

**Giotto's Crucifix** (7), a radically naturalistic and probably very early work (c.1288–90), now hangs in what is thought to be its intended position, poised dramatically over the centre of the nave. Hitherto, it had been hidden away in the sacristy, veiled by a layer of dirt so thick that many scholars refused to recognize it as the work of the master; the attribution is still disputed.

Nothing else in the main part of the church has quite the same resonance as these three works, but the wealth of decoration is astounding. In the right transept lies the **tomb** of the Patriarch of Constantinople (8), who died in the adjoining convent in 1440 after unsuccessful negotiations to unite the Roman and Byzantine churches at the 1439 Council of Florence. Raised above the pavement of the transept, the **Cappella Rucellai** (9) contains a marble *Madonna and Child* by Nino Pisano, and – in the centre of the floor – Ghiberti's superb bronze tomb of the Francesco Leonardo Dati, the head of the Dominican order.

## The Cappella di Filippo Strozzi

In 1486 the chapel to the right of the chancel (11) was bought by Filippo **Strozzi**, a wealthy banker, who then commissioned Filippino Lippi to paint a much-interrupted fresco cycle (1489–1502) on the life of his namesake, St Philip the Apostle. The paintings, a departure from anything seen in Florence at the time, were completed well after Strozzi's death in 1491.

Before starting the project Filippino spent some time in Rome, and the work he carried out on his return displays an archeologist's obsession with ancient Roman culture. The right wall depicts Philip's *Crucifixion* and his *Miracle before the Temple of Mars*. In the latter, the Apostle uses the cross to banish a dragon that had been an object of pagan worship in a Temple of Mars. The enraged temple priests then capture and crucify the saint. The figures swooning from the dragon's stench are almost overwhelmed by an architectural fantasy that's derived from Rome's recently excavated Golden House of Nero. Look carefully in the top right-hand corner and you'll see a minuscule figure of Christ, about the same size as one of the vases behind the figure of Mars.

The left wall depicts *The Raising of Drusiana* and the *Attempted Martyrdom of St John*. The latter scene alludes to the persecutions of the Emperor Domitian, during which John was dipped in boiling oil in an attempt to kill him – the Apostle apparently emerged rejuvenated by the experience. The vaults portray Adam, Noah, Jacob and Abraham and, like the chapel's stained glass and impressive trompe l'oeil decoration, were also the work of Lippi. Behind the altar of this chapel is **Strozzi's tomb** (1491–95), beautifully carved by Benedetto da Maiano.

## The chancel (Cappella Tornabuoni)

The frescoes around the **chancel** (12) and high altar together constitute the masterpiece of **Domenico Ghirlandaio**. Commissioned by **Giovanni Tornabuoni**, a banker and uncle of Lorenzo il Magnifico, the pictures depict scenes from the lives of the Virgin and St John the Baptist, and were designed to replace works on similar themes by Orcagna which were destroyed a century earlier, reputedly by a bolt of lightning. However, they are liberally sprinkled with contemporary portraits and narrative details, with certain illustrious ladies of the Tornabuoni family, for example, present at the births of both the Baptist and the Virgin. Such self-glorification made the frescoes the object of special ire after they were completed, drawing the vitriol of Savonarola during his hellfire and brimstone sermons.

Some later critics have also thought them too superficial for serious comment: John Ruskin, for example, observed that "if you are a nice person, they are not nice enough", and "if you are a vulgar person, not vulgar enough". But there are few frescoes in the city with such immediate charm, and none which are so self-conscious a celebration of Florence at its zenith – indeed, one of the frescoes (S) includes a prominent Latin inscription (on an arch to the right) which reads: "The year 1490, when the most beautiful city renowned for abundance, victories, arts and noble buildings profoundly enjoyed

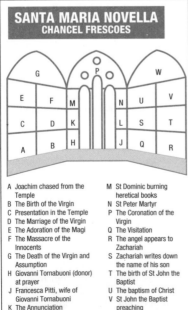

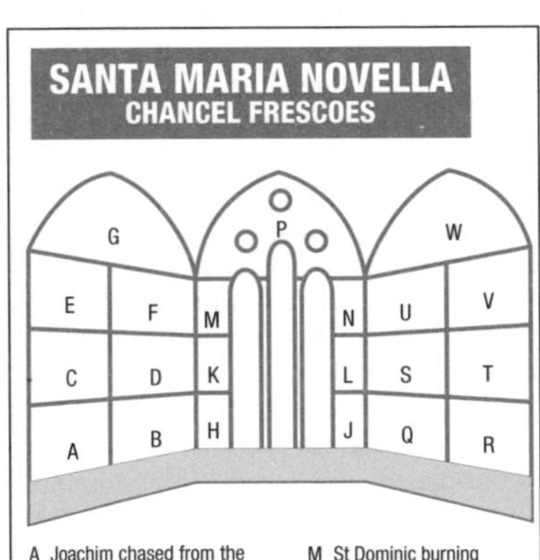

## St Peter Martyr and the Paterenes

In the twelfth century Florence became the crucible of one of the reforming religious movements that periodically cropped up in medieval Italy. The **Paterenes**, who were so numerous that they had their own clerical hierarchy in parallel with that of the mainstream Church, held heretical views very similar to those of the Cathars in southern France, one of their core beliefs being that everything worldly was touched by the Devil. Accordingly they despised the papacy for its claims to temporal power and spurned the adoration of all relics and images. Furthermore, they rejected all forms of prayer and all contracts – including marriage vows – and were staunch pacifists.

Inevitably their campaign against the financial and moral corruption of the Catholic Church brought them into conflict with Rome, and the displeasure of the Vatican eventually found its means of expression in the equally zealous but decidedly non-pacific figure of **St Peter Martyr**. Born in Verona in 1206, to a couple who seem to have been at least sympathetic to the Paterenes, Peter was educated at the university of Bologna, and there, at the age of fifteen, he met St Dominic. Soon afterwards he joined the Dominican order, and subsequently became so fervent an upholder of orthodox doctrine that Pope Innocent IV appointed him as a papal inquisitor. He roamed all over Italy preaching against heresy, but was especially active in Florence, where, operating from the monastery of Santa Maria Novella, he headed the anti-Paterene fraternities known as the Crocesegnati and the Compagnia della Fede, which were in effect his private army. In 1244 he led them into battle across the Piazza Santa Maria Novella, where they proceeded to massacre hundreds of the theological enemy. The epicentre of the carnage is marked by the Croce del Trebbio in Via delle Belle Donne, off the eastern side of the Piazza Santa Maria Novella.

After this, the Dominicans turned to less militant work, founding the charitable organization called the Misericordia, which is still in existence today (see p.60). In 1252 Peter was knifed to death by a pair of assassins in the pay of a couple of Venetians whose property he'd confiscated, which is why he's usually depicted with a blade embedded in his skull. The official version, however, identifies the assassins as Paterene heretics, and relates that the dying man managed to write out the Credo with his own blood before expiring – an incident depicted in the frescoes in Santa Maria Novella's Cappellone degli Spagnoli. Within the year he'd been made a saint.

salubrity and peace." The creator of the frescoes has included a self-portrait in (A), in which Joachim, the Virgin's father, is chased from the temple because he has been unable to have children – Ghirlandaio is the figure in the right-hand group, with hand on hip. In the next fresco (B), the young woman in the white and gold dress leading the group of women is Ludovica, Tornabuoni's only daughter, who died in childbirth aged 15: it's no accident that the scene painted in the fresco depicts the birth of the Virgin. Across the chancel, on the right wall, the **Visitation** (Q) features Giovanna degli Albizi, Tornabuoni's daughter-in-law, who also died in childbirth – she's the first of the three women to the right of the Virgin. The **Birth of St John the Baptist** (T) features Tornabuoni's sister, Lucrezia, the mother of Lorenzo de' Medici: she's in front of the servant bearing fruit on her head.

### The Cappella Strozzi

The next chapel beyond the chancel is the **Cappella Gondi** (13), which houses Brunelleschi's crucifix, the artist's only surviving sculpture in wood, and supposedly carved as a riposte to the uncouthness of Donatello's cross in Santa Croce. Legend has it that Donatello was so startled on seeing his rival's work that he dropped a basket of eggs.

Another great fresco cycle adorns the next chapel but one, the **Cappella Strozzi** (14), which lies above the level of the rest of the church at the end of the north transept. These frescoes (1350–57) were commissioned as an expiation of the sin of usury by Tommaso Strozzi, an ancestor of Filippo Strozzi, patron of the chapel across the church. The pictures are the masterpiece of Nardo di Cione, brother of the better-known Orcagna (Andrea di Cione), with whom Nardo collaborated to design the chapel's stained glass.

Orcagna alone painted the chapel's magnificent high altarpiece, *Christ Presenting the Keys to St Peter and the Book of Wisdom to Thomas Aquinas* (1357), which shows Christ bestowing favour on both St Peter and St Thomas Aquinas, the latter a figure second only to St Dominic in the order's hierarchy. Behind the altar, the central fresco depicts the *Last Judgement*, with Dante featured as one of the saved (in white, third from the left, second row from the top). So, too, are Tommaso Strozzi and his wife, shown being led by St Michael into paradise, with an angel helping the righteous up through a trapdoor. The theme of judgement is continued in the bleached fresco of Dante's *Inferno* on the right wall, faced by a thronged *Paradiso* on the left. The entrance arch features a frieze of saints, while the vaults depict St Thomas Aquinas and the Virtues.

## The Museo di Santa Maria Novella

Further remarkable paintings are to be found in the spacious Romanesque conventual buildings that are now home to the **Museo di Santa Maria Novella** (Mon–Thurs & Sat 9am–5pm; €2.70). The first set of cloisters beyond the entrance, the **Chiostro Verde** (15), dating from 1332 to 1350, features frescoes of *Stories from Genesis* (1425–30) executed by Paolo Uccello and his workshop. The cloister takes its name from the green base *terra verde* pigment they used, and which now gives the paintings a spectral undertone.

The windswept image of **The Flood** (16), the best preserved of the cloister's frescoes, is rendered almost unintelligible by the telescoping perspective and the double appearance of the ark (before and after the flood), whose flanks form a receding corridor in the centre of the picture: on the left, the ark is rising on the deluge, on the right it has come to rest as the waters subside. In the foreground, two men fight each other in their desperation to stay alive; the chequered lifebelt that one of these men has around his neck is a device for demonstrating Uccello's mastery of perspective, a subject he studied with health-jeopardizing devotion – it's a *mazzocchio*, a 72-faceted wicker ring round which a turbanned headdress was wrapped. Another man grabs the ankles of the visionary figure in the foreground – presumably Noah, though he is a much younger Noah than the hirsute patriarch leaning out of the ark on the right to receive the dove's olive branch. In the right foreground there's a preview of the universal devastation, with tiny corpses laid out on the deck, and a crow gobbling an eyeball from one of the drowned.

### The Cappellone degli Spagnoli

Off the cloister opens what was once the chapter house of the immensely rich convent of Santa Maria, the **Cappellone degli Spagnoli** (17), or Spanish Chapel. For a time the headquarters of the Inquisition, it received its name after Eleonora di Toledo, wife of Cosimo I, reserved it for the use of her Spanish entourage. Presumably she derived much inspiration from its majestic fresco cycle (1367–69) by Andrea di Firenze, which was described by Ruskin as "the most noble piece of pictorial philosophy in Italy".

Virtually every patch of the walls is covered with frescoes, whose theme is the role of the Dominicans in the battle against heresy and in the salvation of

Christian souls. The **left wall** as you enter depicts *The Triumph of Divine Wisdom*, with Thomas Aquinas enthroned below the Virgin and Apostles amidst the winged Virtues and the "wise men" of the Old and New Testaments (the so-called Doctors of the Church). Below these are fourteen figures who symbolize the Arts and Sciences, branches of learning brought to fruition by the Holy Spirit (symbolized by the dove above the Virgin) working through the Catholic faith.

The more spectacular **right wall** portrays the "Mission, Work and Triumph of the Dominican Order". Everything here conforms to a strict and logical hierarchy, beginning on the ceiling with the boat of St Peter, a symbol of the Church. At the bottom is Florence's cathedral, imagined one hundred years before the structure was completed. In front of it stand the pope and Holy Roman Emperor, the world's highest spiritual and temporal rulers. Before them stand ranks of figures representing religious orders, among which the Dominicans are naturally pre-eminent. In particular, note St Dominic, the order's founder, unleashing the "hounds of the lord", or *Domini Canes*, a pun on the Dominicans' name: heretics, the dogs' victims, are shown as wolves.

Among the group of pilgrims (in the centre, just below the Duomo) are several portraits, real or imagined: Cimabue (in a large brown cloak); Giotto (beside him in profile, wearing a green cloak); Boccaccio (further right, in purple, holding a closed book); Petrarch (above, with a cloak and white ermine hood); and Dante (alongside Petrarch in profile, with a white cap). Above and to the right, are scenes of young people dancing, hawking, playing music and engaging in other pleasures of the sort that the Dominicans so heartily condemned.

Those able to resist such abominations – the saved – are shown being marshalled by a nearby friar who hears their confession before dispatching them towards St Peter and the Gate of Paradise. Once through the gate, the blessed are shown in adoration of God and the angels with the Virgin at their midst. Foremost among those confessing is the chapel's donor, one Buonamico Guidalotti (shown kneeling), who paid for the chapel in honour of his wife, who died during the 1348 plague. The far wall shows scenes connected with the Crucifixion, while the near (entrance) wall, which is excluded from the frescoes' unified theme, contains scenes from the life of St Peter Martyr, one of the Dominicans' leading lights.

The contemporaneous decoration of the **Chiostrino dei Morti** (18), the oldest part of the complex, has not aged so robustly; it was closed for restoration at the time of writing. The **Chiostro Grande** (19), to the west, is also out of bounds, as it belongs to the carabinieri (Italy's semi-military police force). The small museum adjoining the Chiostro Grande is notable chiefly for some peculiarly glamorous fourteenth- and fifteenth-century reliquary busts, containing alleged remnants of St Ursula and Mary Magdalene, among others.

## The Museo Nazionale Alinari Fotografia

Back at the start of the thirteenth century the colonnaded building that faces Santa Maria Novella across the piazza was the hospital of San Paolo, a refuge for the sick and the destitute, and also the base for the Dominicans before they moved to Santa Maria Novella. At the beginning of the fifteenth century the administration of the hospital passed to the Arte dei Giudici e Notari (the guild of judges and notaries), and it was they who enlarged the building, probably to a design by Michelozzo, whose loggia – the **Loggia di San Paolo** – is a close imitation of Brunelleschi's Spedale degli Innocenti (see p.128). In the 1490s Andrea della Robbia added the attractive terracotta medallions and lunettes, further emphasizing the similarity between the two buildings. One of the lunettes depicts the momentous meeting of Saint Francis (who founded a Franciscan convent next door) and his fellow monastic reformer Saint Dominic, an event that's generally believed to have happened in Rome in 1217, but is said by local folklore to have occurred a little sooner, on this very spot.

In the 1780s the hospital was suppressed and the building became a school for impoverished girls and unmarried young women, which it remained until World War II, when it was used by the Fascists as a prison. After the war it re-opened as a state school, and now, having been handsomely restored, it's home to the **Museo Nazionale Alinari Fotografia** (Mon, Tues, Thurs, Fri & Sun 9.30am–7.30pm, Sat 9.30am–11.30pm; €9). Part of the museum is set aside for one-off photography exhibitions, but most of the space is given over to changing displays drawn from Alinari's archive of more than four million pictures, covering everything from 1840s daguerreotypes to the work of present-day photographers. The technology of the art is featured too, with a variety of cameras on show, plus stereoscopes and camera obscuras. Production values are top-notch, but you might think that the entrance charge is excessive.

# Ognissanti to the Cascine

In medieval times one of the main areas of cloth production – the mainstay of the Florentine economy – was in the western part of the city. **Ognissanti** (daily 7.30am–12.30pm & 4–7.30pm; free), or All Saints, the main church of this quarter, stands on a piazza that might be taken as a symbol of the state of the present-day Florentine economy, dominated as it is by the five-star *Grand* and *Excelsior* hotels.

The church was founded in 1256 by the Umiliati, a Benedictine order from Lombardy whose speciality was the weaving of woollen cloth. In 1561 the Franciscans took over the church, the new tenure being marked by a Baroque overhaul that spared only the medieval campanile. The facade of the church is of historical interest only, as one of the earliest eruptions of the Baroque in Florence, but the building within is well worth a visit for its **paintings** by Domenico Ghirlandaio and Sandro Botticelli.

The young face squeezed between the Madonna and the dark-cloaked man in Ghirlandaio's *Madonna della Misericordia* (1473), over the second altar on the right, is said to be that of Amerigo Vespucci (1451–1512), an agent for the Medici in Seville, whose two voyages in 1499 and 1501 would lend his name to a continent. The altar was paid for by the Vespucci, a family of silk merchants from the Ognissanti district, which is why other members of the clan appear beneath the Madonna's protective cloak. Among them is Simonetta Vespucci (at the Virgin's left hand), the mistress of Giuliano de' Medici and reputedly the most beautiful woman in Florence – she is said to have been the model for Botticelli's *Venus*.

The idea may not be so far-fetched, for Botticelli was born in the Ognissanti parish and lived locally, and the Vespucci and Filipepi families were on good terms. Botticelli is buried in the church, beneath a round tomb slab in the south transept (the slab bears his baptismal name, Sandro Filipepi), and his small fresco of *St Augustine's Vision of St Jerome* (1480) hangs on the same wall as the Madonna, between the third and fourth altars. Facing it is Ghirlandaio's more earthbound *St Jerome*, also painted in 1480; in the same year Ghirlandaio painted the well-preserved *Last Supper* that covers one wall of the **refectory**, reached through the cloister entered to the left of the church (March–June Mon, Tues & Thurs–Sun 9am–5pm; rest of year Mon, Tues & Sat 9am–noon; free).

## The Cascine

Florence's public park, the **Cascine**, begins close to the Ponte della Vittoria and dwindles away 3km downstream, at the confluence of the Arno and the Mugnone, where there's a statue of the Maharajah of Kohlapur – he died in Florence in 1870 and the prescribed funeral rites demanded that his body be cremated at a spot where two rivers met.

Once the Medici dairy farm (*cascina*), then a hunting reserve, this strip of greenery mutated into a high-society venue in the eighteenth century: if there was nothing happening at the opera, all of Florence's *beau monde* turned out to promenade under the trees of the Cascine. A fountain in the park bears a dedication to Shelley, who was inspired to write his *Ode to the West Wind* while strolling here on a blustery day in 1819.

Thousands of people come out here on Tuesday mornings for the **market** beyond the former train station (now an arts centre), and on any day of the week the Cascine swarms with joggers, cyclists and roller-bladers. Parents bring their kids out here too, to play on the grass – a rare commodity in Florence. However, the Cascine is not one of Europe's great urban parks – construction of the new tram line has marred parts of it, and elsewhere it's rather ill-kempt and grubby. And though its clubs bring a lot of people out here at night (see p.198) it's emphatically not a place for a nocturnal stroll, as it has long been a playground for the city's pimps and junkies.

# North of the centre: the San Lorenzo, San Marco and Annunziata districts

A few blocks from the train station and the Duomo lies the San Lorenzo district, the city's main market area, with scores of stalls encircling a vast food hall. The racks of T-shirts and belts almost engulf the church of **San Lorenzo**, a major building that's often overlooked in the rush to the Duomo and the Uffizi. Attached to the church is another key sight, the **Cappelle Medicee** (Medici Chapels). While various of the most important Medici are buried in the main part of San Lorenzo, dozens of lesser lights are interred in these chapels, and two of the least impressive are celebrated by some of **Michelangelo**'s finest sculpture. The Medici also account for the **Palazzo Medici-Riccardi**, with its exquisite fresco-covered chapel, while the most celebrated of all Michelangelo's works in stone – the *David* – can be admired in the nearby **Accademia**. The magnificent paintings of Fra' Angelico fill the nearby **Museo di San Marco**, which is but a stroll away from **Piazza Santissima Annunziata**, one of Florence's most photogenic locales, thanks to Brunelleschi's **Spedale degli Innocenti** and the church of **Santissima Annunziata**, which is notable chiefly for its a beautiful frescoed atrium. The neighbouring **archeological museum** is never going to make Florence's must-do list, but it deserves more visitors than it gets.

## San Lorenzo



Founded in 393 AD, **San Lorenzo** (daily 10am–5.30pm; March–Oct closes Sun 1.30pm; €3.50) has a claim to be the oldest church in Florence. For some three hundred years it was the city's cathedral, before renouncing its title to Santa Reparata, the precursor of the Duomo. By 1060 a sizeable Romanesque church had been constructed on the site, a building which in time became the Medici's parish church, benefiting greatly over the years from the family's munificence.

The Medici were in a particularly generous mood in 1419, when a committee of eight parishioners headed by Giovanni di Bicci de' Medici, founder of the family fortune, offered to finance a new church. **Brunelleschi** was commissioned to begin the project, starting work on the Sagrestia Vecchia (Old Sacristy) before being given the go-ahead two years later to build the entire church. Construction lapsed over the next two decades, hampered by financial problems, political upheavals and Brunelleschi's simultaneous work on the cathedral dome. Giovanni's son, Cosimo de' Medici, eventually gave the work fresh impetus with a grant of 40,000 *fiorini* (florins), at a time when 150 florins would support a Florentine family for a year. Cosimo's largesse saved the day, but was still not sufficient to provide the church with a facade. No less a figure than Michelangelo laboured to remedy the omission, one of many to devote time to a scheme to provide a suitable frontage. None of the efforts was to any avail: to this day the exterior's bare brick has never been clad.

## The interior

When you step inside the church, what strikes you first is the cool rationality of Brunelleschi's design, an instantly calming contrast to the hubbub outside. San Lorenzo was the earlier of Brunelleschi's great Florentine churches (the other is Santo Spirito) but already displays his mastery of classical decorative motifs and mathematically planned proportions.

The first work of art to catch your attention, in the second chapel on the right, is Rosso Fiorentino's **Marriage of the Virgin** (1523; marked 1 on our plan), with its unusually youthful and golden-haired Joseph. There's another arresting painting at the top of the left aisle – Bronzino's enormous fresco of *The Martyrdom of St Lawrence*, painted in 1569 (10) – but it seems a shallow piece of work alongside the nearby bronze pulpits (2) by **Donatello**. The reliefs that cover the pulpits, depicting scenes preceding and following the Crucifixion, were the artist's last works; begun around 1460, they were completed by his pupils as increasing paralysis limited their master's ability to model in wax. Jagged and discomforting, seemingly charged with more energy than the space can contain, these panels are more like brutal sketches in bronze than conventional reliefs. The overpopulated *Deposition*, for example, has demented mourners sobbing beneath crosses which disappear into the void beyond the frame, while in the background a group of horsemen gather on a hill whose contours are implied rather than modelled. Donatello is buried in the nave of the church, next to his patron, Cosimo de' Medici, and commemorated by a **memorial** (8) on the right wall of the chapel in the north transept, close to Filippo Lippi's 1440 altarpiece of the *Annunciation* (9).

On the opposite side of the church, near the right-hand pulpit, there's a fine tabernacle, the **Pala del Sacramento** (3), by Desiderio da Settignano. Round the corner to the right lies a chapel (4) containing a Roman sarcophagus, a fresco fragment of the Virgin, a wooden crucifix by Antonio del Pollaiuolo and two modern works in *pietra dura*, a peculiarly Florentine kind of technicolour marquetry using semi-precious stones. In the centre of the church, the **tomb of Cosimo de' Medici** (5), known as Cosimo il Vecchio, bears the inscription "Pater Patriae" (Father of the Fatherland) – a title once borne by Roman emperors.

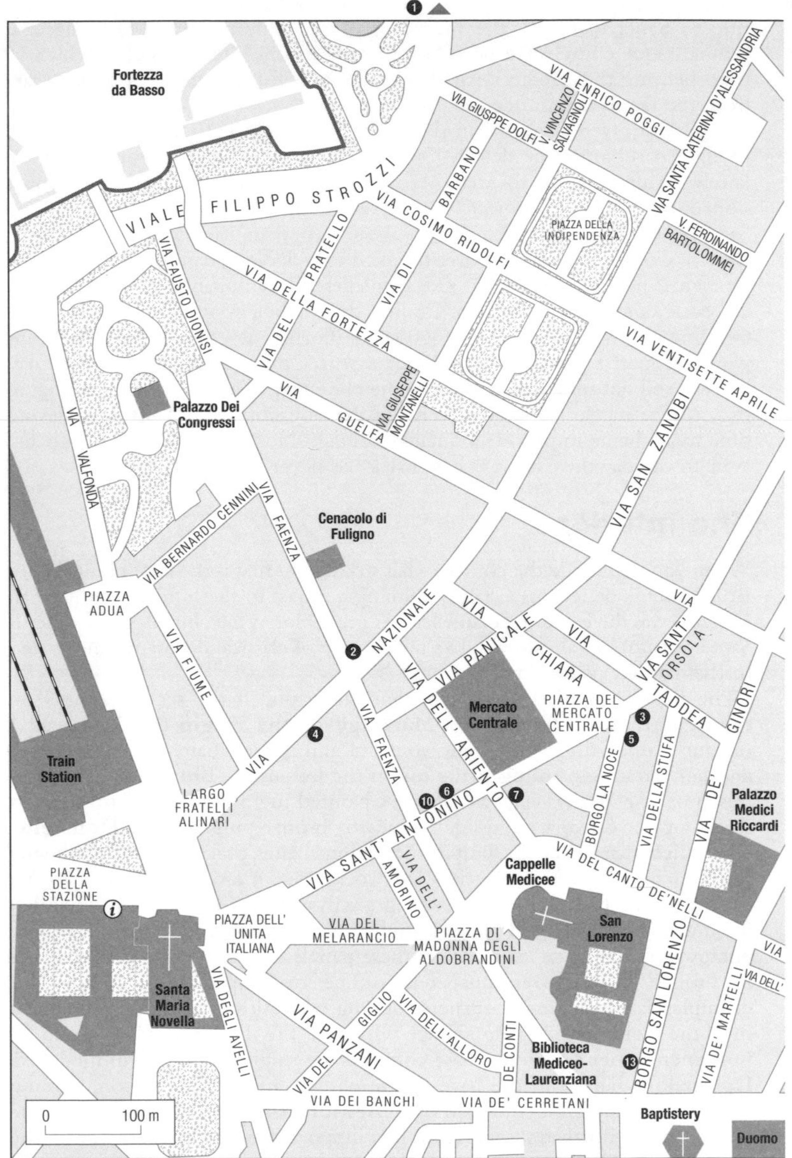


### The Sagrestia Vecchia

Four more leading Medici members lie buried in the neighbouring **Sagrestia Vecchia** (D) or Old Sacristy, a minor architectural masterpiece that is far more than simply a Medici mausoleum. One of Brunelleschi's earliest projects (1421–26) – and the only one completed in his lifetime – the design, a cube and hemispherical dome, could hardly be more simple and yet more perfect. Brunelleschi's biographer, Manetti, wrote that "it astounded all men both of the

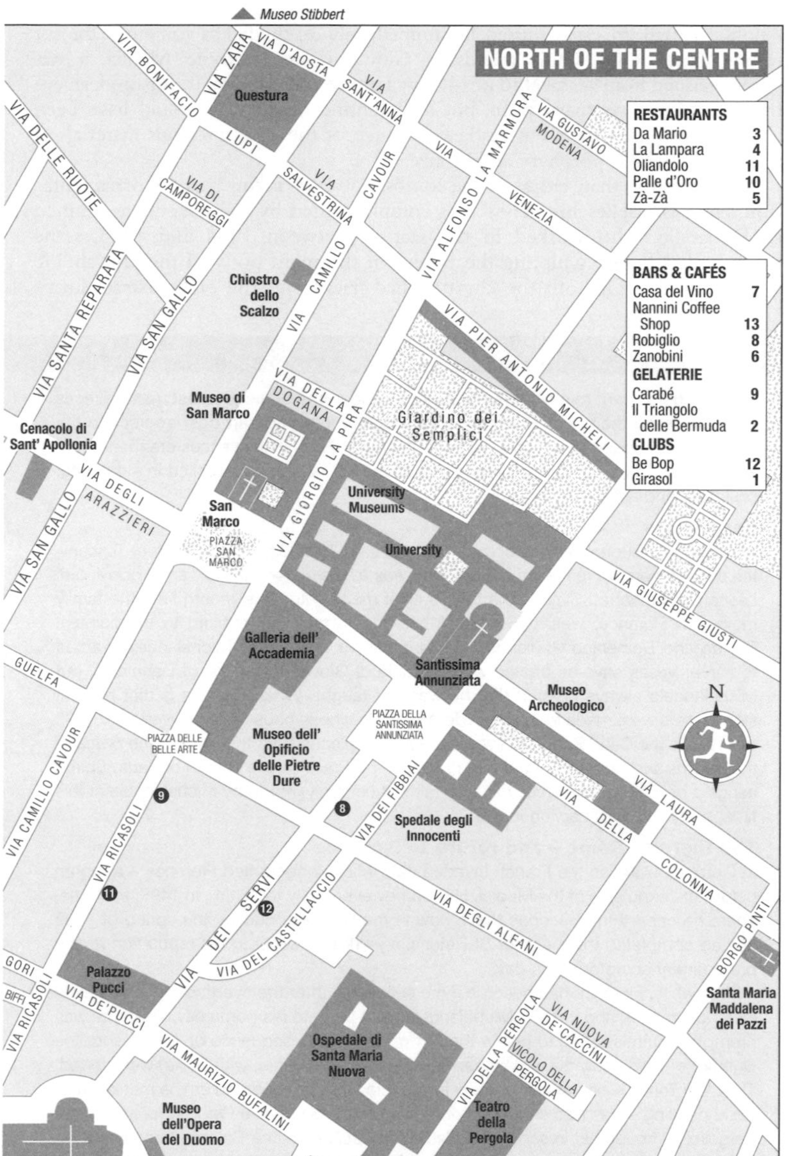


city and foreigners … for its new and beautiful manner. And so many people came continuously that they greatly bothered those who worked there."

The room was commissioned by Giovanni Bicci de' Medici, the principal founder of the Medici fortune, as a private chapel. The dedication is to St John the Evangelist, patron saint of Giovanni (John), but note that it is the Medici *palle* motif (see p.115) that dominates. On his death, Giovanni, along with his wife Piccarda, was buried beneath the massive marble slab at the centre of the **chapel** (7).

Another **tomb** (6), easily missed, lies immediately on the left as you enter: the last resting place of Giovanni's grandsons, Giovanni and Piero de' Medici, it was commissioned from Verrocchio in 1472 by Lorenzo de' Medici. To the modern eye the tomb looks relatively plain, but a Florentine of the day would have been abundantly aware that it was made from three of the most precious materials of antiquity – marble, porphyry and bronze.

More arresting than either of the tombs, however, is the chapel's ornamentation. Here Brunelleschi's genius was complemented by the decorative acumen of Donatello, who worked in the sacristy between 1434 and 1443, some twenty years before sculpting the pulpits in the main body of the church. He was responsible for both the cherub-filled frieze and the eight extraordinary

## Michelangelo

Michelangelo spent much of his life in Rome, and some of his greatest masterpieces are to be seen there, yet Florence is the place where you can best appreciate the extraordinary scope of his achievement, because the city possesses creations from every phase of his life and in every genre of the visual arts he excelled in – painting, sculpture and architecture.

### Early years

Michelangelo Buonarroti was born on March 16, 1475 in Caprese, in eastern Tuscany, the second son of Francesca di Neri (who was to die six years later) and Lodovico di Leonardo Buonarroti Simoni, the town's chief magistrate. One month later the family moved to Florence, where, in 1488, Michelangelo was apprenticed to the painters Davide and Domenico Ghirlandaio. Little is known about how Michelangelo learned to carve: Vasari says he trained with Bertaldo di Giovanni (a pupil of Donatello), but Michelangelo always insisted that he was self-taught. What's certain is that his first stone reliefs were made for Lorenzo de' Medici, in whose household he lived from 1490 to 1492. In the Casa Buonarroti you can see two pieces from this period: the *Battle of the Lapiths and Centaurs* and the *Madonna of the Stairs*. In the church of Santo Spirito hangs a delicate *Crucifix* that was also (almost certainly) made by Michelangelo at this time, and is his only carving in wood.

### The flight to Rome – and return to Florence

In October 1494, as the French invaded Italy, Michelangelo fled Florence – a month before the expulsion of the Medici. His journey eventually took him, in 1496, to Rome. There he carved the *Bacchus* that's now in the Bargello, and by the spring of 1499 he had completed the *Pietà* for St Peter's, a work that secured his reputation as the pre-eminent sculptor of his day.

Meanwhile, Florence had become more peaceable after the overthrow of Savonarola (see box, p.124), and in 1501 Michelangelo went back to his home city, where he was promptly commissioned to create the *David*, and then a sequence of *Apostles* for the Duomo, of which only the *St Matthew* (now in the Accademia, with *David*) was started. The *Doni Tondo* – one of his very few forays into what he regarded as the menial art of easel painting – was also created during this period, as was the *Pitti Tondo*, now in the Bargello. Although his fresco of the *Battle of Cáscina*, for the Palazzo Vecchio, never advanced beyond the cartoon stage, it became the single most influential work of art in the city, with its unprecedented emphasis on the nude male form and its use of twisting figures, a recurrent motif in later Mannerist art.

### 1505–16: Rome

Work on the *Battle of Cáscina* was suspended in 1505 when Michelangelo was called to Rome by Pope Julius II, to create a tomb for him. When completed in 1545, the tomb bore little resemblance to what had been originally planned: it was built not in tondi above it, four of the latter a striking orangey-pink, the rest crafted in a more muted white against grey. The tondi's subjects are the four Evangelists and a quartet of scenes from the life of St John the Evangelist. The terracotta bust of St Lawrence (Lorenzo) is attributed to either Donatello or Desiderio da Settignano.

Two large **reliefs**, also probably by Donatello, adorn the space above the two doors on the end wall: one shows SS Lawrence and Stephen, twin protectors of Florence, the other SS Cosmas and Damian. These last two, twins and early Christian martyrs, were the patron saints of doctors (*medici*) and thus of the Medici, who were probably descended from doctors or apothecaries. By happy coincidence, Cosimo de' Medici, the church's chief patron, was born on the

St Peter's but in San Pietro in Vincoli, and instead of having forty statues it had just seven, only three of them by Michelangelo: *Moses*, *Leah* and *Rachel*. The latter two (both 1542) were the last sculptures that Michelangelo finished; the unfinished *Slaves* in the Accademia was made for another version of the tomb. His relationship with the fiery Julius was always fractious, and in 1506 he returned to Florence. In 1508, however, he was summoned back to the Vatican to commence the most superhuman of all his undertakings – the Sistine Chapel ceiling.

### Final return to Florence

In 1516, with the Sistine ceiling finished, Michelangelo returned to Florence, where his plans for the facade of San Lorenzo church – sponsored by the Medici pope, Leo X – came to nothing. But in 1521 Leo contracted him to design a new sacristy for San Lorenzo, as a Medici mausoleum. Work on this, Michelangelo's first architectural project, was interrupted frequently, and building really only began in 1523, when he was also asked to build a library – the Biblioteca Laurenziana – alongside the church. In the San Lorenzo project Michelangelo created an architectural vocabulary that was to provide the basis of Mannerist design, and he carved a remarkable group of sculptures for the sacristy, but once more what one sees is but a portion of what was planned.

The Medici were expelled from Florence in 1527, and Michelangelo stayed in the city to supervise the defences when it was besieged in 1530 by Emperor Charles V, who then installed the despotic Alessandro de' Medici as his puppet ruler. Once Alessandro was in place, Michelangelo's life in the city was far from easy. In 1534 he left Florence for the last time.

### 1534–64: Rome

He was to spend his last thirty years in Rome, where he was soon appointed architect to St Peter's, which Bramante had begun to rebuild in 1506. The colossal dome was Michelangelo's most spectacular addition to the architecture of the Vatican; he made a similarly profound alteration to the civic fabric of the city, when he remodelled the Campidoglio (the Capitol) in the 1540s. In the earlier part of this final period he also produced the tumultuous *Last Judgement* in the Sistine Chapel (1536–41), and two frescoes for Pope Paul III in the Cappella Paolina, scenes of tortured intensity that are a long way from the contemplative serenity of the early *Pietà*. Some time around 1540 he carved his last secular work, the *Brutus* (now in the Bargello), but the greatest sculptures of his last years are versions of the *Pietà*. One of these – an ensemble that exemplifies the quality that contemporaries termed *terribilità* ("awesome powerfulness" is an approximation) – was intended for his own tomb, and is now in Florence's Museo dell'Opera del Duomo. Michelangelo died in Rome on February 18, 1564; his body was transported to Florence, where it was borne in torchlit procession to Santa Croce.

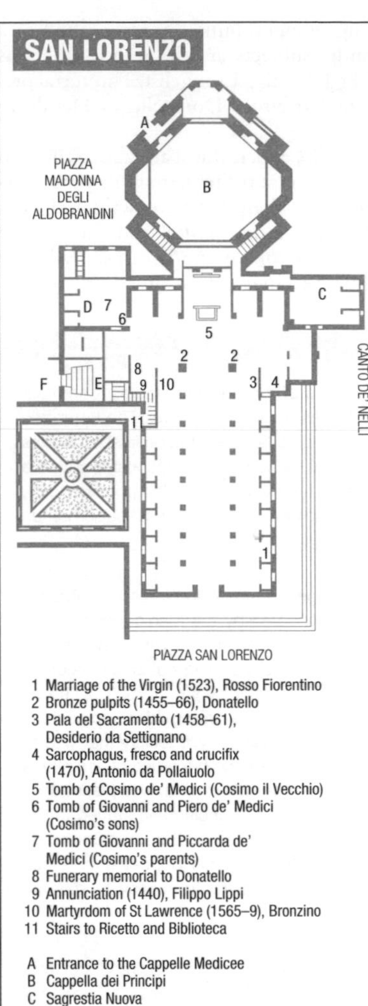


saints' feast day (Sept 27), so the two are often seen in paintings or buildings commissioned or connected with him.

Donatello was also responsible for the two bronze doors below with their combative martyrs to the left, and the Apostles and Fathers of the Church to the right. The chapel beyond the left door has a sublime little marble *lavabo*, probably by Verrocchio: many of its fantastic creatures have Medici connections – the falcon and lamb, for example, are the heraldic symbols of Piero de' Medici, who commissioned the work.

Lastly, the **stellar fresco** on the dome above the recessed altar inevitably draws your eye: opinion differs as to whether the position of the painted stars is synonymous with the state of the heavens on July 16, 1416, the birthday of Piero de' Medici, or on July 6, 1439, the date on which the union of the Eastern and Western churches was celebrated at the Council of Florence.

## The Biblioteca Medicea-Laurenziana

A gateway to the left of the church facade leads through a pleasant cloister and through a doorway (11) up to the **Biblioteca Medicea-Laurenziana** (F) (Mon, Fri & Sat 8.30am–2pm, Tues–Thurs 8am–5pm; €3). Wishing to create a suitably grandiose home for the precious manuscripts assembled by Cosimo and Lorenzo de' Medici, Pope Clement VII – Lorenzo's nephew – asked Michelangelo to design a new Medici library in 1524. The **Ricetto** (E) or vestibule (1559–71) of the building he eventually came up with is a revolutionary showpiece of Mannerist architecture, delighting in paradoxical display: brackets that support nothing, columns that sink into the walls rather than stand out from them, and a flight of steps so large that it almost fills the room, spilling down like a solidified lava flow.

From this bizarre space, you're sometimes allowed into the tranquil **reading room**; here, too, almost everything is the work of Michelangelo, even the inlaid desks. Exhibitions in the connecting rooms draw on the 15,000-piece Medici collection, which includes manuscripts as diverse as a fifth-century copy of Virgil – the collection's oldest item – and a treatise on architecture by Leonardo. Note how the coffered ceiling and terracotta floor mirror each other's designs.

## The Cappelle Medicee

Michelangelo's most celebrated contribution to the San Lorenzo complex forms part of the **Cappelle Medicee** (Tues–Sat 8.15am–5.50pm; first, third and fifth Sun of month and second and fourth Mon of month same hours; €6), entered from Piazza Madonna degli Aldobrandini, at the back of the church. These chapels divide into three sections: the **crypt**, burial place of many minor Medici; the **Cappella dei Principi**, housing the tombs of six of the more major Medici; and the **Sagrestia Nuova**, home to three major sculptural groups by Michelangelo.

### The crypt

Hardly any of the Medici, however humble, suffered the indignity of a modest grave. Some might have expected more, though, than the low-vaulted **crypt** of the Cappelle Medicee, home to the brass-railed tombs of many of the family's lesser lights. Most were placed here in 1791 by Ferdinand III with what appears to have been scant regard for his ancestors: one contemporary recorded how the duke had the corpses thrown "together pell-mell … caring scarcely to distinguish one from the other".

This haphazard arrangement prevailed until 1857, when it was decided – after much controversy – to exhume 49 of the bodies and provide them with a more dignified interment. William Wetmore Story, an American sculptor present at

▲ The Sagrestia Nuova, Cappelle Medicee

the exhumation, described the event with obvious relish: "Dark and parchment-dried faces were seen, with thin golden hair, rich as ever, and twisted with gems and pearls and golden nets … Anna Luisa, almost a skeleton, lay robed in rich violet velvet, with the electoral crown surmounting a black, ghastly face … Francesco, her uncle, lay beside her, a mass of putrid robes and rags."

Since 2004 researchers have been conducting exhumations in another Medici crypt below the church, where they have discovered that the dead Medici are not quite as well ordered as one would have expected: the skeleton of a one-year-old was found in the tomb of Filippino de' Medici (son of Grand Duke Francesco I), who was almost five when he died, and the crypt also contains the remains of eight children who feature on no Medici family tree.



## Cappella dei Principi

After filing through the crypt, you climb steps at its rear into the larger of the chapels, the **Cappella dei Principi** (Chapel of the Princes), a morbid and oppressive marble-plated hall built as a mausoleum for Cosimo I and the grand dukes who succeeded him. The octagonal chapel took as its inspiration the floorplan of no less a building than the Baptistery, and the extent of Medici conceit was underlined by the chapel's intended centrepiece – the Holy Sepulchre of Christ, a prize that had to be forfeited when an expedition sent to Jerusalem to steal it returned empty-handed.

Dismissed by Byron as a "fine frippery in great slabs of various expensive stones, to commemorate rotten and forgotten carcasses", this was the most expensive building project ever financed by the Medici, and the family were still paying for it in 1743 when the last of the line, Anna Maria Ludovica, joined her forebears in the basement. It could have looked even worse than it does – the massive statues in the niches were intended to be made from semi-precious stones, like those used in the heraldic devices set into the walls (the crests are those of Tuscan and other towns within the Medici domain). Captured Turkish slaves formed the bulk of the workforce set to haul and hack the stone into manageable pieces. Only two of the massive statues were ever completed.

Scaffolding has adorned the walls since a section of cornice fell off in 2000, revealing major structural faults.

## The Sagrestia Nuova

Begun in 1520, the **Sagrestia Nuova** (C) was designed by Michelangelo as a tribute to, and reinvention of, Brunelleschi's Sagrestia Vecchia in the main body of San Lorenzo. Architectural experts go into raptures over the sophistication of the architecture, notably the empty niches above the doors, which play complex games with the vocabulary of classical architecture, but the layperson will be drawn to the three fabulous **Medici tombs** (1520–34), two wholly and one partly by Michelangelo. The sculptor was awarded the commissions by Pope Leo X – a Medici – and the pope's cousin, Cardinal Giulio de' Medici, later to become Pope Clement VII.

As you enter, the tomb on the left belongs to **Lorenzo, duke of Urbino**, the grandson of Lorenzo the Magnificent. Michelangelo depicts him as a man of thought, and his sarcophagus bears figures of *Dawn* and *Dusk*, the times of day whose ambiguities appeal to the contemplative mind. Opposite stands the tomb of Lorenzo de' Medici's youngest son, **Giuliano, duke of Nemours**; as a man of action, his character is symbolized by the clear antithesis of *Day* and *Night*. A contemporary writer recorded that the sculptor gave his subjects "a greatness, a proportion, a dignity … which seemed to him would have brought them more praise, saying that a thousand years hence no one would be able to know that they were otherwise". The protagonists were very much otherwise: Giuliano was in reality an easygoing but somewhat feckless individual, while Lorenzo combined ineffectuality with unbearable arrogance. Both died – young and not greatly lamented – of tuberculosis, combined in Lorenzo's case with syphilis.

The two principal effigies were intended to face the equally grand tombs of Lorenzo de' Medici and his brother Giuliano, two Medici who had genuine claims to fame. The only part of the project completed by Michelangelo is the **Madonna and Child**, the last image of the Madonna he ever sculpted. The figures to either side are Cosmas and Damian, patron saints of doctors (*medici*) and the Medici family. Although completed by others, they follow Michelangelo's original design. Wax and clay models exist in the Casa Buonarroti (see p.141) and British Museum of other figures Michelangelo planned for the tomb. Among these were allegorical figures of Heaven and Earth and statues of river gods representing the Tiber and Arno, the last two intended to symbolize the provinces of Tuscany and Lazio, both briefly ruled by Giuliano. Sketches relating to this scheme are visible behind the altar (visitors are allowed to see them, under supervision, every thirty minutes), but the chapel was never completed as Michelangelo intended: in 1534, four years after the Medici had returned to Florence, Michelangelo decamped to Rome, where he stayed for the rest of his life.

## The Palazzo Medici-Riccardi

On the edge of the square in front of San Lorenzo stands the **Palazzo Medici-Riccardi** (9am–7pm; closed Wed; €5), designed for Cosimo de' Medici by Michelozzo between 1444 and 1462. As you'd expect, it's a magnificent structure, but it's considerably more modest than it might have been. Cosimo

### The Medici balls

You come across the **Medici emblem** – a cluster of red balls (*palle*) on a gold background – all over Florence, yet its origins are shrouded in mystery. Legend claims the family was descended from a Carolingian knight named Averardo, who fought and killed a giant in the Mugello, north of Florence. During the encounter his shield received six massive blows from the giant's mace, so Charlemagne, as a reward for his bravery, allowed Averardo to represent the dents as red balls on his coat of arms.

Rival families claimed that the balls had less exalted origins, that they were medicinal pills or cupping glasses, recalling the family's origins as apothecaries or doctors (*medici*). Others claim they are *bezants*, Byzantine coins, inspired by the arms of the *Arte del Cambio*, the moneychangers' guild to which the Medici belonged. In a similar vein, some say the balls are coins, the traditional symbols of pawnbrokers.

Whatever the origin, the number of *palle* was never constant. In the thirteenth century, for example, there were twelve. By Cosimo de' Medici's time the number had dropped to seven, though San Lorenzo's Old Sacristy, a Cosimo commission, strangely has eight, while Verrocchio's roundel in the same church's chancel has six and Grand Duke Cosimo I's tomb, in the Cappella dei Principi, has five. Cosimo il Vecchio was said to be so fond of displaying the *palle* on the buildings he had funded that a rival alleged that even the monks' privies in San Marco were adorned with Medici balls.

initially asked Brunelleschi to design the new family residence, but when he saw the model of what the architect had in mind he rejected the grandiose scheme on political grounds, saying: "envy is a plant one should never water". Brunelleschi, who was notorious for his temper, is said to have smashed the model in rage. The feature of Michelozzo's design that immediately strikes you (other than its scale) is its heavy rustication – the vast, rough-hewn blocks of stone that cover the exterior. Rustication was recommended by Michelozzo for buildings of this sort, as it united "an appearance of solidity and strength with the light and shade so essential to beauty under the glare of an Italian sun", and its use on the Palazzo Medici was to prove very influential – this is the prototype for several major Florentine *palazzi*, including Palazzo Pitti and Palazzo Strozzi.

The palace remained the family home and Medici business headquarters until Cosimo I moved to the Palazzo Vecchio in 1540. In Cosimo de' Medici's prime, around fifty members of the Medici clan lived in the palace, though after the deaths of his son Giovanni and grandson Cosimino, the embittered, gouty old man was said to repeatedly complain that the palace had become "too large a house for so small a family". In its day, Donatello's statue of *Judith and Holofernes* (now in the Palazzo Vecchio) adorned the walled garden, a rarity in Florence; the same artist's *David*, now in the Bargello, stood in the entrance courtyard.

After 1659 the palace was greatly altered by its new owners, the Riccardi, and it now houses the offices of the provincial government. The chief attraction for tourists is the cycle of Gozzoli **frescoes** in the chapel, which a maximum of fifteen people may view at any one time; while you're waiting to go in, you can explore an interactive video version of the chapel in a ground-floor room.

## The Gozzoli frescoes

Today all that survives of the interior of the original palace is Michelozzo's deep, colonnaded courtyard, which closely follows the style established by Brunelleschi in the foundling hospital (see p.128), and the tiny **chapel**, reached by the main staircase from the Cortile d'Onore. Its walls are covered by some of the city's most charming frescoes: **Benozzo Gozzoli**'s sequence depicting *The Journey of the Magi*, painted around 1460 and recently restored to magnificent effect. The landscape scenes to each side of the altar are by the same artist.

Despite the frescoes' ostensible subject, the cycle probably portrays the pageant of the Compagnia dei Magi, the most patrician of the city's religious confraternities, whose annual procession took place at Epiphany. Several of the Medici, inevitably, were prominent members, including Piero de' Medici (Piero il Gottoso – the Gouty), who may have commissioned the pictures. It's known that several of the Medici household are represented in the procession, but putting names to these prettified faces is a problem. The man leading the cavalcade on a white horse is almost certainly Piero, while the figure behind him, in the black cloak, is probably his father, Cosimo il Vecchio. Piero's older son, the future Lorenzo il Magnifico, who was 11 at the time the fresco was painted, is probably the gold-clad young king in the foreground, riding the grey horse detached from the rest of the procession; his brother, Giuliano, is probably the one preceded by the black bowman, to the left of Cosimo il Vecchio. The artist himself is in the crowd at the rear of the procession, his red beret signed with the words "Opus Benotii" in gold. Finally, the bearded characters among the throng might be portraits of the retinue of the Byzantine Emperor John Paleologus III, who had attended the Council of Florence twenty years before the fresco was painted.

### The gallery

Another set of stairs leads from the passageway beside the courtyard up to the **gallery**, where a display case in the lobby contains a *Madonna and Child* painted in the late 1460s by **Filippo Lippi**, one of Cosimo de' Medici's more troublesome protégés. Even as a novice friar at Santa Maria del Carmine, Filippo managed to earn himself a reputation as a drunken womanizer: in the words of Vasari, he was "so lustful that he would give anything to enjoy a woman he wanted … and if he couldn't buy what he wanted, then he would cool his passion by painting her portrait". Cosimo set up a workshop for him in the Medici palace, from which he often absented himself to go chasing women. On one occasion Cosimo actually locked the artist in the studio, but Filippo escaped down a rope of bed sheets; having cajoled him into returning, Cosimo declared that he would in future manage the painter with "affection and kindness", a policy that seems to have worked more successfully.

The gallery ceiling glows with Luca Giordano's enthusiastic fresco of *The Apotheosis of the Medici* (1683), from which one can only deduce that Giordano had no sense of shame. Accompanying Cosimo III on his flight into the ether is his son, the last male Medici, Gian Gastone (d. 1737), who grew to be a man so dissolute and indolent that he could rarely summon the energy to get out of bed in the morning.

## From the Mercato Centrale to the Fortezza da Basso

The **Mercato Centrale** is Europe's largest covered food hall, built in stone, iron and glass by Giuseppe Mengoni, architect of Milan's famous Galleria. Opened in 1874, it received a major overhaul a century later, reopening in 1980 with a new upper level. Butchers, *alimentari*, tripe-sellers, greengrocers, pasta stalls – they're all gathered here under one roof, and all charging prices lower than you'll readily find elsewhere in the city. Get there close to the end of the working day at 2pm and you'll get some good reductions.

Each day from 8am to 7pm the streets around the Mercato Centrale are thronged with **stalls** selling bags, belts, shoes and trousers. Most of the stuff is of doubtful quality, but this is the busiest of Florence's daily street markets, and an immersion in the haggling mass of customers can be fun.

### The Cenacolo di Fuligno

One of Florence's more obscure *cenacoli* (Last Suppers), the **Cenacolo di Fuligno**, is to be found a short distance from the market at Via Faenza 42, in the former Franciscan convent of Sant'Onofrio (Tues, Thurs & Sat 9am–noon; free, but donation requested). Discovered under layers of whitewash and grime in 1840, it was once thought to be by Raphael but was then reassigned to Raphael's mentor Perugino. Latest research indicates that it was painted by a member of Perugino's workshop but designed by the master in the 1490s – the orderliness and wistful tranquillity of the scene is typical of Perugino's style, and the Apostles' poses are drawn from a repertoire of gestures which the artist frequently deployed. A small collection of contemporaneous devotional art hangs on the other walls of the former refectory.

## The Fortezza da Basso

North of Via Faenza, the **Fortezza da Basso** was built to intimidate the people of Florence by the vile Alessandro de' Medici, who ordained himself duke of Florence after the Medici had been forcibly restored by a ten-month siege by the army of Charles V and Pope Clement VII (who was probably Alessandro's father). Michelangelo, the most talented Florentine architect of the day, had played a major role in the defence of the city during the siege; the job of designing the fortress fell to the more pliant Antonio da Sangallo.

Within a few years the cruelties of Alessandro had become intolerable: a petition to Charles V spoke of the Fortezza da Basso as "a prison and a slaughterhouse for the unhappy citizens". Charles's response to the catalogue of Alessandro's atrocities was to marry his daughter to the tyrant. In the end, another Medici came to the rescue: in 1537 the distantly related **Lorenzaccio de' Medici** stabbed the duke to death as he waited for an amorous assignation

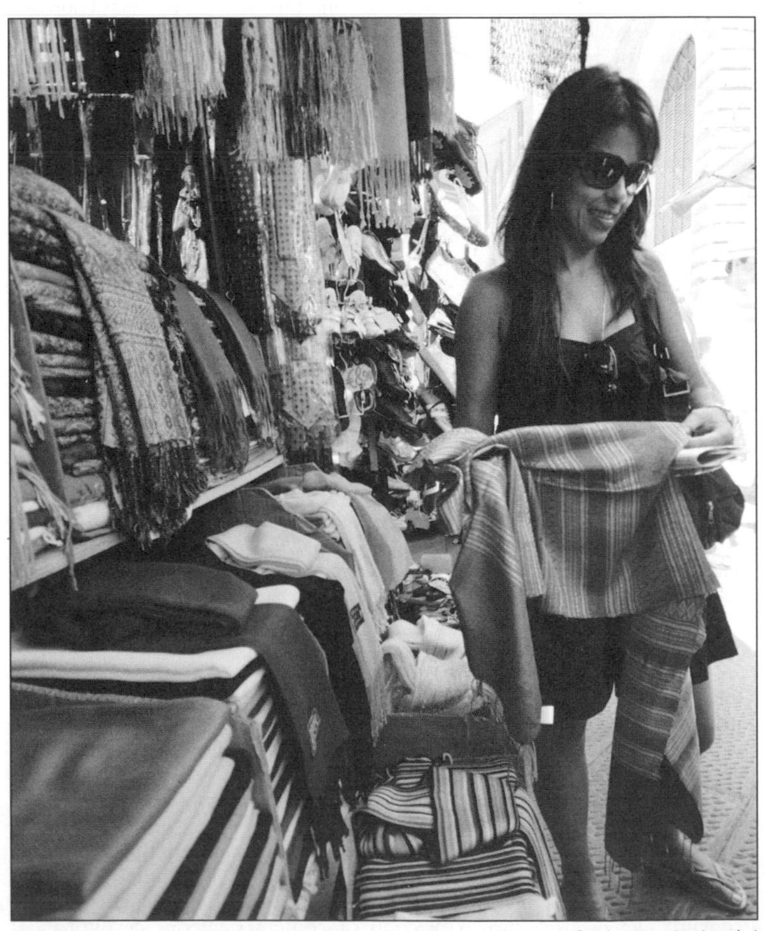

▲ San Lorenzo street market

in Lorenzaccio's house. The reasons for the murder have never been clear but it seems that Lorenzaccio's mental health was little better than Alessandro's: in his earlier years he and Alessandro had regularly launched lecherous sorties on the city's convents, and he had been expelled from Rome after lopping the heads off statues on the Arch of Constantine. The assassination, however, had favourable consequences for the city: as Alessandro died heirless, the council proposed that the leadership of the Florentine republic should be offered to **Cosimo de' Medici**, the great-grandson of Lorenzo il Magnifico.

The Fortezza da Basso served as a gaol and a barracks before falling into dereliction, but since 1978 there's been a vast shed in the centre of the complex, used for trade fairs and shows such as the *Pitti Moda* fashion jamborees in January and July. The public gardens by the walls are fairly pleasant, if you want an open-air spot to relax before catching a train.



## The San Marco district

Much of central Florence's traffic is funnelled along Via Cavour, the thoroughfare connecting the Duomo area to Piazza della Libertà, a junction of the city's *viali* (ring roads). Except as a place to catch buses out to Fiesole and other points north, the street itself has little to recommend it, but halfway along it lies **Piazza San Marco**, home of the **Museo di San Marco**, which is now in effect an immense gallery devoted to a single Renaissance master – Fra' Angelico, a painter in whom a deeply traditional piety was allied to a modern and exquisite sophistication of style. In the same district lies the **Accademia**, a museum that comes second only to the Uffizi in the popularity stakes, because it possesses half a dozen sculptures by **Michelangelo**, among them the *David* – symbol of the city's republican pride and of the illimitable ambition of the Renaissance artist. So great is the public appetite for this one work in particular that you'd be well advised to book tickets in advance (see p.44).

### The Accademia

Florence's first academy of drawing, the Accademia del Disegno, was founded in 1563 by Bronzino, Ammannati and Vasari. Initially based in Santissima Annunziata, it moved in 1764 to Via Ricasoli, and soon afterwards was transformed into a general arts academy, the Accademia di Belle Arti. Twenty years later the Grand Duke Pietro Leopoldo I founded the nearby **Galleria dell'Accademia** (Tues–Sun 8.15am–6.50pm; €6.50), filling its rooms with paintings for the edification of the students. Later augmented with pieces from suppressed religious foundations and other sources, the Accademia has an extensive collection of paintings, especially of Florentine work of the fourteenth and fifteenth centuries.

The **picture galleries** which flank the main sculpture hall are quite small and generally unexciting, with copious examples of the work of "Unknown Florentine" and "Follower of ...". The pieces likeliest to make an impact are Pontormo's *Venus and Cupid* (1532), painted to a cartoon by Michelangelo; a *Madonna of the Sea* (1470) attributed to Botticelli; and the painted fifteenth-century *Adimari Chest*, showing a Florentine wedding ceremony in the Piazza del Duomo. A cluster of rooms near the exit contain gilded religious works from the thirteenth and fourteenth centuries, including an altarpiece of *Pentecost* by Andrea Orcagna (c.1365).

## Michelangelo's David

Commissioned by the Opera del Duomo in 1501, the **David** was conceived to invoke parallels with Florence's freedom from outside domination (despite the superior force of its enemies), and its recent liberation from Savonarola and the Medici. It's an incomparable show of technical bravura, all the more impressive given the difficulties posed by the marble from which it was carved. The four-metre block of stone – thin, shallow and riddled with cracks – had been quarried from Carrara forty years earlier. Several artists had already attempted to work with it, notably Agostino di Duccio, Andrea Sansovino and Leonardo da Vinci. Michelangelo succeeded where others had failed, completing the work in 1504 when he was still just 29.

When they gave Michelangelo his commission, the Opera del Duomo had in mind a large statue that would be placed high on the Duomo's facade. Perhaps because the finished *David* was even larger than had been envisaged, at some point it was decided that it should be placed instead at ground level, in the Piazza della Signoria. Four days and a team of forty men were required to move the statue from the workshop to the piazza; another three weeks were needed to raise it onto its plinth. During the move the statue required protection day and night to prevent it being stoned by Medici supporters who were all too aware of its symbolism. Damage was done a few years later, in 1527, when the Medici were again expelled from the city: a bench, flung from a window of the Palazzo Vecchio by anti-Medici rioters, struck and smashed the left arm, but the pieces were gathered up and reassembled. The statue remained in its outdoor setting, exposed to the elements, until it was sent to the Accademia in 1873, by which time it had lost its gilded hair and the gilded band across its chest. Also missing these days is a skirt of copper leaves added to spare the blushes of Florence's more sensitive citizens.

Thoroughly cleaned in 2004, *David* now occupies a specially built alcove, protected by a glass barrier that was built in 1991, after one of its toes was cracked by a hammer-wielding artist. With his massive head and gangling arms, *David* is something of a graceless lump, but his proportions would not have appeared so graceless in the setting for which it was first conceived, at a rather higher altitude and at a greater distance from the public than the position it occupies in the Accademia's chapel-like space.

## The Slaves

Michelangelo once described the process of carving as being the liberation of the form from within the stone, a notion that seems to be embodied by the remarkable unfinished **Slaves** (or Prisoners). His procedure, clearly demonstrated here, was to cut the figure as if it were a deep relief, and then to free the three-dimensional figure; often his assistants would perform the initial operation, working from the master's pencil marks, so it's possible that Michelangelo's own chisel never touched these stones.

Probably carved in the late 1520s, the statues were originally destined for the tomb of Julius II, intended perhaps to symbolize the liberal arts left "enslaved" by Julius's demise. The tomb underwent innumerable permutations before its eventual abandonment, however, and in 1564 the artist's nephew gave the carvings to the Medici, who installed them in the grotto of the Bóboli garden. Four of the original six statues came to the Accademia in 1909. Two others found their way to the Louvre in Paris.

Close by is another unfinished work, *St Matthew* (1505–06), started soon after completion of the *David* as a commission from the Opera del Duomo; they actually requested a full series of the Apostles from Michelangelo, but this is the only one he ever began. It languished half-forgotten in the cathedral vaults until 1831.

## The Museo dell'Opificio delle Pietre Dure

The **Opificio delle Pietre Dure** (Mon–Sat 8.15am–2pm, Thurs open until 7pm; €2), which occupies a corner of the Accademia building, was founded in 1588 to train craftsmen in the Florentine art of creating pictures or patterns with polished semi-precious stones. The museum elucidates the highly skilled processes involved in the creation of *pietre dure* work, and has some remarkable examples of the genre. If you want to see some more spectacular (and to modern eyes rather gross) specimens, you should visit the Cappelle Medicee or the Palazzo Pitti's Museo degli Argenti. While several local workshops still maintain the traditions of this specialized art form, the Opificio itself has evolved into one of the world's leading centres for the restoration of stonework and paintings.

## The Museo di San Marco

A whole side of Piazza San Marco is taken up by the Dominican convent and church of San Marco, the first of which now houses the magnificent **Museo di San Marco** (Tues–Thurs 8.15am–1.50pm, Fri 8.15am–6pm, Sat 8.15am–7pm; also first, third and fifth Mon of month 8.15am–1.50pm, and second and fourth Sun of month 8.15am–7pm; €4). The Dominicans acquired the site in 1436, after being forced to move from their former home in Fiesole, and the complex promptly became the recipient of Cosimo's most lavish patronage. In the 1430s he financed Michelozzo's enlargement of the conventual buildings, and went on to establish a vast library here. Ironically, the convent became the centre of resistance to the Medici later in the century: Girolamo **Savonarola**, leader of the government of Florence after the expulsion of the Medici in 1494, was the prior of San Marco. In 1537 Duke Cosimo expelled the Dominicans once more, reminding them that it was another Cosimo who had established the building's magnificence in the first place.

As Michelozzo was altering and expanding San Marco, the convent's walls were being decorated by one of its friars and a future prior, **Fra' Angelico**. Born into a wealthy farming family in Vicchio di Mugello (a village in the hills to the northeast of Florence) some time in the late 1390s, Fra' Angelico entered the Dominican monastery of Fiesole aged around 20. Then known as Fra' Giovanni da Fiesole, he was already recognized as an accomplished artist, but really flourished when he came to San Marco in 1436. Here he was encouraged by the theologian Antonino Pierozzi, the convent's first prior and later archbishop of Florence (but best known now as St Antonine). By the time Fra' Giovanni succeeded Pierozzi as prior, the pictures he had created for the monastery and numerous churches in Florence and elsewhere – including the Vatican – had earned him the title "the angelic painter", the name by which he's been known ever since. In 1982 he was beatified (a halfway house to sainthood), thus formalizing the name by which he had long been known, Beato Angelico, or the Blessed Angelico.

### The ground floor

Immediately beyond the **entrance** (marked 1 on the plan) lies the **Chiostro di Sant'Antonino** (2), designed by Michelozzo and now dominated by a vast cedar of Lebanon. Most of the cloister's faded frescoes are sixteenth-century depictions of episodes from the life of Antonino Pierozzi, Angelico's mentor and the convent's first prior. Angelico himself painted the frescoes in its four corners, of which the most striking is the lunette of *St Dominic at the Foot of the Cross* (3).

This weather-bleached work pales alongside the twenty or so paintings by the artist gathered in the **Ospizio dei Pellegrini** (5), or Pilgrims' Hospice, which lies

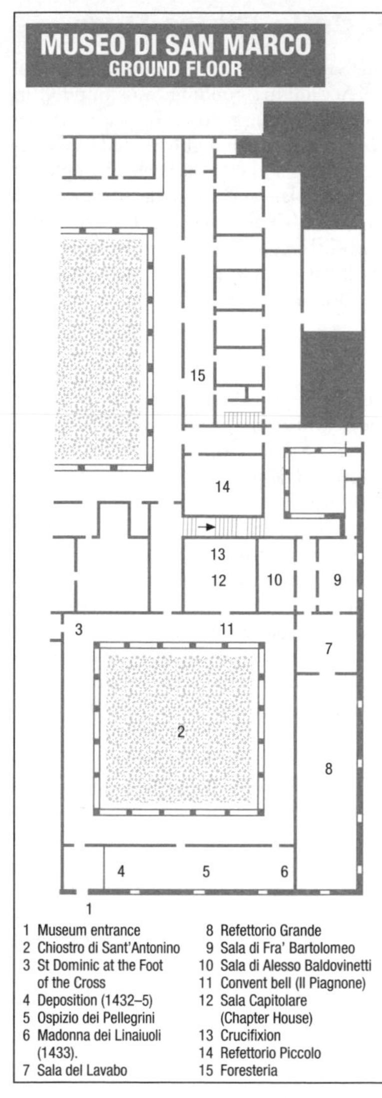


1 Museum entrance
2 Chiostro di Sant'Antonino
3 St Dominic at the Foot of the Cross
4 Deposition (1432–5)
5 Ospizio dei Pellegrini
6 Madonna dei Linaiuoli (1433).
7 Sala del Lavabo
8 Refettorio Grande
9 Sala di Fra' Bartolomeo
10 Sala di Alesso Baldovinetti
11 Convent bell (Il Piagnone)
12 Sala Capitolare (Chapter House)
13 Crucifixion
14 Refettorio Piccolo
15 Foresteria

between the cloister and the piazza. Many of the works – including several of Angelico's most famous – were brought here from churches and galleries around Florence; all display the artist's brilliant colouring and spatial clarity, and an air of imperturbable piety. On the right wall as you enter is a *Deposition* (4), 1432–35, originally hung in the church of Santa Trìnita. Commissioned by the Strozzi family, the painting was begun by Lorenzo Monaco, who died after completing the upper trio of triangular pinnacles, and continued by Fra' Angelico. At the opposite end of the room hangs the *Madonna dei Linaiuoli* (6), Angelico's first major public painting (1433), commissioned by the *linaiuoli* (the flax-workers' guild) for their headquarters; the grandiose marble frame is the work of Ghiberti. Halfway down the room, on the inner wall, the so-called *Pala di San Marco* (1440), though badly damaged by the passage of time and a disastrous restoration, demonstrates Fra' Angelico's familiarity with the latest developments in artistic theory. Its figures are arranged in lines that taper towards a central vanishing point, in accordance with the principles laid out in Alberti's *Della Pittura* (*On Painting*), published in Italian just two years before the picture was executed. The work was commissioned by the Medici as an altarpiece for the church of San Marco, hence the presence of the family's patron saints Cosmas and Damian, who can be seen at work as doctors (*medici*), in the small panel immediately to the right.

Back in the cloister, a doorway in its top right-hand corner opens into the **Sala del Lavabo** (7), where the monks washed before eating. Its entrance wall has a *Crucifixion with Saints* by Angelico, and its right wall two panels with a pair of saints, also by Angelico. The left wall contains a damaged lunette fresco of the *Madonna and Child* by Paolo Uccello, plus part of a predella by the same artist. The impressive room to the right, the **Refettorio Grande** (8), or Large Refectory, is dominated by a large fresco of the *Crucifixion* by the sixteenth-century painter Giovanni Sogliani. Of more artistic interest are the rooms devoted to paintings by **Fra' Bartolomeo** (9) and **Alesso Baldovinetti** (10).

Note in particular Fra' Bartolomeo's suitably intense portrait of Savonarola, and his unfinished *Pala della Signoria* (1512), originally destined for the Salone dei Cinquecento in the Palazzo Vecchio.

Further round the cloister lies the **Sala Capitolare** (12), or Chapter House, which now houses a large conventual bell, the Piagnone (11), which was rung to summon help on Savonarola's arrest on the eve of April 8, 1498: it became a symbol of anti-Medici sentiment ever after. Here, too, is a powerful fresco of the *Crucifixion* (13), painted by Angelico and assistants in 1441. At the rear of this room, entered via a passageway alongside the Chapter House, lies the **Refettorio Piccolo** (14), or Small Refectory, with a lustrous *Last Supper* (1480) by Ghirlandaio. This forms an anteroom to the **Foresteria** (15), home to the convent's former guest rooms, which is cluttered with architectural bits and pieces salvaged during nineteenth-century urban improvement schemes. The corridor provides good views into the (closed) Chiostro di San Domenico.

## The first floor

Stairs off the cloister by the entrance to the Foresteria lead up to the first floor, where almost immediately you're confronted with one of the most sublime paintings in Italy. For the drama of its setting and the lucidity of its composition, nothing in San Marco matches Angelico's **Annunciation** (A). The pallid, submissive Virgin is one of the most touching images in Renaissance art, and the courteous angel, with his scintillating unfurled wings, is as convincing a heavenly messenger as any ever painted. An inscription on this fresco reminds the passing monks to say a Hail Mary as they venerate the image.

Angelico and his assistants also painted the simple and piously restrained pictures in each of the

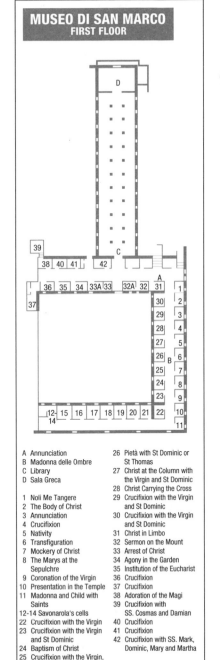

**MUSEO DI SAN MARCO**
**FIRST FLOOR**

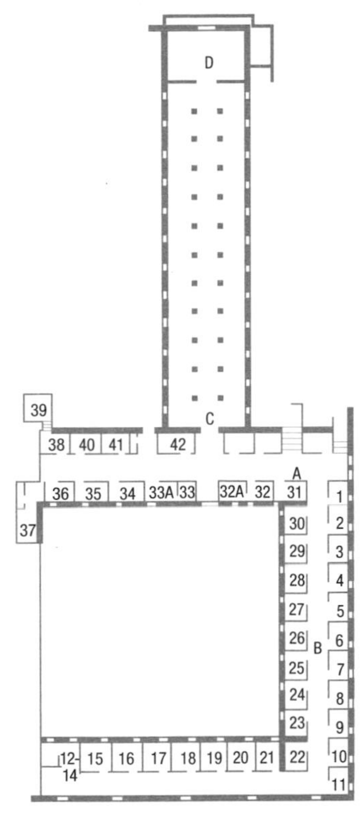


A Annunciation
B Madonna delle Ombre
C Library
D Sala Greca

1 Noli Me Tangere
2 The Body of Christ
3 Annunciation
4 Crucifixion
5 Nativity
6 Transfiguration
7 Mockery of Christ
8 The Marys at the Sepulchre
9 Coronation of the Virgin
10 Presentation in the Temple
11 Madonna and Child with Saints
12-14 Savonarola's cells
22 Crucifixion with the Virgin
23 Crucifixion with the Virgin and St Dominic
24 Baptism of Christ
25 Crucifixion with the Virgin, Magdalen and St Dominic
26 Pietà with St Dominic or St Thomas
27 Christ at the Column with the Virgin and St Dominic
28 Christ Carrying the Cross
29 Crucifixion with the Virgin and St Dominic
30 Crucifixion with the Virgin and St Dominic
31 Christ in Limbo
32 Sermon on the Mount
33 Arrest of Christ
34 Agony in the Garden
35 Institution of the Eucharist
36 Crucifixion
37 Crucifixion
38 Adoration of the Magi
39 Crucifixion with SS. Cosmas and Damian
40 Crucifixion
41 Crucifixion
42 Crucifixion with SS. Mark, Dominic, Mary and Martha

44 **dormitory cells** on this floor, into which the brothers would withdraw for solitary contemplation and sleep. Such privacy was a novelty, permitted only after a papal concession of 1419 that freed the Dominicans from sleeping in dormitories, but privacy came at a price – it's said that the realism of the frescoes, in particular the copious amounts of blood present in some of the Crucifixion scenes, caused some of the more timorous monks to faint. Almost all the outer cells of the corridor on the left (1–11) have works by Angelico himself – don't miss the *Noli Me Tangere* (1), the *Annunciation* (3), the outstanding *Transfiguration* (6) and the *Coronation of the Virgin* (9). The marvellous **Madonna delle Ombre** (B), or Madonna of the Shadows, on the wall facing these cells, is probably also by Angelico. Several of the scenes include one or both of a pair of monastic onlookers, serving as intermediaries between the occupant of the cell and the personages in the pictures: the one with the star above his head is St Dominic; the one with the split skull is St Peter Martyr (see p.101).

At the end of the far corridor is a knot of rooms (12–14) once occupied by Savonarola. These now contain various relics – a belt, a cape, a torn vest – questionably authenticated as worn by the man himself; most dubious of all is the piece of wood from his funeral pyre, which is depicted in a couple of paintings here. If you turn right at the main *Annunciation* and continue to

## Savonarola

Girolamo **Savonarola** was born in 1452, the son of the physician to the Ferrara court. He grew up to be an abstemious and melancholic youth, sleeping on a bare straw mattress and spending much of his time reading the Bible and writing dirges. At the age of 23 he absconded to a Dominican monastery in Bologna, informing his father by letter that he was "unable to endure the evil conduct of the heedless people of Italy".

Within a few years, the Dominicans had dispatched him to preach all over northern Italy, an enterprise which got off to an unpromising start. Not the most attractive of men – he was frail, with a beak of a nose and a blubbery mouth – Savonarola was further hampered by an uningratiating voice and a particularly inelegant way of gesturing. Nonetheless, the intensity of his manner and his message attracted a committed following when he settled permanently in the monastery of **San Marco** in 1489.

By 1491, Savonarola's sermons had become so popular that he was asked to deliver his Lent address in the Duomo. Proclaiming that God was speaking through him, he berated the city for its decadence, for its paintings that made the Virgin "look like a whore" and for the tyranny of its Medici-led government. Following the death of Lorenzo il Magnifico, the rhetoric became even more apocalyptic. "Wait no longer, for there may be no more time for repentance," he told the Duomo congregation, summoning images of plagues, invasions and destruction.

When Charles VIII of France marched into Italy in September 1494 to press his claim to the throne of Naples, Savonarola presented him as the instrument of God's vengeance. Violating Piero de' Medici's declaration of Tuscan neutrality, the French army massacred the garrison at Fivizzano, and Florence prepared for the onslaught, as Savonarola declaimed, "The Sword has descended; the scourge has fallen." With support for resistance ebbing, Piero capitulated to Charles; within days the Medici had fled and their palace had been plundered. Hailed by Savonarola as "the Minister of God, the Minister of Justice", Charles and his vast army passed peacefully through Florence on their way to Rome.

The political vacuum in Florence was filled by the declaration of a **republican constitution**, but Savonarola was now in effect the ruler of the city. Continual decrees were issued from San Marco: profane carnivals were to be outlawed, fasting was to be the end of the corridor you'll come to cells 38 and 39: these more luxuriously appointed retreats were the personal domain of Cosimo de' Medici. The fresco of the *Adoration of the Magi* (38) may well be the work of Angelico's star pupil Benozzo Gozzoli. Its subject may have been suggested by Cosimo himself, who liked to think of himself as a latter-day wise man, or at least as a gift-giving king.

On the way to these VIP cells you'll pass the entrance to **Michelozzo's Library** (C), built in 1441–44 to a design that exudes an atmosphere of calm study, though – as the plaque by the doorway tells you – it was here that Savonarola was finally cornered and arrested in 1498. Cosimo's agents roamed to the Holy Land and beyond, garnering precious manuscripts and books; in turn, Cosimo handed all the religious items over to the monastery, stipulating that they should be accessible to all, making it Europe's first public library. At the far end, a door leads through to the **Sala Greca** (D; usually open for guided visits on the hour), which was added to house a growing collection of Greek codices.

## San Marco church

Greatly altered since Michelozzo's intervention, the church of **San Marco** (Mon–Sat 9.30am–noon & 4–5.30pm; free) is worth a quick visit for two works on the second and third altars on the right: a *Madonna and Saints* painted

observed more frequently, children were to act as the agents of the righteous, informing the authorities whenever their parents transgressed the Eternal Law. Irreligious books and paintings, expensive clothes, cosmetics, mirrors, board games, trivialities and luxuries of all types were destroyed, a ritual purging that reached a crescendo with a colossal **"Bonfire of the Vanities"** on the Piazza della Signoria.

Meanwhile, Charles VIII was installed in Naples and a formidable alliance was being assembled to overthrow him: the papacy, Milan, Venice, Ferdinand of Aragon and the Emperor Maximilian. In July 1495 the army of this Holy League confronted the French and was badly defeated. Charles's army continued northwards back to France, and Savonarola was summoned to the Vatican to explain why he had been unable to join the campaign against the intruder. He declined to attend, claiming that it was not God's will that he should make the journey, and thus set off a chain of exchanges that ended with his **excommunication** in June 1497. Defying Pope Alexander's order, Savonarola celebrated Mass in the Duomo on Christmas Day, which prompted a final threat from Rome: send Savonarola to the Vatican or imprison him in Florence, otherwise the whole city would join him in excommunication.

Despite Savonarola's insistence that the Borgia pope was already consigned to hell, the people of Florence began to desert him. The region's crops had failed, plague had broken out again, and the city was at war with Pisa, which Charles had handed over to its citizens rather than return to Florence's control, as he had promised. The Franciscans of Florence, sceptical of the Dominican monk's claim to divine approval, now issued a terrible challenge. One of their community and one of Savonarola's would walk through an avenue of fire in the Piazza della Signoria: if the Dominican died, then Savonarola would be banished; if the Franciscan died, then Savonarola's main critic, Fra' Francesco da Puglia, would be expelled.

A thunderstorm prevented the trial from taking place, but the mood in the city had anyway turned irrevocably. The following day, Palm Sunday 1498, a siege of the monastery of San Marco ended with Savonarola's **arrest**. Accused of heresy, he was tortured to the point of death, then **burned at the stake** in front of the Palazzo Vecchio, with two of his supporters. When the flames had finally been extinguished, the ashes were thrown into the river, to prevent anyone from gathering them as relics.

in 1509 by Fra' Bartolomeo, and an eighth-century mosaic of *The Madonna in Prayer* (surrounded by later additions), brought here from Constantinople. This had to be cut in half in transit, and you can still see the break across the Virgin's midriff. On the left side of the church you'll find the tomb-slabs of Pico della Mirandola (1463–94) and Poliziano (1454–94), two of the greatest scholar-writers in the circle of Lorenzo il Magnifico – the latter was tutor to Lorenzo's son, and is pictured beside him in the Sassetti chapoel frescoes in Santa Trìnita.



## West and north of Piazza San Marco

Within a couple of minutes' stroll west and north of **Piazza San Marco** are two little-visited art attractions (the Cenacolo di Sant'Apollonia and the Chiostro dello Scalzo), one of the city's more obscure parks and a cluster of specialist museums. The first pair in particular merit a diversion.

### The Cenacolo di Sant'Apollonia

Running off the west side of Piazza San Marco, Via degli Arazzieri soon becomes Via XXVII Aprile, where the former Benedictine convent of **Sant'Apollonia** stands at no. 1 (Tues–Sun 8.15am–1.50pm; second and fourth Sun of month and first, third and fifth Mon of month same hours; free). Most of the complex has now been turned into apartments, but one entire wall of the former refectory houses Andrea del Castagno's *Last Supper*, a very early use of rigorous perspective in Renaissance art and one of the most disturbing versions of the event ever painted. Blood-red is the dominant tone, and the most commanding figure is the diabolic, black-bearded Judas, who sits on the near side of the table. The seething patterns in the marbled panels behind the Apostles enhance the intensity of the scene, in which the state of mind of each Apostle is distinctly delineated at the moment at which Christ announces that one of them will betray him. Painted around 1450 (which makes it the first of the city's Renaissance *cenacoli*), the fresco was plastered over by the nuns before being uncovered in the middle of the nineteenth century. Above the illusionistic recess in which the supper takes place are the faded remains of a *Resurrection, Crucifixion and Deposition* by Castagno, who also painted the lunettes of the *Crucifixion* and *Pietà* on the adjacent walls. Various *sinopie* are on display as well, and opposite the *Last Supper* you'll see the remnants of frescoes painted for the church of Sant'Egidio by Castagno, Piero della Francesca, Domenico Veneziano and Baldovinetti – all that's left now is a row of marbled panels and a gallery of severed feet.

### The Chiostro dello Scalzo

To the north of San Marco, at Via Cavour 69, is **Lo Scalzo**, the home of the Brotherhood of St John, whose vows of poverty entailed walking around barefoot (*scalzo*). The order was suppressed in 1785 and their monastery sold off, except for the **cloister** (Mon, Thurs & Sat 8.15am–1.50pm; free). This was the training ground for Andrea del Sarto, an artist venerated in the nineteenth century as a painter with no imperfections, but now regarded with slightly less enthusiasm on account of this very smoothness. His monochrome paintings of the *Cardinal Virtues* and *Scenes from the Life of the Baptist* occupied him off and on for a decade from 1511, beginning with the *Baptism* and finishing with the *Birth of St John*. A couple of the sixteen scenes – *John in the Wilderness* and *John Meeting Christ* – were executed by his pupil Franciabigio in 1518, when del Sarto was away in Paris.

## The Museo Stibbert

About 1500m north of San Marco, at Via Stibbert 26 (bus #4 from the station), is the loopiest of Florence's museums, the **Museo Stibbert** (Mon–Wed 10am–2pm, Fri–Sun 10am–6pm; guided tour €6). This rambling, murky mansion was the home of the half-Scottish half-Italian Frederick Stibbert, who in his twenties made a name for himself in Garibaldi's army. Later he inherited a fourteenth-century house from his mother, then bought the neighbouring mansion and joined the two together, thus creating a place big enough to accommodate the fruits of his compulsive collecting. The 64 rooms contain over fifty thousand items, ranging from snuffboxes to paintings by Carlo Crivelli and a possible Botticelli.

Militaria were Frederick's chief enthusiasm, and the Stibbert **armour** collection is reckoned one of the world's best. It includes Roman, Etruscan and Japanese examples (the highlight of the whole museum), as well as a fifteenth-century *condottiere*'s outfit and the armour worn by the great Medici commander Giovanni delle Bande Nere, retrieved from his grave in San Lorenzo in 1857. The big production number comes in the great hall, between the two houses, where a platoon of mannequins is clad in full sixteenth-century gear. Also on show are the regalia in which Napoleon was crowned king of Italy.

### The Giardino dei Semplici and the university museums

The **Giardino dei Semplici** or **Orto Botanico** (Mon, Tues, Thurs, Fri & Sun 9am–1pm, Sat 9am–5pm; €4), northeast of San Marco, was set up in 1545 for Cosimo I as a medicinal garden, following the examples of Padua and Pisa. Entered from Via Micheli, it now covers five acres, most of the area being taken up by the original flowerbeds and avenues.

On the south side of the garden, at Via La Pira 4, you'll find the entrance to a number of **museums** administered by the university. The **Museo Botanico** (currently open only to scholars; ⓣ055.275.7462), set up for Leopoldo II of Lorraine, contains over four million botanical specimens, supplemented by plaster mushrooms and remarkable wax models of plants. Masses of rocks are on show in the **Museo di Minerologia e Litologia** (June–Sept Wed & Fri 9am–1pm; Oct–May Tues 9am–1pm & 2–5pm, Wed–Sat 9am–1pm; €6 joint ticket with the next museum), including a 150-kilo topaz from Brazil and a load of worked stones from the Medici collection – snuffboxes, little vases, a quartz boat, etc. The **Museo di Geologia e Paleontologia** (same hours and ticket as above) is one of Italy's biggest fossil shows, featuring such delights as prehistoric elephant skeletons from the upper Valdarno and a skeleton from Grosseto once touted as the missing link between monkeys and *Homo sapiens*. There's a plan to move all these natural history museums into a new home on Via Circondaria, making what will be the largest museum of its kind in Italy, but the project has spent years stuck on the drawing board.

# Piazza Santissima Annunziata

The pedestrianized **Piazza Santissima Annunziata**, with its distinctive arcades, is one of the city's most attractive public spaces and has a special importance for the city too. Until the end of the eighteenth century the Florentine year used to begin on March 25, the Festival of the Annunciation – hence the Florentine predilection for paintings of the Annunciation, and the fashionableness of the

Annunziata church, which has long been the place for society weddings. The festival is still marked by a huge fair in the piazza and the streets leading off it; later in the year, on the first weekend in September, the square is used for Tuscany's largest crafts fair.

Planned by Brunelleschi in the 1420s, the piazza has at its centre an equestrian **statue** of Grand Duke Ferdinand I (1608); this was Giambologna's final work, and was cast by his pupil Pietro Tacca from cannons captured at the Battle of Lepanto. Tacca was also the creator of the bizarre **fountains** (1629), on each of which a pair of aquatic monkeys spit water at two whiskered sea slugs.

## The Spedale degli Innocenti

Piazza Santissima Annunziata is flanked on its eastern side by the **Spedale degli Innocenti**, or Ospedale (Mon–Sat 8.30am–7pm, Sun 8.30am–2pm; €4). Commissioned in 1419 by the *Arte della Seta*, the silk-weavers' guild, it opened in 1445 as the first foundlings' hospital in Europe, and is still an orphanage today. It was largely designed by Brunelleschi (whose activity as a goldsmith, strangely, allowed him membership of the guild), and his nine-arched loggia was one of Europe's earliest examples of the new classically influenced style. The mirror-image building on the other side of the piazza was designed a century later by Antonio da Sangallo and Baccio d'Agnolo as accommodation for the Servite friars who staffed the orphanage.

Andrea della Robbia's blue-backed ceramic tondi (1487) of well-swaddled babies advertise the Spedale's function, but their gaiety belies the misery associated with it. Slavery was part of the Florentine economy as late as the fifteenth century (it's possible that Leonardo da Vinci's mother was a slave), and many of the infants given over to the care of the Innocenti were born to domestic slaves. From 1660 children could be abandoned anonymously in the *rota*, a small revolving door whose bricked-up remains are still visible at the extreme left of the facade; it remained in use until 1875.

▲ Piazza Santissima Annunziata

The building within centres on two beautiful cloisters, Brunelleschi's central **Chiostro degli Uomini** (Men's Cloister) and the narrow, graceful **Chiostro delle Donne** (Women's Cloister) to the right. Stairs from the left-hand corner of the former lead up to the **museum**, a miscellany of Florentine Renaissance art that includes one of Luca della Robbia's most beguiling Madonnas and an *Adoration of the Magi* (1488) by Domenico Ghirlandaio. The latter, commissioned as the altarpiece of the building's church, features a background depicting the *Massacre of the Innocents*. The parallel of the slaughter of Bethlehem's first-born with the orphanage's foundlings, or *innocenti*, was deliberately made.



## Santissima Annunziata

The elegant church of **Santissima Annunziata** (daily 7am–12.30pm & 4–6.30pm; free) is the mother house of the Servites, or Servi di Maria (Servants of Mary), a religious order founded by Filippo Benizzi and six Florentine aristocrats in 1234. From humble beginnings, the order blossomed after 1252, when a painting of the Virgin begun by one of the monks – abandoned in despair because of his inability to create a truly beautiful image – was completed by an angel while he slept. So many people came to venerate the image that by 1444 a new church, financed by the Medici, was commissioned from Michelozzo (who happened to be the brother of the Servites' head prior). The project, completed by Leon Battista Alberti in 1481, involved laying out the present-day Via dei Servi, designed to link Santissima Annunziata and the cathedral, thus uniting the city's two most important churches dedicated to the Madonna.

### The Chiostrino dei Voti

As the number of pilgrims to the church increased, so it became a custom to leave wax votive offerings (*voti*) in honour of its miraculous Madonna. In the early days these were placed around the walls; later they were hung from the nave ceiling. Eventually they became so numerous that in 1447 a special atrium, the **Chiostrino dei Voti**, was built onto the church. In time this came to house some six hundred statues, some of them life-sized depictions of the donor, with a full-sized wax horse in close attendance. The collection was one of the city's great tourist attractions until 1786, when the whole lot was melted down to make candles.

More lasting alterations to the cloister's appearance, in the shape of a major **fresco cycle**, were made in 1516 on the occasion of the canonization of Filippo Benizzi, the Servites' founding father. Three leading artists of the day – Andrea del Sarto, Jacopo Pontormo and Rosso Fiorentino – were involved, together with several lesser painters. Some of the panels are in a poor state – all were removed from the walls and restored after the 1966 flood (see p.135) – but their overall effect is superb.

The entrance wall, together with the right (south) and far (east) walls, depicts scenes from the *Life of the Virgin*, while the remaining two walls portray scenes from the *Life of St Filippo Benizzi*. Moving right around the cloister, the sequence works backwards from the Virgin's death, beginning with an **Assumption** (1) by Rosso Fiorentino, one of his first works, painted when he was aged around 19. The authorities immediately found fault with it (for one thing, the *putti* bearing Mary to heaven seem to be having an unseemly amount of fun), asking Andrea del Sarto to paint a new version over it, but in the event it was never altered.

Alongside lies Pontormo's **Visitation** (2), which was said to have taken some eighteen months to paint; del Sarto's **Journey of the Magi** (5), by contrast, across the atrium, took a little over three months. In the next alcove note Franciabigio's **Marriage of the Virgin** (3), in which the painter is said to have

## SANTISSIMA ANNUNZIATA: CHIOSTRINO DEI VOTI

Chiostro dei Morti

Chiostrino dei Voti

Cappella Pucci

PIAZZA SANTISSIMA ANNUNZIATA

1 Assumption (1513–4), Rosso Fiorentino
2 Visitation (1514–6), Pontormo
3 Marriage of the Virgin (1513), Franciabigio
4 The Birth of the Virgin (1511), Andrea del Sarto
5 Journey of the Magi (1511), Andrea del Sarto
6 Nativity (1460–2), Alesso Baldovinetti
7 Vocation and Investiture of San Filippo Benizzi (1476), Cosimo Rosselli
8 The Saint Covers a Leper with His Shirt (1509–10), Andrea del Sarto
9 The Saint Punishes Blasphemers (1509–10), Andrea del Sarto
10 The Saint Cures a Possessed Woman (1509–10), Andrea del Sarto
11 The Saint Raises a Child (1509–10), Andrea del Sarto
12 The Saint Cures a Sick Child (1509–10), Andrea del Sarto

A Main entrance
B Entrance to Chiostro dei Morti
C Entrance to church

taken a hammer to the Virgin's face: apparently he was angry at the monks for having secretly looked at the work before its completion; after the artist's tantrum no one had the courage to repair the damage.

Before the next lunette comes a fine marble bas-relief of the *Madonna and Child* attributed to Michelozzo, followed by the cloister's masterpiece, Andrea del Sarto's **Birth of the Virgin** (4). To the right of the large church door is the same artist's **Journey of the Magi** (5), which includes a self-portrait in the right-hand corner. Left of the door lies Alesso Baldovinetti's **Nativity** (6), its faded appearance the result of poor initial preparation on the part of the artist. The sequence devoted to Filippo Benizzi begins on the next wall with Cosimo Rosselli's **Vocation and Investiture of the Saint** (7); the five remaining damaged panels (8–12) are all the work of Andrea del Sarto.

### The interior

Few Florentine interiors are as striking at first sight as Santissima Annunziata, but to be sure of seeing it you should visit in the afternoon: this church commands the devotion of a large congregation, and there are Masses every hour all morning. Beyond the startling first impression made by the gilt and stucco gloss that was applied in the seventeenth and eighteenth centuries, the church contains few genuine treasures. One notable exception is the ornate **tabernacle** (1448–61) immediately on your left as you enter, designed by Michelozzo to house the miraculous image of the Madonna. Michelozzo's patron, Piero di Cosimo de' Medici, made sure that nobody remained unaware of the money he sank into the shrine: an inscription reads *Costò fior. 4 mila el marmo solo* ("The marble alone cost 4000 florins"). The painting encased in the marble has been repainted into illegibility, and is usually kept covered anyway. It is further obscured by a vast array of lamps, candles and votive offerings: Florentine brides still traditionally visit the shrine to leave their bridal bouquets with the Madonna.

To the tabernacle's right lies a chapel (1453–63) originally created as an oratory for the Medici, adorned with five panels of inlaid stone depicting the Virgin's principal symbols (sun, moon, star, lily and rose) and a small picture of the *Redeemer* (1515) by Andrea del Sarto. The **Cappella Feroni**, next door, features a restrained fresco by Andrea del Castagno of *Christ and St Julian* (1455–56). The adjacent chapel contains a more striking fresco by the same artist, the *Holy Trinity and St Jerome* (1454). Now restored, both frescoes were obliterated after Vasari spread the rumour that Castagno had poisoned his erstwhile friend, Domenico Veneziano, motivated by envy of the other's skill with oil paint. Castagno was saddled with this crime until the nineteenth century, when an archivist discovered that the alleged murderer in fact predeceased his victim by four years.

Separated from the nave by a triumphal arch is the unusual **tribune**, begun by Michelozzo but completed to designs by Alberti; you get into it along a corridor from the north transept. The chapel at the farthest point was altered by Giambologna into a monument to himself, complete with bronze reliefs and a crucifix by the sculptor. The chapel to its left contains a sizeable *Resurrection* (1550) by Bronzino. Look out, too, for the magnificent **organ** at the head of the aisle; built in 1628, it's the city's oldest and the second oldest in Italy.

The spacious **Chiostro dei Morti** is worth visiting for Andrea del Sarto's intimate *Madonna del Sacco* (1525) over the door that opens from the north transept (if you can't find the sacristan to open it, you may be able to enter the cloister from the street – the entrance is to the left of the main entrance); depicting the Holy Family at rest during their flight into Egypt. The picture takes its curious name from the sack (*sacco*) on which St Joseph is leaning.

## The Museo Archeologico

On the other side of Via della Colonna from Santissima Annunziata, the **Museo Archeologico** (Mon 2–7pm, Tues & Thurs 8.30am–7pm, Wed & Fri–Sun 8.30am–2pm; €4) houses the finest collection of its kind in northern Italy, but struggles to draw visitors for whom the Renaissance is the beginning and end of Florence's appeal. And to tell the truth, it's not the most alluring museum: it suffered terrible damage in the flood of 1966, and in some of the more ramshackle rooms you get the impression that the place still hasn't fully recovered. Nonetheless, the new ground-floor galleries make a good space for one-off exhibitions, and the main collection is slowly being put in better order.

Its special strength is its **Etruscan** collection, much of it bequeathed, inevitably, by the Medici. Most of the Etruscan finds are on the first floor, where there's a large array of funerary figures and two outstanding bronze sculptures. The first of these, the *Arringatore* (Orator), is the only known Etruscan large bronze from the Hellenistic period; made some time around 100 BC, it was discovered near Lago Trasimeno in 1566 and promptly sold to Cosimo I. Nearby is the *Chimera*, a triple-headed monster made in the fourth century BC. Showing the beast wounded in its fight with Bellerophon (it might have been part of a group that included a figure of the hero), the *Chimera* was unearthed on the outskirts of Florence in 1553 and was much admired by Cosimo I's retinue of artists. Legend has it that Benvenuto Cellini recast two of its paws, but this is almost certainly not the case – for one thing, Cellini makes no mention of it in his autobiography, and he was not a man to pass up the opportunity for some boasting.

Numerous dowdy cabinets are stuffed with unlabelled Etruscan figurines, and much of the **Egyptian collection** – the third largest such collection in Italy, after the Vatican's and the Egyptian museum in Turin – is similarly displayed in an uninspiring manner, though some of the rooms were spectacularly decorated in mock-Egyptian style in the late nineteenth century. The single most remarkable object amid the assembly of papyri, statuettes and mummy cases is a Hittite chariot made of bone and wood, dating from the fourteenth century BC.

There are more Etruscan pieces on the top floor (sometimes open only to guided tours, usually hourly), but here the primary focus is on the **Greek and Roman collections**. The star piece in the huge hoard of Greek vases is the large *François Vase*, an Attic *krater* discovered in an Etruscan tomb near Chiusi in 1844; dated to the sixth century BC, it's signed by the potter Ergotimos and the painter Kleitias. Another attention-grabbing item is the life-size bronze torso known as the *Torso di Livorno*, probably a fifth-century BC Greek original, though some argue that it's a Roman copy; incrustations inside the figure show that it was recovered from the sea, but nobody knows precisely when or where it was found. There's some debate also about the large horse's head that's on show in the same room. This fragment of a full-size equestrian statue is probably an early Hellenistic bronze from around 100 BC, but again it may be a Roman copy; what's known for certain is that it was once a feature of the garden of the Palazzo Medici, where it was studied by Donatello and Verrocchio before they began work on their great equestrian statues of Gattemalata (in Padua) and Bartolomeo Colleoni (in Venice). Also on this floor you'll see two beautiful sixth-century BC Greek *kouroi,* dubbed the *Apollo* and *Apollino,* and the bronze statue of a young man known as the *Idilono di Pésaro* – yet again there's some dispute about his origins, but he's generally thought to be a Roman replica of a Greek figure dating from around 100 BC.

Finally, if you're visiting on a Saturday, be sure to take a stroll in the museum garden, which is open only on that day – it's worth a look for its Etruscan tombs, reconstructed here in 1903.

# 5

# East of the centre: Santa Croce to Campo di Marte

The focal point of the eastern side of central Florence is the vast Franciscan church of **Santa Croce**, a building that's compelling both for its architecture and for its frescoes. The Santa Croce district was one of Florence's more densely populated areas before November 4, 1966, when the Arno burst its banks. This had catastrophic consequences for this low-lying zone, which was then packed with tenements and small workshops. Many residents moved out permanently in the following years, but now the more traditional businesses that survived the flood have been joined by a growing number of new and often extremely good bars and restaurants, a transformation that's particularly noticeable around the **Sant'Ambrogio** market. In addition to the great church and its museum, the other main cultural attractions in this part of the city are the **Museo Horne**, a modest but pleasing collection of art treasures, and the **Casa Buonarroti**, a less than entirely satisfying homage to Michelangelo.

## Santa Croce

**Piazza Santa Croce** is one of Florence's largest squares and traditionally one of its main arenas for ceremonials and festivities. Thus when Lorenzo the Magnificent was married to the Roman heiress Clarice Orsini, the wedding was celebrated on this square, with a tournament that was as much a fashion event as a contest of skill: Lorenzo's knightly outfit, for instance, was adorned with pearls, diamonds and rubies. It's still used as the pitch for the Gioco di Calcio Storico (see p.200), a football tournament between the city's four *quartieri*; held three times in St John's week, the game is characterized by incomprehensible rules and a level of violence which the sixteenth-century costumes do little to inhibit.

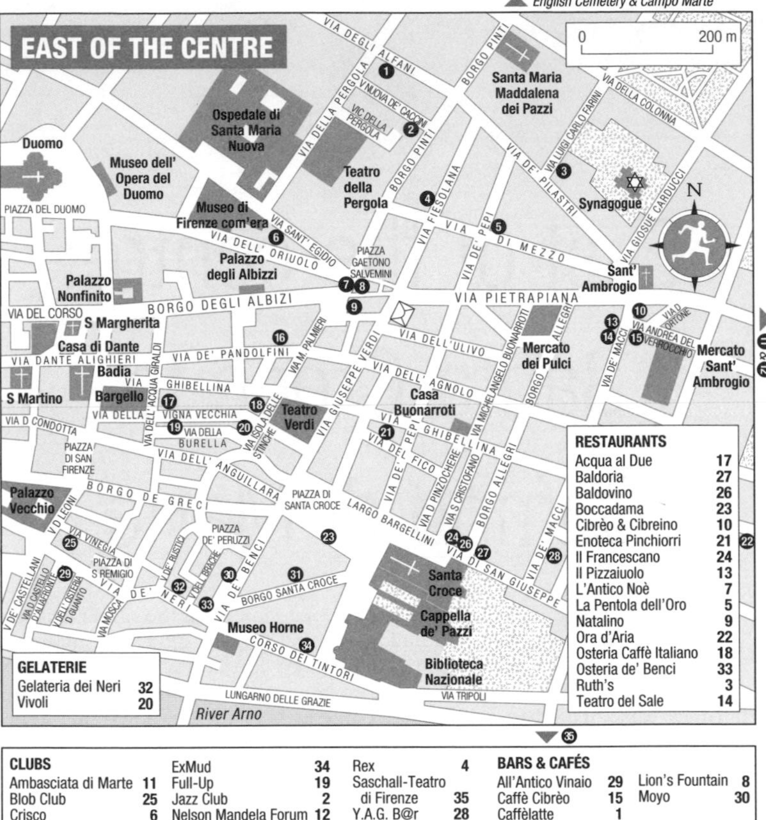


The **church of Santa Croce** (Mon–Sat 9.30am–5.30pm, Sun 1–5.30pm; €5) is the Franciscans' principal church in Florence – a rival to the Dominicans' Santa Maria Novella – and was probably begun seventy or so years after Francis's death, in 1294, possibly to a design by the architect of the Duomo, Arnolfo di Cambio. It replaced a smaller church on the site, a building that had become too small for the vast congregations gathering to hear the Franciscans' homilies on poverty, chastity and obedience in what was then one of the city's poorest areas. Francis – who never became a priest – had intended his monks to live as itinerants, begging for alms when necessary, and preaching without the use of churches, let alone churches the size of Santa Croce. After his death, this radical stance was quickly abandoned by many of his followers, with the backing of a papacy anxious to institutionalize a potentially troublesome mass movement.

Ironically, it was Florence's richest families who funded the construction of Santa Croce, to atone for the sin of usury on which their fortunes were based. Plutocrats such as the Bardi, Peruzzi and Baroncelli sponsored the extraordinary **fresco cycles** that were lavished on the chapels over the years, particularly during the fourteenth century, when artists of the stature of Giotto and the Gaddi family worked here. In further contradiction of the Franciscan ideal of humility, Santa Croce has long served as the national pantheon: the walls and nave floor are lined with the **monuments** to more than 270 illustrious Italians, many of them Tuscan, including Michelangelo, Galileo, Machiavelli, Alberti, Dante and the great physicist Enrico Fermi (though the last two are not buried here).

Of all the events that have happened at Santa Croce, none was more momentous than the **Council of Florence**, held in 1439 in an attempt to reconcile the differences between the Roman and Eastern churches. Attended by the pope, the Byzantine emperor and the patriarch of Constantinople, the council arrived at a compromise that lasted only until the Byzantine delegation returned home. Its more enduring effect was that it brought scores of classical scholars to the city, some of whom stayed on to give further impetus to the Florentine Renaissance.

## Florence's floods

The calamity of the November 1966 flood had plenty of precedents. Great areas of the city were destroyed by a flood in **1178**, a disaster exacerbated by plague and famine. In **1269** the Carraia and Trìnita bridges were carried away on a torrent so heavy that "a great part of the city of Florence became a lake", as a contemporary chronicler put it. The flood of **1333** was preceded by a four-day storm, with thunder and rain so violent that all the city's bells were tolled to drive away the evil spirits thought to be behind the tempest: bridges were demolished and the original *Marzocco* – a figure of Mars rather than the leonine figure that inherited its name – was carried away by the raging Arno. Cosimo I instituted an urban beautification scheme after a deluge put nearly twenty feet of muddy water over parts of the city in **1557**; on that occasion the Trìnita bridge was hit so suddenly that everyone on it was drowned, except for a couple of children who were left stranded on a pillar in midstream, where for two days they were fed by means of a rope slung over from the bank.

It rained continuously for forty days prior to **November 4, 1966**, with nearly half a metre of rain falling in the preceding two days. When the water pressure in an upstream reservoir threatened to break the dam, it was decided to open the sluices. The only people to be warned about the rapidly rising level of the river were the jewellers of the Ponte Vecchio, whose private nightwatchman phoned them in the small hours of the morning with news that the bridge was starting to shake. Police watching the shopkeepers clearing their displays were asked why they weren't spreading the alarm. They replied, "We have received no orders." When the banks of the Arno finally broke, a flash flood dumped around 500,000 tonnes of water and mud on the streets, moving with such speed that people were drowned in the underpass of Santa Maria Novella train station. In all, 35 Florentines were killed, six thousand shops put out of business, more than ten thousand homes made uninhabitable, some fifteen thousand cars wrecked, and countless works of art damaged, many of them ruined by heating oil flushed out of basements.

Within hours an impromptu army of salvagers had been formed, many of them students – to haul pictures out of slime-filled churches and gather fragments of paint in plastic bags. Donations came in from all over the world, but the task was so immense that the restoration of many items is still continuing – scores of precious books from the National Library, which is located next door to Santa Croce and took the brunt of the flood, remain in the laboratories. In total around two-thirds of the three thousand paintings damaged in the flood are now on view again, and two laboratories – one for paintings and one for stonework – are operating full-time in Florence, developing restoration techniques that are often taken up by galleries all over the world. Today, throughout the city, you can see small marble plaques with a red line showing the level the floodwaters reached on that dreadful day in 1966.

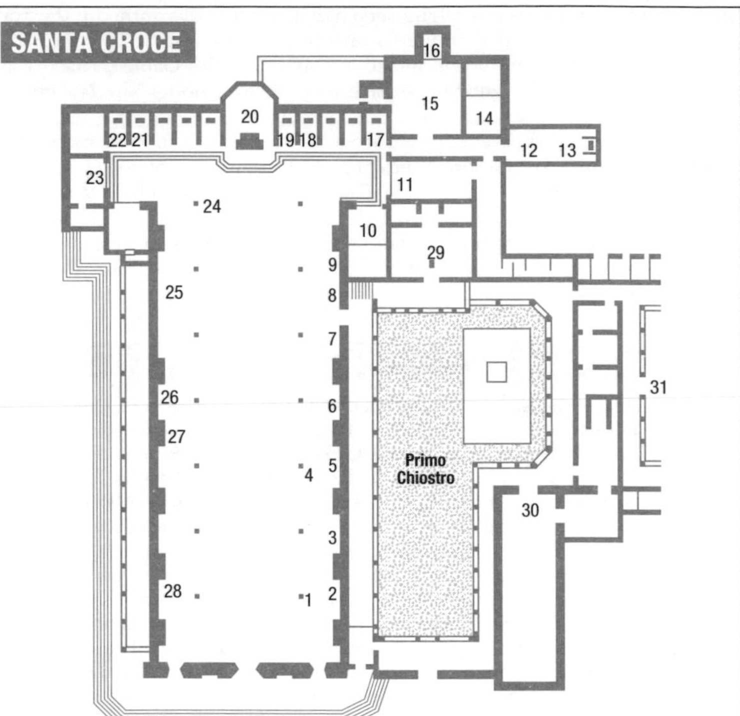

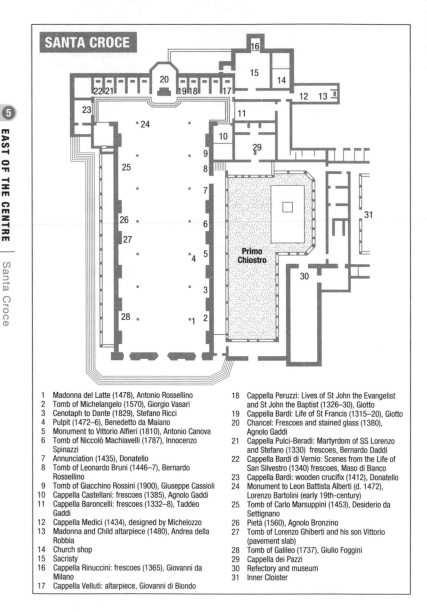

1 Madonna del Latte (1478), Antonio Rossellino
2 Tomb of Michelangelo (1570), Giorgio Vasari
3 Cenotaph to Dante (1829), Stefano Ricci
4 Pulpit (1472–6), Benedetto da Maiano
5 Monument to Vittorio Alfieri (1810), Antonio Canova
6 Tomb of Niccolò Machiavelli (1787), Innocenzo Spinazzi
7 Annunciation (1435), Donatello
8 Tomb of Leonardo Bruni (1446–7), Bernardo Rossellino
9 Tomb of Giacchino Rossini (1900), Giuseppe Cassioli
10 Cappella Castellani: frescoes (1385), Agnolo Gaddi
11 Cappella Baroncelli: frescoes (1332–8), Taddeo Gaddi
12 Cappella Medici (1434), designed by Michelozzo
13 Madonna and Child altarpiece (1480), Andrea della Robbia
14 Church shop
15 Sacristy
16 Cappella Rinuccini: frescoes (1365), Giovanni da Milano
17 Cappella Velluti: altarpiece, Giovanni di Biondo
18 Cappella Peruzzi: Lives of St John the Evangelist and St John the Baptist (1326–30), Giotto
19 Cappella Bardi: Life of St Francis (1315–20), Giotto
20 Chancel: Frescoes and stained glass (1380), Agnolo Gaddi
21 Cappella Pulci-Beradi: Martyrdom of SS Lorenzo and Stefano (1330) frescoes, Bernardo Daddi
22 Cappella Bardi di Vernio: Scenes from the Life of San Silvestro (1340) frescoes, Maso di Banco
23 Cappella Bardi: wooden crucifix (1412), Donatello
24 Monument to Leon Battista Alberti (d. 1472), Lorenzo Bartolini (early 19th-century)
25 Tomb of Carlo Marsuppini (1453), Desiderio da Settignano
26 Pietà (1560), Agnolo Bronzino
27 Tomb of Lorenzo Ghiberti and his son Vittorio (pavement slab)
28 Tomb of Galileo (1737), Giulio Foggini
29 Cappella dei Pazzi
30 Refectory and museum
31 Inner Cloister

## The interior

The church's **facade** is a neo-Gothic sham that dates from as recently as 1863. Santa Croce had languished for centuries without a suitable frontage, a situation remedied when someone claimed to have discovered long-lost plans for the "original" facade; in truth the scheme was no more than a giant-sized pastiche of Orcagna's tabernacle in Orsanmichele. The vast interior is infinitely more satisfying, and feels rather more airy than it would originally have done: a large partition, built to separate the monks' choir from the area reserved for the congregation, used to interrupt the nave. Both the partition and choir were torn down in 1566 on the orders of Cosimo I, acting on Counter-Reformation dictates that proscribed such arrangements. Unfortunately the changes gave Vasari a chance to interfere, opening up the side altars and damaging frescoes by Orcagna, traces of which still adorn parts of the walls.



### The south aisle

If all you want to see are the church's most famous works of art, head towards the high altar and the Giotto-painted chapels to its right. Otherwise, take a more measured walk down the **south aisle**. Against the first pillar stands the tomb of Francesco Nori, one of the victims of the Pazzi Conspiracy (see p.50), surmounted by Antonio Rossellino's lovely relief of the *Madonna del Latte* (marked 1 on our plan). Nearby is Vasari's **tomb of Michelangelo** (2), which is said to have been positioned close to the church's entrance at his own request, so that when the graves fly open on the Day of Judgement, the first thing to catch his eye will be Brunelleschi's cathedral dome.

The Neoclassical **monument to Dante** (3) is a cenotaph rather than a tomb, as the exiled poet is buried in Ravenna, where he died in 1321. Three centuries before Dante finally received this bland nineteenth-century tribute, Michelangelo had offered to carve the poet's tomb – a tantalizing thought. Against the third pillar there's a marvellous **pulpit** (4) by Benedetto da Maiano, adorned with niche statuettes of the Virtues and scenes from the life of St Francis.

Canova's **monument to Alfieri** (5) commemorates an eighteenth-century Italian poet and dramatist as famous for his amatory liaisons as his literary endeavours. The tomb was paid for by his mistress, the so-called Countess of Albany, erstwhile wife of Charles Edward Stuart (aka Bonnie Prince Charlie). The lady herself modelled for the tomb's main figure, an allegory of Italy bereaved by Alfieri's death. The nearby **tomb of Machiavelli** (6), carved 260 years after his death, is unexceptional save for its famous inscription: *Tanto nomini nullum par elogium* ("No praise can be high enough for so great a name"). The side door at the end of the aisle is flanked by Donatello's beautiful gilded limestone relief of the *Annunciation* (7); created around 1430, it was once flanked by a fresco by Domenico Veneziano that's now in the Santa Croce museum.

Beyond the door is Bernardo Rossellino's much-imitated **tomb of Leonardo Bruni** (8), chancellor of the Republic, scholar, biographer of Dante and Petrarch, and author of the first history of the city – his effigy is holding a copy of it. Bruni, who died in 1444, was the first man of any great eminence to be buried in the church, which is a little surprising given his predominantly Humanist rather than Christian beliefs. The tomb, one of the most influential of the Renaissance, makes the point: for the first time the human figure dominates, with the Madonna and Child banished to a peripheral position high in the lunette. The inscription on Bruni's tomb – "After Leonardo departed life, history is in mourning and eloquence is dumb" – was penned by his successor as chancellor, Carlo Marsuppini, who is commemorated by a splendid tomb on the opposite side of the church (see below).

### The Castellani, Baroncelli and Medici chapels, and the sacristy

The **Cappella Castellani** (10), at the end of the south aisle, is strikingly, if patchily, covered in frescoes by Agnolo Gaddi and his pupils. To the right are depicted the stories of St John the Baptist and St Nicholas of Bari: the latter, the patron saint of children – he's the St Nicholas of Santa Claus fame – is shown saving three girls from prostitution and reviving three murdered boys. The left wall features episodes from the lives of St John and St Antony Abbot; the latter gave away his wealth, making him a favourite of the poverty-inspired Franciscans. Also note the chapel's fine tabernacle, the work of Mino da Fiesole, and its funerary monuments, including that of the Countess of Albany.

The adjoining **Cappella Baroncelli** (11) was decorated by Agnolo's father, Taddeo, a long-time assistant to Giotto. Taddeo's cycle, largely devoted to the life of the Virgin, features one of the first night scenes in Western painting, *The Annunciation to the Shepherds*, in which the angel appears amid a blaze of light that's believed to be a representation of Halley's Comet. The main altar painting, the *Coronation of the Virgin*, may also be by Taddeo, though an increasing number of critics now attribute it to his master, Giotto.

The corridor to the right ends at the **Cappella Medici** (12), usually open only for those taking Mass. It's notable for the large terracotta altarpiece by Andrea della Robbia (13) and a nineteenth-century forged Donatello; the chapel, like the corridor, was designed by Michelozzo, the Medici's pet architect. Finely carved wooden doors lead off the corridor into the beautifully panelled **Sacristy** (15), where the highlight is a marvellous *Crucifixion* by Taddeo on the left. The tiny **Cappella Rinuccini** (16), separated from the sacristy by a grille, is impressively covered with frescoes depicting the life of the Virgin (on the left) and St Mary Magdalene (on the right); the Lombard artist responsible, Giovanni da Milano, was one of Giotto's most accomplished followers.

### The east chapels: Giotto's frescoes

Both the **Cappella Peruzzi** (18) and the **Cappella Bardi** (19) – the two chapels on the right of the chancel – are entirely covered with frescoes by Giotto, with some assistance in the latter. Their deterioration was partly caused by Giotto's having painted some of the pictures onto dry plaster, rather than the wet plaster employed in true fresco technique, but the vandalism of later generations was far more destructive. In the eighteenth century they were covered in whitewash, then

▲ Santa Croce

they were heavily retouched in the nineteenth; restoration in the 1950s returned them to as close to their original state as was possible.

Scenes from the lives of St John the Evangelist and St John the Baptist cover the Peruzzi chapel, while a better-preserved cycle of the life of St Francis fills the Bardi. Despite the mutilation caused by a tomb that was once attached to the wall, the *Funeral of St Francis* is still a composition of extraordinary impact, the grief-stricken mourners suggesting an affinity with the lamentation over the body of Christ – one of them even probes the wound in Francis's side, echoing the gesture of Doubting Thomas. The *Ordeal by Fire*, showing Francis about to demonstrate his faith to the sultan by walking through fire, shows Giotto's mastery of understated drama, with the sultan's entourage skulking off to the left in anticipation of the monk's triumph. On the wall above the chapel's entrance arch is the most powerful scene of all, *St Francis Receiving the Stigmata*, in which the power of Christ's apparition seems to force the chosen one to his knees.

Agnolo Gaddi was responsible for the design of the **stained glass** in the lancet windows round the high altar, and for all the chancel **frescoes** (20), which depict the legend of the True Cross – a complicated tale tracing the wood of the Cross from its origins as the Tree of Paradise. The vast polyptych on the high altar is a composite of panels by several artists.

The **Cappella Bardi di Vernio** (22) was painted by Maso di Banco, perhaps the most inventive of Giotto's followers. Following tradition, the frescoes, showing scenes from the life of St Sylvester, portray the saint baptizing Emperor Constantine, notwithstanding Sylvester's death some time before the emperor's actual baptism. The second **Cappella Bardi** (23) houses a wooden crucifix by Donatello, supposedly criticized by Brunelleschi as resembling a "peasant on the Cross". According to Vasari, Brunelleschi went off and created his own crucifix for Santa Maria Novella to show Donatello how it should be done (see p.101).

### The north aisle

As you walk back towards the entrance along the north aisle, the first pillar you pass features a ghastly nineteenth-century **monument to Leon Battista Alberti** (24), the Renaissance architect and artistic theorist whose writings did much to influence Rossellino in his carving of the Bruni tomb across the nave. The Bruni tomb in turn influenced the outstanding **tomb of Carlo Marsuppini** (25) by Desiderio da Settignano. Marsuppini's lack of Christian qualifications for so prominent a church burial is even more striking than Bruni's: he's said to have died without taking confession or communion. The tomb inscription opens with the words, "Stay and see the marbles which enshrine a great sage, one for whose mind there was not world enough."

A *Pietà* (26) by the young Bronzino, a future Mannerist star, briefly disturbs the parade of tombs that follows. A surprisingly modest pavement slab marks the **tomb of Lorenzo Ghiberti** (27) – the artist responsible for the Baptistery's marvellous doors – and his son Vittorio. The **tomb of Galileo** (28) is more ostentatious, though it was some ninety years after his death in 1642 that the "heretic" scientist was deemed worthy of a Christian burial in Florence's pantheon.

## The Cappella dei Pazzi

The door in the south (right) aisle leads through into the church's Primo Chiostro (First Cloister), site of Brunelleschi's **Cappella dei Pazzi** (29), the epitome of the learned, harmonious spirit of early Renaissance architecture. It was commissioned in 1429 as a chapter house for Santa Croce, by Andrea de' Pazzi, a member of a banking dynasty that played a prominent role in the Pazzi Conspiracy (see p.50).

Its exterior remained unfinished at the time of the plot, however, and it seems none of the family was ever buried here. Dogged by financial problems, the construction of the chapel was completed only in the 1470s, some thirty years after the architect's death.

Geometrically perfect without seeming pedantic, the chapel is exemplary in its proportion and in the way its decorative detail harmonizes with the design. The polychrome lining of the portico's shallow cupola is by Luca della Robbia, as is the garland of fruit which surrounds the Pazzi family crest and the tondo of *St Andrew* (1461) over the door; Desiderio da Settignano crafted the frieze of angels' heads. As for the portico itself, it may be the work of Giuliano da Maiano, while the majestic wooden doors (1472) are known to have between a collaboration between Giuliano and his brother Benedetto. Inside, the twelve blue and white tondi of the *Apostles* are by Luca della Robbia, while the four vividly coloured tondi of the *Evangelists* in the upper roundels were produced in the della Robbia workshop, possibly to designs by Donatello and Brunelleschi.



## The Museo dell'Opera di Santa Croce and the inner cloister

The recently extended **Museo dell'Opera di Santa Croce** (30), which flanks the first cloister, houses a sizeable miscellany of works of art, the best of which are gathered in the ex-refectory. Foremost of these is Cimabue's famous *Crucifixion*, very badly damaged in 1966 and now the emblem of the havoc caused by the flood. Other highlights include a detached fresco of the *Last Supper* (1333), considered the finest work by Taddeo Gaddi (end wall), and the earliest surviving example of the many Last Suppers (*cenacoli*) dotted around the city. Also compelling are Donatello's enormous gilded *St Louis of Toulouse* (1424), made for Orsanmichele, and Bronzino's *Descent of Christ into Limbo*. Fragments of Orcagna's frescoes of *The Triumph of Death* and *Hell* (on the side walls), and Domenico Veneziano's *SS John and Francis*, were all salvaged from Santa Croce after Vasari had carried out his supposed improvements. Elsewhere in the museum you'll find more frescoes rescued from the church, plus some excellent della Robbia ceramics.

The spacious **Inner Cloister** (31), another late project by Brunelleschi, was completed in 1453, after the architect's death. It's perhaps the most peaceful spot in the centre of Florence, with a tranquil atmosphere that's enhanced by the slow rhythm of the narrow, widely spaced columns.

# The Museo Horne

On the south side of Santa Croce, down by the river at Via dei Benci 6, stands one of Florence's more esoteric museums, the **Museo della Fondazione Horne** (Mon–Sat 9am–1pm; €5). Its collection was left to the state by the English art historian Herbert Percy Horne (1864–1916), who was instrumental in rescuing Botticelli from neglect with a pioneering biography that was published in 1908. The half-dozen rooms of paintings, sculptures, pottery, furniture and other domestic objects contain few masterpieces, but are diverting enough if you've already done the major collections. With winning eccentricity, the exhibits are labelled with numbers only and you have to carry round a catalogue, which is handed to you at the ticket office. The museum building, the Palazzo Corsi-Alberti (1489), is worth more than a glance even if you're not going into the museum. Commissioned by the Corsi family, it's a typical merchant's house of the period, with huge cellars in which wool would have been dyed, and an open gallery above the courtyard for drying the finished cloth.

The pride of Horne's collection was its drawings, which are now salted away in the Uffizi, though a small display is maintained in the room on the right of the **ground floor**. On the **first floor**, the highlight of Room 1 is a tiny and badly damaged panel (once part of a triptych) by Masaccio, showing *Scenes from the Life of St Julian*; nearby there's an unfinished and age-darkened *Deposition* by Gozzoli, his last documented work. The next room contains the collection's big draw, Giotto's *St Stephen* (a fragment from a polyptych), which was probably painted at around the time that Giotto was at work in Santa Croce. Room 3 has a tondo of the *Holy Family* by Beccafumi, who is also attributed with a *Drunkenness of Noah* on the **second floor**, where you'll also find minor works by Filippo and Filippino Lippi. One of the main exhibits on this storey is a piece of little artistic merit but great historical interest: a copy of part of Leonardo's *Battle of Anghiari*, once frescoed on a wall of the Palazzo Vecchio.

## Casa Buonarroti and the Sant'Ambrogio district

The enticing name of the **Casa Buonarroti**, located north of Santa Croce at Via Ghibellina 70 (daily except Tues 9.30am–2pm; €6.50), is somewhat misleading. Michelangelo Buonarroti certainly owned three houses here in 1508, and probably lived on the site intermittently between 1516 and 1525, but thereafter the properties' associations with the artist become increasingly tenuous. On Michelangelo's death they passed to his nephew, Leonardo, whose son converted them into a single *palazzo*, leaving little trace of the earlier houses (though he built a gallery dedicated to his great-uncle). Michelangelo's last descendant, Cosimo, left the building to the city on his death in 1858. Today the house contains a smart but low-key museum. Many of the rooms are pleasing enough, all nicely decorated in period style and adorned with beautiful furniture, *objets d'art*, frescoed ceilings and the like, but among the jumble of works collected here, only a handful are by Michelangelo: most were created simply in homage to the great man, the most celebrated being Daniele di Volterra's portrait in bronze, which was derived from Michelangelo's death mask.

Etruscan and Roman fragments have been wrested back from the archeological museum to languish on the ground floor once more, but the two main treasures are to be found in the room on the left at the top of the stairs. The **Madonna della Scala** (c.1490–92) is Michelangelo's earliest-known work, a delicate relief carved when he was no older than 16. The similarly unfinished *Battle of the Centaurs* was created shortly afterwards, when he was living in the Medici household. In the adjacent room you'll find the artist's wooden model (1517) for the facade of San Lorenzo. Close by is the largest of all the sculptural models on display, the torso of a **River God** (1524), a work in wood and wax probably intended for the Medici chapel in San Lorenzo. Other rooms contain a frequently changed display of half a dozen Michelangelo drawings, plus an array of small and fragmentary pieces, possibly by the master, possibly copies of works by him.

## The Sant'Ambrogio markets

Two of Florence's markets lie within a few minutes' stroll of the Casa Buonarroti. To the north, the Piazza dei Ciompi is the venue for the **Mercato delle Pulci** or Flea Market (summer Mon–Sat 10am–1pm & 4–7pm; winter Mon–Sat 9am–1pm & 3–7pm; plus same hours on last Sun of month). Much of the junk maintains the city's reputation for inflated prices, though you can find a few interesting items at modest cost – old postcards, posters and so on. Vasari's Loggia del Pesce (1567) gives the square a touch of style; built for the fishmongers of the Mercato Vecchio in what is now Piazza della Repubblica, it was dismantled when that square was laid out, and rebuilt here in 1951.

A short distance to the east, out of the orbit of nearly all tourists, is the **Mercato di Sant'Ambrogio** (Mon–Sat 7am–2pm), a smaller, tattier but nonetheless enjoyable version of the San Lorenzo food hall. The *tavola calda* (snacks and meals stall) here is one of Florence's lunchtime bargains, and – as at San Lorenzo – the stallholders bring their prices down in the last hour of trading.

## The church of Sant'Ambrogio

Nearby **Sant'Ambrogio** (daily 8am–12.30pm & 4–7pm; free) is one of Florence's older churches, having been documented in 988, though rebuilding over the centuries has left it somewhat bland in appearance. Inside you'll find a *Madonna Enthroned with SS John the Baptist and Bartholomew* (second altar on the right), attributed to Orcagna (or the school of Orcagna), and a recently restored triptych in the chapel to the right of the main altar, attributed to Lorenzo di Bicci. More compelling than either painting, though, is the **Cappella del Miracolo**, the chapel to the left of the high altar, and its tabernacle by Mino da Fiesole, an accomplished sculptor whose name crops up time and again across Tuscany. It was completed in 1483, a year before Mino's death, and he's buried close by, in a tomb marked by a pavement slab at the chapel entrance. Another great artist, the multi-talented Verrocchio (d.1488), is buried in the fourth chapel. The narrative **fresco** (1486) alongside Mino's tabernacle alludes to the miracle that gave the Cappella del Miracolo its name. The work of Cosimo Rosselli (best known for his frescoes in Santissima Annunziata), it depicts a procession bearing a chalice in which, during a Mass conducted here in 1230, the communion wine was discovered to have turned into blood. The Florentines believed the chalice saved them from, among other things, the effects of a virulent plague outbreak of 1340. The painting is full of portraits of Rosselli's contemporaries, making it another of Florence's vivid pieces of Renaissance social reportage: Rosselli himself is the figure in the black beret at the extreme left of the picture.

## From the synagogue to the English cemetery

The enormous domed building rising to the north of Sant'Ambrogio church is the **synagogue**, built in the nineteenth century after the ghetto established by Cosimo I was demolished. This extravagant Moorish-Byzantine hybrid contains a **museum** that charts the history of Florence's Jewish population (April–Oct Sun–Thurs 10am–5/6pm, Fri 10am–2pm; Nov–March Sun–Thurs 10am–3pm, Fri 10am–2pm; €4).

West of the synagogue, on Borgo Pinti, stands the church of **Santa Maria Maddalena dei Pazzi** (Mon–Sat 9–11.50am, 5–5.20pm & 6.10–6.50pm, Sun 9–10.45am & 5–6.50pm; free), named after a Florentine nun who was famed for her religious ecstasies: when possessed by the holy spirit she would spew words at such a rate that a team of eight novices was needed to transcribe her inspired dictation. She was also prone to pouring boiling wax over her arms, and was fond of reclining naked on a bed of thorns. This unflinching piety was much honoured in Counter-Reformation Florence: when Maria de' Medici went off to marry Henry IV of France, Maria Maddalena transmitted the news that the Virgin expected her to re-admit the Jesuits to France and exterminate the Huguenots, which she duly did.

Founded in the thirteenth century but kitted out in Baroque style, the church is not itself much of an attraction, but its chapter house – reached by a subterranean passageway that's accessed from the top of the right aisle – is decorated with a radiant **Perugino** fresco of the *Crucifixion* (€1). Based on the terrain around Lago Trasimeno, the scene is painted as a continuous panorama on a

## Crisis and revival at Campo di Marte

In recent years there have been some tough times for the Fiorentina football team, known as the *Viola* after the distinctive violet colour of their shirts. Some fans still shudder at the memory of 1990, when the great **Roberto Baggio** was transferred – for what was then a world-record fee – to Juventus, amid scenes of fervent protest. In 1996, with Argentinian striker Gabriel Batistuta (aka **"Batigol"**) attracting something like the affection that Baggio once commanded, Fiorentina won the Italian cup, and they came close to a league championship in 1999, finishing third. But then Batigol was lured to Roma, sparking demonstrations of such violence that the club's owner, TV and film magnate Vittorio Cecchi-Gori, required police protection. Roma promptly rubbed salt into the wound by becoming champions of Serie A (Italy's top division), but far worse was to come in 2002, when Fiorentina became the most spectacular casualty of the financial crisis that engulfed what used to be the world's wealthiest league. For many years the clubs in Serie A had been paying insupportable salaries on the basis of projected TV revenue, while consistently failing in the lucrative Champions' League. By 2002 the aggregrate debts of the Serie A teams was in the region of 500 million euros, and for Fiorentina the situation was almost terminal: declared **bankrupt**, they were kicked out of Serie A and demoted to Serie C2B – in effect, the bottom of the heap.

The once-great club was reformed, under the new ownership of footwear millionaire Diego della Valle. The star players – Nuno Gomes, Adani, Enrico Chiesa – all exercised their right to a free transfer when the bankruptcy was confirmed, leaving former Juventus and Italy midfielder Angelo di Livio as the linchpin of a team composed mainly of teenagers. Yet the club quickly fought its way back up the leagues, returning to Serie A for the 2004/2005 season (when they just about avoided relegation to Serie B), and despite being further penalized for its involvement in the 2006 match-fixing racket, has now re-established itself in the upper reaches of the league. Yet the whiff of scandal is still in the air, because of the premature deaths of three ex-Fiorentina players between 1987 and 2004, and other cases of severe ill-health (including heart and kidney disease, and cancer) among men who appeared for the club in the 1970s. The suspicion is that players might have been doped with strength-building drugs, administered in the form of a coffee-like drink. Nello Saltutti, who played for the *Viola* from 1972 to 1975 and died of a heart attack in 2003, told an investigator after his first cardiac arrest: "That 'coffee' was very good for us. We all played very well and played twice as fast as usual. The day after, however, we were all destroyed."

Stoked by the fans' long-standing sense of themselves as the unloved outsiders of Italian football, support at the Stadio Franchi is always intense, so **tickets** can be hard to obtain. They cost from as little as €10 and can be bought at the ground itself, or three to four days in advance from various outlets around the city – they're listed on the club website (it.violachannel.tv).

wall divided into three arches, giving the effect of looking out through a loggia onto a springtime landscape. As always with Perugino, there is nothing troubling here, the Crucifixion being depicted not as an agonizing death but rather as the necessary prelude to the Resurrection.

North of the Pazzi church, at the end of Borgo Pinti, lies the **English Cemetery** at Piazza Donatello (daily 9am–noon & 3–6pm). Now a funerary traffic island, this patch of garden is the resting place of Elizabeth Barrett Browning and a number of contemporaneous artistic Brits, among them Walter Savage Landor and Arthur Hugh Clough.



# San Salvi and Campo di Marte

In Via San Salvi, twenty minutes' walk beyond Piazza Beccaria, east of Sant'Ambrogio (or bus #10 from the station, or #6 from Piazza San Marco), is the ex-convent of **San Salvi**, which was reopened in 1982 after the restoration of its most precious possession, a fresco of *The Last Supper* by Andrea del Sarto (Tues–Sun 8.15am–1.50pm; free). As a prelude to this picture, there's a gallery of big but otherwise unremarkable Renaissance altarpieces, a gathering of pictures by various del Sarto acolytes, and the beautiful reliefs from the tomb of Giovanni Gualberto, founder of the Vallombrosan order to whom this monastery belonged. The tomb was smashed up by Charles V's troops in 1530 but they refused to damage the *Last Supper*, which is still in the refectory for which it was painted, accompanied by a pair of del Sarto frescoes brought here from other churches in Florence. Painted between 1520 and 1525, and much influenced by Leonardo's work, the *Last Supper* is the epitome of del Sarto's soft, suave technique – emotionally undernourished for some tastes, but faultlessly carried out.

## The Stadio Comunale

As befits this monument-stuffed city, Florence's football team plays in a stadium that's listed as a building of cultural significance, the **Stadio Comunale** (or Stadio Artemio Franchi) in the district of **Campo di Marte** (bus #11 or #17). Pier Luigi Nervi designed the stadium in 1930, as a consequence of two decisions: to create a new football club for Florence and to stage the 1934 World Cup in Italy. For information on buying **tickets**, see box on p.143.

The stadium was the first major sports venue to exploit the shape-making potential of reinforced concrete, and its spiral ramps, cantilevered roof and slim central tower still make most other arenas look dreary. From the spectator's point of view, however, it's far from perfect: for instance, the peculiar D-shape of the stands – necessitated by the straight 200-metre sprint track – means that visibility from some parts of the ground is awful. But the architectural importance of Nervi's work meant that when Florence was chosen as one of the hosts for the 1990 World Cup there could be no question of simply building a replacement (as was done brilliantly at Bari), nor of radically altering the existing one (as happened at most grounds). Much of the seventy billion lire spent on the refurbishment of the Stadio Comunale was spent ensuring that the improvements did not ruin the clean modernistic lines, and most of the extra space in the all-seater stadium was created by lowering the pitch a couple of metres below its previous level, to insert extra layers of seats where the track had been.

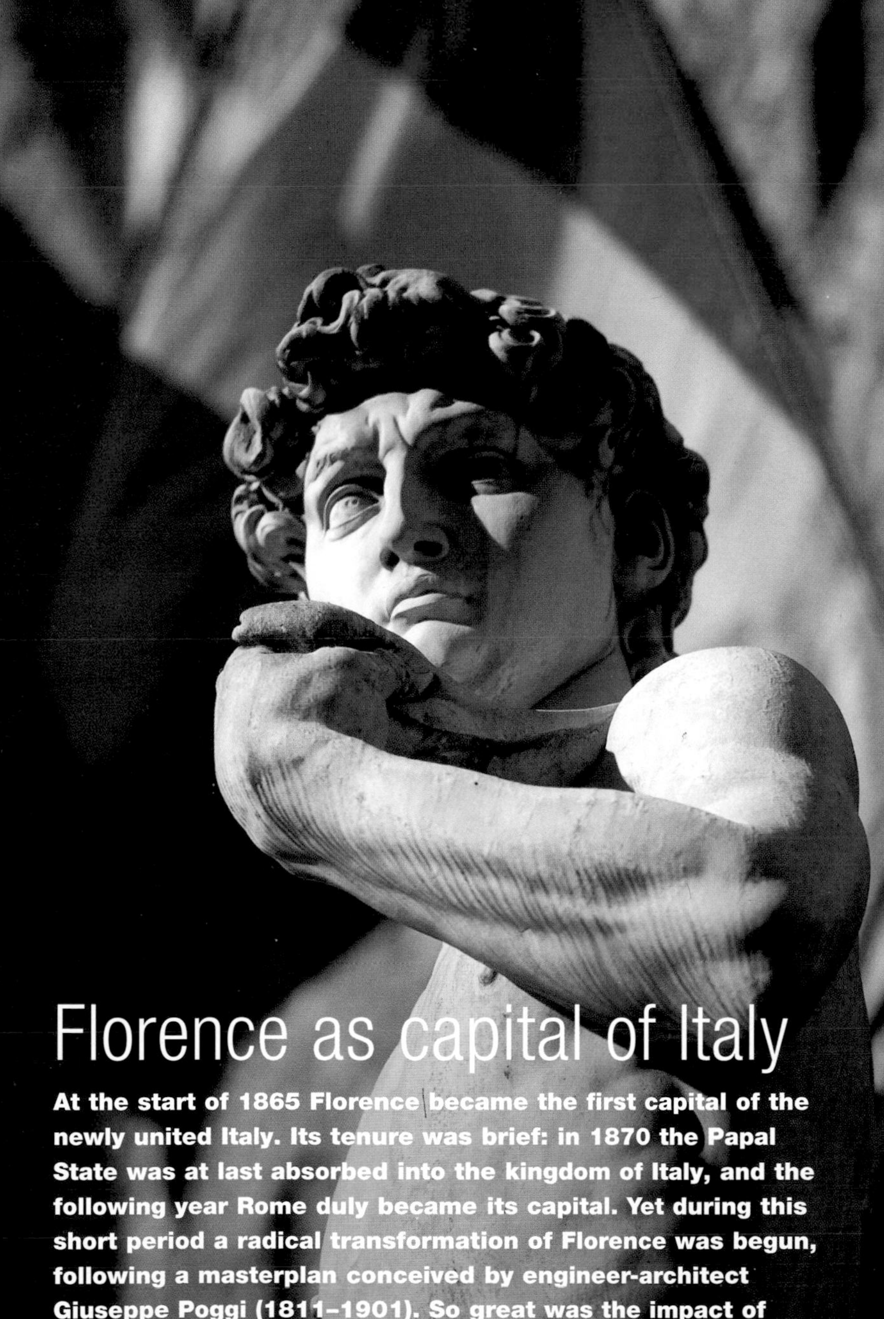

# Florence as capital of Italy

**At the start of 1865 Florence became the first capital of the newly united Italy. Its tenure was brief: in 1870 the Papal State was at last absorbed into the kingdom of Italy, and the following year Rome duly became its capital. Yet during this short period a radical transformation of Florence was begun, following a masterplan conceived by engineer-architect Giuseppe Poggi (1811–1901). So great was the impact of Poggi's scheme that the present-day appearance of Florence owes more to him than to any architect of the Renaissance.**

Aerial view of Piazza Beccaria ▲

Porta San Gallo, Piazza della Libertà ▼

The English cemetery ▼

## The housing crisis

In 1865 Florence had a population of 150,000, so an influx of twenty thousand government employees plus their families created an immediate strain. Finding offices wasn't a problem – while the parliament moved into the Palazzo Vecchio, the ministries requisitioned buildings such as the Uffizi and the Palazzo Medici. But housing had to be built quickly, both for the newcomers and for the Florentines who found themselves priced out of the city centre as rents soared.

Poggi's scheme, which encompassed everything from the water supply to the abattoirs, created new residential quarters on the city's peripheries, such as **Mattonaia**, on the east side. Designed in the Neoclassical style, Mattonaia was focused on **Piazza d'Azeglio**, a square which – with its communal garden set aside for residents – took its inspiration from London's upmarket West End squares.

## The viali

To facilitate new housing projects, Poggi demolished the old city walls on the north side of the Arno and at a stroke changed the city's character – after more than half a millennium of enclosure, Florence now began to sprawl into the countryside. Where the walls had stood, Poggi constructed a belt of wide boulevards or **viali**, in emulation of capitals such as Paris and Vienna. Ancient city gates – notably the **Porta San Gallo** at Piazza della Libertà and the **Porta alla Croce** at Piazza Beccaria – were left marooned on the piazzas that were created at the intersections of the *viali*. The **English cemetery** (see p.144), which for sixty years was on the eastern edge of the city, now became an island in the middle of a major road.

# The city centre

To ease traffic movement between the train station and the Duomo, Poggi widened **Via de' Cerretani** and **Via Panzani**. He also modernized the major shopping streets, including **Via de' Tornabuoni**, and smartened up **Piazza della Signoria**. **Via della Scala** – hitherto an area of open land – was built up, while the riverside streets on the north bank of the Arno were significantly developed. But the most drastic intervention in the centre of town was the removal of the old market, which was full of overcrowded slums, and the establishment of a new market hall near San Lorenzo. In 1869, dozens of buildings were quickly demolished to make way for the iron and glass **Mercato Centrale** (see p.117), designed by Giuseppe Mengoni, architect of the great Galleria Vittorio Emanuele in Milan.

It wasn't until the mid-1880s that the old market was erased, and it wasn't just the market that went: tenements, three churches and several medieval tower-houses were swept away, leaving just a few old structures intact – notably Orsanmichele. Massive blocks were built over the district's ancient alleyways, and a vast new piazza was created, initially named **Piazza Vittorio Emanuele II** after the nation's first monarch, later renamed **Piazza della Repubblica**. Only two features of the old market were preserved: the column on the east side and the fish-vendors' Loggia del Pesce, which was removed to Piazza dei Ciompi. On the west side of the piazza, the arch known as the Arcone was topped with a huge sculpture entitled *Italy Enthroned*; this has now gone, as has the equestrian statue of the king that used to occupy centre stage – it was removed to Piazzale delle Cascine, where Poggi had wanted it.

▲ Loggia in Piazza dei Ciompi

▲ Mercato Centrale

▼ Piazza della Repubblica

Porta San Niccolò, Piazza Poggi ▲

Statue of David, Piazzale Michelangelo ▼

## Piazzale Michelangelo

Perhaps Poggi's most dramatic piece of urban planning was the hill below the church of San Miniato, which was an area of olive groves and cypress woodland before he started work on it. At the foot of the hill, around the medieval Porta San Niccolò, he designed a small piazza (renamed Piazza Poggi after his death), from where a sequence of ramps and steps cuts across the winding Viale Poggi before reaching the spacious **Piazzale Michelangelo**. The *piazzale* was designed by Poggi as a belvedere and as a tribute to Michelangelo, a replica of whose *David* stands in the centre. The loggia that Poggi built here was intended to form part of a Michelangelo museum, but instead became a café – a downsizing that symbolizes the difficulties that beset Florence when it ceased to be capital. By the mid-1870s the population had dropped by more than fifteen percent, and a decade later the local economy was in such dire straits that the *comune* declared itself bankrupt.

## Later developments

Displaced by the demolition of the old market, much of Florence's Jewish population moved to the Santa Croce district, where a huge new synagogue was soon raised. This and the Russian Orthodox church (1899–1903) were the most conspicuous additions to the city prior to the 1930s, when Santa Maria Novella train station and the sports stadium at Campo di Marte were built. In August 1944 the retreating Nazis dynamited tracts of the city on both sides of the Ponte Vecchio, which was the only bridge they didn't destroy. Ponte Trìnita was reconstructed, while the rest were redesigned in modern style.

6

# Oltrarno

Visitors to Florence might perceive the River Arno as a simple interruption in the urban fabric, but some Florentines still talk as though a ravine runs through their city. North of the river is known as *Arno di quà* ("over here"), while the other side, hemmed in by a ridge of hills that rises a short distance from the river, is *Arno di là* ("over there"). More formally, it's known as the **Oltrarno** – literally "beyond the Arno" – a terminology that has its roots in medieval times, when the district was not as accessible as the numerous bridges now make it.

Traditionally an artisans' quarter, the Oltrarno is still home to plenty of small workshops (particularly furniture restorers and leather-workers), and Via Maggio remains the focus of Florence's thriving antiques trade. The ambience is distinctly less tourist-centred here than in the zone immediately across the water, and though the bars and restaurants around **Piazza Santo Spirito** and **Piazza del Carmine** attract their share of outsiders, the conversations you'll overhear are more likely to be in Italian than any other language. Which is not to say that the Oltrarno doesn't have major sights – **Palazzo Pitti**, **Santa Maria del Carmine**, **San Miniato** and **Santo Spirito** are all essential visits.

## Central Oltrarno

The most famous bridge in the city, the **Ponte Vecchio**, links the northern bank to the Oltrarno's central area, home to the **Palazzo Pitti**, a rambling palace complex whose cluster of museums includes the city's second-ranking picture gallery, the **Galleria Palatina**. Close by lies the **Giardino di Bóboli**, Italy's most visited garden, a leafy retreat from the sightseeing. Lesser attractions include the ancient church of **Santa Felìcita**, known for one of the city's stranger paintings, and the extraordinary medical waxworks of **La Specola**.

### The Ponte Vecchio

The direct route from the city centre to the heart of the Oltrarno crosses the Arno via the **Ponte Vecchio**, the last in a line of bridges that stretches back to Etruscan and Roman times. Until 1218, when the Ponte alla Carraia was built, the bridge here was the only one in the city, though the version you see today dates from 1345, and was raised to replace a wooden bridge swept away by floods twelve years earlier. Over its arcades runs Vasari's concealed passageway (see p.77), commissioned by the Medici in 1565 to allow them to pass unobserved from the

Palazzo Vecchio to the Palazzo Pitti. Much later the Ponte Vecchio was the only bridge not mined by the Nazis in 1944 as they retreated before the advancing American Fifth Army; Field Marshal Kesselring is said to have spared it on Hitler's express orders.

The Ponte Vecchio has always been loaded with stores like those now propped over the water. The earliest vendors were butchers and fishmongers, attracted to the site by the proximity of the river, which provided a convenient dumping ground for their waste. Next came the tanners, who used the river to soak their hides before tanning them with horses' urine. The current plethora of jewellers dates from 1593, when Ferdinando I evicted the butchers' stalls and other practitioners of what he called "vile arts". In their place he installed eight jewellers and 41 **goldsmiths**, while taking the opportunity to double the rents. Florence had long revered the art of the goldsmith, and several of its major artists were skilled in the craft: Ghiberti, Donatello and Cellini, for example. The third of this trio is celebrated by a bust in the centre of the bridge, a favourite night-time meeting point.



## Santa Felìcita

**Santa Felìcita** (Mon–Sat 9.30am–12.30pm & 3–6.30pm) might be the oldest church in Florence, having possibly been founded in the second century AD by Greek or Syrian merchants, pioneers of Christianity in the city. It was built close to the Via Cassia over an early Christian cemetery, commemorated by a column (1381) in Piazza della Felìcita. It's known for certain that a church existed on the site by the fifth century (a tombstone dated 405 has been found nearby), by which time it had been dedicated to St Felicity, an early Roman martyr who is

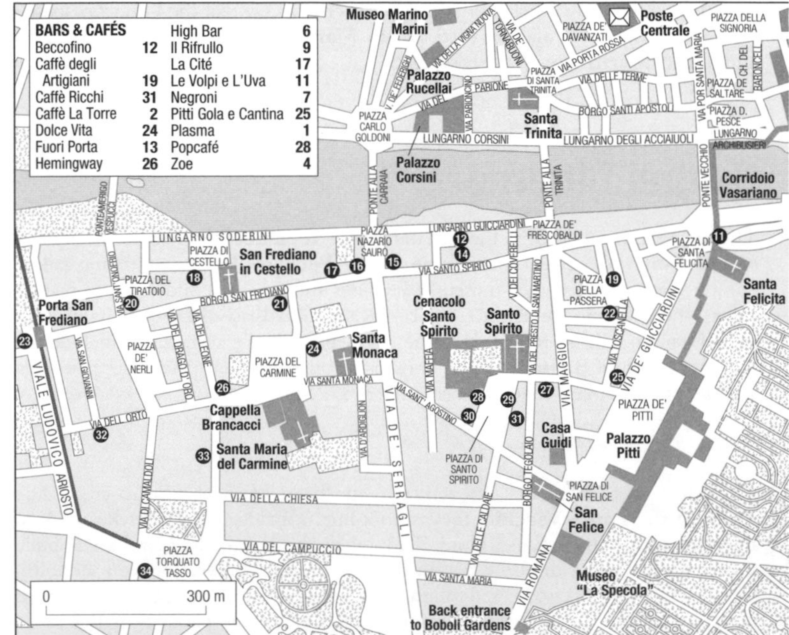

often shown in Renaissance paintings with her seven sons, each of whom was executed in front of her for refusing to renounce his faith (the saint herself was either beheaded or thrown into boiling oil). New churches were built on the site in the eleventh and fourteenth centuries, while in 1565 Vasari added an elaborate portico to accommodate the *corridoio* linking the Uffizi and Palazzo Pitti; an opening in the corridor looks directly into the church. All but the facade was remodelled between 1736 and 1739.

The interior demands a visit for the amazing Pontormo paintings in the **Cappella Capponi**, which lies to the right of the main door, surrounded by obstructive railings. The chapel was designed in the 1420s by Brunelleschi, but subsequently much altered – notably by Vasari, who destroyed the Pontormo fresco in the cupola when building his corridor. Under the cupola are four tondi of the *Evangelists* (painted with help from his adoptive son, Bronzino), while on opposite sides of the window on the right wall are the Virgin and the angel of Pontormo's delightfully simple *Annunciation*, the arrangement alluding to the Incarnation as the means by which the Light came into the world. The low level of light admitted by this window was a determining factor in the startling colour scheme of Pontormo's weirdly erotic **Deposition** (1525–28), one of the masterworks of Florentine Mannerism. Nothing in this picture is conventional: the people bearing Christ's body are androgynous quasi-angelic creatures; billows of gorgeously coloured drapery almost engulf the scene; many of the figures seem to be standing in midair rather than on solid ground; and there's no sign of the cross, the thieves, soldiers or any of the other scene-setting devices usual in paintings of this subject – the only contextual detail is a solitary ghostly cloud. The bearded brown-cloaked figure on the right (Nicodemus) is believed to be a self-portrait of the artist.

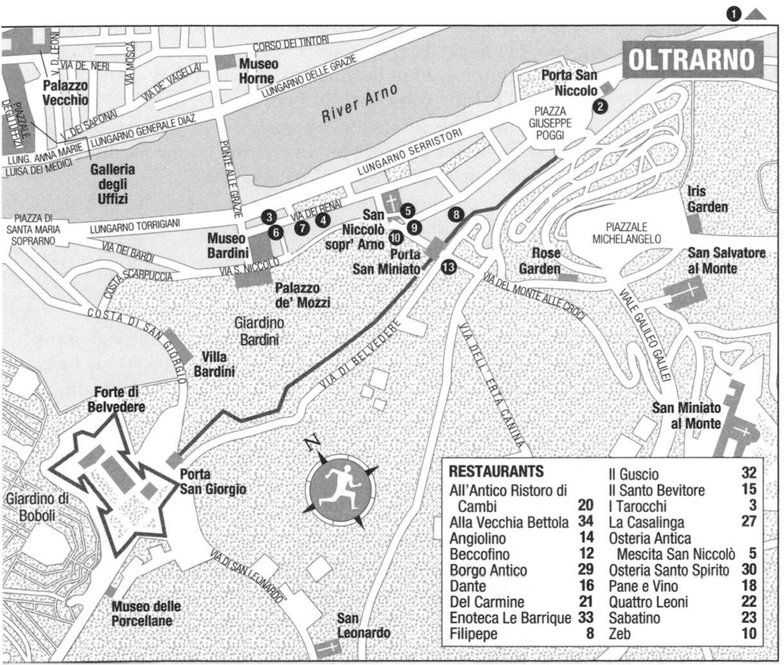

## Jacopo Pontormo

Born near Empoli, Jacopo Carrucci (1494–1556), better known as **Pontormo** after his native village, studied under Andrea del Sarto in Florence in the early 1510s. His early independent works include the frescoes in the atrium of Santissima Annunziata in Florence, which have an edgy quality quite unlike that of his master. In the 1520s he was hired by the Medici to decorate part of their villa at Poggio a Caiano, after which he executed a *Passion* cycle for the Certosa di Galluzzo, to the south of the city. His masterpiece in Florence is the *Deposition* in Santa Felìcita; the major project of his later years, a fresco cycle in San Lorenzo, has been totally destroyed, though some of his other paintings can be seen in the Uffizi.

A crucial figure in the evolution of the hyper-refined Mannerist style, Pontormo was every bit as strange as his bizarre *Deposition* suggests. A chronic hypochondriac – his diary is a tally of the state of his kidneys, bowel disorders and other assorted ailments – he seems to have found the company of others almost intolerable, spending much of his time in a top-floor room that could be reached only by a ladder, which he drew up behind him. So eccentric was his behaviour that he was virtually mythologized by his contemporaries. One writer attributed to him an all-consuming terror of death and called his room a "beast's lair", while another insisted that he kept corpses in a tub as models for a *Deluge* that he was painting – an antisocial research project that allegedly brought protests from the neighbours.

# Palazzo Pitti

Beyond Santa Felìcita, the street opens out at Piazza Pitti, forecourt of the largest palace in Florence, the **Palazzo Pitti**. Banker and merchant Luca Pitti commissioned the palace to outdo his chief rivals, the Medici. Work started around 1457, possibly using a design by Brunelleschi which had been rejected by Cosimo de' Medici for being too overbearing. No sooner was the palace completed, however, than the Pitti's fortunes began to decline, and by 1549 they were forced to sell out to the Medici. The Pitti subsequently became the Medici's base in Florence, growing in bulk until the seventeenth century, when it achieved its present gargantuan dimensions. Later, during Florence's brief tenure as the Italian capital between 1865 and 1870, it housed the Italian royal family.

Today the Palazzo Pitti and the pavilions of the Giardino di Bóboli contain eight museums, of which the foremost is the **Galleria Palatina**, a painting collection second in importance only to the Uffizi.

## The Galleria Palatina and Appartamenti Reali

Many of the paintings gathered by the Medici in the seventeenth century are now arranged in the **Galleria Palatina** (Tues–Sun 8.15am–6.50pm; €8.50, includes admission to the Appartamenti Reali & Galleria d'Arte Moderna), a suite of almost thirty rooms on the first floor of one wing of the palace. The pictures are not arranged in the sort of didactic order observed by most galleries, but are instead hung as they would have been in the days of their acquisition, three or four deep in places, with the aim of making each room pleasurably varied.

The current itinerary takes you straight through into the suite containing mostly less famous works, though some individual paintings are well worth seeking out, notably: **Fra' Bartolomeo**'s *Deposition*; a tondo of the *Madonna and Child with Scenes from the Life of St Anne* by **Filippo Lippi**; his son Filippino's *Death of Lucrezia*; a *Sleeping Cupid* by **Caravaggio**; and Cristofano Allori's *Judith and Holofernes*, for which Allori himself, his mother and his mistress provided the models for the principal characters. Also in this section are the Corridoio del

Volterrano, which houses mainly Florentine works of the seventeenth century, and the Corridoio della Colonna, which has a Flemish theme.

In the second, more captivating part of the gallery, **Andrea del Sarto** is represented in strength, his seventeen works including a beautifully grave *Annunciation*. Even more remarkable is the Pitti's collection of eleven paintings by his great contemporary, **Raphael**. When Raphael settled in Florence in 1505, he was besieged with commissions from patrons delighted to find an artist for whom the creative process involved so little agonizing. In the next three years he painted scores of pictures for such people as Angelo Doni, the man who commissioned Michelangelo's *Doni Tondo* (now in the Uffizi). Raphael's portraits of Doni and his wife, Maddalena (1506–07), display an unhesitating facility and perfect poise; if the Maddalena's pose looks familiar, incidentally, it's because it's copied from Leonardo's *Mona Lisa*. Similar poise illuminates Raphael's splendidly framed 1515 *Madonna della Seggiola*, or Madonna of the Chair, in which the figures are curved into the rounded shape of the panel (which is said to have come from the bottom of a wine barrel), with no sense of artificiality. For centuries this was Italy's most popular image of the Virgin: nineteenth-century copyists had to join a five-year waiting list to study the picture. According to Vasari, the model for the famous *Donna Velata* (Veiled Woman), in the Sala di Giove, was the painter's mistress (possibly his wife), a Roman baker's daughter known to posterity as La Fornarina.

The assembly of paintings by the Venetian artist **Titian** (fourteen in all) includes a number of his most trenchant portraits. The lecherous and scurrilous Pietro Aretino – journalist, critic, poet and one of Titian's closest friends – was so thrilled by his 1545 portrait that he gave it to Cosimo I; Titian painted him on several other occasions, sometimes using him as the model for Pontius Pilate. Also here are likenesses of Philip II of Spain and the young Cardinal Ippolito de' Medici (1532), the illegitimate son of Giuliano di Lorenzo de' Medici. The so-called *Portrait of an Englishman* (1540) scrutinizes the viewer with unflinching sea-grey eyes, and to his left, by way of contrast, is the same artist's sensuous and much-copied *Mary Magdalene* (1531), the first of a series on this theme produced for the Duke of Urbino. In the same room, look out for Rosso Fiorentino's *Madonna Enthroned with Saints* (1522), and the gallery's outstanding sculpture, Canova's *Venus Italica*, commissioned by Napoleon as a replacement for the *Venus de' Medici*, which he had whisked off to Paris.

Much of the rest of the Pitti's first floor comprises the **Appartamenti Reali**, the Pitti's state rooms. They were renovated by the dukes of Lorraine in the eighteenth century, and then by Vittorio Emanuele when Florence became the country's capital, so the rooms display three distinct decorative phases. The gallery leads straight through into the apartments, and after Raphael and Titian it can be difficult to sustain a great deal of enthusiasm for such ducal elegance, notwithstanding the sumptuousness of the furnishings.

## The other Pitti museums

On the floor above the Palatina is the **Galleria d'Arte Moderna** (Tues–Sun 8.15am–6.50pm; joint ticket with Galleria Palatina €8.50), a chronological survey of primarily Tuscan art from the mid-eighteenth century to 1945. The products of the *Macchiaioli*, the Italian division of the Impressionist movement, are of interest; most startling, however, are the sculptures, featuring sublime kitsch such as Antonio Ciseri's *Pregnant Nun*.

The **Museo degli Argenti** (Nov–Feb 8.15am–4.30pm; March closes 5.30pm; April–May & Sept–Oct closes 6.30pm; June–Aug closes 7.30pm; closed first & last

Mon of month; joint ticket with Museo delle Porcellane, Galleria del Costume & Giardino di Bóboli, €7), entered from the main palace courtyard, is a vast museum not just of silverware but of luxury artefacts in general. The lavishly frescoed reception rooms are full of the latter: the first hall, the Sala di Giovanni da San Giovanni, shows Lorenzo de' Medici giving refuge to the Muses; the other three ceremonial rooms have trompe l'oeil paintings by seventeenth-century Bolognese artists. As for the exhibits, the least ambivalent response is likely to be aroused by Lorenzo the Magnificent's trove of antique vases, all of them marked with their owner's name. (His death mask is in the same room.) With many of the pieces, though, you might well be torn between admiring the skills of the craftsman and deploring the extravagant ends to which those skills were employed; by the time you reach the end of the jewellery show on the first floor, you'll have lost all capacity to be surprised or revolted by seashell figurines, cups made from ostrich eggs, rock-crystal vases, impossibly complicated ivory carvings (including a long-haired dog), portraits in stone inlay and the like. Exhibitions are sometimes held here, which can affect the ticket price and opening hours.

Visitors without a specialist interest are unlikely to be riveted by the other Pitti museums that are currently open. In the Palazzina della Meridiana, the eighteenth-century southern wing of the Pitti, the **Galleria del Costume** (same hours & ticket as Museo degli Argenti) provides the opportunity to see the dress that Eleonora di Toledo is wearing in Bronzino's famous portrait of her, and a miscellany of other fine apparel. Also housed in the Meridiana is the **Collezione Contini Bonacossi** (free tours usually Thurs & Sat 9.45am; booking essential a week ahead at the Uffizi ⓣ055.23.885), which is on long-term loan to the Pitti. Its prize pieces are its Spanish paintings, in particular Velázquez's *Water Carrier of Seville*. The well-presented collection of porcelain at the **Museo delle Porcellane** (same hours & ticket as Museo degli Argenti) is located at the top of the Bóboli garden, while the **Museo delle Carrozze** (Carriage Museum) has been closed for years and, despite what the Pitti handouts tell you, will almost certainly remain so for the foreseeable future, to the chagrin of very few.

## The Giardino di Bóboli

The delightful formal gardens of the Palazzo Pitti, the **Giardino di Bóboli** (same hours & ticket as Museo degli Argenti), takes its name from the Bóboli family, erstwhile owners of much of this area, which was once a quarry; the bedrock here is one of the sources of the yellow sandstone known as *pietra forte* (strong stone) that gives much of Florence its dominant hue. Shaped into a rough, boulder-like texture, this stone was also used to "rusticate" the Palazzo Pitti's great facade. When

### The Birth of Opera

The Medici pageants in the gardens of the Pitti were the last word in extravagance, and the palace has a claim to be the birthplace of the most extravagant modern performing art, **opera**. The roots of the genre are convoluted, but its ancestry certainly owes much to the singing and dancing tableaux called *intermedii*, with which high-society Florentine weddings were padded out. Influenced by these shows, the academy known as the Camerata Fiorentina began, at the end of the sixteenth century, to blend the principles of Greek drama with a semi-musical style of declamation. The first composition recognizable as an opera is *Dafne*, written by two members of the Camerata, Jacopo Peri and Ottavio Rinucci, and performed in 1597; the earliest opera whose music has survived in its entirety is the same duo's *Euridice*, premiered in the Pitti palace on the occasion of the proxy marriage of Maria de' Medici to Henry IV.

▲ Giardino di Bóboli

the Medici acquired the house in 1549 they set to work transforming their back yard into an enormous 111-acre garden, its every statue, view and grotto designed to elevate the beauty of nature by the judicious application of art.

Work continued into the early seventeenth century, by which stage this steep hillside had been turned into a maze of statue-strewn avenues and well-trimmed vegetation. Opened to the public in 1766, it is the only really extensive area of accessible greenery in the centre of the city, and can be one of the most pleasant spots for a midday picnic. It's no place to seek solitude, however: some five million visitors annually take time out here, more than at any other Italian garden. If the queues at the main entrance are too daunting, walk about three hundred metres further along the main road, the Via Romana, where you'll find another, invariably quieter, entrance.

Aligned with the central block of the *palazzo*, the garden's **amphitheatre** was designed in the early seventeenth century as an arena for Medici entertainments. The site had previously been laid out by Ammannati in 1599 over an earlier stone quarry as a garden in the shape of a Roman circus. For the wedding of Cosimo III and Princess Marguerite-Louise, cousin of Louis XIV, twenty thousand guests were packed onto the stone benches to watch a production that began with the appearance of a gigantic effigy of Atlas with the globe on his back; the show got under way when the planet split apart, releasing a cascade of earth that transformed the giant into the Atlas mountain. Such frivolities did little to reconcile Marguerite-Louise to either Florence or her husband, and after several acrimonious years this miserable dynastic marriage came to an effective end with her return to Paris, where she professed to care about little "as long as I never have to set eyes on the grand duke again".

Of all the garden's Mannerist embellishments, the most celebrated is the **Grotta del Buontalenti** (1583–88), to the left of the entrance, beyond Giambologna's much-reproduced statue of Cosimo I's favourite dwarf astride a giant tortoise. Embedded in the grotto's faked stalactites and encrustations are replicas of Michelangelo's *Slaves* – the originals were lodged here until 1908. Lurking in the deepest recesses of the cave, and normally viewable only from afar, is Giambologna's *Venus*, leered at by attendant imps. The Grotta is kept locked, but attendants allow small groups in for a look, usually once an hour.

Another spectacular set piece is the fountain island called the **Isolotto**, which is the focal point of the far end of the garden; from within the Bóboli the most dramatic approach is along the central cypress avenue known as the **Viottolone**, many of whose statues are Roman originals. These lower parts of the garden are its most pleasant – and least visited – sections. You come upon them quickly if you enter the Bóboli by the Porta Romana entrance.



## The Casa Guidi

Close to the Pitti, on the junction of Via Maggio and Via Romana, you'll find the home of Robert Browning and Elizabeth Barrett Browning, the **Casa Guidi** (April–Nov Mon, Wed & Fri 3–6pm; free, but donations welcome). It's something of a shrine to Elizabeth, who wrote much of her most popular verse here (including, naturally enough, *Casa Guidi Windows*) and died here. Virtually all the Casa Guidi's furniture went under the hammer at Sotheby's in 1913, and there's just a piano and one oil painting left, though two of the three rooms still manage to conjure up something of the Brownings' spirit. It makes a spectacular place **to stay** – you can rent it through the Landmark Trust but it is booked months ahead and is far from cheap (Ⓦwww.landmarktrust.org.uk).

## La Specola

On the third floor of the university buildings at Via Romana 17 is a museum that can reasonably claim to be the strangest in the city. Taking its name from the telescope (*specola*) on its roof, **La Specola** (daily except Wed 9am–1pm, Sat until 5pm; €4) is a twin-sectioned museum of zoology. The first part is conventional enough, with ranks of shells, insects and crustaceans, followed by a mortician's ark of animals stuffed, pickled and desiccated, including a hippo, given to Grand Duke Pietro Leopardo, which used to reside in the Bóboli garden. Beyond some rather frayed-looking sharks lie the exhibits everyone comes to see, the **Cere Anatomiche** (Anatomical Waxworks). Wax arms, legs and organs cover the walls, arrayed around satin beds on which wax cadavers recline in progressive stages of deconstruction, each muscle fibre and nerve cluster moulded and dyed with absolute precision. Most of the six hundred models – and nearly all of the amazing full-body mannequins – were made between 1775 and 1791 by one Clemente Susini, under the supervision of the physiologist Tommaso Bonicoli, and were intended as teaching aids, in an age when medical ethics and refrigeration techniques were not what they are today.

In a separate room towards the end, after the obstetrics display and a few zoological waxworks, you'll find the grisliest section of La Specola, a trio of tableaux created by **Gaetano Zumbo**, a cleric from Sicily, to satisfy the hypochondriacal obsessions of Cosimo III, a Jesuit-indoctrinated bigot who regarded all genuine scientific enquiry with suspicion. Enclosed in tasteful display cabinets, they depict Florence during the plague: rats teasing the intestines from green-fleshed corpses, mushrooms growing from the mulch of fleshly debris, and the pink bodies of the freshly dead heaped on the suppurating semi-decomposed. A fourth tableau, illustrating the horrors of syphilis, was damaged in the 1966 flood, and now consists of a loose gathering of the dead and diseased. In the centre of the room lies a dissected waxwork head, built on the foundation of a real skull; it's as fastidious as any of Susini's creations, but Zumbo couldn't resist giving the skin a tint of putrefaction, before applying a dribble of blood to the mouth and nose.



## Western Oltrarno

Western Oltrarno is one of the city's earthier districts, though in recent years it's been steadily colonized by bars, restaurants and shops that are turning it into a south-of-the-river equivalent of the upwardly mobile area around Sant'Ambrogio. An indication of the importance of the parish of **Santo Spirito**, the Oltrarno's social and geographical heart, is that when Florence was divided into four administrative *quartieri* in the fourteenth century, the entire area south of the Arno was given its name. The busy piazza in front of Santo Spirito church, with its buzzing cafés and restaurants, encapsulates the genuinely Florentine character of this part of the Oltrarno, an area not hopelessly compromised by the encroachments of tourism, even though there's a steady stream of visitors heading for the great fresco cycle in the church of **Santa Maria del Carmine**.

### Santo Spirito

Designed in 1434 as a replacement for a thirteenth-century church, **Santo Spirito** (Mon, Tues & Thurs–Sun 9.30am–12.30pm & 4–6pm; free) was one of Brunelleschi's last projects, a swansong later described by Bernini as "the most beautiful church in the world". Work began in 1444, but only a single column had been raised by the time the architect died two years later. Brunelleschi had wanted Santo Spirito to enjoy an uninterrupted view of the Arno, but was thwarted by the aristocratic families whose homes would have needed to be demolished. Many of the same families, however, helped pay for the church, whose chief source of income was sponsorship of its many side chapels. One Frescobaldi aristocrat donated a thousand florins, a huge sum at the time, as long as no coat of arms other than that of the Frescobaldi were placed in the sepulchre of his chapel. Funds were supplemented in more modest fashion by Augustinian monks from the neighbouring monastery, who sacrificed a meal a day as a money-raising example to others.

#### The interior

The church is so perfectly proportioned that nothing could seem more artless, yet the plan is extremely sophisticated: a Latin cross with a continuous chain of 38 chapels round the outside and a line of 35 columns running without a break round the nave, transepts and chancel. The exterior wall was originally designed to follow the curves of the chapels' walls, creating a flowing, corrugated effect.

As built, however, the exterior is a plain, straight wall, and even the main facade remained incomplete, disguised today by a simple eighteenth-century plastering job. Inside the church, only the Baroque baldachin, about as nicely integrated as a jukebox in a Greek temple, disrupts the harmonious design and the subtle monochrome of grey stone and off-white plaster.

A fire in 1471 destroyed most of Santo Spirito's medieval works, including frescoes by Cimabue and the Gaddi family, but as a result, the paintings in the many chapels comprise an unusually unified collection, as most were commissioned in the immediate aftermath of the fire. Most prolific among the artists is the so-called **Maestro di Santo Spirito**, but the best paintings – to be found in the transepts – are by others.

In the south transept is Filippino Lippi's **Nerli Altarpiece**, an age-darkened Madonna and Child with saints (second chapel from the left of the four chapels on the transept's south wall); Tanai and Nanna dei Nerli, who commissioned the painting, are portrayed amidst the saints, and their home, the Palazzo dei Nerli near Porta San Frediano, is depicted in the background. Across the church, in the north transept, is an unusual **St Monica and Augustinian Nuns** (1460–70), probably by Verrocchio or Francesco Botticini, that's virtually a study in monochrome, with black-clad nuns flocking round their black-clad paragon; two chapels to the left, the Cappella Corbinelli features a fine sculpted altarpiece (1492) by the young Andrea Sansovino.

A door in the north aisle leads through to Giuliano da Sangallo's stunning vestibule and **sacristy** (1489–93), the latter designed in imitation of Brunelleschi's Pazzi chapel. The meticulously planned proportions and soft tones create an atmosphere of calm that is only disrupted by the botanical carvings of the capitals, some of which were designed by Sansovino. Hanging above the altar is a wooden Crucifix, a tenderly feminized image of uncertain origins. It's known that the young Michelangelo was commissioned by the monks of Santo Spirito to make a Crucifix for the church in the early 1490s, and several scholars believe that this sculpture – discovered in Santo Spirito in 1963 – is the work in question; others, though, think it was made half a century later by Taddeo Curradi, an artist who was known for the gracefulness of his wooden Crucifixes.

### The Chiostro dei Morti and the Cenacolo di Santo Spirito

A glass door at the far end of the vestibule, usually locked, gives out onto the **Chiostro dei Morti**, the only cloister in the complex that is still part of the Augustinian monastery. The 1471 fire destroyed much of the rest of the monastery, with the exception of its refectory (entered to the left of the main church, at Piazza Santo Spirito 29), which is now the home of the **Cenacolo di Santo Spirito** (Sat April–Oct 9am–5pm; Nov–March 10.30am–1.30pm; €2.20), a one-room collection comprising an assortment of carvings, many of them Romanesque, and a huge fresco of *The Crucifixion* (1365) by Orcagna and his workshop.

## Santa Maria del Carmine

Nowhere in Florence is there a more startling contrast between exterior and interior than in **Santa Maria del Carmine**, a couple of blocks west of Santo Spirito in Piazza del Carmine. Outside it's a drab brick box; inside – in the frescoes of the **Cappella Brancacci** (Mon & Wed–Sat 10am–5pm, Sun 1–5pm; €4) – it provides one of Europe's supreme artistic experiences. The chapel is barricaded off from the rest of the Carmine, and visits are restricted to a maximum of thirty people at a time, for just fifteen minutes. The time limit is strictly enforced in high season, but tends to become more flexible as the crowds ebb away. At the time of writing tickets could be obtained only by reserving in advance on ⓣ055.276.8224 or 055.276.8558; this system is so cumbersome, however, that it surely will be replaced by something less visitor-repellent – ask the tourist office about the current situation.

## The Cappella Brancacci

The Cappella Brancacci frescoes were commissioned in 1424 by Felice Brancacci, a silk merchant and leading patrician figure. The decoration of the chapel was begun in the same year by **Masolino** (1383–1447). Alongside Masolino was the much younger Tommaso di Ser Giovanni di Mone Cassai – known ever since as **Masaccio** (1401–28), a nickname meaning "Mad Tom".

Two years into the project Masolino was recalled to Budapest, where he was official painter to the Hungarian court. Left to his own devices, Masaccio began to blossom. When Masolino returned in 1427 the teacher was soon taking lessons from the supposed pupil, whose grasp of the texture of the real world, of the principles of perspective and of the dramatic potential of his biblical texts far exceeded that of his precursors. In 1428 Masolino was called away to Rome, to be followed by Masaccio a few months later. Neither would return. Masaccio died the same year, but, in the words of Vasari, "all the most celebrated sculptors and painters since Masaccio's day have become excellent and illustrious by studying their art in this chapel". (Michelangelo used to come here to make drawings of Masaccio's scenes, and had his nose broken on the chapel steps by a young sculptor whom he enraged with his condescension.) Any thought of further work ceased in 1436, when Brancacci (married to the daughter of Palla Strozzi, leader of the city's anti-Medici faction) was exiled by Cosimo de' Medici. The Carmelite monks in charge of the chapel and its frescoes promptly removed all portraits and other references to the disgraced donor.

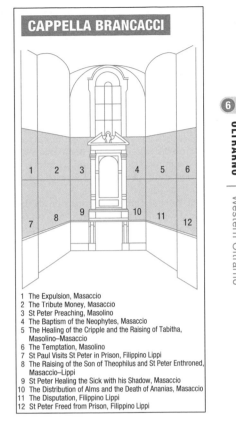

Work resumed between 1480 and 1485, when the paintings were completed by **Filippino Lippi**, who mimicked Masaccio's style to perfection. By the late seventeenth century public taste had changed so much that the demolition of the entire chapel was proposed. That suggestion was over-ruled, though alterations were made which destroyed frescoes in the lunettes. The surviving scenes were blurred by smoke from a fire that destroyed much of the church and convent in 1771, and subsequent varnishings damaged them so much that when

### CAPPELLA BRANCACCI

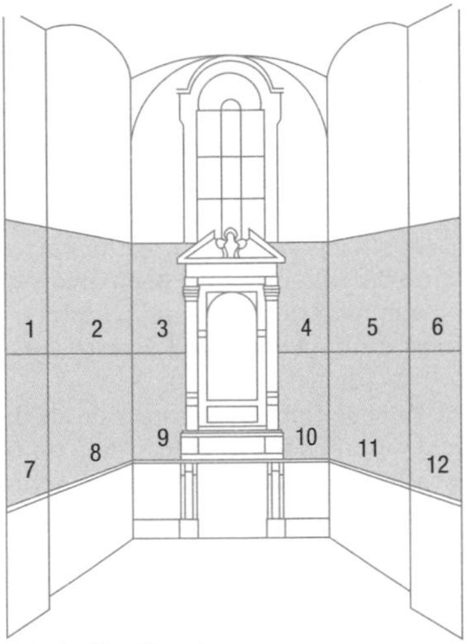

1 The Expulsion, Masaccio
2 The Tribute Money, Masaccio
3 St Peter Preaching, Masolino
4 The Baptism of the Neophytes, Masaccio
5 The Healing of the Cripple and the Raising of Tabitha, Masolino–Masaccio
6 The Temptation, Masolino
7 St Paul Visits St Peter in Prison, Filippino Lippi
8 The Raising of the Son of Theophilus and St Peter Enthroned, Masaccio–Lippi
9 St Peter Healing the Sick with his Shadow, Masaccio
10 The Distribution of Alms and the Death of Ananias, Masaccio
11 The Disputation, Filippino Lippi
12 St Peter Freed from Prison, Filippino Lippi

Bernard Berenson saw the frescoes in 1930 he described them as "dust-bitten and ruined". Then, in 1932, part of an altar that had been installed in the eighteenth century was moved, revealing areas of almost pristine paint; half a century later, work finally got under way to restore the chapel to the condition of the uncovered patch.

The small scene on the left of the entrance arch is the quintessence of Masaccio's art. Plenty of artists had depicted **The Expulsion of Adam and Eve** (1) before, but none had captured the desolation of the sinners so graphically: Adam presses his hands to his face in bottomless despair, Eve raises her head and screams. The monumentalism of these naked figures – whose modesty was preserved by strategically placed sprigs of foliage prior to the restoration – reveals the influence of Donatello, who may have been involved in the planning of the chapel. In contrast to the emotional charge and sculptural presence of Masaccio's couple, Masolino's almost dainty **Adam and Eve** (6) on the opposite arch, pose as if to have their portraits painted.

St Peter is chief protagonist of all the remaining scenes. It's possible that the cycle was intended as propaganda on behalf of the embattled papacy, which had recently resolved the bitter Great Schism, during which one pope held court in Rome and another in Avignon. By celebrating the primacy of St Peter, the rock upon whom the Church is built, the frescoes by implication extol the apostolic succession from which the pope derives his authority.

Three scenes by Masaccio are especially compelling. First off is the **Tribute Money** (2), most widely praised of the paintings and the first monumental fresco of the Renaissance. The narrative is complex, with three separate events portrayed within a single frame. The central episode shows Christ outside the gates of Capernaum being asked to pay a tribute owing to the city. To the left, St Peter fetches coins from the mouth of a fish in order to pay the tribute, Christ in the central panel having pointed to where the money will be found. The third scene, to the right, depicts Peter handing over the money to the tax official.

Masaccio's second great panel is **St Peter Healing the Sick** (9), in which the shadow of the stern and self-possessed saint (followed by St John) cures the infirm as it passes over them, a miracle invested with the aura of a solemn ceremonial. The third panel is **The Distribution of Alms and Death of Ananias** (10), in which St Peter instructs the people to give up their possessions to the poor. One individual, Ananias, retains some of his wealth with the knowledge of his wife, Sapphira. Rebuked by Peter, Ananias dies on the spot, closely followed by a similarly castigated Sapphira.

Filippino Lippi's work included the completion of Masaccio's **Raising of Theophilus's Son and St Peter Enthroned** (8), which depicts St Peter raising the son of Theophilus, the Prefect of Antioch (after he'd been dead for fourteen years). The people of Antioch, suitably impressed by the miracle, build a throne from which St Peter can preach, shown as a separate episode to the right. The three figures to the right of the throne are thought to be portraits of Masaccio, Alberti and Brunelleschi, who made a trip to Rome together. Masaccio originally painted himself touching Peter's robe, a reference to the enthroned statue of Peter in Rome, which pilgrims touch for good luck. Lippi considered the contact of the artist and saint to be improper and painted out the arm; his over-painting has been allowed to remain, but you can see where the arm used to be.

Lippi left another portrait in the combined scene of **St Peter in Disputation with Agrippa** (or Nero) and his crucifixion (11): the central figure looking out from the painting in the trio right of the crucifixion is Botticelli, the painter's teacher, while Filippino himself can be seen at the far right.

# Eastern Oltrarno

As happened on the opposite bank of the river, **Eastern Oltrarno** was badly damaged in 1944, when blocks of historic buildings were destroyed by the Nazis to hamper the Allied advance. Some characterful parts remain, however, notably the medieval Via de' Bardi and its continuation, Via San Niccolò. These narrow, *palazzo*-lined streets will take you past the **Bardini garden and museum**, and the medieval church of **San Niccolò**, all of which can be visited as part of the walk up the hill to **San Miniato al Monte**, one of the most beautiful Romanesque churches in Italy.

## The Bardini museum, garden and villa

The best way to reach the Bardini museum from the Ponte Vecchio and elsewhere in the Oltrarno is to take Via de' Bardi, known in the Middle Ages as the Borgo Pitiglioso – the "miserable" or "flea-bitten" street. Partway down the street on the left, beyond the small Piazza di Santa Maria Soprarno, you'll pass the tiny church of **Santa Lucia dei Magnoli**, founded in 1078. Pop inside if you're lucky enough to find it open: the first altar on the left has a panel of *St Lucy* by the Sienese master Pietro Lorenzetti.

The **Museo Bardini**, which stands at the end of the street at Piazza de' Mozzi 1, is like the Museo Horne just across the Arno, in that it was built around the bequest of a private collector. **Stefano Bardini** (1836–1922) was once the most important art dealer in Italy; his tireless activity, at a time when Renaissance art was relatively cheap and unfashionable, laid the cornerstone of many important modern-day European and American collections. Determined that no visitor to his native city should remain unaware of his success, he ripped down a church that stood here and built a vast house for himself, studding it with fragments of old buildings. Doorways, ceiling panels and other orphaned pieces are strewn all over the place: the first-floor windows of the main facade, for instance, are altars from a church in Pistoia. Musical instruments, carvings, ceramics, armour, furniture, carpets, paintings – Bardini snapped them all up, and bequeathed the whole lot to the city. For several years the museum has been under restoration, a process that is allegedly soon to be concluded; the next paragraph is a summary of the place as it was before its closure.

On the **ground floor**, Tino da Camaino's *Charity* (Room 7) stands out, but the most interesting items are upstairs. Room 10 is a display of funerary monuments arranged as if in a crypt, with an enamelled terracotta altarpiece attributed to Andrea della Robbia. Beyond several rooms of weapons, three pieces in Room 14 also grab the attention: a polychrome terracotta of the *Madonna and Child* by Donatello; an extraordinarily modern-looking stucco, mosaic and glass relief of the *Madonna dei Cordai* (1443), also probably by Donatello; and a terracotta *Madonna and Child with St John* by Benedetto da Maiano. Room 16 has some lovely *cassoni* (painted chests) and several of the museum's many depictions of the Madonna and Child, a subject with which Bardini appears to have been obsessed. Other highlights of the final rooms include Domenico Beccafumi's *Hercules at the Crossroads between Vice and Virtue*, Michele Giambono's *St John the Baptist*, a painted relief in terracotta from the workshop of Jacopo della Quercia, a *St Michael* by Antonio del Pollaiuolo and a beautiful terracotta *Virgin Annunciate*, an anonymous piece from fifteenth-century Siena.

When the museum reopens, the top floor will house the **Galleria Corsi**, a collection of seven hundred paintings dating from the fourteenth to the nineteenth century, donated to the city in 1937 by Fortunata Carobbi Corsi.

## The Giardino Bardini and Villa Bardini

Close to the Bardini museum, at Via de' Bardi 1r, is an entrance to the **Giardino Bardini** (same hours and ticket as the Giardino di Bóboli), which was opened to the public for the first time in 2007. The garden occupies the slope that was formerly the olive grove of the **Palazzo dei Mozzi**, a colossal house that was built in the late thirteenth century by the Mozzi family, at that time one of the richest families in Florence. After Stefano Bardini bought the property in 1913 he set about creating a semi-formal garden that has now been restored to the appearance he gave it, with a neo-Baroque staircase and terraces dividing the fruit-growing section from the miniature woodland of the *bosco Inglese*. At the summit of the garden, reached by a lovely long pergola of wisteria and hortensia, a colonnaded belvedere gives a splendid view of the city.

If you're coming from the Bóboli gardens you can enter the garden at the top, from Costa di San Giorgio, where you'll find the **Villa Bardini** (daily 10am–4pm; closed first & last Mon of month; €5), which was built as the Villa Manadora and extended by Stefano Bardini. Having been thoroughly restored, the villa now houses two somewhat non-essential collections. One is dedicated to **Pietro Annigoni** (1910–88), a vehemently anti-modernist painter who was best known for his technically accomplished but sterile portraits of luminaries such as Pope John XXIII, the Shah of Iran and Queen Elizabeth II. Fashionistas may enjoy the villa's exhibition of clothes created by **Roberto Capucci** (born 1930). Dubbed the "Givenchy of Rome" by his admirers, Capucci made his name with frocks that seemed intent on upstaging their wearer – one of his most celebrated creations was a nine-layered dress that became famous when worn by a model in Cadillac ads in the 1950s, and another was assembled from plastic quilts filled with coloured liquid.

# From San Niccolò to Piazzale Michelangelo

Beyond the Museo Bardini, Via San Niccolò swings past **San Niccolò sopr'Arno** (daily 8.30–10am & 5.30–7pm), which has been here since the eleventh century but was rebuilt towards the end of the fourteenth. Restoration work after the 1966 flood uncovered several frescoes underneath the altars, but none is as appealing as the fifteenth-century fresco in the sacristy; known as *The Madonna of the Girdle*, it was probably painted by Baldovinetti.

In medieval times the church stood on the edge of the city, and two of Florence's fourteenth-century gates still stand in the vicinity: the diminutive **Porta San Miniato**, set in a portion of the walls, and the huge **Porta San Niccolò**. From either of these gates you can begin the climb up to San Miniato: the path from Porta San Niccolò weaves up through **Piazzale Michelangelo**, with its replica *David* and bumper-to-bumper tour coaches; the more direct path from Porta San Miniato offers a choice between the steep Via del Monte alle Croci or the stepped Via di San Salvatore al Monte, both of which emerge a short distance uphill from Piazzale Michelangelo. (If you don't fancy the climb, take **bus** #12 or #13 to the Piazzale.)

In spring you can break the walk by visiting one of the gardens on the slopes just below the Piazzale: to the west, on Via di San Salvatore al Monte, is the pleasant Rose Garden and Japanese Garden (May to mid-June daily 8am–8pm; free), but more striking is the **Iris Garden** (3 weeks in May daily 10am–12.30pm & 3–7pm; free), whose entrance lies at the southeast corner of the Piazzale. The iris is one of the city's many symbols, and in May the garden hosts the Italian Iris Society's Florence Prize, an international competition that turns this olive grove into a mass of colour.

## San Miniato al Monte

Arguably the finest Romanesque structure in Tuscany, **San Miniato al Monte** (summer daily 8am–7pm; winter Mon–Sat 8am–noon & 3–6pm, Sun 3–6pm; free) is also the oldest surviving church building in Florence after the Baptistery. Its brilliant multicoloured facade lures troops of visitors up the hill from Oltrarno, and the church more than fulfils the promise of its distant appearance.



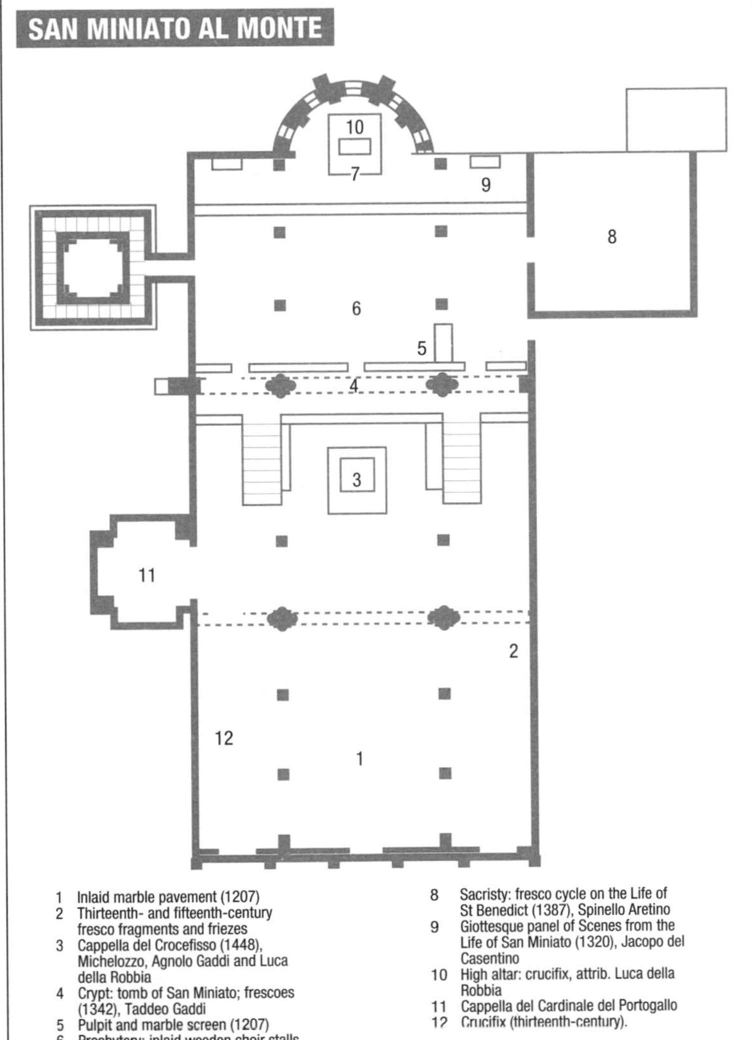


1 Inlaid marble pavement (1207)
2 Thirteenth- and fifteenth-century fresco fragments and friezes
3 Cappella del Crocefisso (1448), Michelozzo, Agnolo Gaddi and Luca della Robbia
4 Crypt: tomb of San Miniato; frescoes (1342), Taddeo Gaddi
5 Pulpit and marble screen (1207)
6 Presbytery: inlaid wooden choir stalls (1466–70)
7 Apse: mosaic of Christ Pantocrator between the Virgin and San Miniato (1260–1297)
8 Sacristy: fresco cycle on the Life of St Benedict (1387), Spinello Aretino
9 Giottesque panel of Scenes from the Life of San Miniato (1320), Jacopo del Casentino
10 High altar: crucifix, attrib. Luca della Robbia
11 Cappella del Cardinale del Portogallo
12 Crucifix (thirteenth-century).

The church's patron saint, **St Minias**, was Florence's first home-grown martyr. Possibly a Greek merchant or the son of an Armenian king, he made a pilgrimage to Rome before moving to Florence in around 250 AD, where he became caught up in the anti-Christian persecutions of the Emperor Decius. Legend has it that after being decapitated close to the site of Piazza della Signoria, the saintly corpse was seen to carry its severed head over the river and up the hill to this spot, an area where he'd previously lived as a hermit: a shrine was subsequently erected on the slope. The hill, known as **Mons Fiorentinus**, was already the site of pagan temples and a secret oratory dedicated to Peter the Apostle.

A chapel dedicated to St Minias is known to have stood on the site in the eighth century, and construction of the present building began in 1013. It was raised by Alibrando, bishop of Florence, and endowed by Emperor Henry II "for the good of his soul". Initially run as a Benedictine foundation, the building passed to the Cluniacs until 1373, and then to the **Olivetans**, a Benedictine offshoot, who reside here still. The monks sell their famous liquors and honeys from the shop next to the church, as well as souvenirs and various unguents, proof against complaints ranging from anxiety to varicose veins.



## The exterior

San Miniato's gorgeous marble **facade** alludes to the Baptistery in its geometrical patterning, and, like the Baptistery, the church was often mistaken for a structure of classical provenance during the later Middle Ages. The lower part of the facade is possibly eleventh-century, while the upper levels date from the twelfth century onwards, and were financed in part by the *Arte di Calimala* (cloth merchants' guild), the body responsible for the church's upkeep from 1288. Their trademark, a gilded copper eagle clutching a bale of cloth, perches on the roof, above the mosaic of *Christ between the Virgin and St Minias*, which dates from 1260. The original **bell tower** collapsed in 1499 and was replaced in the 1520s by the present structure. During the 1530 siege of Florence it was used as an artillery post, thus attracting the attention of enemy gunners. Michelangelo, then advising on the city's defences, had it wrapped in woollen mattresses to protect it from cannon balls.

## The interior

With its choir raised on a platform above the large crypt, the sublime **interior** of San Miniato is like no other in the city, and its general appearance has changed little since the mid-eleventh century. The main additions and decorations in no way spoil its serenity, though the nineteenth-century recoating of the marble columns is a little lurid: the columns' capitals, however, are Roman and Byzantine originals removed from older buildings, while the intricately patterned panels of the **pavement** (1) are dated 1207.

The lovely tabernacle, or **Cappella del Crocefisso** (3), which dominates the middle of the nave, was designed in 1448 by Michelozzo. The date is significant, for the piece is one of the few works commissioned by Piero de' Medici, or Piero il Gottoso (the Gouty), during his brief tenure as head of the Medici dynasty. The marble medallion to the rear and other parts of the work are adorned with Piero's motto (*Semper*) and several Medici symbols – the eagle holding three feathers and a diamond ring, the latter a symbol of durability. The chapel originally housed the miraculous crucifix associated with St Giovanni Gualberto (see p.94), which was moved to Santa Trìnita in 1671. Today it contains painted **panels** by Agnolo Gaddi depicting the *Annunciation*, *Stories of the Passion* and *SS Giovanni Gualberto and Miniato* (1394–96). These were originally arranged in the form of a cross to act as a frame for the now vanished crucifix. Maso di Bartolomeo crafted the twin eagles (1449), symbols of the *Calimala*, to stress that although Piero was the work's sponsor, the guild was responsible for overseeing all stages of its construction. The terracotta in the barrel vault is by Luca della Robbia.

Steps either side of the cappella lead down to the **crypt** (4), the oldest part of the church, where the original high altar still contains the bones that Bishop

▲ San Miniato al Monte

Alibrando confirmed as those of St Minias in the eleventh century (ignoring a well-founded belief that the real bones had been removed to Metz by a relic-obsessed German). The vaults, supported by 36 wonderfully mismatched pillars, contain gilt-backed frescoes (1341) of the saints, martyrs, prophets, virgins and Evangelists by Taddeo Gaddi.

Back in the main body of the church, steps beside the Cappella del Crocefisso lead to the raised **choir** and **presbytery** (6), where there's a magnificent Romanesque **pulpit** (5) and screen dating from 1207. The great **mosaic** (7) in the apse was created in 1297, probably by the same artist who created the facade mosaic, as their subjects are identical – *Christ Pantocrator* enthroned between the Virgin and St Minias. The **crucifix** (10) above the high altar is attributed to Luca della Robbia. Off the presbytery lies the **sacristy** (8; €1 entrance), whose walls are covered by a superlative fresco cycle by Spinello Aretino (1387), devoted to the life of St Benedict.

Back in the lower body of the church, the **Cappella del Cardinale del Portogallo** (11), dating from a few years after the Cappella del Crocefisso, is one of the masterpieces of Renaissance chapel design and a marvellous example of artistic collaboration. Completed in 1473, it was built as a memorial to Cardinal James of Lusitania, the nephew of King Alfonso V of Portugal, who died in Florence in 1459, aged a mere 25. Close to death in the city, he asked to be buried in San Miniato. The cardinal's aunt and his humanist friends and admirers jointly sponsored his tomb. Aside from that of Minias himself, this is – remarkably – the church's only tomb.

The chapel's basic design was the work of Antonio di Manetto (or Manetti), a pupil and biographer of Brunelleschi, who borrowed heavily from his master's work in San Lorenzo's Sagrestia Vecchia. The **tomb** itself was carved by Antonio and Bernardo Rossellino; their elder brother Giovanni oversaw the chapel's construction after Manetto's death. Antonio Rossellino's tondo of the *Madonna and Child* keeps watch over the deceased.

The chapel's architectural and sculptural work was followed in 1466 by carefully integrated frescoes and **paintings**: an *Annunciation* (to the left) and the *Evangelists* and *Doctors of the Church* by Alesso Baldovinetti (lunettes and beside the arches). Antonio and Piero del Pollaiuolo produced the **altarpiece** depicting the cardinal's patron saint, St James, with SS Vincent and Eustace: the present picture is a copy; the original is in the Uffizi. The ceiling's tiled decoration and four glazed terracotta medallions, perhaps the finest such work in the city, were provided by Luca della Robbia.

All the decorative details were carefully designed to complement one another and create a unified artistic whole. Thus Rossellino's tondo of the *Madonna and Child*, for example, echoes the round windows of the walls; the colours in Baldovinetti's *Annunciation* deliberately echo the tones of the surrounding porphyry and serpentine inlays; and the curtain held aside by angels on the cardinal's tomb is repeated in a similar curtain half-shielding the altar.

## From the Forte di Belvedere to San Leonardo in Arcetri

The **Forte di Belvedere**, standing on the crest of the hill above the Bóboli garden, was built by Buontalenti on the orders of Ferdinando I between 1590 and 1595, ostensibly to protect the city, but in fact to intimidate the grand duke's subjects. The urban panorama from here is superb, and ambitious exhibitions are often held in and around the shed-like palace in the centre of the fortress, as are occasional summer-evening film screenings.

In the past it has sometimes been possible to get up to the fort from the Bóboli gardens, but if you want to be certain of getting in, approach the fort from the **Costa di San Giorgio**, a lane which you can reach by backtracking slightly from the Museo Bardini, or pick up directly from the rear of Santa Felìcita. Look out for the villa at no. 19, home to Galileo between 1610 and 1631.

East from the Belvedere stretches the best-preserved section of Florence's fortified **walls**, running parallel to Via di Belvedere. South of the Belvedere, Via San Leonardo leads past olive groves to the church of **San Leonardo in Arcetri**, site of a beautiful thirteenth-century pulpit brought here from a church that is now incorporated into the Uffizi. Dante and Boccaccio are both said to have preached from the spot. The church is usually open only for Mass at weekends, but the sacristan at no. 25 can let you in.

7

# Fiesole



The hill-town of **FIESOLE**, which spreads over a cluster of hills above the Mugnone and Arno valleys some 8km northeast of Florence, is conventionally described as a pleasant retreat from the crowds and heat of summertime Florence. Unfortunately, its tranquillity has been so well advertised that in high season it's now hardly less busy than Florence itself; you'd be pushed to detect much climatic difference between the two on an airless August afternoon.

That said, Fiesole offers a grandstand view of the city, has something of the feel of a country village, and bears many traces of its history – which is actually lengthier than that of Florence. First settled in the Bronze Age, then later by the Etruscans, and then absorbed by the Romans, it rivalled its neighbour until the early twelfth century, when the Florentines overran the town. From that time it became a satellite town, favoured as a semi-rural second home for wealthier citizens such as the ubiquitous Medici.

Fiesole is an easy short trip from central Florence: city **bus** #7 makes the half-hour journey from Santa Maria Novella train station to Fiesole's central Piazza Mino da Fiesole three times an hour. Fiesole's **tourist office** (March–Oct Mon–Sat 9am–6pm, Sun 10am–1pm, 2–6pm; Nov–Feb Mon–Sat 9am–5pm, Sun 10am–4pm; ⓣ055.598.720, ⓦwww.comune.fiesole.fi.it) is nearby at Via Portigiani 3/5, next to the entrance to the archeological site.

## The Town

When the Florentines wrecked Fiesole in 1125, the only major building spared was the **Duomo** (daily: summer 7.30am–noon & 3–6pm; winter 7.30am–noon & 2–5pm) on the edge of Piazza Mino. Nineteenth-century restorers subsequently managed to ruin the exterior, which is now notable only for its lofty campanile. The most interesting part of the bare interior is the raised choir: the altarpiece is a polyptych, painted in the 1440s by Bicci di Lorenzo, and the Cappella Salutati, to the right, contains two fine pieces carved around the same time by Mino da Fiesole – an altar frontal of the Madonna and Saints and the tomb of Bishop Salutati. Fiesole's patron saint, St Romulus, is buried underneath the choir in the ancient crypt. Behind the Duomo at Via Dupré 1, the **Museo Bandini** (Oct–March 10am–6pm, closed Tues & Wed; April–Sept 10am–7pm, closed Tues; joint ticket, valid one day, covering all Fiesole's museums €13) possesses a collection of glazed terracotta in the style of the della Robbias, the odd piece of Byzantine ivory work and a few thirteenth- and fourteenth-century Tuscan pictures, none of them inspiring.

Across the road from the museum are the town's other museums: the **Teatro Romano** and the **Museo Archeologico** (same times and ticket as Museo Bandini). Built in the first century BC, the three-thousand-seat theatre was excavated towards the end of the nineteenth century and is in such good repair that it's used for performances during the Estate Fiesolana festival (see p.202). Parts of the site may be closed as excavation work continues. Most of the exhibits in the site's small **museum** were excavated in this area and encompass pieces from the Bronze Age to Roman occupation.

Fiesole's other major churches, Sant'Alessandro and San Francesco, are at the top of the steep Via San Francesco, which runs past the **Oratorio di San Jacopo** (Sat & Sun 10am–7pm; same ticket as the museums), a little chapel containing a fifteenth-century fresco and some ecclesiastical treasures. A little further up, a terrace offers a knockout view of Florence. **Sant'Alessandro** (summer Mon–Sat 9am–6pm, Sun 10am–1pm & 2–6pm; winter Mon–Sat 9am–5pm, Sun 10am–4pm) was founded in the sixth century on the site of Etruscan and Roman temples; repairs have rendered the outside a whitewashed nonentity, but the beautiful *marmorino cipollino* (onion marble) columns of the basilical interior make it the most atmospheric building in Fiesole. Again, restoration has not improved the Gothic **San Francesco** (daily: April–Sept 9am–noon & 3–7pm; Oct–March closes 6pm; free), which occupies the site of the acropolis: the interior is a twentieth-century renovation, but the tiny cloisters are genuine. The church itself contains an *Immaculate Conception* by Piero di Cosimo (second altar on the right), and below the church is a small museum featuring material gathered mainly by missions to the Far East, much of it from China, as well as a piece of Etruscan wall. From the front of San Francesco a gate opens into a wooded public park, the most pleasant descent back to Piazza Mino.

If you want to wring every last drop of historical significance from central Fiesole, you could follow the signposts from here up the hill to the east of the Teatro, to the ruins of a couple of **Etruscan tombs** from the third century BC.

## To San Domenico

The most enjoyable excursion from Fiesole is to wander down the narrow Via Vecchia Fiesolana, which passes the **Villa Medici** – built for Cosimo il Vecchio by Michelozzo – on its way to the hamlet of **SAN DOMENICO**, a little over

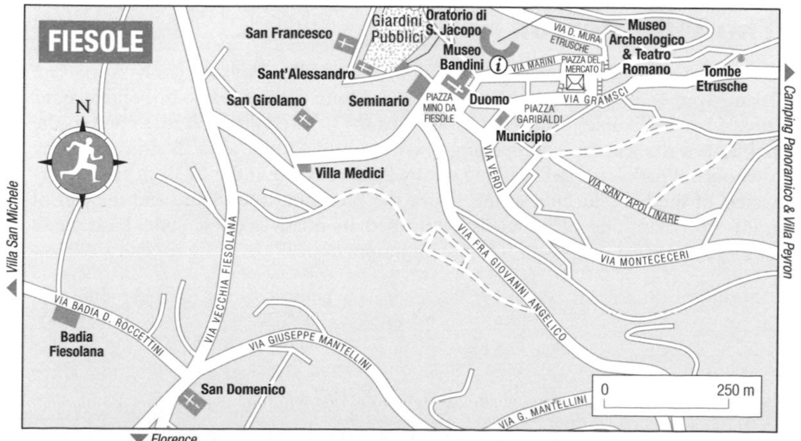

▲ Badía Fiesolana

a kilometre southwest of Fiesole. Fra' Angelico was once prior of the Dominican **monastery** at this village and the church (daily: summer 7.30am–12.30pm & 4.30–6.30pm; winter 8.30am–noon & 4–6pm; free) retains a *Madonna and Angels* by him, in the first chapel on the left. The chapter house also has a Fra' Angelico fresco of *The Crucifixion* (ring at no. 4 if you find the church closed).

Five minutes' walk northwest from San Domenico stands the **Badìa Fiesolana** (Mon–Fri 8.30am–6.30pm), Fiesole's cathedral from the ninth century to the eleventh. Cosimo il Vecchio had the church altered in the 1460s, a project which kept the magnificent Romanesque facade intact while transforming the interior into a superb Renaissance building.

## The Villa Peyron

Garden aficionados shouldn't miss out on the **Villa Peyron** (daily April–Oct 10am–1pm & 3–7pm; Nov–March 10am–3.30pm; €10) at Bosco di Fontelucente, 2.5km east of Fiesole (from Fiesole take bus #47). The villa itself isn't open to the public, but the garden – comprising a sequence of formal terraces surrounded by a woodland park – is a delight. Laid out by Paolo Peyron in the 1930s, it's fed by the waters of the Fontelucente spring, hence the plethora of fountains and the pair of miniature lakes, one of which is landscaped in quasi-Japanese style. Fine views of Florence add a nice garnish to the experience.

# Listings

# Listings


8 Accommodation ........................................ 169

9 Eating and drinking ........................................ 183

10 Nightlife and cultural events ........................................ 197

11 Shopping ........................................ 204

12 Directory ........................................ 210

8

# Accommodation



Accommodation in Florence can be a problem: hotels are plentiful, but demand is almost limitless, which means that prices are high and some hoteliers are less than scrupulous. The tourist invasion has very few slack spots: low season is defined by most hotels as meaning mid-July to the end of August (the weeks during which nearly all Italians head for the beaches or the mountains), and from mid-November to mid-March, except for the Christmas and New Year period. Between March and October you'll need to book your room well in advance or reconcile yourself to staying some distance from the centre. If you're considering a package deal, check the location of your hotel carefully. There's a handful of **hostels** and a couple of **campsites**.

The tourist office can find you a hotel (for a fee), but you'd be mad to roll into town without having somewhere already booked. If none of our recommended places has a room, search the listings on the official tourism website, Ⓦwww.firenzeturismo.it. Never respond to the touts who hang around the train station: their hotels are likely to be expensive, or remote, or unlicensed private houses.

For more general information on accommodation, see p.24. Central Florence accommodation is marked on the map on pp.170–171, while more outlying places are shown on the map on pp.176–177.

## Hotels

**Hotels** in Italy are graded on a scale running from one-star to five-star, but bear in mind that prices in Florence are higher than anywhere else in the country except Venice: one-star establishments in this city cost as much as two-star or even three-star places. elsewhere in Tuscany.

The main concentration of lowish-cost hotels is to the east of the station, centred on Via Faenza and Via Nazionale, with a smaller cluster along Via della Scala, which extends westwards from Piazza della Stazione. Neither of these zones is very pleasant: the Faenza/Nazionale area has a sizeable night-time population of assorted lowlife, while Via della Scala is a major traffic artery and feels a little more remote from the heart of the city. Note also that some of the places in these areas are unlicensed. Our reviews are grouped by district, with subdivisions by price: "Inexpensive" hotels are those which have doubles for under €100 in high season; "Moderate" means €100–200; "Expensive" means €200–350; and in our "Very Expensive" hotels you'll be paying upwards of €350.

Many hotels in Florence drop their prices considerably in low season, and our reviews make it clear which places offer substantial **reductions**. (Wherever you see a line like "Doubles are €120–240", the first figure indicates low-season minimum, and the latter high-season maximum.)

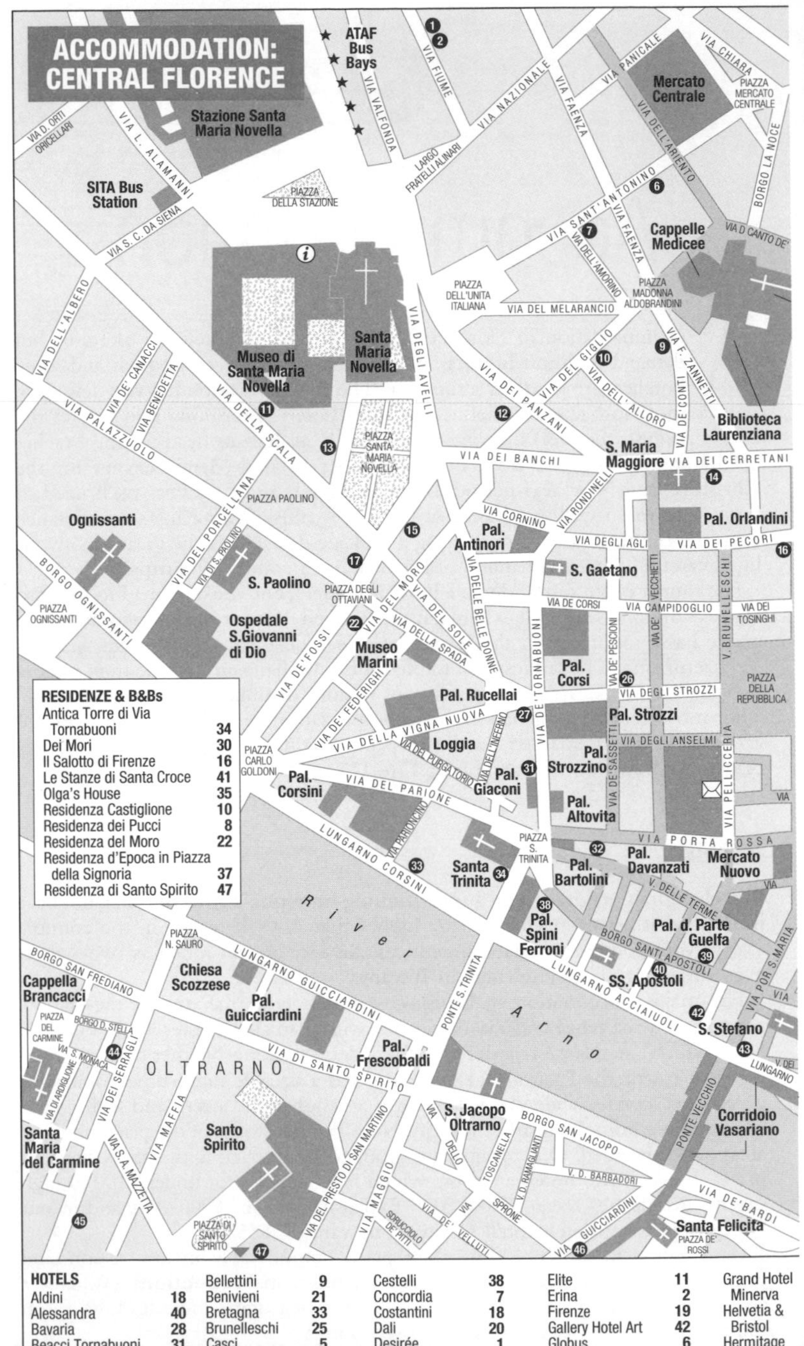


**RESIDENZE & B&Bs**

| | |
|---|---|
| Antica Torre di Via Tornabuoni | 34 |
| Dei Mori | 30 |
| Il Salotto di Firenze | 16 |
| Le Stanze di Santa Croce | 41 |
| Olga's House | 35 |
| Residenza Castiglione | 10 |
| Residenza dei Pucci | 8 |
| Residenza del Moro | 22 |
| Residenza d'Epoca in Piazza della Signoria | 37 |
| Residenza di Santo Spirito | 47 |

**HOTELS**

| | |
|---|---|
| Aldini | 18 |
| Alessandra | 40 |
| Bavaria | 28 |
| Beacci Tornabuoni | 31 |
| Bellettini | 9 |
| Benivieni | 21 |
| Bretagna | 33 |
| Brunelleschi | 25 |
| Casci | 5 |
| Cestelli | 38 |
| Concordia | 7 |
| Costantini | 18 |
| Dali | 20 |
| Desirée | 1 |
| Elite | 11 |
| Erina | 2 |
| Firenze | 19 |
| Gallery Hotel Art | 42 |
| Globus | 6 |
| Grand Hotel Minerva | |
| Helvetia & Bristol | |
| Hermitage | |

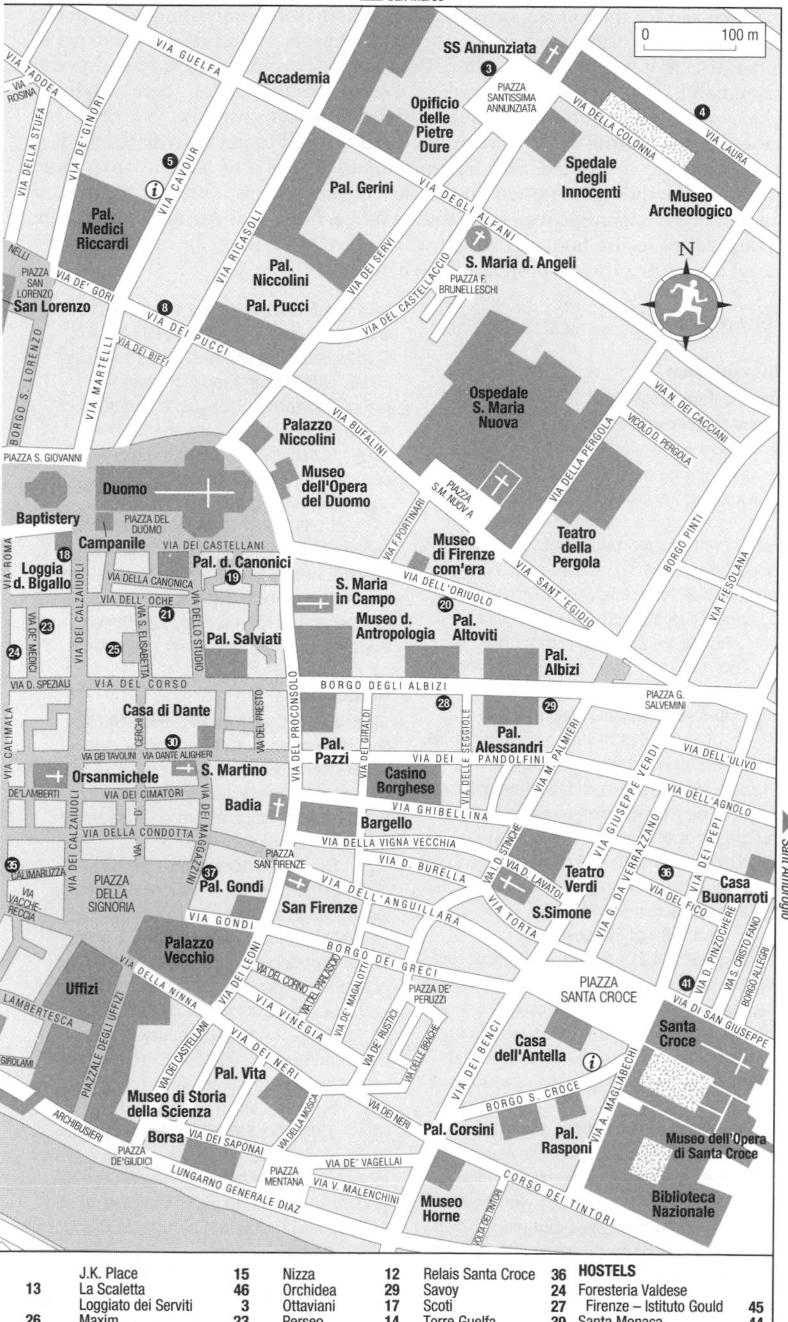


| | | | | | | | | | |
|---|---|---|---|---|---|---|---|---|---|
| | J.K. Place | 15 | Nizza | 12 | Relais Santa Croce | 36 | **HOSTELS** | |
| 13 | La Scaletta | 46 | Orchidea | 29 | Savoy | 24 | Foresteria Valdese | |
| | Loggiato dei Serviti | 3 | Ottaviani | 17 | Scoti | 27 | Firenze – Istituto Gould | 45 |
| 26 | Maxim | 23 | Perseo | 14 | Torre Guelfa | 39 | Santa Monaca | 44 |
| 43 | Morandi alla Crocetta | 4 | Porta Rossa | 32 | | | | |

Watch out for the hidden extra cost of breakfast: some hotels include it in the room price, but many don't; it's nearly always cheaper and usually nicer to eat in a bar or café if you have the option. Prices for rooms may also vary within the same hotel, so if the first price you're quoted seems high, ask if there's anything cheaper – rooms without a private bathroom always cost less. As ever in big cities, **single rooms** are at a premium: you'll do well to get away with less than two-thirds the cost of a double. The maximum cost of a room, plus any charge for breakfast, should be posted on the back of the door; if it isn't, or if you have any other complaints, contact the tourist office. Note that many hotels require a **deposit** to secure booking, which will involve sending credit card details; if a hotel demands a cash deposit, go elsewhere.



## City centre

### Inexpensive

**Bavaria Borgo degli Albizi 26 ⓣ055.234.0313, ⓦwww.hotelbavariafirenze.it.** A simple and decent one-star near the city centre (second floor, no lift) with just nine rooms, including some palatial chambers on the upper floor, and a couple of inexpensive rooms with shared bathroom. The hotel occupies part of a sixteenth-century *palazzo* built for a follower of Eleonora di Toledo. It has a range of prices: doubles with shower for €70–90, with bathroom for €80–110, and there are cheaper rooms with shared bathrooms as well. ❷

**Bretagna Lungarno Corsini 6 ⓣ055.289.618, ⓦwww.hotelbretagna.net.** This one-star riverfront hotel has a superb location and rococo-style breakfast and living rooms. The management has increased to six the number of rooms overlooking the Arno, and most of the 24 rooms are en suite with a/c. Doubles with shared bathroom €45–85, en suites €55–115. ❷

**Cestelli Borgo SS Apostoli 25 ⓣ055.214.213, ⓦwww.hotelcestelli.com.** Spotlessly maintained by its young Florentine-Japanese owners, this eight-roomed one-star occupies part of a house that once belonged to a minor Medici, whose bust adorns the facade. The rooms are a good size, and most are en suite. ❷

**Dali Via dell' Oriuolo 17 ⓣ055.234.0706, ⓦwww.hoteldali.com.** One of the least expensive one-star options close to the centre. The nine rooms, three with bath, are plain and rather basic, but the location – on the top floor of a *palazzo* built in 1492 – helps, as does the view from the back rooms of the giant magnolia in the garden. The friendly young owners speak good English. ❷

**Maxim entrances at Via dei Calzaiuoli 11 (lift) and Via de' Medici 4 (stairs) ⓣ055.217.474, ⓦwww.hotelmaximfirenze.it.** Few two-star hotels offer a better location than this friendly 26-room place just a minute from the Duomo. The doubles are good value at €70–110; all have a/c and the quietest look onto a central courtyard. ❷

**Orchidea Borgo degli Albizi 11 ⓣ055.248.0346, ⓦwww.hotelorchideaflorence.it.** On the first floor of a lovely twelfth-century building (said to have been the birthplace of Dante's wife), this place has seven big rooms, including three doubles, one with a shower in the room. ❷

### Moderate

**Aldini Via dei Calzaiuoli 13 ⓣ055.214.752, ⓦwww.hotelaldini.it.** A two-star at a very convenient address on the corner of Piazza Duomo. Of its fourteen somewhat functional rooms, all the doubles are en suite, as are some of the singles. ❸

**Alessandra Borgo Santi Apostoli 17 ⓣ055.283.438, ⓦwww.hotelalessandra.com.** One of the best and friendliest of the central two-stars, with 27 rooms (most with bathroom) occupying a sixteenth-century *palazzo* and furnished in a mixture of antique and modern styles. En-suite doubles are €150–190 – the more expensive ones overlook the river; you pay €110 for those with shared bathrooms. ❸

**Costantini Via dei Calzaiuoli 13 ⓣ055.213.995, ⓦwww.hotelcostantini.it.** This fourteen-room two-star shares a great location with the *Aldini*, on the city's main pedestrian street, close to the Duomo and Piazza della Signoria. En-suite doubles for €80–140. ❸

**Firenze Piazza dei Donati 4 ⓣ055.214.203, ⓦwww.albergofirenze.net.** A clean and central no-frills two-star hotel. It has 57 rooms, so there's a better chance of finding space here than in some of the smaller places. Most rooms are doubles; all have private bathrooms. Rooms on top floors enjoy a touch more daylight. 3

**Perseo Via de' Cerretani 1 ⓣ055.212.504, ⓦwww.hotelperseo.it.** Not one to pick if you need peace and quiet, but this twenty-room three-star couldn't be more central, and a radical renovation in 2006 has made it very attractive, with unfussy modern decor and furnishings in warm organic tones. In low season doubles cost around €100; in high season €160. 4

**Scoti Via de' Tornabuoni 7 ⓣ055.292.128, ⓦwww.hotelscoti.com.** Located opposite the Palazzo Strozzi, this is the best inexpensive option on a notoriously expensive street, with doubles from as low as €70 in off season, excluding breakfast. Just eleven rooms, all with bathrooms and all recently renovated. 3

**Torre Guelfa Borgo SS Apostoli 8 ⓣ055.239.6338, ⓦwww.hoteltorreguelfa.com.** Twenty tastefully furnished rooms are crammed onto the third floor of this ancient tower, the tallest private building in the city. Guests can enjoy the marvellous views all over the city from the small roof garden. There are also six cheaper doubles on the first floor (no TV and more noise from the road). Very charismatic (if slightly shabby in places), very popular, and quite pricey too – as much as €260 for the best room in high season (it has a small terrace), though a room on the first floor costs some €100 less. 4

### Expensive

**Beacci Tornabuoni Via de' Tornabuoni 3 ⓣ055.212.645, ⓦwww.tornabuonihotels.com.** With 28 rooms occupying the top two floors of a fifteenth-century *palazzo*, this is a beguilingly antiques-stuffed three-star hotel, perfectly placed on Florence's poshest shopping street. The roof garden is superb, especially in spring, when the jasmine is blossoming. A few more rooms are available in the adjoining *Residenza Tornabuoni* and *Relais Tornabuoni*. Doubles cost up to €300 in high season, but around half that amount in low season – and special offers are sometimes available on the website. 6

**Benivieni Via delle Oche 5 ⓣ055.238.2133, ⓦwww.hotelbenivieni.it.** This small, friendly and family-run three-star is situated between the Duomo and Piazza della Signoria, tucked away on a quiet backstreet. Fifteen smallish rooms are ranged around two floors of a former synagogue; the rooms on the upper floor are brighter but all are simple, modern and in perfect condition. Doubles usually cost around €220, but they sometimes have discounts. 5

**Hermitage Vicolo Marzio 1/Piazza del Pesce ⓣ055.287.216, ⓦwww.hermitagehotel.com.** Pre-booking is recommended at any time of year to secure one of the 28 rooms in this superbly located three-star hotel right next to the Ponte Vecchio, with unbeatable views from some rooms as well as from the flower-filled roof garden. The service is friendly and rooms are cosy, decorated with the odd antique flourish; bathrooms are small but nicely done. Double-glazing has eliminated the noise problems once suffered by the front rooms, and you'll need to book many months in advance to secure one of these. Rooms from the former *Archibusieri* hotel, now incorporated into the *Hermitage*, are slightly less appealing. Doubles (with jacuzzi) are around €250 in high season, but only half that in low season. 6

**Porta Rossa Via Porta Rossa 19 ⓣ055.287.551, ⓦwww.hotelportarossa.com.** Florence's most venerable three-star hotel, the 78-room *Porta Rossa* has been in business since the beginning of the nineteenth century and has hosted, among others, Byron and Stendhal. You come here for character and nineteenth-century ambience rather than luxurious modern touches, though the hotel should be looking rather more sleek after its year-long refurbishment. Doubles used to cost around €200 in summer, or around twice that for one of the two tower rooms; the tariffs will probably be a little higher when it reopens. 5

### Very expensive

**Brunelleschi Piazza Santa Elisabetta 3 ⓣ055.27.370, ⓦwww.hotelbrunelleschi.it.** Designed by leading architect Italo Gamberini, this four-star hotel is built around a Byzantine chapel and fifth-century tower. A small in-house museum displays Roman and other fragments found during building work. Decor is simple and stylish, with the original brick and stone offset by lots of wood. The 96 rooms and suites are spacious – the best, on the fourth floor, have views of the Duomo and Campanile.

The rack rate for a double is upwards of €380, but there are often special deals to be had. ❼

**Gallery Hotel Art** **Vicolo dell'Oro 5 ⓣ055.27.263, ⓦwww.lungarnohotels.com.** This immensely stylish four-star is unlike any other hotel in central Florence. A member of the Design Hotels group, it has a sleek, minimalist and hyper-modern look – lots of dark wood and neutral colours – and tasteful contemporary art displayed in the reception and all 74 rooms. There is a small but smart bar, a sushi restaurant and an attractive lounge with art-filled bookshelves and comfortable sofas. The location is perfect, in a small, quiet square ten seconds' walk from the Ponte Vecchio. Doubles are normally around €300–400, but special online promotions sometimes offer rooms for as little as €200. ❼

**Helvetia & Bristol** **Via dei Pescioni 2 ⓣ055.266.51, ⓦwww.royaldemeure.com.** In business since 1894 and very expensively refitted in the 1990s, this is one of Florence's very finest five-star hotels. The public spaces and 67 bedrooms and suites (each unique) are faultlessly designed, mixing antique furnishings and modern facilities – such as jacuzzis in many bathrooms – to create a style that evokes the Belle Epoque without being suffocatingly nostalgic or twee. If you're going to treat yourself, this is a leading contender. Doubles start at around €400, without breakfast. ❽

**Savoy** **Piazza della Repubblica 7 ⓣ055.27.351, ⓦwww.roccofortehotels.com.** The *Savoy* had become something of a decrepit old dowager before being taken in hand by the Rocco Forte group. Now it's once again one of the city's very best hotels, having been completely refurbished in discreetly luxurious modern style, with plenty of bare wood, stone-coloured fabrics and peat-coloured marble. And the location could not be more central. Basic doubles are around €300, but most are in the €350–500 range. ❼

## Santa Maria Novella district

### Inexpensive

**Elite** **Via della Scala 12 ⓣ055.215.395, ⓦwww.hotelelitefirenze.com.** A basic ten-room two-star run by one of the most pleasant managers in town. Most doubles have private bathrooms; quieter rooms are at the back. ❷

**Ottaviani** **Piazza degli Ottaviani 1 ⓣ055.239.6223, ⓔpensioneottaviani@hotmail.com.** The best of this one-star's twenty rooms (only two with private bathrooms) overlook Piazza Santa Maria Novella; others aren't so good, but still remain inexpensive and convenient. No credit cards. ❶

### Moderate

**Grand Hotel Minerva** **Piazza Santa Maria Novella 16 ⓣ055.27.230, ⓦwww.grandhotelminerva.com.** A big four-star with large rooms, many of them overlooking the piazza. The decor is fairly bland, but the location is good, and the bar and swimming pool on the roof are major pluses. Doubles cost as little as €150, but you're more likely to pay around €200 – still a very good price in this category. ❹

**Nizza** **Via del Giglio 5 ⓣ055.239.6897, ⓦwww.hotelnizza.com.** A smart eighteen-room family-run two star, with helpful staff and in a very central location. All rooms are en suite, and are better furnished and decorated than many in this category. In high season the maximum price is €140 for an en-suite double; in low season you might get a room for half that. ❸

### Very expensive

**J.K. Place** **Piazza Santa Maria Novella 7 ⓣ055.264.5181, ⓦwww.jkplace.com.** One of the newest and most appealing of Florence's designer hotels occupies a fine eighteenth-century building on Piazza Santa Maria Novella. *J.K. Place*'s big idea is to create a homely rather than hotel-like atmosphere, with a hostess rather than a receptionist, a bar from which you help yourself, and a communal breakfast table where you can chat with fellow guests. The twenty rooms bear designer Michele Bönan's elegant stamp, and have DVD players and flat-screen TVs. Doubles €350–500; the top-of-the-range Penthouse suite is €800. ❼

## Station and San Lorenzo district

### Inexpensive

**Erina** **Via Fiume 17 ⓣ055.288.294, ⓦwww.hotelerina.it.** A three-star hotel located on the third floor of an old *palazzo*, very close to the station. Has fourteen spacious and recently refurbished double rooms, which – if you book online and well in advance – cost less than €100 throughout the year, which makes the *Erina* one of the cheapest three-stars in the city. ❷

**Kursaal Ausonia Via Nazionale 24 ⓣ055.496.324, ⓦwww.kursonia.com.** Welcoming and recently refurbished three-star near the station, formed in 2007 by the merger of two formerly separate hotels. If you book online and well in advance, you can pick up a "superior" double for less than €100 in summer; the price of a "standard" room can go as low as €55 in off season. ❷

**Marcella Via Faenza 58 ⓣ055.213.232.** The furnishings are somewhat basic and miscellaneous, and it's quite a haul up to the third floor, but the staff at the one-star *Marcella* are welcoming and the seven bedrooms are clean and very inexpensive – as low as €50 in off season. No credit cards; midnight curfew. ❷

**Nazionale Via Nazionale 22 ⓣ055.238.2203, ⓦwww.nazionalehotel.it.** Completely overhauled in 2007, this small family-run one-star is equidistant from the train station and the San Lorenzo market. It's not exactly charismatic, but it's better than many at this end of the scale. Doubles with en-suite bathroom are €80–120 and singles start at a mere €50. ❸

**Nella Via Faenza 69 ⓣ055.265.4346, ⓦwww.hotelnella.net.** Small, tidy and cheap, much like the *Giovanna* at the same address (ⓣ055.238.1353). Both have just seven rooms each, some with private bathrooms. ❷

**Via Faenza 56** Several budget hotels are crammed into this address near the station – note there is no lift. On the top floor is the *Paola* (ⓣ055.213.682, ⓦwww.albergopaola.com), which is in effect a small hostel, with a four-bed en-suite room and four six-bed mini-dorms, all painted in bright colours (there's a lot of bright orange). Whichever you choose, you'll pay around €30 per person. On the same floor is the one-star *Merlini* (ⓣ055.212.848, ⓦwww.hotelmerlini.it; ❷), which has ten rooms, most with private bathrooms (€60–100; rooms without bathroom are €40–70). On the first floor you'll find the one-star *Armonia* (ⓣ055.211.146, ⓔarmonia1962@libero.it; ❷), which has seven rooms (none with private bathroom). Also on this floor is the two-star *Azzi* (ⓣ055.213.806, ⓦwww.hotelazzi.com; ❸), which has fifteen bedrooms and is by far the nicest place in the building, with garden views from most of its rooms (€80–130 per double).

### Moderate

**Bellettini Via dei Conti 7 ⓣ055.213.561, ⓦwww.hotelbellettini.com.** The warm welcome of owner Signora Gina counts for much in this 27-room two-star, close to San Lorenzo; so too do her copious breakfasts. Most of the simple rooms have private bathrooms and all have TVs and a/c. ❸

**Concordia Via dell'Amorino 14 ⓣ055.213.233, ⓦwww.albergoconcordia.it.** An extremely convenient first-floor hotel (no lift), located at the back of San Lorenzo church. There are sixteen rooms, all with private bathrooms. All the rooms have been given a warm, tastefully coloured look, as part of an upgrade to two-star status. ❸

**Desirée Via Fiume 20 ⓣ055.238.2382, ⓦwww.desireehotel.com.** Located one block east of the station, this two-star features stained-glass windows, simulated antique furniture and a bath in each of the eighteen rooms. There are better-situated hotels at this price, but it's nonetheless a reasonable choice. Doubles €80–140. ❸

**Globus Via Sant'Antonino 24 ⓣ055.211.062, ⓦwww.hotelglobus.com.** Formerly a one-star, the *Globus* has recently been drastically restyled (wenge furniture and natural tones throughout) and has consequently moved up two grades. The 23 a/c rooms start from as little as €70 in off season, rising to around €170 for the best room in peak season. ❹

## San Marco and Annunziata districts

### Moderate

**Casci Via Cavour 13 ⓣ055.211.686, ⓦwww.hotelcasci.com.** It would be hard to find a better two-star in central Florence than this 26-room hotel, which occupies part of a building in which Rossini once lived. Only two (soundproofed) rooms face the busy street: the rest are quiet, clean and neat, and they're well priced at around €150 for a double in high season (falling to €100 in off season). The welcome is warm and the owners are unfailingly helpful and courteous. The big buffet breakfast under the frescoed ceiling of the reception area is a major plus, as is free internet access. ❹

**Cimabue Via Bonifacio Lupi 7 ⓣ055.471.989, ⓦwww.hotelcimabue.it.** This sixteen-room three-star is in a somewhat remote location, but the family atmosphere is

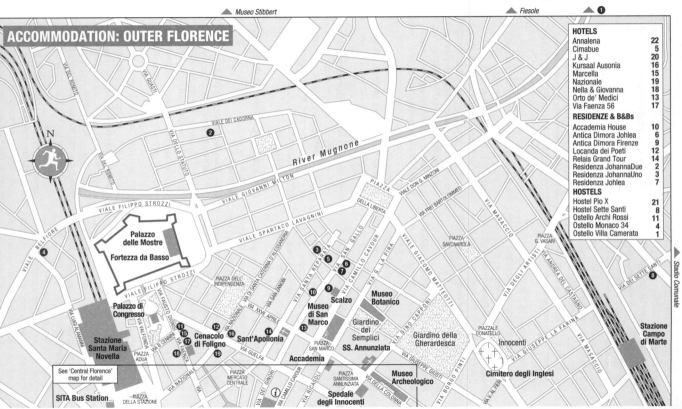

# ACCOMMODATION: OUTER FLORENCE

**HOTELS**

- Annalena 22
- Cimabue 5
- J & J 20
- Kursaal Ausonia 16
- Marcella 15
- Nazionale 19
- Nella & Giovanna 18
- Orto de' Medici 13
- Via Faenza 56 17

**RESIDENZE & B&Bs**

- Accademia House 10
- Antica Dimora Johlea 6
- Antica Dimora Firenze 9
- Locanda dei Poeti 12
- Relais Grand Tour 14
- Residenza JohannaDue 2
- Residenza JohannaUno 3
- Residenza Johlea 7

**HOSTELS**

- Hostel Pio X 21
- Hostel Sette Santi 8
- Ostello Archi Rossi 11
- Ostello Monaco 34 4
- Ostello Villa Camerata 1

Museo Stibbert
Fiesole
1
Prato & Pistoia
Stadio Comunale
N
VIA DEL ROMITO
VIA GUASTI
VIALE DEI CADORNA
VIA DELLO STATUTO
River Mugnone
VIALE GIOVANNI MILTON
VIALE FILIPPO STROZZI
VIALE BELFIORE
VIALE SPARTACO LAVAGNINI
PIAZZA DELLA LIBERTA
VIALE DON G. MINZONI
VIA FREI BARTOLOMMEO
VIA MASACCIO
PIAZZA SAVONAROLA
PIAZZA G. VASARI
VIA DEGLI ARTISTI
VIA ANDREA DEL CASTAGNO
VIA DEI SETTE SANTI
Palazzo delle Mostre
Fortezza da Basso
PIAZZA DELL' INDIPENDENZA
VIA DI SANTA CATERINA D'ALESSANDRIA
VIA SAN ZANOBI
VIA SANTA REPARATA
VIA SAN GALLO
VIA CAMILLO CAVOUR
VIA G. LA PIRA
VIALE GIACOMO MATTEOTTI
Museo Botanico
Scalzo
Museo di San Marco
Giardino dei Semplici
VIA GINO CAPPONI
Giardino della Gherardesca
PIAZZALE DONATELLO
Innocenti
VIA GIUSEPPE LA FARINA
Stazione Campo di Marte
Palazzo di Congresso
VIA FAUSTO DIONISI
VIA VALFONDA
VIA B CENNINI
VIA FAENZA
Cenacolo di Foligno
VIA NAZIONALE
VIA XXVII APRILE
Sant'Apollonia
VIA GUELFA
PIAZZA SAN MARCO
SS. Annunziata
Accademia
VIA GIUSEPPE GIUSTI
VIA BORGO PINTI
Cimitero degli Inglesi
VIA V. AL FIERI
VIA LUIGI ALAMANNI
Stazione Santa Maria Novella
PIAZZA ADUA
See 'Central Florence' map for detail
SITA Bus Station
PIAZZA DELLA STAZIONE
PIAZZA MERCATO CENTRALE
VIA DEI GINORI
VIA CAMILLO CAVOUR
VIA RICASOLI
PIAZZA SANTISSIMA ANNUNZIATA
VIA DELLA COLONNA
Museo Archeologico
Spedale degli Innocenti

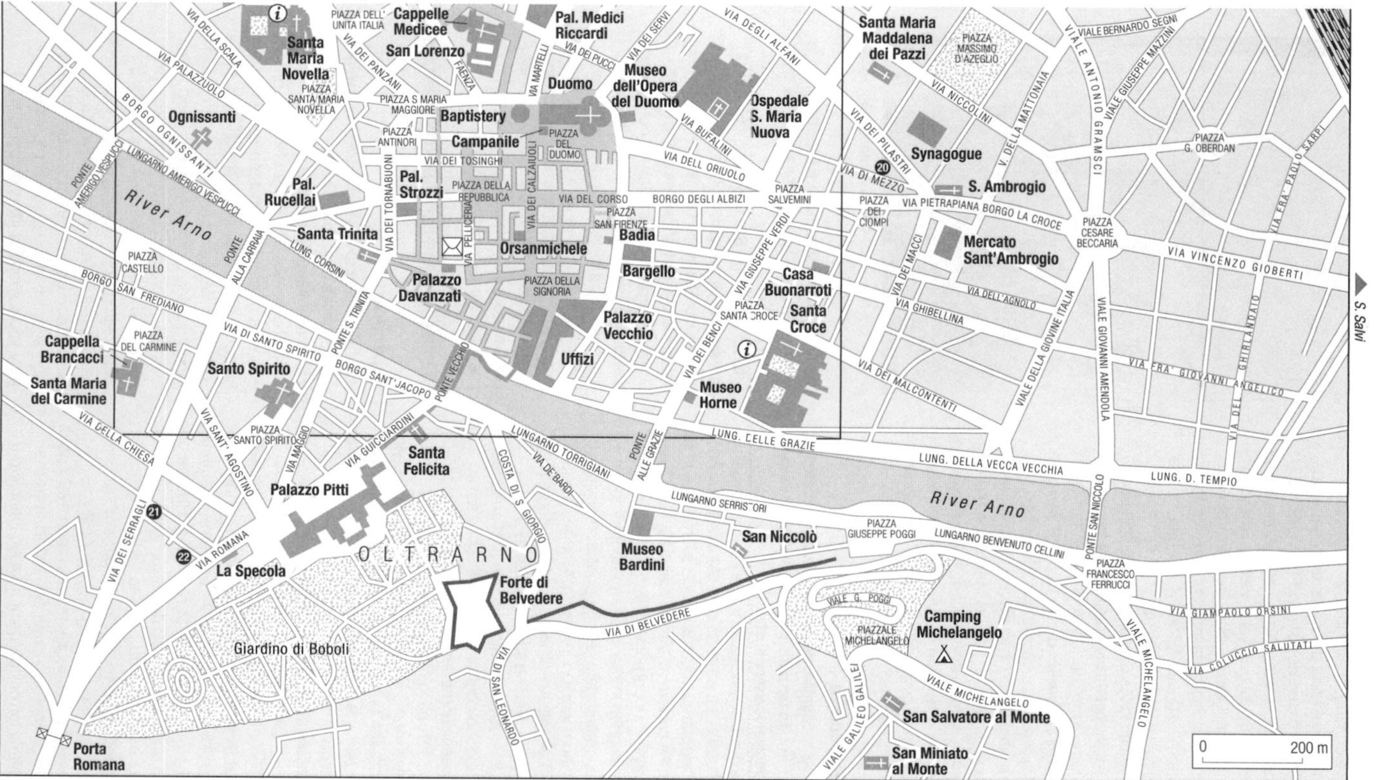
S. Salvi
200 m
Santa Maria Maddalena dei Pazzi
Synagogue
S. Ambrogio
Mercato Sant'Ambrogio
Piazza Massimo D'Azeglio
Viale Antonio Gramsci
Viale Giuseppe Mazzini
Viale Bernardo Segni
Piazza G. Oberdan
Via Fra' Paolo Sarpi
Via Vincenzo Gioberti
Via del Ghirlandaio
Via Fra' Giovanni Angelico
Piazza Cesare Beccaria
Viale Giovanni Amendola
Lung. D. Tempio
Via Giampaolo Orsini
Via Coluccio Salutati
Viale Michelangelo
Piazza Francesco Ferrucci
Ponte San Niccolo
Lungarno Benvenuto Cellini
Lung. della Vecca Vecchia
River Arno
Viale della Giovine Italia
Via dell'Agnolo
Via Ghibellina
Via dei Malcontenti
Via dei Macci
Via Pietrapiana
Borgo la Croce
V. della Mattonaia
Via Niccolini
Via dei Pilastri
Via di Mezzo
Piazza dei Ciompi
Camping Michelangelo
San Salvatore al Monte
San Miniato al Monte
Piazzale Michelangelo
Viale G. Poggi
Viale Galileo Galilei
Piazza Giuseppe Poggi
San Niccolò
Museo Bardini
Via di Belvedere
Forte di Belvedere
Via di San Leonardo
Costa di S Giorgio
Via de' Bardi
Lungarno Torrigiani
Ponte alle Grazie
Museo Horne
Santa Croce
Casa Buonarroti
Via Giuseppe Verdi
Via dei Benci
Piazza Salvemini
Ospedale S. Maria Nuova
Via degli Alfani
Via Bufalini
Via dell Oriuolo
Borgo degli Albizi
Museo dell'Opera del Duomo
Via dei Servi
Pal. Medici Riccardi
Via dei Pucci
Duomo
Piazza del Duomo
Via del Corso
Piazza San Firenze
Badia
Bargello
Palazzo Vecchio
Uffizi
Orsanmichele
Piazza della Signoria
Via dei Calzaiuoli
Via Martelli
Campanile
Baptistery
Cappelle Medicee
San Lorenzo
Faenza
Via dei Tosinghi
Piazza della Repubblica
Via Pellicceria
Palazzo Davanzati
Ponte Vecchio
Santa Felicita
Oltrarno
Via Guicciardini
Borgo Sant'Jacopo
Palazzo Pitti
Giardino di Boboli
Piazza dell' Unità Italia
Via dei Panzani
Piazza S Maria Maggiore
Piazza Antinori
Pal. Strozzi
Via dei Tornabuoni
Santa Maria Novella
Piazza Santa Maria Novella
Pal. Rucellai
Santa Trinita
Lung. Corsini
Ponte S. Trinita
Via Maggio
Via di Santo Spirito
Santo Spirito
Piazza Santo Spirito
Ponte alla Carraia
Via Sant' Agostino
La Specola
Via Romana
Ognissanti
Via della Scala
Via Palazzuolo
Borgo Ognissanti
Lungarno Amerigo Vespucci
Ponte Amerigo Vespucci
Piazza Castello
Borgo San Frediano
Piazza del Carmine
Cappella Brancacci
Santa Maria del Carmine
Via della Chiesa
Via dei Serragli
Porta Romana

welcoming, the rooms are immaculate and the breakfasts are more than generous. Some of the double and triple rooms have frescoed ceilings, and all are kitted out with antiques and classy fabrics. The smaller "Classic" doubles are around €160 in high season (€80 in low); the more luxurious "Liberty" doubles cost a maximum of €180. ④

**Panorama Via Cavour 60 ⓣ055.238.2043, ⓦwww.hotelpanorama.fi.it.** Taking its name from the top-floor veranda, which gives fine views of the city, the 31-room *Panorama* occupies two storeys of a nineteenth-century *palazzo* in the university area just north of San Marco, on the city's main north-running road. The two-star accommodation is somewhat functional, but the management is very friendly and the prices fair. ③



### Expensive

**Loggiato dei Serviti Piazza Santissima Annunziata 3 ⓣ055.289.592, ⓦwww.loggiatodeiservitihotel.it.** This elegant, extremely tasteful and well-priced three-star hotel is situated on one of Florence's most celebrated squares. Its 38 rooms (five in the new annexe at Via dei Servi 49) have been stylishly incorporated into a structure designed in the sixteenth century to accommodate Servite priests, many of whom worked in the orphanage opposite. Their relative plainness reflects something of the building's history, but all are decorated with fine fabrics and antiques, and look out either onto the piazza or peaceful gardens to the rear: top-floor rooms have glimpses of the Duomo. The five rooms in the annexe are similarly styled, but the building doesn't have the same charisma. Doubles in high season cost from around €200, but there are often special offers at around half that price. ⑤

**Morandi alla Crocetta Via Laura 50 ⓣ055.234.4747, ⓦwww.hotelmorandi.it.** An intimate three-star gem, whose small size and friendly welcome ensure a home-from-home atmosphere. Rooms are tastefully decorated with antiques and old prints, and vivid carpets laid on parquet floors. Two rooms have balconies opening onto a modest garden; the best room – with fresco fragments and medieval nooks and crannies – was converted from the site's former convent chapel. Doubles in

▲ Morandi alla Crocetta

high season cost around €230, but in winter there are sometimes offers as low as €120. ⑤

**Orto de' Medici Via San Gallo 30 ⓣ055.483.427, ⓦwww.ortodeimedici.it.** A 31-room frescoed and antique-furnished three-star, occupying a quiet and very handsome *palazzo* in the university area. Via San Gallo is not the most attractive street in Florence, but the hotel has been recently and impressively refurbished, and there is a nice breakfast terrace. Prices vary a lot with the seasons, ranging from less than €100 to around €250 in the busiest weeks; the best room has a balcony, overlooking the hotel's garden. ⑤

## Santa Croce and Sant'Ambrogio districts

### Expensive

**J & J Via di Mezzo 20 ⓣ055.263.121, ⓦwww.jandj.hotelinfirenze.com.** The bland exterior of this former fifteenth-century convent, located very close to Piazza Sant'Ambrogio, conceals a romantic nineteen-room four-star hotel. Some rooms are vast split-level affairs – but all have charm and are furnished with modern fittings, attractive fabrics and a few antiques. Common areas are decked with flowers, and retain frescoes and vaulted ceilings from the original building. In summer breakfast is served in the convent's lovely old cloister. Doubles from around €280 in high season; in the quietest months you may find a room at fifty percent less. ⑥

### Very expensive

**Relais Santa Croce Via Ghibellina 87 ⓣ055.234.2230 ⓦwww.relaisantacroce.com.** This magnificent five-star shares a lobby with the mind-blowingly expensive *Pinchiorri* restaurant, and is a similarly top-flight establishment. The grandiose public rooms are a very slick amalgam of the historic and the contemporary, with modern sofas set on acres of gleaming parquet, surrounded by eighteenth-century stucco panels. Contemporary and understated luxury prevails in the bedrooms. Doubles from around €500; the suites are in the "if you have to ask the price you can't afford it" category. ❽

## Oltrarno

### Moderate

**Annalena Via Romana 34 ⓣ055.222.402, ⓦwww.hotelannalena.it.** Situated a short way beyond Palazzo Pitti (and right by an entrance to the Bóboli gardens), this twenty-room three-star, once owned by the Medici, passed to a young Florentine noblewoman (Annalena) who retired from the world after a disastrous love affair and bequeathed the building to the Dominicans. The best rooms open onto a gallery with garden views, and a sprinkling of antiques lend a hint of old-world charm. Doubles cost around €175 in summer, but in low season they can drop to €75. ❹

**La Scaletta Via Guicciardini 13 ⓣ055.283.028, ⓦwww.lascaletta.com.** Some of the rooms in this tidy and recently refurbished sixteen-room two-star give views across to the Bóboli gardens; rooms on the Via Guiccardini side are double-glazed against the traffic. Drinks are served on the rooftop terraces, where you look across the Bóboli in one direction and the city in the other. All rooms are en suite and nicely decorated in cool milky tones. Low-season minimum price is about half of high-season maximum. ❹

## Fiesole

**Villa San Michele Via Doccia 4 ⓣ055.567.8200, ⓦwww.villasanmichele.orient-express.com.** The astronomically expensive *Villa San Michele* is one of Italy's most sybaritic hotels. Occupying a former monastery that was designed in part by Michelangelo, it's surrounded by gorgeous parkland, offers terrific views of Florence, and boasts a great restaurant. A once-in-a-lifetime kind of place. Doubles from around €900. ❽

# Affitacamere and residenze

To be classified as a hotel in Florence, a building has to have a minimum of seven bedrooms. Places with fewer rooms operate under the title *affitacamere* ("rooms for rent") or *residenze d'epoca* (if occupying a historic building) – though, confusingly, a *residenze d'epoca* might have as many as a dozen rooms. Some *affitacamere* are nothing more than a couple of rooms in a private house (and, though calling themselves "bed and breakfast", may not actually offer breakfast), but several – and most *residenze d'epoca* – are in effect small hotels in all but name, and some of the city's *residenze d'epoca* are among the most charismatic accommodation you can find in Florence. What follows is our pick of the small-scale places to stay; for full listings of accredited *affitacamere*, *residenze* and all other types of accommodation, go to ⓦwww.firenzeturismo.it. One thing to bear in mind: like the budget hotels, *affitacamere* are often on the upper floors of large buildings, and usually can be reached only by stairs.

## City Centre

**Antica Torre di Via Tornabuoni Via Tornabuoni 1 ⓣ055.265.816, ⓦwww.tornabuoni1.com.** Arranged over the top three floors of a thirteenth-century tower virtually next door to the church of Santa Trìnita, this high-class *residenza* offers twelve rooms (more are planned) for €150–300. The rooms are somewhat bland, but they are generally spacious and several have private terraces; the main attraction, though, is the shared terrace on the roof, which gives a fabulous 360° vista of the city. ❼

**Dei Mori Via Dante Alighieri 12 ⓣ055.211.438, ⓦwww.deimori.it.** *Dei Mori* was one of the first B&Bs to open in Florence, and is still one of the best. Five rooms, all with bathroom (though some of the bathrooms are across the hall, rather than en suite), for €80–120, with discounts for stays of more than three days. ❸

**Il Salotto di Firenze Via Roma 6 ⓣ055.218.347, ⓦwww.ilsalottodifirenze.it.** Six well-appointed rooms, four of them doubles (three overlooking Piazza del Duomo). Not a good choice if you're a light sleeper, but the standard of accommodation is high, prices low and the location absolutely central. ❸

**Olga's House Via Calimaruzza 4 ⓣ330.883.421, ⓦwww.olgashouse.com.** *Olga's House* is in effect a four-room micro-hotel. The sleek modern decor is a refreshing change from the usual bygone style, and the owners are extremely pleasant. Some might find the eighty-step staircase a bit of a slog, though. Doubles €80–160. ❹

**Residenza d'Epoca in Piazza della Signoria Via dei Magazzini 2 ⓣ055.239.9546, ⓦwww.inpiazzadellasignoria.com.** This luxurious *residenza d'epoca* has ten spacious bedrooms, several of them giving a view of the piazza. The style is antique, but tastefully restrained, and the management is very friendly. Doubles €200–280. ❻

## Santa Maria Novella district

**Residenza del Moro Via del Moro 15 ⓣ055.264.8494, ⓦwww.residenzadelmoro.com.** Occupying the *piano nobile* of a fresco- and stucco-laden sixteenth-century *palazzo*, this must be the most spectacular *residenza* in the city. The eleven suites and rooms have canopied beds with cashmere blankets, marble-clad bathrooms and expensive fabrics all over the place – even big-name modern art on the walls. There's a very nice garden too. Prices are, unsurprisingly, sky-high: €400–1000. ❽

## San Lorenzo district

**Locanda dei Poeti Via Guelfa 74 ⓣ055.488.701, ⓦwww.locandadeipoeti.com.** Run by an actor and his partner, this small B&B has a poetry theme, as you might have guessed. Various parts of the building are dedicated to different poets, and poems are written on some of the walls. The wackiness doesn't extend to the four bedrooms, however, which are individually decorated in styles ranging from pseudo-antique to vaguely Japanese. Doubles €90–160. ❹

**Relais Grand Tour Via Santa Reparata 21 ⓣ055.283.955, ⓦwww.florencegrandtour.com.** The very hospitable owners have done a great job in turning two floors of this old *palazzo* into a superb guesthouse, with three large bedrooms (around €100) on the second floor and three suites (around €150) on the floor above. Each room's decor is unique – one is replete with Neapolitan majolica tiles, another has a gold-leaf wooden ceiling, and a third is loaded with mirrors ("suitable for a couple", as the website has it). ❸

**Residenza Castiglioni Via del Giglio 8 ⓣ055.239.6013, ⓦwww.residenzacastiglioni.com.** Run by the same team as runs the *Torre Guelfa*, this is a discreet and hugely stylish hideaway that has just six spacious en-suite doubles (three of them frescoed), on the second floor of a *palazzo* very close to San Lorenzo church. Doubles €80–180. ❹

**Residenza dei Pucci Via dei Pucci 9 ⓣ055.264.314, ⓦwww.residenzadeipucci.com.** Located very close to the Duomo, the *Residenze dei Pucci* occupies a fine nineteenth-century town house and offers six beautifully furnished and decorated rooms. Doubles €80–170. ❹

## San Marco and Annunziata districts

**Accademia House Via San Gallo 61 ⓣ055.484.879, ⓦwww.accademiahouse.com.** This B&B has three rooms ("modern", "antique" and "classic") in a beautifully restored sixteenth-century building. Doubles as low as €60 in low season. ❸

**Residenza Johanna Uno Via Bonifacio Lupi 14 ⓣ055.481.896, ⓦwww.johanna.it.** A genteel place that feels very much a "residence" rather than a hotel, hidden away in an unmarked apartment building in a very quiet, leafy corner of the city, 5min walk north of San Marco; ring the bell on the brass plaque by the wrought-iron gates. Rooms are cosy and well kept, there are books and magazines, and the two *signore* who run the place are as friendly and helpful as you could hope for. The very similar *Residenza Johanna Due* (ⓣ055.473.377; same website) is located further from the main sights, at Via Cinque Giornate 12, to the north of the Fortezza da Basso. *Johanna Uno* costs in the region of €100–130 a night; *Due* is a little cheaper. ❸

**Residenza Johlea Via San Gallo 76** ⓣ**055.463.3292,** ⓦ**www.johanna.it**. Another venture from the people who created the nearby *Residenza Johanna*, offering the same low-cost, high-comfort package, with the same level of hospitality. At nearby Via San Gallo 80 you'll find the *Antica Dimora Johlea* (ⓣ055.461.185; same website), which is a somewhat plusher version of the *Residenza*, with deluxe doubles for around €125–150 and a nice roof terrace. The same team runs the similarly upmarket *Antica Dimora Firenze* at Via San Gallo 72 (ⓣ055.462.7296, ⓦwww.anticadimorafirenze.it), which has six very comfortable rooms (some with four-poster beds) in the same price range as the *Dimora Johlea*. ❸

## Santa Croce district

**Le Stanze di Santa Croce Via delle Pinzochere 6** ⓣ**347.259.3010,** ⓦ**www.viapinzochere6.it.** This excellent B&B has four comfortable and brightly decorated rooms (though one of them has skylights rather than windows) and very hospitable owners. ❹

## Oltrarno

**Residenza Santo Spirito Piazza Santo Spirito 9** ⓣ**055.265.8376,** ⓦ**www.residenzasspirito.com.** A well-presented B&B with two large double rooms (both with fantastic frescoed ceilings, and both overlooking the piazza) and a two-roomed suite. The doubles cost around €120–150; the suite is about €100 more. ❸



# Hostels

Florence has only a handful of **hostels** and the best of these is some distance from the centre. To help matters a little, there are a number of places run by religious bodies, plus student institutions which provide beds for non-natives at the city universities. Out of term time (June–Oct) some of these places are open to young tourists, and a few even have accommodation throughout the year. In addition to the houses listed below, there are also a number of *Case dello Studente*, which are run by the university authorities and occasionally made available to visitors; for latest information on these, ask at the tourist office.

**Foresteria Valdese Firenze – Istituto Gould Via dei Serragli 49** ⓣ**055.212.576,** ⓦ**www.istitutogould.it.** Run by the Waldensian church, this hostel-cum-evangelical college occupies part of a former seventeenth-century *palazzo* (the doorbell is easily missed). The hostel's 97 beds are extremely popular, so it's wise to book in advance, especially during the academic year. Street-front rooms can be noisy (rear rooms are better – and a little more expensive) but the old courtyard, terracotta floors and stone staircases provide atmosphere throughout. Open for check-in Mon–Fri 8.45am–1pm & 3–7.30pm, Sat 9am–1.30pm & 2.30–6pm, but closed Sun. Singles €44; doubles €56–64; triples €75; quads €84–92. Nearly all rooms have private bathroom. No curfew.

**Hostel Pio X Via dei Serragli 106** ⓣ**055.225.044,** ⓦ**www.hostelpiox.it.** One of the cheapest options in town, often booked up by school groups. Don't be put off by the huge picture of Pope Pius X at the top of the steps; the management is friendly and the atmosphere relaxed. Get there by 9am, though, as the 64 beds are quickly taken. Showers are free. Beds in doubles, triples, quads and quintuples cost around €18 per person, a few euros more with en-suite bathrooms; minimum stay two nights, maximum five. Open all day throughout the year; midnight curfew; no reservations by phone.

**Hostel Sette Santi Viale dei Mille 11** ⓣ**055.504.8452,** ⓦ**www.7santi.com.** This new hostel occupies a converted convent on a main road just over 1km northeast of the city centre. There are 160 beds in total, some in dorms, but with 32 private en-suite rooms, plus ten others with shower and nineteen with shared bath on the same floor. Sheets and towels are provided, as is a buffet breakfast. Doubles €40–60, dorm beds around €20. Bus #17 from the station goes past the door; #11 takes you to within one block.

**Ostello Archi Rossi Via Faenza 94r** ⓣ**055.290.804,** ⓦ**www.hostelarchirossi.com.** A 5min walk from the train station, this privately owned guesthouse/hostel is spotlessly clean and decorated with guests' wall-paintings and graffiti. It's popular – the

96 places fill up quickly – and has a pleasant garden and terrace. Evening meals are available at extra cost; there's a spacious dining room with satellite TV. Single rooms around €30. Dorm beds €20–25, depending on size of dorm (4–9 beds) and whether or not there's an internal bathroom; all prices include breakfast and 30min internet time. Disabled access rooms available. Curfew at 2am for dorms.

**Ostello Monaco 34** **Via Guido Monaco 34 ⓣ055.321.018, ⓦwww.ostellomonaco34.com.** This well-managed and smart private hostel has fifty beds in eighteen rooms spread over five floors, with two bathrooms, a living room and a kitchen on each floor; wi-fi and TVs in all rooms add to the attractiveness of the package. The big downside is that the locale – on a very busy main road some way to the north of the train station – is very far from ideal. Around €20–50 per person per night.

**Ostello Villa Camerata** **Viale Augusto Righi 2–4 ⓣ055.601.451, ⓦwww.ostellionline.org.** An HI hostel tucked away in a beautiful park to the northeast of the city, 5km from Santa Maria Novella station. This is one of Europe's most attractive hostels, a sixteenth-century house with frescoed ceilings, fronted by lemon trees in terracotta pots. There are 322 dorm places, and a few family rooms. Breakfast and sheets are included, but there are no kitchen facilities; optional supper costs about €10. Films in English are shown every night. Dorm beds €20; two/three/four-bed rooms €32.50/25/22 per person. Doors open at 2pm; if you'll arrive later, call ahead to make sure there's space – bookings by email or fax only. Midnight curfew. Bus #17b from the train station takes about 30min.

**Santa Monaca** **Via Santa Monaca 6 ⓣ055.268.338, ⓦwww.ostello.it.** Privately owned hostel in Oltrarno, close to Santa Maria del Carmine. Has 115 beds, arranged in a dozen dorms with between four and twenty beds. Kitchen facilities (no utensils), washing machines, free hot showers and a useful noticeboard with information on lifts and onward travel. Dorm beds €17–20; credit cards accepted. Open for check-in 6am–2am. Curfew 2am, and the bedrooms have to be vacated between 10am and 2pm. It's a 15min walk from the station, or take bus #11, #36 or #37 to the second stop after the bridge.

## Campsites

The situation for **camping** isn't very good: in summer, you're almost certain to find that the only available spaces are at the *Area di Sosta*, an emergency accommodation area sometimes set aside by the city authorities, which usually amounts to a patch of ground sheltered by a rudimentary roof, with a shower block attached. Contact the tourist offices for details, if any, of the current location.

**Camping Internazionale Firenze** **Via San Cristofano 2 ⓣ055.237.4704, ⓦwww.florencecamping.com.** Located 5km south of Florence in the hills a short distance to the south of the Certosa di Galluzzo, this well-equipped three-star site offers four-berth bungalows (around €30 per person per night) in addition to places for tents. Other facilities include an open-air pool, kitchen facilities, a play area for kids, and an internet point. Take #37 bus from the station – ask for the "Bottai" stop. Open all year.

**Camping Michelangelo** **Viale Michelangelo 80 ⓣ055.681.1977, ⓦwww.ecvacanze.it.** A 240-pitch site that's always crowded, owing to its superb hillside location in an olive grove overlooking the city centre. Kitchen facilities and well-stocked, if expensive, shop nearby. Take #13 bus from the station. Open April–Oct.

**Camping Panoramico** **Via Peramondo 1, Fiesole ⓣ055.559.069, ⓦwww.florencecamping.com.** Located in Fiesole, a 15min ride on bus #7 from Florence train station, this 120-pitch three-star site is as slick as *Camping Internazionale*, with a bar, restaurant, pool and small supermarket. Open all year.

**Villa Camerata** **Viale Augusto Righi 2–4 ⓣ055.601.451, ⓦwww.ostellionline.org.** Basic 55-pitch all-year site in the grounds of the *Villa Camerata* HI hostel.

9

# Eating and drinking



As you'd expect in a major tourist city, Florence has plenty of **cafés, bars and restaurants** – but since a large number of them are aimed squarely at visitors, standards are often patchy. Some of the locals will swear there's scarcely a single genuine Tuscan place left in the Tuscan capital – an exaggeration, of course, but a reflection of a general feeling that too much has been lost to tourism. Yet the situation is nowhere near as bad as some reports would have it: in fact, it's been improving in recent years, with the appearance of several stylish and good-value restaurants, alongside some superb wine bars. As a general rule, quality and value increase the further you go from Piazza della Signoria and Piazza del Duomo, and there are several eateries in those hotspots that should be avoided at all costs. But even here, right in the thick of the crowds, there are some genuinely Florentine places to eat and drink.

## Restaurants

In Italian gastronomic circles, **Florentine cuisine** is accorded almost as much reverence as Florentine art, yet Florentine food has always been characterized by modest raw materials and simple technique: beefsteak (*bistecca*), tripe (*trippa*) and liver (*fegato*) are typical ingredients, while grilling (*alla Fiorentina*) is a favoured method of preparation. It's an unpretentious style that clearly shows its peasant origins, and on every menu you'll find dishes that could have been found on any Tuscan farmer's table hundreds of years ago, such as white beans (*fagioli*), served either on their own, garnished with liberal quantities of olive oil, or as the basis of such dishes as *ribollita*.

There aren't many decent **restaurants** where you can get away with spending less than €30 per person for three courses excluding wine, although Florence does have a few good **low-budget places**, and even the simplest trattoria should offer *bistecca alla Fiorentina* – though note that this dish is priced per hundred grams, so your bill will be considerably higher than the figure written on the menu. And, of course, if your budget is tight, there's always the option of a pizzeria: Florence has several very good ones.

The restaurants are organized by area. Very roughly, the cheapest places tend to be near the station and San Lorenzo market, while the main concentrations of mid-range and top-class restaurants are around Santa Croce and Sant'Ambrogio and over in the Oltrarno. Any place displaying the **Slow Food** sign is likely to be good; founded in 1986, the Slow Food movement promotes the use of fresh local food and well-executed cooking.

Many restaurants are **closed on Sunday**, so if you want to be sure of a table it's always a good idea to make a reservation for that night. In high season it's a

## Snacks and picnic supplies

If you want to put together a picnic, an obvious place to shop is the **Mercato Centrale** by San Lorenzo church (Mon–Sat 7am–2pm, plus Sat 4–8pm in winter), which offers a bewildering variety of bread, ham, cheese, fruit, wine and ready-made sandwiches. The **Mercato Sant'Ambrogio** over by Santa Croce (Mon–Fri 7am–2pm) is smaller but of comparable quality. For a hearty sit-down lunchtime snack, each of the two markets has an excellent *tavola calda*, serving meatballs, pasta, stews, soups and sandwiches: *Nerbone* (Mon–Sat 7am–2pm) in the Mercato Centrale, and *Tavola Calda da Rocco* (Mon–Sat noon–2.30pm), in the Mercato di Sant'Ambrogio.

Every district has its **alimentari**, which in addition to selling the choicest Tuscan produce will often make sandwiches to order. For great local produce, you can't beat these three *alimentari*:'Ino, very close to the Uffizi at Via de' Georgofili 3–7r; Mariano, near Santa Maria Novella at Via del Parione 19r; and Olio e Convivium, at Via Santo Spirito 4, in Oltrarno. Nearly all **wine** bars sell bottles to take away, but you'll get a far better selection at a specialist shop such as Millesimi, at Borgo Tegolaio 35r, or Obsequium, at Borgo San Jacopo 17 – they're both in Oltrarno. Chocoholics should check out *Vestri*, at Borgo degli Albizi 11r, which offers deliciously thick **chocolate** to drink (hot or cold depending on the season) and a mouth-watering array of chocolate products, including ice cream.

If you really want to go native, you could join the throng of office workers around the **tripe** stall in Piazza dei Cimatori (Mon–Fri 8.30am–8.30pm; closed four weeks in July/Aug). Its speciality is the local delicacy called *lampredotto*: hot tripe served in a bun with a spicy sauce. (Or rather, two cuts of tripe – *gala*, famed for its delicate, pink-crested ridges and supposedly exquisite taste, and the fattier, heavier *spannocchia*.) The stall also sells wine, so you can wash the taste away should you realize you've made a horrible mistake. There's a similar operation – Da Sergio e Pierpaolo – parked outside the *Cibrèo* restaurant in Via de' Macci, close to the Sant'Ambrogio market (Mon–Sat 7.15am–3pm).

good idea to reserve a table on any night of the week. And bear in mind that simple meals – not just snacks – are served in many Florentine bars, so if you're exploring a particular area of the city and fancy a quick bite to eat rather than a full-blown restaurant meal, take a look at the relevant section in the "Cafés and bars" and "Wine bars" listings on p.193.

### Piazza della Signoria

The listings in this section are marked on the map on p.63.

**Antico Fattore Via Lambertesca 1–3r ⓣ055 .288.975.** Simple Tuscan dishes dominate the menu, and the soups are particularly good. The nearest thing you'll find to a genuine trattoria within a short radius of the Uffizi (mains cost around €10–14), though it's a tad grander than it used to be before the refurbishment that was needed after the 1993 Uffizi bombing, which badly damaged the place. Mon–Sat 12.15–3pm & 7.15–10.30pm; closed Aug.

**Da Ganino Piazza dei Cimatori 4r, off Via Dante Alighieri ⓣ055.214.125.** One of only a handful of recommendable places close to the Signoria. Produces good home-made pasta and desserts, though the prices reflect the locale as much as the quality of the kitchen – mains from €10. In summer, when tables are moved out onto the tiny square, it's essential to book. Mon–Sat 7pm–1am.

**Gustavino Via della Condotta 37r ⓣ055.239.9806, ⓦwww.gustavino.it.** With its steel chairs and glass-topped tables, this *enoteca con cucina* is the antithesis of the faux-rustic style that's still prevalent in Florence. Some might find it a bit too clinical, but it has a fine selection of wines, and the kitchen (which is on full view, both from the tables and from the street) turns out some very interesting dishes – such as black *tagliolini* with sea urchin and zucchini-flower pesto. Main courses are in the region of €20–25. Less pricey snacks and light meals are offered at its excellent wine shop next door, called *Canova*. *Gustavino* is open daily 7.30–11.30pm, plus Sat & Sun 12.30–3pm; *Canova* is open daily noon–11.30pm.

## West of the centre

The listings in this section are marked on the map on pp.90–91.

**Belle Donne Via delle Belle Donne 16r.** A tiny, convivial, faux-rustic trattoria, where you sit elbow-to-elbow on bare benches and stools, under swags of foliage, drinking your wine from a tumbler. Not a place to linger, but it's honest food, cheerfully presented at honest prices (main courses around €10), and serves up seasonal specialities such as *baccelli* (raw broad beans in their pods) with pecorino. Daily noon–3pm & 7–11pm; closed Aug.

**Coco Lezzone Via del Parioncino 26r, corner of Via del Purgatorio ☎055.287.178.** Stumble on this backstreet place and you'd swear you'd found one of the great old-world Florentine *trattorie*. The prices are moderate (three courses for around €35), the food is sometimes good and sometimes not, and the service is frequently offhand – this place has been fashionable for so long that the proprietors often seem to think they don't need to make an effort any more. Mon & Wed–Sat noon–2.30pm & 7–10pm, Tues noon–2.30pm; closed mid-July to mid-Aug.

**Hostaria Bibendum Via dei Pescioni 2.** Belle Epoque–styled restaurant/bar in the same relaxed deluxe style as the *Helvetia & Bristol* hotel to which it's attached. Good wine list, excellent "H&B" cocktails and an interesting menu that's strong on fish and has an excellent dish of cheeses and truffled honey. It's expensive if you go à la carte (main courses around €30), but offers a fine set lunch at €25, coffee included. Kitchen open 11am–2.30pm & 7.30–10.30pm; bar open until 1am.

**Il Contadino Via Palazzuolo 71r.** Small, popular place with simple black-and-white interior and fascinating large photos of old Florence on the walls. Fast and friendly service, shared tables (no booking), and very cheap but good fare: the three-course lunch and dinner menu costs a mere €10. No written menu: the four or so choices for each course are recited rapidly. Mon–Fri noon–9.30pm.

**Il Latini Via dei Palchetti 6r ☎055.210.916.** Once a trattoria of the old school, the quasi-legendary *Latini* is now something of a caricature of itself. It still looks the part – hams hanging from the ceiling, family photos on the wall, simple tables and old rush chairs. Food quality, though, is often no better than average, whereas prices are above those of most comparable *trattorie* – around €40 per head. Old regulars still eat here, but you'll find the queues in the evenings are full of foreigners. And there's always a queue, as bookings aren't taken in the evening. Tues–Sun 12.30–2.30pm & 6–10.30pm.

**La Spada Via della Spada 62r ☎055.218.757.** This very congenial *rosticceria* specializes in plain roast meats, but also does some excellent pasta dishes. One of the best-value places to eat in the centre of the city – you'll eat well for around €20. Daily noon–3pm & 6–10.30pm.

**Marione Via della Spada 27r ☎055.214.756.** Simple, good-value Tuscan cooking, at prices that are a pleasant surprise for this location, a stone's throw from Via Tornabuoni. Mains from just €6. Daily noon–3pm & 7–11.30pm. Closed first two weeks of Aug.

**Oliviero Via delle Terme 51r ☎055.240.618.** *Oliviero* has a welcoming and old-fashioned feel – something like an Italian restaurant of the 1960s – and the menu, though predominantly Tuscan, includes dishes from other regions of Italy. Fresh fish, when available, tends to feature strongly – something of a rarity in Florence. It's not inexpensive, but neither is it overpriced for cooking of this calibre: expect to pay upwards of €50, without wine. Mon–Sat 7pm–midnight. Closed Aug.

## North of the centre

The listings in this section are marked on the map on pp.108–109.

**Da Mario Via Rosina 2r ☎055.218.550.** Located very close to the Mercato Centrale, *Da Mario* has probably been packed out every lunchtime since the Colsi family started running the place in 1953. For earthy Florentine cooking at very low prices, there's nowhere better. It's just a pity it isn't open in the evenings. Mon–Sat noon–3.30pm; closed most of Aug.

**La Lampara Via Nazionale 36r ☎055.215.164.** The narrow entrance to this trattoria-pizzeria is deceptive: this is a huge place that goes back and back and has a garden terrace, too, at the rear. Don't be put off by the multilingual menus: the food is good, the prices moderate and the waiters attentive. Daily noon–midnight.

**Oliandolo** **Via Ricasoli 38–40r** Ⓣ**055.211.296.** A small, fast and very cheap spot (dishes from €5) that's extremely popular with locals at lunchtime – you'll probably have to queue if you come after 12.30pm. Good roast pork and beans, and excellent baked cheesecake. Mon–Sat 8am–6pm.

**Palle d'Oro** **Via Sant'Antonino 43r** Ⓣ**055.288.383.** Close to San Lorenzo market, this is the plainest possible type of trattoria, serving very good fare at very good prices – there are plenty of main courses for less than €10. Besides full meals, they do sandwiches to take away. Mon–Sat noon–2.30pm & 6.30–9.45pm.

**Zà-Zà** **Piazza del Mercato Centrale 26r** Ⓣ**055.210.756,** Ⓦ**www.trattoriazaza.it.** In business for more than thirty years, *Zà-Zà* is one of the best of several *trattorie* close to the Mercato Centrale. In recent years it has raised its profile to the extent that booking is virtually obligatory in summer. The interior is dark, stone-walled and brick-arched, with a handful of tables – though in summer there are plenty more tables on the outside terraces. There's usually a set-price menu for around €15 that offers a choice of three or four pastas and main courses; otherwise you'll pay around €30 per head. The omelette with a creamy truffle sauce is exquisite and the mixed antipasti are generous. Daily 11am–11pm; closed Aug.

## East of the centre

The listings in this section are marked on the map on p.134.

**Acqua al Due** **Via dell'Acqua 2r/Via della Vigna Vecchia 40r** Ⓣ**055.284.170.** Always packed (often with foreigners but with Italians too), chiefly on account of its offbeat decor, lively atmosphere and *assaggio di primi* – a succession of pasta dishes shared by everyone at the table. A three-course meal, excluding wine, should cost around €40. Daily 7pm–1am.

**Baldoria** **Via San Giuseppe 18r.** An offshoot of the excellent *Baldovino* across the road, this bright modern bistro has a bar area out front, where you can sample some top-quality wine, and a small dining room at the back (plus a small terrace) for those who prefer to sit down for a quick light meal or pizza. Summer daily noon–midnight; winter Tues–Sun noon–4pm & 6pm–midnight.

**Baldovino** **Via San Giuseppe 22r** Ⓣ**055.241.773,** Ⓦ**www.baldovino.com.** This superb place, run by an imaginative Scottish couple, is renowned above all for its pizzas (made in a wood-fired oven according to Neapolitan principles), but the main menu (which changes monthly) is full of good Tuscan and Italian dishes, with mains around €12–17 – although you pay the usual premium for the succulent *bistecca alla Fiorentina*. Portions are very generous. April–Oct daily 11.30am–2.30pm & 7–11.30pm; rest of year closed Mon.

**Boccadama** **Piazza Santa Croce 25–26r** Ⓣ**055.243.640.** *Boccadama* used to function chiefly as a wine bar, offering vintages from all over the country and a good selection of snacks. Nowadays, although some people stop here just for a drink, it's essentially a restaurant – not one of Florence's very best, but certainly the top choice on Piazza Santa Croce. You'll pay about €30 a head. Summer daily 8am–midnight; winter closes 3pm Mon, 11pm all other days.

**Cibrèo** **Via de' Macci 118r** Ⓣ**055.234.1100.** Fabio Picchi's *Cibrèo* restaurant – which has now spawned a café, trattoria and a canteen-cum-theatre – is the first Florentine port-of-call for many foodies, having achieved fame well beyond the city. The recipe for success is simple: superb food with a creative take on Tuscan classics, in a tasteful dining room with friendly and professional service. You'll need to book days in advance for a table in the main part of the restaurant, but next door there's a small, somewhat spartan and sometimes overly busy trattoria section (*Cibreino*) where the food is virtually the same (though the menu is smaller), no bookings are taken and the prices are much lower: around €15 for the main course, as opposed to €35 in the restaurant. Both *Cibrèo* and *Cibreino* are open Tues–Sat 12.30–2.30pm & 7–11.15pm. Closed Aug.

**Enoteca Pinchiorri** **Via Ghibellina 87** Ⓣ**055.242.777,** Ⓦ**www.enotecapinchiorri.com.** No one seriously disputes the *Pinchiorri*'s claim to be Florence's best restaurant, certainly not Michelin, who've given it three of their coveted stars. The food is as magnificent as the plaudits suggest, but the ceremony that surrounds its presentation might strike you as excessive (jackets are compulsory for men), and the prices are wicked – you could easily spend in excess of €300 per person, excluding wine, though there are two fabulous eight-course set menus for a mere €225 per person. As for the wine list, it has no equal in Italy, with some 150,000 bottles lying in the *Pinchiorri* cellars; bottles start at about €60, rising beyond €20,000 for a 1945 Pétrus. Tues & Wed 7.30–10pm, Thurs–Sat 12.30–2pm & 7.30–10pm; closed Aug & Dec 15–27.

**Il Francescano Largo Bargellini 16 ⓣ055.241.605.** *Francescano* began life as a sibling of *Baldovino*, and though it is now independently owned, still offers similarly good food in an easy-going, clean-cut setting. The menu is simpler (no pizzas), smaller and a little less expensive than at *Baldovino* (mains €10 and up), but it's reliably good – and all its desserts are home-made. Daily noon–2.30pm & 7–11pm.

**Il Pizzaiuolo Via de' Macci 113r ⓣ055.241.171.** The Neapolitan pizzas here are among the best in the city. Wines and other menu items also have a Neapolitan touch, as does the atmosphere, which is friendly and high-spirited. Booking is a good idea, at least in the evening. The kitchen stays open until a little after midnight. 12.30–3pm & 7pm–1am. Closed Sun & Aug.

**L'Antico Noè Volta di San Piero 6r ⓣ055.234.0838.** Situated next door to the *vinaio* of the same name, this tiny trattoria has a very insalubrious setting (the Volta di San Piero is the one place in Florence where you're guaranteed to see a drunk or two), but the food is fine and the prices low – mains from €9. Mon–Sat noon–3pm & 7–11pm.

**La Pentola dell'Oro Via di Mezzo 24r ⓣ055.241.821.** Run by Giuseppe Alessi, the owner of a fine upmarket restaurant in Fiesole, *La Pentola* has one of the more imaginative menus in Florence, mingling the innovative with the profoundly traditional (some recipes date back to the sixteenth century). The main basement restaurant isn't the cosiest of dining rooms, but the quality is difficult to match for the price. Expect to pay upwards of €35, or a little less in the more informal ground-floor section, which focuses on traditional rather than aristocratic cuisine. Mon–Sat noon–3.30pm & 9pm–midnight.

**Natalino Borgo degli Albizi 17r ⓣ055.289.404.** Slighly pricier than your average trattoria, but it has excellent food, is untouristy for the location and has outside tables. The truffled courgettes with pecorino are astounding. Tues–Sun noon–3pm & 7–11pm.

**Ora d'Aria Via Ghibellina 3c/r ⓣ055.2001.699.** Marco Stabile, the young boss of *Ora d'Aria*, has quickly established a high reputation with this stylish venture, which offers a high-quality mix of the traditional and the innovative, with an unusual emphasis on fish and seafood dishes. The tasting menus (from €50) are very good value; à la carte, main courses are around €30. The cool, pale and spacious dining room is one of the most relaxing in the city. Mon–Sat 7.30–11.30pm.

**Osteria Caffè Italiano Via Isola delle Stinche 11–13r ⓣ055.289.368.** The high vaulted ceilings lend a medieval touch to this café, wine bar and restaurant, but the clientele are smart but relaxed Florentines. The cuisine is typically Tuscan – lots of beef, veal and wild boar – and first-rate; expect to pay upwards of €40 per head. Pizzas are served in a tiny annexe at number 19r, while round the corner, at Via della Vigna Vecchia 4r, you'll find *Sud*, a bistro offshoot where the menu draws on the cuisine of southern Italy, as the name suggests. All are open Tues–Sun; *Caffè Italiano* is open continuously 10am–1am, whereas the other two are open for lunch and dinner sittings.

**Osteria de' Benci Via de' Benci 13r ⓣ055.234.4923.** A modern, busy and reasonably priced *osteria*, with café-bar attached. The interior is pretty and pleasant, and is augmented by outside tables when it's warm enough – in summer it attracts big crowds. The tables have paper tablecloths and you eat off chunky ceramic plates. The moderately priced menu offers well-prepared standards plus innovative Tuscan cuisine. The strawberry risotto is an unexpected and delicious starter (€9) and the *goloso* and *piccante* steaks are very good. Staff are young, and the atmosphere friendly. Restaurant open Mon–Sat 1–2.45pm & 7.30–10.45pm; café-bar open 8am–midnight.

**Ruth's Via Luigi Carlo Farini 2a ⓣ055.248.0888.** Next to the synagogue, this is a fine kosher vegetarian restaurant, with an emphasis on Middle Eastern and North African dishes. Mains €9–18. Mon–Thurs 12.30–2.30pm & 7.30–10.30pm, Fri 12.30–3.30pm.

**Teatro del Sale Via dei Macci 111/r ⓣ055.200.1492, ⓦwww.teatrodelsale.com.** Run by Fabio Picchi, the chef/owner of *Cibrèo*, this is a fabulous and utterly unique place – a combination of restaurant and cultural centre. You pay €10 annual membership (valid for one guest too), and then an extra amount to help yourself to the amazing buffets: €7 for breakfast (9–11am), €20 for lunch (12.30-2.15pm), and €30 for dinner (7–8.45pm), when Picchi himself is often on duty in the open kitchen, announcing the dishes as they're put out. At 9.45pm guests are treated to a show, which might be anything from stand-up comedy to a piano recital or a dance group (the website has details of coming events). If you don't want to eat, you can just hang out, drinking coffee and browsing through the books and magazines that are lying around. Needless to say, it's very popular, and reservations are advisable in the evenings. Tues–Sat 9am–3pm & 6pm–midnight.



## Oltrarno

The listings in this section are marked on the map on pp.146–147.

**All'Antico Ristoro di Cambi Via Sant'Onofrio 1r ⓣ055.217.134, ⓦwww.anticoristorodicambi.it.** Run by the same family since the 1940s, this rough-and-ready trattoria is particularly good for meaty Florentine standards such as wild boar and steak, and has an excellent wine list. It's vast, but nonetheless gets packed on a Sat night, when even the large terrace fills up. Main dishes from around €10. Mon–Sat noon–10.30pm.

**Alla Vecchia Bettola Viale Lodovico Ariosto 32–34r ⓣ055.224.158.** Located on a major traffic intersection a couple of minutes' walk from the Carmine, this place – with its long marble-topped tables – has something of the atmosphere of an old-style drinking den, which is what it once was; nowadays it boasts a good repertoire of Tuscan meat dishes, with main courses reasonably priced from €10. Excellent choice of wines by the glass as well. Tues–Sat noon–2.30pm & 7.30–10.30pm.

**Angiolino Via Santo Spirito 36r ⓣ055.239.8976.** Long a no-nonsense Oltrarno favourite, with a menu that's short and to the point, featuring Tuscan classics such as *bistecca*, *ribollita* and *pappa al pomodoro*. Some nights it's as good as any restaurant in its price range – mains are €12–15 – but quality can be erratic and service problematic. April–Sept daily noon–3pm & 7–11pm; Oct–March closed Mon.

**Beccofino Piazza degli Scarlatti 1r ⓣ055.290.076.** A sleek and austerely stylish venture from David Gardner (the Scottish boss of *Baldovino* – see p.186), *Beccofino* was once one of the city's most fashionable restaurants. It's lost some of its lustre recently, but it's still worth its place on anyone's roster of Florence's gastronomic highlights. Prices are in the region of €15–22 for *secondi*, which is reasonable for the quality – chef Roberto Pepin learned his craft with the great Alain Ducasse. If you'd like to test the waters first, have a drink at the attached wine bar. Tues–Sun 7–11.30pm.

**Borgo Antico Piazza di Santo Spirito 6r ⓣ055.210.437.** The spartan chic of *Borgo Antico*'s white-tile and pink-plaster decor reflects the increasingly trendy character of this once notoriously sleazy Oltrarno piazza, and there's no Oltrarno restaurant trendier than this place. It's usually very crowded and very noisy, though in summer the tables outside offer relative quiet. Choose from a menu of pizzas or a range of Tuscan standards at reasonable prices (€13–18). Salads here are good, and there's often a selection of fresh fish and seafood pastas. Servings – on the restaurant's famous huge plates – are generous. Open daily noon–midnight.

**Dante Piazza Nazario Sauro 10r ⓣ055.219.219.** *Dante* is another Oltrarno institution, popular mainly for its pizzas (€7), though it also offers a menu of pasta, fish and meat dishes (from €10 for mains). Closed Wed & last 2 weeks of Aug.

**Del Carmine Piazza del Carmine 18r ⓣ055.218.601.** Years ago this was an unsung local trattoria; now the tourists have taken over, but it hasn't altogether lost its soul. Uncomplicated Florentine cooking, with a frequently changing menu. You'll pay in the region of €35 per person. Mon–Sat noon–3pm & 6.30–10.30pm.

**Enoteca Le Barrique Via del Leone 40r ⓣ055.224.192.** Formerly a wine bar, *Le Barrique* has mutated into a good mid-range restaurant, with a small and simple menu that's essentially classic Tuscan. Duck breast in vin santo is something of a speciality, and the home-made pasta dishes are good as well. The wine list is extensive, and is more international than most in Florence. Tues–Sun 7.30–11pm.

**Filipepe Via San Niccolò 39r ⓣ055.200.1397.** A well-priced and imaginative place, with a menu that's markedly different from most of the competition – it markets itself as a "Mediterranean Restaurant", and offers delicious food drawn from a variety of Italian regional cuisines. The wine list is similarly wide-ranging, and the decor offbeat and attractive. You'll pay in the region of €40 per person. Daily 7.30pm–1am; closed 2 weeks in Aug.

**I Tarocchi Via dei Renai 12r ☎055.234.3912.** There are a few simple dishes on the menu, but this is essentially a pizzeria – and one of the best in the city. Tues–Fri 12.30–2.30pm & 7pm–1am, Sat & Sun 7pm–1am only.

**Il Guscio Via dell'Orto 49 ☎055.224.421.** A long-established upper-range Oltrarno favourite: high-quality Tuscan meat dishes (and some excellent fish and seafood in summer), home-made pasta and superb desserts, plus a wide-ranging wine list. Expect to pay around €50 per head. Mon–Fri noon–2pm & 8–11pm, Sat 8–11pm; closed 2 weeks in Aug.

**Il Santo Bevitore Via Santo Spirito 64–66r ☎055.211.264.** The Holy Drinker is an airy and stylish "gastronomic *enoteca*" with a small but classy menu (around €30 for a meal without drinks) to complement its enticing wine list. Daily 12.30–2.30pm & 7.30–11.30pm. Closed 3 weeks in Aug.

**La Casalinga Via del Michelozzo 9r ☎055 .218.624.** Located in a side street off Piazza di Santa Spirito, this long-established family-run trattoria serves up some of the best low-cost Tuscan dishes in town (€10 for a *secondo*). No frills – paper tablecloths, so-so house wine by the flask and brisk service – but most nights it's filled with regulars and a good few outsiders. By 8pm there's invariably a queue. Mon–Sat noon–2.30pm & 7–10pm; closed 3 weeks in Aug.

**Osteria Antica Mescita San Niccolò Via San Niccolò 60r ☎055.234.2836.** This genuine old-style Oltrarno *osteria* has a small menu of robust and well-prepared Florentine staples (*ribollita*, *lampredotto*, etc), at around €10 for main courses; there's also a good lunchtime buffet for a mere €10. The downstairs dining room was formerly a crypt of the adjacent church of San Niccolò. Mon–Sat 12.30–3pm & 7pm–1am; closed Aug.

**Osteria Santo Spirito Piazza di Santo Spirito 16r ☎055.238.2383.** Run by the owners of the *Borgo Antico* (see opposite), this informal and modern *osteria* serves hearty Tuscan dishes with contemporary flair, and at good prices: pasta dishes from €6, mains from €12, and there's a lunchtime set menu for €12. In summer you can eat outdoors on the piazza. Daily 12.30–2.30pm & 8pm–midnight.

**Pane e Vino Piazza di Cestello 3r ☎055.247.6956.** *Pane e Vino* began life as a bar (over by San Niccolò), so it's no surprise that the wine list is excellent and well priced, with bottles from around €15. In its new home, the ambience is stylish yet relaxed and the menu small and consistently excellent (*secondi* €15–20), featuring two very enticing set menus (€35 & €45). Small TV screens in the dining area show the chefs beavering away in the kitchen, producing some of the best food in town – the ravioli with asparagus in a lemon cream melts in your mouth. Mon–Sat 8pm–midnight; closed 2 weeks in Aug.

▲ Pane e Vino

**Quattro Leoni Via dei Vellutini 1r/Piazza della Passera ☎055.218.562, ⓦwww.4leoni.com.** Occupying a three-roomed medieval interior, this is a young, relaxed place with wooden beams and splashy modern paintings strung across the rough stone walls. In summer you can also eat al fresco under vast canvas umbrellas in the tiny Piazza della Passera

– one of the most appealing outdoor eating venues in the city. It's popular with visiting stars – Dustin Hoffman and Sting feature on the walls, and Anthony Hopkins ate here while filming *Hannibal*. You can eat very well for around €40 a head. Noon–2.30pm & 7–11pm; closed Wed lunch.

**Sabatino Via Pisani 2r ⓣ055.225.955.** Situated right by Porta San Frediano, this old-fashioned long-running family *osteria* is not a gourmet venue, but it's absolutely authentic and ridiculously cheap (main courses from just €5). Mon–Sat noon–3pm & 7pm–midnight; closed Aug.

**Zeb Via San Miniato 2r.** If you're not in the mood for something as hefty as a full meal, *Zeb* might be just the ticket. The name stands for "*zuppa e bollito*", so soups are a speciality, but it also serves fine cheeses and cold cuts, as well as panini; seating is on high stools around the food counter, so it's not a place for taking your time. Mon, Tues & Thurs–Sun 8am–8pm.



## Cafés and bars

As elsewhere in Italy, the distinction between Florentine bars and cafés can be tricky to the point of impossibility, as almost every café serves alcohol and almost every bar serves coffee. It's really just a question of degrees of emphasis: in some cafés, most of the custom comes first thing in the morning, as people on their way to work stop off for a dash of caffeine and a brioche; in others, the tables are busiest late at night, when people drop by after an evening out, to relax over a Campari or a glass of wine.

The distinction between bars and clubs is getting vaguer too, with many of Florence's hotter bars now aiming to keep the punters on the premises all night, by serving free snacks with the *aperitivi* (usually from about 7pm to 9 or 10pm) before the music kicks in – either live or (more often) courtesy of the in-house DJ. Bars where **music** is the main attraction are reviewed in "Nightlife" (see p.198), but at many of the places listed below you'll get good sounds too.

There's one category of bar that's quite distinct from cafés, and that's the **enoteca**, where the enjoyment of wine is the chief point of the exercise – though in this case the complicating factor is that almost all *enoteche* serve food, and in some instances they've evolved into restaurants with huge wine lists. You'll find the wine-centred *enoteche* and more humble drinking dens reviewed in the "Wine bars" section (see p.193).

### Piazza del Duomo

The listings in this section are marked on the map on p.46.

**Astor Caffè Piazza del Duomo 20r.** From its modest street-front opposite the northeast corner of the Duomo you wouldn't guess that this was the hottest spot on the piazza, but inside you'll find a glitzy and spacious three-storey set-up. Food is served in the upstairs restaurant, while in the basement you get DJs playing anything from hip-hop to Brazilian music most nights, and in the ground-floor bar you sip cocktails with the city's gilded youth. Daily noon–2am.

**Caffè Gilli Piazza della Repubblica 36–39r.** Founded in 1733, this most appealing of this square's expensive cafés moved to its present site in 1910. The lavish Belle Epoque interior is a sight in itself (there are rumours of an imminent modernization), but most people choose to sit on the big outdoor terrace. On a cold afternoon try the famous hot chocolate – it comes in five blended flavours: almond, orange, coffee, *gianduia* and cocoa. 8am–midnight; closed Tues.

**Chiaroscuro Via del Corso 36r.** Nice cakes, but caffeine's the main draw, as you might guess from the coffee-related paraphernalia in the window. Also a good place for a quick, cheap lunch – choose food at the bar and take it to tables at the back. Mon–Sat 8am–9.30pm, Sun 3–8.30pm.

**Robiglio Via Tosinghi 11r.** Renowned for its pastries and chocolates, *Robiglio* also specializes in a hot chocolate drink that's so thick it's barely a liquid. Mon–Sat 8am–8pm.

## Piazza della Signoria

The listings in this section are marked on the map on p.63.

**Caffè Italiano Via della Condotta 56r.** Located one block north of the piazza, this is a combination of old-fashioned stand-up bar and smart café, with lots of dark wood, silver teapots and superb cakes, coffees and teas. Lunch is inexpensive and excellent, as you'd expect from a place owned by Umberto Montano, boss of the outstanding *Osteria Caffè Italiano* (see p.187). Mon–Sat 8am–8pm, Sun 11am–8pm; closed 2 weeks in Aug.

**Mayday Via Dante Alighieri 16r.** For years there's been a vaguely "alternative" bar at this central address; *Mayday*, the current encumbent, is a members-only joint (membership is free on the door), which has something of an art-school vibe – the ceiling is adorned with dozens of old radios, while the soundtrack has a bias towards jazz. Mon–Sat 8pm–2am; closed 2 weeks in Aug.

**Rivoire Piazza della Signoria 5r.** If you want to people-watch on Florence's main square, this is where to do it, and the outside tables are invariably packed. Founded in 1872, the café started life specializing in hot chocolate, still its main claim to fame. Ice creams are also fairly good, but the sandwiches and snacks are overpriced and poor: this is a place for one pricey beer or cappuccino, just to say you've done it. Tues–Sun 8am–midnight.

## West of the centre

The listings in this section are marked on the map on pp.90–91.

**Art Bar Via del Moro 4r.** A fine little bar near Piazza di Carlo Goldoni. The interior looks like an antique shop, while the club-like atmosphere attracts a studenty crowd. Especially busy at happy hour (7–9pm), when the low-priced cocktails are in heavy demand. The after-hours ambience is also ideal for a laid-back nightcap. Mon–Thurs 7pm–1am, Fri & Sat 7pm–2am; closed 3 weeks in Aug.

**Bar Curtatone Borgo Ognissanti 167r.** Despite the name, this big and slick establishment is more a café than a bar; a good place to recharge over an espresso and a slab of cake. Mon, Wed–Fri & Sun 7am–1am, Sat 7am–2am; closed Aug.

**Caffè Amerini Via della Vigna Nuova 63r.** A straightforward café that serves good sandwiches, salads and snacks – and charges only a small premium for sitting down. Mon–Sat 8am–8pm.

**Mariano Via Parione 19r.** It just says *Alimentari* above the door, but this is also a smartish local café-bar that does brisk lunchtime business with its freshly prepared sandwiches and snacks, including *panini tartufati.* Mon–Fri 8am–3pm & 5–7.30pm, Sat 8am–3pm.

**Noir Lungarno Corsini 12–14r.** Recently revamped in moody nocturnal tones, the bar formerly known as *Capocaccia* has been voted the Florentines' favourite night-time hangout several times, and it remains out in front. The well-designed interior is roomy and has plenty of tables and stools; there's a DJ every night; and you'll be mixing almost entirely with fashionable locals, especially later on – if you have neither youth nor beauty on your side, however, you'd best stay away. Sunday brunch (12.30–3.30pm) is excellent, as is the nightly *aperitivo* buffet (7.30–10.30pm). Open daily noon–2am.

▲ DJ in Noir

**Procacci Via de' Tornabuoni 64r.** Famous café that doesn't serve coffee, just wine and cold drinks. Its reputation comes from the extraordinary and delicious *tartufati*, or truffle-butter brioche – from Oct–Dec, when truffles are in season, the wood-lined interior of *Procacci* is a swooningly aromatic spot. Mon–Sat 10.30am–8pm; closed Aug.

**Slowly Via Porta Rossa 63r.** This extremely trendy bar, with its neat little banquettes and candle lanterns, tends to attract a showy, beautifully dressed young crowd, who while away the hours chatting over pricey cocktails and bar snacks (the *aperitivo* buffet is one of the best in Florence). The atmosphere is pretty laid-back, even when the DJ gets to work. Time will tell whether its appearance in all the designer magazines will lead to style tourists edging out the Florentines. Mon–Sat 7pm–2am.

## North of the centre

The listings in this section are marked on the map on pp.108–109.

**Nannini Coffee Shop Via Borgo San Lorenzo 7r.** The Florentine outpost of Siena's *Nannini* operation, famed for its superb coffee and tooth-wrecking *panforte*, an extremely dense and delicious cake. Open 7.30am–7.30pm; open until 8.30pm Sat.

**Robiglio Via dei Servi 112r.** The smaller branch of this famed café – see p.190. Mon–Sat 8am–8pm.

## East of the centre

The listings in this section are marked on the map on p.134.

**Caffè Cibrèo Via Andrea del Verrocchio 5r.** Possibly the prettiest café in Florence, *Caffè Cibrèo* opened in 1989, but the wood-panelled interior gives it the look of a place that's at least two hundred years older. Cakes and desserts are great, and the light meals bear the culinary stamp of the *Cibrèo* restaurant kitchens opposite. Tues–Sat 8am–1am.

**Caffèlatte Via degli Alfani 39r.** The one-room *Caffèlatte* began life in the 1920s, when a milk-and-coffee supplier opened here. Nowadays, it's expanded its operation to include an organic bakery, which produces delicious breads and cakes; the vegetarian brunch is excellent too. The speciality drink, as you'd expect, is caffè latte, served in huge bowls. Laid-back music and temporary exhibitions of paintings and photographs enhance the atmosphere. Daily 8am–midnight.

**Moyo Via de' Benci 23r.** A young crowd flocks to this bar every evening – the food's pretty good (come for the early-evening *aperitivo* buffet), the free wi-fi access is a plus (it was the first place in Florence to offer it), but it's the buzz that really brings them in. With *Osteria de' Benci* just down the road (see p.187), this is one of the city's sparkiest corners. Open daily noon–4pm & 8pm–2am (Fri & Sat 3am).

## Oltrarno

The listings in this section are marked on the map on pp.146–147.

**Caffè degli Artigiani Via dello Sprone 16r.** Slightly ramshackle and very welcoming café on a delightful small square near the Ponte Vecchio, much used by local students. Serves salads and sandwiches. May–Sept Mon 8am–4pm, Tues–Sat 8am–midnight; Oct–April Mon–Sat 8.30am–10.30pm.

**Caffè La Torre Lungarno Cellini 65r.** This bar changes its decor every year, which is one reason it has managed to remain one of the most fashionable bars in Florence. The other is its superb location, in the shadow of the tower of the Porta San Niccolò, close to the Arno, with lots of outdoor seating. There's live music many nights, and excellent cocktails. Daily 10.30am–3am.

**Caffè Ricchi Piazza di Santo Spirito 9r.** The smartest of the cafés on this square. Menus change daily, and there's a good selection of cakes, ice cream and sandwiches. Summer Mon–Sat 7am–1am; winter closes 10pm. Closed 2 weeks in Feb & 2 weeks in Aug.

**Dolce Vita Piazza del Carmine 6r.** This smart and extremely popular bar-club has been going for more than a decade and has stayed ahead of the game through constant updating. Take a seat on one of the aluminium bar stools and preen yourself with Florence's beautiful young things. Live music (often Latin or jazz) on Wed and Thurs, 7.30–9.30pm; *aperitivi* every night 7.30–9.30pm, then the DJ gets to work. Tues–Sun 5pm–2am.

**Hemingway Piazza Piattellina 9r, off Piazza del Carmine.** Self-consciously trendy, but don't let that put you off – there's nothing else like it in Florence. Choose from one of countless speciality teas, sample over twenty coffees, or knock back one of the "tea cocktails". Owners Paul de Bondt and Andrea Slitti are members of the Compagnia del Cioccolato, a chocolate appreciation society – and it shows: the handmade chocolates are sublime. Mon–Thurs 4.30pm–1am, Fri & Sat 4.30pm–2am, Sun 3.30pm–1am. Closed mid-June to mid-Sept.

**High Bar Via dei Renai 27a.** Run by the ever-friendly Luigi and Laura, the *High Bar* is a relaxed and unpretentious alternative to its super-hip neighbours *Zoe* and *Negroni*. They serve good snacks at *aperitivo* time, and have a garden out back, as well as tables out front. Free wi-fi too, plus table football. Mon 8.30am–10pm, Tues–Thurs 8.30am–1am, Fri 8.30am–2am, Sat 6pm–2am.

**Il Rifrullo Via San Niccolò 53–57r.** New owners have smartened and expanded this bar, which is a very nice place to unwind after the hike up to San Miniato, or for a nightcap. Lying to the east of the Ponte Vecchio–Pitti Palace route, it attracts fewer tourists than many Oltrarno café-bars. Serves delicious snacks with the early evening *aperitivi* (when the music gets turned up), as well as larger dishes, and it's always packed out for Sunday brunch. Has a pleasant roof terrace, too. Daily 8am–2am. Closed 2 weeks in Aug.

**La Cité Borgo San Frediano 20r.** With its huge windows, mezzanine balcony and shelves of books (to buy or browse), this café-bar-bookshop has an arty ambience that's as much Parisian as Florentine. An area is set aside for live performances (usually music), and food-tastings are regular occurrences too. Sun & Mon 3.30pm–midnight, Tues–Sat 10.30am–midnight.

**Negroni Via dei Renai 17r.** Set back from the banks of the Arno, on the south side of the grassy Piazza Demidoff, *Negroni* has been a fixture on the Florentine scene for years. It takes its name from the Negroni cocktail (gin, vermouth and Campari), created on this spot for Count Camillo Negroni way back at the start of the last century. Cocktails are still a major attraction, along with the early-evening *aperitivo* buffet and the music – there's a DJ almost every night. Small exhibitions of art and photography usually adorn the walls. Mon–Sat 8am–2.30am, Sun 6pm–2am. Closed 2 weeks in Aug.

**Plasma Piazza Ferrucci 1r.** Owned and designed by a theatre director, this self-styled "cocktail bar and video galley", is so cool it almost hurts, with fibre-optic lighting throughout, a red resin bar on the lower floor, and loads of big plasma screens in the big vaulted room upstairs – where, in addition to another bar, there's also a waterfall. The sound system is state of the art as well. It's some way out of the centre, about 1500m east of Ponte Vecchio, but for many style-conscious Florentines no night is complete without at least a cocktail here. Wed–Sun 7pm–2am.

**Popcafé Piazza Santo Spirito 18a/r Ⓦwww.popcafe.it.** This new café has proved to be a big hit with the locals, thanks to the music (often live – details on the website) and Boho vibe. Another aspect of its appeal is the vegetarian food: lunch from Mon–Sat, brunch on Sun (12.30–3pm), and lashings of vegetarian *aperitivi* every evening (7.30–9.30pm). Daily noon–2am.

**Zoe Via dei Renai 13r.** Like the neighbouring *Negroni, Zoe is* perennially popular for summer evening drinks, but it attracts lots of young Florentines right through the day – 8am–noon is breakfast time, lunch is noon–3pm, then it's "Aperitif" from 6–10pm, when the "American Bar" theme takes over (the Crimson Zoe cocktail is notorious). Does good snacks and simple meals. There's a DJ in the back room, and – like *Negroni* – it's something of an art venue too. Mon–Thurs 8am–1.30am, Fri & Sat 8am–2am, Sun 6pm–1am.

## Wine bars

As you'd expect in a city that lies close to some of the best vineyards in the country, Florence has plenty of bars dedicated to the wines of Chianti and other Tuscan producers. At one end of the scale there's the endangered species known as the **vinaio** (see box, p.194), which consists of little more than a niche with a few shelves of generally workaday wines, plus a counter of snacks. At the opposite pole there's the **enoteca**, which is a wine-bar-cum-restaurant; all *enoteche* have vast wine menus, but in some cases – such as *Il Santo Bevitore* and *Boccadama* – the kitchen has come to play so large a role in the operation that the place is now more a restaurant than a bar, which is why you'll find some *enoteche* listed in our restaurant section.

### Piazza del Duomo

**Fiaschetteria Nuvoli Piazza dell'Olio 15 (see map, p.46).** It's something of a surprise to find such a traditional place so close to the Duomo. The tiny, dark, bottled-lined shop is dominated by a counter laden with cold meats, *crostini* and other snacks, plus a few opened wine bottles. There's room inside to eat sitting down, but most of the customers are content with a quick glass at the bar. Mon–Sat 8am–8pm.

## Piazza della Signoria

**Cantinetta dei Verrazzano Via dei Tavolini 18–20r (see map, p.63).** Owned by Castello dei Verrazzano, a major Chianti vineyard, this wood-panelled place near Orsanmichele is part-bar, part-café and part-bakery, making its own excellent pizza, *focaccia* and cakes. A perfect spot for a light lunch or an early evening drink. July & Aug Mon–Sat 8am–4pm; Sept–June Mon–Sat 8am–9pm.

## North of the centre

The listings in this section are marked on the map on pp.108–109.

**Casa del Vino Via dell'Ariento 16r.** Located a few yards south of the Mercato Centrale, and passed by hordes of tourists daily – yet probably visited by only a handful. Patrons are mostly Florentines, who pitch up for a drink, a chat with owner Gianni Migliorini and an assault on various panini, *crostini*, and saltless Tuscan bread and salami. Mon–Fri 9.30am–5.30pm, Sat 10am–3.30pm; closed Aug.

**Zanobini Via Sant'Antonino 47r.** Like the *Casa del Vino*, its rival just around the corner, this is an authentic Florentine bar, whose feel owes much to the presence of locals and traders from the nearby Mercato Centrale. Offers acceptable snacks, but most people are simply here for a chat over a glass of wine. Mon–Sat 8am–2pm & 3.30–8pm.

## Oltrarno

The listings in this section are marked on the map on pp.146–147.

**Beccofino Piazza degli Scarlatti 1r.** Like the restaurant to which it's attached, this *enoteca* is a stylish establishment – the selection of wines is terrific, and there's a menu of innovative dishes from the restaurant's kitchen, at somewhat lower prices. Tues–Sun 7pm–midnight.

**Fuori Porta Via del Monte alle Croci 10r ⓣ055.234.2483.** If you're climbing up to San Miniato you could take a breather at this superb and justly famous wine *enoteca-osteria*. There are over four hundred wines to choose from by the bottle, and an ever-changing selection of wines by the glass,

## Vinaii

The *vinaio* was once a real Florentine institution. These tiny places with no seating would typically see customers lingering for no more than a couple of minutes – long enough to down a tumbler of basic red wine and exchange a few words with the proprietor. The number of *vinaii* has declined markedly in recent years; the following are the notable survivors.

**All'Antico Vinaio Via dei Neri 65r (see map, p.134).** Though recently revamped, this place – located between the Uffizi and Santa Croce – preserves much of the rough-and-ready atmosphere that's made it one of Florence's most popular wine bars for the last hundred years. Also serves coffee, rolls and plates of pasta. Tues–Sat 8am–8pm, Sun 8am–1pm; closed 3 weeks in late July & early Aug.

**I Fratellini Via dei Cimatori 38r (see map, p.63).** In business since 1875, this minuscule dirt-cheap stand-up bar (there's nothing more to it than a counter and some shelves) is somehow clinging on in the immediate vicinity of the high-rent Via dei Calzaiuoli. Serves decent panini and local wines. Mid-June to Aug Mon–Fri 8am–5pm; Sept to mid-June daily 8am–8pm.

**L'Antico Noè Volta di San Piero 6r (see map, p.134).** A long-established stand-up wine bar, tucked into an uninviting little alley to the north of Santa Croce, at the eastern end of Borgo degli Albizi. Mon–Sat noon–3pm & 7pm–midnight.

**Quasigratis Piazza del Grano 10 (see map, p.63).** Little more than a window in a wall at the back of the Uffizi, and it doesn't say *Quasigratis* ("Almost free") anywhere – just "Vini". Rolls, nibbles and wine – in tiny glasses called *rasini* – are consumed standing up. Daily 10am–11pm; closed Jan–Feb.

### Pubs

Every Italian town of any size now has at least one pub, generally with an Irish theme, in which the clientele tends to be a mix of local lads and students sipping slowly at their half-pints, and British tourists showing them how it's really done. Florence has an increasing number of such places, of which the following pair are more convincing than most of the rest.

**Fiddler's Elbow Piazza di Santa Maria Novella 7r (see map, pp.90–91).** Part of an Italy-wide chain, with just one smoky, dark and wood-panelled room, invariably heaving with homesick foreigners – fortunately there's also seating out on the piazza. Women travellers are likely to find themselves the object of concerted attention from packs of Guinness-sozzled Italians. Daily noon–2am.

**Lion's Fountain Borgo degli Albizi 34r (see map, p.134).** Background music isn't traditional, but it's inoffensive; the decor is pseudo-Irish, and the bar staff and atmosphere are generally friendly. Food is simple and good – lots of salads and sandwiches – and you can catch big sporting events on the TVs. Drinks are reasonably priced, and include a good range of cocktails as well as the ubiquitous Guinness. Daily 6pm–2am.

as well as a wide selection of grappas and malt whiskies. Bread, cheese, ham and salami are available, together with a choice of pasta dishes and tasty salads. Has a summertime terrace and large dining area, but it's still wise to book if you're coming here to eat. Mon–Sat 12.30–3.30pm & 7pm–12.30am; closed 2 weeks in mid-Aug.

**Le Volpi e L'Uva Piazza dei Rossi 1r, off Piazza di Santa Felìcita.** This discreet, friendly little *enoteca*, just over the Ponte Vecchio, does good business by concentrating on the wines of small producers and providing tasty cold meats and snacks to help them down (the selection of cheeses in particular is tremendous). At any one time you can choose from at least two dozen different wines by the glass. In summer the shady terrace is a very pleasant refuge from the heat. Mon–Sat 11am–9pm.

**Pitti Gola e Cantina Piazza Pitti 16.** A small and friendly wine bar, very handily placed for a glass of Chianti after a slog around the Pitti museums. Tues–Sun: summer 10am–midnight; winter 12.30–4pm & 7–9pm. Closed 2 weeks in Aug.

## Gelaterie

Devotees of Italian **ice cream** will find that Florence offers plenty of opportunities to indulge: the city has several superb *gelaterie*, and some would claim that *Vivoli* is one of the top purveyors in the country.

The procedure is the same wherever you buy. First decide whether you want a cone (*un cono*) or a cup (*una coppa*) – though some of the more upmarket *gelaterie* don't believe in cones. Then decide how much you want to pay: cone and cup sizes tend to start around €2, going up in €1 increments. Unless you plump for the smallest size you'll usually be able to choose a combination of two or three flavours. You may be asked if you want a squirt of cream (*panna*) on top – it's usually free.

**Café delle Carozze Piazza Pesce 3r (see map, p.63).** Good outlet right by the Ponte Vecchio. Daily except Wed 11am–8pm.

**Caffè Ricchi Piazza di Santo Spirito 9r (see map, pp.146–147).** Excellent ice cream at a popular location – flavours include English trifle (*zuppa inglese*).

**Carabé Via Ricasoli 60r (see map, pp.108–109).** Wonderful Sicilian ice cream made with Sicilian ingredients as only they know how. Also serves a variety of cakes. May–Oct daily 9am–1am; rest of year daily 9am–8pm, but closed mid-Dec to mid-Jan.

**Festival del Gelato Via del Corso 75r (see map, p.46).** Around seventy varieties of ice cream, with some very exotic combinations. Tues–Sun 10am–midnight.

**Gelateria dei Neri Via dei Neri 20–22r (see map, p.134).** Small place in contention for the best ice cream in town. Close to the Uffizi but away from the crowds. The range of flavours is fantastic – fig and walnut, Mexican chocolate (very spicy), rice and they also have some non-dairy ice cream. Daily 11am–midnight.

**Grom Via del Campanile (see map, p.46).** Founded in Turin in 2003, *Grom* is a retro-styled but very slick operation, concocting fabulous *gelati* from top-quality ingredients gathered from all over Italy. The house speciality is Crema di Grom, made from organic eggs, soft *meliga* biscuits and Ecuadorian chocolate. Daily April–Oct 10.30am–midnight, rest of year closes 11pm.

**Il Triangolo delle Bermuda Via Nazionale 61r (see map, pp.108–109).** The Bondi family make some of the most unusual concoctions in town, such as cinnamon, Oreo (made from the American biscuit) and Mars bar. Closed Mon.

**Perchè No! Via de' Tavolini 19r (see map, p.63).** Superb *gelateria*, in business since the 1930s; go for the classic *crema*, the chocolate or the gorgeous pistachio. Mon, Wed–Sun 11am–11pm, Tues noon–8pm; closed Nov.

**Vivoli Via Isola delle Stinche 7r (see map, p.134).** Operating from deceptively unprepossessing premises in a side street close to Santa Croce, this café has long been rated one of the best ice cream-makers in Florence – the very best, in the opinion of many. Tues–Sun: summer 7.30am–midnight; winter closes 9pm. Closed 2 weeks in Aug.

10

# Nightlife and cultural events

Florence has something of a reputation for catering primarily to the middle-aged and affluent, but like every university town it has its pockets of **nightlife** activity, not to mention the added buzz generated by thousands of young tourists. Details of the city's club and live music venues are given below, but for up-to-the-minute **information** about what's on, call in at the tourist office in Via Cavour or at Box Office, which is to the northwest of the train station at Via Alamanni 39 (ⓣ055.210.804; Mon 3–7.30pm, Tues–Sat 10am–7.30pm). Tickets for most events are available at Box Office (credit cards not accepted); otherwise, keep your eyes peeled for advertising posters, or pick up the monthly *Firenze Spettacolo*, which has an English section as well as a map of places open after midnight.

## Clubs

Florence has a decent **club** scene, even if clubs in Italy often don't resemble their equivalents in London or other big cities: most Florentines aren't in clubs to dance or drink – they're there to see and be seen, and dress up to the nines. Foreigners are a different matter, and one or two – mostly central – clubs have a slightly more sweaty and familiar atmosphere as a result.

Faced with a low income from the bar (Italians don't go in for binge-drinking), most clubs charge a fairly stiff **admission**: reckon on €15–25 for the bigger and better-known places. This is not quite as bad as it sounds, as the admission often includes a drink. Prices at the bar after that are usually quite steep. Some clubs operate a system where you're given a card on entry that gets stamped every time you spend money at the bar; if by the end of the night you haven't spent a specified minimum amount, you have to pay a charge before the bouncers will let you out. Alternatively, the card may be used just to keep tabs

> The streets of central Florence are generally safe at night, but women should be wary of strolling through the red-light districts alone: the area northeast of the **station** (notably Via Faenza and around) has a particularly dodgy reputation, and kerb-crawling is not unknown. Unaccompanied tourists of either sex should stay well clear of the **Cascine park** at night: if you're going to one of the clubs located there, get a taxi there and back.

## Gay and lesbian Florence

*Florenzer* was, during the seventeenth century at least, German slang for gay, and the city remains for the most part tolerant towards gay and lesbian visitors. The leading gay bar is **Crisco**, a short distance east of the Duomo at Via Sant'Egidio 43r (see map, p.134; ⓣ055.248.0580; Mon, Wed, Thurs & Sun 11pm–3am, Fri & Sat 10pm–6am), but the ambience can be a bit heavy for some tastes. **Piccolo**, at Borgo Santa Croce 23r (see map, p.134; ⓣ055.200.1057; daily 8pm–2.30am), has a more chilled-out atmosphere and draws a mixed gay and lesbian crowd, as does the stylish **Y.A.G. B@r**, also near Santa Croce at Via de' Macci 8r (see map, p.134; ⓣ055.246.9022, ⓦwww.yagbar.com; daily 8pm–3am). The key bar-club is the pioneering **Tabasco**, which has been going for more than 35 years at Piazza Santa Cecilia 3r (see map, p.63; ⓣ055.213.000, ⓦwww.tabascogay.it; Tues–Sun 10pm–6am). For lesbian contacts, check the noticeboard at the women's bookshop Libreria delle Donne, at Via Fiesolana 2b (Mon 3.30–7.30pm, Tues–Sat 9.30am–1pm & 3.30–7.30pm).



on your drinks, with the bill settled at the end of the evening. Payment always has to be in cash.

In addition to the places listed below, plenty of **temporary clubs** spring into existence in the summer months, often as open-air venues on the edge of town, in spots such as Piazza della Libertà and the Cascine. From June to the beginning of September keep an eye out for posters and flyers, or check the listings in *Firenze Spettacolo*.

One other thing to bear in mind is that in recent years more and more of Florence's trendier bars have taken to employing DJs later in the evening, and serving **complimentary snacks** with drinks before that (usually from about 7 to 9/10pm), to lure the customers in. Whereas a good night out in Florence used to begin with cocktails at a bar at around 10pm, before moving on to a club, a lot of locals decamp to bars such as *Noir* or *Dolce Vita* quite early, fill up at the free *aperitivo* buffet, then stick around for the music. So for the complete picture of Florence's club scene, skim through our listings in the "Bars" section as well as what's listed below.

### West of the centre

The listings in this section are marked on the map on pp.90–91.

**Central Park Via Fosso Macinante 2, Parco delle Cascine ⓣ335.818.3400.** One of the city's biggest and most commercial clubs, with adventurous, wide-ranging and up-to-the-minute music on several dance floors from DJs who know what they're doing and have access to a superb sound system. A card system operates for drinks, and the first drink is included in the admission – around €20–25 after midnight, usually free before. Summer Tues–Sat 11.30pm–4.30am; winter Fri & Sat same hours.

**Meccanò Viale degli Olmi 1/Piazzale delle Cascine ⓣ055.331.371.** People flock here for a night out from across half of Tuscany. The place is labyrinthine, with a trio of lounge and bar areas, and a huge and invariably packed dance floor playing mostly house music. In summer, when the action spills out of doors, you can cool off in the gardens bordering the Cascine. The €15–20 admission includes your first drink. Summer Tues–Sat 11.30pm–4am; winter Thurs–Sat same hours; closed Nov & two weeks in Aug.

**Space Electronic Via Palazzuolo 37 ⓣ055.293.082.** You'll find all the disco clichés of a big Continental club here – glass dance floors and mirrored walls – and one or two less familiar features, such as the piranha tank in the downstairs bar, near the karaoke area. Cooler-than-thou clubbers might be sniffy about its popularity with youthful tourist coach parties and local lads on the pull, but it's fine if all you want to do is dance, and the music can be surprisingly good. Admission around €15 with one free drink. Mon–Fri & Sun 10pm–2.30am, Sat 10pm–3am; winter closed Mon.

**Yab Via Sassetti 5r ⓣ055.215.160.** This long-established basement club (full name: You Are Beautiful) has been popular for years, and is known throughout the country for Monday's Yabsmoove – Italy's longest-running hip-hop night. Thursday is deep house night. On other nights it doesn't have the most up-to-the-minute playlist in the world, but still offers probably the most relaxed and reliable night's clubbing in central Florence. You're given a card and pay on leaving if you've spent less than €15 at the bar; if you've spent more, there's no extra charge. Mon, Tues & Thurs–Sat 9pm–4am; closed June–Sept.

### East of the centre

The listings in this section are marked on the map on p.134.

**Blob Club Via Vinegia 21r ⓣ055.211.209.** A favourite with Florentine students, possibly on account of its free admission and the 6–10pm happy hour. Seating upstairs, bar and tiny dance floor downstairs, but don't expect to do much dancing – later on, especially on weekend nights, *Blob* gets packed to the rafters with a very happy and very drunken crowd. Quieter in the summer months. Daily 6pm–4am.

**Doris Via de' Pandolfini 26r ⓣ055.246.6775.** Recently given a stylish overhaul, *Doris* is one of the best clubs in central Florence. The bar is open 7–10pm for drinks and snacks, with the club kicking into action from 11.30pm until 4am. Admission €10. Closed Mon.

**ExMud Corso dei Tintori 4 ⓣ055.263.8583.** Formerly *Mood*, this subterranean Santa Croce club rocks to drum 'n' bass, house and garage, as well as more experimental Italian electronica. Admission €10. Tues–Sat 11.30pm–4am.

**Full-Up Via della Vigna Vecchia 25r ⓣ055.293.006.** Situated close to the Bargello, this club has been going so long it's become something of an institution. The best nights are usually Thurs (hip-hop) and Fri (house). *Aperitivi* from 10.30pm each night; the music begins an hour later. If you're a non-Italian student you get in free. Tues–Sat 10.30pm–4am. Closed June–Sept.

**Rex Via Fiesolana 25r ⓣ055.228.0331, ⓦwww.rexcafe.it.** One of the city's big night-time fixtures, this is a friendly bar-club with a varied and loyal clientele. Vast curving lights droop over the central bar, which is studded with turquoise stone and broken mirror mosaics. Big arched spaces to either side mean there's plenty of room, the cocktails and DJs are good, and the snacks excellent – the *aperitivi* session is 7–9.30pm. Mon, Wed–Sun 6pm–3am. Closed June–Aug.

### Perètola

**Tenax Via Pratese 46 ⓣ055.632.958, ⓦwww.tenax.org.** Florence's biggest club, pulling in the odd jet-setting DJ. Given its location in the northwest of town, near the airport (there's usually a shuttle bus from the train station – otherwise, take a taxi), you'll escape the hordes of *internazionalisti* in the more central clubs. With two large floors, it's a major venue for concerts, as well. Admission €20–25. It's also the city's longest-running venue for new and established bands, as well as big-name international acts. Thurs–Sat 10.30pm–4am. Closed mid-May to mid-Sept.

## Live music

Florence's **live music** scene isn't the hottest in Italy, but there's a smattering of venues for small-time local outfits, and a couple of big stages for visiting stars. In addition to the recommendations below, a few of the places reviewed under "Bars and cafés" and "Clubs" put on live sessions from time to time: check listings magazines for one-off events.

### West of the centre

The listings in this section are marked on the map on pp.90–91.

**Eskimo Via dei Canacci 12r ⓣ055.715.794.** A small, well-established club close to Santa Maria Novella with live music every night. Its long-standing status as the prime lefty bar is reflected in the music, which has a leaning towards thoughtful Italian singer-songwriters. The atmosphere is welcoming and you may catch the odd cultural event.

Members only, but you can get annual membership on the door, for around €7. Daily 9pm–3am; closed June–Sept.

**Loonees Via Porta Rossa 15 ⓣ055.212.249, ⓦwww.loonees.it.** Set up by a former biker from Birmingham, this sweltering subterranean bar is a favourite with the city's students. The music is loud right through the night, and live from Wed–Sat. Free entry. Mon–Sat 9pm–3am.

**Sintetika Via Alamanni 4 ⓣ333.359.1575, ⓦwww.sintetikalive.it.** A new venue that primarily promotes local indie bands, but has managed to attract a few prestigious outsiders too, such as Bonnie Prince Billy. Entry by membership – €8 on the door. Days vary; usually open 11pm–4am.

## North of the centre

The listings in this section are marked on the map on pp.108–109.

**Be Bop Via dei Servi 76r.** A nice and rather classy rock, jazz and blues bar with bow-tied bar staff and faux Art Nouveau decor. Located close to the university district, and often full of students as a result. No dance floor as such; this is more a place to sit and chill out to the music. Daily 5pm–2am.

**Girasol Via del Romito 1 ⓣ055.474.948, ⓦwww.girasol.it.** Florence's liveliest Latin bar, located on a minor road due north of the Fortezza da Basso, is hugely popular. Rather than relying solely on salsa classes, cocktails and the usual vinyl suspects – although it does all these – the place draws in some surprisingly good live acts, with different countries' sounds each day of the week, from Brazilian bossa nova to Cuban son. Tues–Sun 7pm–2am.

## East of the centre

The listings in this section are marked on the map on p.134.

**Ambasciata di Marte Via Mannelli 2 ⓣ055.655.0786, ⓦwww.ambasciatadimarte.org.**

## Florence's festivals

Florence's main cultural festivals are covered in the "Classical music" section overleaf; what follows is a rundown on its more folkloric events.

### Scoppio del Carro

The first major folk festival of the year is Easter Sunday's **Scoppio del Carro** (Explosion of the Cart), which commences with two costumed parades. The smaller one sets off from Santi Apostoli, bearing a flame lit from the church's sacred flints (see p.92); the larger procession accompanies a huge and elaborate cartload of fireworks which is hauled by six white oxen from the Porta a Prato to the Duomo. At 11am, during the Gloria of the midday Mass, the fireworks are set off by a "dove" that whizzes down a wire from the high altar. The origins of this incendiary descent of the Holy Spirit lie with one Pazzino de' Pazzi, leader of the Florentine contingent on the First Crusade. On getting back to Florence he was entrusted with the care of the flame of Holy Saturday, an honorary office which he turned into something more festive by rigging up a ceremonial wagon to transport the flame round the city. His descendants continued to manage the festival until the Pazzi conspiracy of 1478, which lost them the office. Since then, the city authorities have taken care of business.

### Festa del Grillo

On the first Sunday after Ascension Day (forty days after Easter), the **Festa del Grillo** (Festival of the Cricket) is held in the Cascine park. In among the stalls and the picnickers you'll find people selling tiny wooden cages containing mechanical crickets. Until quite recently real crickets were used – a ritual that may have harked back to the days when farmers had to scour their land for locusts, or to the time when men used to place a cricket on the door of their lovers to serenade them.

### St John's Day and the Calcio Storico

The saint's day of **John the Baptist**, Florence's patron, is June 24 – the occasion for a massive fireworks display up on Piazzale Michelangelo, and for the final of the Calcio Storico on Piazza Santa Croce. Played in sixteenth-century costume to perpetuate the memory of a game played at Santa Croce during the siege of 1530, this uniquely

This self-styled "centre for creative development" is the city's new showcase for local bands; it has a bookshop and gallery space too. It's in the Campo di Marte area, and buses #3, #6, #10, #20 and #44 go close.

**Jazz Club Via Nuova de' Caccini 3 ⓣ055.247.9700, ⓦwww.jazzclubfirenze.com.** Florence's foremost jazz venue has been a fixture for years. The €9 "membership" fee gets you down into the medieval brick-vaulted basement, where the atmosphere's informal and there's live music most nights. Mon night is usually a jam session. Cocktails are good, and you can also snack on bar nibbles and *focaccia*. Mon–Fri 9pm–2am, Sat 9pm–3am. Closed July & Aug.

**Nelson Mandela Forum Viale Pasquale Paoli 3 ⓣ055.678.841, ⓦwww.mandelaforum.it.** Along with the *Saschall* and *Tenax* (see p.199), this 7000-capacity hall – located at Campo di Marte – is the city's main venue for big-draw mainstream acts, such as Lenny Kravitz and Zucchero. Bus #3 takes you there.

**Saschall-Teatro di Firenze Via Fabrizio de André 3 ⓣ055.650.4112, ⓦwww.saschall.it.** Holding around four thousand people, the new and well-designed *Saschall* is used for acts that don't quite have the following to pack out the *Mandela Forum*. It's by Lungarno Aldo Moro, a couple of kilometres east of the city centre – bus #14 is the one you need.

## Il Poggetto

**Auditorium FLOG Via Michele Mercati 24b ⓣ055.490.437, ⓦwww.flog.it.** One of the city's best-known mid-sized venues, and a perennial student favourite – with a suitably downbeat studenty look and feel – for all forms of live music (and DJs), but particularly local indie-type bands. It's usually packed, despite a position way out in the northern suburbs at Il Poggetto; to get there take buses #4, #8, #14, #20 or #28.

Florentine mayhem is a three-match series, with two matches in early June preceding the bedlam of June 24. Each of the four historic quarters fields a team of 27 players, with Santa Croce in green, San Giovanni in red, Santa Maria Novella in blue and Santo Spirito in grossly impractical white. The prize for the winning side is a calf, which gets roasted in a street party after the tournament and shared among the four teams and the inhabitants of the winning quarter.

The Calcio Storico has been undergoing something of a crisis since the 2006 event, when the semi-final between Santa Croce and Santo Spirito became so violent that the game was stopped. The 2007 event was then cancelled, and revisions to the rules are now being introduced – under the traditional rules, players were allowed to tackle any other player, regardless of whether or not he had the ball, and virtually any method of tackling short of outright murder was permitted. And although the players are supposed to be residents of the quarter for which they are playing, it's not been unknown for teams to draft in professional boxers and wrestlers to help with the dirty work. It's hoped that such skulduggery will now cease.

### Festa delle Rificolone

The **Festa delle Rificolone** (Festival of the Lanterns) takes place on the Virgin's birthday, September 7, with a procession of children to Piazza Santissima Annunziata, where a small fair is held. Each child carries a coloured paper lantern with a candle inside it – a throwback to the days when people from the surrounding countryside would troop by lantern light into the city for the Feast of the Virgin. The procession is followed by a parade of floats and street parties.

### Festa dell'Unità

October's **Festa dell'Unità** is part of a nationwide celebration run by the Italian communists. Florence's is the biggest event after Bologna's, with loads of political stalls and restaurant-marquees. Box Office will have details of venues, while news about the Feste and other political events in Florence can be found in *Anteprima*, a local supplement published with Friday's edition of the communist daily *L'Unità*.

## Classical music

The **Maggio Musicale**, Italy's oldest and most prestigious music festival, is the most conspicuous sign of the health of the city's classical music scene, though it should be said that the fare tends towards the conservative. In addition to this and the festival in Fiesole (see below), the **Amici della Musica** hosts a season of chamber concerts from September to April with top-name international performers, mostly in the Teatro della Pergola, occasionally in the Teatro Goldoni. From March to October the **Orchestra da Camera Fiorentina** (Florence Chamber Orchestra; Ⓦwww.orcafi.it) plays concerts, often in Orsanmichele, and Tuscany's major orchestra, the **Orchestra della Toscana** (Ⓦwww.orchestradella toscana.it), performs once or twice a month between November and May in the Teatro Verdi, often including contemporary pieces in their programmes. The Lutheran church on Lungarno Torrigiani regularly holds free chamber music and organ recitals.

**Teatro Comunale Corso Italia 16 Ⓣ055.213.535.** Florence's main municipal theatre, out to the west of Santa Maria Novella, hosting many of the city's major classical music, dance and theatre events in its main auditorium, the Teatro del Maggio Musicale Fiorentino. It has its own orchestra, chorus and dance company, and attracts top-name international guest performers. The main season for dance and opera runs from Oct–Dec, with classical music concerts taking over from Jan until the start of the Maggio Musicale festival, when there's a rich mix of opera and concerts on offer. Chamber music and other small-scale events are held in the theatre's Teatro Piccolo, and there are theatre productions in the months between the dance, opera and concert seasons.

**Teatro Goldoni Via Santa Maria 15 Ⓣ055.210.804.** This exquisite little eighteenth-century theatre, located a little way past the Palazzo Pitti, is occasionally used for chamber music and opera performances, but lately it has hosted more dance productions than anything else.

**Teatro della Pergola Via della Pergola 18 Ⓣ055.226.4353, Ⓦwww.pergola.firenze.it.** The beautiful little Pergola was built in 1656 and is Italy's oldest surviving theatre – Verdi's *Macbeth* was first performed here. During the season, that runs from Oct–April, it plays host to chamber concerts, small-scale operas, and some of the best-known Italian theatre companies.

**Teatro Verdi Via Ghibellina 99–101 Ⓣ055.212.320, Ⓦwww.teatroverdifirenze.it.** Home to the Orchestra della Toscana, this is another of the city's premier music venues. It also puts on plays, similar to the mainstream fare of the Teatro Comunale, though you may also catch the odd musical.

### Music festivals

**Estate Fiesolana Ⓦwww.estatefiesolana.it.** Slightly less exclusive than the Maggio Musicale, concentrating on chamber music, orchestral music and jazz. It's held in Fiesole every summer, usually from mid-June to late Aug or early Sept. Films and theatre are also featured, and most events are held in the open-air Teatro Romano.

**Maggio Musicale Fiorentino Ⓦwww.maggiofiorentino.com.** The highlight of Florence's cultural calendar and one of Europe's leading festivals of opera and classical music; confusingly, it isn't restricted to May (*Maggio*) but lasts for a couple of months from late April or early May. Events are staged at the Teatro Comunale, the Teatro della Pergola, the Palazzo dei Congressi, the Teatro Verdi and occasionally in the Bóboli gardens. Information and tickets can be obtained from the Teatro Comunale.

## Theatre and dance

Should your Italian be up to a performance of the plays of Machiavelli or Pirandello in the original, Florence's **theatres** offer year-round entertainment. In addition to the places listed below, various halls and disused churches are enlisted for one-off performances.

**Stazione Leopolda** Viale Fratelli Rosselli 5 ⓣ055.212.622, ⓦwww.stazione-leopolda.com. New contemporary arts centre in Florence's first railway station, 1km west of Santa Maria Novella. Built in 1848 and closed down in 1861, the old station is a fine Neoclassical space for dance, arts events and occasional concerts.

**Teatro Comunale** see opposite.

**Teatro Le Laudi** Via Leonardo da Vinci 2r ⓣ055.572.831. Located northeast of the centre, a few minutes' walk from San Marco; stages a fair amount of modern work.

**Teatro della Pergola** see opposite.

**Teatro Verdi** see opposite.

## Cinema

In Italy the vast majority of English-language films are dubbed, but **Odeon Original Sound**, at Via de' Sassetti 1 (ⓣ055.214.068; closed Aug), screens films in their original language (*versione originale*) once a week, generally on Monday, for most of the year, plus Tuesday and Thursday in summer. The opening of the eleven-screen **Warner Village** out on Via Cavallaccio, on the south side of the river about 4km west of the city centre, was the death-knell for Florence's older cinemas, which had already been struggling to stay afloat; the Odeon is the only notable survivor.

Florence and Fiesole have a few small **film festivals**, notably the **Premio Fiesole ai Maestri del Cinema** (July/Aug), in which the films of a single director are screened in Fiesole's Roman theatre, and the somewhat earnest **Festival dei Popoli** (2 weeks in Nov or Dec), run by an academic institution concerned with documentary film. In addition, in summer there are often **open-air screens** at the Forte Belvedere and the Palazzo dei Congressi (near the train station).

# Shopping



Florence is known as a producer of luxury items, notably **gold jewellery** and top-quality **leather goods**. The whole Ponte Vecchio is crammed with goldsmiths, but the city's premier shopping thoroughfare is **Via de' Tornabuoni**, where you'll find not only expensive jewellery and shoe shops but also the showrooms of Italy's top **fashion designers**: Prada, Gucci, Armani and Dolce e Gabbana are all here, as well as the main outlets for the top three Florentine fashion houses – Pucci, Roberto Cavalli and Ferragamo. Younger and more left-field designers tend to cluster in and around Via Matteo Palmieri (not far from Santa Croce), while for cheaper items there's the plethora of street stalls around the San Lorenzo market. If you want everything under one roof, try the handful of **department stores**. Marbled paper is another Florentine speciality, and, as you'd expect in this arty city, Florence is also a great place to pick up **books** on Italian art, architecture and culture. For delicatessens and **food** stores, see the box on p.184.

## Books and maps

**BM Borgo Ognissanti 4r ⓣ055.294.575.** English-language bookshop, with particular emphasis on Italian literature in translation, as well as books on Italian art, cookery and travel in Italy. Mon–Sat 9.30am–7.30pm.

**Edison Piazza della Repubblica 27r ⓣ055.213.110.** This US-style operation is arranged on four floors, with English-language books on the top; the stock is impressive, as are the opening hours. Mon–Sat 9am–midnight, Sun 10am–midnight.

**Feltrinelli Via de' Cerretani 30r ⓣ055.238.2652.** This branch of the Feltrinelli chain, a short distance west of the Duomo, is best for Italian titles, maps and guides. Mon–Fri 9am–7.30pm, Sat 10am–8pm, Sun 10.30am–1.30pm & 3.30–7.30pm.

**Feltrinelli International Via Cavour 12–20r ⓣ055.219.524.** Bright and well staffed, this has a good stock of English and other foreign-language books, plus newspapers, videos, posters, cards and magazines. Mon–Sat 9am–7.30pm.

**McRae Via de' Neri 32r ⓣ055.238.2456, ⓦwww.mcraebooks.com/shop.** Located not far from Santa Croce, this small bookshop has one of the finest collections of English-language books in town: guides, cookery books, literature and art are all covered. Daily 9am–7.30pm.

**Melbookstore Via de' Cerretani 54r ⓣ055.287.339.** Displaced from its famous location on Via de' Tornabuoni, the venerable Seeber bookshop has mutated into this modern megastore. It's lost all the soul of Seeber, but the stock is vast. Mon–Wed 9am–8pm, Thurs–Sat 9am–midnight, Sun 10am–midnight.

**Paperback Exchange Via delle Oche 4–6r ⓣ055.293.460.** Located just a few metres south of the Duomo, this shop has a good stock of English and American books, with the emphasis on Italian-related and second-hand titles; also exchanges secondhand books and has informative and friendly staff. Mon–Fri 9am–7.30pm, Sat 10am–7.30pm.

## Markets

**Cascine** Parco del Cascine. The biggest of all Florence's markets happens Tuesday morning (8am–1pm) at the Cascine park near the banks of the Arno (bus #1, #9, #12 or #17c), where hundreds of stallholders set up an al fresco budget-class department store. Fewer tourists make it out here than to San Lorenzo, so prices are keener. Clothes (some secondhand) and shoes are the best bargains, though for cheaper still, you should check out the weekday-morning stalls at Piazza delle Cure, just beyond Piazza della Libertà (bus #1 or #7; Tues 8am–1pm).

**San Lorenzo** Piazza di San Lorenzo. Another open-air warehouse of cheap clothing. San Lorenzo is as well organized as a shopping mall: huge waterproof awnings ensure that the weather can't stop the trading, and some of the stallholders even accept credit cards. You'll find plenty of leather jackets, T-shirts and other cheap clothes. For anything pricey, you could try haggling, but bear in mind that these traders aren't exactly desperate for customers. Daily 8am to 7pm.

**Mercato Centrale** Piazza del Mercato Centrale. Europe's largest indoor food hall is situated at the heart of the stall-filled streets around San Lorenzo, and is well worth a visit whether you intend to buy or not. Its popularity as a tourist sight has pushed prices up, but it's still unbeatable for picnic supplies. Monday to Saturday 7am to 2pm, plus Saturday 4 to 8pm in winter.

**Mercato Nuovo** Loggia del Mercato Nuovo. Just to the west of Piazza della Signoria (and also known as the Mercato del Porcellino), this is the main emporium for straw hats, plastic *Davids* and the like. Mid-February to mid-November daily 9am to 7pm; mid-November to mid-February Tuesday to Saturday 9am to 5pm.

**Mercato delle Pulci** Piazza dei Ciompi. A flea market stacked with antiques and bric-a-brac, pitched every day near the Sant'Ambrogio food market. Monday to Saturday 9am to 7pm. More serious antique dealers swell the ranks on the last Sunday of each month (same hours). On the second Sunday of each month there's a smaller flea market on Piazza Santo Spirito, from 8am to 6pm.

**Mercato Sant'Ambrogio** Piazza Ghiberti. Big, cheap market just beyond Santa Croce, with food stalls in the central hall, as well as cheap clothes and leather. Monday to Saturday 7am to 2pm.



# Clothing

**Ferragamo Via de' Tornabuoni 14r ⓣ055.292.123, ⓦwww.salvatoreferragamo.it.** The one Florentine designer whose name is known far and wide, Salvatore Ferragamo emigrated to the US at the age of 14 and became the most famous shoemaker in the world. Managed by his widow and children, Ferragamo now produces ready-to-wear outfits, but the company's reputation still rests on its beautiful shoes. The shop, occupying virtually the entire ground floor of a colossal *palazzo* on Piazza Santa Trìnita, is unbelievably grandiose, and even has a shoe museum. Mon–Sat 10am–7.30pm.

**Il Guardaroba Via Giuseppe Verdi 28r ⓣ055.247.8250.** Outlet for the previous season's designer lines, at sizeable discounts. Mon 3.30–7.30pm, Tues–Sat 9.30am–7.30pm.

**Luisa at Via Roma Via Roma 19–21r ⓣ055.217.826, ⓦwww.luisaviaroma.com.** A

▲ Flaunting the label on Via de' Tornabuoni

long-standing fixture at this address, with a host of different labels every season. Mon–Sat 10am–7.30pm, Sun 11am–7pm.

**Poncif Borgo Albizi 35r ⓣ055.263.8739.** Florentine design tends to be somewhat conservative, but the clothes and costume jewellery at Poncif – the work of a variety of youngish talents – are both elegant and contemporary. Mon 3.30–7.30pm, Tues–Thurs 10am–1.30pm & 3.30–7.30pm, Fri & Sat 10am–7.30pm.

**Raspini Via Por Santa Maria 70r & Via Roma 25r ⓣ055.213.077, ⓦwww.raspini.com.** Florence's biggest multi-label clothes shop, with a good stock of diffusion lines. These are the two main branches, and there's a third one at Via de' Martelli 5–7r. Leftovers from previous season are sold at big discounts at Raspini Vintage, at Via Calimaruzza 17r, very close to the Via Por Santa Maria branch. Mon 3.30–7.30pm, Tues–Sat 9.30am–7.30pm, plus last Sun of month 10am–7pm.



## Department stores

**Coin Via dei Calzaiuoli 56r (but with entrances on all four sides of the block) ⓣ055.280.531, ⓦwww.coin.it.** Clothes-dominated chain store in a central position. Quality is generally high, though styles are fairly conservative except for one or two youth-oriented franchises on the ground floor. Also a good place for linen and other household goods. Mon–Sat 10am–8pm, Sun 11am–8pm.

**La Rinascente Piazza della Repubblica 1 ⓣ055.239.8544, ⓦwww.rinascente.it.** Like Coin, Rinascente is part of a national chain, though this store, opened in 1996, is a touch more upmarket than its nearby rival. Sells clothing, linen, cosmetics, household goods and other staples. The rooftop café isn't one of the city's best, but it has a fabulous location. Mon–Sat 10am–9pm, Sun 10.30am–8pm.

### Fashion factory outlets

Tuscany is the powerhouse of the country's textile industry, and the Arno valley – in particular the area between Incisa Val d'Arno and Pontassieve – is the home of many of the factories that manufacture clothes for the top labels. Several of these factories have retail outlets alongside, in which the season's leftovers (sometimes the previous season's) are sold at discounts as high as sixty percent. The best of these shops are listed below.

**Dolce e Gabbana Via Pian dell'Isola 49, localita Santa Maria Maddalena, Incisa Val d'Arno ⓣ055.833.1300.** This two-storey shed, a few kilometres north of Incisa Val d'Arno, is packed with clothes, accessories and household items from the main Dolce e Gabbana range, plus cheaper stuff from the D&G diffusion label. Mon–Sat 9am–7pm, Sun 3–7pm.

**Fendi, Loewe & Cellini Via Pian dell'Isola 66, Rignano sull'Arno ⓣ055.834.7155.** Situated a short distance north of Dolce e Gabbana, the Fendi/Loewe/Cellini warehouse is best for bags and other leather accessories. Mon–Sat 10am–7pm, Sun 3–7pm.

**The Mall Via Europe 8, Leccio Regello ⓣ055.865.7775.** Located between the Fendi and Dolce e Gabbana outlets, The Mall contains separate outlets for Gucci, Bottega Veneta, Sergio Rossi, Loro Piana and Armani. Gucci is the dominant presence, with a huge range of bags, shoes, sunglasses and other accessories. Daily 10am–7pm.

**Space Levanella, Montevarchi ⓣ055.91.901.** Located just outside Montevarchi, on a small industrial estate in the Levanella district (on the SS69), this unmarked concrete shed is the busiest of all the factory outlets, as it's stacked with clothes from the ineffably stylish Prada label, as well as items from the scarcely less trendy Jil Sander and Helmut Lang, both of which are now subsidiaries of Prada. Also on sale is a good selection from Miu Miu, Prada's mid-priced diffusion range. Mon–Sat 9.30am–7.30pm, Sun 10am–7pm.

# Jewellery

**Alessandro Dari Via San Nicolò 115r ⓣ055.244.747, ⓦwww.alessandrodari.com.** Goldsmith Alessandro Dari produces jewellery that combines remarkable craftsmanship with a sort of neo-Baroque New Age fantasy, in which motifs such as spiders, butterflies, musical instruments and imaginary animals frequently recur. The showroom-cum-workshop – converted from a sixteenth-century loggia in which cloth used to be dyed – is pretty spectacular in itself. Mon–Sat 9.30am–1.30pm & 4–7.30pm.

**Dettagli per donzelle, comari e sognatori Borgo degli Albizi 40r ⓣ055.234.0333.** Funky, brightly coloured handmade jewellery and accessories at reasonable prices. Mon 3.30–7.30pm, Tues–Sat 10am–7.30pm.

**Gatto Bianco Borgo SS Apostoli 12r ⓣ055.282.989.** Strange combinations of precious and everyday materials are the signature of this outlet, one of the city's more adventurous jewellery workshops. Mon 3.30–7.30pm, Tues–Sat 9.30am–1pm & 3.30–7.30pm.

**Moltissimo Via Matteo Palmieri 27r ⓣ055.242.038.** Inventive jewellery and accessories made from non-precious materials, though there's a dash of silver in some of the pieces. You could pick up a bracelet or a pair of earrings here for around €20. Mon–Sat 10.30am–7.30pm.

**Torrini Piazza del Duomo 10r ⓣ055.230.2401, ⓦwww.torrini.com.** Torrini registered its trademark – a distinctive half-clover leaf with spur – as early as 1369. Seven centuries later this store remains one of the best places to buy Florentine jewellery: gold predominates, but all manner of classic and modern pieces are available, at a price. Mon 3–7pm, Tues–Sat 10am–1.30pm & 2.30–7pm.

# Music

**Alberti Via de' Pucci 16r ⓣ055.284.346 & Borgo San Lorenzo 45–49r ⓣ055.294.271.** Founded in 1873, this is the city's leading supplier of domestic hi-fi, DVDs, records and CDs. The Borgo San Lorenzo store is good for opera, classical and jazz, while the Via de' Pucci shop (a couple of blocks to the east) concentrates on contemporary music (dance, rock, etc). Mon 3.30–7.30pm, Tues–Sat 9am–7.30pm.

**Data Records 93 Via de' Neri 15r ⓣ055.287.592.** Huge collection of new and secondhand albums covering rock, pop, reggae, jazz, punk, heavy metal, etc. Mon 3.30–7.30pm, Tues–Sat 10am–1pm & 3.30–7.30pm.

**Ricordi Media Store Via Brunelleschi 8–10r ⓣ055.214.104.** The city's biggest general CD store, just off Piazza della Repubblica. Mon–Sat 9.30am–7.30pm, plus last Sun of month 3–7.30pm.

# Paper, stationery and artists' materials

**Giulio Giannini e Figlio Piazza Pitti 36r ⓣ055 .212.621, ⓦwww.giuliogiannini.it.** Established in 1856, this paper-making and book-binding firm has been honoured with exhibitions dedicated to its work. Once the only place in Florence to make its own marbled papers, it now offers a wide variety of diaries, address books and so forth as well. Mon–Sat 10am–7.30pm, Sun 10.30am–6.30pm.

**Pineider Piazza della Signoria 13r ⓣ055.284.655, ⓦwww.pineider.com.** Pineider sell briefcases, picture frames and other accessories for the home and office, but their reputation rests on their calling cards, handmade papers and envelopes – as used by Napoleon, Stendhal, Byron and Shelley, to name just a few previous customers. Daily 10am–7pm.

**Il Torchio Via de' Bardi 17 ⓣ055.234.2862.** A marbled-paper workshop using manufacturing techniques known only to the owner. Desk accessories, diaries, albums and other items in paper and leather are also available. Mon 2.30–7pm, Tues–Sat 10am–1.30pm & 2.30–7.30pm.

**Zecchi Via della Studio 19r.** A very good stock of paints, brushes and all artistic equipment, close to the Duomo. Mon–Fri 8.30am–7.30pm, Sat 8.30–12.30am.

# Perfume and toiletries

**Farmacia Santa Maria Novella Via della Scala 16 ⓣ055.216.276.** Occupying the pharmacy of the Santa Maria Novella monastery, this sixteenth-century shop was founded by Dominican monks as an outlet for their potions, ointments and herbal remedies. Many of these are still available, including distillations of flowers and herbs, together with face-creams, shampoos and other, more esoteric, products. The shop's as famous for its wonderful interior as for its goods, which are sold worldwide. Mon–Sat 9.30am–7.30pm, Sun 10.30am–6.30pm; closed Sun in Feb & Nov.

**Spezieria Erborista Palazzo Vecchio Via Vaccherccia 9r ⓣ055.239.6055.** A celebrated old pharmacy-cum-cosmetics shop, selling its own natural remedies and a range of unique perfumes, such as Acqua di Caterina de' Medici. July & Aug Mon–Fri 9am–7.30pm, Sat 9am–5pm; Sept–June Mon–Sat 9.30am–7.30pm, first and last Sun of month 1.30–7pm.

# Prints and photos

**Alinari Largo Alinari 15 ⓣ055.239.51, ⓦwww.alinari.com.** Founded in 1852, this is the world's oldest photographic business. Owners of the largest archive of old photographs in Italy, they will print any image you choose from their huge catalogue. They also publish books, calendars, posters and cards. Mon–Fri 9am–1pm & 2–6pm; closed two weeks in mid-Aug.

**Giovanni Baccani Via della Vigna Nuova 75r ⓣ055.214.467.** The richest selection of prints and engravings in Florence is at Baccani, a beautiful old shop that's crammed with all manner of prints, frames and paintings. Prices range from a few euros to wallet-busting sums. Mon 3.30–7.30pm, Tues–Sat 9am–1pm & 3.30–7.30pm; July closed Sat afternoons; closed first three weeks of Aug.

# Shoes, bags, gloves and hats

**Il Bisonte Via del Parione 31–33r ⓣ055.215.722, ⓦwww.ilbisontefirenze.com.** Beautiful and robust bags, briefcases and accessories, many of them made from vacchetta, a soft cow-hide which ages very nicely. Mon–Sat 9.30am–7pm.

**Bojola Via de' Rondinelli 25r ⓣ055.211.155, ⓦwww.bojola.it.** Founded in 1892, still operating from its original shop and still run by the Bojola family, this firm produces very high-quality bags, cases and wallets. Mon 3.30–7.30pm, Tues–Sat 9am-7.30pm.

**Bologna Piazza San Giovanni 13–15r ⓣ055.290.545.** Probably the best-known shoe shop in the city; trendy men's and women's footwear at relatively sane prices. Mon–Sat 9.30am-7.30pm, Sun 3–7pm.

**Cellerini Via del Sole 37r ⓣ055.282.533, ⓦwww.cellerini.it.** Bags, bags and more bags. Everything here is made on the premises under the supervision of the firm's founders, the city's premier exponents of the craft; bags don't come more elegant, durable – or costly. Summer Mon–Fri 9am–1pm & 3–7pm, Sat 9am–1pm; winter Mon 3–7pm, Tues–Sat 9am–1pm & 3–7pm.

**Francesco da Firenze Via Santo Spirito 62r ⓣ055.212.428.** Handmade shoes for men and women at relatively reasonable prices (under €200). Classical footwear combined with striking designs. Mon–Sat 9am–1pm & 3.30–7.30pm; Aug closed Sat afternoon.

**Madova Via Guicciardini 1r ⓣ055.239.6526, ⓦwww.madova.com.** The last word in gloves – every colour, every size, every style. Prices from around €35. Mon–Sat 9.30am–7.30pm.

**Mannina Via Guicciardini 16r ⓣ055.282.895, ⓦwww.manninafirenze.com.** This famed Oltrarno shoemaker has been going for donkey's years, producing beautifully made and sensible footwear at prices that are far from extravagant. Mon–Sat 9.30am–7.30pm, Sun 10.30am–1pm & 2–6pm.

**Saskia Via di Santa Lucia 22–24r ⓣ055 .293.291.** Trained in Hamburg and Florence, Vivian Saskia Wittmer produces exquisite and durable made-to-measure shoes in classic designs. Her workshop, located near Ognissanti, specializes in men's footwear, but makes a few pieces for women too. The quality is comparable to Stefano Bemer, but the prices are less agonizing. Mon–Sat 9am–1pm & 3.30–7.30pm.

**Scuola del Cuio Via San Giuseppe 5r ⓣ055.244.533, ⓦwww.scuoladelcuio.com.** This academy for leather-workers – located at the back of Santa Croce church – sells bags, jackets, belts and other accessories at prices that compare very favourably with the shops. You won't find any startlingly original designs here, but the quality is very high and the staff are knowledgeable and helpful. Mon–Sat 9.30am–6pm, Sun 10am–6pm.

**Sol Gabriel Via Matteo Palmieri 6r ⓣ055.718.9648, ⓦwww.solgabriel.com.** As a change from all that Florentine leather, here's a shop that makes beautiful bags from all sorts of fabrics; at least three different materials go into every bag (cotton, vinyl and silk are favourites), and every one is unique. Most are less than €100. Tues–Sat 10.30am–1.30pm & 2.30–7pm.

**Stefano Bemer Borgo San Frediano 143r ⓣ055.211.356.** If you're in the market for made-to-measure Italian shoes, there's no better place than this. Another branch, close by at Via Camaldoli 10r, is an outlet for Bemer'S [sic], the off-the-peg (but still expensive) footwear designed by Stefano and his brother Mario. Mon–Sat 9am–1pm & 3.30–7.30pm.

# Directory

**Banks and exchange** Florence's main bank branches are on or around Piazza della Repubblica, but exchange booths (*cambio*) and ATM cash card machines (*bancomat*) can be found across the city. Banks generally open Mon–Fri 8.20am–3.35pm, though some are open longer hours and some close for an hour in the middle of the day.
**Bike, scooter & moped rental** Alinari, Via Guelfa 85r to Via Zanobi 38r ⓣ055.280.500, ⓦwww.alinarirental.com; Florence by Bike, Via San Zanobi 120–122r ⓣ055.488.992, ⓦwww.florencebybike.it (they also do repairs).
**Bus information** City buses are run by ATAF ⓣ800.424.500, ⓦwww.ataf.net.
**Car rental** Avis, Borgo Ognissanti 128r ⓣ055.213.629; Europcar, Borgo Ognissanti 53 ⓣ055.290.438; Hertz, Via Maso Finiguerra 33r ⓣ055.239.8205; Italy by Car, Borgo Ognissanti 134r ⓣ055.293.021; Maggiore, Via Maso Finiguerra 31r ⓣ055.290.164.
**Consulates** UK, Lungarno Corsini 2 ⓣ055.284.133; US, Lungarno Amerigo Vespucci 38 ⓣ055.239.8276.
**Doctors** The Tourist Medical Service is a private service used to dealing with foreigners; they have doctors on call 24hr a day on ⓣ055.475.411 (ⓦwww.medicalservice.firenze.it), or you can visit their clinic at Via Lorenzo il Magnifico 59 (Mon–Fri 11am–noon & 5–6pm, Sat 11am–noon). Note that you'll need insurance cover to recoup the cost of a consultation, which will be at least €50. Florence's central hospital is on Piazza Santa Maria Nuova.
**Internet cafés** Many hotels and hostels now offer free internet access, but if you need to find a computer your best bet is a branch of Internet Train (ⓦwww.internettrain.it), which has seven outlets in the city, including Via de Benci 36r, Via Guelfa 54/56r, Via Porta Rossa 38r and Piazza Stazione 14 – they're open Mon–Sat 10am–midnight, Sun 3–11pm. The tourist office has a full list of current internet points.
**Laundry** Florence has plenty of self-service *lavanderie* costing around €3–4 for a complete wash, with the main concentration being near the one-star hotels of the station and San Lorenzo districts. Wash & Dry has seven branches, open 8am–10pm daily: Via dei Servi 105r, Via della Scala 52–54r, Via Ghibellina 143r, Via dei Serragli 87r, Viale Morgagni 21r, Via Orsini 39r and Via Nazionale 129r.
**Left luggage** Santa Maria Novella station by platform 16 (daily 6am–midnight). Around €4 for first 5hr, then around €0.60 for each additional hour.
**Lost property** Lost property handed in at the city or railway police ends up at Via Circondaria 17b (Mon–Sat 9am–noon; ⓣ055.367.943; take bus #23 to Viale Corsica). There's also a lost property office at Santa Maria Novella station, on platform 16 next to left luggage.
**Pharmacies** The Farmacia Comunale, on the train station concourse, is open 24hr, as is All' Insegna del Moro, at Piazza San Giovanni 20r, on the north side of the Baptistery, and Farmacia Molteni, at Via dei Calzaiuoli 7r. All pharmacies display a roster in their window, showing the nearest pharmacy that's open through the night on that particular day; from midnight to 8.30am these pharmacies (but not the trio of 24hr places) impose a surcharge of around €3.
**Police** Emergency ⓣ112 or 113. To report a theft or other crime, go to the Carabinieri at Borgo Ognissanti 48 (open 24hr), or the city police, at Via Pietrapiana 50r (Mon–Fri 8.30am–7.30pm, Sat closes 1.30pm) – you're likelier to find an English-speaker at the latter. When reporting an incident you will have to fill out a form (*una denuncia*): this may be time-consuming, but it's essential if you want to make a claim on your travel insurance.
**Post office** The main central post office is near Piazza della Repubblica at Via Pellicceria 3 (Mon–Sat 8.15am–7pm); the poste restante section is through the door immediately on the left as you enter. If you're having mail sent to you poste restante, make sure it's marked for Via Pellicceria, otherwise it will go to Florence's biggest post office, at Via Pietrapiana 53–55 (Mon–Fri 8.15am–7pm, Sat 8.15am–12.30pm).
**Toilets** Public toilets are usually open 10am–6pm daily and cost €0.50–60; otherwise, for the price of a coffee, you can use the facilities of any bar.

# Tuscany

# The best of Tuscany


13 Prato and Pistoia ........ 213

14 Pisa and Lucca ........ 227

15 Chianti ........ 250

16 Siena ........ 257

17 Sienese hill-towns ........ 297

18 San Gimignano and Volterra ........ 316

19 Arezzo and Cortona ........ 327

# Prato and Pistoia

The busy commercial centre of Prato – the second-largest city in Tuscany – and the provincial capital of Pistoia are close enough to Florence to make fine day-trips: trains from Florence to Prato run every thirty minutes (20min) and hourly to Pistoia (30–45min). Taking its name from the meadow (*prato*) where the ancient settlement's market used to be held, **Prato** has been Italy's chief textile centre since the early Middle Ages, and despite the rise in competition from Asian producers it's still doing well, with thousands of local companies involved in the production and marketing of cloth. It might not feature on a list of the prettiest places in Tuscany, but it makes a bracing change from tourist-inundated Florence, and its longtime wealth has left a fair legacy of buildings and art, including an unequalled collection of paintings by Filippo Lippi, whose frescoes adorn the Duomo. Sitting in the shadow of the Apennines, well-preserved **Pistoia** is notable for a number of handsome Romanesque churches, in which you'll find some superb sculpture – and it has a handful of excellent restaurants too. It's the quieter of the two towns, except in July, when the **Luglio Pistoiese** features a month-long programme of concerts and events (including the international Pistoia Blues festival of jazz and blues), culminating in the Giostra dell'Orso.



## Prato

Florence's close connection with **PRATO** goes back to 1350, when the latter was besieged by its neighbour, which was alarmed at the economic threat of Prato's cloth mills. The year after, Florence bought the titles to the town from its Neapolitan rulers, thus sealing their union. Thereafter, political events in the capital were mirrored here, a relationship that was to cost Prato dear after Savonarola's example led the Pratese to join him in rejecting the Medici. Under the direction of Leo X, the imperial army sacked Prato in 1512 as a warning to the rebellious Florentines. A more pacific relationship developed, and Florence limited its bullying to quotas on Prato's factories. Today the balance has shifted: while Florence struggles to find some alternative to a service-based economy, Prato is a self-sufficient city with the highest per capita income in Tuscany. Unsurprisingly, Prato's most well-appointed museum is devoted to textiles, but it also has a good art gallery, the **Museo di Pittura Murale**, while superb frescoes are to be seen in the **Duomo**, which has work by Paolo Uccello as well as the celebrated cycle by Filippo Lippi. In addition, Prato has a fine Renaissance church, **Santa Maria delle Carceri**, which stands in the lee of the thirteenth-century **castle** walls.

## Arrival and information

**Buses** from Florence run direct to the Piazza del Duomo; if you're coming from the main **train** station it's basically a question of following your nose – cross the Ponte della Vittoria over the Bisenzio River, and Viale Vittorio Veneto leads you through the walls at Piazza San Marco. Prato's **tourist office** (Mon–Sat 9am–1.30pm & 2.30–7pm, Sun 10am–1pm; ⓣ0574.24.112, ⓦwww.prato.turismo.toscana.it) is opposite the Carceri church in Piazza delle Carceri.

## Accommodation

Most of Prato's hotels are featureless concrete blocks catering for business visitors, but there's a handful of places in the historic centre offering decent accommodation at good prices.

**Flora Via Cairoli 31 ⓣ0574.33.521, ⓦwww.hotelflora.info.** The 31-room *Flora* occupies a handsome nineteenth-century *palazzo* very close to the Piazza del Comune. It may not be a contender for any shortlist of hip Tuscan hotels, but this well-run three-star is the pick of central Prato's accommodation. ❹

**Il Giglio Piazza San Marco 14 ⓣ0574.37.049, ⓦwww.albergoilgiglio.it.** This little two-star, tucked against the city walls, has been offering simple and functional rooms for forty years now, and the styling hasn't changed greatly in the interim. All rooms are en suite and a/c, however, and the prices are low. ❷

**La Toscana Piazza Ciardi 3 ⓣ0574.28.096, ⓦwww.hoteltoscana.prato.it.** Founded back in the nineteenth century, the eighteen-room Toscana is today a modest, tidy and bland two-star hotel. High-season doubles are about €10 pricier than at the *Giglio* – otherwise, location and history are pretty well the only things that distinguish them. ❷

## The City

The historic centre remains enclosed within its hexagon of grey stone walls, making orientation very straightforward. At the centre of the hexagon lie the two most important squares, **Piazza del Duomo** and **Piazza del Comune**; on the east side, the castle guards the gate at Piazza San Marco, which is a short distance south of the huge market square; on the west side, the main art gallery – the **Museo di Pittura Murale** – is the chief focus.

### The Castello area

Walking from the train station, if you turn left at the far side of Piazza San Marco (where the traffic swirls around a large Henry Moore sculpture), you'll pass under the **Cassero**, a fortified corridor built in the middle of the fourteenth century to link the castle to the city walls; the entrance to it is on Viale Piave (daily 10am–1pm & 4–7pm; free). A short distance beyond, in Via Santa Chiara, you'll come to the former Campolmi factory, a huge nineteenth-century textile mill that has been converted into an impressive home for the **Museo del Tessuto** (Mon & Wed–Fri 10am–6pm, Sat 10am–2pm, Sun 4–7pm; €6, free on Sun). Tracing the city's rise from rags to riches, the museum also displays a collection of more than five thousand fabrics from all over the world, ranging right back to the third century AD. It's also a venue for one-off exhibitions on textile- or fashion-related themes.

Five minutes' walk away stands the city's signature building, the white-walled **Castello dell'Imperatore** (9am–1pm & 4–7pm; closed Tues; €2.50, or joint ticket with Museo dell'Opera del Duomo & Museo di Pittura Murale €6.50), built in the 1230s for Emperor Frederick II as a base for his representative in

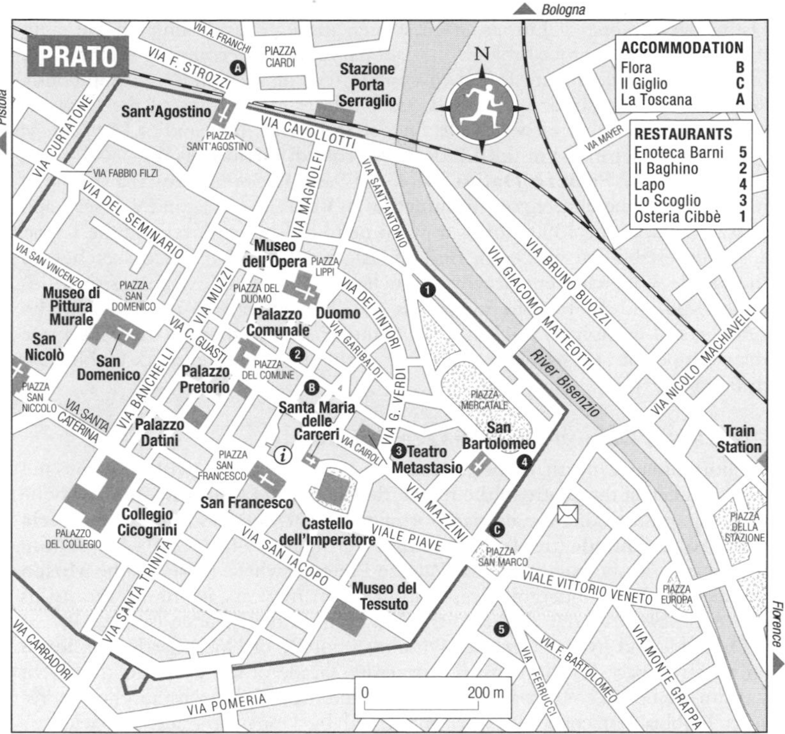




the city and as a way-station for imperial progresses between Germany and his domains in southern Italy and Sicily. The castle is heavily restored and empty except for the rooms used for temporary exhibitions, but you can wander around the ramparts for views over the old city and its industrial suburbs.

Round the back is Prato's major Renaissance monument, Giuliano da Sangallo's church of **Santa Maria delle Carceri** (daily 7am–noon & 4–7pm), built to honour a miraculous talking image of the Virgin that was painted on the walls of the jail here – hence the name "Mary of the Prisons". With its perfect proportions and uncluttered lines, the church is a rather severe demonstration of the correctness of the Brunelleschian style, though the exterior makes a decorative gesture towards the Romanesque with its half-completed bands of green and white marble. The interior – lightened by Andrea della Robbia's tondi of the Evangelists and ceramic frieze – is designed so that on the exact anniversary of the moment at which the Virgin spoke (3.18pm on July 15) a beam of light shines through the top of the cupola and strikes the centre of the altar.

Twin-coloured marble cladding also features on the facade of the thirteenth-century church of **San Francesco** (daily 8am–noon & 4–7pm; free), which presents its back to the far side of the square. Inside are a couple of fine monuments: on the left wall of the single aisle you'll find Bernardo Rossellino's worn-down tomb of Gemignano Inghirami, and set into the floor near the high altar is the slab of Francesco di Marco Datini (1335–1410), Prato's most celebrated citizen. The subject of Iris Origo's classic study, *The Merchant of Prato*,

Datini became one of Europe's richest men through his dealings in the cloth trade, and played a crucial role in the rationalization of accounting methods: on his death, his offices were found to contain tens of thousands of scrupulously kept ledgers, all inscribed "To God and profit". Off the cloister, the Cappella Migliatori has lovely frescoes of *The Lives of St Anthony Abbot* and *St Matthew and The Crucifixion*, painted in the 1390s by Niccolò di Pietro Gerini.

Datini's house, **Palazzo Datini** (Mon–Sat 9am–12.30pm; free), is a couple of minutes from the church, on the junction of Via Rinascelda and Via Ser Lapo Mazzei. Built in the 1390s, this is now home to the city archives and the *Ceppo*, a charity established by Datini himself. The barely legible fresco sketches on the facade – which were heavily retouched in 1910 – show scenes from his life; the ground floor of the interior is also frescoed, mostly with fleur-de-lys ceilings and engagingly cack-handed hunting scenes, though there's a more than competent *St Christopher* at the foot of the stairs, another work by Niccolò di Pietro Gerini.



## Piazza del Comune and Piazza del Duomo

A short distance north of here, Datini is commemorated with a statue and bronze reliefs at the centre of the trim little **Piazza del Comune**. Inevitably, he crops up again among the myriad portraits of local worthies in the **Quadreria Palazzo Comunale** (free by appointment – ring ☎0574.616.220). Across from the *palazzo* sits the huge medieval Palazzo Pretorio, whose museum, the **Museo Civico**, has been undergoing restoration for many years; in the meantime, its contents have been transferred to the Museo di Pittura Murale (see p.218).

The wide and lively Piazza del Duomo, a couple of blocks farther in, forms an effective space for the Pisan-Romanesque facade of the **Duomo** (Mon–Sat 7.30am–7pm, Sun 7.30am–noon & 3–7pm; free), distinguished by another Andrea della Robbia terracotta over the portal and by Donatello's and Michelozzo's beautiful **Pulpit of the Sacred Girdle**. This unique addition was constructed for the ceremonial display of the girdle of the Madonna, a garment allegedly dropped into the hands of the apostle Thomas at her Assumption. The girdle (or *Sacro Cingolo*) was supposedly bequeathed by Thomas to a priest, one of whose descendants married a Crusader from Prato, who in turn brought it back to his home town in 1141. Replicas have replaced the Donatello reliefs of gambolling children; the originals are now housed in the cathedral museum. The girdle itself is displayed five times a year: on Easter Sunday, May 1, August 15, September 8 and Christmas Day.

**Filippo Lippi**'s famous frescoes, around the high altar, were completed over a period of fourteen years (1452–66) and depict the lives of John the Baptist and St Stephen. These are marvellously sensuous paintings in which even the Baptist's wilderness looks quite enticing, a whisked-up landscape like a confectioner's fantasy. Lippi's characteristic tenderness is much in evidence too, notably in the attendants kissing the feet of the dead St Stephen, and in the scene depicting John taking his leave of his parents. High drama, however, was not his forte: in the *Feast of Herod* the decapitation seems like a regrettable incident that needn't ruin the party. There's a scandalous story to the creation of these pictures: during the period of their creation, Lippi – himself a friar, at least in name – became so besotted with a young nun named Lucrezia Buti that he abducted her as she was preparing to attend the ceremony of the girdle. Later to become the mother of Filippino Lippi, Lucrezia is said to have been the model for the dancing Salome. Her lover is also believed to have depicted himself among the superb gallery of portraits around the body of St Stephen: it's most likely that he's the third mourner from the right.

After several years of restoration, the Lippi cycle is now once again on show (Mon–Sat 10am–5pm, Sun 3–5pm; €3). Your ticket also gives you access to the scenes from the lives of the Virgin and St Stephen in the chapel to the right of the high altar. Some believe – though studies of the underpainting have cast

▲ Piazza del Duomo, Prato

doubt on the attribution – that these were begun by Paolo Uccello in 1435, a year before he was called away to Florence to paint the Hawkwood monument in the Duomo, having finished just the vault and the lunettes of *The Birth of the Virgin*, *The Birth of St Stephen* and *The Stoning of St Stephen*; the lower part of the chapel was painted by Andrea di Giusto.

Housed alongside the Duomo, around the cloister of the bishop's palace, the **Museo dell'Opera del Duomo** (Mon & Wed–Sat 9.30am–12.30pm & 3.30–6.30pm, Sun 9.30am–12.30pm; €4, or joint ticket with Castello & Museo Pittura Murale €6.50) contains the Donatello panels from the great pulpit; they are badly cracked and stained by exhaust fumes but their sculpted *putti* make a sprightly contrast with the lumbering little lads on Maso di Bartolomeo's tiny silver *Reliquary for the Sacred Girdle*, the museum's other main treasure. Also on show is Filippino Lippi's plucky *St Lucy*, unperturbed by the gigantic sword lodged in her neck, and the magnificent painting that Filippo Lippi produced to demonstrate his suitability for the fresco commission, *The Death of Jerome*. A doorway on the far side of the cloister opens into the Duomo's frescoed **crypt**; beside the altar is the head of one of the city's main wells, which – as the inscription records – was choked with corpses left by the imperial invaders in 1512.



### The Museo di Pittura Murale

A five-minute walk west of the Duomo, in the ex-monastery adjoining the mainly fourteenth-century church of San Domenico, the **Museo di Pittura Murale** (Mon, Wed, Thurs & Sun 9am–1pm, Fri & Sat 9am–1pm & 3–6pm; €4, or joint ticket with Museo dell'Opera & Castello €6.50) currently houses one of the town's star attractions – Filippo Lippi's *Madonna del Ceppo*. The painting contains portraits of the five men who financed the picture; Datini coughed up more than the other four, so he's the one depicted large-scale. Among the other Lippi pieces on show is a tender *Nativity with SS George and Vincent Ferrer*: the Madonna and Christ were probably modelled on Lucrezia and their son. There are works by Filippino here as well, plus – among a variety of fourteenth-century altarpieces – a predella by Bernardo Daddi narrating the story of the Girdle of the Madonna.

## Eating and drinking

Unpretentious Prato has several good and inexpensive restaurants, most of which are to be found on or near to the market square. While you're in town, you might want to sample the best-known Prato speciality, the *Biscotto di Prato*, a very hard yellow biscuit, made a touch less resistant by dipping in wine or coffee. The best outlet for these and other Prato pastries is Antonio Mattei, which has been in existence at Via Ricasoli 22 (very close to Piazza San Francesco) since 1858.

**Enoteca Barni Via Ferrucci 22 ⓣ0574.607.845.** An excellent family-run restaurant/wine bar, where you'll spend in the region of €40–50 a head. Closed lunchtime Sat & Sun.

**Il Baghino Via dell'Accademia 9 ⓣ0574.27.920.** A long-standing local favourite, serving Prato specialities in a traditional atmosphere. Closed Sun eve & Mon lunch.

**Lapo Piazza Mercatale 141 ⓣ0574.23.745.** One of two very good *trattorie* on the city's largest square. Closed Sun.

**Lo Scoglio Via Verdi 42 ⓣ0574.22.760.** Pizzas and inexpensive fish dishes. Closed Mon.

**Osteria Cibbè Piazza Mercatale 49 ⓣ0574.60.759.** Like *Lapo* at the opposite end of the piazza, this is a good no-nonsense trattoria, catering mainly for local traders. Closed Sun.

# Pistoia

The provincial capital of **PISTOIA** is one of the least visited cities in Tuscany, an unjustified neglect for this quiet, well-preserved medieval settlement at the base of the Apennines. Just 35 minutes or so by train from Florence (about the same by bus), it is an easy and enjoyable day-trip – and also forms an attractive approach to Lucca and Pisa, with both of which it has strong architectural links. In terms of art attractions, its appeal lies in a sequence of Romanesque churches and medieval sculptures, and one of the masterpieces of the della Robbia workshop.

The town's **Roman** forerunner, Pistoria, was where Catiline and his fellow conspirators against the republic were finally run to ground; the town later went on to earn itself a reputation as a lair of malcontents after its conquest by Florence in 1254 led to internecine fighting among the victorious Guelphs. Such was Pistoia's reputation for mayhem, Dante found it entirely appropriate that this should have been the home of Vanni Fucci, a thuggish factional leader whose exploits included stealing the silver from the cathedral; he's encountered in the *Inferno*, enmeshed in a knot of snakes and cursing God.

Except for a brief spell at the start of the fourteenth century, when Castruccio Castracani held the city for Lucca, Pistoia remained a **Florentine** fief, yet for centuries the mythology of murderous Pistoia endured, and Michelangelo spoke for many when he referred to the Pistoiese as the "enemies of heaven". It's therefore fitting that, according to one school of thought, the word **pistol** should be derived from this violent town; meaning "from Pistoia", a *pistole* was originally a dagger, but the name was transferred to the first firearms made here in the sixteenth century. These days, Pistoia maintains its industrial tradition with a large rail plant, but is better known for the acres of garden nurseries on the slopes around.

The liveliest time to be in Pistoia is July, for the **Luglio Pistoiese**, a month-long programme of concerts and events (including the Pistoia Blues music festival featuring major international jazz and blues artists), and culminating in the Giostra dell'Orso (see box, p.222).

## Arrival and information

The **train station** and adjacent **bus stops** are just a couple of minutes' walk south of the historic centre: Viale XX Settembre points the way through the city walls, which were raised in the fourteenth century and reinforced by the Medici. Pistoia's central **tourist office** is at Piazza del Duomo 4 (Mon–Sat 9am–1pm & 3–6pm, Sun 10am–1pm & 3–6pm; ⓣ0573.21.622, ⓦwww.comune.pistoia.it).

## Accommodation

As with Prato, the city's low tourist profile means a shortage of accommodation – but there are three decent options in the city centre, plus another on the fringes.

**Autisti Viale Pacinotti 43 ⓣ0573.21.771.** This clean and friendly place is Pistoia's only one-star. The location isn't great (it's out on the southern stretch of the city's ring road), but a double room is some €40 cheaper than any other place in Pistoia. ❶

**Firenze Via Curtatone e Montanara 42 ⓣ0573.231.141, ⓦwww.hotel-firenze.it.** The twenty-room *Firenze* is Pistoia's only two-star and it offers good value for money – all bedrooms have a/c and en-suite bathroom, and all are brightly turned-out. ❷

**Leon Bianco Via Panciatichi 2 ⓣ0573.26.675, ⓦwww.hotelleonbianco.it.** The thirty-room *Leon Bianco* is a long-established and inexpensive three-star, right in the heart of the city. It would benefit from a dash of renovation, but for every guest who finds it dowdy, another might find it homely. ❸

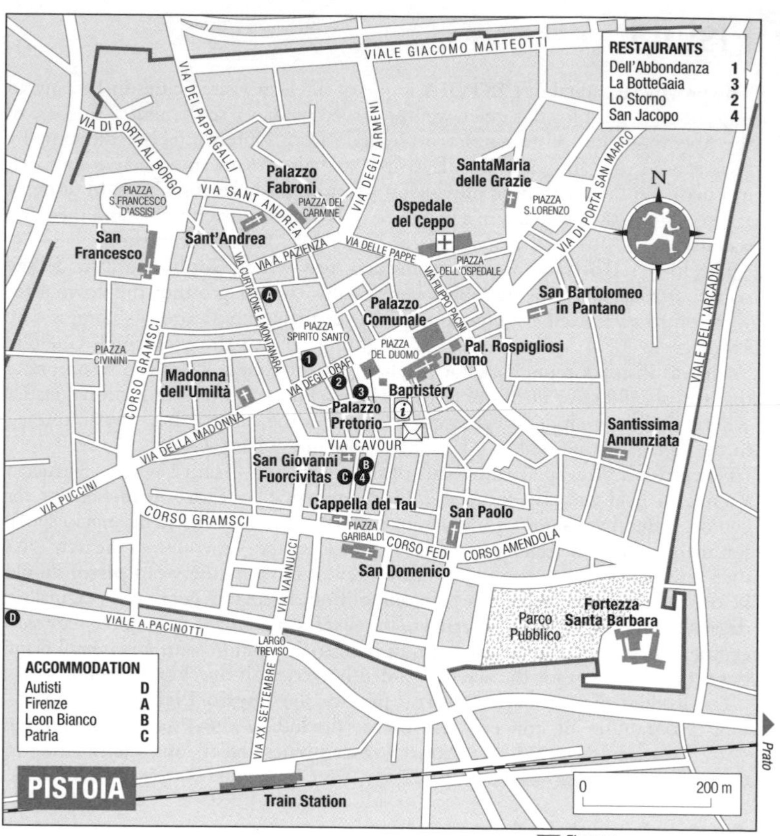


**Patria** Via Crispi 6–8 ⓣ0573.25.187, ⓦwww.patriahotel.com. Like the nearby and very similar *Leon Bianco*, the chief selling points of the three-star *Patria* are its centrality and low prices. ❸

## The City

The interesting part of the city begins one block north of Largo Treviso, at the junction with the centre's widest avenues, Corso Gramsci and Corso Fedi. Just follow your nose and you'll come to **Piazza del Duomo**, where the main monuments and museums are concentrated; the other main sights are just a few minutes' walk away – **San Giovanni Fuorcivitas** to the south, the **Ospedale del Ceppo** and **Sant'Andrea** to the north, and **San Bartolomeo** to the east.

### Around Piazza Garibaldi

In Piazza Garibaldi you'll find the thirteenth-century church of **San Domenico** (daily 7.30am–noon & 4.30–6pm, Sun closes 8pm; free), rebuilt in the 1970s after terrible damage during World War II. Scraps of medieval frescoes remain inside, but the most arresting feature is the Rossellino brothers' tomb of the teacher Filippo Lazzari, on the right near the door. In the cloister (entered from the aisle) there are remnants of a fresco of *The Journey of the Magi* by Benozzo Gozzoli, who died of the plague in Pistoia and is buried here.

Opposite San Domenico, the **Cappella del Tau** (Mon–Sat 9am–1pm; free), or Sant'Antonio Abate, preserves a chaos of mainly fourteenth-century frescoes depicting the Creation (in the vault), the life of St Anthony Abbot, and the story of the Sacred Girdle (see p.216). Next door, in the Palazzo del Tau, is the **Museo Marino Marini** (Mon–Sat: April–Sept 10am–6pm; Oct–March closes 5pm; €3.50, or €6.50 joint ticket), showing a selection of work by Pistoia's most famous modern son. Marini (1901–80) found an early influence in the realism of Etruscan sarcophagi, expressed in the sculptures of horses and riders that he churned out throughout his life. In the 1940s he diversified into portraiture – subjects here include Thomas Mann, Henry Miller and Marc Chagall.

On the same side of the Cappella del Tau, a couple of minutes' walk east, looms the late thirteenth-century facade of **San Paolo**; the front of greenish stone with dark green and white inlays is topped by a statue of St James, possibly by Orcagna.

### San Giovanni Fuorcivitas and Madonna dell'Umiltà

All streets north from Piazza Garibaldi link with Via Cavour, now the main street of the city's inner core but once the settlement's outer limit – as the name of the majestic **San Giovanni Fuorcivitas** (Saint John Outside the Walls) proclaims. The church (daily 7.30am–noon & 5–6.30pm; free) was founded in the eighth century, but rebuilt between the twelfth and fourteenth centuries, when it received the dazzling green and white flank that serves as its **facade**. Rather than being the focal point of the wall, the doorway is just a brief interruption in the infinitely repeatable pattern of the triple arcade and bands of contrasting marble, a colour scheme echoed in the oratory across the alleyway (now a shop). This is one of three Pistoia churches distinguished by pulpits that rank among the most sophisticated sculptures produced in thirteenth-century Tuscany. The **pulpit** here was carved in 1270 by a pupil of Nicola Pisano, whose son, Giovanni, executed the equally impressive holy water stoup, with its figures of the cardinal and theological virtues. On the opposite side of the church is a life-size terracotta *Visitation*, probably by Luca della Robbia.

From here, a turn up Via Roma is the quickest way into the central square, but if you want to make sure you don't miss any of Pistoia's architectural sights, follow the westward arc of Via Cavour into Via Buozzi until you come to **Madonna dell'Umiltà** (daily 7.45am–noon & 4–7pm; free). This handsome church was designed by a pupil of Bramante and finished off by Vasari with a dome so heavy that the walls had to be reinforced to prevent the building from collapsing.

#### Pistoia's museums

Entry to each of Pistoia's museums is €3.50, except for the Palazzo Fabroni, which costs €6. For €6.50 you can buy a joint ticket for the Museo Marini and the museums of the Palazzo Communale (which contains a couple of collections that are counted as one) and Palazzo Rospigliosi (three collections counted as one). You can also get a €8 ticket that covers Palazzo Fabroni plus any two museums, and a €10 ticket for all three plus the Fabroni.

## Piazza del Duomo

The direct path from Via Cavour to Piazza del Duomo crosses the market square, Piazza della Sala. A marginally more long-winded alternative is to walk through the minuscule Piazza San Leone, a few blocks east; this was the centre of the ancient Lombard settlement, and its stocky tower was later the bolt hole of Vanni Fucci (see p.219).

The medieval complex of the **Piazza del Duomo** is a superb and slightly eccentric ensemble, reversing the normal priorities of the Italian central square: the ornate baptistery lurks in a recess off one corner and the Duomo faces it, turning its sparsely adorned side to the open space and leaving the huge campanile and monolithic civic buildings to take the limelight. There's something odd about the expanse of the piazza too, as if it were conceived for a town considerably larger than present-day Pistoia. Once a year, though, the square is packed to capacity for the **Giostra dell'Orso** (see box below), Pistoia's answer to the medieval shenanigans of Siena's Palio.



### The Duomo

If you've come from Pisa or Lucca, the style of Pistoia's **Duomo**, the Cattedrale di San Zeno (daily 8am–12.30pm & 3.30–7pm; free), will be immediately familiar, with its tiered arcades and distinctive Pisan-Romanesque decoration of striped black and white marble. Set into this soberly refined front is a tunnel-vault portico of bright terracotta tiles by Andrea della Robbia, creator also of the *Madonna and Child* above the door.

The **interior** has an outstanding array of sculptural pieces, one of which is part of the entrance wall – a marvellous font designed by Benedetto da Maiano, showing incidents from the life of the Baptist. Close by, on the wall of the right aisle, is the monument to Dante's friend, the diplomat, teacher and poet Cino da Pistoia; it is said that Boccaccio is one of the pupils to whom he's shown lecturing in the bottom panel.

### The Giostra dell'Orso

The earliest forerunner of the **Giostra dell'Orso** was a peculiar ritual mentioned in a chronicle of 1300. On March 10 of that year, the feast day of San Francesca Romana, a dozen knights fought a ceremonial battle against a bear dressed in the town's coat of arms. The precise form of this joust changed many times over the following centuries but some version of it was fought every year until 1666, when it seems suddenly to have been abandoned. In 1947 it was revived in more humane form and now takes place on July 25, feast of the city's patron, St James. It forms the centrepiece of the festival season known as the Luglio Pistoiese (Pistoia July).

The fun begins with a procession of around three hundred standard bearers, trumpeters, knights, halberdiers and assorted costumed extras from the Porta Lucchese to the Piazza del Duomo. These characters represent the villages around Pistoia, the city's crafts and trades, and the four districts of the historic centre. Each of these four districts is represented in the joust by three knights, their regalia bearing the heraldic emblems of the Lion, the Stag, the Griffon and the Dragon. Having led the procession into the arena laid out on the piazza, the knights are separated into pairs, who then ride against each other around the track, scoring points by hitting the two highly stylized "bears" set on bales on opposite sides of the circuit. Points are awarded according to which parts of the target are hit with the lance, and at the end of the day two prizes are awarded – to the highest-scoring district and the highest-scoring knight.

The *giostra* is always a sell-out; to be sure of tickets, you should contact the regional tourist office at least a month in advance (Ⓣ0573.21.622; Ⓦwww.giostradellorso.it).

Just beyond this monument is the **Cappella di San Jacopo** (€2), now incorporated into the cathedral museum, which boasts one of the richest pieces of silverwork to be seen in Italy, the **Altarpiece of St James**. Weighing almost a ton and populated with 628 figures, it was begun in 1287 and completed in the fifteenth century, when Brunelleschi cast the two half-figures of prophets on the left-hand side. The length of time taken on the work is clear if you compare the scenes on the front with the bolder figures in the scenes from the life of St James on the left-hand flank, where an extra suppleness and vitality is evident. The artist responsible for these latter panels was a certain Leonardo di Ser Giovanni, who immediately after completing them was given the commission to begin another remarkable piece of silverwork – the altarpiece now in Florence's Museo dell'Opera del Duomo.

The Duomo's adjacent **Campanile** was originally a Lombard watchtower, then was spruced up with Romanesque arcades in the twelfth century and a Gothic turret in the sixteenth. On Saturdays and Sundays the campanile is often open for guided tours, usually at 11am, noon, 4pm and 5pm; the tourist office will have the latest details.

### Around Piazza del Duomo

You'll have to book at the tourist office in order to see inside the partly clad Palazzo dei Vescovi, now home of the small **Museo di San Zeno** (guided tours Tues, Thurs & Fri 8.30am, 10am, 11.30am & 3.30pm, plus Fri 2.30pm & 4.45pm; €3.60), where the chief exhibit is Ghiberti's reliquary of St James. The basement has an even more modest archeological collection, with relics from the Roman settlement.

Opposite is the dapper Gothic **Baptistery** (Tues–Sun 10am–6pm), designed by Giovanni Pisano and completed in the mid-fourteenth century by Cellino di Nese, creator of the Duomo's monument to Cino da Pistoia. Commercial art shows sometimes fill the space around the font.

Though its interior is closed to the public, you can take a look at the courtyard of the **Palazzo del Podestà** (or Palazzo Pretorio), the law-court building to the side of the baptistery. From the stone benches half-sheltered by the portico the Pistoian judges used to pronounce sentences notorious for their severity; a grimly humorous speciality was to sentence the guilty to be elevated to the ranks of the nobility – thus depriving them of any civic rights under the town's republican constitution.

On the far side of the square, the flaking pale limestone facade of the **Palazzo Comunale** contains the **Museo Civico** (April–Sept Tues & Thurs–Sat 10am–6pm, Wed 4–7pm, Sun 11am–6pm; Oct–March Tues & Thurs–Sat 10am–5pm, Wed 3–6pm, Sun 11am–5pm; €3.50, or €6.50 joint ticket), where the customary welter of run-of-the-mill medieval and Renaissance pieces is counterweighted by an impressive showing of Baroque hyperactivity – including a couple of hideous battle scenes by the evidently disturbed Ciccio Napoletano. Attached to the museum is a display devoted to Pistoia-born architect **Giovanni Michelucci**, featuring models and photographs of his major buildings and some nine hundred of his drawings.

The Palazzo Rospigliosi, in Ripa del Sale (down the right-hand side of the Palazzo Comunale), houses the combined **Museo Diocesano**, **Museo Rospigliosi** and **Museo del Ricamo** (Tues–Sat 10am–1pm & 3–6pm, plus same hours on second Sun of month; €3.50, or €6.50 joint ticket), where much of the space is occupied by chalices, censers, crosses, miscellaneous ecclesiastical accoutrements, mediocre paintings and various pieces of furniture. Many of these items were bequeathed by Pope Clement IX, another illustrious native of Pistoia, who occupied the papal throne from 1667 to 1669. The last museum of the trio is a two-room showcase for some remarkably elaborate embroidery, a skill for which Pistoia was long renowned.

## The northern quarters

At the back of the Palazzo Comunale, Via Pacini is the obvious route to take to explore the northern part of the town. Across this road, on Piazza San Bartolomeo, is the **Abbazia di San Bartolomeo in Pantano** ("St Bartholomew in the Swamp"), named after the marshy ground on which it was raised in the eighth century. The semi-complete facade is as appealing as any of the city's more polished fronts, and inside (daily 8.30am–noon & 4–6pm; free) is the earliest of Pistoia's trio of notable pulpits. Executed in 1250 by Guido da Como, and reconstructed from its dismantled parts, it comprises a rectangular box whose principal scenes are filled with figures arrayed in level ranks like a crowd in a stadium.

The most photographed element of the Pistoia townscape is not a church but a hospital in a square at the end of Via Pacini – the thirteenth-century **Ospedale del Ceppo**, which takes its name from the hollowed-out tree stump (*ceppo*) in which alms were traditionally collected. Emblazoned along its length is the feature that makes it famous, Giovanni della Robbia's painted terracotta **frieze** of the *Theological Virtues* and the *Seven Works of Mercy*. Completed in the early sixteenth century, it is a startlingly colourful panoply of Renaissance types and costume: pilgrims, prisoners, the sick, the dead.

A couple of minutes' walk over to the west, at Via Sant'Andrea 18, stands **Palazzo Fabroni** (Mon–Sat noon–6pm, Sun 2–6pm; €6), a recently opened venue for exhibitions which also houses a permanent collection of modern art, based on work from the Museo Civico's collection and augmented with pieces bought from or donated by various Italian artists; it's a moderately engaging assembly, but the special events are generally of greater interest. The street takes its name from the twelfth-century church **Sant'Andrea** (daily 8am–12.30pm & 3–6.30pm; free), which has a typically Pisan facade with a pair of Romanesque lions and a panel of *The Journey of the Magi* stuck onto it. The murky

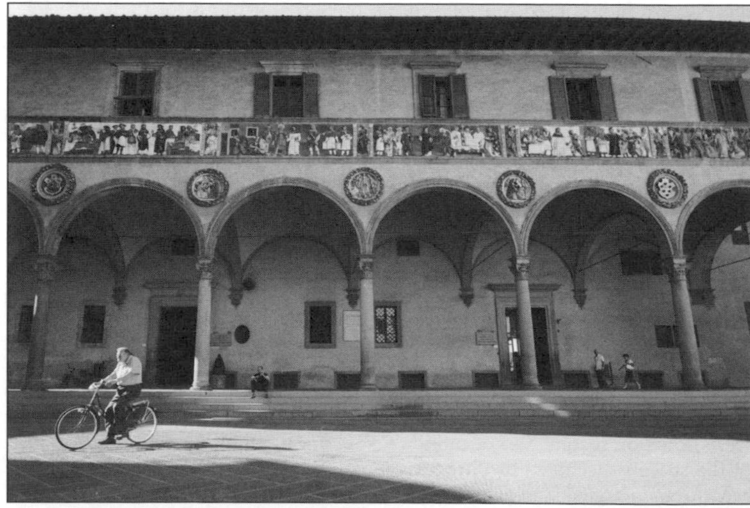

▲ Ospedale del Ceppo, Pistoia

## Vinci – Leonardo's birthplace

Sitting amid vineyards and olive groves on the southern slopes of Monte Albano, 11km north of Empoli, **VINCI** might be a torpid little place but it's overrun with tourists thanks to its association with **Leonardo da Vinci**, who in April 1452 was born nearby and baptized in Vinci's church of Santa Croce. (If you're reliant on public transport, take a COPIT bus from Pistoia to Empoli, and change there for a bus to Vinci.) Vinci preserves a mighty thirteenth-century castle, the Castello dei Conti Guidi, which houses the main part of the **Museo Leonardiano** (daily 9.30am–6pm; €6) – the ticket office is in the smaller section of the museum, the Palazzina Uzielli, in Via Rossi. Opened on the five-hundredth anniversary of Leonardo's birth, the museum is dedicated to Leonardo the inventor and engineer rather than Leonardo the artist, with a large and fairly imaginative display of models – tanks, water cannon, flying machines, looms and gear mechanisms – all reconstructed from his notebook drawings, which are reproduced alongside the relevant contraptions. Leonardo's **birthplace** (same hours; free) is in **Anchiano**, some 2km farther north into the hills, a pleasant walk past fields of poppies. The house was owned by his father, a Florentine clerk called Ser Piero; Leonardo's mother is generally believed to have been a *contadina* (peasant girl), but it's been argued that she was in fact an Arab slave – the only things that are known for certain is that her name was Caterina and she didn't marry his father, possibly because Ser Piero was already betrothed. Placard-size captions and a couple of reproduction drawings are pretty well all there is to see inside the house.



and corridor-slim aisle contains a **pulpit** carved in 1297 by Giovanni Pisano, based on his father's design for the Pisa baptistery pulpit. It shows scenes from the life of Christ and the Last Judgement, the figures carved in such deep relief that they seem to be surging out of a limitless depth. Giovanni was the first to appreciate the glory of his achievement; Nicola Pisano had boasted of being the greatest living sculptor, and Giovanni's inscription brags that he has now surpassed his father. The church also has a second piece by Giovanni – the Crucifix mounted on the wall of the right aisle.

The plainest of the city's churches, the Franciscans' **San Francesco al Prato** (daily 7.30am–noon & 4–6.30pm; free), is a little farther to the west, on the edge of one of the main bus terminals. Tattered fourteenth-century frescoes are preserved in the single nave, and some healthier specimens adorn the chapels at the east end, where there's a fine *Triumph of Augustine* in the chapel to the left of the high altar. To the side of the church there's an unusual memorial to Aldo Moro, the Italian prime minister killed by the terrorist group the Red Brigades on May 7, 1978; the bronze plaques are imprinted with the newspaper headlines from the day his body was found.

### Fattoria di Celle

Some 4km east of Pistoia at Santomato, the **Fattoria di Celle**, once a farm, now holds a remarkable private art collection, established in 1982 to give Italy an international forum for contemporary art comparable to such centres as the Kröller-Müller in the Netherlands. Everything here, in the rooms and park of the Villa Celle, could be described as environmental art: the large-scale outdoor pieces are conceived as interactions with the natural world, while the smaller installations inside take their cue from the enclosing space of the rooms.

Artists from all over Europe and the United States have contributed to the **sculpture park**, devising a variety of responses to its woodlands and grassy slopes, and to the wider cultural environment of Tuscany. Alice Aycock's steel constructions recall such Renaissance mechanisms as the astrolabe, but are built on a scale to echo the curves and angles of the landscape. A labyrinth of polished green and white marble by Robert Morris recalls the Romanesque churches of the region, and is so perfectly placed on the gradient of the hill that it seems to be a single mass of stone until you come to the entrance. An artificial stream and grotto laid out in the nineteenth century has been used by Anne and Patrick Poirier to evoke the epic struggle between Zeus and the Titans, with steel lightning flashes and fragments of huge marble heads littering the water course. In high-tech contrast, Dennis Oppenheim's massive contraption of steel towers, immovable pulleys and functionless wires looks like a visual pun on the ski-lifts of the winter resorts north of Pistoia. Most of the installations date from the inaugural year, but new pieces are being commissioned all the time, maintaining the Fattoria di Celle's status as one of the most vital art centres in the country.

The centre is open for guided tours only (May–Sept Mon–Fri) and visitors must first write for an appointment, to Fattoria di Celle, 51030 Santomato di Pistoia (Ⓕ0573.479.486; Ⓔgoricoll@tin.it). The entrance gate is not signposted, but signalled by a huge spherical metal ribcage construction by Alberto Burri.



## Eating and drinking

There are several excellent **places to eat** in the centre of Pistoia, with four of the top recommendations to be found very close to Piazza del Duomo.

**Dell'Abbondanza Via Dell'Abbondanza 10 Ⓣ0573.368.037.** A superb trattoria, with main courses around €15. Open 12.15–2.15pm & 7–10.30pm; closed all Wed & Thurs lunch.

**La BotteGaia Via del Lastrone 4 Ⓣ0573.365.602.** A good-value *osteria* (around €30 a head), very close to Piazza della Sala, with an enticing *menú degustazione*, main courses from €10 and a terrific wine list. Closed Sun lunch & Mon.

**Lo Storno Via del Lastrone 8 Ⓣ0573.26.193.** Serves robust local dishes at similar prices to *La BotteGaia*. Open Mon–Sat noon–3pm & 7.30–9.30pm.

**San Jacopo Via Crispi 15 Ⓣ0573.27.786.** A straightforward, inexpensive and good-quality Tuscan menu. Closed Sun evening & all Mon.

14

# Pisa and Lucca



Flying into Tuscany you'll most likely arrive at **Pisa**, a city which – thanks to the Leaning Tower – is known, at least in name, to every visitor to Italy. Thousands of tourists pour into Pisa every day in summer (hourly trains from Florence take one hour), take a look at the tower and then promptly jump back on the bus. But Pisa warrants more than a whistle-stop visit: it isn't one of those Tuscan towns with a photo-opportunity on every corner, but in addition to the stupendous monuments of the Campo dei Miracoli, it has a scattering of fine churches and museums, and during the month-long Giugno Pisano festival there's a real buzz about the place.

**Lucca**'s proximity to Pisa – half an hour by road or rail – makes it an excellent first or last Tuscan stop if you're flying in or out of that city's airport. Trains to Lucca also connect hourly from Florence (1–2hr), Pistoia (40min) and Prato (1hr). The town is the most graceful of Tuscany's provincial capitals, set inside a ring of Renaissance walls fronted by gardens and huge bastions. It's quiet without being dull, absorbs its tourists with ease, has a peaceful, self-contained historic centre and offers a range of good restaurants. Henry James's eulogy – "a place overflowing with everything that makes for ease, for plenty, for beauty, for interest and good example" – still holds true.

Above all, Lucca is a delightful town simply to wander through: it's one of the few places in Tuscany where many locals ride bikes, and as a result much of the old centre is refreshingly free of traffic. The city is reputed to have once had seventy churches, and even today you can hardly walk for five minutes without coming upon a small piazza and marble-fronted church facade. Although you could see the best part of the town in a day – with the Duomo, a couple of museums and the churches of San Michele and San Frediano the key targets – the charm of the place is such that you'd be well advised to stay at least one night, preferably two.

## Pisa

**PISA**'s tower is the tourist magnet, but it's just one element of the **Campo dei Miracoli**, where the Duomo, Baptistery and Camposanto complete an unrivalled quartet of medieval masterpieces. These buildings belong to Pisa's golden age, from the eleventh to the thirteenth century, when the city, then still a port, was one of the great powers of the Mediterranean. Decline set in early, however, with defeat at sea by the Genoese in 1284 followed by the silting up of the harbour. From 1406 Pisa was governed by Florence, whose Medici rulers re-established the

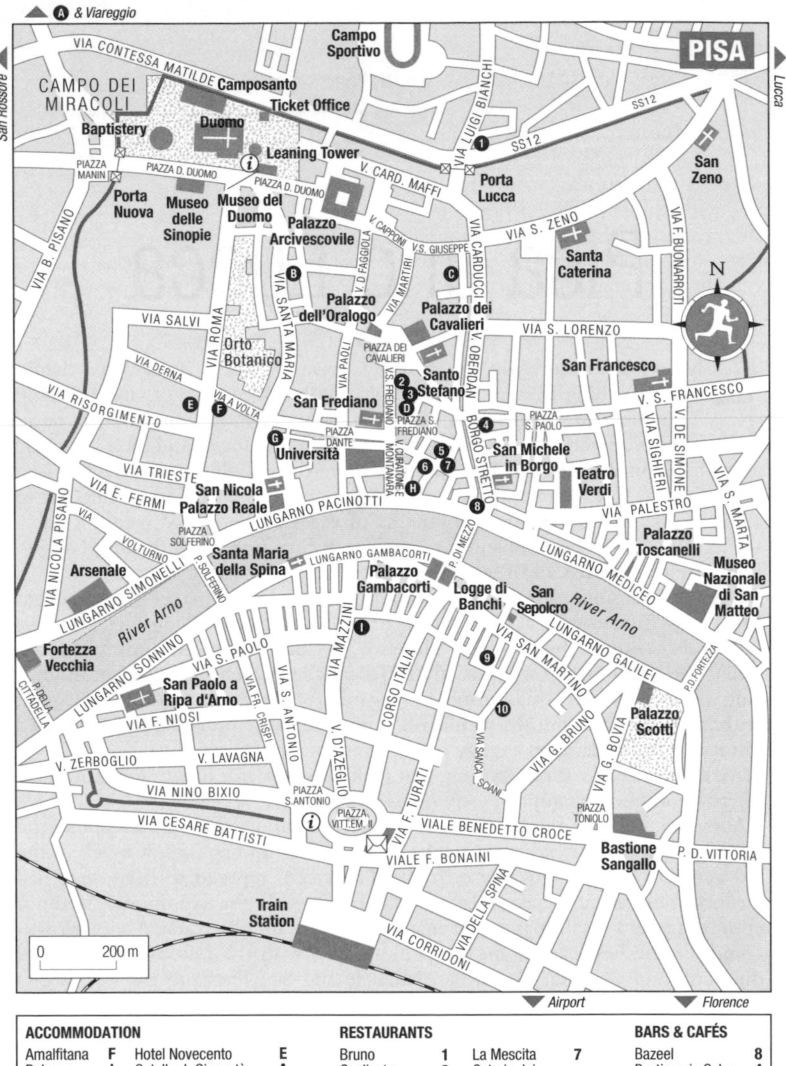


| ACCOMMODATION | | | | RESTAURANTS | | | | BARS & CAFÉS | |
|---|---|---|---|---|---|---|---|---|---|
| Amalfitana | F | Hotel Novecento | E | Bruno | 1 | La Mescita | 7 | Bazeel | 8 |
| Bologna | I | Ostello d. Gioventù | A | Cagliostro | 3 | Osteria dei Cavalieri | 2 | Pasticceria Salza | 4 |
| Di Stefano | C | Rinascente | D | Da Cucciolo | 9 | San Omobono | 5 | | |
| Galileo | G | Royal Victoria | H | Il Campano | 6 | | | | |
| Helvetia | B | | | La Cereria | 10 | | | | |

University of Pisa, which remains one of Italy's major universities; **Galileo**, Pisa's most famous native, was a teacher there. Subsequent centuries saw the city fade into provinciality – its state when the Shelleys and Byron decamped to the city, forging what Shelley termed their "paradise of exiles". Since World War II – when it suffered heavy damage – Pisa has been revitalized by the airport and industrial development in the suburbs, and of course by tourism, but that dominates just one small enclave of this gritty city – away from the Campo dei Miracoli, Pisa just gets on with its own business.

## Arrival and information

**Trains** arrive at Pisa Centrale station, about 1km south of the River Arno. **Buses** come into the nearby Piazza San Antonio. From either, the Campo dei Miracoli is about twenty-five minutes' walk north (up the pedestrianized Corso Italia and across the Ponte di Mezzo), or a five-minute ride on bus #1 from outside the train station; bus tickets are sold at a kiosk outside the station.

There are two **tourist offices**, giving information on Pisa province as well as the city: a short way north of the train station, at Piazza Vittorio Emanuele 13 (Mon–Fri 9am–7pm, Sat 9am–1.30pm; Ⓣ050.42.291); and inside the Museo dell'Opera del Duomo (see p.234). For online information, go to Ⓦwww.pisaturismo.it.

## Accommodation

Finding accommodation in Pisa is less troublesome than in Tuscany's more overtly attractive towns, but if you want to be sure of a room in a particular hotel it always pays to reserve in advance in high season. Budget accommodation is easier to find on the south side of the river, but this is the less enticing part of town, especially the area close to the train station.

**Amalfitana Via Roma 44 Ⓣ050.29.000, Ⓕ050.25.218.** Pleasant 21-room two-star, 5min walk south of the Campo dei Miracoli. ❷

**Bologna Via Mazzini 57 Ⓣ050.502.120, Ⓦwww.hotelbologna.pisa.it.** Located close to Santa Maria della Spina, this smart and well-managed hotel – by far the best on the south side of the Arno – has recently refurbished its rooms to bring it up to four-star standard. ❻

**Di Stefano Via Sant'Apollonia 35 Ⓣ050.553.559, Ⓦwww.hoteldistefano.pisa.it.** This tidy three-star hotel, located in a quiet street just off Piazza dei Cavalieri, occupies two buildings – the better rooms are in a heavily restored eleventh-century tower and cost around €180 in high season. Other rooms are considerably less expensive, and special offers are frequent, so check the website before booking. ❹

### Pisa airport

Pisa's **Galileo Galilei airport** (Ⓣ050.849.300, Ⓦwww.pisa-airport.com), most visitors' point of entry to Tuscany, lies about 3km south of the city centre. It has an impressive turnout of **car-rental** firms, though on-the-spot deals are more expensive than those arranged in advance. All require a deposit to cover a full tank of fuel: usually you just leave your credit card details. When you return the car, you'd do well to refuel before getting to the airport, since petrol is pricier here than elsewhere. The **drive** to Florence is straightforward (an airport slip road takes you directly onto the motorway), but the road into Pisa is so confusing that, without directions from the car-rental desk, you may well end up getting lost.

Terravision **buses** to Florence are scheduled to synchronize with incoming budget airline flights and leave from in front of the terminal; they take 70min to reach Florence's Santa Maria Novella station, and tickets (€8 single) are sold at the stand right in front of you as you come out into the airport concourse.

**Trains** from the airport station are cheaper (€5.40), if often slower; there are only six direct trains daily (6.40am–10.20pm), but every 30min a shuttle runs from the airport to Pisa Centrale (5min), where you can change to one of the regular services to Florence – there's rarely more than 30min between trains, and the journey time is between an hour and 80min. The last train from Pisa Centrale to Florence is at 10.30pm, with services resuming at around 4am. Train tickets can be bought from the office at the opposite end of the concourse from the station.

## Tickets for Pisa's museums & monuments

There are two **ticket offices** for the **Campo dei Miracoli** sights: on the north side of the Leaning Tower (the only one that sells tickets for the tower itself) and inside the Museo delle Sinopie. Tickets for the museums and monuments of the Campo dei Miracoli – the Duomo, Baptistery, Museo dell'Opera, Camposanto and Museo delle Sinopie – can be bought only at these two offices. Admission to the Duomo costs €2, except from November 1 to March 1, when it's free. Single admission to the other sights costs €5. Admission to any two sights (including the Duomo) is €6, to any four is €8.50, and to all five is €10; these combined tickets are valid for the day of issue only.

There's a separate ticket (€15) for the **Leaning Tower**: groups of thirty are allowed in for half an hour, and you should expect a long wait in high season. For an extra €2 you can pre-book your visit online at Ⓦwww.opapisa.it, as long as you're making your reservation between forty-five and fifteen days in advance. Children under the age of 8 are not allowed into the tower.

Finally, there is also a joint €8 ticket for the Museo Nazionale di San Matteo and the Museo di Palazzo Reale, plus a €2.50 ticket for the Torre Guelfa della Cittadella Vecchia and Santa Maria della Spina. It's worth pointing out, however, that Pisa's multiple tickets are notoriously changeable.



**Galileo Via Santa Maria 12 Ⓣ&Ⓕ050.40.621.** Nine big – and in some cases very nicely decorated – one-star rooms, with and without private bathrooms; not the quietest hotel in town, but central and good value. ❷

**Helvetia Via Don G. Boschi 31 Ⓣ050.553.084.** Spotless and friendly one-star off Piazza Arcivescovado offering doubles with or without private bathroom. ❷

**Novecento Via Roma 37 Ⓣ050.500.323, Ⓦwww.hotelnovecento.pisa.it.** This new three-star *residenza d'epoca* occupies a handsome old town house, but the rooms are immaculately modern in style. The rates are very reasonable, the location convenient and it has a nice garden as well. ❺

**Ostello della Gioventù Via Pietrasantina 15, Madonna dell'Acqua Ⓣ050.890.622, Ⓦwww.pisaonline.it/AlbergoDellaGioventu.** This non-HI hostel is 1km from Campo dei Miracoli: if you don't want to walk, take bus #3 from the station or the airport. Make sure you have mosquito repellent in summer, as the hostel is right by a swamp, although it benefits from a nearby supermarket, pizzeria and burger joint. Reception opens 6pm. Dorm bed €16; double room €21.

**Rinascente Via del Castelletto 28 Ⓣ050.580.460, Ⓦwww.pisaonline.it/hotelrinascente.** This very popular one-star occupies an old *palazzo* hidden away a short distance south of Piazza dei Cavalieri – follow the signs from Via San Frediano. Shared or private bathrooms. ❷

**Royal Victoria Lungarno Pacinotti 12 Ⓣ050.940.111, Ⓦwww.royalvictoria.it.** Run by the same family since its foundation in 1837, this old-fashioned and appealingly frayed three-star is the most characterful of central Pisa's hotels – and the best value. The public rooms, with their musty engravings and antique furniture, are redolent of the place's history (there's even a music room, with piano), but if you're deterred by wobbly door-handles and crudely patched-up ceiling frescoes, it's not the hotel for you. ❸

# The Campo dei Miracoli

The name of the **Campo dei Miracoli** (Field of Miracles) comes from the notoriously over-excitable writer Gabriele D'Annunzio, but the label is no mere bombast – the ecclesiastical centre of Pisa is a stunning spectacle, from which the inevitable array of kitsch-selling stalls can barely detract. Nowhere else in Italy are the key religious buildings – the cathedral, baptistery and bell-tower – so perfectly harmonious, and nowhere else is there so beautiful a contrast of stonework and surrounding meadow. And the mere existence of such enormous structures on this spot is remarkable in itself, because beneath the pavements and the turf lies a soggy mix of sand and silt, whose instability accounts for the angle of the Leaning Tower and the lesser tilt of its companions: take a close look at the Baptistery and you'll see that it's inclined some way out of the vertical, while the facade of the Duomo is a few degrees out of true as well.

## The Leaning Tower

The **Leaning Tower** (Torre Pendente) has always been a leaning tower. Begun in 1173, it started to subside when it had reached just three of its eight storeys, but it tilted in the opposite direction to its present one. Odd-shaped stones were inserted to correct this deficiency, whereupon the tower lurched the other way. Over the next 180 years a succession of architects continued to extend the thing upwards, each one endeavouring to compensate for the angle, the end result being that the main part of the tower is slightly bent. Around 1350, Tommaso di Andrea da Pontedera completed the magnificent stack of marble and granite arcades by crowning it with a bellchamber, set closer to the perpendicular than the storeys below it, so that it looks like a hat set at a rakish angle.

By the end of the twentieth century, the tower was leaning 4.5m from the upright and nearing its limits, and in 1990 it was shut to the public. Soon after the closure, steel bands were wrapped round the lowest section of the tower to prevent the base from buckling under the weight of the fifteen thousand tonnes of marble above. Various schemes aimed at arresting the effects of gravity were discussed, and in the end it was decided to place more than nine hundred tonnes of lead ingots at its base to counterbalance the force of the leaning stonework. In 1998, when it was clear that the weights had stabilized the structure, the project entered its second phase with a delicate drilling operation – supervised by Professor John Burland of London's Imperial College – to remove water and silt from beneath the tower's northern foundations. The resulting subsidence corrected the building's southwards tilt by ten percent, bringing it back to the angle by which it was tilting in the first half of the nineteenth century; to ensure that it stayed that way for the foreseeable future (three hundred years, according to Professor Burland) the foundations were strengthened and steel reinforcement bars were inserted into the walls of the tower. Eleven years and tens of millions of euros later, the tower was officially reopened to the public in November 2001. Now that the building has been made safe, work has begun on cleaning up the stonework – restoration is projected to continue until 2010.

The ascent to the bellchamber takes you up a dark and narrow spiral staircase of 294 steps, at a fairly disorientating five-degree angle. It's not for the claustrophobic or those afraid of heights, but you might think the steep admission fee is worth it for the privilege of getting inside one of the world's most famous and perilous buildings. The **opening hours** are extremely complicated, but the briefest opening period is from November to February, when tours begin at 10am and finish around 4pm; for most of the summer (April–Sept) they run from 8.30am to 7.50pm, but from June 17 to September 5 the last tour departs at around 10.20pm.

## The Duomo

The **Duomo** (daily: March 10am–6pm; April–Sept Mon–Sat 10am–8pm; Oct 10am–7pm; Nov–Feb 10am–1pm & 2–5pm; no admittance to tourists before 1pm on Sun; €2, or combined ticket; free from Nov 1 to March 1) was begun a century before its campanile, in 1064. With its four levels of variegated colonnades and its subtle interplay of dark grey marble and white stone, it's the archetype of the Pisan-Romanesque style, a model often imitated but never surpassed. Squares and discs of coloured marble are set into the magnificent facade, but the soberly graceful effect of the primary grey and white is such that you notice the other tones only when you look closely.

Inside, the impact of the crisp black and white marble of the long arcades – recalling Moorish architecture – is slightly diminished by the incongruous gilded ceiling, the fresco in the squashed circle of the dome, and the massive air vents that have been bunged through the upper arches. Much of the interior was

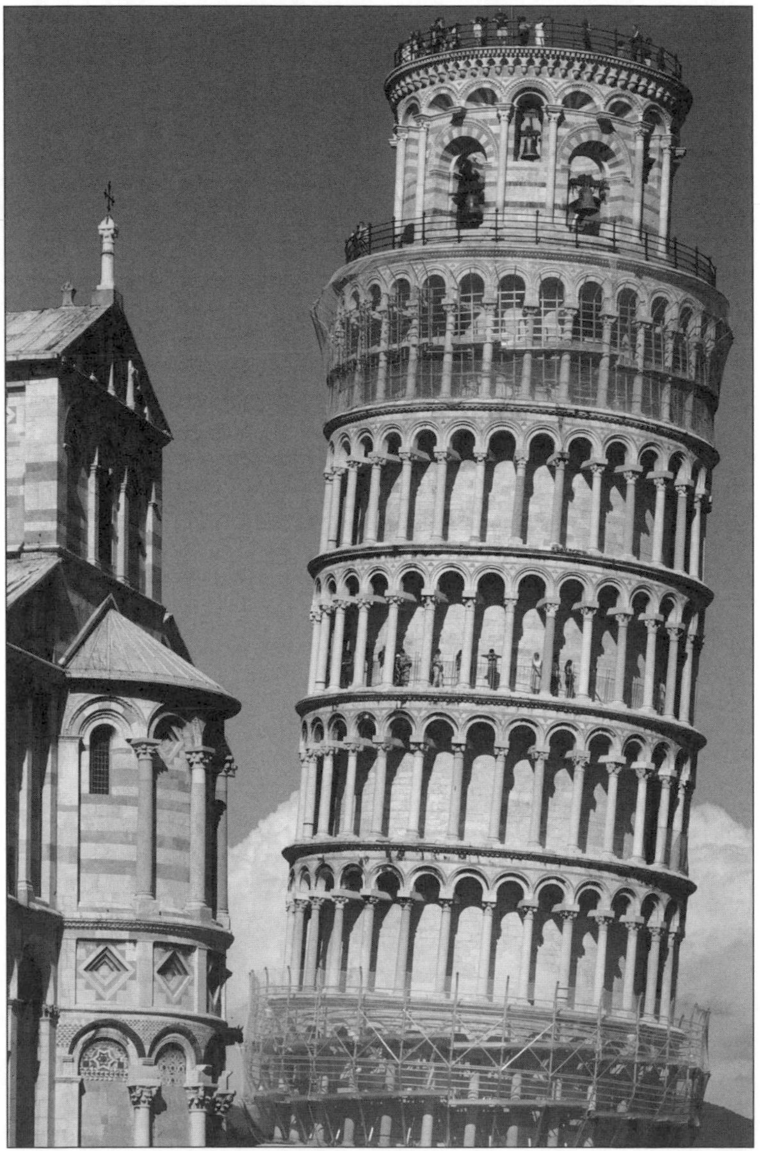

▲ The Leaning Tower

redecorated, and some of the chapels remodelled, after a fire in 1595, so most of the paintings and sculpture are Renaissance or later. (The Duomo's huge bronze doors – a panoply of high-Renaissance detail – were also made after the fire, in Giambologna's workshop.)

The magnificent apse mosaic of *Christ in Majesty* is one of the survivors of the blaze. It was completed by Cimabue in 1302, the year Giovanni Pisano began to sculpt the cathedral's extraordinary **pulpit**. The last of the great series of pulpits created in Tuscany by Giovanni and his father Nicola (the others are in Siena and Pistoia), it is a work of amazing virtuosity – indeed, the Latin inscription celebrates Giovanni as "superior to all other sculptors ... incapable of creating clumsy and ungraceful figures". The whole surface is animated with figures almost wholly freed from the block, and its narrative density demands close attention: the entire story of the Passion, from Judas's betrayal to the scourging of Christ, for instance, is condensed into a single panel.

In the right transept is the mummified body of Pisa's patron saint, **Ranieri**, and (set into the east wall) the tomb of the Holy Roman Emperor **Henry VII**, who died in 1313 (aged just 38) near Siena – probably from malaria, though some said from eating a poisoned wafer at Mass. After laying Siena to waste, the pro-imperial Pisans bore the body of their hero back home, where Tino da Camaino carved this fine image. The Pisans weren't the only ones to revere the young emperor – Dante saw *alto Arrigo* as a man who could unite Italy within a new Christian empire, and in the *Divine Comedy* accorded him a throne of honour in heaven (hence the quotation from Dante below the sarcophagus). The tomb was originally placed in the centre of the transept, but was later broken up; only in 1921 were the effigy and sarcophagus placed in their current position, with other pieces of the tomb being transferred to the Museo dell'Opera del Duomo.



## The Baptistery

The third building of the Miracoli ensemble, the **Baptistery** (daily: March 9am–6pm; April–Sept 9am–8pm; Oct 9am–7pm; Nov–Feb 10am–5pm; €5, or combined ticket), was begun in 1152 by a certain Diotisalvi ("God save you"), who left his name on the column to the left of the door. Lack of money – caused mainly by Genoa's incursions into the Pisan trade network – prevented its completion in the style in which it had been started. In the second half of the thirteenth century the Gothic top storeys and attendant flourishes were applied by Nicola and Giovanni Pisano, who rounded off the job with a glorious gallery of statues – the originals of which are now displayed in the Museo dell'Opera del Duomo.

This is the largest baptistery in Italy, and the plainness of the vast interior is immediately striking, with its unadorned arcades and bare dome. The acoustics are astonishing too, as is regularly demonstrated by the custodian. At the centre, a huge mosaic-inlaid **font** by Guido da Como (1246) is overlooked by Nicola Pisano's splendid **pulpit**, which was sculpted in 1260, half a century before his son's work in the cathedral. This was the sculptor's first major commission and – though the architectural details recall the stonework of French Gothic churches – and it clearly shows the influence of classical models: the seated Virgin in the *Adoration of the Magi* is obviously derived from a Roman image, while the nude figure of Daniel (underneath the *Adoration*) is evidently Hercules under an alias. For good views out over the Campo dei Miracoli, climb the **stairs** to the upper gallery.

## The Camposanto

The screen of sepulchral white marble running along the north edge of the Campo dei Miracoli is the perimeter wall of what has been called the most beautiful cemetery in the world, the **Camposanto** (same hours as Baptistery; €5, or combined ticket). According to Pisan legend, at the end of the twelfth century the city's archbishop brought back from the Crusades five shiploads of soil from Golgotha, in order that eminent Pisans might be buried in holy earth. The building enclosing this sanctified site was completed almost a century later.

The Camposanto takes the form of an enormous Gothic cloister, each of whose long sides is as big as a cathedral nave. Since the fourteenth century the arcades have housed a large array of Roman sarcophagi, some of which were re-used for local dignitaries. Later tombs constitute a virtual encyclopedia of the various ways in which death has been accommodated, ranging from pavement slabs that record the occupant's name, dates and nothing else, to the opposite extreme, where the focus of interest is not on the deceased but on those left behind – as in the monument surmounted by a woman identified merely as "The Inconsolable".

However, when Ruskin described the Camposanto as one of the three most precious buildings in Italy (along with the Sistine Chapel and the Scuola di San Rocco in Venice), it was not its tombs but rather its **frescoes** that he was praising. Paintings once covered more than two thousand square metres of cloister wall, but incendiary bombs dropped by Allied planes on July 27, 1944 set the roofing on fire and drenched the frescoes in a river of molten lead, and the masterpieces of **Benozzo Gozzoli** were all but destroyed – just a few patches of his Old Testament scenes remain. Recent restoration work (the first stage of a planned restoration of all the Camposanto frescoes) has sparked a fierce dispute over a cleaning technique which, some experts say, has permanently bleached the pigments. Alongside another picture that came through the bombing: a fascinating fourteenth-century *Theological Cosmograph*, showing the concentric spheres of the universe and the tripartite division of the Earth into Europe, Asia and Africa.

The most important surviving frescoes, however, are a remarkable cycle that's been put on show in a room opposite the entrance, beyond a photographic display of the Camposanto before the bombing. Some experts attribute this work to an artist called **Buonamico Buffalmacco**, though others assign it to an anonymous *Maestro del Trionfo della Morte*, the "Master of the Triumph of Death". There's also some dispute about the date: the frescoes are labelled as having been created in 1336–41, but many argue that they were painted after the Black Death of 1348, a pestilence which hit Tuscany so badly that it was known throughout Europe as the Florentine Plague. The most famous episode of the *Triumph* shows a trio of aristocratic huntsmen stopped in their tracks by a trio of coffins, the contents of which are so putrescent that one of the riders has to pinch his nose. Over to the right, squadrons of angels and demons bear away the souls of the dead, whose final resting place is determined in the terrifying *Last Judgement* and *Inferno* at the far end of the room.

## The Campo's museums and the city walls

A sizeable array of statuary from the Duomo and Baptistery, plus ecclesiastical finery, paintings and other miscellaneous pieces are displayed in the **Museo dell'Opera del Duomo** (same hours as Baptistery; €5, or combined ticket), at the southeast corner of the Campo.

The first masterpieces you encounter are the extraordinary bronze doors made for the Duomo by **Bonanno Pisano** (first architect of the Leaning Tower) in 1180. (Replicas are now in place at the **Portale di San Ranieri**, opposite the tower.) The panels depict the life of Christ in powerfully schematic scenes: the Massacre of the Innocents, for example, is represented by the smallest possible cast – Herod, one mother, one soldier and three babies. In the next room, exhibits dating from the period of the Duomo's construction illustrate the various influences at work in Pisan culture of the time. There's stonework from a Roman basilica, adapted for use in the cathedral, and items showing how Islamic influences came to filter into the city's art – notably in the marble inlays from the Duomo facade. A large bronze griffon is a more direct borrowing from Islam, having been thieved from the Middle East by a Pisan war party in the eleventh century. The most striking work, however, is from Burgundy, source of the strange painted wooden Crucifix, a gigantic figure with a tiny head and mantis-thin arms.

Sculptures by the various Pisanos are the high points of the museum, but the first pieces you encounter – Nicola and Giovanni's figures from the Baptistery – are too eroded to give more than an approximate idea of their power. Room 7, which is given over to works by **Giovanni Pisano**, contains the most affecting statue in Pisa, the *Madonna del Colloquio*, so called because of the intensity of the gazes exchanged by the Madonna and Child. Giovanni's great pupil, **Tino da Camaino**, monopolizes the next room, where fragments from the tomb of Emperor Henry VII are assembled; the magnificent figures of the emperor and his counsellors may have come from the tomb as well.

**Nino Pisano** – no relation to Nicola and Giovanni – is the subject of room 9, where his monuments to archbishops Giovanni Scherlatti and Francesco Moricotti show the increasing suavity of Pisan sculpture in the late fourteenth century. Giovanni Pisano returns in the **treasury**, with an intense wooden Crucifix and an ivory *Madonna and Child* that shows remarkable ingenuity in the way it exploits the natural curve of the tusk from which it's carved. The other priceless object here is the *Pisan Cross*, which – legend has it – was carried by the Pisan contingent on the First Crusade.

Upstairs, large altarpiece paintings take up a lot of room, none of them as impressive as the museum's remarkable examples of intarsia, the art of inlaid wood. The strangest objects on view are the two ancient parchment rolls known as **Exultets**, from the opening word of the chant on the eve of Holy Saturday. It was during this service that the cantor would unfurl these scrolls from the pulpit, so that the congregation could follow his words through the pictures painted on them. Beyond a small collection of **Roman and Etruscan** pieces, where a thin-lipped bust of Julius Caesar commands attention, the museum closes with a sequence of engravings by **Carlo Lasinio,** whose efforts were instrumental in rescuing the Camposanto from ruin at the beginning of the nineteenth century; his fastidious record of the now-lost frescoes is one of the most poignant items on show.

Part of the south side of the Campo is occupied by the **Museo delle Sinopie** (same hours as Baptistery; €5, or combined ticket). After the catastrophic damage wreaked on the Camposanto by the bombers, the building's restorers removed its *sinopie* (monochrome sketches for the frescoes). These great plates of plaster are now hung from the walls of this high-tech museum, where raised galleries give you the chance to inspect the painters' preliminary ideas at close range, but it's a rather scholastic enterprise. You're not likely to get much greater reward from taking a stroll on the small portion of the **city walls** that border the northwest corner of Campo (March–Oct 10am–1pm & 3–6pm; €4).

## The rest of the city

Within a short radius of the Campo dei Miracoli, Pisa takes on a quite different character, because very few tourists bother to explore the squares and streets of the city centre. While it's true that nothing in Pisa comes close to having the impact of the Campo, a tour of its lesser churches and other monuments could easily fill up a day.

### Piazza dei Cavalieri and the eastern districts

The **Piazza dei Cavalieri**, an obvious first stop after the Campo, opens unexpectedly from the narrow backstreets. Perhaps the site of the Roman forum, it was the central civic square of medieval Pisa, before Vasari remodelled it as the headquarters of the Knights of St Stephen. This order was established by Cosimo I, ostensibly for crusading, though in reality they amounted to little more than a gang of licensed pirates, given state sanction to plunder Turkish shipping. Their palace, the sgraffiti-covered **Palazzo dei Cavalieri** (now home to the Scuola Normale Superiore, which was founded in 1810 by the Napoleonic regime), is fronted by a statue of Cosimo and adjoins the order's church of **Santo Stefano**, which was largely designed by Vasari and houses banners captured from the Turks.

On the other side of the square is the Renaissance-adapted **Palazzo dell'Orologio**, with its archway and clock tower. This was a medieval palace, in whose tower the military leader Ugolino della Gherardesca was starved to death in 1288, along with his sons and grandsons, as punishment for his alleged duplicity with the Genoese enemy – a grisly episode described in Dante's *Inferno* and Shelley's *Tower of Famine*.

Northeast from here, across the wide Piazza dei Martiri della Libertà, stands the Dominican church of **Santa Caterina**, whose Romanesque lower facade dates from the year of its foundation, 1251. Inside, there's an *Annunciation* and a tomb by Nicola Pisano, and a fourteenth-century painting of the *Triumph of Thomas Aquinas*. Nearby, in front of the **Porta Lucca** – the main northern gate of medieval Pisa – you can see the unimpressive remnants of the city's Roman baths, while tucked into the northeast corner of the city walls is the church of **San Zeno**, parts of which go back to the fifth century.

### Borgo Stretto and the Museo Nazionale di San Matteo

Heading from Piazza dei Cavalieri towards the Arno, Via Dini swings into the arcaded **Borgo Stretto** – pedestrianized to create a traffic-free route that extends across the river and down Corso Italia, this is Pisa's smartest street. On the west side of Borgo Stretto you'll find Pisa's market area (Mon–Fri mornings & Sat all day), with fruit, vegetable, fish, meat and clothing stalls filling Piazza Vettovaglie, Piazza San Ombono and the neighbouring lanes.

Past the Romanesque-Gothic facade of **San Michele** – built on the site of the Roman temple to Mars – the Borgo meets the river at Piazza Garibaldi, which opens onto **Ponte di Mezzo**, the city's central bridge. A left turn along Lungarno Mediceo takes you past the **Palazzo Toscanelli** (now the city archives), which was rented by Byron in 1821–22 after his expulsion from Ravenna for seditious activities. Slightly farther along the *lungarno* is the **Museo Nazionale di San Matteo** (Tues–Sat 9am–7pm, Sun 9am–2pm; €5), where most of the major works of art from Pisa's churches are now gathered. Fourteenth-century religious paintings make up most of the collection, with a Simone Martini polyptych and work by Antonio Veneziano outstanding in the early sections. Later on, there's a stash of Middle Eastern ceramics pilfered by Pisan adventurers, a panel of *St Paul* by Masaccio, Gozzoli's strangely festive *Crucifixion* and Donatello's reliquary bust of the introspective *St Rossore*. Also housed in the museum are the antique armour and wooden shields used in the annual Gioco del Ponte pageant (see p.238).

### West of Ponte di Mezzo

The faculty buildings of Pisa's university are scattered all over the city, but the main concentration is to the west of the Ponte di Mezzo, around **Piazza Dante**. Immediately north of Piazza Dante, the bare stone nave of the eleventh-century

**San Frediano** preserves some capitals from that period. West of here, off Via Santa Maria, lies the university's **Orto Botanico** (Mon–Sat 8.30am–1pm; free); founded in 1591, this is the oldest botanical garden in the world. At the southern end of Via Santa Maria rises Pisa's second leaning tower, the thirteenth-century campanile of **San Nicola**. Cylindrical at its base, mutating into an octagon then a hexagon, it contains a majestic spiral staircase that was Bramante's inspiration for his grand Belvedere staircase in the Vatican. Inside the church, the Crucifix in the first chapel on the left is attributed to Giovanni Pisano, while Nino Pisano is credited with the wooden *Madonna and Child* in the fourth chapel on this side. In a chapel on the other side of the nave, there's a painting showing Pisa around 1400, being protected from the plague by St Nicholas of Tolentino.

Alongside San Nicola, fronting the Arno at Lungarno Pacinotti 46, is the **Museo Nazionale di Palazzo Reale** (Mon–Fri 9am–2.30pm, Sat 9am–1.30pm; €5), displaying artefacts that once belonged to the Medici, Lorraine and Savoy rulers of the city, who successively occupied the house. Lavish sixteenth-century Flemish tapestries share space with antique weaponry, ivory miniatures, porcelain and a largely undistinguished picture collection, featuring a version of Bronzino's famous portrait of Cosimo I's wife, Eleanora di Toledo.

Further along the river, on Lungarno Simonelli, lies the **Arsenale Mediceo**. Built by Cosimo I, it is now being converted into a home for the sixteen Roman ships that have been excavated since 1998 from the silt at nearby San Rossore, which was a port for the Roman colony at Pisa. Almost perfectly preserved in mud for two millennia, the cargo-laden fleet includes what experts believe could be the oldest Roman warship ever found.

Just west of the arsenal rises the **Torre Guelfa della Cittadella Vecchia**, or **Fortezza Vecchia** (Jan, Feb, Nov & Dec Sat & Sun 2–5pm, plus 10am–1pm on second Sun of month; rest of year Fri–Sun 3–7pm; €2). This ancient fortress, originally built in the thirteenth century, once stood guard over Pisa's harbour but now punctuates an otherwise little-explored district; the view from the tower is spectacular.

## South of the river

The more down-at-heel districts south of the Arno are popularly known as the *mezzogiorno*, the name more widely used in Italy to refer to the under-developed south of the country. On the second Sunday and the preceding Saturday of each month both banks are linked by a big **street market**, with earrings, candles and other craft stuff filling the lower reaches of Borgo Stretto, and furniture and general bric-a-brac around the **Logge di Banchi** on the south bank. Formerly the city's silk and wool market, this vast and usually deserted loggia stands at the top of the main shopping street of the *mezzogiorno*, the pedestrianized Corso Italia.

East along the Lungarno Galilei, the only real sight is the octagonal **San Sepolcro**, built for the Knights Templar by Diotisalvi, first architect of the Baptistery. A short way past here is the ruined **Palazzo Scotti**, Shelley's home during the period when Byron was in residence on the other side of the river.

Along the **lungarni** to the west of the Ponte di Mezzo, the rather monotonous line of *palazzi* – mirroring those on the facing bank – is suddenly enlivened by the oratory of **Santa Maria della Spina** (March–Oct Tues–Fri 10am–1.30pm & 2.30–6pm, Sat & Sun 10am–1.30pm & 2.30–7pm; rest of year Tues–Sun 10am–2pm, except second Sun of month 10am–7pm; €1.50).

### The Gioco del Ponte and other festivals

Pisa's big traditional event is the **Gioco del Ponte**, held on the last Sunday of June, when twelve teams from the north and south banks of the city stage a series of "push-of-war" battles, shoving a seven-tonne carriage over the Ponte di Mezzo. First recorded in 1568, the contest and attendant parades are still held in Renaissance costume. Other celebrations – concerts, regattas, art events – are held around the same time, and the city has a festive feel for most of June (the Giugno Pisano), with banners and pavement drawings brightening the streets. Most spectacular of the ancillary shows is the **Luminara di San Ranieri** (June 16), when buildings along both riverbanks are lit by seventy thousand candles in honour of Pisa's patron saint. At 6.30pm the following evening, the various quarters of the city compete in the **Palio di San Ranieri**, a boat race along the Arno.

Italy's four great maritime republics (Amalfi, Pisa, Genoa and Venice) take turns to host the **Regata delle Antiche Repubbliche Marinare**, which next comes round to Pisa in late May/early June 2010. Four eight-man crews from each of the cities race against each other on the Arno, in between festivities and parades.



Founded in 1230 but rebuilt in the 1320s by a merchant who had acquired one of the thorns (*spine*) of Christ's crown, this spry little church is the finest flourish of Pisan-Gothic. Originally built closer to the water, it was moved here for fear of floods in 1871. The single-naved interior has lost most of its furnishings, but contains a trio of statues by Andrea and Nino Pisano.

Farther west again, **San Paolo a Ripa d'Arno** probably occupies the site of Pisa's very first cathedral. The arcaded facade was built in imitation of the present cathedral in the twelfth century; the interior, badly damaged in World War II, has a handsome Roman sarcophagus and a finely carved capital (second on left). Behind the church is the octagonal **Cappella di Sant'Agata**, also built in the twelfth century.

## Eating and drinking

Pisa's proximity to the coast means that **seafood** is the staple of its restaurant menus, with *baccalà alla Pisana* (dried cod in tomato sauce) and *pesce spada* (swordfish) featuring prominently. Avoid the temptation to eat at one of the plethora of places in the vicinity of the Campo dei Miracoli – aimed squarely at the tourist trade, they are generally of poor quality. It's in the backstreets of Pisa, especially in the market area to the west of Borgo Stretto, that you'll find the best of the city's restaurants. Pisa doesn't have the range of trend-setting or long-established cafés and bars that you'll find in Florence – most of the bars are fairly indistinguishable set-ups, catering for an ever-changing and impecunious student clientele. That said, you'll find decent places to drink on and near Pizza Garibaldi, where the *Bottega del Gelato*, at no. 11, sells terrific ice creams, as does *De' Coltelli*, just round the corner at Lungarno Pacinotti 23.

### Cafés and bars

**Bazeel Piazza Garibaldi 15.** This stylish bar is currently Pisa's most favoured hang-out – the interior is cool and spacious, but when the weather's good the punters prefer the outside tables, or even the parapet overlooking the river. DJs on Fri & Sat, live music Thurs & Sun. Daily 5pm–2am.

**Pasticceria Salza Borgo Stretto 46.** The best-known café-*pasticceria* in Pisa; it has a restaurant section at the back, but the food isn't as good as you'll find elsewhere. Tues–Sun 8am–8.30pm.

### Restaurants

**Bruno Via L. Bianchi 12 ☎050.560.818.** Simple and hearty Pisan dishes have kept this place well regarded for years. Reckon on around €35 a head. Closed Tues.

**Cagliostro Via del Castelletto 26–30 9 ☎050.575.413.** Tucked away in an obscure alley parallel to Via San Frediano, alongside the *Rinascente* hotel, *Cagliostro* is an extremely good restaurant-wine bar, offering a small but classy menu that offers classic Pisan dishes and others with an innovative twist – such as Tuscan leek soup with stilton. The dining room is spectacular too. Expect to pay about €40 per person. Closed Sun, Mon lunchtime & Tues.

**Da Cucciolo Vicolo Rosselmini 9 ☎050.26.086.** The family-run *Cucciolo* has been in business for forty years and is always reliable, offering unfussy, delicious traditional meals (with an emphasis on organically produced food), with main courses in the €10–15 range. Closed Sun eve & Mon.

**Il Campano Via Domenico Cavalca 19 ☎050.580.585.** Home-made pasta and gnocchi, and local seafood, are the big things at this first-rate trattoria – though they also do meaty Tuscan classics, including a one-kilo Fiorentino steak (to share, of course). This may also be the only Pisan restaurant with ostrich on the menu. Extremely good selection of wines, too. Closed all Wed & Thurs eve.

**La Cereria Via Pietro Gori 33 ☎050.20.336.** Popular, unpretentious restaurant tucked away in a courtyard a short distance south of the river. Excellent seafood and pasta dishes, superb pizzas (the best in the city, some reckon) and a pleasant garden. Closed Tues.

**La Mescita Via Domenico Cavalca 2 ☎050.544.294.** This wine bar/restaurant, located on the edge of the Piazza Vettovaglie market, has established a good reputation with its ever-changing Tuscan menu and excellent cellar. You'll pay around €35 per person. Closed Sat & Sun eve, Mon & 3 weeks in Aug.

**Osteria dei Cavalieri Via San Frediano 16 ☎050.580.858.** Outstanding quality, good prices (about €30 per person) and a nice atmosphere. The fish is exquisite, Tuscan meat and game dishes are expertly prepared and their vegetarian options are excellent. Closed Sat lunch & Sun, plus most of Aug.

**San Omobono Piazza San Omobono 6 ☎050.540.847.** This city-centre trattoria serves terrific authentic Pisan home cooking, featuring dishes such as *brachette alla renaiaola* – pasta in a purée of greens and smoked fish. Closed Sun & 2 weeks in Aug.

# Lucca

**LUCCA** lies at the heart of one of Italy's richest agricultural regions and has prospered since the Romans, whose gridiron orthodoxy is still obvious in the layout of the streets. Under the **Lombards** it was the capital of Tuscia (Tuscany), though its heyday was between the eleventh and fourteenth centuries, when banking and the silk trade brought wealth and, for a time, political power. In a brief flurry of military activity Lucca lost its independence to Pisa in 1314, but regained it under the command of a remarkable adventurer, **Castruccio Castracani**, who went on to forge an empire covering much of western Tuscany. Pisa and Pistoia both fell to the Lucchesi, and but for Castracani's untimely death from malaria, Florence might have followed. In subsequent centuries the city remained largely independent – if fairly inconsequential – until passing to **Napoleon** (and rule by his sister, Elisa Baciocchi), the Bourbons, and, just short of Italian unification, to the Grand Duchy of Tuscany.

Today the city is reckoned among the wealthiest in Tuscany, a prosperity gained largely through **silk** that was produced here by scores of small family businesses, and on the region's high-quality **olive oil** and other produce. There is, too, a tradition of decorum, traceable to eighteenth- and nineteenth-century court life; up until the turn of the twentieth century, smart Italian

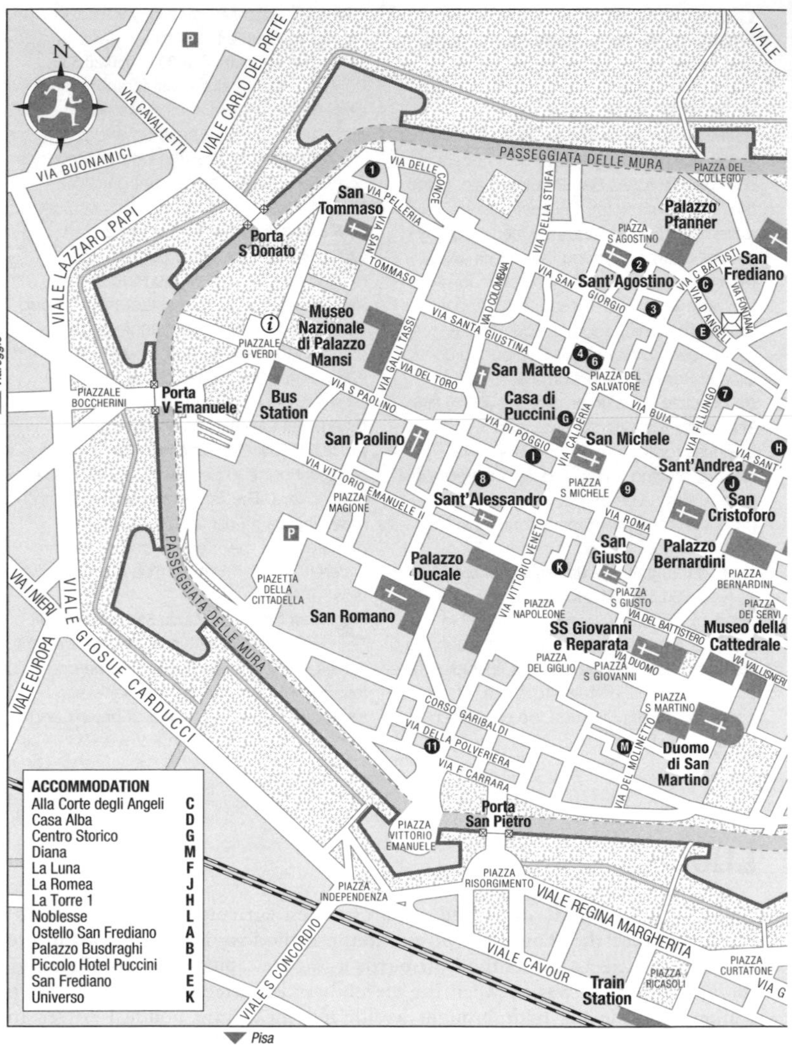


families sent their daughters to Lucca to pick up the better manners presumed to prevail here.

The town is easily reached and easily seen, with **Piazza San Michele**, focus of the historic core, and its eponymous church an obvious starting point. From here, head to Piazza del Duomo, home to the **cathedral**, which contains several major works of art, including one of Tuscany's most touching – and accomplished – Renaissance sculptures. From here, any meandering route north towards **Piazza Anfiteatro**, a medieval piazza that preserves the shape of the earlier Roman amphitheatre on the site, will reveal numerous evocative corners and several Pisan-Romanesque churches. The most of important of these, **San Frediano**, is moments from the piazza and easily seen before attending to Lucca's two key art

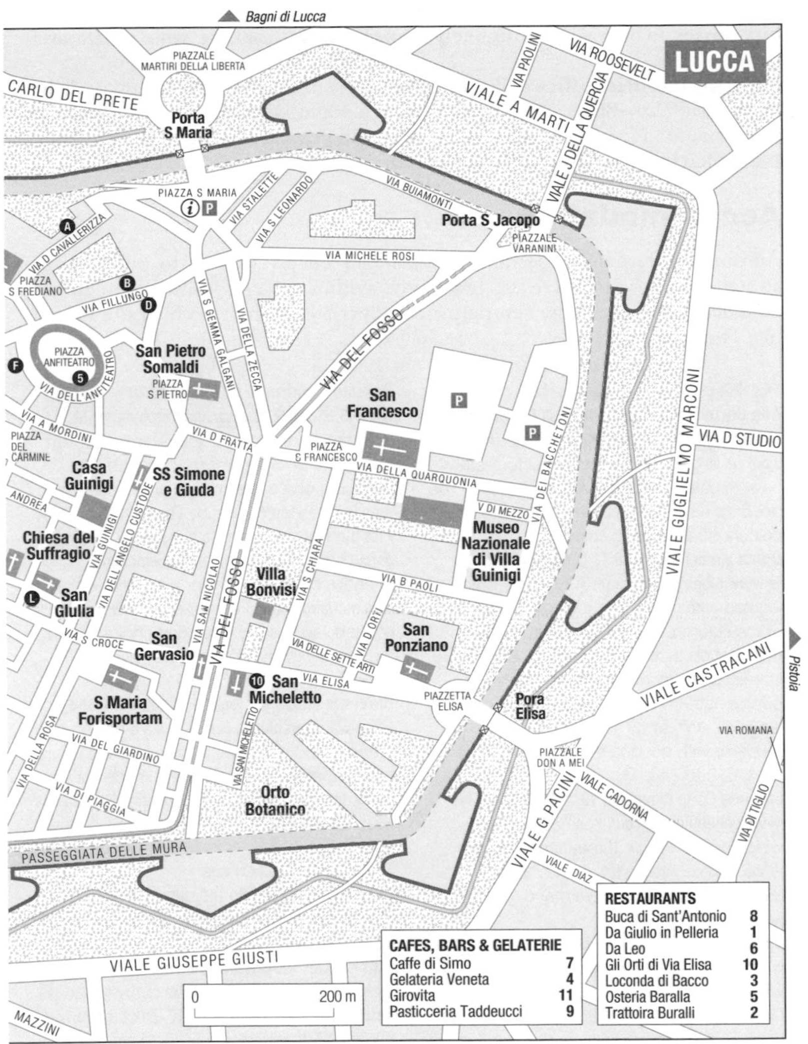


galleries, the Palazzo Mansi and Villa Guinigi. Finally, be sure to walk or cycle all or part of the town's remarkable **walls** (bikes are easily rented at several points in the city, notably Piazza Santa Maria).

## Arrival and information

The **train station** is on Piazza Ricasoli, a short way outside the walls to the south, and is served by roughly half-hourly services from Pisa Centrale (journey time is 30min) and the odd direct train from Pisa Aeroporto. **Buses** to and from the same destinations (trains are invariably quicker and more convenient) arrive just inside the western stretch of walls, in Piazzale Giuseppe Verdi, while

**city buses** (which you are unlikely to need) leave from the same piazza and Corso Garibaldi.

The main **tourist office** is Piazza Santa Maria in the north of the town (daily: April–Oct 9am–8pm; Nov–March 9am–6.30pm; ⓣ0583.919.931, ⓦwww.luccaturismo.it), with another large office at Piazzale Verdi (daily 9am–7pm; Nov–March closes 6pm; ⓣ0583.583.150).

## Accommodation

Accommodation always seems in demand in Lucca: it's wise to book ahead at any time of year. There are few hotels within the city walls so you might consider staying in a more centrally located private room or B&B, or the *Ostello San Frediano*.

### Hotels and hostels

**Alla Corte Degli Angeli Via degli Angeli 23 ⓣ0583.469.204, ⓦwww.allacortedegliangeli.com.** A bright, airy and colourful four-star hotel situated inside the medieval walls. The decor of each room is inspired by the colours of different flowers. ❹

**Diana Via del Molinetto 11 ⓣ0583.492.202, ⓦwww.albergodiana.com.** A two-star hotel located within the walls a block west of the Duomo and only 500m from the train station. Rooms are plain, but clean, spacious and comfortable, and all have private bathrooms. Those in the *dipendenza* (annexe) 40m away are a little more modern, with good bathrooms, and cost an extra €13 to €44. ❷

**La Luna Corte Compagni 12 ⓣ0583.493.634, ⓦwww.hotellaluna.com.** A smart and welcoming 29-room three-star within the walls, with characterful rooms ranged around an internal courtyard and free parking. Closed Jan. ❹

**La Romea Vicolo delle Ventaglie 2 ⓣ0583.464.175, ⓦwww.laromea.com.** A welcoming three-star hotel, 30m from the Guinigi Tower, with only five rooms. It's run by a young couple and is on the first floor of a fourteenth-century building. ❺

**Noblesse Via Sant'Anastasio 23 ⓣ0583.440.275, ⓦwww.hotelnoblesse.it.** Lucca's long-term lack of a five-star hotel has been remedied by this 13-room gem at the heart of the old city, a converted eighteenth-century *palazzo* over three floors with period furniture, antiques, Persian rugs and a warm, intimate atmosphere. ❼

**Ostello San Frediano Via della Cavallerizza 12 ⓣ0583.469.957, ⓦwww.ostellolucca.it.** Conveniently located HI hostel just within the walls, with a midnight curfew. Dorm beds €19.

**Palazzo Busdraghi Via Fillungo 170 ⓣ0583.950.856, ⓦwww.apalazzobusdraghi.it.** An intimate and central four-star hotel, with only seven rooms, all furnished with fine antiques; one of the rooms even boasts a wardrobe once owned by Puccini. ❼

**Piccolo Hotel Puccini Via di Poggio 9 ⓣ0583.55.421, ⓦwww.hotelpuccini.com.** Friendly, central three-star with fourteen rooms. It's located almost beside San Michele, so is an obvious first choice – and thus definitely needs booking. Private parking for an extra €15. ❸

**Universo Piazza del Giglio 1 ⓣ0583.954.854, ⓦwww.universolucca.com.** Lucca's not-so-grand grand old hotel: a three-star with sixty rooms that lacks atmosphere, made up for by its location bang on the central Piazza Napoleone. ❸

### Private rooms

**Casa Alba Via Fillungo 142, second floor ⓣ0583.495.361, ⓦwww.casa-alba.com.** Five clean, pleasant rooms (doubles and singles) with or without private bathroom on Lucca's main street, just north of Piazza Anfiteatro. ❷

**Centro Storico Corte Portici 16 ⓣ0583.490.748, ⓦwww.affittacamerecentrostorico.com.** Six convenient rooms, four with bathroom, located on a courtyard off Via Calderia just northwest of Piazza San Michele. ❷

**La Torre 1 Via del Carmine 11 ⓣ0583.957.044.** Five nice double rooms with or without bathroom; located off Piazza del Carmine south of Piazza Anfiteatro. ❸

**San Frediano Via degli Angeli 19 ⓣ0583.469.630, ⓦwww.sanfrediano.com.** Six rooms, including singles and doubles with a choice of private and shared bathrooms. Situated on a street between Via Fillungo and Via C. Battisti just southeast of San Frediano. ❸

## The City

Confined within its walls, Lucca is an easy place to get your bearings. The centre of town is ostensibly **Piazza Napoleone**, a huge expanse carved out by the Bourbons to house their administration. From here the main **Via Fillungo** – the "long thread" – heads north through the heart of the medieval city. You're most likely to gravitate to **Piazza San Michele**, home to the church of San Michele, the apotheosis of the Pisan-Romanesque style. From here, you might want to potter around the streets to the west, or head south to the **Duomo**, another Romanesque gem, with one of Italy's most sublime funerary sculptures. Further east, the Fosso ("ditch") cuts off the quarter around **San Francesco**, while to the north is **Piazza Anfiteatro**, built over the old Roman arena, and **San Frediano**, the third of the city's trio of outstanding churches. A trip to Lucca is not complete without strolling part of the panoramic and tree-lined promenade atop the **walls**, accessed from almost any part of the city.



### San Michele

Head to the historical heart of Lucca and you come to the site of the Roman forum, now the square surrounding **San Michele in Foro** (daily: summer 7.40am–noon & 3–6pm; winter 9am–noon & 3–6pm; closed during services; free), a church with one of Tuscany's most exquisite facades. The building is first mentioned in 795, but most of the present structure dates from between 1070 and the middle of the twelfth century (you can see the date 1143 marked on a pillar on the left side of the main portal's triumphal arch). The structure is unfinished, however, money having been diverted to the **facade**, begun in the thirteenth century; funds ran out before the rest of the church could be raised to a similar standard. The effect is wonderful, the upper loggias and the windows fronting air, like the figure of the archangel at their summit. Each of its many columns is different – some twisted, others sculpted or candy-striped. The impressive twelfth-century **campanile** is the city's tallest.

It would be hard to match the facade's architectural display, and the **interior** barely tries. On the rear wall is a statue of the *Madonna and Child* by local sculptor Matteo Civitali, previously on the facade, but the best work of art is a beautifully framed painting of *SS Jerome, Sebastian, Roch and Helena* by Filippino Lippi, at the end of the right-hand nave.

### The western quarter

The birthplace and family home of Giacomo Puccini, the **Casa di Puccini** (currently closed; Ⓦ www.puccini.it), is in Corte San Lorenzo 9, off Via di Poggio, very close to San Michele – where the composer's father and grandfather both played the organ. Today the house is a school of music, and contains a small museum displaying scores, photographs and even the Steinway on which he wrote *Turandot*.

To the west is the **Museo Nazionale di Palazzo Mansi**, at Via Galli Tassi 43 (Tues–Sat 8.30am–7.30pm, Sun 8.30am–1.30pm; €4; joint ticket with Museo Guinigi €6.50). This seventeenth-century building is worth seeing for its magnificently over-the-top Rococo decor; from a vast, frescoed music salon, you pass through three drawing-rooms hung with seventeenth-century Flemish tapestries to a spectacularly gilded bridal suite. Rooms 11–14 in the far wing house the **Pinacoteca Nazionale**, an eclectic grouping of pictures whose real highlights are a Pontormo portrait, possibly of Alessandro de' Medici; Bronzino's portrait of Cosimo I (the artist painted several versions); two male portraits by Tintoretto; and works by the Sienese Mannerists Beccafumi and Rutilio Manetti. Also worth seeing is the section of the museum that traces the development of Lucca's important **textile** industry, in particular its silks and damasks.

## Duomo di San Martino

It needs a double-take before you realize what's odd about the **Duomo di San Martino** (mid-March to Oct Mon–Fri 9.30am–5.45pm, Sat 9.30am–6.45pm, Sun 9–10.45am & noon–5pm; rest of the year closes 4.45pm Mon–Fri and 6pm Sun; free). The building is fronted by a severely asymmetric facade, its right-hand arch and loggias squeezed by the bell-tower, which was already in place from an earlier building. Nonetheless, little detracts from its overall grandeur, created by the repetition of tiny columns and loggias and by the stunning **atrium**, whose bas-reliefs are some of the finest sculptures in the city.

It's worth looking closely at these carvings, some dated as early as the fifth century, which were executed by a variety of mainly Lombard artists, most of them unknown. Part of the sculpture is attributed to **Nicola Pisano**, and may well be his first work after arriving in Tuscany from Apulia. His are probably the offerings around the left-hand door: the *Deposition* (in the lunette), *Annunciation*, *Nativity* and *Adoration of the Magi*.

The panels of the *Life of St Martin* (1204–10), between the doors, are the masterpiece of the architect, **Guidetto da Como**, responsible for the upper facade's three tiers of arcades.

### The interior

The Duomo's **interior** is best known for the contribution of **Matteo Civitali** (1435–1501). He's represented here by a couple of water stoups near the entrance, the pulpits and several tombs and altars – notably the tomb of Pietro da Noceto, secretary to Pope Niccolo V (right wall of the south transept), and the altar of San Regolo, on the chancel wall immediately right of the apse.

Civitali's most famous work is the **Tempietto**, the gilt and marble octagon encountered halfway down the church. Some fanatically intense acts of devotion are performed by worshippers in front of it, directed at the **Volto Santo** (Holy Face), Lucca's most famous relic. A cedarwood Crucifix, it's said to be a true effigy of Christ carved by Nicodemus, an eyewitness to the Crucifixion, but is probably a thirteenth-century copy of an eleventh-century copy of an eighth-century original. Legend has it that the *Volto Santo* came to Lucca of its own volition in 782, first journeying by boat from the Holy Land, and then brought by oxen guided by divine will – a story similar to the ecclesiastical sham of St James's bones at Santiago di Compostela in Spain. The effigy attracted pilgrims from all over Europe and inspired devotion in all who heard of it: King William Rufus of England used to swear by it ("Per sanctum vultum de Lucca!").

Elsewhere in the church the works of art are of less disputed origin. The finest of them is the **Tomb of Ilaria del Carretto** (1407–10), housed in the **sacristy** entered midway down the south nave (Ⓦwww.museocattedralelucca.it; mid-March to Oct Mon–Fri 9.30am–5.45pm, Sat 9.30am–6.45pm, Sun 9.30am–10.45pm; rest of the year Mon–Fri 9.30am–4.45pm, Sat 9.30am–6.45pm, Sun noon to 6pm; €2 or €6 with Museo della Cattedrale and church of San Giovanni). Considered the masterpiece of Sienese sculptor Jacopo della Quercia, it consists of a dais and the sculpted body of Ilaria, second wife of Paolo Guinigi, one of Lucca's leading medieval nobles. In a touching, almost sentimental gesture, the artist has carved the family dog at Ilaria's feet, a symbol of fidelity. Also within the sacristy is a superb *Madonna Enthroned with Saints* by Domenico Ghirlandaio.

Other pictorial highlights of the cathedral include a *Madonna and Child* in the enclosed chapel to the left of the high altar in the north transept, painted in

1509 by **Fra Bartolommeo**. In the main part of the Duomo, the first chapel on the left has a *Presentation of the Virgin* by Alessandro Allori (1598), and the third altar on the right a *Last Supper* (1592) by **Tintoretto.**

## Around the Duomo

Occupying a converted twelfth-century building across Via Arcivescovato from the cathedral is the **Museo della Cattedrale** (mid-March to Oct daily 10am–6pm; Nov to mid-March Mon–Fri 10am–2pm, Sat & Sun 10am–5pm; €4, or €6 with the cathedral sacristy & San Giovanni). The museum's four floors are home to a collection of ecclesiastical and other ephemera interspersed with the occasional artistic gem.

▲ Street scene, Lucca

On the north side of the square stands the large basilica of **SS Giovanni e Reparata** (same hours; €2.50; joint ticket with cathedral sacristy and Museo della Cattedrale or €6), Lucca's original cathedral until 715. Rebuilt many times, it preserves a lion-flanked carved Romanesque portal, saved during restructuring of the facade in 1589. Inside, excavations have uncovered a tangle of architectural remains, embracing a wide range of much earlier buildings on the site.

A short distance east is the twelfth-century **Santa Maria Forisportam** ("outside the gate"), signalling the limit of the Roman and medieval city until 1260. The facade sports just two unfinished tiers and none of its relatives' decorative columns, but it's appealing for all that, with a few carvings above the doors and the usual jutting animals high on the front.

### North to San Frediano

North of the Duomo, **Via Fillungo** cuts through Lucca's luxury shopping district, a tight huddle of streets and alleys where medieval fragments and bricked-up loggias compete with Art Nouveau shop fronts and lunchtime and early-evening throngs. Amid the crowds it's easy to miss the gorgeous facade of **San Cristoforo**, the deconsecrated church at the southern end; inside, the left-hand wall is completely covered in writing – the names of Lucca's dead in the two world wars. Farther on is the **Torre delle Ore**, the city's clock tower since 1471; then at no. 58 there's the famous *Caffè di Simo*, a bar worth the price of a drink just for the early twentieth-century ambience. Beyond, the street branches into a warren of lanes that lead to **Piazza San Frediano**.

### San Frediano

The church of **San Frediano** (Mon–Sat 8.30am–noon & 3–5.30pm, Sun 9–11.30am & 3–5.30pm; closed during services; free) is again Pisan-Romanesque, built between 1112 and 1147 on the site of a sixth-century basilica of San Vincenzo but orientated back to front (west-facing), probably because the old entrance would have been blocked by the new set of medieval city walls nearby. In place of the characteristic multiple loggias of Lucca's other great facades is a magnificent thirteenth-century mosaic of *The Ascension* with the apostles gathered below.

The **interior** lives up to the facade's promise – a delicately lit, hall-like basilica, with subtly varied columns and capitals and some fine treasures. Immediately facing the door is one of the best, the **Fonte Lustrale**, a huge twelfth-century font executed by three different craftsmen. The first, an unknown Lombard, carved the stories of Moses on the outer slabs of the basin, including a superb *Crossing of the Red Sea*, with the Egyptian soldiers depicted as medieval knights. The second, one Maestro Roberto, added the Good Shepherd and six prophets on the other two basin slabs, their enframing arches showing a clear Byzantine influence. To the third sculptor, an unknown Tuscan, is owed the decoration of the Apostles and the Months on the cup above the basin and the beautiful fantasy masks from which the water is disgorged. Set behind the font is an *Annunciation* attributed to Matteo della Robbia, festooned with trailing garlands of ceramic fruit.

A figure of St Bartholomew by Andrea della Robbia is to be found lower down to the left, close to the left-hand of the two chapels behind the font, the Cappella Fatinelli, which houses the incorrupt body of **St Zita** (died 1278). A Lucchese maidservant, Zita achieved sainthood from a fortuitous white lie: she used to give bread from her household to the poor and when challenged one day by her boss as to the contents of her apron, replied "only roses and flowers" – into which the bread was duly transformed. She is commemorated

## A walk around the walls

Climbing up at any of the bastions, some of which are signposted, you can follow the four-kilometre circuit of the city **walls**, either by bike or on foot. The mid-afternoon shutdown is perhaps the best time to walk their broad promenade, which is lined successively with plane, lime, ilex and chestnut trees. Bikes can easily be **rented** from a cluster of outlets on Piazza Santa Maria, by the tourist office.

Construction of the walls started around 1500, prompted by the need to replace medieval ramparts rendered inadequate by advances in weapon technology. By 1650 the work was completed, with eleven bastions to fortify walls that were 30m wide at the base, 12m high and surrounded by moats 35m across. There were originally just three gates. Perhaps the best feature, from the present-day perspective, was the destruction of all trees and buildings within a couple of hundred metres of the walls, creating a green belt of lawns that has shielded the old town from the ugliness that's sprouted on the outside.

Ironically, having produced a perfect set of walls, Lucca was never called on to defend them. The only siege was against the floodwaters of the River Serchio in 1812, when the gates were sealed against the deluge that had flooded the countryside. Napoleon's sister and city governor, Elisa Baciocchi, one of the last people allowed in, had to be winched over the ramparts by crane. Marie Louise of Bourbon, her successor, had the walls transformed to their present garden aspect, arranging them, as the local tourist handout puts it, "with unparalleled good taste and moderation".

on April 27 by a flower market outside the church and by the Lucchesi freeing her of her finery and bringing her out to touch.

Moving to the top of the church, note the wonderful twelfth-century Cosmati marble pavement of the presbytery, while on the left are fragments of the original **tomb of San Frediano**, an Irish monk who is said to have brought Christianity to Lucca in the sixth century. Moving back down the left (north) nave from the high altar, the first chapel, the **Cappella Trenta**, contains a superb carved altarpiece with niche statues of the Madonna, Child and Saints by Jacopo della Quercia.

The best **frescoes** in the city adorn the Cappella di Sant'Agostino, the next chapel but one: Amico Aspertini's *The Arrival of the Volto Santo* and *The Baptism of St Augustine* on the left wall, and *The Miracle of St Frediano* on the right, the last depicting the River Serchio in flood being diverted by the saint's crib. Dating from the early sixteenth century, the murals are painted in a style that is much influenced by the realism of Flemish and German painters.

### Piazza Anfiteatro and around

East of San Frediano is the remarkable **Piazza Anfiteatro**, aerial shots of which feature in just about all of Lucca's tourist literature. A ramshackle circuit of medieval buildings, it incorporates elements of the Roman amphitheatre that once stood here. Much of the original stone was carted off in the twelfth century to build the city's churches, while parts of the old structure were used as a medieval prison and salt warehouse, but arches and columns can still be seen embedded in some of the houses, particularly on the north side of the outer walls. Medieval slums used to occupy the centre of the arena, but these were cleared in 1830 on the orders of the Bourbon ruler, Marie Louise.

A couple of blocks east is **San Pietro Somaldi**, its delicate facade dating from 1248 – this time stone on the lower levels, topped with two tiers of Pisan marbling and tiny columns. Above the lovely portal is a good carved frieze executed by Guido da Como in 1203, *Jesus Giving the Keys to St Peter*, and the customary pair of lions, common symbols for the Resurrection in medieval art – after the belief that cubs, when born, lay dead for three days until a male lion brought them to life by breathing in their faces.

### Torre Guinigi

The **Torre Guinigi** (daily: June–Sept 9am–midnight; Nov–Feb 9.30am–5pm; March 9am–5pm; April 9.30am–9pm; May & Oct 10am–6pm; €3.50), south of San Pietro in Via Sant'Andrea, is the strangest sight in Lucca's cityscape. This battlemented tower, attached to the fifteenth-century **Casa Guinigi**, town house of Lucca's leading medieval family, is surmounted by an ancient holm oak whose roots have grown into the room below. You can climb the 44-metre tower, entering on Via Sant'Andrea, for a close-up of the tree and easily the best view over the city. The adjacent fortress, which has some wonderful austere medieval details, fronts a startling number of streets.



### The eastern quarter

The city's canal and parallel road, the **Via del Fosso**, mark the entry to Lucca's more lacklustre eastern margins. The most attractive part of this quarter is the **Orto Botanico** (Mon–Fri 9.30am–12.30pm; April–Oct also Sat & Sun 9.30am–12.30pm & 3.30–6.30pm; €3) at the southern end of Via del Fosso, an extensive patch of green laid out in 1820 that neatly complements the ramparts.

Across the street from the plain-faced church of San Francesco is the much-restored Villa Guinigi, built to supplement the family's medieval town house. It's now home to Lucca's major museum, the **Museo Nazionale di Villa Guinigi** (Tues–Sat 8.30am–7.30pm, Sun 8.30am–1.30pm; €4; joint ticket with Palazzo Mansi €6.50), an extremely varied collection of painting, sculpture, furniture and applied arts. The lower floor is mainly sculpture and archeological finds, with numerous Romanesque pieces and works by della Quercia and Matteo Civitali. Upstairs, the gallery moves on to paintings, with lots of big sixteenth-century canvases, and more impressive works by early Lucchese and Sienese masters, as well as fine Renaissance offerings from artists such as Fra' Bartolommeo.

## Eating and drinking

As a wealthy, gastronomic centre, Lucca has some high-quality restaurants. **Local specialities** often feature *zuppa di farro*, a thick soup of *farro*, an ancient variety of grain grown in the Garfagnana; other dishes include roast mountain goat (*capretto*) and puddings based on chestnut flour, such as *castagnaccio*.

### Cafés, bars and gelaterie

**Caffè di Simo Via Fillungo 58.** Lucca's most famous café-bar was Puccini's favourite haunt and retains an appealing late nineteenth-century ambience. It serves a decent array of cakes as well as a few simple hot dishes for €6–8. Closed Mon.

**Gelateria Veneta Via Vittorio Veneto 74.** It's been serving some of Lucca's best ice cream since 1927 and is open conveniently late. Closed mid-Jan to mid-Feb and Tues in winter.

**Girovita Piazza Antelminelli 2.** With tables outside in the quiet piazza opposite the cathedral, trendy *Girovita* is the place to come for an *aperitivo* or a lengthy afternoon coffee. Closed Mon.

**Pasticceria Taddeucci Piazza San Michele 34 ⓣ0583.494.933.** A stunning interior of wood-panelling and mosaic tiles match the selection of cakes and great coffee.

### Restaurants

**Buca di Sant'Antonio Via della Cervia 3 ⓣ0583.55.881.** Lucca's finest restaurant has been around for over two hundred years and still retains some of its old-world charm.

Excellent service, top-quality meat or fish menu and delicious house pasta and desserts such as *semifreddo Buccellato*. Around €30 a head. Closed Sun eve & Mon; booking essential.

**Da Giulio in Pelleria** **Via della Conce 45** **☏0583.55.948.** A lively trattoria always packed in the evenings – the food is not exceptional, but the prices are very reasonable (*primi* from €5, *secondi* €5 and up) and the atmosphere makes it worth it. Closed Sun.

**Da Leo** **Via Tegrimi 1** **☏0583.492.236.** Another good-value family-run place near Piazza San Michele that preserves the authentic look and feel of an old-fashioned trattoria. Closed Sun evening.

**Gli Orti di Via Elisa** **Via Elisa 17** **☏0583.491.241.** Popular pizzeria/trattoria with wonderful risottos and some vegetarian dishes, open evenings only. Closed Wed.

**Locanda Di Bacco** **Via San Giorgio 36** **☏0583.493.136.** This restaurant with lovely wood-panelled interior does quality food at good prices (around €20 for a full meal). Specialities include salt cod with chickpeas. Closed Tues.

**Osteria Baralla** **Via Anfiteatro 5** **☏0583.440.240.** Something of an institution in Lucca, this traditional *osteria* serves simple local food at moderate prices. Occasional live music. Closed Sun.

**Trattoria Buralli** **Piazza Sant'Agostino 10** **☏0583.950.611.** Traditional trattoria with a wide choice of home-style local cooking and a selection of wines from the Lucchesi hills. Closed Wed.

# Chianti

One region of Tuscany exemplifies the stereotypical image of rural Italy as an idyll of vineyards, soft hills and ancient villages, and that's **Chianti**, the area that stretches between Florence and Siena, the two cities that contested ownership of much of this region until Siena's final capitulation in 1557. To the outsider, every aspect of life in Chianti seems in perfect balance: the landscape is the sort of harmoniously varied terrain beloved of painters evoking any mythical Golden Age; the climate for most of the year is balmy; and on top of all this there's the **wine**, the one Italian vintage that's familiar to just about everyone.

The British and other northern Europeans long ago took note of Chianti's charms, and the rate of immigration has been so rapid since the 1960s that the region is now popularly known as "Chiantishire". With up to a million visitors a year, **tourism** has overtaken wine to become the region's most important cash crop, and has helped push property prices beyond the reach of the local population – thus altering the tone of certain parts irreparably. Although foreign residents still account for only five percent of Chianti's 45,000 inhabitants and tourist handouts still talk of the unsullied charm of Chianti's medieval hamlets, many of these villages are places where history has become a commodity and where newly varnished shutters remain closed for much of the off season. There is, nonetheless, much to enjoy in Chianti – quiet back roads, hundreds of acres of woodland, and of course the vineyards.

**Buses** from Florence and Siena connect with the main Chianti towns, but the best way to really get to know the region is **by car**. There's no better way to experience the village life of Chianti than to drive along the **Chiantigiana road (SS222)**, which cuts right across the hills from Florence to Siena, connecting with a tangle of minor roads that traverse the most unspoilt parts of the region. If you put your foot down, its twists and turns can be negotiated in only a little more time than the major N2 road to the west, but this is a route to dawdle along, taking turnings on a whim and dropping by at any vineyard that takes your fancy. If you want to see the best of Chianti in a single day, devise an itinerary that takes in **Greve** and **Radda**, two of the region's most alluring little towns.

Hotels in Chianti are rarely inexpensive, but this is prime **agriturismo** territory, with scores of farms offering rooms or apartments (or even self-contained mini-villas), generally for a minimum period of one week, which for an extended stay can provide a good-value alternative to hotel accommodation. There are already far too many agriturismi in Chianti to list here, and with every passing month a new operation starts up, but you can find a good choice of properties at Ⓦwww.agriturismo.net, Ⓦwww.agriturismo.it and Ⓦwww.chiantishire.org/agriturismi.htm. The Chiantishire website, despite its dreadful name, is a good source of topical information on the area.

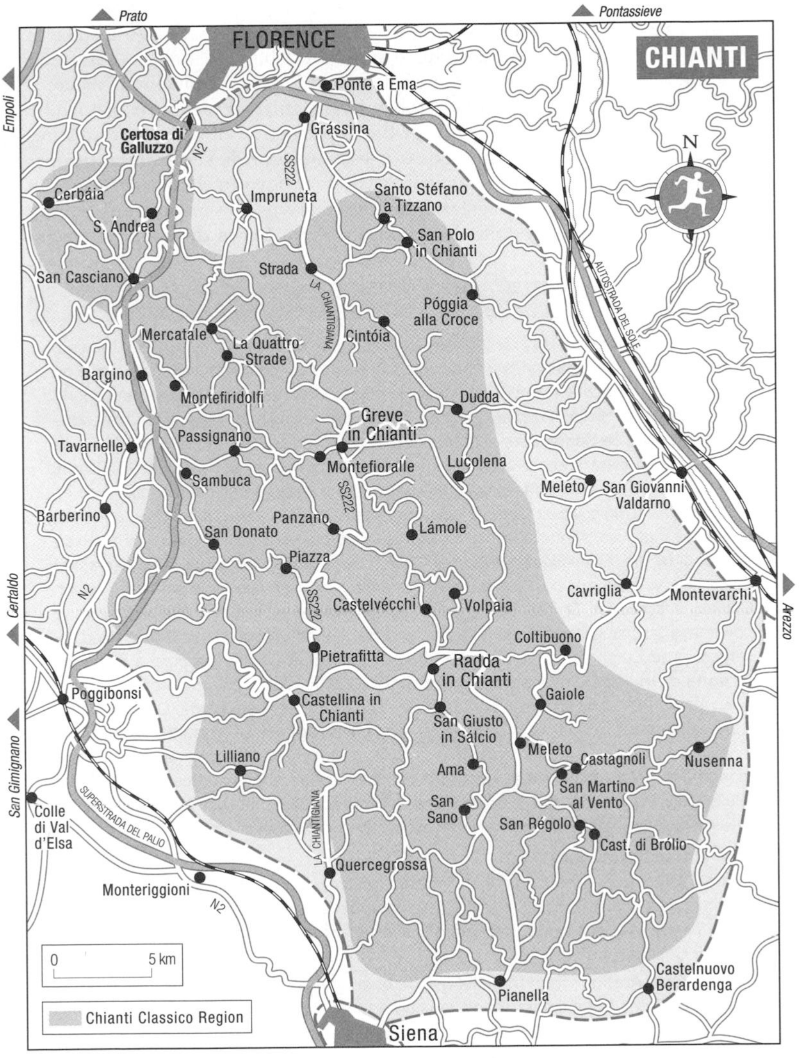


# Greve and around

The venue for Chianti's biggest **wine fair** (the Rassegna del Chianti Classico, usually held during the second weekend in September), **GREVE** is a town with wine for sale on every street: two of the best outlets are the Enoteca di Gallo Nero, at Piazzetta Santa Croce 8, and the Cantina di Greve in Chianti, at Piazza delle Cantine 6, which claims to have the biggest selection of Chianti Classico wines in the whole region. SITA runs about thirty **bus** services a day from Florence to Greve, taking a little over an hour; if you're reliant on public transport, places south of Greve are best approached from Siena. Greve itself is around 20km south from Florence along the SS222.

Though razed to the ground in 1325 by Castruccio Castracani (the ruler of Lucca), by the fifteenth century Greve had re-established itself as a thriving mercantile town, focused on the funnel-shaped **Piazza Matteotti**, where a Saturday morning market is still held today. Its irregular arcades are explained by the fact that various merchants paid for the construction of their own stretches of colonnade. The statue in the centre is of Giovanni da Verrazzano, the first European to see what became Manhattan; he was born in the nearby Castello di Verrazzano. Other than the piazza, the Greve townscape has just one feature that might be classified as a sight: the **Museo d'Arte Sacra di San Francesco**,

## Chianti wines

**Chianti** became the world's first officially defined wine-producing area in 1716, the year Cosimo III drew the boundaries within which vineyards could use the region's name on their product. Modern Chianti dates from the 1860s when Bettino Ricasoli, the second prime minister of unified Italy, established the classic formula for the wine at his estate at Brolio, based on **Sangiovese** – central Italy's predominant red grape. White *Malvasia bianca* grapes were another component of Ricasoli's recipe, but since 1995 Chianti growers have been allowed to produce wines with no white grapes in the mix.

There was a time when Chianti was synonymous with low-grade wine, and had an image that was symbolized by the squat straw-covered bottle known as a *fiasco* – indeed, by the 1950s the reputation of Chianti had sunk so low that it was suggested that many vineyards should be returned to pasture. Given the wide area over which Chianti is produced, it can never be a consistent wine, but the overall quality is nowadays far higher than it used to be, and the kitschy *fiasco* is no longer used by serious producers, whose number has burgeoned since Chianti became a **Denominazione d'Origine Controllata e Garantita (DOCG)** in 1984. The area's total output is now about 100 million litres per annum, making it Italy's highest-volume DOCG by far.

The wine-growing area is split into seven classified **regions**, of which the most highly regarded are Chianti Classico and Chianti Rúfina. Many Chiantis are fine when young, though the better wines take at least four years to mature; the best recent vintages are 1997, 1999, 2001, 2004 and 2006, but one to avoid is 2002 – the worst Chianti summer in living memory, with torrential rain that rotted the vines all over the region.

### The Chianti districts

**Chianti Classico** – the original delineated district, accounting for a third of the Chianti produced. In 1924 Chianti Classico took as its trademark the black cock (*Gallo Nero*) that was once the heraldic symbol of the baronial alliance called the Lega di Chianti.

**Chianti Colli Aretini** – from the hills on the east side of the Arno valley, to the north of Arezzo. Tends to be lighter than Classico and is best drunk young.

**Chianti Colli Fiorentini** – from the area immediately south and east of Florence, and along the Arno and Pesa valleys. Good quaffing wine and staple *Rosso* of many a restaurant in Florence.

**Chianti Colli Senesi** – the largest Chianti zone, split into three distinct districts: around Montalcino, around Montepulciano, and south of the Classico region east of San Gimignano. Variable quality, with the name of the producer all-important.

**Chianti Colline Pisane** – the lightest Chianti comes from this region, southeast of Pisa, around Casciana Terme.

**Chianti Montalbano** – from the hills west of Florence and south of Pistoia; the wines are usually soft and scented.

**Chianti Rúfina** – from the lower Sieve valley, northeast of Florence, producing some of the most refined and longest-living Chiantis. Not to be confused with the big Chianti producer Ruffino.

at Via San Francesco 4 (April–Sept Thurs & Fri 10am–1pm, Sat & Sun 4–8pm; Oct–March Thurs & Fri 10am–1pm, Sat & Sun 3.30–6.30pm; €3), a minor museum where the chief exhibit is a painted terracotta *Lamentation*, created in the 1530s, and thus one of the last examples of a genre that originated with Luca della Robbia more than a century earlier.

As the chief town of the *Gallo Nero* region, Greve is equipped with an efficient **tourist office**, tucked into a corner of Piazza Matteotti at Via delle Capanne 11 (Mon–Fri 10.30am–2pm & 3–6pm; ⓣ055.854.5243), which can give information on vineyards, accommodation in local farmhouses and trekking in Chianti. A couple of three-star **hotels** on Piazza Matteotti offer comfortable accommodation: the *Del Chianti* at no. 86 (ⓣ055.853.763, ⓦwww.albergodelchianti.it; ❷) and *Da Verrazzano* at no. 28 (ⓣ055.853.189, ⓦwww.albergoverrazzano.it; ❸). The latter is slightly more characterful and also has a good **restaurant** (closed Mon & mid-Jan to mid-Feb), with a terrace overlooking the piazza; expect to pay around €40 for a full meal. Alternatively, the *Gallo Nero*, just off the piazza at Via Cesare Batisti 6 (closed Thurs), is a perfectly acceptable bar-trattoria-pizzeria.

## Montefioralle

Five minutes' drive from Greve, west up a steep zigzagging road, lies the much restored hamlet of **MONTEFIORALLE**, where a single elliptical street – Via di Montefioralle – encompasses a few tower-houses and a pair of Romanesque churches. This street has one of the best simple **trattorie** in Chianti, the *Taverna del Guerrino* (ⓣ055.853.106; winter open Thurs–Sun for lunch & dinner; summer open daily for dinner, Thurs–Sun for lunch). Very close to Montefioralle, at Via San Cresci 31–32 in Mezzuola, you'll find one of the best **hotels** in Chianti – the *Villa Bordoni* (ⓣ055.884.0004, ⓦwww.villabordoni.com; ❺), a magnificent country house that was rescued from dereliction by David and Catherine Gardner, the owners of *Baldovino* and *Beccofino* in Florence. Each of the ten bedrooms and suites is uniquely and beautifully furnished, and the restaurant is fine as well; a pool and open-air fitness pavilion complete the package.

## Panzano

About 8km south of Greve along the *Chiantigiana*, the hill-top town of **PANZANO** overlooks a circle of hills known as the Conca d'Oro (Golden Valley) because of their sun-trap properties; the local wines can be sampled at the Enoteca del Chianti Classico, at Via Giovanni da Verrazzano 8. Signposted down a branch road, the Romanesque **Pieve di San Leolino**, 1km south of the village, is one of the oldest churches in Chianti, and traces its origins to the first Christian settlers; the most notable of its paintings is a *Madonna with SS Peter and Paul*, created in the mid-thirteenth century.

Panzano is best known, however, as the home of the **Antica Macelleria Cecchini**, perhaps the most famous butcher's shop in the country, though it stands in relation to ordinary butcher's shops in the same way as a Ferrari relates to a Fiat van – it even has a downstairs room for wine tastings, art shows and concerts. In existence at Via XX Luglio 11r for 250 years, it's nowadays run by Dario Cecchini, a charismatic and eloquent champion of Tuscan carnivorous cuisine and Chianti traditions in general. He's recently opened a terrific restaurant opposite the shop – called *Solociccia* ("only meat"), it has sittings at 7pm and 9pm from Thursday to Saturday, and at 1pm on Sunday, and reservations are compulsory (ⓣ055.852.727). There's no menu: you pay €30 person and you get what you're given; the price excludes wine, which you're encouraged to bring along. Dario has recently announced plans to open a Tuscan fast-food place as well, selling burgers, which of course will be the best in Italy. Panzano also has a very nice three-star **hotel**, the *Villa Sangiovese* (Ⓣ055.852.461; Ⓦwww.villasangiovese.it; open mid-March to mid-Dec; ❸); located on Piazza Bucciarelli, it has an excellent restaurant too (closed Wed).

## Castellina

The summit of the next main hill, 15km south, is occupied by well-heeled **CASTELLINA IN CHIANTI**, which formerly stood on the front line of the continual wars between Florence and Siena. The walls, fortress and the covered walkway known as the **Via delle Volte** – a kind of gallery looking east from underneath the town (it was originally open, but houses were later built over it) – all bear testimony to an embattled past. Traces of a more distant era can be seen at the **Ipogeo Etrusco di Montecalvario** (open daylight hours; free), a complex of subterranean sixth-century BC Etruscan burial chambers, carved into the summit of a small hill that's five minutes' walk to the north of the village. The area's distant history is illuminated in the **Museo del Chianti Senese** (10am–1pm & 3.30–6.30pm; closed Wed; €5), which also gives you access to the town's tower, but neither the Etruscans nor Castellina's one sizeable church – the neo-Romanesque San Salvatore (notable only for a single fifteenth-century fresco and the mummified remains of the obscure St Fausto) – are what brings in the tourists. Wine is of course Castellina's primary attraction, as is evident from the power-station bulk of the **wine co-operative** on the main road; the local vintages (and olive oil) can be sampled at several places in town.

The very helpful Castellina **tourist office** is at Via Ferruccio 40 (daily 9am–1pm & 2.30–6.30pm). Pick of the **hotels** in town is the three-star *Palazzo Squarcialupi*, which occupies the upper floors of a vast fifteenth-century *palazzo* at Via Ferruccio 22 (Ⓣ0577.741.186, Ⓦwww.palazzosquarcialupi.com; ❸); the rooms are large, and there's a sauna in the basement and a pool in the garden, which commands a wonderful view. Another good three-star, the rustic *Colle Etrusco Salivolpi*, is located at Via Fiorentina 89, a short distance northwest of Castellina on the road to San Donato (Ⓣ0577.740.484, Ⓦwww.hotelsalivolpi.com; ❸); surrounded by a beautiful garden, it has an outdoor pool and large timber-ceilinged bedrooms. The two best **restaurants** in Castellina are *La Torre*, an unspoilt and well-priced Tuscan trattoria at Piazza del Comune 15 (Ⓣ0577.740.236; closed Fri), and *Il Gallopapa*, at Via delle Volte 16 (Ⓣ0577.742.939; closed Mon), which has a range of excellent and imaginative set menus from €50 to €75 per person, excluding drinks.

# Radda and around

The best of Chianti lies east of Castellina and the *Chiantigiana*, in the less domesticated terrain of the **Monti del Chianti** – the stronghold of the Florence-affiliated military alliance known as the Lega di Chianti, whose power bases were Castellina itself and the two principal settlements of this craggy region, Radda and Gaiole. The nearer of these, the ancient Etruscan-founded town of **RADDA IN CHIANTI**, became the league's capital in 1384, and the imprint of the period is perhaps stronger here than anywhere else in Chianti. The street plan of this minuscule but historic centre is focused on Piazza Ferrucci, where the frescoed and shield-studded Palazzo Comunale faces a church raised on a

▲ Chianti farmhouse

high platform. Neither is an outstanding building on its own, but taken together they form an impressive ancient core that gives Radda its appeal. There are around five **buses** a day from Siena to Radda, taking just under an hour.

The **tourist office** lurks behind the church, on the corner of Piazza del Castello (Mon–Sat 10am–1pm & 3–7pm, Sun 10.30am–12.30pm). Stylish **accommodation** is on offer at the three-star *Hotel Podere Le Vigne* (Ⓣ0577.738.640; Ⓦwww.tuscany.net/vigne; ③), a converted farmhouse located a kilometre outside Radda, just off the road between Radda and the hamlet of Villa a Radda. *Le Vigne* also has some plainer (and much cheaper) but still very pleasant rooms in the centre of Radda, and there's a good restaurant at the main site, where you'll pay around €40 per person. At Via Roma 33 you'll find the *Hotel Palazzo Leopoldo* (Ⓣ0577.735.603, Ⓦwww.palazzoleopoldo.it; ⑤), which was founded as a pilgrims' hostel, then converted into a magnificent town house prior to becoming an extremely elegant four-star hotel, with a great restaurant. At the top of the range lies the *Relais Vignale*, on the edge of the village at Via Pianigiani 9 (Ⓦwww.vignale.it; Ⓣ0577.738.012; ⑤); it has a wine bar in the cellars, and a restaurant that's a touch pricier than *Le Vigne* (Ⓣ0577.738.094; daily March–Nov). There are no low-cost hotels in Radda, but you can **eat** cheaply and well at the *Da Michele* trattoria-pizzeria (closed Mon) – it's at the end of the car park below the town walls, and is prominently signposted off the main road.

About 7km north of Radda lies the unspoilt village of **VOLPAIA**, which from the tenth to the sixteenth century was an important military lookout over the valley of the Pesa. The medieval donjon still stands, but the most interesting structure is the deconsecrated Commenda di Sant'Eufrosino, designed by Michelozzo, and now used as a *cantina* and exhibition space by the vast Castello di Volpaia wine estate (Ⓦwww.volpaia.it).

## Badìa a Coltibuono

Heading east from Radda and taking the first turning left after the *Villa Miranda*, you pass the foot of the hill on which stands the **Badìa a Coltibuono**. This abbey was founded on the site of an eighth-century hermitage, and its church of San Lorenzo, built in 1050, is one of Tuscany's finest Romanesque buildings. The monastic complex is now owned by one of the biggest wine estates in the region, whose vintages are served at the famous *Badìa a Coltibuono* **restaurant**, adjoining the abbey (Ⓣ0577.749.424, Ⓦwww.coltibuono.com; Nov–April closed Mon; also closed Jan to early March) – a meal here will cost in the region of €50 per head. The Bàdìa is also celebrated for its lavish residential cookery courses, detailed on its website, and since 2005 – when it began marketing itself as Italy's first "wine resort" – has been offering accommodation in eight beautifully converted monastic cells (❹). There are some good Club Alpino **walks** laid out through the oak and pine woods on the surrounding slopes.



## Gaiole, Meleto and Brolio

Modern times have caught up with the third of the Lega di Chianti triad, **GAIOLE**, 5km south of Coltibuono. Now a brisk market town, it has a **wine co-operative** at Via Mulinaccio 10 that offers splendid tasting opportunities, as does the Enoteca Montagnani, at Via Bandinelli 13–17, which has a superlative range of Chianti Classico. The most impressive sights in the immediate area are the ruins of the **Castello di Vertine**, occupying the heights 3km west of the village, and the fortified village of **Barbischio**, up a winding little road to the east.

A couple of kilometres south of Gaiole, the towers of the **Castello di Meleto** (Ⓦwww.castellomeleto.it) peer from behind a screen of cypresses over the road leading to Castagnoli. Meleto was founded by the monks of Coltibuono, but by 1269 it was in the hands of the Ricasoli family, who built its massive fortifications in the fifteenth century. The highlights of the guided tour (Mon–Sat at 11.30am, 3pm & 4.30pm, Sun 11.30am, 4.30pm & 5pm) are the delicate eighteenth-century theatre and the visit to the *cantina*, where you can sample the Meleto estate's olive oil, wine or food (the price of the tour varies according to which option you choose). Meleto has **accommodation** too, ranging from B&B (from around €60 per person) to seven-bed agriturismo apartments (up to €2000 per week).

The busiest Chianti *cantina* is that of the **Castello di Brolio** (Ⓦwww.ricasoli.it), just outside the nearby village of **BROLIO**. This building passed to the Ricasoli family as far back as the twelfth century, and was the object of frequent tussles between the Florentines and the Sienese. Demolished by the Sienese army, it was rebuilt in the sixteenth century, then converted in the nineteenth century into a colossal mock-medieval country residence by the vinicultural pioneer **Baron Bettino Ricasoli**, who allegedly moved here to keep his attractive young wife away from her admirers in Florence. The castle's garden and the baron's apartments can be visited on a tour of the house (daily 10am–noon & 3–6pm; €3), but a far more rewarding experience is to buy some Castello di Brolio wine at the estate's *enoteca* (Mon–Sat 9am–6pm, plus Sun 11am–7pm in summer), or sample it as an accompaniment to a meal in the excellent but expensive *Osteria del Castello* **restaurant**, one of the best places to eat in Chianti (Ⓣ0577.747.277; closed Thurs).

16

# Siena

Self-contained and still partly rural behind its medieval walls, **SIENA**'s attraction lies in its cityscape: a majestic Gothic whole that could be enjoyed without venturing into a single museum. In its great scallop-shaped piazza, **Il Campo**, it has the loveliest of all Italian public squares; in its zebra-striped **Duomo**, a religious focus to match; and the city's whole construction, on three ridges, presents a succession of beautiful vistas over medieval cityscapes to the bucolic Tuscan countryside on all sides. It is also a place of immediate charm: airy, easy-going and pedestrianized, it is startlingly untouristed away from the few centres of day-trip sightseeing. Eating out here is as good as anywhere in Tuscany, albeit without the variety and choice of Florence, and while shopping is low-key, there are several outstanding food shops ranged along Via di Città, one of the main streets. Perhaps most important of all, though, Siena is host to the undisputed giant of Italian festivals, the **Palio**, a bareback horse race around the Campo, whose sheer excitement and unique importance to the life of the community is reason enough to plan your holiday around one of the two race dates – July 2 and August 16.

Above all, however, Siena is a city of art and architecture. The city's **Duomo**, **Baptistery** and **Palazzo Pubblico** are three of the purest examples of Italian Gothic, and the finest of the city's paintings – of which many are collected in the Palazzo's **Museo Civico** and the separate **Pinacoteca Nazionale** – are in the same tradition. Other outstanding Sienese painting remained stamped with Byzantine, Romanesque and Gothic influences long after classical humanism had transformed Florence. Its traditions were shaped by a group of artists working in the last half of the thirteenth century and the first half of the fourteenth: Duccio di Buoninsegna, Simone Martini and the brothers Ambrogio and Pietro Lorenzetti. Arguably the greatest of all Siena's paintings belongs to the first of these, a magnificent *Maestà* housed in another of Siena's outstanding galleries, the **Museo dell'Opera del Duomo**. Another supreme work, the fresco cycle of Domenico di Bartolo, an artist working on the cusp of the Renaissance, fills part of **Santa Maria della Scala**, the city's hospital for some eight hundred years, now one of its premier exhibition spaces.

As a provincial capital, Siena has good **transport links** with some of the finest sights and countryside of Tuscany. Florence, in particular, 78km distant, is easily reached by train (either direct or with a change at Empoli) in a couple of hours and there are regular express bus services between the two cities (see box on p.263 for full details of getting between the two cities). Siena also makes a good base for much of the territory covered in the following two chapters, with numerous bus services to most towns and villages, including Montalcino and San Gimignano, while to the north, the wine heartland of Chianti is also within reach.

## Some history

Though myth attributes its origins to Senius and Acius, sons of Remus (hence the she-wolf emblem of the city), **Siena** was in fact founded by the Etruscans and refounded as a Roman colony – Saena Julia – by Augustus in the first century BC. Over the course of the next millennium it grew to be an independent republic, and in the thirteenth and fourteenth centuries was one of the major cities of Europe. It was almost the size of Paris, controlled most of southern Tuscany and its flourishing wool industry, dominated the trade routes from France to Rome, and maintained Italy's richest banks. The city also developed a highly sophisticated civic life, with its own written constitution and a quasi-democratic council – the *comune*. It was in this great period that the city was shaped, and in which most of its art and monuments are rooted.

This golden era, when the Republic of Siena controlled a great area of central and southern Tuscany, reached an apotheosis with the defeat of a much superior Florentine army at the **Battle of Montaperti** in 1260. Although the result was reversed nine years later, shifting the fulcrum of political power towards Florence, Siena's merchants and middle classes – the so-called *Popolo Grasso* – embarked on an unrivalled urban development; from 1287 to 1355, under the rule of the **Council of Nine**, the city underwrote first the completion of the **Duomo** and then the extraordinary **Campo**, with its exuberant **Palazzo Pubblico**.

Prosperity and innovation came to an abrupt halt with the **Black Death**, which reached Siena in May 1348. By October, when the disease had run its

### Siena's contrade

Within the fabric of the medieval city, Siena preserves its ancient division into wards, or **contrade**. These are integral to the competition of the Palio (see p.261) and sustain a unique neighbourhood identity, clearly visible as you wander around the streets. Each of the seventeen *contrade* has its own church, social centre and museum, as well as a flag and heraldic **animal motif**, after which most of them take their names. The animals – giraffe, snail, goose, porcupine and others – can be seen all around the city on wall plaques and are represented in a series of modern fountains near the *contrada* churches or headquarters, in each of the city's three *terzi*:

**Aquila** – Eagle (Città). Casato di Sotto ⓣ0577.288.086, ⓦwww.contradadellaquila.it.

**Bruco** – Caterpillar (Camollia). Via del Comune 44 ⓣ0577.44.842.

**Chiocciola** – Snail (Città). Via San Marco 37 ⓣ0577.45.455, ⓦmembers.xoom.alice.it/chiocciola_1.

**Civetta** – Owl (San Martino). Piazzetta del Castellare ⓣ0577.285.505.

**Drago** – Dragon (Camollia). Piazza Matteotti 19 ⓣ0577.40.575, ⓦwww.contradadeldrago.it.

**Giraffa** – Giraffe (Camollia). Via delle Vergini 18 ⓣ0577.287.091, ⓦwww.contadellagiraffa.com.

**Istrice** – Porcupine (Camollia). Via Camollia 87 ⓣ0577.48.495, ⓦwww.istrice.org.

**Leocorno** – Unicorn (San Martino). Via di Follonico 15 ⓣ0577.288.549.

**Lupa** – She-Wolf (Camollia). Via di Vallerozzi 71/73 ⓣ0577.270.777.

**Nicchio** – Shell (San Martino). Via dei Pispini 68 ⓣ0577.49.600, ⓦwww.nobilecontradadelnicchio.it.

**Oca** – Goose (Camollia). Vicolo del Tiratoio 11 ⓣ0577.285.413, ⓦwww.contradadelloca.it.

**Onda** – Wave (Città). Via Giovanni Dupré 111 ⓣ0577.48.384, ⓦwww.contradacapitanadellonda.it.

course, the population had dropped from 100,000 to 30,000. The city was never to recover fully (the population today is around 60,000) and its politics, always factional, moved into a period of intrigue and chaos. The chief figures in these war-ridden and anarchic years were the city's two nationally renowned saints, **Caterina** (1347–80) and **Bernardino** (1380–1444), who both exercised enormous influence amid two further outbreaks of the plague.

As the sixteenth century opened, a period of autocratic rule brought a further military victory over Florence, but ended with the city embroiled in ever-expanding intrigues involving the Borgias, the Florentines, the papacy, the French and the empire of **Charles V**. The last proved too big to handle for the Sienese; imperial troops imposed a fortress and garrison, and laid siege to the city and the surrounding countryside. The effects of the siege (1554–55) proved more terrible even than the Black Death, with the population plummeting from 40,000 to as few as 8000. The republic was over in all but name.

Two years after the siege, Philip II, Charles's successor, gave up Siena to **Cosimo I**, Florence's Medici overlord, in payment for war services, the city subsequently becoming part of Cosimo's Grand Duchy of Tuscany. This was the death knell. For sixty years the Sienese were forbidden even to operate banks, while control of what was by now an increasingly minor provincial town reverted, under Medici patronage, to the nobles.

Siena's swift decline from republican capital to little more than a market centre explains the city's astonishing state of medieval preservation. Little was built and



**Pantera** – Panther (Città). Via San Quirico ⓣ0577.48.468.

**Selva** – Forest (Città). Piazzetta della Selva ⓣ0577.45.093, ⓦwww.contradadellaselva.it.

**Tartuca** – Turtle (Città). Via Tommaso Pendola 21 ⓣ0577.49.448, ⓦwww.tartuca.it.

**Torre** – Tower (San Martino). Via Salicotto 76 ⓣ0577.222.181, ⓦwww.contradadellatorre.it.

**Valdimontone** – Ram (San Martino). Via di Valdimonte 6 ⓣ0577.222.590, ⓦwww.valdimontone.it.

There were once social distinctions between the *contrade*, and although today these are blurred to the point of extinction, allegiance to one's *contrada* – conferred by birth – remains a strong element of social life. After a conventional church baptism, anyone born in a ward division is baptized for a second time in their *contrada* fountain. Subsequently, the *contrada* plays a central role in activities: for kids in the flag-twirling and drumming for the Palio and local *contrada* festivals, for adults in the social clubs – a mix of bar and dining club – and in the attendance of a herald at marriages and funerals. *Contrade* also dispense social assistance to needy members. The respect accorded to the institution of *contrade* is said to have a significant effect on the city's social cohesion. Certainly, for a city of its size, Siena has remarkably low levels of crime and drug usage. Indeed, the only violence tolerated is during the Palio, when *contrada* members may get into fights with their ancient rivals.

For an insight into the workings of the *contrade*, it is worth paying a visit to one of their **museums**, each of which gives pride of place to its displays of Palio trophies. All the museums are open to visitors during the build-up to the Palio and at other times by appointment; ask the tourist office to phone. Each *contrada* also has its own **annual celebration**, accompanied by parades and feasts. And at almost any time of year, you'll see groups practising flag-waving and drum-rolling in the streets.

▲ The Palio

still less demolished, while allotments and vineyards occupied the spaces between the ancient quarters, as they do today. This near-pristine state also reflects its escaping war damage in 1944 and 1945; Siena was taken, unopposed, by the French Expeditionary Force on July 3, 1944.

Since the last war, however, Siena has again become prosperous, partly due to **tourism**, partly to the resurgence of the **Monte dei Paschi di Siena**. This bank, founded in Siena in 1472, is one of the major players in Italian finance and in its home base is one of the city's largest employers.

## The Siena Palio

The **Siena Palio** (ⓦpalio.comune.siena.it) is the most spectacular festival event in Italy: a twice-yearly bareback horse race around the Campo, preceded by days of preparation, medieval pageantry and chicanery. Only ten of the seventeen *contrade* can take part in any one race; these are chosen by lot, and their horses and jockeys are also assigned at random. The seven that miss out are automatically entitled to run in the following year's race. The only rule is that riders cannot interfere with each other's reins. Otherwise, anything goes: each *contrada* has a traditional rival, and ensuring that it loses is as important as winning oneself. Jockeys may be bribed to throw the race or whip a rival or a rival's horse; *contrade* have been known to drug horses and even to ambush a jockey on his way to the race. This is primarily a show for the Sienese; for visitors, in fact, the undercurrent of brutality and the bragging, days-long celebration of victory can be quite a shock.

The race has been held since at least the thirteenth century. Originally it followed a circuit through the town, but since the sixteenth century it has consisted of three laps of the **Campo**, around a track covered with sand and padded with mattresses to minimize injury to riders and horses (though this does occur, and the Palio is a passionate subject for animal-rights supporters). There are two Palios a year, with the following build-up:

**June 29 and August 13**: The year's horses are presented in the morning at the town hall and drawn by lot. At 7.15pm the first trial race is held in the Campo.

**June 30 and August 14**: Further trial races at 9am and 7.45pm.

**July 1 and August 15**: Two more trial races at 9am and 7.45pm, followed by a street banquet in each of the *contrade*.

**July 2 and August 16**: The day of the Palio opens with the *messa del Fantino* (jockeys' mass), held by the archbishop in the chapel beside the Palazzo Pubblico, before a final trial at 9am. In the early afternoon each *contrada* takes its horse to be blessed in its church (it's a good omen if the horse shits). At around 5pm the Palazzo Publico's bell begins to ring and riders and *comparse* – equerries, ensigns, pages and drummers in medieval costume – proceed to the Campo for a display of flag-twirling and other pageantry. The **race** itself begins at 7.45pm on July 2, or 7pm on August 16, and lasts little more than ninety seconds. There's no PA system to tell you what's going on. At the start (in the northwest corner of the Campo) all the horses except one are penned between two ropes; the free one charges the group from behind, when its rivals least expect it, and the race is on. It's a hectic and violent spectacle; a horse that throws its rider is still eligible to win. The jockeys don't stop at the finishing line but keep going at top speed out of the Campo, pursued by a frenzied mass of supporters. The **palio** – a silk banner – is subsequently presented to the winner.

There are viciously expensive stands for dignitaries and the rich (booked months ahead), but most spectators crowd for free into the centre of the Campo. For the **best view**, you need to have found a position on the inner rail by 2pm (ideally at the start/finish line), but be prepared to stand your ground; people keep pouring in right up until a few minutes before the race, and the swell of the crowd can be quite overwhelming. Toilets, shade and refreshments are minimal, and you won't be able to leave the Campo until at least 8.30pm. **Hotel rooms** are extremely difficult to find, and if you haven't booked, reckon on either staying up all night or travelling in from a neighbouring town. The races are shown live on national TV and repeated endlessly all evening.

The Cinema Moderno on Piazza Tolomei (May–Oct Mon–Sat) regularly screens a twenty-minute **film** explaining the history and drama of the race, dubbed into various languages.

# Arrival and information

Most **intercity buses** arrive in the city centre on Viale Federico Tozzi, the road running alongside Piazza Gramsci, or at La Lizza nearby, but note that some stop near the church of San Domenico, while others avoid the centre altogether and terminate at the train station. Ticket offices beneath Piazza Gramsci have information on all routes. The bus company serving Siena and its hinterland is called TRA-IN (ⓣ0577.204.246 or toll-free in Italy 800.570.530, ⓦwww.trainspa.it).

Siena's **train station** (ⓦwww.trenitalia.it) is inconveniently sited at Piazza Fratelli Rosselli, down in the valley 2km northeast of town. Its foyer has a small train information office, exchange facilities, basic tourist information and a counter selling city bus tickets. To get into town, take just about any city bus – #3, #9 to Tozzi; #4, #7, #8, #14, #17, #77 to Garibaldi/Sale; #10 to Gramsci. All these drop at various points on or near Piazza Matteotti or Piazza Gramsci on the northern edge of the centre. If in doubt, ask at the information desk. Local **city taxis** are to be found at ranks by the train station (ⓣ0577.44.504) and on Piazza Matteotti (ⓣ0577.289.350), or can be called elsewhere between 7am and 9pm by phone (ⓣ0577.49.222). Note, however, that in Siena it's virtually impossible to book taxis in advance and you should allow plenty of time for cabs to reach you.

**Parking** in Siena can be a problem. Parking **garages** (ⓦwww.sienaparcheggi.com) are clearly signposted, secure and affordable, but the two biggest are misleadingly named: "Parcheggio Il Campo" is a long way from the Campo, just inside the Porta Tufi, and "Parcheggio Il Duomo" is just within Porta San Marco, nowhere near the Duomo. **Street-parking** outside the city walls is free; inside the walls, it can be expensive and hard to find. Follow signs to the *centro* and try at one of the following: around Piazza Gramsci or the large triangle of La Lizza; opposite San Domenico in the car park alongside the stadium; off the Viale Manzoni, which loops around the northeast wall of the city; or around the Porta Romana. Viale Manzoni is free parking; at the others a machine or an attendant issues tickets, usually by the hour. If you know you'll be driving in, you'd do well to arrange parking with your hotel in advance. You can drive through the old town alleys only in order to load or unload baggage at your hotel. Note that you cannot park around La Lizza on Wednesday mornings (8am–2pm), when the market takes place; offending cars are towed away.

Siena's main **tourist office** is at Piazza del Campo 56 (Mon–Sat 9am–7pm; ⓣ0577.280.551, ⓦwww.terresiena.it). It provides hotel lists, a town map and a range of information booklets.

# Accommodation

Securing a hotel room in Siena for any time between Easter and October requires booking six months in advance. If you arrive without a booking and find that all the establishments listed below are full, make your way to the **Siena Hotels Promotion** booth (Mon–Sat 9am–8pm; winter closes 7pm; ⓣ0577.288.084, ⓦwww.hotelsiena.com), opposite the church of San Domenico on Piazza Madre Teresa di Calcutta. The staff here are generally very helpful and can book rooms in any of the city's hotels. The city's second specialist agency, **Vacanze Senesi**,

## Transport from Florence

From Florence, hourly or more frequent TRA-IN **buses** bound for Siena depart from the bus station on Via di Caterina da Siena just west of the main train station; be sure to jump on a *Corse Rapide* or *Rapido* (about 1hr 15min; €6.50 bought in advance, €8 on board), as some buses (misleadingly called *Corse Dirette* or *Diretta*) are much slower and run via Colle di Val d'Elsa and Poggibonsi (1hr 35min; €4.50 in advance, €6 on board). Both services arrive at La Lizza-Piazza Gramsci. Some **trains** run direct to Siena (fastest journey 1hr 27min), but many involve changing at Empoli (about 1hr 40min). By **car**, the two cities are linked by a highway that starts from the Firenze Certosa junction on the A1 autostrada, 6km south of Florence; from central Florence, head through the Oltrarno to the Porta Romana and follow "Certosa" signs.

is situated in the tourist office at Piazza del Campo 56 (Mon–Fri 9am–7pm; ⓣ0577.45.900, ⓦwww.vacanzesenesi.it).

All accommodation reviewed in this section is located on a map: places south of the Campo are on pp.266–267, places north of the Campo are on p.289.



### Hotels

**Antica Residenza Cicogna** Via dei Termini ⓣ0577.285.613, ⓦwww.anticaresidenzacicogna.it. A little-known B&B in a perfect, if tucked-away location near the *Osteria del Ficomezzo*. The owner, Elisa Trefoloni, is charming, and there are five en-suite rooms, all frescoed, delightfully appointed and recently restored – the "Liberty" and "Leoni" rooms are especially nice. wi-fi is available. Breakfast is taken in an extraordinary, high-ceilinged room with colossal beams. ❷

**Antica Torre** Via Fieravecchia 7 ⓣ0577.222.255, ⓦwww.anticatorresiena.it. By far the nicest and most intimate of the three-star places: just eight smallish rooms squeezed into an old medieval tower. Top rooms have views. ❸

**Bernini** Via della Sapienza 15 ⓣ0577.289.047, ⓦwww.albergobernini.com. Nine inexpensive but rather pokey one-star rooms, most en suite. ❷

**Cannon d'Oro** Via Montanini 28 ⓣ0577.44.321, ⓦwww.cannondoro.com. A stylish thirty-room two-star hotel tucked down an alleyway just beyond where Banchi di Sopra becomes Via Montanini. Friendly and well maintained, this is the best choice among the central mid-price hotels. ❷

**Centrale** Via Cecco Angiolieri 26 ⓣ0577.280.379. Just seven large two-star rooms on an upper floor in a quiet street as central as the name suggests, a block north of the Campo. ❷

**Certosa di Maggiano** Via Certosa 82 ⓣ0577.288.180, ⓦwww.certosadimaggiano.com. A former monastery in the countryside 1km southeast of Siena that offers luxurious comfort in its few, tasteful rooms (€590 plus per night, though web and other deals can bring down this price) and an alluring retreat from worldly affairs in its library, cloister and tranquil terrace. ❽

**Chiusarelli** Viale Curtatone 15 ⓣ0577.280.562, ⓦwww.chiusarelli.com. A nice old three-star villa hotel with 49 rooms and a garden at the back, but it's on a busy street near the bus stops – ask for one of the back rooms, several of which are very large and comfortable. Also has some private parking. ❸

**Duomo** Via Stalloreggi 34 ⓣ0577.289.088, ⓦwww.hotelduomo.it. Rooms are reliable but unexceptional – apart from those with views of the Duomo – but this is nonetheless the best located of the city's three-star hotels. ❹

**Grand Hotel Continental** Via Banchi di Sopra 85 ⓣ0577.56.011, ⓦwww.royaldemeure.com. For years Siena had no luxury five-star hotel – until the hugely expensive restoration of this former palace in a perfect location. The public spaces, especially the grand salon, are astounding, with frescoes and a large covered courtyard. The best rooms and suites are also exceptional – vast, entirely frescoed and with stunning views of the Duomo. Other rooms are still excellent and superbly appointed, but mostly lack the fabulous period details you'll see in the brochures or on the website. This is a first choice for a treat or if money is no object: be prepared to say goodbye to around €900 nightly (less with special deals), less for upper rooms (or with online deals) under the eaves, or if you go through a tour operator. ❽

**La Perla** Via delle Terme 25 ⓣ0577.47.144, ⓦwww.hotellaperlasiena.com. Regular one-star with thirteen rooms (all with bathroom), in a very central location, two blocks north of the Campo. Curfew 1am. ❷

**La Toscana** Via Cecco Angiolieri 12 ⓣ0577.46.097, ⓕ0577.270.634. Big, well-priced 41-room three-star in an atmospheric and central location, on an alley behind Piazza Tolomei. Rooms with and without bathrooms – unusual in this category. ❷

**Locanda Garibaldi** Via Giovanni Dupré 18 ⓣ0577.284.204. A good, no-nonsense seven-room two-star (four shared bathrooms), sited above one of the city's better low-cost restaurants, just south of the Campo. Midnight curfew. ❷

**Palazzo Ravizza** Pian dei Mantellini 34 ⓣ0577.280.462, ⓦwww.palazzoravizza.it. This elegant 35-room three-star, located in a pleasant area near San Niccolò al Carmine, has been run by the same family since opening for business in the 1920s, and has recently been renovated in a way that has freshened the place without sacrificing its period charm. The rooms are sparingly and tastefully furnished with antiques, with ceiling frescoes in several of them. In high season, reservations are accepted on a half-board basis only; at other times of the year they have doubles from around €270. The little garden at the back is a charming place for afternoon tea. ❻

**Piccolo Hotel Etruria** Via Donzelle 3 ⓣ0577.288.088, ⓦwww.hoteletruria.com. A very neat two-star and deservedly popular: advance booking for high season is a must to secure one of its thirteen rooms. ❷

**Piccolo Hotel Il Palio** Piazza del Sale 19 ⓣ0577.281.131, ⓦpiccolohotelilpalio.it. Perfectly located for bus arrivals, right near all the bus stops, 200m north of the centre. Clean, good-sized rooms and friendly, helpful staff. ❸

**Santa Caterina** Via Piccolomini 7 ⓣ0577.221.105, ⓦwww.hscsiena.it. A nineteen-room three-star 10min walk from the Campo, on the street that leads out of town from Porta Romana. Has a/c and parking. ❹

**Tre Donzelle** Via Donzelle 5 ⓣ0577.280.358, ⓕ0577.223.933. Excellent one-star option right in the heart of town, just off Banchi di Sotto, north of the Campo. Good, clean rooms, some with private bath, but has a curfew of 12.30am and its 27 rooms are often booked solid. ❷

**Villa Scacciapensieri** Via di Scacciapensieri 10 ⓣ0577.41.441, ⓦwww.villascacciapensieri.it. Four-star country villa 3km north of Siena, with every luxury including a pool. ❺

### Hostels

**Alma Domus** Via Camporegio 31 ⓣ0577.44.177. An old pilgrim hostel behind San Domenico, with doubles from €60, all with private bathrooms. Triple and quad rooms are also available. Curfew 11.30pm. Bookings taken only Mon–Sat 1–3pm.

**Ostello della Gioventù "Guidoriccio"** Via Fiorentina 89, Lo Stellino ⓣ0577.52.212, ⓦwww.ostellionline.org. Rather sterile and uninspiring HI hostel with 111 beds, located 4km northwest of the centre. Take bus #15 from Piazza Gramsci, or, if you're coming from Florence, ask to be let off at "Lo Stellino", just after the Siena city sign. Has several double rooms, a restaurant (meals €9) and a bar. Curfew 11.30pm. Dorm beds €14.45, including breakfast. Doubles are €28.90.

### Long-stay accommodation

For long-stay budget accommodation, call in at the tourist office, which has lists of **rooms** (*affittacamere*) available in private houses. These are offered mainly to students, either at the university or on the numerous language and art courses held in the city, but some are willing to offer shorter lets. They're certainly worth a try if you're staying for a week or more; rates are around €25 per person per night, usually for a shared room (less for long-term lets).

The annual accommodation booklet (*Guida alla Hospitalità*) issued by the tourist office also has full lists of the agriturismo options in the area.

▲ Piazza del Campo



# The City

The centre of Siena is its great square, the **Campo**, built at the intersection of a Y-shaped configuration of hills and the convergence of the city's principal roads, the **Banchi di Sopra**, **Banchi di Sotto** and **Via di Città**. Each of these roads leads out across a ridge, straddled by one of the city's three medieval districts, or *terzi* (literally "thirds"): the **Terzo di Città** to the southwest, the **Terzo di San Martino** to the southeast, and the **Terzo di Camollia** to the north.

This central core – almost entirely medieval in plan and appearance – is initially a little disorientating, though with the Campo as a point of reference you won't go far wrong. Movement around is also made easier by the fact that the city centre has been effectively pedestrianized since the 1960s. Everywhere of use or interest in the city is within easy walking distance, with the exception of St Bernardino's monastic retreat, L'Osservanza, the *Guidoriccio* hostel and the campsite.

## The Campo

**The Campo** is the centre of Siena in every sense: the main streets lead into it, the Palio takes place around its perimeter, and in the evenings it is the natural place to gravitate towards, for visitors and residents alike. Four hundred years ago, Montaigne described it as the most beautiful square in the world – an assessment that still seems pretty fair.

With its amphitheatre curve, the Campo appears an almost organic piece of city planning. In fact, when the Council of Nine began buying up land in 1293, they were adopting the only possible site – the old marketplace, which lay at the convergence of the city quarters but was a part of none (the old Roman forum probably also occupied the site). To build on it, it was necessary to construct an enormous buttress beneath the lower half of the square, where the Palazzo Pubblico was to be raised. The piazza itself was completed in 1349, when the council laid its nine segments of paving to commemorate their highly civic rule and pay homage to the Virgin, the folds of whose cloak it was intended to symbolize.

From the start, the stage-like Campo was a focus of city life. As well as its continuing role as the city's marketplace – for livestock as well as produce – it was the scene of executions, bullfights, communal boxing matches, and, of course, the Palio. St Bernardino preached here, too, holding before him the monogram of Christ's name in Greek ("IHS"), which he urged the nobles to adopt in place

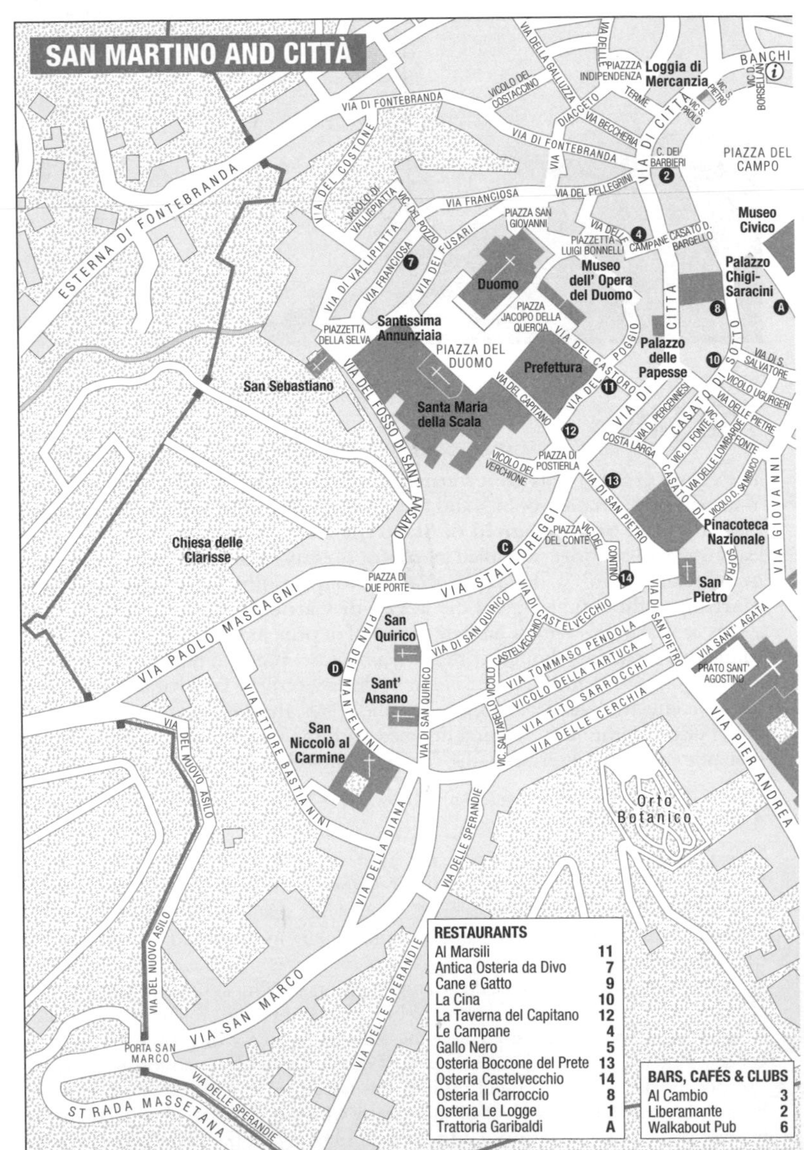

of their own vainglorious coats of arms. A few did so (the monogram is to be seen on various *palazzi*) and it was adopted by the council on the facade of the **Palazzo Pubblico**, alongside the city's she-wolf symbol, which is a reference to Siena's legendary foundation by the sons of Remus.

At the highest point of the Campo is the Renaissance **Fonte Gaia** ("Gay Fountain"), designed and carved by Jacopo della Quercia in the early fifteenth century. Its panels are poor, nineteenth-century reproductions but they give

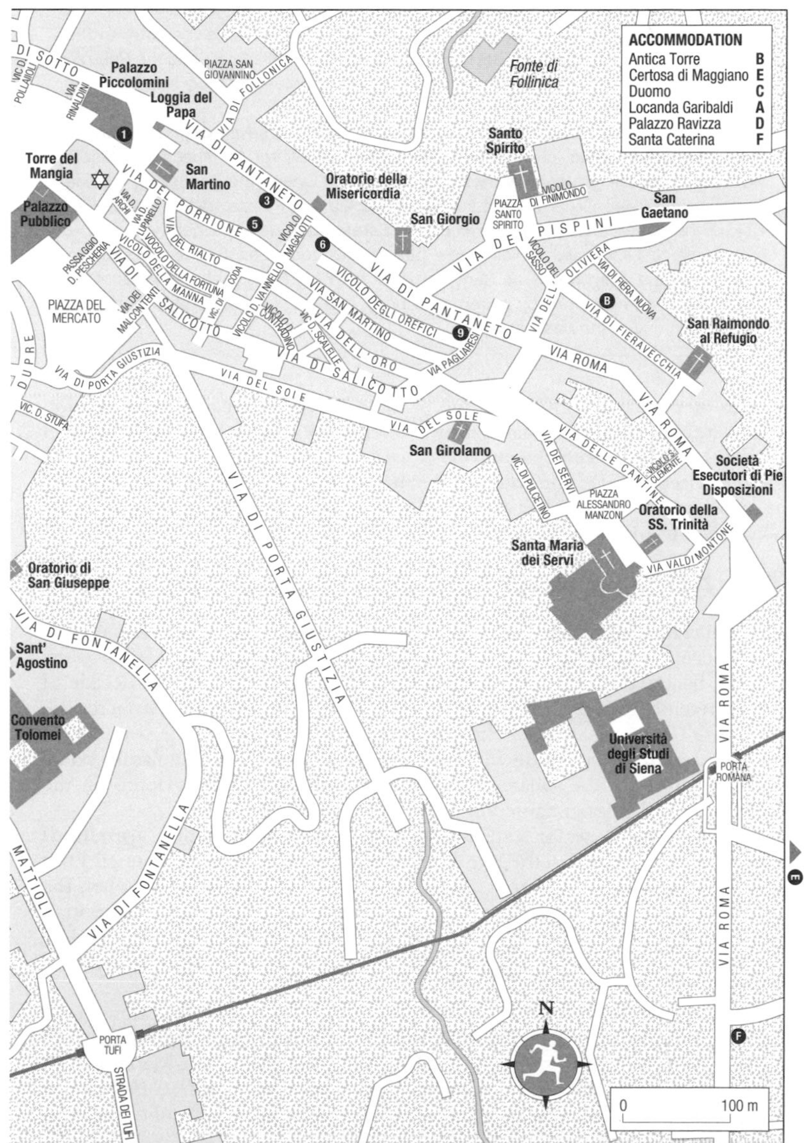


16

**SIENA** | The City

## Siena museum admission

Rather than paying admission at each attraction, it's a good idea to pick up a **pass** or **joint ticket** (*biglietto cumulativo*) covering entry to several sites. Siena has an array of these, though they have a tendency to change from year to year. Usually they are available at any of the participating museums. All, though, permit only a single entry to each attraction.

The **cathedral authorities** have an "Opera" pass which gives entry to the Museo dell'Opera, the Baptistery and San Bernardino for €10 and is valid for three days. The **civic museum authorities** have their own two-day pass, which gives entry to the Museo Civico (but not the Torre del Mangia), Santa Maria della Scala and the Palazzo delle Papesse for €10. A joint ticket covering only the Museo Civico and Torre del Mangia costs €12.

Finally, there are seasonal versions of an all-encompassing seven-day "Art Itinerary" pass – the **SIA Inverno**, or **Itinerario d'Arte Inverno** (Winter Art Itinerary; available Nov to mid-March), covering entry to the Museo dell'Opera, the Baptistery, Libreria Piccolomini, Museo Civico, Santa Maria della Scala and Palazzo delle Papesse for €14; or the **SIA Estate**, or **Itinerario d'Arte Estate** (Summer Art Itinerary; available mid-March to Oct), valid for all these plus the Oratorio San Bernardino, Museo Diocesano and the church of Sant'Agostino for €17. Note that the Pinacoteca Nazionale is administered by a separate body from all the above, and so is not included on any of the passes.



an idea of what was considered one of the city's masterpieces. Its conception – the Virgin at the centre, flanked by the Virtues – was a conscious emulation of the Lorenzetti frescoes on *Good and Bad Government* in the Palazzo Pubblico (see p.271). The fountain's name comes from festivities celebrating its inauguration in 1419, the climax of a long process that began in the 1340s, when masons managed to channel water into the square.

# The Palazzo Pubblico and Museo Civico

The **Palazzo Pubblico**, bristling with crenellations and glorious medieval detail, occupies virtually the entire south side of the Campo, loomed over by its giant belltower, the **Torre del Mangia**. Built largely in the first decade of the fourteenth century, the palace's lower level of arcading is characteristic of Sienese Gothic, as are the columns separating the windows. The council was so pleased with this aspect of the design that they ordered its emulation on all other buildings on the square – and it was indeed gracefully adapted on the twelfth-century Palazzo Sansedoni on the north side.

The other main exterior feature of the Palazzo Pubblico is the **Cappella di Piazza**, a stone loggia set at the base of the tower, which the council built after the Plague in 1348. Funds came slowly, however, and by 1376, when the chief mason at the cathedral turned his hand to its design, new Florentine ideas were already making their influence felt. The final stage of construction, a century later, when the chapel was heightened and a canopy added, was wholly Renaissance in concept.

In the days of the *comune*, the lower floors of the Palazzo Pubblico housed the city accounts, and the upper storeys, as today, the council. Nowadays, its principal rooms have been converted into the **Museo Civico** (daily: mid-March to Oct 10am–7pm; Nov & Feb to mid-March 10am–6pm; Dec & Jan 10am–5.30pm; €7.50, or €12 with Torre del Mangia), entered through the courtyard to the right of the Cappella di Piazza.

The museum starts on the first floor of the *palazzo*. At the top of the stairs you're directed through a disappointing, miscellaneous five-room picture collection, whose nineteenth-century hunting scenes are enough to put you off eating *cinghiale* (wild boar) for the rest of your visit. You then wind round into the **Sala del Risorgimento** (1878–90), painted with scenes commemorating Vittorio Emanuele, first king of Italy. These depict various battle campaigns, the king's coronation and his earlier meeting with Garibaldi and his army on the road to Capua, where he refused Garibaldi governorship of the Neapolitan provinces, instead inflicting a decade of martial rule.

## Sala di Balia

The first of the rooms of any real interest is the **Sala di Balia** (or Sala dei Priori), frescoed by Spinello Aretino and his son, Parri, in 1407 with episodes from the life of Siena-born Pope Alexander III – in particular his conflict with Frederick Barbarossa, the German Holy Roman Emperor. The story is a complex one. The pope and emperor came into dispute following Barbarossa's destruction of Milan in 1162, an event that caused the formation of a Lombard League of Italian states, supported by the Vatican and the Venetians. Barbarossa entered Rome in 1166, whereupon the pope fled to Venice (where he is depicted, disguised as a monk, but recognized by a French pilgrim). The scenes include a superbly realized naval conflict – in which the Venetians are shown capturing the emperor's son and the Germans desperately trying to rescue him – and the pope's eventual reconciliation with Barbarossa, in a procession led by the doge of Venice.

## Anticamera and Sala del Concistoro

Beyond is the **Anticamera del Concistoro** (or Sala dei Cardinali). A detached fresco, *Three Saints and Donor*, attributed to Ambrogio Lorenzetti, graces the wall by the entrance door. It was transferred here in the nineteenth century and was probably once part of a much larger work depicting the *Madonna and Child*: in

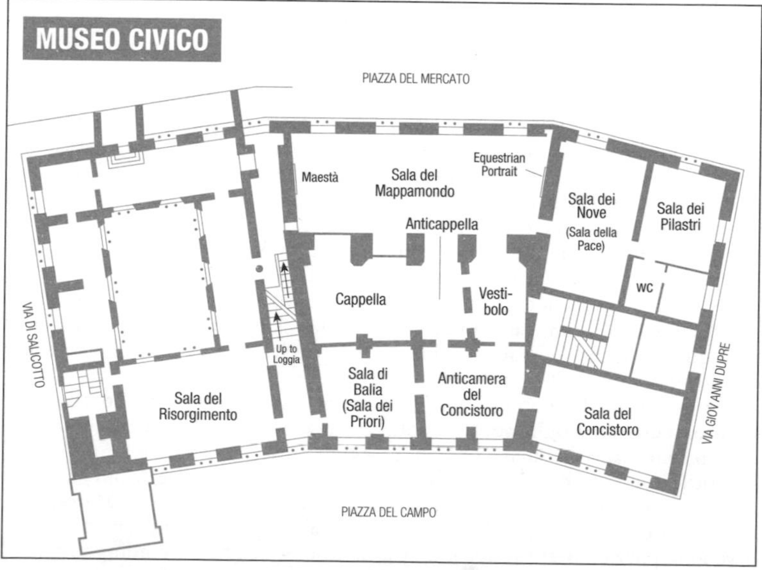

such pictures the donor – the individual responsible for commissioning the picture – would have been shown kneeling at the feet of the Madonna. In the centre of the left wall is a beautiful *Madonna and Child* attributed to Matteo di Giovanni, whose Madonna has the unquiet look typical of this painter: his propensity for the unsettling found expression in several grisly depictions of the *Massacre of the Innocents*, one of which is on display in another room of the museum.

The next room is the **Sala del Concistoro**, entered via an ornate marble doorway (1448) by Bernardo Rossellino, the sculptor and architect responsible for redesigning much of the southern Tuscan town of Pienza (see p.304) for Pope Pius II. Mannerist star Domenico Beccafumi superbly frescoed the room's vault between 1529 and 1535. The panels are either allegories or describe events from Greek and Roman history, but, like virtually every painting in the *palazzo*, deliberately evoke parallels with the civic virtues or historical achievements of Siena itself.

## Vestibolo, Anticappella and Cappella

Doors from the Anticamera behind you lead on into the **Vestibolo**, which contains a damaged fresco of the *Madonna and Child* (1340) by Ambrogio Lorenzetti and a gilded bronze of the *She-Wolf Suckling Romulus and Remus* (1429), an allusion to the city's mythical foundation by Senius, son of Remus. On the left is the more interesting **Anticappella**, decorated between 1407 and 1414 by Taddeo di Bartolo, the last major exponent of Siena's conservative Gothic style, with a vast *St Christopher* and frescoes – like those in the Sala del Concistoro – whose Greek and Roman themes reflect Siena's own civic concerns. Taddeo also frescoed the **Cappella** alongside with episodes from the *Life of the Virgin* (1407–08), work overshadowed by Sodoma's altarpiece, as well as the vast wrought-iron screen (1435–45) – attributed to Jacopo della Quercia – and the exceptional set of inlaid choir stalls (1415–28).

## Sala del Mappamondo

All these works, though, are little more than a warm-up for the **Sala del Mappamondo**, one of the great set pieces of Italian art. Taking its name from its now scarcely visible ceiling fresco of a map of the cosmos, executed by Ambrogio Lorenzetti, the room was used for several centuries as the city's law court and contains one of the greatest of all Italian frescoes, **Simone Martini**'s fabulous and recently restored *Maestà*, a painting of almost translucent colour, which was the *comune*'s first major commission for the palace. Its political dimension is apparent in the depiction of the Christ Child holding a parchment inscribed with the city's motto of justice, and the inscription of two stanzas from Dante on the steps below the throne, warning that the Virgin will not intercede for those who betray her or oppress the poor. It is one of Martini's earliest known works, painted in 1315 at the age of 30; before this extraordinary debut not a thing is known of him. Martini's great innovation was the use of a canopy and a frieze of medallions which frame and organize the figures – a sense of space and hint of perspective that suggest a knowledge of Giotto's work.

The fresco on the opposite wall, the marvellous **Equestrian Portrait of Guidoriccio da Fogliano**, is a motif for medieval chivalric Siena, and was, until recently, also credited to Martini. Showing the knight setting forth from his battle camp to besiege a walled hill-town (thought to be Montemassi, a village southwest of Siena near Roccastrada), it would, if it were by Martini, be accounted one of the earliest Italian portrait paintings. Art historians, however, have long puzzled over the apparently anachronistic castles: according to some, they are of a much later architectural style than the painting's supposed date of 1328. The work would also seem to be part-painted over a fresco to the right by Lippo Vanni, which is dated 1364. In the mid-1980s the waters were further muddied when, during restoration, another apparently anachronistic fresco was found – the painting now beneath the equestrian portrait showing two men in front of a castle, believed to be the one at Arcidosso in southern Tuscany; it has been variously attributed to Martini, Duccio, Pietro Lorenzetti and Memmi di Filippuccio.

The current state of the debate is confused, with a number of historians – led by the American Gordon Moran (whom the council for a while banned from the Palazzo Pubblico and accused of belonging to the CIA) – interpreting the *Guidoriccio* as a sixteenth-century fake, and others – including an Italian commission of experts – maintaining that it is a genuine Martini overpainted by subsequent restorers. Much rests on a scrupulous analysis of Siena's vast archives in the Palazzo Piccolomini: details contained in the records of payments for various paintings of the period may help solve the mystery. The only other option – often suggested but not yet countenanced – is to strip away all the frescoes concerned to study exactly what overlays what.

At least there's no problem with the coffered figures to the right and left of the uncovered fresco beneath the equestrian portrait; these are a pair of saints by Sodoma dating from 1529. The other large frescoes in the room also depict Sienese military victories, namely the *Victory at the Val di Chiana* (1364) by Lippo Vanni (on the long wall) and the *Victory at Poggio Imperiale* (1480) by Christoforo Ghini and Francesco d'Andrea. Don't miss the figures on the pilasters below the latter, which from left to right are Sodoma's *Blessed Tolomei* (1533), founder of the abbey at Monte Oliveto Maggiore; *St Bernardino* (1450) by Sano di Pietro; and *St Catherine of Siena* (1461) by Vecchietta.

### Sala dei Nove (Sala della Pace)

The Palazzo Pubblico's most important and interesting frescoes adorn the **Sala dei Nove** (or **Sala della Pace**) next door; these are Ambrogio Lorenzetti's **Allegories of Good and Bad Government**, commissioned in 1338 to remind the councillors of the effects of their duties, and widely considered one of Europe's most important surviving cycles of secular paintings. The walled city they depict is clearly Siena, along with its countryside and domains, and the paintings are full of details of medieval life: agriculture, craftwork, trade and building, even hawking and dancing. They form the first-known panorama in Western art and show an innovative approach to the human figure – the beautiful, reclining Peace (Pax) in the *Good Government* hierarchy is based on a Roman sarcophagus still on display in the Palazzo Pubblico. An odd detail is that the "dancing maidens" in *Good Government* are probably young men: women dancing in public, according to the historian Jane Bridgeman, would have been too shocking in medieval Siena, and the figures' short hair and slit skirts were characteristic of professional male entertainers.

The moral theme of the frescoes is expressed in a complex iconography of allegorical virtues and figures. *Good Government*, painted on the more brightly lit walls and better preserved, is dominated by a throned figure representing the *comune* (he is dressed in Siena's colours), flanked by the Virtues (Peace – from which the room takes its name – is the nonchalantly reclining figure in white) and with Faith, Hope and Charity buzzing about his head. To the left, on a throne, Justice (with Wisdom in the air above) dispenses rewards and punishments, while below her throne Concordia advises the republic's councillors on their duties. All hold ropes, symbol of agreement. *Bad Government* is ruled by the figure of Fear (or the Devil), whose scroll reads: "Because he looks for his own good in the world, he places justice beneath tyranny. So nobody walks this road without Fear: robbery thrives inside and outside the city gates." Fear is surrounded by figures symbolizing the Vices.

Ironically, within a decade of the frescoes' completion, Siena was engulfed by the Black Death – in which Lorenzetti and his family were among the victims – and the city was under tyrannical government. However, the paintings retained an impact on the citizenry: St Bernardino preached sermons on their themes.

### Sala dei Pilastri and loggia

The room adjoining the Sala della Pace, the **Sala dei Pilastri** (or delle Colonne) displays panel paintings from the thirteenth to the fifteenth century, whose conservatism and strict formulaic composition points up the scale of Lorenzetti's achievement. Notable among them is one of the earliest Sienese masterpieces, Guido da Siena's gripping thirteenth-century *Maestà*, for which Duccio repainted the Virgin's face; a fascinating picture of *St Bernardino Preaching in the Campo* by Neroccio di Bartolomeo (note how the men and women in the crowd are separated by a white cloth); and a graphically violent *Massacre of the Innocents* removed from Sant'Agostino, painted by Matteo di Giovanni – one of four he completed in the city. The stained-glass figure of St Michael in one of the windows is attributed to Ambrogio Lorenzetti.

Backtracking through the museum, it is worth climbing the stairs between the Sala del Risorgimento and Sala di Balia to the rear **loggia**, where you can enjoy a view over the Piazza del Mercato, now mainly a car park with a belvedere-like platform and a pleasant café-pizzeria and restaurant. It is here you realize how abruptly the town ends: buildings rise to the right and left for a few hundred metres along the ridges of the Terzo di San Martino and Terzo di Città, but in the centre the land drops away to a rural valley.

### The Torre del Mangia

Within the Palazzo Pubblico's courtyard, opposite the entrance to the Museo Civico, is separate access to the 97-metre **Torre del Mangia** (daily: March to mid-Oct 10am–7pm; rest of the year 10am–4pm; €7 or €12 with the Museo Civico). Climb the 388 steps and you have fabulous, vertigo-inducing views across the town and countryside. Built between 1338 and 1348 – the cresting was designed by Lippo Memmi – the tower takes its name from its first watchman, a spendthrift (*mangiaguadagni*) named Giovanni di Balduccio, who is commemorated by a statue in the courtyard. It was the last great project of the *comune* before the Black Death and exercised a highly civic function: its bell was rung to order the opening of the city gates at dawn, the break for lunch, the end of work at sunset and the closing of the city gates three hours later.

## Piazza del Duomo

Dominating the hill on which it stands, visible from many parts of the city, Siena's mighty **Duomo** is the focus of an ensemble of art and architecture arrayed around the **Piazza del Duomo**. The southwest side of the square is occupied by the medieval complex of **Santa Maria della Scala**, Siena's main hospital for over eight hundred years and now a museum and arts complex displaying some staggering medieval frescoes. Two floors below it is the **Museo Archeologico**, a modest but well-presented collection, and part of a scheme that will see the former hospital turned into Siena's principal exhibition space. The other sides of the square continue the history of Sienese power, with the

# Tuscan food and wine

**At first glance, art and culture might appear to be the chief attractions of Florence and Tuscany, but the food and wine can be just as seductive: a long lunch on a vine-covered terrace or a glass of Chianti under a starry summer sky provide experiences as memorable as any museum visit. Tuscans have a long association with their land and the natural ingredients it provides, and have consequently developed a world-class cuisine in which poverty has been the mother of culinary invention.**

## A simple art

Other Italians call the Tuscans *mangiafagioli*, or "beaneaters" – a slightly unfair label, but one that hints at the region's humble culinary roots and its inhabitants' perchant for earthy, no-nonsense food. For centuries, cooking across much of Italy was based on peasant traditions – the so-called *cucina povera* ("cooking of the poor") and Tuscany was no exception. Tomatoes, olives, pasta, pulses, cheese, fruit and vegetables were the region's staples. Today, affluence has brought a few changes – more meat in particular, notably the famous *bifstecca all fiorentina* (a vast, grilled T-bone steak) but for the most part tradition and a preference for simplicity prevail. Better still, in this age of air-freighted, year-round availability, most Tuscan food remains resolutely seasonal: fruits mature, appear for a few weeks in shops and on tables, and then disappear for another year.

Garlic hanging in Mercato Centrale, Florence ▲

Diners at the Quattro Leoni in Florence ▼

Traditional bottega selling artisanal foods ▼

## French gifts

Not all Tuscan food has humble roots. Florentines, for example, claim they invented many of the classic dishes of French cuisine, pointing to the marriage in 1534 of Caterina de' Medici to Henri of Valois, the future King Henri II. The prospect of French food is said to have appalled Caterina, who embarked for Paris accompanied by a retinue of Tuscan chefs. Which is why, say the Florentines, the French have *canard à l'orange* (duck in orange sauce), a simple variation on Tuscany's *papero melarancia*. And why Gallic vol-au-vents are but pale replicas of the *turbanate di sfoglia* you'll find in any Tuscan pastry shop. Caterina also introduced the French to two essentials of the civilized table – the fork and the napkin.

## Rich variety

The classic Florentine meal will quickly become familiar during a visit: bruschetta (toasts) to start, or piquant hams and salamis, accompanied by the region's distinctive saltless bread; pasta or soups, notably *ribollita*, so thick as to be almost a stew; and then grilled meat, possibly the *bifstecca* for a treat, but more usually lamb. To finish, stay with fresh fruit or ice cream – if an Italian meal is to disappoint, the chances are it will be at the end. But there are numerous regional variations, plus a huge variety of pastas, soups, hams and cheeses, as you'll discover when you visit any *alimentatri* (food shop) or market. The best of the latter are in Florence, notably the Mercato Centrale, Europe's largest covered food hall, offering a cornucopia of gastronomic treats from Tuscany and beyond.

## Festivals

Restaurants offer an obvious range of local and regional dishes, but for some specialities – and what will be a fun experience – make a point of tracking down some of the many food festivals that take place across the region. Virtually all of them involve a degree of eating or drinking, but the word *sagra* usually signifies an event devoted to a single food product, often accompanied by dancing, fireworks, a local brass band – and lots of eating. Such events are often only advertised locally on fliers, but tourist offices carry lists. And it's not just in high season that you'll find the festivals: early autumn, during the grape harvest and when sweet chestnuts ripen, or when truffles begin to appear, is also a busy time.

▲ The traditional feast before the Palio race in Siena

▼ Gelateria di Piazza, San Gimignano

Wine tasting in Montepulciano ▲

Vineyard and cypresses near Montalcino ▼

Bottle of Montepulciano wine ▼

## Tuscan Wines

Tuscan wine used to mean Chianti, made from the humble Sangiovese grape, but in the last twenty years the region's viticulture has been transformed, producing numerous excellent new wines. Now there are hundreds of Chiantis, good and bad – wines from the Chianti Classico area are some of the best: look for the Gallo Nero (black cockerel) logo on bottles. Chianti, though, is often overshadowed by the Vino Nobile wine from around Montepulciano and the best of the traditional wines, Brunello di Montalcino and Rosso di Montalcino (the former aged for longer).

Tuscan whites have lagged behind the region's reds – victims of trebbiano, the region's bland, traditional grape. A few brave souls are experimenting, though, so look out for wines made from the vermintino grape, or chardonnay and sauvignon blanc blends. Many estates across the region are open for tours and tasting, especially in Chianti. Simply follow the signs or inquire at local tourist offices.

### Super Tuscans

For centuries, Tuscan wines were made in the same way and from the same handful of native grape varieties. All this changed in the 1960s, when innovative producers began to create wines using modern methods and "non-Italian" grapes such as syrah, merlot, cabernet franc and cabernet sauvignon. The result was the so-called Super Tuscans, which initially came from small estates on the coast near Bolgheri in southwest Tuscany. There are now many such wines, but the originals – Tignanello, Solaia, Sassicaia and Ornellaia – are still some of the best.

Palazzo dei Vescovi (Archbishop's Palace), the Palazzo del Magnifico built for Petrucci in 1508, and the Palazzo Granducale, erected later the same century for the Medici. More interesting than any of these, though, is the **Museo dell'Opera del Duomo**, home to Siena's single greatest work of art – Duccio's *Maestà* – and a range of other significant sculptures and paintings.

## The Duomo

Few buildings reveal so much of a city's history and aspirations as Siena's **Duomo** (March–May & Sept–Oct Mon–Sat 10.30am–5.30pm, Sun 1.30–5.30pm; June–Aug Mon–Sat 10.30am–8pm, Sun 1.30–6pm; Nov–Feb Mon–Sat 10.30am–6.30pm, Sun 1.30–5.30pm; €3; €6 during the summer uncovering of the marble pavement; Ⓦwww.operaduomo.siena.it). Completed to virtually its present size around 1215, the Duomo was subjected to constant plans for expansion throughout the city's years of medieval prosperity. A project at the beginning of the fourteenth century attempted to double its extent by building a baptistery on the slope below and using this as a foundation for a rebuilt nave, but the work ground to a halt as the walls gaped under the pressure. For a while, the chapter pondered knocking down the whole building and starting from scratch to the principles of the day, but eventually they hit on a new scheme to re-orientate the cathedral instead, using the existing nave as a transept and building a **new nave** out towards the Campo. Again cracks appeared, and then in 1348 came the Black Death. With the population halved and funds suddenly cut off, the plan was abandoned once and for all. The part-built extension still stands at the north end of the square, a vast structure that – had it been completed – would have created the largest church in Italy outside Rome.

Despite all the grand abandoned plans, the Duomo is still a delight. Its style is an amazing conglomeration of Romanesque and Gothic, delineated by bands of black and white marble, an idea adapted from Pisa and Lucca – though here with much bolder and more extravagant effect. The lower part of the **facade** was designed by the Pisan sculptor Giovanni Pisano, who from 1284 to 1296 created, with his workshop, much of its statuary – the philosophers, patriarchs and prophets, now removed to the Museo dell'Opera and replaced by copies.

In the next century the **Campanile** was added, its windows multiplying at each level, as was the Gothic **rose window** above the doors. Thereafter work came to a complete halt, with the **mosaics** designed for the gables having to wait until the nineteenth century, when money was found to employ Venetian artists. Immediately above the central door, note St Bernardino's bronze monogram of Christ's name.

### The pavement

The facade's use of black and white decoration is echoed by the Duomo's great marble **pavement**, or floor, which begins with geometric patterns and a few scenes outside the church and takes off into a startling sequence of 56 figurative panels within. These were completed between 1349 and 1547, with virtually every artist who worked in the city trying his hand on a design. The earliest employed a simple *sgraffito* technique, which involved chiselling holes and lines in the marble and then filling them in with pitch; later tableaux are considerably more ambitious, worked in multicoloured marble. Unfortunately, the whole effect can only be seen for about a month in August (dates vary); the rest of the year, most of the panels are rather unimaginatively protected by underfoot boarding.

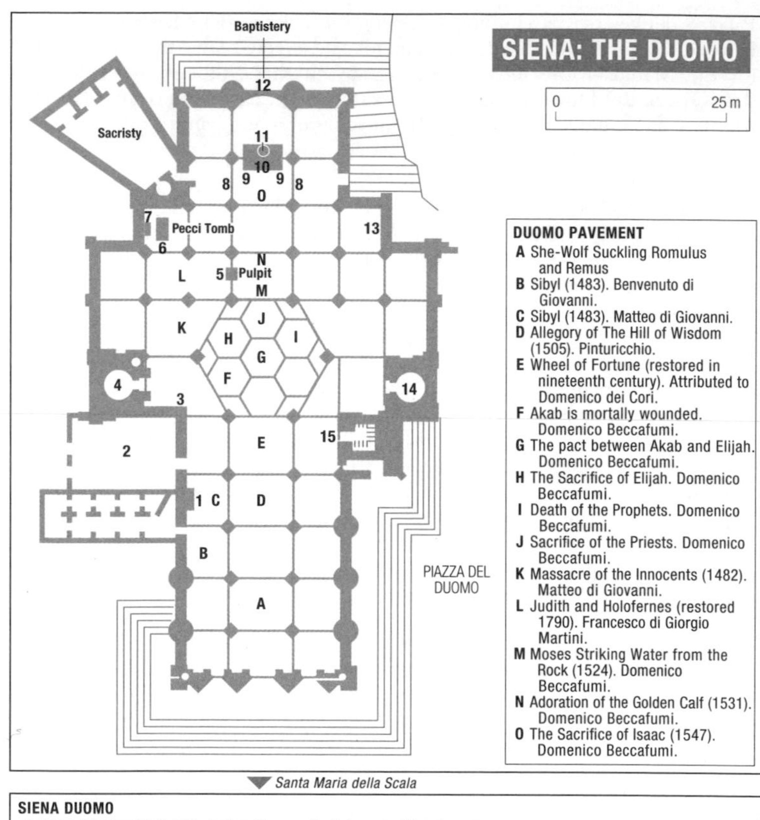

SIENA: THE DUOMO
0
25 m
Baptistery
Sacristy
Pecci Tomb
Pulpit
PIAZZA DEL DUOMO
Santa Maria della Scala
DUOMO PAVEMENT
A She-Wolf Suckling Romulus and Remus
B Sibyl (1483). Benvenuto di Giovanni.
C Sibyl (1483). Matteo di Giovanni.
D Allegory of The Hill of Wisdom (1505). Pinturicchio.
E Wheel of Fortune (restored in nineteenth century). Attributed to Domenico dei Cori.
F Akab is mortally wounded. Domenico Beccafumi.
G The pact between Akab and Elijah. Domenico Beccafumi.
H The Sacrifice of Elijah. Domenico Beccafumi.
I Death of the Prophets. Domenico Beccafumi.
J Sacrifice of the Priests. Domenico Beccafumi.
K Massacre of the Innocents (1482). Matteo di Giovanni.
L Judith and Holofernes (restored 1790). Francesco di Giorgio Martini.
M Moses Striking Water from the Rock (1524). Domenico Beccafumi.
N Adoration of the Golden Calf (1531). Domenico Beccafumi.
O The Sacrifice of Isaac (1547). Domenico Beccafumi.


**SIENA DUOMO**

**1** Altare Piccolomini (1491). Andrea Bregno. Sculptures by Michelangelo.
**2** Libreria Piccolomini. Frescoes on the life of Pope Pius II (1505–07) by Pinturicchio.
**3** Flagpole from the Battle of Montaperti.
**4** Cappella di San Giovanni Battista. Frescoes (1501–04) by Pinturicchio; bronze by Donatello of St John the Baptist (1457).
**5** Pulpit. Nicola Pisano and assistants (1268).
**6** Tomb of Bishop Pecci of Grosseto (1426–7). Donatello.
**7** Tomb of Cardinal Riccardo Petroni (1314–18). Tino da Camaino.
**8** Bronze candleholders (1548–50). Domenico Beccafumi.
**9** Bronze candleholders (1497–99). Francesco di Giorgio Martini.
**10** High altar (1532). Baldassare Peruzzi.
**11** Ciborio (1467–72). Vecchietta.
**12** Stained glass (1288). To a design by Duccio.
**13** Cappella del Sacramento. Bas-reliefs (1425) by Domenico dei Cori.
**14** Cappella Chigi (1659–62). To a design by Gian Lorenzo Bernini.
**15** Tomb of Tommaso Piccolomini (1484–5). Neroccio di Bartolomeo Landi. Below: bas-reliefs of Episodes from the Life of the Virgin (1451) by Urbano da Cortona.

The subjects chosen for the panels are a strange mix, incorporating biblical themes, secular commemorations and allegories. The most ordered part of the scheme are the ten Sibyls – mythic prophetesses who foretold the coming of Christ – on either side of the main aisle. Fashioned towards the end of the fifteenth century, when Sienese painters were still imprinting gold around their conventional Madonnas, they are totally Renaissance in spirit. Between them, in the central nave, are the much earlier *Sienese She-wolf Enclosed by the Republic's Twelve Cities* (marked as A on our plan) and the *Wheel of Fortune* (E), along with Pinturicchio's *Allegory of Virtue* (D), a rocky island of serpents with a nude posed between a boat and the land. Moving down the nave, the central hexagon is dominated by Domenico Beccafumi's *Stories from the Life of Elijah* (F–I). Beccafumi worked intermittently on the pavement from 1518 to 1547, also designing the vast friezes of *Moses Striking Water from a Rock and on Mount Sinai* (M) and *The Sacrifice of Isaac* (O). To the left of the hexagon is a *Massacre of the Innocents* (K), almost inevitably the chosen subject of Matteo di Giovanni.

It's interesting also to note the **choir stalls**, in the context of the pavement. These use intarsia techniques of a superb standard and again were made between the mid-fourteenth and mid-sixteenth centuries.

### The pulpit, sculptures and chapels

The rest of the cathedral interior is equally arresting, with its zebra-stripe bands of marble, and the line of **popes' heads** – including several Sienese – set above the pillars. These stucco busts were added through the fifteenth and sixteenth centuries and many seem sculpted with an apparent eye to their perversity: the same hollow-cheeked scowls crop up repeatedly.

The greatest individual artistic treasure is the **pulpit**. This was completed by Nicola Pisano in 1268, soon after his pulpit for the Baptistery at Pisa, with help from his son Giovanni and Arnolfo di Cambio. The carving's distance from the Byzantine world is perhaps best displayed by the statuette of the *Madonna*, whose breast is visible beneath the cloak for the first time in Italy, and by the *Last Judgement*, with its mastery of the human figure and organization of space. Come equipped with plenty of coins for lighting.

Almost all the sculpture is of an exceptional standard. Near the pulpit in the north transept are Tino di Camaino's *Tomb of Cardinal Petroni* (1318), a prototype for Italian tomb architecture over the next century, and, in front, **Donatello**'s bronze pavement *Tomb of Bishop Pecci* (1426). The Renaissance high altar is flanked by superb candelabra-carrying angels by Beccafumi. In the **Piccolomini Altarpiece**, the young **Michelangelo** also makes an appearance. He was commissioned to carve the whole series of fifteen statues here, but after completing saints Peter, Paul, Pius and Gregory in the lower niches he left for a more tempting contract in Florence – the *David*.

There are further Renaissance sculptural highlights in the two circular transept chapels. The **Cappella di San Giovanni Battista**, on the left, focuses on a bronze statue of the *Baptist* by Donatello, cast in 1457. The frescoes in this chapel, with their delightful landscape detailing, are by Pinturicchio.

The **Cappella Chigi**, or Cappella del Voto, was the last major addition to the Duomo, built at the behest of Pope Alexander VII, another local, in 1659. It was designed by Bernini as a new setting for the *Madonna del Voto*, a thirteenth-century painting that commemorated the Sienese dedication of their city to the Virgin on the eve of the Battle of Montaperti. The style of the chapel is pure Roman Baroque, most notably seen in the four niche statues, two of which are by Bernini himself – wild, semi-clad figures of Mary Magdalene and St Jerome, the latter holding a cross in ecstasy like some 1970s rock guitarist. Outside the chapel, the walls are covered in a mass of devotional objects – silver limbs and hearts, *contrada* scarves, even the odd Palio costume and crash helmet.

### Libreria Piccolomini

Midway along the nave, on the left, Pinturicchio's brilliantly coloured fresco of the *Coronation of Pius II* marks the entrance to the **Libreria Piccolomini**, well worth a visit for the beautiful fresco cycle within. The frescoes and library were commissioned by Francesco Piccolomini (who for ten days was Pope Pius III) to house the books of his uncle, Aeneas Sylvius Piccolomini (Pius II). Pius II, born at nearby Pienza in 1405, was the archetypal Renaissance man, writing poetry, a geography and the *Commentaries*, a deeply humanist work in which he enthuses over landscape, antiquity and architecture and describes the languages, customs and industries encountered on his travels.

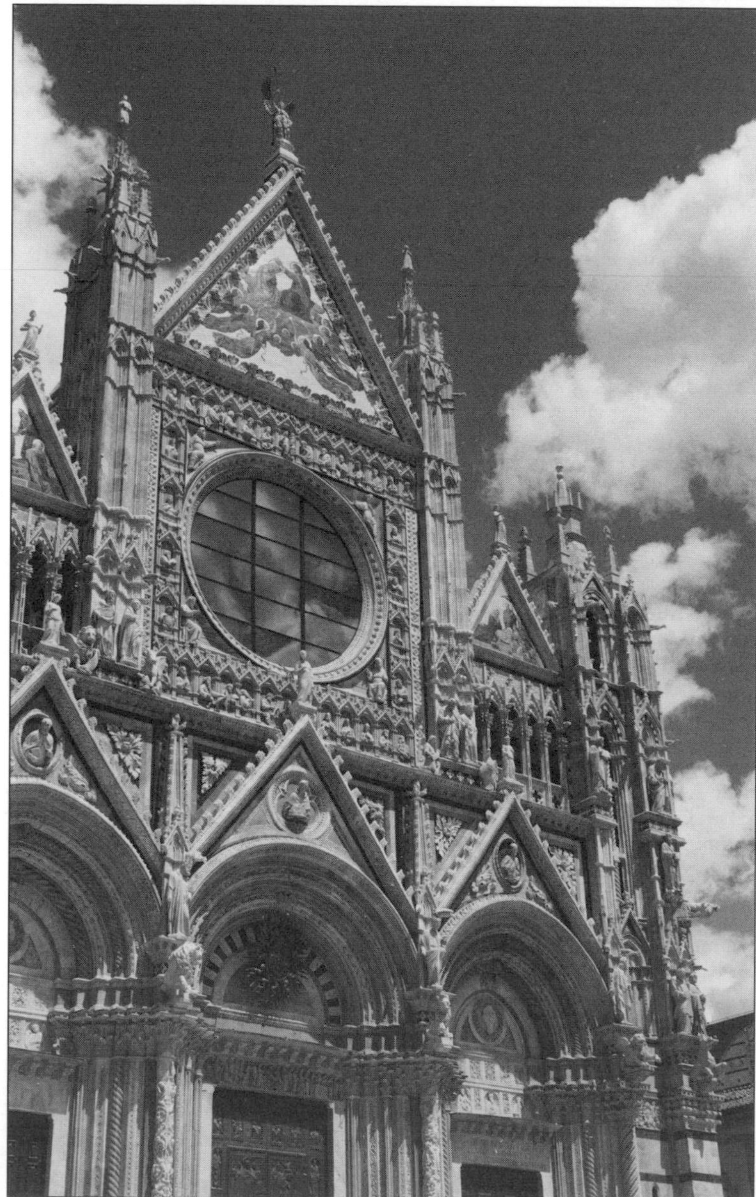

▲ Facade of the Duomo

**Pinturicchio's frescoes**, painted with an equal love of nature and classical decor as well as a keen sense of drama, commemorate the whole gamut of Pius's career. The cycle begins to the right of the window, with Aeneas's secular career as a diplomat: attending the Council of Basle as secretary to an Italian bishop (panel 1); presenting himself as an envoy to James II of Scotland (panel 2); being crowned poet laureate by the Holy Roman Emperor, Frederick III (panel 3); and then representing Frederick on a visit to Pope Eugenius IV (panel 4). Aeneas subsequently returned to Italy and took orders, becoming first Bishop of Trieste and then of Siena, in which role he is depicted presiding over the meeting of Frederick III and his bride-to-be, Eleonora of Portugal, outside the city's Porta Camollia (panel 5).

In 1456 Aeneas was made a cardinal (panel 6) and just two years later was elected pope (panel 7), taking the title Pius II. In political terms, his eight-year rule was not a great papacy, despite his undoubted humanism and diplomatic skill, with much of the time wasted in crushing the barons of Romagna and the Marche. The crusade he called in 1456 at Mantua (panel 8) to regain Constantinople from the Turks – who took the city in 1453 – came to nothing, and the last picture of the series (panel 10) shows his death at Ancona, where he had gone to encourage the troops. It was said that his death was brought on by grief for the failure to get the crusade off the ground, or possibly by poisoning by the troops, eager to terminate their pledge. Between these two panels is the event for which Siena most remembers him – the canonization of St Catherine.

The library is now used to display the cathedral's **choirbooks**, illuminated by Sano di Pietro and other Sienese Gothics. At the centre of the room is a Roman statue of the **Three Graces**, supposedly copied from a lost Greek work by Praxiteles. It was bought by the Piccolomini nephew and was used as a model by Pinturicchio and Raphael.

## The Baptistery

The cathedral **Baptistery** (daily: March–May & Sept 9.30am–7pm; June–Aug hours vary, but usually 9am–8pm; Oct 9am–6pm; rest of year 10am–1pm & 2–5pm; €3 or €10 with joint ticket) contains one of the city's great Renaissance works – a hexagonal **font** with scenes illustrating the Baptist's life. It's unusual in being placed beneath the main body of the church: to reach it, turn left out of the Duomo, follow the walls left and then take the flight of steps leading down behind the cathedral.

The cathedral chapter responsible for the font (1417–30) must have had a good sense of what was happening in Florence at the time, for they managed to commission panels by **Ghiberti** (*Baptism of Christ* and *John in Prison*) and **Donatello** (*Herod's Feast*), as well as by the local sculptor **Jacopo della Quercia** (*The Angel Announcing the Baptist's Birth*). Jacopo also executed the marble tabernacle above, and the summit statue of *John the Baptist* and five niche statues of the Prophets. Of the main panels, Donatello's scene, in particular, is a superb piece of drama, with Herod and his cronies recoiling at the appearance of the Baptist's head.

The lavishly frescoed **walls** almost overshadow the font, their nineteenth-century overpainting removed after a vigorous assault by the restorers. With your back to the entrance, the best include (on the left arched vault lunette) a fresco of scenes from the life of St Anthony (1460) by Benvenuto di Giovanni, a pupil of Vecchietta; scenes from the life of Christ by Vecchietta himself (inside left wall of the central stepped chapel); and the same artist's *Prophets*, *Sibyls* and *Articles of the Creed* (the main vaults), the last a repeat of a theme he would use in Santa Maria della Scala (see p.278).

## Santa Maria della Scala

The complex of **Santa Maria della Scala** (daily: mid-March to Oct 10am–6.30pm; rest of year 10.30am–4.30pm; €6; for joint tickets see p.268; Ⓦ santamaria.comune.siena.it), opposite the Duomo, served as the city's hospital for over eight hundred years, listing among its charitable workers St Catherine and St Bernardino. Its closure in 1995 aroused mixed feelings, for the functioning building gave a sense of purpose to the cathedral square, which won't be matched by its use as a cultural and museum space. At the same time, the *comune*'s grandiose plans for the enormous building – which include a new home for the Pinacoteca Nazionale – mean that some extraordinary works, long hidden from all but the most determined visitors, are now on public view for the first time in centuries.

While some of the complex still remains off-limits, the last few years have seen the restoration and opening of the church of **Santissima Annunziata**; the **Cappella del Sacro Chiodo** with its highly acclaimed fresco cycle by Vecchietta; a beautiful Beccafumi fresco in the **Cappella del Manto**; the **Oratorio di Santa Caterina della Notte**, a finely decorated subterranean chapel used by, among others, St Catherine; and, adjacent to this, Jacopo della Quercia's original marble panels from the Fonte Gaia in the **Fienile**. Best of all, in the **Sala del Pellegrinaio**, is a vast secular fresco cycle by Domenico di Bartolo, a work now talked of as third only to the frescoes in the Duomo and Palazzo Pubblico in Siena's artistic pantheon. Siena's **Museo Archeologico** occupies the converted basement of the building.



### Santissima Annunziata and the Cappella del Manto

To the left of the ticket desk, and also with its own door onto Piazza del Duomo, is the church of **Santissima Annunziata**, wholly within the complex of Santa Maria della Scala. Remodelled in the fifteenth century, the church is disappointingly bland, but worth a look for the high altar's marvellous bronze statue of the *Risen Christ* by Vecchietta, its features so gaunt the veins show through the skin. Before the church's remodelling, frescoes by Vecchietta had entirely covered its walls, a loss as tantalizing as the missing Martini and Lorenzetti frescoes on the hospital's exterior.

The other way from the ticket office leads into a small vestibule known as the **Cappella del Manto**, which contains an arresting and beautifully restored fresco of *St Anne and St Joachim* (1512), the earliest major work in Siena by the Mannerist Domenico Beccafumi. The protagonists depicted are the parents of the Virgin, whose story – popular in Tuscan painting – is told in the apocryphal gospels, biblical adjuncts reintroduced to the medieval world in the *Golden Legend* by Jacopo da Voragine. Having failed to conceive during twenty years of marriage, they are each told by an angel to meet at Jerusalem's Golden Gate. Here they kiss (the scene depicted in the fresco), a moment which symbolizes the Immaculate Conception of their daughter.

### Sala del Pellegrinaio

You turn left from the Cappella del Manto into a vast hall, a majestic white-washed space typical of the "longitudinal" architectural elements introduced into Italy by French Cistercians travelling the Via Francigena, and now partly used as a bookshop. Turning immediately left (rooms off to the right are used for temporary exhibitions) brings you into another similarly elongated space, the **Sala del Pellegrinaio**, its walls completely covered in a fresco cycle of episodes from the history of Santa Maria della Scala by Domenico di Bartolo and Vecchietta. Incredibly, this astounding space was used as a hospital ward until relatively recently.

## A history of Santa Maria della Scala

According to legend, the hospital of Santa Maria della Scala was founded by **Beato Sorore**, a ninth-century cobbler-turned-monk who worked among orphans, a story given credence by the reputed discovery of his "tomb" in 1492. Sorore was almost certainly mythical, his name a corruption of *suore*, or nuns, who for centuries tended the sick as a part of their vocation. The hospital was probably founded by the cathedral's canons, the first written record of its existence appearing in 1090. Its development was prompted by the proximity of the **Via Francigena**, a vital trade and pilgrimage route between Rome and northern Europe, which in the early Middle Ages replaced the deteriorating Roman consular roads used previously. Its route passed below Siena's walls, giving rise to the growth of numerous rest-places (*ospedali*) where travellers and pilgrims could seek shelter and succour. Some forty of these grew up in Sienese territory alone, the most important of which was Santa Maria della Scala. Initially pilgrims were the main concern: hospital work, in the modern sense, came later: "hospitality rather than hospitalization" was the credo.

The foundation was one of the first European examples of the **Xenodochium**, literally an "abode", a hospital that not only looked after the sick but could also be used as a refuge and food kitchen for an entire town in times of famine and plague. This role made it a vital part of the city's social fabric, its importance leading to a long-running and ill-mannered tussle between lay and secular authorities. In time it passed from the cathedral canons into the hands of hospital friars, and in 1404, after an intense dispute, into the care of the *comune*, who appointed its rectors and governing body. Alms and bequests of money over the centuries kept it richly endowed, the Sienese taking to heart St Paul's stricture that charity was the most important of the three Cardinal Virtues.

Some of the donated funds were diverted away from humanitarian concerns and into artistic and architectural commissions: as early as 1252, Siena's bishop gave permission for Santa Maria's abbot to build a **church**, the precursor of the present Santissima Annunziata. In 1335 the hospital commissioned Simone Martini and Pietro and Ambrogio Lorenzetti, the city's three leading painters, to fresco the building's exterior facade (works that have since been lost to the elements). In 1359 it paid an exorbitant sum to acquire from Constantinople a nail used during the Passion, a piece of the True Cross, and a part of the Virgin's girdle, along with a miscellany of **saints' relics**. In 1378 it financed the setting of a stone bench along the length of the hospital's exterior, its original purpose being to provide the hospital's dignitaries with somewhere to sit during the city's interminable religious and civic ceremonies – and still much used today as a shady spot from which to view the facade of the Duomo.

The ward was built around 1380 and the frescoes begun in 1440, their aim being to not only record scenes from the hospital's history, but also to promote the notion of charity towards the sick and – in particular – the orphaned, whose care had been a large part of the hospital's early function. Their almost entirely **secular** content was extraordinary at the time they were painted, still some years short of the period when Renaissance ideas would allow for non-religious narratives. It's well worth taking the trouble to study the eight major panels in detail – each is full of insights into the Sienese daily life of the time – along with the two paintings on the end wall by the window. The cycle starts at the left end of the left wall and moves clockwise.

The **first panel**, *The Dream of the Mother of Beato Sorore*, is by Vecchietta. It depicts in part a dream in which the mother of Sorore, the hospital's mythical founder, foresees her son's destiny. Her vision focuses on the abandoned children of the hospital, the *gettatelli* (from *gettare*, to throw away), who are shown ascending to Paradise and the waiting arms of the Madonna. Sorore is shown twice: on the right of the painting with upraised hand receiving the first *gettatello*, and kneeling at the foot of the child-filled ladder. This ladder (*scala*) is the key to the Santa Maria della Scala, which may take its name from this part of the legend. Another version of the story suggests that a three-runged ladder, a symbol of the Trinity, was found during the hospital's construction. Whatever the origins, a three-runged ladder surmounted by a cross is the symbol you now see plastered all over the museum's literature and displays.

The **second panel**, *The Building of the Hospital*, depicts a mounted bishop of Siena at the head of a procession passing the hospital, which is in the process of being built. Note the buildings, a strange mixture of Gothic and Renaissance that bear little relation to anything in Siena, and the rector of the hospital, portrayed behind the ladder on the right doffing his hat to the visiting dignitaries. The **third panel**, the weakest of the cycle, is by Priamo della Quercia, brother of the more famous Jacopo, and shows the *Investiture of the Hospital Rector by the Blessed Agostino Novello*, the latter traditionally, but erroneously, credited as being the author of the hospital's first statute. The **fourth panel** shows one of Santa Maria's defining moments, when in 1193 Pope Celestine III gave the hospital the right to elect its own rector, thus transferring power from the religious to lay authorities. For the rest, the fresco is an excuse to portray day-to-day life in Siena – note, for example, the preponderance of oriental merchants.

The paintings on either side of the **end wall** are late sixteenth-century pieces, but illustrate two fascinating aspects of the hospital's work. The vast number of orphans taken in meant that an equally large number of wet nurses, or *baliatici*, were needed to feed the infants. At one time their numbers were such that feeding took place in the vast hall now occupied by the bookshop. The pictures here show the nurses in action, and the payment for their services: in grain (on the left wall) and hard cash (on the right).

On the long right wall, the **fifth panel**, the most famous in the cycle, shows *The Tending of the Sick*, a picture crammed with incident, notably the close scrutiny being given to a urine sample by two doctors on the left, the youth with a leg wound being washed, and the rather ominous scene on the right of a monk confessing a patient prior to surgery.

The **sixth panel** shows *The Distribution of Charity*, one of the hospital's main tasks, an event that takes place in the old hospital church (now replaced by Santissima Annunziata) with the central door of the Duomo just visible in the background. Bread is distributed to beggars, pilgrims and children (one of whom passes it on to his mother); at the centre an orphan puts on clothes that it has been given. On the left, meanwhile, the hospital's rector is shown doffing his hat, possibly to Sigismondo.

The **seventh panel** illustrates further work of the hospital, underlining the vital part it played in maintaining the social fabric of the city. It shows the reception, education and marriage of one of the female orphans, who were provided with a small grant designed to enable them to marry, stay on in the hospital or join a convent. Also included are details that suggest how the hospital not only took in children, but committed itself to caring for them over a long period. Thus the wet nurses are shown in action on the table to the left, along with scenes to suggest weaning, education and play.

The final **eighth panel**, which details the feeding of the poor and the elderly, is less engaging than the rest, partly because of the awkwardly sited window, reputedly built by a nineteenth-century superintendent so that he could survey the sick from his upper-floor office without the bother of having to go down into the ward.

### The Cappella del Sacro Chiodo

Some idea of what was lost in the remodelling of Santissima Annunziata can be grasped in Vecchietta's fresco cycle (1446–49) in the **Cappella del Sacro Chiodo**, so named because it once housed the nail (*chiodo*) from the Passion and other holy relics; it's also known as the **Sagrestia Vecchia**, reached through the small Cappella della Madonna beside the Sala del Pellegrinaio. Some art critics pay these frescoes more attention than the Bartolo cycle in the Sala del Pellegrinaio, but for the casual viewer they are less easy to interpret, principally because the subject matter – an illustration of the *Articles of the Creed* – requires some theological knowledge. If you can manage the Italian, however, the various panels and vaults are well described. Each lunette illustrates one or more articles, the figure of one of the Apostles to the right holding the text of the article in question, the scenes below or to the left depicting an episode from the Old Testament which embodies the article's meaning.

The frescoes are extremely unusual, partly in that they illustrate a written text – something that remained rare until much later in the Renaissance – and partly in that they revolve around the figure of Christ (depicted twice in the main vaults). The latter was a strange choice in a city dedicated to the Madonna, where virtually every work of note either eulogizes Siena itself or includes Christ only as an adjunct to the Virgin. It's thought that the choice was suggested by the *chiodo* contained in the chapel, a relic with obvious relevance to the story of Christ.

Domenico di Bartolo's **high altarpiece**, the *Madonna della Misericordia* (1444), is more intelligible than much of the cycle, and shows the Madonna casting a protective cloak over various of Siena's inhabitants (a common theme in Sienese and other central works). The fresco once graced the Cappella del Manto (see p.278), the Virgin's cloak (*manto*) having given the chapel its name. It was detached and fixed here in 1610, its side parts torn away to fit the dimensions of the new altar; in 1969, however, the discarded fragments were found and reattached.

### The rest of Santa Maria della Scala

Stairs lead down to the **Fienile**, the hospital's old hayloft, now housing Jacopo della Quercia's original marble panels from the Fonte Gaia (1409–19), transferred here from the Palazzo Pubblico. With their serious state of erosion it's hard to appreciate that Jacopo della Quercia was rated by Vasari on a par with Donatello and Ghiberti, with whom he competed for the commission of Florence's Baptistery doors. Michelangelo, too, was an admirer, struck perhaps by the physicality evident in the *Expulsion of Adam and Eve*.

Adjacent is the **Oratorio di Santa Caterina della Notte**, which belonged to one of a number of the medieval confraternities who maintained oratories in the basement vaults of the hospital. It's a dark and strangely spooky place, despite the wealth of decoration; you can easily imagine St Catherine passing nocturnal vigils down here. Even if you prove immune to the atmosphere, it's worth a visit for Taddeo di Bartolo's sumptuous triptych of the *Madonna and Child with SS Andrew and John the Baptist* (1400).

Stairs lead down again to the lavishly decorated **Compagnia della Madonna sotto le Volte**, the oratory and meeting-room of the Società di Esecutori di Pie Diposizioni, the oldest of the lay confraternities, where you'll find a wooden crucifix said to be the one that inspired St Bernardino to become a monk.

From the small columned courtyard (**Corticella**) back on the Fienile level you enter the medieval storerooms – now used for temporary exhibitions – from where stairs lead down into the spacious labyrinth of the **Museo Archeologico**, which houses private collections from the late nineteenth century and plenty of local finds from excavation work in and around Siena, Chianti, the upper Val d'Elsa and Etruscan Murlo.

## The Museo dell'Opera del Duomo

Tucked into a corner of the proposed – and abandoned – new nave of the Duomo is the impressive **Museo dell'Opera del Duomo** (daily March to May & Sept–Oct 9.30am–7pm; June–Aug 9.30am–8pm; Nov–Feb 10am–5pm; €6; Ⓦwww.operaduomo.siena.it), which offers the bonus of some fine views over Siena.

On the ground floor, in the **Galleria delle Statue**, the statuary by Giovanni Pisano (1250–1314) seems a little bizarre when displayed at eye level: the huge, elongated, twisting figures are obviously adjusted to take account of the original viewing position, which was ranged across the Duomo's facade. They are totally Gothic in conception, and for all their subject matter – philosophers from antiquity are represented alongside Old Testament prophets and other characters – show little of his father Nicola's experiment with classical forms on the cathedral pulpit. In marked contrast is Donatello's ochre-coloured *Madonna and Child*, a delicate piece in the centre of the room (removed from the door of the Duomo's south transept), alongside a bas-relief by Jacopo della Quercia of *St Anthony Abbot and Cardinal Antonio Casini*.

Upstairs, a curator admits you to the **Sala di Duccio**, curtained and carefully lit to display the artist's vast and justly celebrated **Maestà**. Originally painted on both sides, it depicts the *Madonna and Child Enthroned* (or *Maestà*) and the *Story of the Passion*. The four saints in the front rank of the main painting, the *Maestà*, are Siena's patron saints at the time, Ansano, Savino, Crescenzio and Vittore, while the ten smaller figures at the rear of the massed ranks represent ten of the Apostles. On its completion in 1311 the work was, as far as scholars can ascertain, the most expensive painting ever commissioned, and had occupied Duccio for almost four years. It was taken in a ceremonial procession from Duccio's studio around the Campo and then to a special Mass in the Duomo; everything in the city was closed and virtually the entire population attended. It then remained on the Duomo's high altar until 1505.

The *Maestà* – the Virgin as Queen of Heaven surrounded by her "court" of saints – was a Sienese invention, designed as a "sacrifice" to the Virgin, the city's patron (the consecration took place in 1260), a quality emphasized by the lavish use of gold.

The altarpiece was dismembered in 1771 and removed to the museum in 1887. Only a handful of panels are missing and – to quite understandable local disgust – will not be released by their owners to the city: two are in Washington, three in London's National Gallery and three in the Frick and Rockefeller collections in New York.

Also in the room is a *Madonna di Crevole*, an early work by Duccio, and Pietro Lorenzetti's triptych of the *Nativity of the Virgin*, the latter remarkable for breaking with the tradition of triptych painting by running a single scene across two of the painting's three panels. In the room behind the Sala is a fascinating nineteenth-century drawing of the cathedral pavement, providing a unified view impossible on the spot.

For the art that followed Duccio, and some that preceded him you need to make your way upstairs again. Here you enter the **Sala di Tesoro**, featuring amid its reliquaries the head of St Galgano and a startling *Christ on the Cross* (1280), an important early work in wood by Giovanni Pisano in which Christ is shown on a Y-shaped tree growing out of the skull of Adam. The latter symbolizes the Tree of Life, or Tree of Knowledge, which grew from a sprig planted in the dead

Adam's mouth and would – in the apocryphal story – eventually yield the wood used to crucify Christ.

Beyond the Sala di Tesoro you reach the **Sala della Madonna dagli Occhi Grossi**. The work that gives its name to this room is the cathedral's original, pre-Duccio altarpiece – a stark, haunting Byzantine icon (literally the "Madonna of the Big Eyes") in the centre of the room. It occupies a special place in Sienese history, for it was before this painting that Siena's entire population came to pray before their famous victory over the Florentines at Montaperti in 1260. Around it are grouped a fine array of panels, including works by Simone Martini, Pietro Lorenzetti and Sano di Pietro. Note the panels flanking Sano's *Madonna and Child*: one shows St Bernardino preaching in the Campo and Piazza San Francesco (the latter now home to the saint's oratory; see p.292); the other shows St Apollonia, patron saint of dentists, martyred in Alexandria in the fourth century for refusing to make sacrifices to pagan gods.

Don't miss the tiny entrance to the so-called **Panorama dal Facciatone**: this leads to steep spiral stairs that climb out of the building, up within the walls of the abandoned nave. The sensational view from the top over the city and surrounding hills is definitely worth the two-stage climb, but be aware that the topmost walkway – teetering along the very summit of the abandoned nave walls – is narrow and scarily exposed.



## Terzo di San Martino

Banchi di Sotto, the main thoroughfare through the **Terzo di San Martino**, leads southeast from the Campo past the imposing Renaissance buildings of **Palazzo Piccolomini** and the **Loggia del Papa** towards the medieval Servite order's huge monastic base, **Santa Maria dei Servi**. Students outnumber tourists in this university-dominated area that ends at the south gate of the city, **Porta Romana**, but there is plenty of scope for aimless wandering through the quiet backstreets off Via Pantaneto with a loop back to the centre via the church of **San Martino**.

### Loggia di Mercanzia

Marking the start of Banchi di Sotto, the main thoroughfare through Terzo di San Martino, is the **Loggia di Mercanzia** (or Loggia dei Mercanti), designed for merchants to do their deals. The structure was the result of extraordinary architectural indecision by the city authorities, the chronicles recording that "on one day they build in a certain way and on the following destroy and rebuild in a different manner". It was completed in 1421 in accordingly hesitant style, with Gothic niches for the saints carved by Vecchietta and Antonio Federighi, two of the city's leading Renaissance sculptors.

### Palazzo Piccolomini

Following Banchi di Sotto from the loggia, you pass the more committed Renaissance buildings of the **Palazzo Piccolomini** (at Banchi di Sotto 52) and the **Loggia del Papa**, commissioned in the 1460s by Pope Pius II, the Pienza-born Aeneas Sylvius Piccolomini. Pius was the city's great Renaissance patron and an indefatigable builder. The loggia was built in 1462 by Federighi. The palace – one of three the pope built for his family in the city – was designed by Bernardo Rossellino, architect of Piccolomini's famous "new town" of Pienza (see p.304); note the half-moon symbols, Pius's coat of arms, insinuated across much of the facade.

The Palazzo Piccolomini now houses the **Archivio di Stato**, the city's archives (guided visits Mon–Sat at 9.30am, 10.30am & 11.30am; free, no booking required), a fascinating detour, but one made by probably one visitor in five hundred to the city. You're taken through corridors of archives – great bundles of vellum and leather-bound documents for each of the towns and villages in Siena's domain, each one labelled in ancient medieval script with the year in question: a quite overwhelming amount of information for any potential historian, and most of it still unread. If you're lucky you'll also be able to pop out onto the palace's terrace, which offers a rarely seen view of the Campo.

Eventually you come to the **Museo delle Tavolette di Biccherna**, containing the city's account books, tax records (the *Gabelle*) and hallowed manuscripts dating back to the earliest days of Siena's recorded history. The chief exhibits, though, are the *Tavolette*, fascinating painted wooden panels designed as covers for civic records and accounts: what makes them more interesting still is the fact that the *comune* commissioned some of the leading painters of the day to execute the beautifully detailed vignettes. Among those employed were Sano di Pietro and Ambrogio Lorenzetti, who painted the 1344 *Gabella* with a version of his *Good Government* fresco in the Palazzo Pubblico. The paintings began with religious themes, but soon moved towards secular images of city life, providing a record of six centuries of Sienese history. Later panels were designed to be hung as pictures in the council offices, rather than mounted on the books. The city is depicted frequently in the background, protected by the Virgin and mushrooming with towers – much like San Gimignano today. Early panels include several pictures of the *camerlingo* (a duty always filled by a Cistercian monk from San Galgano) doing the audits. Later ones move into specific events: victories over the Florentines; Pius's coronation as pope (1458); entrusting the city keys to the Virgin in the Duomo (1483); the demolition of the Spanish fortress (1552); the fall of Montalcino, the Sienese Republic's last stand (1559), and the entry into Siena of Cosimo I (1560); war with the Turks (1570); and subsequent Medicean events.

## San Martino

From the Palazzo Piccolomini and the Loggia, Via di Pantaneto, Via del Porrione or Via di Salicotto take you quickly away from the bustle around the Campo towards the Porta Romana. Before setting off, however, Mannerist fans should spend a couple of minutes in the church of **San Martino**, founded in the eighth century or earlier, but now a pale Baroque shadow of its former self. The third altar on the left (north) wall features an outstanding *Nativity* (1522–24) by Domenico Beccafumi, a work painted at the same time as the artist was working on the Duomo's pavement, and one which encapsulates his passion for bizarre structures and peculiar light effects. The Virgin's strange gesture, in which she covers the Infant Jesus with a veil, prefigures the Crucifixion, at which she also covers Christ's naked body.

## Santa Maria dei Servi

Via di Salicotto or Via San Martino bring you southeast into the Valdimontone *contrada*, whose museum (Ⓣ0577.222.590, Ⓦwww.valdimontone.it), fountain and parish church are in Via di Valdimontone, alongside the massive brick church and campanile of **Santa Maria dei Servi**, the Servites' monastic base. The church (closed 12.30–3pm; free), which is well worth the walk, is set in a quiet piazza, approached by a row of cypresses and shaded by a couple of spreading trees – good for a midday picnic or siesta. It also offers tremendous views across the city.

The Renaissance-remodelled **interior** is remarkable for a variety of top-notch paintings. The first, above the first main altar on the right (south) wall, is the so-called *Madonna di Bordone* (1261) by **Coppo di Marcovaldo**, a Florentine artist captured by the Sienese at the Battle of Montaperti and forced to paint this picture as part of his ransom for release. The next altar to the left features the *Nativity of* *the Virgin* (1625) by Rutilio Manetti, Siena's leading follower of Caravaggio. Two altars down, in the last altar of the left aisle, is Matteo di Giovanni's *Massacre of the Innocents* (1491), one of two versions of this episode in the church, and one of four in the city by the infanticide-obsessed Matteo. The popularity of this subject in the late fifteenth century may have been due to the much-publicized massacre of Christian children by the Saracens at Otranto in 1480.

Cheek-by-jowl violence also characterizes Pietro Lorenzetti's much earlier version of the *Massacre*, which is found on the right wall of the second chapel to the right of the high altar. (Note Herod watching the carnage from a balcony on the left.) The serene *Madonna and Child* to the right is by Segna di Bonaventura, nephew of the great Duccio. Lorenzetti is further represented by damaged frescoes of the *Banquet of Herod* and the *Death of John the Baptist*, located on the right wall of the second chapel to the left of the high altar. A fine *Adoration of the Shepherds* (1404) by one of Lorenzetti's followers, Taddeo di Bartolo, hangs in the same chapel.

Down the north aisle towards the entrance, the last altar before the rear wall contains the small but eye-catching *Madonna del Belvedere* (1363), one of only a handful of works attributed to Jacopo di Mino, a pupil of Lippo Memmi.



### Porta Romana

From Santa Maria dei Servi, you're just 100m from the **Porta Romana**, the massively bastioned south gate of the city. Its outer arch has a fragmentary fresco of the *Coronation of the Virgin*, begun by Taddeo di Bartolo and completed by Sano di Pietro. If you leave the city here, and turn left along Via Girolamo Gigli, you could follow the walls north to the **Porta Pispini**, another impressive example of defensive architecture and again flanked by a fresco of the Virgin, this time a Renaissance effort by Sodoma.

Just within the Porta Romana, opposite the huge ex-convent of San Niccolò (which now houses a psychiatric hospital), is the little church of **Santuccio**, worth looking into for its seventeenth-century frescoes depicting the life of St Galgano. In the adjacent sacristy, at Via Roma 71, are the premises of the **Società Esecutori di Pie Disposizioni** (the Society of Benevolent Works, formerly the Society of Flagellants). This medieval order, suppressed in the eighteenth century and later refounded along more secular lines, maintains a small collection of art works (open on request Mon–Fri 9am–1pm; free), including a triptych of the *Crucifixion, Flagellation and Burial of Christ* attributed to Duccio, and a semicircular tablet, with wonderful Renaissance landscape, of *St Catherine of Siena Leading the Pope Back to Rome*.

## Terzo di Città

Via di Città, one of Siena's key streets, cuts across the top of the Campo through the city's oldest quarter, the **Terzo di Città**, the area around the cathedral. The street and its continuation, Via di San Pietro, are fronted by some of Siena's finest private *palazzi*, including the Buonsignori, home to the **Pinacoteca Nazionale**, Siena's main picture gallery. The district is also worth exploring for its own sake, with a variety of options taking you in loops past churches such as **Sant'Agostino** and some of the city's tucked-away corners.

### Palazzo Chigi-Saracini and Palazzo delle Papesse

Walking to the Pinacoteca, you pass the **Palazzo Chigi-Saracini** at Via di Città 82, a Gothic beauty, with its curved facade and back courtyard. Although the palace is closed to the public, it houses the **Accademia Chigiana** (Ⓦwww.chigiana.it), which sponsors music programmes throughout the year and maintains a small art collection, including exceptional works by Sassetta, Botticelli and Donatello. It was from this palace that the Sienese victory over the Florentines at Montaperti was announced, the town herald having watched the battle from the tower.

Almost opposite, at Via di Città 126, is a second Palazzo Piccolomini, this one built in 1460 by Bernardo Rossellino as a residence for Pius II's sister, Caterina. Known as the **Palazzo delle Papesse**, it now houses Siena's museum of contemporary art (Tues–Sun 11am–7pm; €5; joint tickets see p.268; Ⓦwww.papesse.org). Its four airy floors house excellent temporary exhibits covering anything from architecture to video art, displayed in rooms, some with nineteenth-century frescoes, that still conserve many of their original Renaissance structural and decorative features.

## Pinacoteca Nazionale

Via di Città continues to a small piazza, from where Via San Pietro leads left (south) to the fourteenth-century Palazzo Buonsignori, now the home of the superb **Pinacoteca Nazionale** (Mon 8.30am–1.30pm, Tues–Sat 8.15am–7.15pm, Sun 8.15am–1.30pm; €4). Its collection is a roll of honour of Sienese Gothic painting, and if your interest has been spurred by the works by Martini in the Palazzo Pubblico or Duccio in the cathedral museum, a visit is the obvious next step. The collection offers an unrivalled chance to assess the development of art in the city from the twelfth century through to late Renaissance Mannerism.

The main rooms are arranged in chronological order, starting on the second floor. **Room 1** begins with the earliest known Sienese work, an altar frontal dated 1215 of *Christ Flanked by Angels*, with side panels depicting the discovery of the True Cross. The figures are clearly Romanesque; the gold background – intricately patterned – was to be a standard motif of Sienese art over the next two centuries. The first identified Sienese painter, Guido da Siena, makes an appearance in this room and covers the same subject in **room 2**, though the influences on his work – dated around 1280 – are distinctively Byzantine rather than Romanesque, incorporating studded jewels amid the gold.

Duccio di Buoninsegna (1260–1319), the dominant figure in early Sienese art, is represented along with his school in **rooms 3 and 4**. The painter's advances in composition are best assessed in his *Maestà*, in the Museo dell'Opera del Duomo. Here Duccio simply shows that he "fulfilled all that the medieval mind demanded of a painter", in the words of Berenson: his dual purpose being to demonstrate Christianity to an illiterate audience and make an offering (the painting) to God.

Sienese art over the next century has its departures from Duccio, but the patrons responsible for commissioning works generally wanted more of the same: decorative paintings, whose gold backgrounds made their subjects stand out in the gloom of medieval chapels. As well as specifying the required materials and composition, the Sienese patrons – bankers, guilds, religious orders – would often nominate a particular painting as the model for the style they wanted.

Even within the conventions required by patrons, however, there were painters whose invention and finesse set them apart. One such was Simone Martini. Though his innovations – the attention to framing and the introduction of a political dimension – are perhaps best seen in the Palazzo Pubblico, there are several great works on show here, mainly in **room 5**, housing one of his masterpieces, the *Blessed Agostino Novello and Four of his Miracles*. Perhaps more rewarding, however, are the works by the Lorenzetti brothers, Pietro and Ambrogio, in **rooms 7 and 8**. Pietro's include a marvellous *Risen Christ*, which could almost hold company with Masaccio, and the *Carmine*

*Altarpiece*, whose predella has five skilful narrative scenes of the founding of the Carmelite order. Attributed to Ambrogio, or, more likely, to Sassetta, are two tiny panels in room 12, *City by the Sea* and *Castles by a Lake*, which the art historian Enzo Carli claims are the first ever "pure landscapes", without any religious purpose. They are thought to have been painted on a door, one above the other.

In **rooms 9 to 11** you come to the major Sienese artists Bartolo di Fredi (1353–1410) and his pupil Taddeo di Bartolo (1362–1422). Bartolo is best known for the New Testament frescoes in San Gimignano, whose mastery of narrative is reflected in his *Adoration of the Magi*. Taddeo, painter of the chapel in the Palazzo Pubblico, has archaic elements – notably the huge areas of gold around a sketch of landscape – but makes strides in portraiture and renders one of the first pieces of dynamic action in the museum in his *Stoning of SS Cosmas and Damian*.

These advances are taken a stage further in Sassetta's *St Anthony Beaten by Devils* (no. 166), where Siena seems at last to be entering the mainstream of European Gothic art, and taking note of Florentine perspective. The influence of the patrons, however, is still prevalent in the mass of stereotyped images – gold again very much to the fore – by Giovanni di Paolo (1403–82), which fill most of **rooms 12 and 13**, and the exquisite Madonnas by Sano di Pietro (1406–81) and Matteo di Giovanni (1435–95) in **rooms 14 to 18**. It is astonishing to think that their Florentine contemporaries included Uccello and Leonardo. Subsequent rooms include some sublime paintings by Beccafumi, Siena's leading Mannerist artist, and works by Antonio Bazzi (better known as Sodoma) and Bernardino Mei, the last an increasingly studied and admired seventeenth-century artist.

The **third floor** of the museum – not always open – presents the self-contained **Collezione Spannocchi**, a miscellany of Italian, German and Flemish works, including a Dürer, a fine Lorenzo Lotto *Nativity*, Paris Bordone's perfect Renaissance *Annunciation*, and Sofonisba Anguissola's *Bernardo Campi Painting Sofonisba's Portrait* – the only painting in the museum by a female artist. Anguissola, who is mentioned by Vasari as a child prodigy, painted at the height of Mannerism; this work is a neat little joke, the artist excelling in her portrait of Campi, but depicting his portrait of her as a flat, stereotyped image.

## Sant'Agostino and a loop to the Duomo

South of the Pinacoteca is the church of **Sant'Agostino**, open some years, closed others, where – if you are lucky – you can admire a *Crucifixion* (1506) by Perugino (second altar of the south aisle), an *Adoration of the Magi* (1518) by Sodoma and a lunette fresco of the *Madonna and Child with Saints* by Ambrogio Lorenzetti (both in the Cappella Piccolomini), and two monochrome lunette medallions by Luca Signorelli (Cappella Bichi, south transept). The church **piazza** is quite a pleasant space, with a kids' playground and usually a few football games in progress. Along with the Campo, this square was the site of violent medieval football matches – *ballone*, as they called it – which were eventually displaced in the festival calendar by the Palio.

An interesting walk from Sant'Agostino is to loop along the **Via della Cerchia**, a route that takes you past some good neighbourhood restaurants to the Carmelite convent and church of **San Niccolò al Carmine** (or Santa Maria del Carmine) in a predominantly student-populated section of the town. The church, a Renaissance rebuilding, contains a sensational *St Michael* by Domenico Beccafumi (midway down the south wall), painted following the monks' rejection of his more intense Mannerist version of the subject in the Pinacoteca (deemed to contain too many nudes for comfort). A hermaphrodite St Michael is shown at the centre of the crowded painting, looked down on by God, who has ordered the saint to earth to dispatch the Devil; the Devil's extraordinary face can be seen at the base of the picture. To the painting's left is a fragment of an *Annunciation* attributed to Ambrogio Lorenzetti.

If you follow the **Via del Fosso di San Ansano**, north of the Carmine square, you find yourself on a country lane, above terraced vineyards and allotments, before emerging at the Selva (wood) *contrada*'s square and **museum** (ⓣ0577.45.093, ⓦwww.contradadellaselva.it) and church of **San Sebastiano**. Climb up the stepped Vicolo di San Girolamo from here and you come out at the Duomo. Alternatively from Sant'Agostino, you could cut back to the Campo along **Via Giovanni Dupré**, where the Onda (wave or dolphin) *contrada* has its base at no. 111; to visit the **museum** you need to make an appointment at least a week in advance (ⓣ0577.48.384, ⓦwww.contradacapitanadellonda.it). The Onda church is San Giuseppe, at the Sant'Agostino end of the street.

## Terzo di Camollia

The northern **Terzo di Camollia** is flanked, to west and east, by the churches of the most important medieval orders, the **Dominicans** and **Franciscans**: vast brick piles which rear above the city's outer ridges. Each has an important association with Siena's major saints, the former with **Catherine**, the latter with **Bernardino**. Bernardino's pilgrim trail also leads out of the city to the north, to the **Osservanza** monastery, his principal retreat.

The central part of the Camollia takes in the main thoroughfare of **Banchi di Sopra**, the base of the **Monte dei Paschi** – long the city's financial power. North from here, you move into a quiet residential quarter, all the more pleasant for its lack of specific sights or visitors. To the west, interestingly detached from the old city, is the **Fortezza di Santa Barbara**.

### San Domenico

The Dominicans founded their monastery in the city in 1125. Its church, **San Domenico** (daily: April–Oct 7am–1pm & 3–6.30pm; Nov–March 9am–1pm & 3–6pm; free), begun in 1226, is a vast, largely Gothic building, typical of the austerity of this militaristic order. The Catherine association is immediately asserted. On the right of the entrance is a kind of raised chapel, the **Cappella delle Volte**, with a contemporary portrait of her by her friend and disciple Andrea Vanni, who according to tradition captured her likeness from life during one of her ecstasies in 1414; below are steps and a niche, where she received the stigmata, took on the Dominican habit, and performed several of her miracles. The saint's own chapel, the **Cappella di Santa Caterina** (erected in 1488), is located midway down the right (south) side of the church. Its entrance arch has images of saints Luke and Jerome by Sodoma, while the marble tabernacle on the high altar (1466) encloses a reliquary containing Catherine's head (other parts of her body lie dotted across Italy). The church's highlights, however – frescoes by Sodoma (1526) – occupy the walls to the left and right of the altar and, respectively, depict her swooning and in ecstasy. Just to the left of the chapel, above the steps to the crypt, is a detached fresco of the *Madonna and Child, John the Baptist and Knight* by Pietro Lorenzetti.

Other notable paintings are found in some of the other chapels, especially the first to the right of the high altar, which contains a Matteo di Giovanni triptych of the *Madonna and Child with SS Jerome and John the Baptist* and fragments of detached frescoes by Lippo Memmi and Andrea Vanni. The high altar boasts

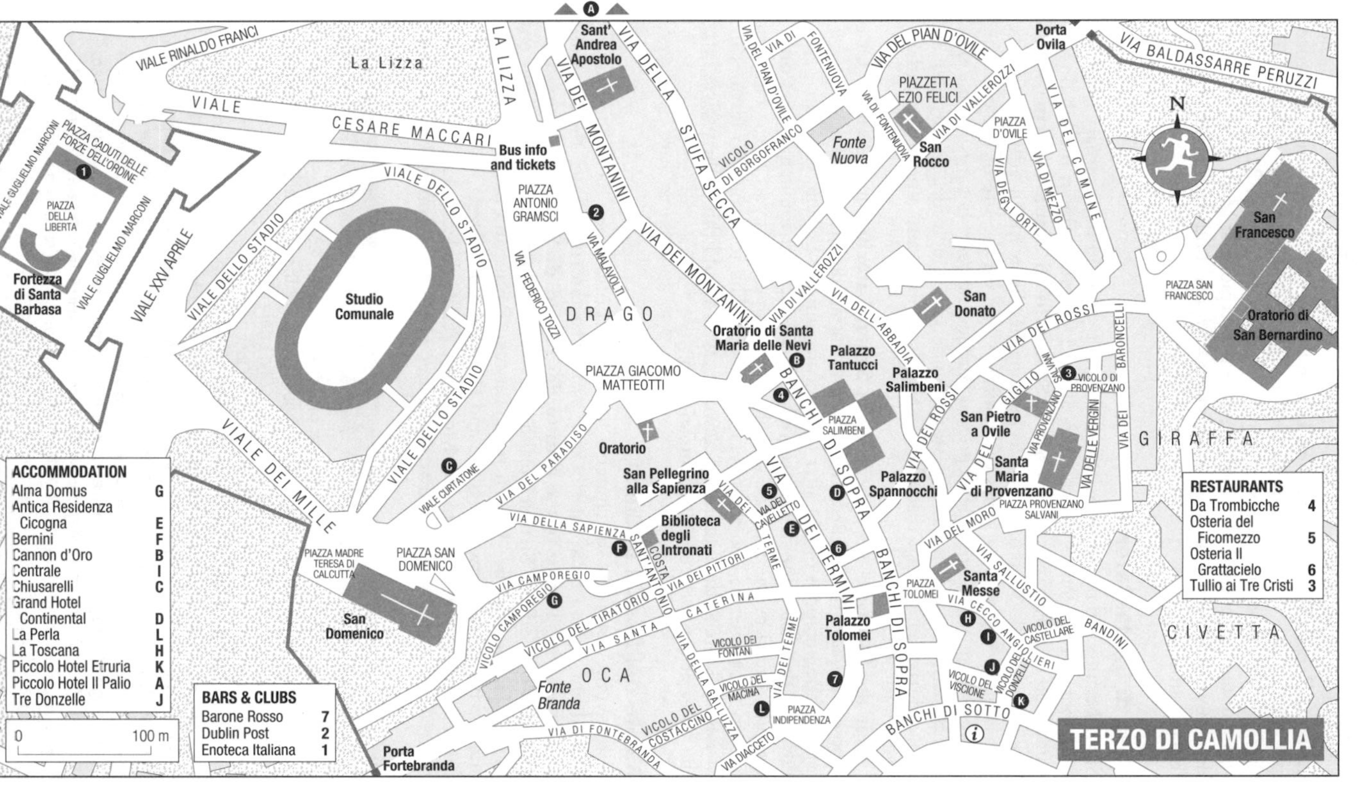
TERZO DI CAMOLLIA
ACCOMMODATION
Alma Domus G
Antica Residenza Cicogna E
Bernini F
Cannon d'Oro B
Centrale I
Chiusarelli C
Grand Hotel Continental D
La Perla L
La Toscana H
Piccolo Hotel Etruria K
Piccolo Hotel Il Palio A
Tre Donzelle J
0 100 m
BARS & CLUBS
Barone Rosso 7
Dublin Post 2
Enoteca Italiana 1
RESTAURANTS
Da Trombicche 4
Osteria del Ficomezzo 5
Osteria Il Grattacielo 6
Tullio ai Tre Cristi 3
N
La Lizza
VIALE RINALDO FRANCI
LA LIZZA
VIALE CESARE MACCARI
Bus info and tickets
Sant' Andrea Apostolo
VIA DELLA STUFA SECCA
VIA DEI MONTANINI
VIA DEL PIAN D'OVILE
VIA DI FONTENUOVA
VICOLO DI BORGOFRANCO
Fonte Nuova
PIAZZETTA EZIO FELICI
VIA DI FONTENUOVA
San Rocco
VIA DI VALLEROZZI
Porta Ovila
VIA BALDASSARRE PERUZZI
PIAZZA D'OVILE
VIA DEGLI ORTI
VIA DI MEZZO
VIA DEL COMUNE
San Francesco
PIAZZA SAN FRANCESCO
Oratorio di San Bernardino
PIAZZA CADUTI DELLE FORZE DELL'ORDINE
VIALE GUGLIELMO MARCONI
PIAZZA DELLA LIBERTA
Fortezza di Santa Barbasa
VIALE XXV APRILE
VIALE DELLO STADIO
Studio Comunale
PIAZZA ANTONIO GRAMSCI
VIA MALAVOLTI
VIA FEDERICO TOZZI
DRAGO
VIA DELL'ABBADIA
San Donato
Oratorio di Santa Maria delle Nevi
Palazzo Tantucci
Palazzo Salimbeni
PIAZZA SALIMBENI
BANCHI DI SOPRA
VIA DEI ROSSI
BARONCELLI
VIA DEL GIGLIO
SALVANI
VICOLO DI PROVENZANO
San Pietro a Ovile
VIA PROVENZANO
VIA DELLE VERGINI
VIA DEI
Santa Maria di Provenzano
PIAZZA PROVENZANO SALVANI
GIRAFFA
PIAZZA GIACOMO MATTEOTTI
Oratorio
VIA DEL PARADISO
VIALE CURTATONE
VIALE DEI MILLE
San Pellegrino alla Sapienza
Biblioteca degli Intronati
VIA DELLA SAPIENZA
COSTA SANT'ANTONIO
VIA DEL CAVELLETTO
VIA DEI TERMINI
VIA DELLE TERME
Palazzo Spannocchi
VIA DEL MORO
Santa Messe
VIA SALLUSTIO BANDINI
PIAZZA TOLOMEI
VIA CECCO ANGIOLIERI
VICOLO DEL CASTELLARE
VICOLO DEI DONZELLE
VICOLO DEL VISCIONE
BANCHI DI SOTTO
CIVETTA
PIAZZA MADRE TERESA DI CALCUTTA
PIAZZA SAN DOMENICO
San Domenico
VIA CAMPOREGIO
VICOLO CAMPOREGIO
VIA DEI PITTORI
VICOLO DEL TIRATORIO
VIA SANTA CATERINA
Palazzo Tolomei
VICOLO DEI FONTANI
VICOLO DEL MACINA
PIAZZA INDIPENDENZA
VIA DELLA GALLUZZA
VIA DIACCETO
OCA
Fonte Branda
VICOLO DEL COSTACCINO
VIA DI FONTEBRANDA
Porta Fortebranda

a fine marble tabernacle and two sculpted angels (1465) by the sculptor and architect Benedetto da Maiano, best known for the Palazzo Strozzi in Florence and several fine works in San Gimignano. The second chapel to the left of the high altar houses *St Barbara, Angels and SS Catherine and Mary Magdalene* surmounted by an *Epiphany*, considered the masterpiece of Matteo di Giovanni, though its effect is somewhat undermined by the odd eighteenth-century frescoes around it.

## Casa di Santa Caterina

St Catherine's family home, where she lived as a Dominican tertiary – of the order but not resident – is just south of San Domenico, down the hill on Via Santa Caterina. Known as the **Casa e Santuario di Santa Caterina** (daily 9am–12.30pm & 3–6pm; free), the building has been much adapted, with a Renaissance loggia and a series of oratories – one on the site of her cell. The paintings here are mostly unexceptional Baroque canvases but it is the life that is important (not that the over-restored house give much idea of this life): an extraordinary career that made her Italy's patron saint and among the earliest women to be canonized.

Near the Santuario are the church of **Santa Caterina**, home of the Oca (goose) *contrada* (Ⓣ0577.285.413, Ⓦwww.contradadelloca.it) – known as *gli infami* ("the infamous ones") after their record number of Palio victories – and, down in the valley, the best-preserved of Siena's several fountains, the **Fonte Branda**. Aided by the fountain's reliable water supply, this part of the city was an area for tanneries into the twentieth century. The fountain also features in Sienese folklore as the haunt of werewolves, who would throw themselves into the water at dawn to return to human form.

## Monte dei Paschi di Siena

Between the two monastic churches lies the heart of business Siena, the **Piazza Salimbeni**, whose three interlocking *palazzi* have formed, since the fifteenth century, the head office of the **Monte dei Paschi di Siena**. Banking was at the heart of medieval Sienese wealth, the town capitalizing on its position on the Via Francigena, the "French road" between Rome and northwest Europe, and the main road between Rome and Florence and Bologna. In the fifteenth century the Republic set up the Monte dei Paschi di Siena as a lending and charitable institution, to combat the abuses of usury. It consolidated its role

### St Catherine of Siena

Born Caterina Benincasa, the daughter of a dyer, on March 25, 1347 – Annunciation Day – **St Catherine** had her first visions aged 5 and took the veil at age 8 (16 in some versions), against strong family opposition. She spent three years in silent contemplation, before experiencing a mystical "Night Obscure". Thereafter she went out into the turbulent, post-Black Death city, devoting herself to the poor and sick, and finally turning her hand to politics. She prevented Siena and Pisa joining Florence in rising against Pope Urban V (then absent in Avignon) and proceeded to bring him back to Rome. It was a fulfilment of the ultimate Dominican ideal – a union of the practical and mystical life. Catherine returned to Siena to a life of contemplation, visions and stigmata, retaining a political role in her attempts to reconcile the later schism between the popes and anti-popes. She died in Rome in 1380 and was canonized by Pius II (as depicted in the cathedral) in 1460. She joined St Francis as a patron saint of Italy in 1939. John Paul II declared her co-patron of Europe in 1999.

under Medici rule and slowly moved into more strictly banking activities. In the twentieth century it merged with other Tuscan and Umbrian banks to become one of the key financial institutions in Italy.

There is some historical interest in the exteriors of the bank's *palazzi*: the **Spannocchi**, on the right, was the first great Renaissance palace built in Siena (1473) and the prototype for the Palazzo Strozzi in Florence, while the **Salimbeni**, in the centre, was a last flourish of Gothicism. However, to appreciate the role of the *Monte* in Siena you need to **tour** the building. In 1972, Pierluigi Spadolino undertook a radical restructuring, encasing the building's interior medieval and Renaissance features within an ultramodern and high-tech framework. This is a sight in itself, but it also provides a wonderful showcase for the bank's **art collection** – the bulk of which is housed in the deconsecrated church of San Donato, linked by an underground passage with the main *palazzi*. The paintings here include some of the finest Gothic works in Siena, among them an exquisitely coloured *Madonna* by Giovanni di Paolo, a *Deposition* by Sano di Pietro and a *Crucifixion* by Pietro Lorenzetti. Also displayed are a series of paintings depicting the Palio and its sixteenth-century bullfighting precursor in the Campo. The bank sometimes exhibits its art collections during banking hours and occasionally by appointment only (details from the tourist office). With any luck, you will be shown the archives and major halls of the bank, as well as the paintings, and the visit ends with a trip up to the tower for a view over the Campo.

## To Porta Camollia and the Fortezza

Heading north from the Piazza Salimbeni, Banchi di Sopra changes name to **Via Montanini** and then **Via di Camollia**, which run through the less monumental parts of the Terzo di Camollia, good for regular shopping and largely untouristed bars and restaurants.

Two churches are worth a brief look on this street, though both are rarely open. **Santa Maria delle Nevi** contains a famous altarpiece – *Our Lady of the Snows* (1477) – by Matteo di Giovanni, while **San Bartolomeo** fronts one of the nicest *contrada* squares in the city, home of the Istrici (porcupine); the *contrada* has its museum at Via Camollia 87 (visits to be booked a week in advance: ⓣ0577.48.495, ⓦwww.istrice.org). At the end of the street is the Renaissance **Porta Camollia**, inscribed on its outer arch "Siena opens her heart to you wider than this gate." It was here that a vastly superior Florentine force was put to flight in 1526, following the traditional Sienese appeal to the Virgin.

A short distance east of Banchi di Sopra – reached by a circuitous network of alleys – is another of the city's fountains, the **Fonte Nuova**. A further, highly picturesque fountain, the **Fonte Ovile**, is to be seen outside the Porta Ovile, a hundred metres or so beyond. Both were built at the end of the twelfth century. Near Fonte Nuova, in Via Vallerozzi, is the church of **San Rocco**, home of the Lupa (she-wolf) *contrada*; its museum is at nos. 71–73 (visits by appointment; ⓣ0577.270.777).

Away to the west, behind the church of Santo Stefano, the gardens of **La Lizza** – taken over on Wednesdays by the town's large market – lead up to the walls of the **Forte di Santa Barbara** (free access). The fortress was built initially by Charles V after the siege of 1554–55, but subsequently torn down by the people, and had to be rebuilt by Cosimo I, who then moved his troops into the garrison. Its Medicean walls resemble the walls of Lucca, designed by the same architect. Occasional summer concerts are held within the fort, which is also a permanent home to the wine collections and bar of the *Enoteca Italiana* (see p.295).

## San Francesco

St Bernardino, born in the year of Catherine's death, began his preaching life at the chill monastic church of **San Francesco**, across the city to the east. A huge, hall-like structure, like that of the Dominicans, it has been heavily restored after damage by fire in 1655 and subsequent use as a barracks. Its remaining art works include fragmentary frescoes by Pietro and Ambrogio Lorenzetti: a *Crucifixion* (1331) by Pietro in the first chapel to the left of the high altar and two collaborative frescoes in the third chapel (the latter depicting *St Louis of Toulouse becoming a Franciscan* and the graphic *Martyrdom of Six Franciscans at Ceuta in Morocco*). It's also worth hunting down the detached fresco right of the entrance door, its choir of angels part of a *Coronation of the Virgin* (1447) by Sassetta that once decorated the city's original Porta Romana. It was completed by Sano di Pietro, a pupil of Sassetta, after the master contracted a fatal chill while working outdoors on the fresco.

If you walk to the end of the right (south) aisle, you'll find the fourteenth-century **Tomba dei Tolomei**, the best of the church's many funerary monuments. It houses various scions of the Tolomei, one of Siena's grandest medieval families. The clan provided numerous of the city's bankers, as well as some of its leading churchmen, among them Bernardo Tolomei, founder of the abbey at Monte Oliveto Maggiore (see p.298). Also buried here is Pia de' Tolomei, first wife of Baldo Tolomei who came to live in Siena after his marriage to his second wife. Pia died, consumed with jealousy, in a castle in the Maremma, prompting Dante's famous reference to her in the *Purgatorio*: *Siena me fé, disfecemi Maremma* ("Siena made me, the Maremma unmade me").



## Oratorio di San Bernardino and Museo Diocesano

In the piazza to the right of San Francesco as you face the church, adjoining the cloisters, is the **Oratorio di San Bernardino** (mid-March to Oct Mon–Sat 10.30am–1.30pm & 3–5.30pm; closed the rest of the year; €3, joint tickets see p.268). The best art works here are in the beautifully wood-panelled upper chapel: fourteen large frescoes by Sodoma, Beccafumi and Girolamo del Pacchia on the *Life of the Virgin*, painted between 1496 and 1518 when the former pair were Siena's leading painters. In the lower chapel are seventeenth-century scenes of the saint's life, which was taken up by incessant travel throughout Italy, preaching against usury, denouncing the political strife between the Italian city-states and urging his audience to look for inspiration to the monogram of Christ. Sermons in the Campo, it is said, frequently went on for the best part of a day. Bernadino's actual political influence was fairly marginal but he was canonized within six years of his death in 1444, and remains one of the most famous of all Italian preachers. His dictum on rhetoric – "make it clear, short and to the point" – was rewarded in the 1980s with his adoption as the patron saint of advertising.

Attached to the Oratorio is the **Museo Diocesano** (same hours and tickets), which contains an array of devotional art from the thirteenth to the seventeenth century; the pieces are beautifully displayed, but as a collection it ranks well below the Museo dell'Opera del Duomo.

## L'Osservanza

If your interest in Bernardino extends to a short pilgrimage, take bus #12 from Piazza Matteotti to Madonnina Rossa (10–15min), from where it's a short walk uphill to the monastery of **L'Osservanza** (daily 9am–1pm & 4–7pm; free). This was founded by Bernardino in 1423 in an attempt to restore the original

Franciscan rule, by then corrupted in the cities. Much rebuilt since, the monastery has a small museum and a largely Renaissance church, whose features include an Andrea della Robbia *Annunciation* and a triptych by Sano di Pietro.

# Eating and drinking

Siena feels distinctly provincial after Florence. The main action of an evening is the *passeggiata* from Piazza Matteotti along Banchi di Sopra to the Campo – and there's not much in the way of nightlife to follow. For most visitors, though, an evening in one of the city's **restaurants** provides diversion enough, while the presence of the university ensures a bit of life in the **bars**, as well as a cluster of cheaper *trattorie* alongside the restaurants.

## Restaurants

Siena used to have a poor reputation for restaurants but over the last few years things have improved, with a range of imaginative *osterie* opening up and a general hike in standards. The only place you need surrender gastronomic ideals is for a meal out in the Campo: the posh restaurant here, *Il Campo*, isn't worth the money – though it's the one to go for if you want to eat in style in the square – which leaves a choice of routine but reasonably priced *pizzerie*. For cheaper meals, you'll generally do best walking out a little from the centre, west towards San Niccolò al Carmine, or north towards the Porta Camollia.

▲ Café, Piazza del Campo

**Local specialities** include *pici* (noodle-like pasta with toasted breadcrumbs), *salsicce secche* (dried sausages), *finocchiona* (minced pork flavoured with fennel), *capolocci* (spiced loin of pork), *pappa col pomodoro* (bread and tomato soup), *tortino di carciofi* (artichoke omelette) and *fagioli all'uccelletto* (bean and sausage stew). The city is also famous for a whole range of **cakes and biscuits**, including the ubiquitous *panforte*, a dense and delicious wedge of nuts, fruit and honey that originated with pilgrimage journeys, *cavallucci* (aniseed, nut and spice biscuits), *copate* (nougat wafers) and rich, almond *ricciarelli* biscuits.

All these restaurants are located on the map on pp.266–267.

**Al Marsili Via del Castoro 3 ⓣ0577.47.154, ⓦwww.ristorantealmarsili.it.** A large, elegant and upmarket restaurant with good local dishes (including some choice for vegetarians) and attentive service. The *risotto al limone* is worth dallying over, plus they have plenty of more exotic dishes such as guinea fowl with prunes, pine nuts and almonds. Around €40 buys a memorable meal.

**Antica Osteria Da Divo Via Franciosa 29 ⓣ0577.286.054.** A close second behind *Osteria Le Logge* for ambience, thanks to its extraordinary subterranean cellar dining rooms. Upstairs is pretty, too, and the food is well above average, with starters at around €8–12 and mains at €15–24. Closed Tues.

**Cane e Gatto Via Pagliaresi 6 ⓣ0577.220.751.** Don't be put off by the un-Sienese Art Nouveau-style decor: this friendly restaurant serves superb Tuscan *cucina nuova*, featuring seven courses on its *menù degustazione*, or tasting menu: this will cost you around €75, with a selection of wines included. Located southeast of the Campo, off Via di Pantaneto. Open evenings only; closed Thurs.

**Da Trombicche Via delle Terme 66 ⓣ0577.288.089.** A tiny, youthful no-nonsense trattoria with a limited menu of glorified snacks – soup, cheese, salami and meat stews – accompanied by rough wine served straight from the barrel. Light meals from €10. Closed Sun.

**Gallo Nero Via del Porrione ⓣ0577.284.356, ⓦwww.gallonero.it.** Quirky, vaulted place, offering a Tuscan menu for around €18, or a six-course medieval menu for twice that, boasting dishes such as bittersweet duck with cheese ravioli and chicken in sweet wine with fruit. Daily except Mon from Nov–Feb.

**La Cina Casato di Sotto 56 ⓣ0577.283.061.** Quiet, affordable Chinese restaurant 150m from the Campo. The food is adequate, and makes a change from Tuscan cooking. It's also cheap – around €10–15 for a decent selection of dishes.

**La Taverna del Capitano Via del Capitano 8 ⓣ0577.288.094.** A stone's throw from the Duomo, this is a serene dining room with a medieval vaulted ceiling and straight-down-the-line Tuscan cooking: *panzanella* (bread salad), *pici*, *pappardelle*, *bistecche* and the like. Reports suggest the once impeccable food and service can slip in the face of large numbers of would-be diners. Closed Tues.

**Le Campane Via delle Campane 6 ⓣ0577.284.035.** High-quality and innovative Sienese cuisine, with an emphasis on fish and seafood, at a small, formal restaurant just below the Duomo. Set menus – *di terra* or *di mare* – cost around €45. Closed Mon.

**Osteria Boccone del Prete Via di San Pietro 17 ⓣ0577.280.388.** One of Siena's newer restaurants, near the Pinacoteca Nazionale, serving delicious *crostini*, salads and pasta dishes in a stylish setting. Reckon on €25 for a meal. Closed Sun.

**Osteria Castelvecchio Via di Castelvecchio 65 ⓣ0577.49.586.** Adventurous, first-rate and nicely informal *osteria* – a good bet for vegetarians (plus plenty of meat dishes and home-made pasta too). Moderately priced menus change daily. Sited off Via San Pietro, near the Pinacoteca Nazionale. Closed Tues & July.

**Osteria del Ficomezzo Via dei Termini 71 ⓣ0577.222.384.** A small, simple *osteria* a touch off the tourist track with a cool, pastel interior: good value set-price menus at lunch, with innovative Tuscan food (menus change weekly), and pricier à la carte in the evening. Closed Sun.

**Osteria Il Carroccio Via del Casato di Sotto 32 ⓣ0577.41.165.** Just 50m from the Campo, though many tables – room for forty inside and twenty outside. Serves fine Tuscan food in a welcoming informal atmosphere. Menus change weekly. Around €25 should buy you a good lunch or dinner. Closed Wed.

**Osteria Il Grattacielo Via Pontani 8** ⓣ**0577.289.326.** A very local *vinaio* serving wine and snacks, this minuscule cafe-*osteria* – ironically named "The Skyscraper" – makes a popular lunch stop for its marinated anchovies, Tuscan beans and salami. Dishes cost just a few euros each. Closed Sun.

**Osteria Le Logge Via del Porrione 33** ⓣ**0577.48.013.** The best-looking restaurant in central Siena, occupying a fine old cabinet-lined *farmacia* off the Campo by the Loggia del Papa. Good pasta and some unusual *secondi*, but the quality of food – once exceptional – is these days merely above average. Closed Sun.

**Trattoria Garibaldi Via Giovanni Dupré 18.** A cheap and basic trattoria sited alongside the hotel of the same name, just south of the Campo. Closed Sat.

**Tullio ai Tre Cristi Vicolo Provenzano 1** ⓣ**0577.280.608.** A Sienese institution since 1830, this is the traditional neighbourhood restaurant of the Giraffa *contrada* – though its prices these days are those of a top-end estalishment. A good, if smart place for a romantic meal or treat. Serves an ambitious, predominantly fish and seafood menu. Terrace tables in summer. Closed Wed.

### Bars and clubs

There are pleasant neighbourhood **bars** in most *contrade* and plenty of neon-lit modern establishments scattered around the city for quick refreshment. The *Enoteca Italiana* (Mon noon–8pm, Tues–Sat noon–1am; ⓣ0577.288.497, ⓦwww.enoteca-italiana.it; free), inside the Fortezza di Santa Barbara, is Italy's largest national **wine** collection. Its cellar stocks and exhibits every single Italian winc (almost a thousand of them), and there's a bar where you can order a glass of any of the cheaper wines, or buy any bottle. You need to head to the *Dublin Post*, uninspiringly situated on Piazza Gramsci, or *Barone Rosso*, at Via dei Termini 9, for a pint of beer, the latter open in the evenings only with live music until late. Of the terrace cafés ringing the Campo, the small *Liberamente* at the corner of Casato dei Barbieri has more charm than most.

**Club** life is fairly limited in Siena but for a glimpse of the smart Sienese on the dance floor try *Al Cambio*, at Via di Pantaneto 48 – a dark, moody place with conventional dance music and a steep entrance fee; somewhat livelier is the pub/disco *Barone Rosso*, the local haunt of foreign students and Sienese army boys, with a fair selection of beers and a range of dance music. The *Walkabout Pub*, at Via di Pantaneto 90, is a predictable "Aussie" pub with Sky TV for big sports events and Australian and British beers.

## Entertainment

City **events and festivals** are advertised on posters around Piazza Matteotti and in the Campo backstreets; the website ⓦwww.terresiena.it is also a good source of information. Classical music tastes are the most likely to be rewarded, as the Monte dei Paschi and Accademia Chigiana (ⓣ0577.22.091, ⓦwww.chigiana.it) sponsor impressive concerts throughout the year. The Siena supplement of *La Nazione* newspaper (ⓦwww.lanazione.it) has a what's on section. The most prestigious classical music festival – often featuring a major opera production – is July and August's **Estate Musicale Chigiana**. Other cultural events include **Siena Jazz** (ⓣ0577.271.401, ⓦwww.sienajazz.it) in late July and August (concerts are held in venues around the city and local towns and villages) and the modest but increasingly popular **Siena Film Festival** (ⓣ0577.222.999, ⓦwww.sienafilmfestival.it) in September.

# Listings

**Bike rental** DF Bike, some way from the centre at Via Massetana Romana 54 ☎0577.271.905, ⓦwww.dfbike.it; €15 daily, €85 weekly. Also Perozzi Automotocicli, at Via del Gazzani 16 ☎0577.223.157, ⓦwww.perozzi.it; €10 daily, €50 weekly.
**Car rental** Avis, at Via Simone Martini 36 ☎0577.270.305; Hertz, at Viale Sardegna 37 ☎0577.45.085.
**Guided tours** Walks and tours around the city and beyond can be booked through Siena Hotels Promotion, at Piazza Madre Teresa di Calcutta (☎0577.288.084, ⓦwww.hotelsiena.com).
**Hospital** Loc. Le Scotte ☎0577.585.111.
**Internet access** Internet Train, at Via di Città 121 and Via Pantaneto 54; MegaWeb, at Via Pantaneto 132; Interfast Net, at Via Casato di Sotto 1. All have long opening hours and charge around €1.50 for 15min (less for students).
**Laundry** Wash & Dry, at Via Pantaneto 38 (daily 8am–9pm); OndaBlu, at Casato di Sotto 17 (daily 8am–10pm); both are self-service.
**Left luggage** At the TRA-IN bus information centre below Piazza Gramsci (daily 7am–7.45pm; €3.50 per piece for one day only). At the train station, there are self-service lockers on platform 1.
**Lost property** Comune di Siena, at Casato di Sotto 23 (Mon–Fri 9am–12.30pm, Tues & Thurs also 3–5pm).
**Market** A huge weekly market sprawls over La Lizza (Wed 8am–1pm).
**Police** The *Questura* is on Via del Castoro ☎0577 201.111.
**Post office** Piazza Matteotti 1 (Mon–Sat 8.15am–7pm).
**Taxi** Radio Taxi ☎0577.49.222; taxis wait on Piazza Matteotti.

# Sienese hill-towns

The region south of Siena is Tuscany at its best: an infinite gradation of hills, trees and cultivation that encompasses the vineyards of Montepulciano and Montalcino, and the crete Senesi. The **crete**, especially, is fabulous: a sparsely populated region of pale clay hillsides, dotted with sheep, cypresses and the odd monumental-looking farmhouse.

The towns on the whole live up to this environment. **Montepulciano** is the most elegant, with its independent hill-town life, acclaimed Vino Nobile wine and backdrop of Renaissance buildings and public spaces that includes the stunning Piazza Grande and an art-filled Duomo. **Montalcino**, too, is an excellent base, filled with churches, museums and overlooked by an imposing Medici fortress. Like Montepulcinao, it also has some highly appealing wines (its Brunello is regarded as Tuscany's finest vintage) and a classic hill-town appearance. **Pienza** is smaller but perhaps even more charming, though it's often too busy with visitors in high season for its own good. A unique Renaissance monument, it is a town created by the great humanist pope, Pius II, though your most enduring memories of the place are likely to be of the glorious views from Pienza's walls over the crete.

**Monasteries** are a major attraction of the area, and feature some of the greatest houses of the medieval Italian orders, notably the Benedictine **Monte Oliveto Maggiore** and **Sant'Antimo**. Both are tremendous buildings, encompassing some of the best Romanesque and Gothic church architecture in Italy.

**Getting around** the region by public transport is relatively easy, at least by **bus**: regular services from Siena serve Pienza (5 daily; 1hr 30min), Montalcino (6 daily; 1hr 10min) and Montepulciano (7–8 daily; 1hr 45min). Around seven buses daily also run between the three towns, though for services to and from Montalcino you usually have to change at Buonconvento, which is also the main axis of the **rail** network locally. About ten trains daily (30min) run to the town from Siena, though it is easier to reach Montepulciano by train from Florence and the regular services from the Tuscan capital to Chiusi, from where there are good bus connections to Montepulciano.

## Montalcino

**MONTALCINO**, 37km south of Siena, is a classic Tuscan hill-town, set within a full circuit of walls and watched over by a castle of almost fairy-tale perfection. A quiet, immediately likeable place, affluent in an unshowy way, it is scarcely changed in appearance since the sixteenth century. It looks wonderful from below, its walls barely sullied by any modern building, and once up in the town

## Monte Oliveto Maggiore

The **Abbazia di Monte Oliveto Maggiore** is Tuscany's grandest monastery, sited 26km southeast of Siena in one of the most beautiful tracts of Sienese countryside, and home to one of the most absorbing Renaissance **frescoes** you'll find anywhere. It can be seen en route to Montalcino, or as part of a meandering but very scenic drive between Montalcino and Pienza. If you are using **public transport**, the nearest you can get to the abbey is Buonconvento, 9km to the southwest, which you can reach by bus or train from Siena or points to the south such as Montalcino.

When Pope Pius II visited in 1463, it was the overall scene that impressed him: the architecture, in honey-coloured Sienese brick, merging into the woods and gardens that the **Olivetan** or White Benedictine monks had created from the eroded hills of the crete. Within six years, the pope recognized the order and over the following two centuries this, their principal house, was transformed into one of the most powerful monasteries in the land. It was only in 1810, when the monastery was suppressed by Napoleon, that it fell from influence. Today it's maintained by a small group of Olivetan monks, who supplement their state income with a high-tech centre for the restoration of ancient books. At the gatehouse, an avenue of cypresses leads to the abbey. Signs at the bottom of the slope direct you along a walk to **Blessed Bernardo's grotto** – a chapel built on the site where the founder lived as a hermit.

The **abbey** (daily 9.15am–noon & 3.15–6pm; winter closes 5pm; free) is a huge complex, though much of it remains off-limits to visitors. The entrance leads to the **Chiostro Grande**, covered by a series of frescoes depicting the Life of St Benedict, the man traditionally regarded as the founder of Christian monasticism. The cycle begins on the east wall, just on the right of the door into the church, and was begun in 1497 by Luca Signorelli, who painted nine panels in the middle of the series that start with the depiction of a collapsing house. The colourful Antonio Bazzi, known as Il Sodoma, painted the remaining 27 scenes between 1505 and 1508. He was by all accounts a lively presence, bringing with him part of his menagerie of pets, which included badgers, depicted at his feet in a self-portrait in the third panel. There's a sensuality in many of the secular figures, especially the young men – as befits the artist's nickname – but also the "evil women" (originally nudes, until the abbot protested). The **church** (entered off the Chiostro Grande) was given a Baroque remodelling in the eighteenth century and some superb stained glass in the twentieth. Its main treasure is the choir stalls, inlaid by Giovanni di Verona and others with architectural, landscape and domestic scenes (including a nod to Sodoma's pets with a cat in a window). Stairs lead from the cloister up to the **library**, again with carving by Giovanni; sadly, it has had to be viewed from the door since the theft of sixteen of its twenty codices in 1975.

the rolling hills, vineyards, orchards, olive groves and ancient oaks below look equally lovely in turn.

### Some history

Montalcino has probably been inhabited since Paleolithic or Etruscan times. No one is quite sure where its name comes from, though its coat of arms – a holm oak atop six hills – suggests that it derives from the Latin **Mons Ilcinus** (the Mount of the Holm Oak). The first reference to the town appears in 814, when it is mentioned in a list of territories ceded to the abbey of Sant'Antimo by Louis the Pious, the son of Charlemagne (see p.302).

Though independent for much of its early medieval history, the town succumbed to **Sienese rule** in 1260 after the Battle of Montaperti. Its finest hour came in 1555, when on April 21 the venerable Sienese Republic was forced, once and for all, to capitulate to the Medici. A group of Sienese exiles, supported by the French, then formed a last bastion of Sienese power in Montalcino, flying the flag of the old Republic for four years in the face of almost constant attack. This heroic interlude is acknowledged at the Siena Palio, where the Montalcino contingent, under their medieval banner proclaiming "The Republic of Siena in Montalcino", still takes place of honour.

In the following centuries, the town declined to a poor, malaria-stricken village. Although the malaria was eradicated in the nineteenth century, in the 1960s Montalcino was still the poorest locality in Siena. Now it is the second-richest, its change in fortunes due principally to the revival and marketing of its wines, notably the **Brunello**, which is reckoned by many to be the finest in Italy.

## Arrival and information

All roads up to Montalcino, perched 567m above sea level, wind through bucolic swathes of vineyards and pastoral countryside (note the decorative roses grown at the end of many rows of vines): views to all sides are stupendous. Once up at the town, you find yourself on a road that rings the walls. **Buses** from Siena and points in between will stop just below the Rocca if you wish, but terminate in Piazza Cavour at the northern end of Via Mazzini, the main street: either point is convenient for Piazza del Popolo, the centre of town. If you're driving, aim to park either in the small pay **car park** by the Rocca (take the narrow road which strikes through the arch – the Porta al Cassero – in the castle walls) or, alternatively, use the large, free car park below the fortress (take the second turning on the right at the mini-roundabout below the Rocca).

The small **tourist office** is located just up from Piazza del Popolo at Costa del Municipio 8 (Tues–Sun 10am–1pm & 2–5.40pm; ⓣ0577.849.331, ⓦwww.prolocomontalcino.it). Montalcino's weekly **market** is held on Fridays (7am–1pm) in Viale della Libertà.

## Accommodation

Accommodation is severely limited and it's wise to book ahead at almost any time of year. There is only a handful of hotels, though if you have transport you could try one or two tempting places in the countryside nearby. **Private rooms** are more numerous, less expensive and a far better option than in many other places. There are also numerous private rooms and agriturismo rooms in the countryside immediately around town. Details are available from the tourist office.

**Albergo Il Giglio Via Soccorso Saloni 5 ⓣ0577.848.167, ⓦwww.gigliohotel.com.** A long-established hotel in a central, sixteenth-century town house that had seen better days, but has been spruced up and offers pleasant, clean rooms, some with terraces. ❷

**Castello di Velona Località Castello di Velona, Castelnuovo dell'Abate ⓣ0577.800.101, ⓦwww.castellodivelona.it.** Until 2001 this twelfth-century "castle" was little more than a pile of rubble: now it is a superb twenty-room, four-star hotel, isolated in lovely open countryside on its own hill and ringed by cypresses. It's close to Castelnuovo dell'Abate and Sant'Antimo, about 10km south of Montalcino. Expensive, but rates drop to €210 In low season and there are often web deals. ❽

**Dei Capitani Via Lapini 6 ⓣ0577.847.227, ⓦwww.deicapitani.it.** A good three-star choice, with the bonus of a small swimming pool. The 29 rooms vary, however: some are smallish and have no view; others look out over marvellous countryside. Ask to see a selection. ❹

**Vecchia Oliviera Via Landi 1 ⓣ0577.846.028, ⓦwww.vecchiaoliviera.com.** Like *Dei Capitani*, a relatively new three-star hotel, but more expensive and not quite as central as its rival. However, it has a pool, its patio has excellent views, and the eleven fine rooms form part of a well-restored former olive mill close to Porta Cerbaia and the walls. Rooms, however, can suffer from noise from the road nearby. ❹

## The Town

Wherever you end up staying, the triangular **Piazza del Popolo** lies only a few minutes' walk away. An odd little square, it is set beneath the elongated medieval tower of the **Palazzo dei Priori**, or Palazzo Comunale (1292), apparently modelled on Siena's Palazzo Pubblico. Crests of long-forgotten dignitaries dot the walls, while the statue (1564) beneath the portico, surprisingly, represents the reviled Medici ruler, Cosimo I – it was sculpted just five years after Montalcino had surrendered to the Florentines.

Occupying other sides of the square are an elegant Renaissance double **loggia**, almost a reprimand in proportional architecture, and a wonderful

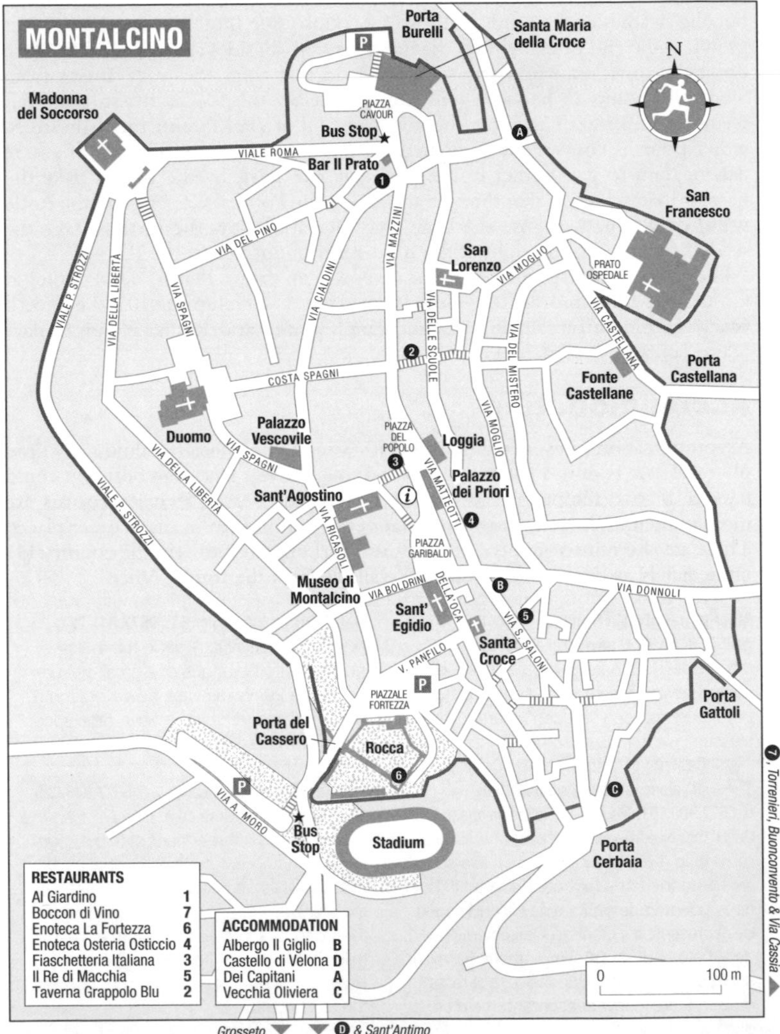


| RESTAURANTS | |
|---|---|
| Al Giardino | 1 |
| Boccon di Vino | 7 |
| Enoteca La Fortezza | 6 |
| Enoteca Osteria Osticcio | 4 |
| Fiaschetteria Italiana | 3 |
| Il Re di Macchia | 5 |
| Taverna Grappolo Blu | 2 |

| ACCOMMODATION | |
|---|---|
| Albergo Il Giglio | B |
| Castello di Velona | D |
| Dei Capitani | A |
| Vecchia Oliviera | C |

▲ View from Montalcino

nineteenth-century **café**, the *Fiaschetteria Italiana* (closed Thurs Nov–Feb). The café is the heart of town life and the focus, inevitably, of the *passeggiata* along Via Mazzini.

## The Rocca

Following Via Mazzini's continuation, Via Matteotti, or Via Ricasoli, and curving up to the right, you emerge at the south end of town by the **Rocca** fortress (April to last Sun in Oct daily 9am–8pm; Nov–March Tues–Sun 9am–6pm; free). The castle was begun in 1361 on the orders of the Sienese, but by the end of the fifteenth century the advent of artillery had left it all but redundant – not that this discouraged those who defended it during sieges in 1526, 1553 and 1555. The ramparts were added by Cosimo I in 1571, together with the large Medici crest (a shield with six balls), whose present peripheral position – tucked away at the back above the road junction – is surely no accident.

Impressively intact, the walls enclose a public park and in-house **enoteca** (Ⓦ www.enotecalafortezza.it) – a reasonable place to sample some of the famed Brunello along with bread, cheese and salami (though at times it becomes hectic and uncomfortably clogged with tourists). The *enoteca* also sells tickets for access to the **ramparts** (€4, joint ticket with Museo Civico €6) and a glimpse of the famous banner. The castle view is said to have inspired Leonardo's drawing of a bird's-eye view of the earth; the Val d'Órcia is easily made out and on a clear day you can even see Siena.

## The Museo di Montalcino

Heading north down Via Ricasoli brings you to the excellent **Museo di Montalcino e Raccolta Archeologica Mediovale e Moderna** (Tues–Sun: April–Dec 10am–6pm; Jan–March 10am–1pm & 2–5.30pm; €4.50, or €6 joint ticket with the Rocca), built in the former seminary of Sant'Agostino. Like many galleries in the region, the quality of the paintings on show is out of all proportion to the size of the town. Montalcino's begins with a superb *Crucifixion* dating from the end of the twelfth century – one of the oldest pieces of Sienese art in existence. An anonymous work, it was originally hung in the abbey at Sant'Antimo. Bartolo di Fredi has two works on show: an oddly narrow *Deposition* and a more conventional *Coronation of the Virgin*. There's also a *Madonna and Child* by Bartolo's collaborator, Luca di Tommè.

One of the gallery's most interesting works is the *Madonna dell'Umiltà* (Madonna of Humility) by Sano di Pietro, a comparatively rare subject, in which the Virgin is shown sitting or kneeling on a simple cushion rather than poised on a throne or chair. Its appearance dates from the early fourteenth century, and coincided with the ideas promulgated by radical Franciscans, who advocated a return to the more rigorous and humble outlook of the first Franciscans. Two paintings by Girolamo di Benvenuto (1470–1524) also merit a close look: an *Adoration of the Shepherds* (with ugly shepherd and fractious Child) and the more spectacular and unusual *Madonna della Cintola*. The latter concerns the Apostle Thomas, who according to legend cast doubt on the Assumption into Heaven of the Virgin (hence "doubting Thomas"). To assuage his worries he opened her tomb, which he found covered in flowers – beautifully depicted in this painting. Casting his eyes upwards, he then saw the Virgin, who removed her belt, or girdle (*cintola*), and let it fall into the hands of the kneeling Thomas. The subject was particularly popular in Tuscany – Agnolo Gaddi, for example, devoted an entire fresco cycle to the theme in Prato, which claims to have the girdle in question (see p.216).



## Sant'Antimo

It's a moot point which of Tuscany's many abbeys is the most beautiful, has the most fascinating history, or boasts the loveliest setting, but many would put the **Abbazia di Sant'Antimo** (Mon–Sat 10.15am–12.30pm & 3–6.30pm, Sun 9.15–10.45am & 3–5pm; free; www.antimo.it) near the top of their list. You really need a car to get here, though there are very occasional buses along the Sant'Antimo road (usually two a day Monday–Friday, one on Saturday) from Montalcino. It's a glorious, isolated Benedictine monastery a short distance from the hamlet of Castelnuovo dell'Abate, 10km south of Montalcino. Splendidly isolated in a timeless landscape of fields, olive groves and wooded hills, the abbey stood empty for some five hundred years, and is today maintained by a small group of French monks who celebrate Mass several times daily in haunting Gregorian chant.

Tradition ascribes the foundation of the abbey to **Charlemagne**, who, while returning with his army from Rome in 781, halted in the nearby Starcia valley. If this sounds too good to be true, it is known that the abbey existed in 814, when Charlemagne's son, **Louis the Pious**, enriched it with vast tracts of land and privileges. Over the two centuries that followed, the abbey's importance grew, thanks in part to its location close to the intersection of several of central Italy's most important medieval trade and pilgrimage routes.

Sant'Antimo's heyday dates from 1118, when an enormous bequest allowed work to begin on the main body of the present church and a complex of monastic buildings (now largely lost). The grant's original deed – a document many hundreds of words long – was engraved in the steps of the altar, where it survives to this day. With new-found funds, the abbey authorities now had access to expertise from elsewhere in Europe, and looked for inspiration to the great Benedictine mother house at Cluny, in Burgundy, and to **French architects**, whose plans for the new church appear to have been based on the abbey church of Vignory (begun in 1050) in the Haute-Marne. After 1492, however, when Montalcino's bishops opted to live in the town instead, the complex was largely abandoned, its buildings ransacked for stone for use in Castelnuovo and Montalcino. What remained was bought by the state in 1867.

### Churches

Walking a few paces up Via Ricasoli from the museum brings you to the church of **Sant'Agostino**, a severe Gothic-Romanesque affair begun in 1360. The barn-like single nave is dotted with patches of fresco, the most extensive of which cover the arched presbytery, and are probably the work of Bartolo di Fredi. The most interesting pictures, however, are two anonymous panels of *Scenes from the Passion*. One, on the left wall, shows St Anthony Abbot sharing bread with a curiously attired St Augustine; the second, to the right of the side entrance, is an almost surreal collection of disembodied heads and symbols. Note the moon and sun, which in paintings of the Passion or Crucifixion serve, among other things, to symbolize the anguish of all creation at the death of Christ.

To the northwest, Via Spagni takes you past the **Duomo**, or San Salvatore, an eleventh-century Romanesque church, horrendously remodelled in Neoclassical style between 1818 and 1832; its interior is unarresting, save for an impressive little pyramid of reliefs in the baptistery chapel salvaged from the original church. Via Spagni continues to emerge in front of the distinctive Renaissance **Santuario della Madonna del Soccorso**, a seventeenth-century sanctuary built over an ancient chapel; its chief appeal is the sensational view from the adjoining park. Drop down Viale Roma to Piazza Cavour and pop into **Santa Maria della Croce**, a hospital founded in the thirteenth century, more recently appropriated by the local council. Just inside the main entrance is the former pharmacy, still covered in a pretty little array of original frescoes. Nearby, facing the Porta Castellana, is

#### The church

The twelfth-century **church** is in excellent repair and is one of the most outstanding examples of Italian Romanesque, built in a soft, creamy stone and perfectly proportioned. The main **portal** contains a twelfth-century lintel whose Latin text alludes to one Azzo, a monk who may have been one of the original architects of the church. Otherwise the capitals, frieze and fluted arch are all lifted directly from French (Languedoc) models. Around the corner, on the left (north) wall, the little filled-in doorway and lintels survive from the earlier ninth-century church.

The French flavour becomes more marked in the lovely **interior**, whose basilican plan – with an ambulatory and radiating chapels – is unique in Tuscany. The **high altar** features a polychrome statue of the crucified Christ, an outstanding Romanesque work dating from the end of the twelfth century. Note the inscription on the altar steps.

The **capitals** on the pillars of the ambulatory display some exquisite carving, a feature for which the abbey is particularly celebrated. Many are carved in lustrous alabaster, lending a beautifully subtle tone to the walls and sculpture. The finest capital sits atop the second column on the right of the nave. It depicts *Daniel in the Lions' Den*, the protagonist – arms raised in prayer – a study of calm while his fellow prisoners are crushed and eaten by rampant beasts. Clearly superior to anything else in the abbey, it is the work of the so-called **Master of Cabestany**, a sculptor of French or Spanish origin whose distinctive style has been identified in abbeys across France, Catalonia and Italy.

The **sacristy** occupies part of the ninth-century Carolingian church, entered (when open), from a door in the right aisle. It features an array of primitive black-and-white frescoes with such details as a rat looking up attentively at St Benedict, and a pair of copulating pigs. Further frescoes are to be found in some of the rooms built around the **women's gallery**, fitted out in the fifteenth century by the bishops of Montalcino: it's approached from the nave by a circular stairway, though here, too, access is often restricted.

a medieval washhouse, the **Fonte Castellane**, and beyond it the deconsecrated church of **San Francesco**, graced with pleasant cloisters, della Robbia school terracottas and an annexe that was once a medieval hospital.

## Eating and drinking

Montalcino is remarkably blessed with good **restaurants**, and you'll be hard-pushed to have a bad meal in any of them. In summer it's worth booking a table at any of the following places. It's even more blessed with small **wine bars** where you can sample and buy Brunello and other local wines. Be warned, though, that the rate of turnover is high, with more opening (and closing) each year.

**Al Giardino** **Piazza Cavour 1 ⓣ0577.849.076, ⓦwww.ristorantealgiardino.it.** Pleasant interior, with good local cooking that has won the approval of the Slow Food movement: the chef is the owner. You'll spend about €30 for a three-course meal, excluding wine. Closed Sun.

**Boccon Di Vino** **Località Colombaio Tozzi 201 ⓣ0577.848.233.** A kilometre east of town on the Torrenieri road, this is a great wine bar and restaurant with superb views and a lovely summer terrace. It's housed in an old rural property, and the dining rooms have a rustic air. Food, though, is more refined – and expensive: reckon on €40 or so for a full meal. Closed Tues.

**Enoteca Osteria Osticcio** **Via G. Mattteotti 23 ⓣ0577.848.271, ⓦwww.osticcio.com.** The smartest of Montalcino's many wine bars, but worth paying a little over the odds for your glass of Brunello and light meal simply to enjoy the spectacular views over the Tuscan countryside. Closed Sun.

**Fiaschetteria Italiana** **Piazza del Popolo 6 ⓣ0577.849.043.** This central wine bar, popular with locals, has been around for years – well before Brunello's rise to fame – and is still one of the most convenient and easy-going places for a glass of wine and a light snack.

**Il Re di Macchia** **Via Soccorso Saloni 21 ⓣ0577.846.116.** Montalcino's swankiest restaurant. While the food is usually excellent, its sometimes pretentious *cucina nuova* leanings may not be to all tastes. Meals from around €30–35. Closed Thurs.

**Taverna Grappolo Blu** **Via Scale di Moglio 1 ⓣ0577.847.150.** Located in a little alley off Via Mazzini. The old stone-walled interior is cool and appealing, and the pastas are excellent. Meals from around €25.

## Moving on

TRA-IN **buses** (ⓣ0577.204.111, ⓦwww.trainspa.it) run more or less hourly from Piazza Cavour and Viale P. Strozzi to Buonconvento and Siena via Torrenieri. At Torrenieri you can pick up one of six daily buses to San Quírico, Pienza and Montepulciano. There are four local buses daily from Montalcino to Sant'Angelo Scalo (ⓦwww.bargagliautolinee.it). Bus tickets are available from tobacconists around town, and from the *Bar Il Prato* on the corner ofViale Roma and Piazza Cavour.

For **train connections** to Siena, head to Buonconvento, Torrenieri or Sant'Angelo.

# Pienza

**PIENZA**, 20km east of Montalcino, is as complete a Renaissance creation as any in Italy, conceived as a Utopian "New Town" by **Pope Pius II**, Aeneas Sylvius Piccolomini (see p.275). The site Pius chose was the village of Corsignano where he was born in 1405, the first of eighteen children of a noble family exiled from Siena in 1385 (the village, at least in part, formed part of the Piccolominis' traditional feudal domain). Today there's little to see beyond Pius's central Renaissance piazza – the pope's death marked the end of his beloved project – though few places in Tuscany have as much immediate charm. There are also some extraordinary **views** from the walls, a scattering of good bars and restaurants, and a range of accommodation – including a fine historic hotel – if you want to stay.

### A brief history

The construction of Pienza began in 1459, less than a year after Pius's election to the papacy. His architect on the project was **Bernardo Rossellino**, who worked on all the major buildings here under the guidance of Leon Battista Alberti, the great theorist of Renaissance art, building and town planning.

Rossellino's commission was to build a cathedral, papal palace and town hall, but Pius instructed the various cardinals who followed his court to build their own residences too, turning the project into nothing less than a Vatican in miniature. Astonishingly, the cathedral, the papal and bishop's palaces, and the core of the town were completed in just three years. Limited though it was, it constituted the first "Ideal City" of the Renaissance to become a reality.

After consecration of the cathedral, Pius issued a papal bull rechristening the "city" Pienza, in his own honour, and stipulating that no detail of the cathedral or palaces should be changed. The wish was fulfilled rather more easily than he could have expected, for he died within two years, and of his successors only Pius III, his nephew, paid Pienza any regard. The city, intended to spread across the hill, never grew beyond a couple of blocks to either side of the main Corso, and its population remained scarcely that of a village.

## Arrival and information

Pienza is a pleasant place to stay, but there's not much life after dark, so it might also be considered as a day-trip from Montepulciano. TRA-IN **buses** cover the routes to Buonconvento and Siena (7 daily) and Montepulciano (9 daily); for details of times, call in at the helpful **tourist office** (ⓣ0578.749.305, ⓦwww.comunepienza.it; mid-March to Oct Mon–Sat 10am–1pm & 3–6pm or later; Nov to mid-March Sat & Sun 10am–1pm, 3–5/6pm) on the Corso in the Museo Diocesano.

## Accommodation

Accommodation is limited: the *Ristorante dal Falco* at Piazza Dante 8 (ⓣ0578.748.551; ❷) has six rooms, each with bathroom, but they're quickly snapped up. Much more expensive is the modern but very pleasant three-star *Hotel Il Corsignano*, at Via della Madonnina 11, about 150m west of the piazza on the left (ⓣ0578.748.501, ⓦwww.corsignano.it; ❸): rooms at the back have little terraces and something of a view. If you're doing Tuscany in style, or fancy a treat, the obvious choice is the three-star *Il Chiostro di Pienza*, at Corso Rossellino 26 (ⓣ0578.748.400, ⓦwww.relaisilchiostrodipienza.com; ❺), though it often has large groups staying. The only in-town hotel, it's an extremely stylish conversion – complete with frescoes, vaults and other medieval trappings – which has been infiltrated into the old cloister and buildings of a Franciscan monastery.

## The Town

It's easy to find your way around Pienza. Roads, buses and cars converge on the **Piazza Dante**, just outside the Porta al Murello, main entrance gate to the papal

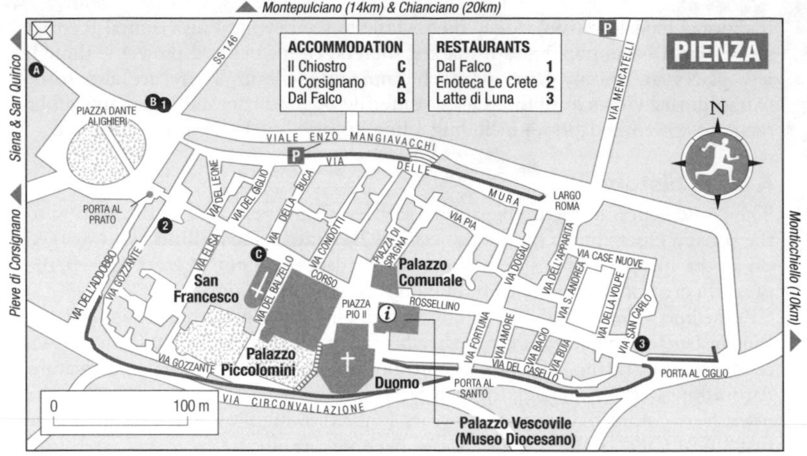




town. From here the Corso Rossellino leads to Rossellino's centrepiece, **Piazza Pio II**, enclosed by the Duomo, Palazzo Piccolomini, Palazzo Comunale and Palazzo Vescovile.

## Piazza Pio II

The juxtaposition of civic and religious buildings in the **Piazza Pio II** was deliberate, and aimed to underline the balance between Church and town through architectural harmony. Apart from the Palazzo Comunale, based on the medieval Palazzo Vecchio in Florence, the ensemble is entirely Renaissance in conception. If it all seems a little cramped, it's partly because Rossellino wished to retain the existing east–west axis of Corsignano's main street, and partly because of Pius's insistence that his palace loggia should command a view and that the Duomo should be flooded with light, meaning that the piazza's two key buildings had to be orientated towards the valley to the rear. For the Duomo, in particular, this was to have near-disastrous structural consequences.

The piazza's small well, the **Pozzo dei Cani**, sets the tone, its twin columns and classical frieze a perfect miniature of Renaissance ambitions.

## The Duomo

The **Duomo**, or Santa Maria Assunta (daily 8.15am–12.30pm & 2.30–7.30pm; closed during services; free), has one of the earliest Renaissance facades in Tuscany, its three-tiered veneer of Istrian marble surmounted by a vast garland of fruit enclosing Pius's papal coat of arms. The **campanile**, rocked to its foundations by an earthquake in 1545, was virtually rebuilt in 1570.

On Pius's orders, the **interior** took inspiration from Franciscan Gothic churches and the German *Hallenkirchen*, or hall-churches, which he had seen on his pre-papal travels as a member of the Curia. The hall-churches, as here, were distinguished by naves and aisles of equal height. The tall windows were also a papal whim, designed to produce a *domus vitrea* (hall of glass), whose flood of light was intended to symbolize the age's humanist enlightenment.

To satisfy Pius's whims, and to fit the cramped site, Rossellino had to build on sandstone with a substratum of clay. Before completion a crack appeared, and following an earthquake in the nineteenth century it has required progressively more buttressing and ties. The nave dips crazily towards the back of the church – still shifting at an estimated rate of a millimetre a year – and alarming cracks are still all too obvious, tagged by small glass ties designed to reveal further movement.

Several outstanding and contrasting **altarpieces** – the church's highlights – still fill the principal chapels, each commissioned by the pope and his architect from some of the major painters of the age. Pius's choice of artists was deliberate: each was Sienese, as was he (at least by family origin) – Rossellino, it's worth noting, was from Settignano, just outside Florence. This partisan choice, however, rather undermined Pius's Renaissance credentials, for Florentine painters by this time were far ahead of their more backward-looking Sienese counterparts. Pius's choice of each subject – the Madonna, to whom the church was dedicated – was equally considered, as was the choice of saints included in each painting. Thus St Sabina in Giovanni di Paolo's work was featured because Pius was titular head of the Basilica di Santa Sabina in Rome; St Peter appeared because he was the first pope; and SS Catherine and Bernardino achieved prominence through their Sienese connections.

The first painting, midway down the right (south) wall, is Giovanni di Paolo's *Madonna and Child with SS Bernardino, Anthony Abbot, Francis and Sabina* with a *Pietà* above. The first apse chapel features Matteo di Giovanni's *Madonna and Child with SS Catherine of Alexandria, Matthew, Bartholomew and Lucy* with the *Flagellation*. The next apse contains a travertine tabernacle attributed to Rossellino, behind whose little central door is a **reliquary** containing bones alleged to be those of St Andrew, Pienza's patron saint. Another work by Rossellino, a vast **font**, can be seen in the crypt, along with Romanesque fragments recovered from Santa Maria, the former church near the site. The central apse – normally containing the high altar – is empty, Pius having stipulated that nothing should block the light coming from the central windows. Instead he commissioned the choir (1462), with the telltale papal shield appearing at the top of the central bishop's throne.

The fourth chapel houses a triptych of the *Assumption with SS Agatha, Callistus, Pius I and Catherine of Siena* by Vecchietta, born in nearby Castiglione dell'Órcia: it's considered one of his masterpieces and is by far the finest of the church's altarpieces. The fifth chapel features Sano di Pietro's *Madonna and Child with SS Philip, James, Anne and Mary Magdalene*.

## Palazzo Piccolomini

Pius's residence, the **Palazzo Piccolomini**, to the right of the Duomo, was modelled on Alberti's Palazzo Rucellai in Florence, and built by Rossellino over the demolished remains of the Piccolomini's former feudal holding in the village. All three main facades are identical, novelty being provided by the imaginative addition of a triple-tiered loggia at the back, making it the first Italian building to be designed specifically to afford views over a swathe of countryside. Its cost was astronomical: Rossellino spent fifty thousand gold florins, five times his allotted budget.

For wonderful views, walk into the superb courtyard at any time of day and through (on the left) to the original "hanging garden" behind; it has remained unchanged over the centuries and is the perfect embodiment of the Renaissance concept that gardens form an intermediary between nature and architecture. The loggia, with its three orders of Classical columns (Ionic, Doric and Corinthian), owes a clear debt to the great imperial buildings of ancient Rome.

For a glimpse of the splendour envisaged for Pius, however, you need to climb the steps in the courtyard to the first-floor **papal apartments** (Ⓦ www.palazzopiccolominipienza.it; Tues–Sun mid-March to mid-Oct 10am–6.30pm; rest of the year 10am–4pm, but closed mid-Feb to end of Feb and mid-Nov to end of Nov; open Mon on public holidays; €7), occupied until 1962 by the Piccolomini family.

Guided tours conduct you to Pius II's dining room, library and music room, each filled with furniture, books, carpets and manuscripts. The highlights, though, are the papal bedroom – complete with a gloriously vulgar canopied bed – and the cavernous Sala d'Armi, filled with rows of fearsome pikes and other weapons.

## Palazzo Vescovile and Museo Diocesano

The **Palazzo Vescovile**, or Palazzo Borgia, to the left of the Duomo, now home to the Museo Diocesano, began as a single-storey Gothic palace but was given to Roderigo Borgia by Pius, on condition that he would demolish and rebuild it in a more modern manner. Borgia, then a cardinal, would later become the infamous Pope Alexander VI and father four children, among them the notorious Lucrezia and Cesare Borgia. Showing the astuteness, if not the meanness, that would characterize his papacy, Borgia refrained from knocking down the palace, but saved money by altering a few superficial details and adding an extra storey. Thus on the ground floor – clearly of different vintage – you can still see the outlines of the old Gothic windows, bricked in to form tiny square windows more in keeping with Renaissance ideas. Still more visible are the holes that pockmark the upper part of the building, the legacy of a mortar bombardment during World War II that also knocked chunks out of the cathedral's apse. The highest marks are even older, inflicted by the artillery of Charles V and the Medici during their assault on the Sienese Republic between 1552 and 1559. How much time Borgia spent in the palace is uncertain – though the Borgia arms are clearly visible on the shield on the corner of the building. In any event, it appears he made a gift of the building in 1468, when it became the Palazzo Vescovile, or Bishop's Palace.

Like many small southern Tuscan museums, the **Museo Diocesano** (Wed–Mon mid-March to Oct 10am–1pm & 3–7pm; Nov to mid-March Sat & Sun 10am–1pm & 3–6pm; €4.10), deserves more attention than it receives. Its star attraction is a superb thirteenth- or fourteenth-century *piviale*, or **cope**, an English work of fantastically embroidered silk embellished with scenes from the life of the Virgin and St Catherine of Alexandria, together with various saints and apostles (originally the cope would also have been studded with pearls and precious stones).

The museum also contains superb tapestries, crosiers, miniatures, illuminated manuscripts, choir books with miniatures by Sano di Pietro and a whole slew of top-notch **paintings**. Look out in particular for the *Madonna dell'Umiltà and SS Elizabeth of Hungary and John the Baptist*, an anonymous work (by the "Maestro dell'Osservanza"), so-called because its Madonna is shown seated on a simple oriental carpet rather than the more usual ornate throne. Also outstanding is a famous *Madonna della Misericordia* (c.1364) by Bartolo di Fredi, his first signed and dated work; among the figures sheltered by the vermilion-robed Madonna are the Emperor Charles IV (in red cloak and crown on the right), who visited Siena in 1355 en route for Rome, together with the pope (alongside) and Charles's queen (to the left, crowned, in pink). It seems likely that Siena's Council of Twelve, then in thrall to the emperor, commissioned the work to commemorate the visit.

More eye-catching still is a magnificent 48-panel painting whose tiny anonymous miniatures depict scenes from the life of Christ. It was one of only a handful of surviving "portable" paintings once used by mendicant monks as a preaching aid during their perambulations around the countryside. The picture was brought here from the castle of Spedaletto in the Val d'Órcia, together with a painting often regarded as the first Renaissance Sienese painting: Vecchietta's seminal polyptych of the *Madonna and Child with SS Blaise, Florian, John the Baptist and Nicholas* (1462).

### The rest of the town

A short way down the main street from Piazza Pio II stands the church of **San Francesco**, one of two churches to survive from the original Corsignano, and the only significant medieval building remaining in Pienza. Its walls were once entirely covered in fourteenth-century frescoes, only a few of which (scenes from the life of St Francis) survive in the apse. More remains of the large *Crucifix* on the right, a fourteenth-century work by a follower of Duccio, and the arresting *Madonna della Misericordia* on the left, attributed to Luca Signorelli.

Be certain to take the alley to the left of the church – or those to either side of the Duomo – to gain access to Pienza's **walls**, rebuilt after being razed by the armies of the Medici and Charles V of Spain in 1559. You can see why Pius wanted his loggia, for the views from here are some of the finest from any town in Tuscany. Head east past the Duomo and you come to a lovely series of little **lanes** leading back into the village, each with impossibly twee names – notably Via dell'Amore (street of love) and Via del Bacio (street of the kiss): the names were altered from more warlike ones in the nineteenth century to be more in keeping with the village's Renaissance idea of itself. In the other direction a more rural lane runs out of Piazza Dante along a level ridge past public gardens.

Not to be missed is the ten-minute downhill walk from Piazza Dante (signed off the south side) to the **Pieve di Corsignano** (or San Vito), the village's original parish church, and the place where Pius was baptized. Extremely ancient, it probably dates from the tenth century, and is one of the best Romanesque churches for miles around. The cylindrical tower – used to shelter the townspeople during bandit raids – is highly unusual, as are the carvings above the main and side doors. You can get the key from the farmhouse just behind the church – leave a small tip.

## Eating and drinking

Of the **restaurants**, the best are *Dal Falco* in Piazza Dante (closed Fri), a simple trattoria which offers superb gnocchi and a filling *pecorino alla griglia* (hot cheese wrapped in prosciutto), at around €23 for a full meal; and the excellent, friendly and moderately priced *Latte di Luna*, at Via San Carlo 2–4 (☎0578.748.606; closed Tues and periods in Nov & Feb), blessed with a small terrace for outdoor eating and an ancient well incorporated into the old interior. You can get light meals at the *Enoteca le Crete* in Piazza Martiri, and there's no shortage of **picnic food**: Pienza is the centre of a region producing *pecorino* sheep's cheese, and has gone overboard on *alimentari* and "natural food" shops.

# Montepulciano

One of the highest of the Tuscan hill-towns, **MONTEPULCIANO** is built along a narrow tufa ridge, with a long main street and alleys that drop away to the walls. It's a stunningly good-looking town, full of vistas, odd squares and corners, and endowed with dozens of Renaissance *palazzi* and churches, which embody the state of architecture fifty years after Bernardo Rossellino's pioneering work at Pienza. Largely forgotten in subsequent centuries, the town today makes most of its money from its wine industry, based on the famed **Vino Nobile**, though its tourist profile becomes higher with each passing year.

## Some history

Montepulciano's unusually consistent array of Renaissance *palazzi* and churches is a reflection of its remarkable development after 1511, when, following intermittent alliance with Siena, the town finally threw in its lot with Florence. In that year the Florentines sent **Antonio da Sangallo the Elder** to rebuild the town's gates and walls, which he did so impressively that the council took him on to work on the town hall and a series of churches. The local nobles meanwhile

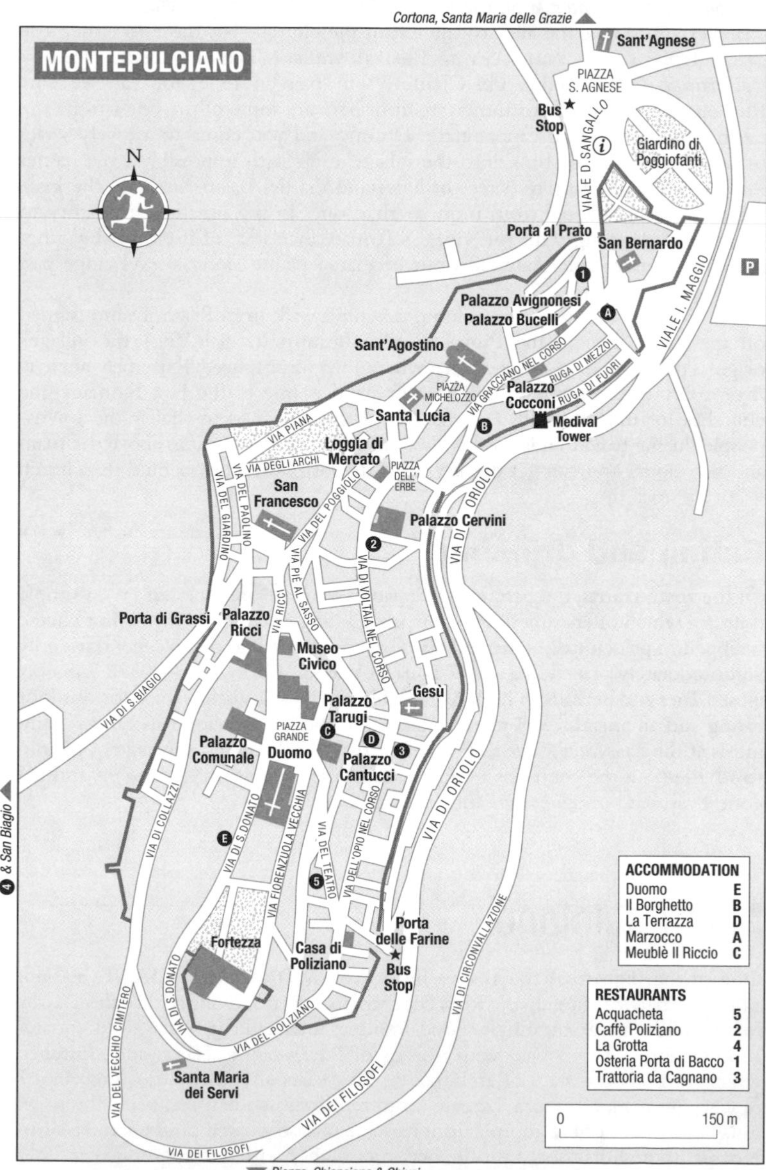

hired him, his nephew, and later the Modena-born architect **Vignola** – a founding figure of Baroque – to work on their own *palazzi*. The work of this trio, assured in both its conception and execution, makes a fascinating comparison with Rossellino's work at Pienza.

## Arrival and information

Montepulciano is on the main **bus** route between Siena and Chiusi, with around fourteen buses daily from the latter (journey time around 45min) and eight daily from the former (1hr 45min). Its **train station** is on the Siena–Chiusi line too, but you'll need a (not always connecting) bus for the 10km trip into town. Regular buses also link with more frequent main-line trains at Chiusi, not much farther away, and a much more efficient way of reaching the town from Florence (there are numerous trains from the city to Chiusi). The buses stop in town at both the north and south gates, the **Porta al Prato** and **Porta di Farine**.

The **tourist office** is towards the lower end of town, close to Sant'Agostino at Via Gracciano nel Corso 59a (April–Oct Mon–Sat 9.30am–12.30pm & 3–7/8pm, Sun 9.30am–12.30pm; Nov–March Mon–Sat 9.30am–12.30pm & 3–6pm, Sun 9.30am–12.30pm; ⓣ0578.757.341, ⓦwww.prolocomontepulciano.it).

## Accommodation

Accommodation is sparse and well worth booking ahead. If you can't get into any of our recommendations, try contacting the tourist office to check on the availability of private rooms or agriturismo options.

**Duomo** **Via San Donato 14 ⓣ&ⓕ0578.757.473, ⓦwww.montepulcianohotels.it/duomo.** A friendly welcome, thirteen spacious and comfortable rooms, three-star facilities and a nice setting off the Piazza Grande make this the town's best upmarket hotel. ❷

**Il Borghetto** **Via Borgo Buio 7 ⓣ0578.757.535, ⓦwww.ilborghetto.it.** Montepulciano's grandest three-star hotel, in a very tastefully refurbished old house off Via Gracciano nel Corso. Just eleven rooms, so be sure to book. ❸

**La Terrazza** **Via Piè al Sasso 16 ⓣ0578.757.440.** Pleasant two-star rooms in an ancient house near the Duomo. ❷

**Marzocco** **Piazza Giralomo Savonarola 18 ⓣ0578.757.262, ⓦwww.albergoilmarzocco.it.** The smartest hotel in town, an elegant nineteenth-century inn with a full-size billiard table. Very courteous owners, but loses out to the *Duomo* on position. ❷

**Meublè Il Riccio** **Ivana Migliorucci, Via Talosa 21 ⓣ0578.757.713, ⓦwww.ilriccio.net.** Five private double rooms, each with private bathroom, TV and phone, off Piazza Grande. ❸

## The Town

The Prato and Farine gates are equally convenient starting points for exploring the town; our account begins at the Porta al Prato. Between the two gates runs the town's main street, the **Corso**, whose name is appended in turn to Via Gracciano, Via di Voltaia and Via dell'Opio. The town's main focus is the **Piazza Grande**, home to the **Duomo** and an ensemble of palaces. To see the town's other big sight, the Renaissance church of **San Biagio**, requires a pleasant ten-minute stroll (downhill) to the west of town.

### The Corso: Porta al Prato to the Fortress

Sangallo's first commission was Montepulciano's main gate, the **Porta al Prato**, at the north end of town. Before embarking on the climb up, you should visit the church of **Sant'Agnese**, named in honour of a local Dominican abbess,

▲ Piazza Grande, Montepulciano

Agnese Segni (1268–1317), who was canonized in 1726 and is buried in the church. The first chapel on the right contains the *Madonna di Zoccoli*, attributed to Simone Martini (or his school), while the second altar on the left features a fourteenth-century Sienese fresco of the *Madonna del Latte*.

Inside the Porta al Prato the **Corso** begins, the *palazzi* immediately making clear the town's allegiance to Florence. In the first square, beside the *Albergo Marzocco*, is the **Colonna del Marzocco**, a stone column bearing the heraldic lion (*marzocco*) of Florence. Across the street further lion heads decorate the **Palazzo Avignonesi** (no. 91), probably the work of Vignola. Sangallo makes a second appearance with the **Palazzo Cocconi** (no. 70), virtually opposite the **Palazzo Bucelli** (no. 73), whose base is strikingly inset with Roman and Etruscan reliefs.

Just beyond this crop of *palazzi* is the eye-catching church of **Sant'Agostino**, designed around 1427 by the earlier Medici protégé, Michelozzo – who also carved the terracotta relief of the *Madonna and Child* above the door; within are a *Crucifixion* on the third altar on the left wall by Lorenzo di Credi and an equally good *St Bernardino* by Giovanni di Paolo on the right wall. Pride of place goes to a polychrome *Crucifix* on the high altar attributed to Donatello. Across the street a medieval **tower-house**, a rare survival in Montepulciano, is surmounted by a *commedia dell'arte* figure of a clown, the **Pulcinella**, who strikes out the hours on the town clock; most un-Tuscan, it is said to have been put up by an exiled bishop from Naples.

About a hundred metres farther along you reach the Renaissance **Loggia di Mercato** and a fork in the roads: turn right here if you want to make straight for the Piazza Grande. The Corso continues to the left past further *palazzi*, including the **Palazzo Cervini**, attributed to Sangallo. Begun for the doomed Marcellus II before he became pope, it is now occupied by a bank, and has the grand civic gesture of an external courtyard. Beyond this, you pass the church of **Gesù**, remodelled in Baroque style by Andrea Pozzo (as are many other churches in the town and region), before the road turns the corner and rambles outside the town walls. Just prior to the turn – at no. 5 – is the **Casa di Poliziano**, birthplace of the Renaissance humanist and poet Angelo Ambrogini (Poliziano), who translated many of the Greek classics under the patronage of Lorenzo de' Medici, as well as teaching the Medici children.

Via di Poliziano loops outside the walls to the Gothic-fronted **Santa Maria dei Servi**, another Baroque interior job by Pozzo. Inside it's visited by devout locals eager to prostrate themselves before the much venerated *Madonna della Santoreggia*, a fifteenth-century fresco (second altar on the left). The only other attention-grabbing work is a *Madonna and Child*, oddly inserted into a larger painting (third altar on the right) by a follower of Duccio. Via di Poliziano then re-enters town by the old **Fortezza**, now partly occupied by houses. At the end of Via di San Donato, the last quiet stretch back into town, you'll find yourself in the cathedral and town hall square, Piazza Grande.

## Santa Lucia, Via del Poggio and the Museo Civico

A quicker approach to Piazza Grande at the Loggia di Mercato would be to head right. A block to the north of here, a beautiful little piazza fronts the church of **Santa Lucia**, built in 1633, which has a fabulous, if damaged, *Madonna* by Luca Signorelli in a chapel on the right, though the church is rarely open. Turning instead to the south, Via del Poggio runs down to the church of **San Francesco**: note the ruined pulpit to the side of the facade, from which St Bernardino of Siena is supposed to have preached. The imposing Via Ricci takes over for the last stretch to the Piazza Grande; it is flanked on one side by the Renaissance **Palazzo Ricci**, and on the other by the Sienese-Gothic **Palazzo Neri-Orselli**.

The latter is home to the town's **Museo Civico** (April–July Tues–Sun & Sept–Oct Tues–Sat 10am–1pm & 3–7pm; Aug daily 10am–7pm; rest of year Tues–Sun 10am–1pm & 3–6pm; €4.13), an extensive collection of small-town Gothic and Renaissance paintings.

## The Piazza Grande

The **Piazza Grande**, Montepulciano's theatrical flourish of a main square, is built on the highest point of the ridge, providing the obvious site for the town's Duomo. Its most distinctive building, however, is the **Palazzo Comunale**, a thirteenth-century Gothic palace to which Michelozzo added a tower and rustication in imitation of the Palazzo Vecchio in Florence. The tower is occasionally open, offering views that on the clearest days stretch to Siena, 65km northwest.

Two of the *palazzi* on the square were designed by Sangallo. The **Palazzo Nobili-Tarugi**, by the lion and griffon fountain, is a highly innovative building, with a public loggia cut through one corner; it originally had an extension on the top floor, though this has been bricked in. The **Palazzo Cantucci**, one of many buildings scattered about the town that serve as *cantine* for the **wine trade**, offers *degustazione* and sale of the Vino Nobile.

## The Duomo

Sangallo and his contemporaries never got around to building a facade for the **Duomo** (daily 9am–1pm & 3.30–7pm; free), whose plain brick pales against the neighbouring *palazzi*. Begun in 1680 by Ippolito Scalzi, the building was raised over an earlier church, of which the ugly fourteenth-century campanile is virtually the only reminder.

The **interior** boasts an elegant Renaissance design, and has several outstanding works of art dotted around its rather foreboding walls. The first of these are fragments of the **tomb of Bartolomeo Aragazzi** (1427–36) by the multi-talented Michelozzo, a monument that was criminally dismembered in the nineteenth century. Aragazzi was born in Montepulciano, and achieved prominence as the secretary to Pope Martin V (pontiff from 1417 to 1431), the first pope to occupy the Holy See in Rome after the Grand Schism (1378–1417) divided the papacy between Rome and Avignon.

Bas-reliefs from the tomb can now be seen at the base of the first two columns on either side of the nave (right and left), and the effigy of Aragazzi himself is mounted on the rear (west) wall to the right of the door. At the other end of the church, two of the tomb's statues surmount the high altar.

Aragazzi also commissioned a painting that would be a highlight of this or any other church: **Taddeo di Bartolo**'s iridescent high altarpiece of the *Assumption*, perhaps the supreme rendition of a subject that was a favourite among Siena's leading artists. Note the apostles gathered around the Virgin's tomb in the main painting: Doubting Thomas is shown receiving the Madonna's girdle (see p.216), while a grief-stricken St John views her flower-decked sepulchre.

Elsewhere in the church, hunt out a work by Vecchietta, best known as a painter but here represented by an excellent piece of sculpture: the marble **ciborium** in the chapel to the right of the high altar. On the left (north) wall of the church, opposite the pillar of the third nave, is a poetic *Madonna del Pilastro* (Madonna of the Pillar) by Sano di Pietro. At the bottom of the north aisle, close to the main remnants of Aragazzi's tomb, the first chapel – the **Baptistery** – contains a wealth of eye-catching art: the font and its six bas-reliefs (1340) are by Giovanni d'Agostino; the riot of glazed terracotta on the wall, the so-called **Altare dei Gigli** (Altar of the Lilies), is by Andrea della Robbia – it frames a relief of the *Madonna and Child* attributed to Benedetto da Maiano.

### San Biagio

Antonio da Sangallo's greatest commission came in 1518, when he was invited by the town's Ricci nobles to design the pilgrimage church of **San Biagio** (daily 9am–noon & 3–6pm) on the hillside below the town. The model for this was his brother Giuliano's design for the facade of San Lorenzo in Florence, which was never built. The Montepulciano project was more ambitious – the only bigger church project of its time was St Peter's in Rome – and occupied Antonio until his death in 1534. He lived to see its inauguration, however (in 1529), with the ceremony performed by the Medici pope Clement VII. To reach the church, follow Via San Biagio out from the Porta di Grassi; it's about fifteen minutes' walk.

The church, built over an earlier chapel to San Biagio (St Blaise), is one of the most harmonious Renaissance creations in Italy, constructed inside and out from a porous travertine, whose soft honey-coloured stone blends perfectly with its niche in the landscape.

## Eating and drinking

**Vino Nobile di Montepulciano** has been acclaimed since medieval times and today boasts a top-rated DOCG mark; something the townspeople have not been shy in exploiting. Montepulciano's streets are filled with wine shops selling gift sets, and local vineyards often offer tastings in the town (generally free, but usually requiring advance notice). Every restaurant can provide a range of vintages, the cheapest of which will still set you back at least €20. The tourist office has a complete list of the town's wine outlets, and can organize a **wine-tasting** ramble. Some of the many places to check out include the venerable *Contucci*, at Via San Donato 15 (ⓣ0578.757.006, ⓦwww.contucci.it), which can trace the family line in Montepulciano back a thousand years, and the *Cantina Del Redi*, at Via di Collazi 5 (ⓣ0578.716.092, ⓦwww.cantinadelredi.com).

**Acquacheta** **Via del Teatro 22 ⓣ0578.758.443, ⓦwww.acquacheta.eu.** A bustling, rustic-look *osteria* that offers hearty Tuscan food, including plenty of meat, sausage and salami options. Expect to pay around €20 for a couple of courses with house wine. Closed Tues.

**Caffè Poliziano** **Via di Voltaia nel Corso 27.** An 1868 tearoom restored to a classic Art Nouveau design; it serves pastries and pots of tea, while its adjoining restaurant, *Il Grifin d'Oro*, serves somewhat pricey meals (at around €25), such as *pici* (fat spaghetti) with wild boar *ragù*, and offers great views from a small terrace. Daily 7am–midnight.

**La Grotta** **Via di San Biagio ⓣ0578.757.607.** Opposite San Biagio church, about 1km outside the city walls, brick-vaulted *La Grotta* serves pricey classic Tuscan cuisine in a sixteenth-century building with its own garden. Closed Wed.

**Osteria Porta di Bacco** **Via di Gracciano nel Corso 106 ⓣ0578.757.948.** Just inside the Porta al Prato, this quiet, characterful old stone-arched place is one of a clutch of moderately priced options, offering a set three-course menu for €12. Closed Tues.

**Trattoria di Cagnano** **Via dell Opio Nel Corso 30 ⓣ0578.758.757.** Popular and bustling, this offers a wide range of pizzas, from the simple €5 *margherita* to the €7.50 *estate* (mozzarella, tomatoes, rocket, prosciutto and parmesan), as well as outside seating. Closed Mon.

18

# San Gimignano and Volterra



San **Gimignano**, 27km northwest of Siena, is perhaps the best-known village in Italy. Its stunning skyline of towers, built in aristocratic rivalry by the feuding nobles of the twelfth and thirteenth centuries, evokes the appearance of medieval Tuscany more than any other sight. And its image as a "Medieval Manhattan" has for decades caught the tourist imagination, helped along by its convenience as a day-trip from Florence or Siena.

The town is all that it's cracked up to be: quietly monumental, very well preserved, enticingly rural and with a fine array of religious and secular frescoes. However, from Easter until October, San Gimignano has very little life of its own and a lot of day-trippers, who don't always respect the place: antisocial behaviour and litter are starting to become a problem. If you want to get any feel for the town, beyond the level of art treasures or quaintness, you really need to come well out of season. If you can't, then aim to spend the night here: in the evenings San Gimignano takes on a very different pace and atmosphere.

Few historic Italian towns could provide as stark a contrast to San Gimignano as **Volterra**, 29km to the west, which has a bleak, isolated appearance – a surprise after San Gimignano's sunny medievalism and the pastoral countryside. D.H. Lawrence wrote, accurately, that "it gets all the wind and sees all the world … a sort of inland island, still curiously isolated and grim." However, its small, walled medieval core certainly merits a stop, with its cobbled and austere stone streets, dark stone *palazzi* and walled gateways. There are great views from the windswept heights, enjoyable walking, and one of the country's most important Etruscan museums.

San Gimignano is easy to reach by **bus** from Florence (about 12 daily; 1hr 15min) or Siena (10 daily; 1hr). Some services from Siena require a change at Poggibonsi, which has the closest **train** station (trains hourly from Siena or Florence; 25min or 1hr 15min respectively). You may also need to change bus at Poggibonsi (or Colle di Val d'Elsa) if you coming from or heading to Volterra (4 daily; 1hr 30min). Services terminate at Piazzale dei Martiri di Monte Maggio, just outside Porta San Giovanni, the town's southern gateway.

# San Gimignano

**SAN GIMIGNANO** was a force to be reckoned with in the early Middle Ages. It was controlled by two great families – the Ardinghelli and the Salvucci – and its population of fifteen thousand (twice the present number) prospered on agricultural holdings and its position on the Lombardy to Rome pilgrim route. At its heyday, the town's walls enclosed five monasteries, four hospitals, public baths and a brothel. Feuds, however, had long wreaked havoc: the first Ardinghelli–Salvucci conflict erupted in 1246. Whenever the town itself was united, it picked fights with Volterra, Poggibonsi and other neighbours. These were halted only by the **Black Death**, which devastated the population and, as the pilgrim trade collapsed, the economy. Subjection to Florence broke the power of the nobles and so their tower-houses, symbolic in other towns of real control, were not torn down; today, fifteen of the original 72 survive. At the beginning of the nineteenth century, travellers spoke of San Gimignano as "miserably poor"; its postwar history, however, has been one of ever-increasing affluence, thanks to **tourism** and the production of an old-established but recently rejuvenated white **wine**, Vernaccia.

## Arrival and information

Although tour buses arrive throughout the day from Siena, San Gimignano welcomes very few direct public **buses** from anywhere other than Colle Val d'Elsa and the ugly industrial town of Poggibonsi: you're likely to have to transfer from those. There's an hourly connecting bus from Poggibonsi train station (on the Florence–Empoli–Siena line) that drops off at both of San Gimignano's main gates, **Porta San Giovanni** in the south and **Porta San Matteo** in the north. From each, the main streets Via San Giovanni and Via San Matteo climb to meet in the middle of town at the interlocking squares of **Piazza Duomo** and **Piazza della Cisterna**, where you'll find the Pro Loco **tourist office**, at Piazza Duomo 1 (daily 9am–1pm & 3–7pm; ⓣ0577.940.008, ⓦwww.sangimignano.com).

## Accommodation

Accommodation is bookable for free from the tourist office or through a branch of Siena Hotels Promotion, located just inside the southern gate at Via San Giovanni 125 (Mon–Sat: summer 9am–7pm; winter 9.30am–12.30pm & 3–6pm, but may close some weekday mornings; ⓣ0577.940.809, ⓦwww.hotelsiena.com). It can also give details of **private rooms**, an especially good option for those looking for cheaper accommodation, which is otherwise thin on the ground.

**Bel Soggiorno** Via San Giovanni 91 ⓣ0577.940.375, ⓦwww.hotelbelsoggiorno.it. Twenty-one smallish but beautifully appointed rooms on the town's main shopping drag. ❹

**Casolare Le Terre Rosse** Località San Donato ⓣ0577.9021, ⓦwww.hotelterrerosse.com. A great choice out of town, in the hamlet of San Donato 4km to the southwest on the road to Castel San Gimignano. The three-star hotel has 42 rooms in a classic Tuscan country house and a lovely rural setting; the big pool is a summer draw. Closed Nov–Feb. ❹

**Foresteria del Monastero San Girolamo** ⓣ0577.940.573, ⓕ0577.940.573. Nine rooms available in a convent run by Benedictine nuns just behind Porta San Jacopo. Rooms are €25 per person including breakfast; half that for children. ❶

**Il Boschetto di Piemma** Santa Lucia ⓣ0577.940.352, ⓦwww.boschettodipiemma.it. The nearest campsite to town, with a bar, restaurant and pool. Located 3km downhill

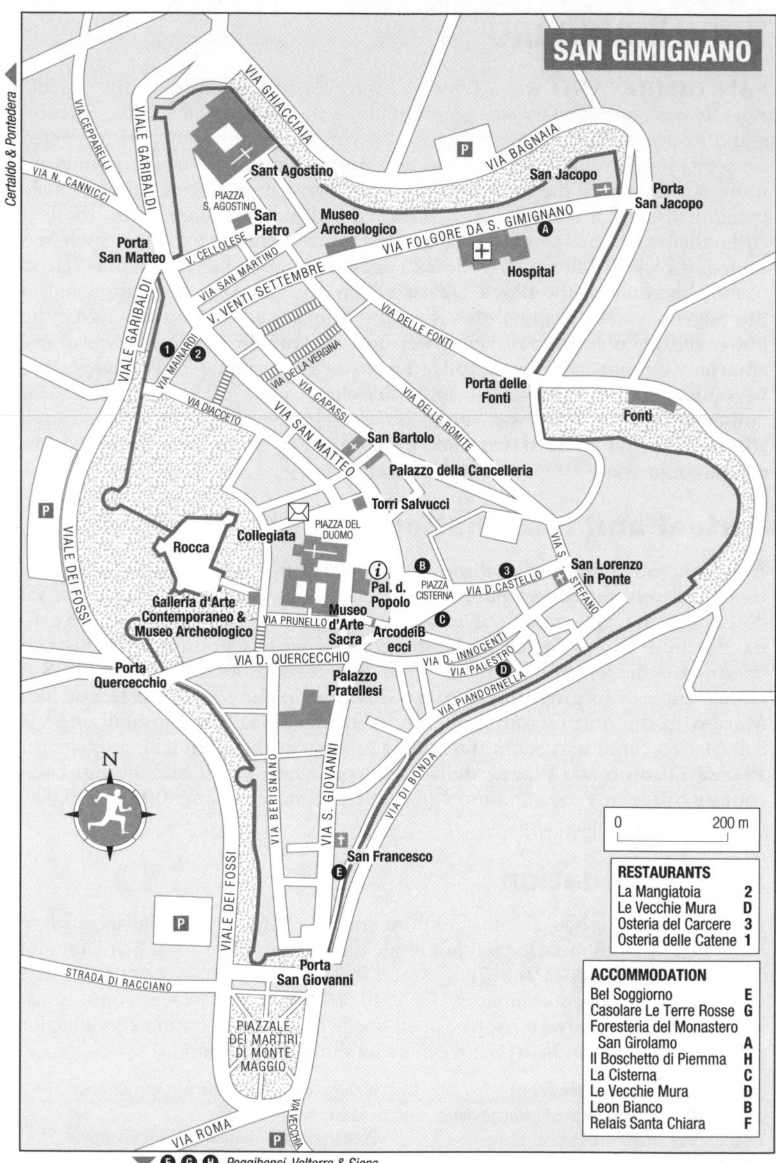




from Piazzale Martiri di Monte Maggio, off the Volterra road.

**La Cisterna** **Piazza Cisterna 24**
**☎ 0577.940.328, Ⓦ www.hotelcisterna.it.**
Elegant ivy-clad hotel (established 1919), built into a medieval ensemble; some rooms have views onto the piazza or over the valley. Good restaurant called *Le Terrazze*. ❸

**Le Vecchie Mura** **Via Piandornella 13**
**☎ 0577.940.270, Ⓦ www.vecchiemura.it.** Three doubles above a restaurant with superb views over vineyards and rolling Tuscan countryside. Free parking on the other side of town. ❷

**Leon Bianco** Piazza Cisterna 13 ⓣ0577.941.294, ⓔleonbianco@joli.it. Tasteful three-star hotel in a fourteenth-century town mansion opposite the *Cisterna*. Also with a roof terrace for breakfast, drinks and lounging. Rooms without a view are considerably cheaper. ❹

**Relais Santa Chiara** Via G. Matteotti 1 ⓣ0577.940.701, ⓦwww.rsc.it. A smart four-star hotel with 41 rooms, a pool and spacious grounds in a panoramic position on the Poggibonsi road 500m east of town. Breakfast and lunch are served, but there's no restaurant. ❺

# The Town

You could walk from one end of San Gimignano to the other in about twenty minutes. It deserves at least a day, however, both for its frescoes and for its lovely surrounding countryside. From the southern gate, **Porta San Giovanni**, the *palazzo*-lined **Via San Giovanni** leads to the interlocking main squares, the Piazza del Duomo and the Piazza della Cisterna, home to the Collegiata, the town's former cathedral, and the superb Museo Civico and picture gallery. You enter the **Piazza della Cisterna** through another gateway, the **Arco dei Becci**, part of the original fortifications built before the town expanded in the twelfth century. The square itself is flanked by an anarchic cluster of towers and *palazzi*, and is named after the thirteenth-century public cistern, still functioning in the centre. Northwest of the square is one of the old Ardinghelli towers; a Salvucci rival rears up behind. An arch leads through to the more austere **Piazza del Duomo**, with further towers and civic *palazzi*. At the town's northern edge, up Via San Matteo, is the church of Sant'Agostino, home, among other things, to a ravishing fresco cycle by Benozzo Gozzoli.

## The Collegiata

The plain facade of the Duomo, or more properly the **Collegiata**, since San Gimignano no longer has a bishop, could hardly provide a greater contrast with its interior (April–Oct Mon–Fri 9.30am–7pm, Sat 9.30am–5pm, Sun 12.30–4.40pm; March & Nov to mid-Jan Mon–Sat 9.30am–5.10pm, Sun 12.30–5.10pm; mid-Jan to Feb open for religious celebrations only; €3.50). This is one of the most comprehensively frescoed churches in Tuscany, with cycles of paintings filling every available space, their brilliant colours set off by Pisan-Romanesque arcades of black-and-white-striped marble. Entrance is from the side courtyard, where you'll also find the small **Museo d'Arte Sacra** (April–Oct Mon–Fri 9.30am–7.10pm, Sat 9.30am–5.10pm, Sun 12.30–5.10pm; Nov–March Mon–Sat 9.30am–4.40pm, Sun 12.30–4.40pm; €3). Less spectacular than the Collegiata, it's nevertheless worth a look for its rescued religious art.

The Collegiata's three principal **fresco cycles** fill the north and south walls, plus two short side walls that protrude from the east (exit) wall of the facade. The **Old Testament** scenes on the north wall, completed by Bartolo di Fredi around 1367, are full of medieval detail in the costumes, activities and interiors. They are also quirkily naturalistic: there are few odder frescoes than the depiction of Noah exposing himself in a drunken stupor. The cycle (which reads from left to right, top to bottom) follows the story of the Flood with those of Abraham and Lot (their trip to Canaan), Joseph (his dream; being let down the well; having his brothers arrested, and being recognized by them), Moses (changing a stick into a serpent before the Pharaoh; the Red Sea; Mount Sinai) and Job (temptation; the Devil killing his herds; thanking God; being consoled). Above, note the beautiful fresco depicting the Creation of Eve, in which Eve emerges from the rib of the sleeping Adam.

The **New Testament** scenes opposite (begun 1333) have a disputed attribution – either Barna da Siena or Lippo Memmi. They impress most by the intensity of their emotional expression: in *The Kiss of Judas*, the focus of eyes is startlingly immediate. One of the most dramatic scenes is the *Resurrection of Lazarus*, in which a dumbstruck crowd witnesses the removal of a door to reveal the living Lazarus in the winding bandages of burial. An altogether different vision pervades Taddeo di Bartolo's *Last Judgement* (1410), with paradise to the left and hell to the right. This is one of the most gruesome depictions of a customarily lurid subject, with no-holds-barred illustrations of the Seven Deadly Sins.

On the north side of the Collegiata, San Gimignano's most important Renaissance art work is the superb fresco cycle made by Domenico Ghirlandaio for the small **Cappella di Santa Fina**. The subject is a local saint, born in 1238, who was struck by a dreadful and incurable disease at the age of 10. She gave herself immediately to God, repented her sins (the worst seems to have been accepting an orange from a boy) and insisted on spending the five agonizing years until her death lying on a plank on the floor. The fresco of the right-hand lunette shows Fina experiencing a vision of St Gregory. Opposite it is an even more accomplished work, the *Funeral of St Fina* – Raphael is said to have been especially impressed with it – showing the saint on her deathbed with the towers of San Gimignano in the background. Ghirlandaio left a self-portrait: he's the figure behind the bishop saying Mass.

## The Museo Civico and Pinacoteca

The Palazzo Popolo, the other key component of the Piazza del Duomo, is partly given over to council offices, but most of the building is devoted to the combined Museo Civico and **Pinacoteca** (picture gallery) and the **Torre Grossa**, the only one of San Gimignano's towers which you can climb for great views of the Val d'Elsa (both daily: March–Oct 9.30am–7pm; Nov–Feb 10am–5.30pm; €5).

The lovely courtyard was built in 1323. A loggia opens on the right, from which judicial and public decrees were occasionally proclaimed (hence the subject matter of its frescoes). Stairs lead up to a picturesque little balcony and the ticket office. The first room, frescoed with hunting scenes, is the **Sala di Dante** – the poet visited as Florence's ambassador to the town in 1299, making a plea here for Guelph unity. Most of the paintings are Sienese in origin or inspiration, and the highlight is Lippo Memmi's *Maestà* (1317).

Highlights upstairs include two outstanding tondi by Filippino Lippi. Rooms off to the right hold a triptych by Taddeo di Bartolo, the *Scenes from the Life of St Gimignano* (1393) – with the saint holding the eponymous town on his lap – and Lorenzo di Niccolò's *Scenes from the Life of St Bartholomew* (1401), which includes a graphic depiction of the saint being flayed alive. The most enjoyable paintings are hidden away in a small room off the stairs, frescoes of wedding scenes completed in the 1320s by the Sienese painter Memmo di Filipuccio that are unique in their subject matter: they show a tournament where the wife rides on her husband's back, followed by the lovers taking a shared bath and then climbing into bed – the man managing to retain the same red hat throughout.

## The rest of the town

Via di Castello continues east past the Romanesque **San Lorenzo in Ponte** (with fragments of a dramatic fresco of the Last Judgement) to a rural lane that winds down between vineyards to the city walls; just beyond the public wellhouse or **Fonti** stretches open countryside. A signposted lane leads from Piazza Duomo up to the **Rocca**, the old Florentine fortress, with its one surviving tower and wonderful views. Nowadays it encloses an orchard-like public garden, with figs, olives and a central well.

**Via San Matteo** is one of the grandest and best preserved of the city streets, running north from Piazza Duomo to the main **Porta San Matteo** gate. Before the gate, Via Venti Settembre heads east to the former convent of Santa Chiara, which now houses both the **Galleria d'Arte Contemporaneo**, with work by nineteenth- and twentieth-century Tuscan artists, and the interesting **Museo Archeologico** (both open daily 11am–5.30pm; closed from Jan–March & Oct–Dec; €3). In the same complex is the **Spezieria di Santa Fina**, fragrant halls filled with exhibits from the sixteenth-century spice and herb pharmacy of the town's Santa Fina hospital.

In the north of the town is the large church of **Sant'Agostino** (daily 7am–noon & 3–7pm; Nov–March closes 6pm; free), with a fresco cycle behind the high altar by Benozzo Gozzoli, the *Life of St Augustine* (1465), which provides an amazing record of life in Renaissance Florence. When read from low down on the left, the panels depict the saint – who was born in what is now Tunisia in 354 AD – being taken to school and flogged by his teacher, studying grammar at Carthage university, crossing the sea to Italy, teaching in Rome and Milan and being received by Emperor Theodosius. Then comes the turning point, when he hears St Ambrose preach and, while reading St Paul, hears a child's voice extolling him "*Tolle, lege*" (take and read). After this, he was baptized and returned to Africa to found a monastic community.

## Eating and drinking

San Gimignano isn't famous for its **food** – there are too many visitors and too few locals to ensure high standards. However, the tables set out on the car-free squares and lanes, and the good local wines, make for pleasant dining. The recommended places below are all moderately priced. Good **bars** are similarly thin on the ground, though there are one or two on each of the main piazzas that are decent enough places from where to watch the world go by.

The little but extraordinarily popular *Gelateria di Piazza*, at Piazza della Cisterna 4 (closed mid-Nov to mid-Feb), has arguably the best **ice cream** in Tuscany. Owner Sergio has certainly won enough competitions, including the *Gelato del Mondo* in 2006. Framed plaudits cover the walls. His incomparable pistachio flavour is made from finest-quality Sicilian nuts, and his trademark *crema di Santa Fina* is perfumed with saffron, but you'd be hard-pushed on a hot afternoon to beat the trio of peach, champagne with grapefruit, and *vernaccia*, the last a fragrant sorbet made from the crisp local white wine.

**La Mangiatoia** **Via Mainardi 2 ⓣ0577.941.528.** Popular restaurant with good Tuscan staples (mains €10–13, pasta €7–9) and a garden open in the summer. Closed Tues.

**Le Vecchie Mura** **Via Piandornella 15 ⓣ0577.940.270.** Housed in an old vaulted stable within the structure of the city walls; follow the sign off Via San Giovanni. Good atmosphere and reasonable value, with starters at €5–8, pasta from €8 and mains around €13. Be sure to book. Closed Tues.

**Osteria del Carcere** **Via del Castello 13 ⓣ0577.941.905.** A relatively new and informal *osteria* with young owners, a few steps from Piazza del Duomo. Excellent hams and salami, plus Tuscan cooking with an innovative edge. Reckon on around €25–30 for three courses; booking is advised. Closed Wed.

**Osteria delle Catene** **Via Mainardi 18 ⓣ0577.941.966.** A thoroughly reliable place for straightforward Tuscan food. The wine list – over a hundred choices – is good, too. A full lunch will cost around €30, dinner €10–15 more. Closed Wed.

# Volterra

**VOLTERRA** may have few standout sights – the excellent **Museo Etrusco Guarnacci** aside – but like most Tuscan towns it has something of passing medieval or Renaissance interest at virtually every turn. Start your exploration at the central **Piazza del Popolo**, home to the Duomo and a cluster of historic palaces, and then walk a short way north to the **Pinacoteca Nazionale**, known for a painting by Rosso Fiorentino that features high in the Mannerist canon. The walk east from here takes in the **Museo Etrusco Guarnacci** and the pleasures of the park below the old Medici fortress, an unexpected green sanctuary in this otherwise brooding town. To see the **Balze**, Volterra's striking cliffs, requires more application, with a walk of about two kilometres west from the town centre.

## Some history

Volterra lies at the heart of a mining region that yields **alabaster** (every other shop sells artefacts) as well as a variety of minerals. The mines – and the easily defended site – made it one of the largest **Etruscan** settlements, called Velathri, and ensured its survival through the **Roman** era as Volaterrae. During the Dark Ages it became an important Lombard centre, and even sheltered the Lombard kings for a time. In the Middle Ages, however, the mines proved Volterra's downfall as the **Florentines** began to cast a covetous eye over their wealth. Florence took control of the town from 1360, and in 1472 – anxious to secure the town's alum deposits, vital for Florence's dyeing industry – crushed all pretensions to independence with a terrible siege and pillage by Lorenzo de' Medici and the Duke of Urbino, one of the three principal crimes Lorenzo confessed to Savonarola on his deathbed.

Subsequently, Volterra was a Florentine fief, unable to keep pace with changing and expanding patterns of trade and sliding into provincial obscurity. It was to remain part of the Grand Duchy of Tuscany until Italian unification in 1860. Physically, the town also began to subside, its walls and houses slipping away to the west over the Balze. Today, Volterra occupies less than a third of its ancient extent.

# Arrival and information

Irregular **buses** run to Volterra from Pisa and Siena (sometimes with a change at Colle Val d'Elsa or Poggibonsi) with connections from San Gimignano. Four buses daily run from San Gimignano to Volterra (again, with possible changes at Poggibonsi), except on Sunday, and the journey takes ninety minutes. All arrive on the south side of the walls at Piazza Martiri della Libertà, from where it's a two-minute walk to the central Piazza dei Priori. The **tourist office** is at Via

### Volterra's alabaster

**Alabaster** is a form of crystallized chalk that has a delicate, milky texture and lends itself to the sculpture of fine, flowing lines and close ornamental detail. In even quite large blocks, it is translucent. The Etruscans and Romans extensively mined Volterra's alabaster for sculpting and up until the 1960s, there were large alabaster factories throughout the town centre, but – not least because of the quantity of dust they threw up – large-scale production was moved to outlying areas. These days, only about a dozen artisans are permitted to maintain workshops in the centre of town, and Volterra's famous art school is the only one in Europe to train students to work alabaster.

You'll spot plenty of alabaster shops dotted around the centre – most are outlets for factories that produce machined pieces from the tasteful to the tacky.

▲ View over rooftops of Volterra



Giusto Turazza 2 (daily: April–Oct 9am–1pm & 2–7pm; Nov–March 10am–1pm & 2–6pm; ⓣ 0588.86.150, ⓦ www.provolterra.it). The **post office** is in the main Piazza dei Priori. There are free **car parks** on the northern side of the walls, and a pay-by-the-hour underground car park just to the south.

## Accommodation

Accommodation options include a hostel, a campsite, several relatively upmarket options and a good villa hotel just outside the old town. Ask about apartments and agriturismo stays at the tourist office, which has a free accommodation service.

**Convento Sant'Andrea ⓣ 0588.86.028.** On the northeast outskirts of the town; follow the road out of Porta Marcoli. There are beautiful views from the old cells, now let as private rooms – to both single women and men, and couples. €18 per person in a room with private bathroom; €14 in a room with shared bathroom.

**Etruria Via Matteotti 32 ⓣ&ⓕ 0588.87.377.** Best value of the hotels proper – and located on the main street, right in the centre – this restored eighteenth-century building has 22 comfortable rooms and a private garden. ❷

**La Locanda Via Guarnacci 24–28 ⓣ 0588.81.547, ⓦ www.hotel-lalocanda.com.** The *San Lino* (see below) had its own way for years among Volterra's top hotels, but the recently opened four-star *La Locanda*, smartly converted from a former nunnery, has stolen its thunder. It also has the advantage of a slightly more central position, north of Piazza dei Priori near the Porta Fiorentina. ❸

**Le Balze Via Mandringa ⓣ 0588.87.880.** Well-equipped and nicely positioned campsite 1km west of the centre, outside Borgo San Giusto (follow signs for the *Balze*). Has a pool and tennis courts; riding can also be arranged. Open April–Sept.

**Nazionale Via dei Marchesi 11 ⓣ 0588.86.284, ⓦ www.hotelnazionale-volterra.it.** In the heart of town, this three-star hotel is the inn D.H. Lawrence stayed at when researching *Etruscan Places* – the medieval *palazzo* was transformed into a hotel in 1860. Now much modernized, with 36 mostly tiny rooms, all with bathroom. ❷

**San Lino Via San Lino 26 ⓣ 0588.85.250, ⓦ www.hotelsanlino.com.** Volterra's grandest hotel until the arrival of *La Locanda*, this four-star place with 43 rooms and pool is still a good bet. It's located on the street leading in from Porta San Francesco. ❸

**Villa Nencini Borgo Santo Stefano 55 ⓣ 0588.86.386, ⓕ 0588.80.601.** Attractive three-star hotel in a seventeenth-century building, with a pool and garden, sited just outside Porta San Francesco on the town's northwest edge. ❷

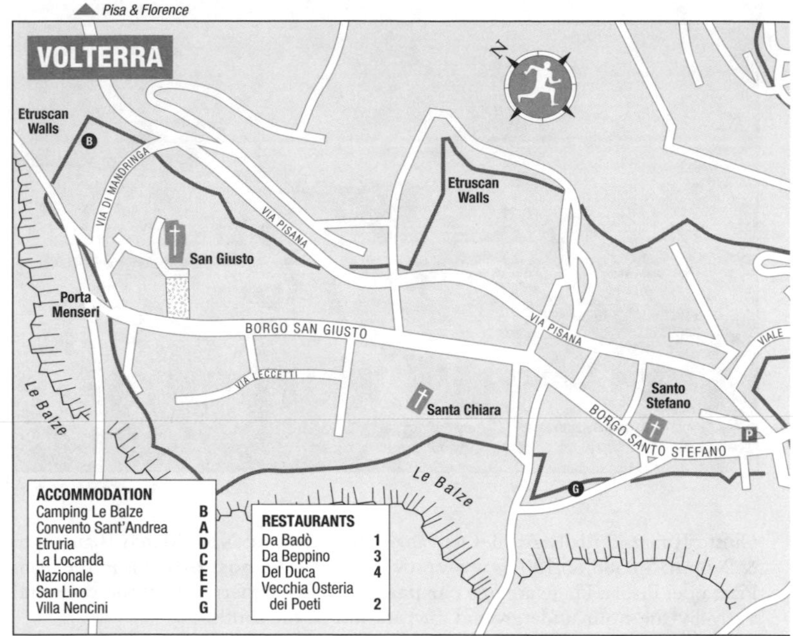


## The Town

Dominating the almost totally medieval square of **Piazza dei Priori**, the **Palazzo Pretorio** is the oldest town hall in Tuscany, begun in 1208, which may have served as the model for Florence's Palazzo Vecchio. Upstairs inside the *palazzo* (mid-March to Oct daily 10.30am–5.30pm; Nov to mid-March Sat & Sun 11am–5pm; €1) is the **Sala del Consiglio**, used as the town's council chamber without interruption since 1257. Its end wall features a huge *Annunciation* by Orcagna.

Leaving the square west past the tourist office, you come to a crossroads overlooked by the **Torre Buomparenti**. South (left) at Via Roma 13 is the **Museo d'Arte Sacra**, a rich four-room collection (daily: mid-March to Oct 9am–1pm & 3–6pm; Nov to mid-March 9am–1pm; joint ticket with Museo Guarnacci and Pinacoteca €8), which includes a silver reliquary bust of St Ottaviano by Antonio del Pollaiuolo. Via Roma continues into the slightly down-at-heel cathedral square, with the Pisan-Romanesque **Duomo**, consecrated in 1120 (daily 8am–12.30pm & 3–5/6pm; free) and **Baptistery** (late-thirteenth century). The best of the Duomo's works is a sculpture of the *Deposition* (1228) in the south transept, disarmingly repainted in its original bright colours. Behind the baptistry is an old foundling's hospital decorated by della Robbia.

Via Marchesi heads south uphill to a lush area of grass, trees and shade known as the **Parco Archeologico** (daily 8.30am–dusk; free). There's not much archeology about the place – a few odd lumps of rock, said to be part of a Roman bathhouse – but it's a beautiful part of the town to walk around for a few hours. Overlooking the park to the east is the Medicean **Rocca**, with rounded bastions and a central tower; it's one of the great examples of Italian military architecture and for the last 150 years has been a prison. The first turning off Via Marchesi is Via Porta dell'Arco, which runs downhill to the **Arco Etrusco**, an Etruscan gateway, third-century BC in origin, built in cyclopean blocks of stone. The gate

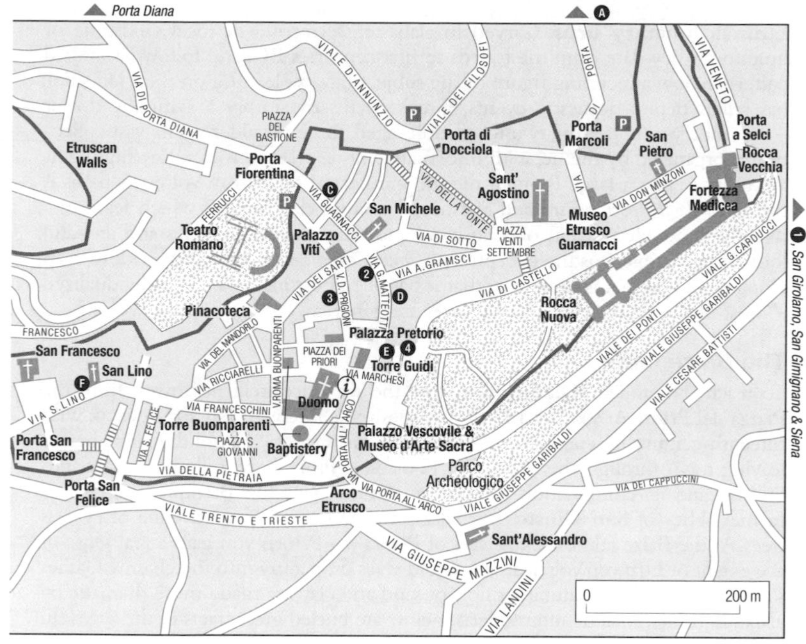


was narrowly saved from destruction in World War II during a ten-day battle between the partisans and Nazis. If you turn north instead off Via Marchesi, and follow Via Matteotti and its continuation, Via Guarnacci, you reach the Porta Fiorentina. Just to the west of the gate, below the road, is an area of excavations including a **Roman theatre** (now restored for use in the summer theatre festival) and a **bath complex** with mosaic floors.

North from the Torre Buomparenti at Via dei Sarti 1 is the beautiful Renaissance Palazzo Minucci-Solaini, now housing the **Pinacoteca e Museo Civico** (daily: mid-March to Oct 9am–7pm; Nov to mid-March 9.30am–1.30pm; €8 joint ticket with Museo Guarnacci and Museo d'Arte Sacra). The key works are Florentine: Ghirlandaio's marvellous *Christ in Glory*, Luca Signorelli's *Annunciation* and, best of all, Rosso Fiorentino's extraordinary *Deposition*. This is one of the masterpieces of Mannerism: its figures, without any central focus, creating an agitated tension from sharp lines and blocks of discordant colour. The building also contains the **Eco-Museo dell'Alabastro** (April–Oct daily 11am–5pm; Nov–March Sat & Sun 9am–1.30pm; €3), which provides an overview of alabaster craftsmanship in the area from Etruscan times to the present day and has a replica sculptor's workshop.

On the same street as the Pinacoteca is **Palazzo Viti**, at Via dei Sarti 41 (April–Oct daily 10am–1pm & 2.30–6.30pm; Nov–March by appointment only; €5; ⓣ0588.840.47), an extensively frescoed Renaissance mansion filled with alabaster, everything from two-metre-high candelabras to tiles laid in the floor of the ballroom.

## The Museo Etrusco Guarnacci

The **Museo Etrusco Guarnacci**, 500m east of Piazza dei Priori at Via Don Minzoni 15 (same hours and ticket as Pinacoteca), is one of Italy's major archeological museums. On display are entirely local finds, including some six hundred

Etruscan **funerary urns**. Carved in alabaster, terracotta or local sandstone or limestone, they date from the fourth to first centuries BC, and follow a standard pattern: below a reclining figure of the subject (always leaning on their left side), bas-reliefs depict domestic events, Greek myths or simply a symbolic flower – one for a young person, two for middle-aged, three for elderly. The vast collection is organized by theme, with informative notes in each room. Key highlights are upstairs: past a large Roman mosaic transferred here from Volterra's baths is the *Urna degli Sposi*, a rare and artistically unique clay urn lid which features a disturbing double portrait of a husband and wife, all piercing eyes and dreadful looks. The star piece is the exceptional *Ombra della Sera* ("Evening Shadow"), an elongated nude that is unique in that it has been personalized and individualized – most of the figurines in nearby cases are generic.

### The Balze cliffs

To reach the eroded **Balze** cliffs, follow the Via Ricciarelli northwest from the Piazza dei Priori. As Via San Lino, this passes the church of **San Francesco**, with fifteenth-century frescoes of the *Legend of the True Cross* by Cenni di Cenni, before leaving town through the Porta San Francesco. From here, follow Borgo Santo Stefano and its continuation, Borgo San Giusto, past the Baroque church and former abbey of **San Giusto**, its striking facade framed by an avenue of cypress trees. At the Balze (almost 2km west of Piazza dei Priori) you gain a real sense of the extent of Etruscan Volterra, whose old walls drop away into the chasms. Gashes in the slopes and the natural erosion of sand and clay are made more dramatic by alabaster mines, ancient and modern. Below are buried great tracts of the Etruscan and Roman city, and landslips continue – as evidenced by the ruined eleventh-century **Badia** monastery ebbing away over the precipice.

## Eating and drinking

Volterra's restaurant menus are dominated by **wild boar** (*cinghiale*), which is hunted locally. You see stuffed heads of the unfortunate beasts throughout town, and the meat is packaged as salamis or hams, as well as roasted in the restaurants, along with hare (*lepre*) and rabbit (*coniglio*).

**Restaurants** listed below cover the best of a similarly priced bunch. Cheaper options include a few *pizzerie*, such as the central *Da Nanni* at Via delle Prigioni 40.

**Da Badò Borgo San Lazzaro 9 ☎0588.86.477.** Excellent local trattoria on the SS68 Florence–Siena road, run by two amiable brothers (with mother in the kitchen) which has made a name for itself in national foodie guides. Serves up delicious *crostini* and Volterran game staples such as *pappardelle alla lepre*. Reckon on €25–35 for a full meal. Closed Wed & periods in July & Sept.

**Da Beppino Via delle Prigioni 13–21 ☎0588.86.051.** Reliable, established and family-run restaurant in the heart of the old town, with lots of space. Serves home-made pasta, pizzas and plenty of game dishes, with an emphasis on truffles and mushrooms. Closed Thurs Nov–March & around mid-Nov to mid-Dec.

**Del Duca Via di Castello 2, corner of Via dei Marhesi ☎0588.81.510.** On the edge of the old centre, this small restaurant is currently the best place in town, thanks to its lovely setting (high ceilings and impressive *cantina*), surprisingly fair prices and fine Tuscan food with a creative twist. Closed periods in late Jan and mid-Nov plus Tues except July–Sept.

**Vecchia Osteria dei Poeti Via Matteotti 55–57 ☎0588.86.029.** One of the most popular and welcoming restaurants in town – and they don't stint on portions. A central location, with one dining room and a rustic appearance that retains many features of the original medieval building. Around €30 should buy you a full meal. Closed mid-Jan to mid-Feb & Thurs except in Aug.

# Arezzo and Cortona

Upstream from Florence, the Arno valley – the **Valdarno** – is a fairly industrialized district, with warehouses and manufacturing plants enclosing many of the small towns strung along the train line. Some of the villages up on the valley sides retain an appealing medieval square or a cluster of attractive buildings but there's no very compelling stop until you reach the provincial capital of the upper Arno region, **Arezzo**, one hour's train ride from Florence. This solidly bourgeois city has its share of architectural delights – including one of the most photogenic squares in central Italy – though the droves of visitors who travel to Arezzo come to see just one thing: the stupendous fresco cycle by **Piero della Francesca** in the church of San Francesco. To the south of Arezzo stretches the agricultural plain of the Valdichiana (the valley of the River Chiana), where the ancient hill-town of **Cortona** is the major attraction; its steep streets forming a distinctive urban landscape and giving an unforgettable view over Lago Trasimeno and the Valdichiana. North of Arezzo lies the beautiful uplands of the **Casentino**, while to the east of the city, in **Monterchi** and **Sansepolcro**, further masterpieces by della Francesca invite a detour.

**Trains** on the Florence–Rome rail line run up the Arno valley, through Arezzo (hourly from Florence; 1hr) and on down the Valdichiana: for Cortona the nearest station on this line is Camucia (roughly hourly from Florence; 1hr 20min), about eight kilometres away, though more services stop at the slightly more distant Terontola, which is on the line to Perugia. For the Casentino, there's the LFI private rail line that runs every hour to the head of the valley, via Poppi (55min), from the main station at Arezzo, but to get to the great monastery at La Verna you'll need a car. Arezzo and Cortona are the centres of overlapping **bus** networks, which between them cover most of Arezzo province. For smaller places such as Monterchi, however, the services are too sporadic to be very useful.

## Arezzo

Maecenas, the wealthy patron of Horace and Virgil, was born in **AREZZO** and it's still a place with the moneyed touch, thanks in large part to its jewellers and goldsmiths, who are so numerous that the city has the world's largest gold manufacturing plant. Topping up the coffers are the proceeds of Arezzo's antiques industry: in the vicinity of the Piazza Grande there are shops filled with museum-quality furniture, and every month the **Fiera Antiquaria** turns the piazza into a vast showroom. Though Arezzo is now making more of an effort to market

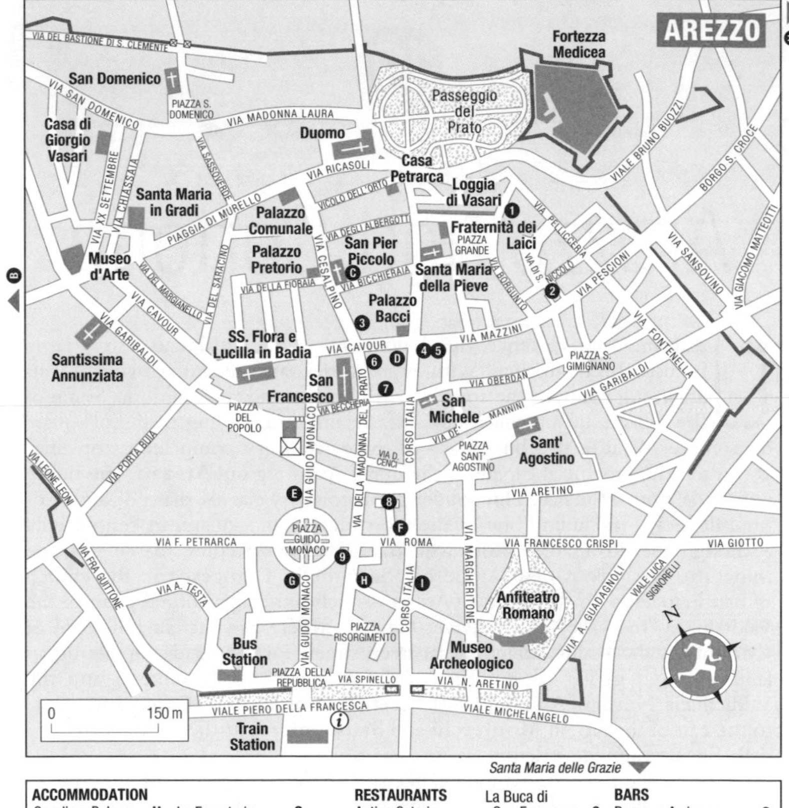


| ACCOMMODATION | | | | RESTAURANTS | | | | BARS | |
|---|---|---|---|---|---|---|---|---|---|
| Cavaliere Palace | H | La Foresteria | C | Antica Osteria L'Agania | 5 | La Buca di San Francesco | 6 | Bacco e Arrianna | 3 |
| Cecco | I | La Toscana | B | I Tre Bicchieri | 8 | La Torre di Gnicche | 1 | Fiaschetteria de' Redi | 7 |
| Continentale | G | Ostello Villa Severini | A | Il Cantuccio | 9 | Miseria e Nobiltà | 2 | | |
| I Portici | F | Vogue Hotel | E | Il Saraceno | 4 | | | | |
| Il Patio | D | | | | | | | | |

itself to visitors (as is reflected in the improving quality of the accommodation on offer), this is still very much a self-sufficient city.

Occupying a site that controls the major passes of the central Apennines, Arezzo was one of the most important settlements of the Etruscan federation. It maintained its pre-eminence under Roman rule, and was a prosperous independent republic in the Middle Ages until, in 1289, its Ghibelline allegiances brought about a catastrophic defeat by the Guelph Florentines at the Battle of Campaldino. Arezzo temporarily recovered from this reversal under the leadership of **Bishop Guido Tarlati**, whose bellicosity eventually earned him excommunication. Subjugation came about in 1384, when Florence paid the ransom demanded of Arezzo by the conquering army of Louis d'Anjou. When the French departed, the city's paymaster was left in power.

Even as a mortgaged political power, Arezzo continued to be a major cultural force. Already renowned as the birthplace of the man known as Guido d'Arezzo or Guido Monaco (c.991–1050), who is widely regarded as the inventor of modern musical notation, Arezzo was brought further prestige by Petrarch (1304–74), and then by the writer Pietro Aretino (1492–1556) and the artist-architect-biographer Giorgio Vasari (1511–74). Yet it was an outsider who gave Arezzo its greatest monument – Piero della Francesca, whose frescoes for the church of San Francesco belong in the same company as Masaccio's cycle in Florence and Michelangelo's in Rome.

## Arrival and information

The main **tourist office** is on the edge of the **train station** forecourt, at Piazza della Repubblica 28 (summer daily 9am–1pm & 3–7pm; winter closed Sun, except first Sun of month; ⓣ0575.377.678, ⓦwww.apt.arezzo.it). The helpful staff speak English and have masses of information on Arezzo and its province. There are **car parks** by the train station and the archeological museum, but you'll more easily find spaces in the new car park outside the northern stretch of the city walls (near San Domenico), in the streets to the south of the rail line, or near Santa Maria delle Grazie.

## Accommodation

Accommodation is not plentiful at any time of year, and almost impossible to come by on the first weekend of every month, because of the antiques fair. In addition the town is booked solid at the end of August and beginning of September, when the Concorso Polifonico Guido d'Arezzo and the Giostra del Saracino (see p.32) follow in quick succession. At the time of going to press, the city's **youth hostel**, the *Ostello Villa Severi* (some way north of the centre at Via Francesco Redi 13) was closed for rebuilding; check the tourism website for the latest situation.

**Cavaliere Palace Via della Madonna del Prato 83 ⓣ0575.26.836, ⓦwww.cavalierehotels.com.** Formerly a one-star, now renamed and rebuilt as a 27-room four-star, this is one of the most comfortable hotels in central Arezzo. ❹

**Cecco Corso Italia 215 ⓣ0575.20.986, ⓦwww.hotelcecco.com.** Very central two-star, above a restaurant of the same name; spacious if slightly institutional in feel. Rooms without private baths cost almost €20 less than the rest. ❷

**Continentale Piazza Guido Monaco 7 ⓣ0575.20.251, ⓦwww.hotelcontinentale.com.** Large old three-star with restaurant right on the hub of the lower town. The rooms are generally characterless, but there are excellent views from the roof terrace. ❸

**I Portici Via Roma 18 ⓣ0575.403.132, ⓦwww.hoteliportici.com.** This sizeable town house has recently been converted into a very comfortable old-style four-star hotel, with just five doubles, one single and a couple of suites. ❺

**Il Patio Via Cavour 23 ⓣ0575.401.962, ⓦwww.hotelpatio.it.** Another small, welcoming and not overly expensive new four-star, just a minute's stroll from San Francesco. As with *I Portici*, the decor reflects Arezzo's love of antiques, but *Il Patio* wears the style more brightly. ❺

**La Foresteria Via Bicchieraia 32 ⓣ0575.370.474.** The nicest budget accommodation in central Arezzo, *La Foresteria* comprises a dozen unfussy and well-decorated rooms in the former convent of the church of San Pier Piccolo. No credit cards. ❷

### Arezzo's biglietto unico

A €12 ticket gives you a single admission to the following monuments and museums in Arezzo: the Museo Archeologico, the Museo Statale d'Arte Medievale e Moderna, the Casa Vasari and the della Francesca frescoes in San Francesco. The ticket can be bought at any of these four locations, but bear in mind that immediate admission to San Francesco may not be possible (see p.331).

**La Toscana** Via M. Perennio 56 ⓣ0575.21.692. One-star with seventeen rooms (nearly all with private bathroom) on the main road coming in from the west; it's no one's idea of a romantic retreat, but if you're counting every euro it's a choice between this and the hostel. ❶

**Vogue Hotel** Via Guido Monaco 54 ⓣ0575.24.361, ⓦwww.voguehotel.it. The new four-star *Vogue* has 26 rooms, each uniquely styled, but all with a sleekly modern look that makes a refreshing change from the retro atmosphere favoured by the city's other higher-end hotels. ❹

## The City

There are two distinct parts to Arezzo: the **older quarter**, at the top of the hill, and the business-like **lower town**, much of which remains hidden from day-trippers, as it spreads behind the train station and the adjacent bus terminal. From the station forecourt, go straight ahead for Via Guido Monaco, the traffic axis between the upper and lower town. The parallel **Corso Italia**, now pedestrianized, is the route to walk up the hill.

### San Francesco

Off to the left of the Corso, on Via Cavour, not far from its summit, stands the building everyone comes to Arezzo to see: the basilica of **San Francesco** (summer Mon–Fri 9am–7pm, Sat 9am–6pm, Sun 1–6pm; winter closes Mon–Fri 6pm, Sat & Sun 5.30pm; free). Built in the 1320s, the shabby brick basilica earned its renown in the early 1450s, when the Bacci family commissioned Piero della Francesca to continue the decoration of the choir. The project had been started by Bicci di Lorenzo, who had painted only the Evangelists (in the vault) and part of the Last Judgement (on the arch outside the chapel) before he died. For the wall paintings, Piero's patrons nominated a subject with rather fewer dramatic possibilities, but which suited the contemplative personality of the artist perfectly.

The theme chosen was **The Legend of the True Cross**, a story in which the physical material of the Cross forms the link in the cycle of redemption that begins with humanity's original sin. The literary source for the cycle, the *Golden Legend* by Jacopo de Voragine, is a very convoluted story, and the way the episodes are arranged adds to the opacity, as Piero preferred to organize the scenes symmetrically rather than in chronological order: thus the two battle scenes face each other across the chapel, rather than coming where the story dictates. Smaller-scale symmetries are present in every part of the work: for example, the retinue of the Queen of Sheba appears twice, in mirror-image arrangement, and the face of the queen is exactly the same as the face of the Empress Helena. This all-pervasive orderliness, combined with the pale light and the statuesque quality of the figures, creates an atmosphere that's unique to Piero, and a sense of each incident as a part of a greater plan.

Our plan is a basic guide to the events depicted. The images of the *Annunciation* and two prophets on the window wall (Isaiah – painted by one of Piero's assistants – to the left; Jeremiah to the right) have nothing to do with the legend, but relate to the theme of the redemptive significance of the Cross, a point underlined by the cruciform plan of the *Annunciation*, which in turns echoes the plan of the *Vision of Constantine* on the other side of the window, where the tent pole and the rim of the tent form a cross.

Damp has badly damaged areas of the chapel and some bits have peeled away, partly as a result of Piero's notoriously slow method of working, but most of the rest has emerged in magnificent condition after a decade's restoration work. You can see the frescoes from the nave of the church, but you need to get closer to really appreciate them, and you're not allowed any closer than the altar steps unless you've bought a **ticket** (€6): visits are limited to 25 people at time (same hours as the church), and to thirty minutes per group. You are encouraged to book tickets in advance by phone (Ⓣ0575.352.727) or online (Ⓦwww.apt.arezzo.it). However, you can make a reservation in person at the ticket office beside the church, and even in high season you may not have to wait long before getting in; in winter there's rarely any wait at all.

### The Pieve di Santa Maria and Piazza Grande

Farther up the Corso from San Francesco stands one of the finest Romanesque structures in Tuscany, the twelfth-century **Pieve di Santa Maria** (daily: summer 8am–1pm & 3–7pm; winter 8am–noon & 3–6pm). Its arcaded facade belongs to a type associated more with Pisa and western Tuscany, and is doubly unusual in presenting its front to a fairly narrow street rather than to the town's main square. Known locally as "the tower of the hundred holes", the campanile was added in the fourteenth century. The most notable adornments to the exterior are the thirteenth-century carvings of the months over the portals. The oldest section of the chalky grey **interior** is the raised sanctuary, where the altarpiece is Pietro Lorenzetti's *Madonna and Saints* polyptych, painted in 1320. The unfamiliar saint on the far left, accompanying Matthew, the Baptist and John the Evangelist, is St Donatus, the second bishop of Arezzo, who was martyred in 304 AD. His relics are in the crypt, encased in a beautiful gold and silver bust made in 1346 by local goldsmiths known only as Pietro and Paolo.

## THE LEGEND OF THE TRUE CROSS

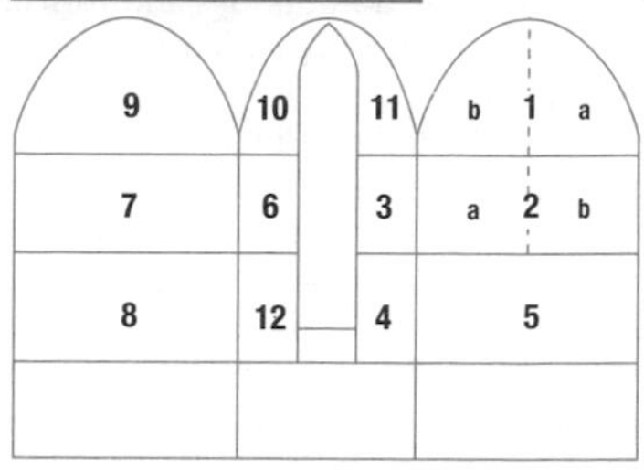


**1a**. Adam announces his death and implores Seth, his son, to seek the oil of mercy from the Angel of Eden.

**1b**. Instead the Angel gives Seth a sprig from the Tree of Knowledge, which is planted in the dead Adam's mouth.

**2a**. Solomon orders a bridge to be built from a beam fashioned from the tree that grew from Adam's grave. The Queen of Sheba, visiting Solomon, kneels in prayer before the bridge, sensing the holiness of the wood.

**2b**. The Queen of Sheba foresees that the beam will later be used to crucify a man, and that the death will bring disgrace to the Jews; she tells Solomon of her prophecy.

**3**. Solomon orders the beam to be buried.

**4**. The Emperor Constantine has a vision of the Cross, hearing a voice that declares: Under this sign shall you be victorious.

**5**. Constantine defeats the rival emperor Maxentius, and then is baptized. The figure of Constantine — the first emperor to rule Byzantium — may be a portrait of John Paleologus, the penultimate Byzantine emperor, who had been in Florence in 1439 to attend the Council of Florence.

**6**. The Levite Judas, under torture, reveals to the servants of St Helena — mother of Constantine — the burial place of the three crosses from Golgotha.

**7**. The crosses are excavated; the true Cross is recognized when it brings about a man's resurrection. Arezzo — serving as Jerusalem — is shown in the background.

**8**. The Persian king Chosroes, who had stolen the Cross, is defeated by the Emperor Heraclius. On the right he kneels awaiting execution; behind him is visible the throne into which he had incorporated the Cross.

**9**. Heraclius returns the Cross to Jerusalem.

**10**. Isaiah.

**11**. Jeremiah.

**12**. The Annunciation.

Opposite the Pieve, occupying the fourteenth-century Palazzo del Capitano del Popolo, the **Casa-Museo Ivan Bruschi** (Tues–Sun 10am–1pm & 3–7pm; €4) commemorates the man who started Arezzo's antiques fair. Bruschi's collection of sculptures, armour, books and miscellaneous *objets d'art* are nicely displayed in a simulated jumble, but it's a museum to leave until you've seen the rest of the city's sights.

The steeply sloping **Piazza Grande**, on the other side of the Pieve, is generally a peaceful spot, but it really comes alive for the Fiera Antiquaria and – more raucously – for September's Giostra del Saraceno. A diverting assortment of buildings encloses the space, with the wooden balconied apartments on the east side facing the apse of the Pieve, the Baroque Palazzo dei Tribunali and the **Palazzetto della Fraternità dei Laici**, which has a Renaissance upper storey and a Gothic lower. The upper level is adorned by a relief of the *Madonna della Misericordia* and niche statues, all carved by Bernardo Rossellino in 1434; below, there's a lunette fresco of the *Pietà* by Spinello Aretino, dating from the 1370s. The piazza's northern edge is formed by the arcades of the **Loggia di Vasari**, occupied by shops that in some instances still retain their original sixteenth-century stone counters.

## The Duomo and around



At the highest point of the town rises the large and unfussy **Duomo** (daily 7am–12.30pm & 3–7pm; free), whose harmonious appearance belies the protracted process of its construction. Begun in 1278, it was virtually finished by the start of the sixteenth century, but the campanile dates from 1859 and the facade from 1914.

The stained-glass windows, a rarity in Italy, were made around 1520 by Guillaume de Marcillat, an Arezzo-based Frenchman who also contributed some frescoes to San Francesco; the coloured panes let in so little light that his other contributions to the interior – the paintings on the first three bays of the nave – are virtually impossible to see. Off the left aisle, separated from the nave by a huge screen, the Cappella della Madonna del Conforto has terracottas by the della Robbia family, but the best of the building's art works lie farther down the aisle. Just beyond the organ is the **tomb of Bishop Guido Tarlati** (died 1327), head of the *comune* of Arezzo during its resurgence in the early fourteenth century; the monument, plated with marble reliefs showing scenes from the militaristic bishop's career, was possibly designed by Giotto. The small fresco nestled against the right side of the tomb is **Piero della Francesca**'s *Magdalene*, his only work in Arezzo outside San Francesco. In the chapel closest to the *Magdalene* lies Pope Gregory X, who died in Arezzo in 1276; a plaque on the wall invites you to consider his remarkable life, which overlapped with the lives of many other outstanding individuals, such as St Thomas Aquinas and St Bonaventure (who both taught him in Paris), St Francis, St Dominic, the Emperor Frederick II, Dante and Marco Polo.

The small and overpriced **Museo Diocesano** (Mon & Wed–Sun 10am–1pm & 2–6pm; €5), alongside the Duomo, won't make anyone's day, but the **Passeggio del Prato**, which extends from the east end of the Duomo to the Fortezza Medicea, is a good place to take a picnic. Cosimo I's fortress here was demolished in the eighteenth century, leaving only the ramparts.

## From San Domenico to the Badía

A short distance north of the Duomo you'll come across the church of **San Domenico** (daily 8am–7pm; free), constructed mostly in the late thirteenth century but with a Gothic campanile. Inside there are tatters of fifteenth- and sixteenth-century frescoes on the walls, while above the high altar hangs a dolorous *Crucifix* by Cimabue (1260), painted when the artist would have been about 20.

From here signs point the way to the **Casa Vasari** (Mon & Wed–Sat 8.30am–7pm, Sun 8.30am–1pm; €2) at Via XX Settembre 55, designed by Vasari himself. Born in Arezzo in 1511, Giorgio Vasari was taught to paint by his distant relative Luca Signorelli, and went on to become court painter, architect and general artistic supremo to Cosimo I. His major contribution to Western culture, however, is his *Lives of the Most Excellent Italian Architects, Painters and Sculptors*, the first attempt to relate artists' work to their social context, and a primary source for all histories of the Renaissance. The industrious Vasari frescoed much of his house with portraits and mythological characters, a decorative scheme that makes this one of the brashest domestic interiors in Tuscany. Portraits include his wife as the muse of conjugal love (in the Chamber of Apollo) and Michelangelo and Andrea del Sarto (in the Chamber of Fame). Work by other minor artists are strewn all over the place, proof that Giorgio was far from the most inept painter of his day.

At the foot of the hill, at Via San Lorentino 8, the fifteenth-century Palazzo Bruni-Ciocchi houses the **Museo d'Arte Medievale e Moderna** (Tues–Sun 8.30am–7pm; €4), containing a collection of minor paintings by local artists and majolica pieces from the thirteenth to the eighteenth centuries, generously spread over three floors.

If you follow Via Cavour from the Museo d'Arte, a huge Baroque tower soon signals the presence of the hulking **Badia di SS Flora e Lucilla** (Mon–Sat 8am–noon & 4–7pm, Sun 7am–12.30pm). The interior was extensively remodelled by Vasari, who also contributed the monstrous main altarpiece, designed as a monument to his family.

## The Museo Archeologico and Santa Maria delle Grazie

Nearly all the principal sights are in the upper part of Arezzo. One exception is the **Museo Archeologico** (daily 8.30am–7.30pm; €4), which occupies part of an abandoned Olivetan monastery built into a wall of the town's Roman

### Arezzo festivals

Arezzo's premier folkloric event is the **Giostra del Saracino**, which was first recorded in 1535 and is nowadays held in the Piazza Grande on the first Sunday in September. The day starts off with various costumed parades; at 5pm the action switches to the jousting arena in the piazza, with a procession of some three hundred participants leading the way. The piazza is the junction of the four quarters of the city and the sides of the square are decked with flags to mark their affiliations. Each quarter is represented by a pair of knights on horseback, who do battle with a wooden effigy of a Saracen king. In one hand it holds a shield marked with point scores, a bit like a dartsboard; in the other it has a cat-o'-three-tails which swings round when the shield is hit, necessitating nifty evasive action from the rider. A golden lance is awarded to the highest-scoring rider. In the days immediately preceding the joust you'll see rehearsals taking place, and in recent years the event has become so popular that a reduced version of the show is now held on the penultimate Saturday of June; check at the tourist office for the latest information on dates and ticket availability.

The musical tradition that began with Guido d'Arezzo is kept alive chiefly through the international choral competition that bears his name: the **Concorso Polifonico Guido d'Arezzo**, held in the last week of August. The less ambitious **Pomeriggi Musicali** is a season of free concerts held in various churches, museums and libraries; on average there's one concert a week from mid-January to June.

The **Fiera Antiquaria** takes over the Piazza Grande on the first Sunday of each month and the preceding Saturday. The most expensive stuff is laid out by the Vasari loggia, with cheaper pieces lower down the square and in the side streets.

amphitheatre, to the east of the station on Via Margaritone. The remains of the amphitheatre (entrance free) amount to little more than the base of the perimeter wall, largely because Cosimo I used the site as a quarry for the fortress up by the Duomo. More impressive are the museum's marvellously coloured coralline vases; produced here in the first century BC, they show why Arezzo's glassblowers were renowned throughout the Roman world as consummate craftsmen.

Ten minutes' walk away, south of the city centre at the end of Viale Mecenate, stands Arezzo's most exquisite church, **Santa Maria delle Grazie** (daily 8am–7pm). In the sixth century BC the Etruscans held fertility rites here, beside a spring in the midst of the woods that covered this area. At the instigation of St Bernardino the site was purged of its pagan associations by the plugging of the spring and the construction of the church, which still has a Carmelite convent attached to it. Fronted by a tiny pine-ringed meadow that's flanked by a pair of arcades, the church is entered through a delicate portico built by Benedetto da Maiano in the 1470s. The church is essentially a single room, containing little more than a few seats and an altarpiece by Parri Spinello, painted on the instructions of St Bernardino; the beautiful marble and terracotta altar that encases it was created by Andrea della Robbia.



## Eating and drinking

Arezzo's **restaurants** are of a generally high standard, and you'll find some nice **cafés** around piazzas Guido Monaco, Grande and San Francesco, and along Corso Italia. For **ice cream**, the first choice is *Il Gelato*, off Corso Italia at Via de' Cenci 24, while for picnic provisions you can't do better than Sbarbacipolle, at Via Garibaldi 120.

**Antica Osteria L'Agania** **Via Mazzini 10 ⓣ0575.25.381.** A very good and informal trattoria with welcoming atmosphere and local dishes (special emphasis on truffles and mushrooms in season), at around €35 per head; it draws much of its clientele from the antiques dealers. Closed Mon & part of June.

**Bacco e Arrianna** **Via Cesalpino 10.** A terrific *enoteca* very close to San Francesco, with delicious food too. Closed Mon & July.

**Fiaschetteria de' Redi** **Via de' Redi 10.** Busy little *osteria* with a superb range of vintages and decent simple meals. Closed Mon.

**I Tre Bicchieri** **Piazzetta Sopra i Ponti 3–5 ⓣ0575.265.57.** A classy and imaginative restaurant, with a notably extensive wine list. You'll pay in the region of €40–50 per head. Closed Wed.

**Il Cantuccio** **Via Madonna del Prato 76 ⓣ0575.26.830.** Good-value food served in a pleasant vaulted cellar. The home-made pasta dishes are particularly delicious. Expect to pay in the region of €30 per person. Closed Wed.

**Il Saraceno** **Via Mazzini 6 ⓣ0575.27.644.** Family-run trattoria, founded in 1946, with a good wine cellar and menus of traditional Aretine specialities (notably duck) at around €35 per head; good wood-oven pizzas too. Closed Wed & part of Jan.

**La Buca di San Francesco** **Via San Francesco 1 ⓣ0575.23.271.** Though it's right next to the main tourist attraction in Arezzo, this place is a genuine mid-range Tuscan trattoria: it's been in business since 1929 and the subterranean interior preserves parts of an Etruscan-Roman pavement and medieval frescoes. Closed Mon evening, Tues & 2 weeks in July.

**La Torre di Gnicche** **Piaggia San Martino 8.** Located off the northerneastern corner of the Piazza Grande, this place is perfect for a simple and inexpensive meal, washed down with a glass from its huge selection of local Colli Aretini and other Italian wines. Closed Wed & 2 weeks in Jan.

**Miseria e Nobiltà** **Via Piaggia di San Bartolomeo 2 ⓣ0575.21.245.** With its enticing pan-Italian menu and its medieval vaulted dining room, this very stylish (but not expensive) restaurant is one of the best in town. Tues–Sun 7–11.30pm.

## Around Arezzo: the Piero trail & The Casentino

Arezzo is the springboard for one of Tuscany's most rewarding art itineraries: the **Piero della Francesca trail**, which extends east of the city to Monterchi and Sansepolcro (the artist's birthplace) and continues via Perugia, where you'll find a stunning Piero altarpiece in the main art gallery, through Urbino and on to Rimini.

The farming village of **Monterchi**, 25km east of Arezzo, is famed for the **Madonna del Parto**, Piero's gracefully solemn depiction of the pregnant Virgin, who places her hand on the upper curve of her belly, her eyes downcast as if preoccupied with a foreknowledge of the course of the child's life. It's housed in a former school (Tues–Sun 9am–1pm & 2–7pm; winter closes 6pm; €3), which was converted into a museum solely to house the Madonna. Fifteen kilometres further on, the Museo Civico at **Sansepolcro** houses several works by Piero, the most notable of which are the **Madonna della Misericordia**, which is his earliest known painting, and the stupendous *Resurrection*, once dubbed by Aldous Huxley as "the greatest painting in the world". You can stay at Sansepolcro's three-star *Fiorentino*, which has been in business at Via Luca Pacioli 60 since 1807 (ⓣ0575.740.350, ⓦwww.albergofiorentino.com; ❷); the rooms are small and functional, but the hotel has friendly owners, its prices are low and it has a very good **restaurant** (closed Fri), in which you can expect to pay around €35 a head.

North of Arezzo, beyond the city's textile factories, lies the lush upper valley of the Arno, a largely agricultural area known as the **Casentino**, whose unshowy little towns see few tourists, even though much of the area has now been designated a national park. The most attractive town is tiny **Poppi**, which is dominated by the castle of the Guidi family, who once ruled the area. The seclusion of the forested and mountainous flanks of the Casentino fostered a strong monastic tradition, and the communities at **Camáldoli** and at **La Verna** continue to be important centres for their respective orders. The latter is the mountaintop retreat where St Francis received his stigmata, which is why it's one of Italy's major pilgrimage sites; it's open every day from 6am to 8.30pm, though in winter the road is sometimes closed by snow. The best place to stay in this area is Poppi's plain, homely and inexpensive three-star *Casentino* (ⓣ0575.529.090, ⓦwww.albergocasentino.it; ❸), which has a nice courtyard garden, a bar and a very popular restaurant (closed Wed).

# Cortona

From the floor of the Chiana valley, a five-kilometre road winds up through terraces of vines and olives to the hill-town of **CORTONA**, whose heights survey a vast domain: the agricultural plain of the Valdichiana stretching westwards, with Lago Trasimeno visible over the low hills to the south. The steep streets of Cortona are more or less untouched by modern building: limitations of space have confined almost all later development to the lower suburb of Camucia, which is where the approach road begins. Even without its monuments and art treasures, this would be a good place to rest up, with decent hotels, excellent restaurants and an amazing view at night, with the villages of southern Tuscany twinkling like ships' lights on a dark sea. In recent years, though, Cortona's tourist traffic has increased markedly, in the wake of Frances Mayes' *Under the Tuscan Sun* and *Bella Tuscany*, books that continue to entice coachloads of her (mainly American) readers to the place where Mayes realized the expat dream of the good life in Tuscany. Accordingly, if you're thinking of visiting any time between Easter and late September, it's advisable to book your accommodation in advance.

Folklore has it that Cortona was founded by Dardanus, later to establish the city of Troy and give his name to the Dardanelles. Whatever its precise origins, there was already a sizeable Umbrian settlement here when the **Etruscans** took over in the eighth century BC. About four hundred years later it passed to the **Romans** and remained a significant Roman centre until its destruction by the Goths. By the eleventh century it had become a free *comune*, constantly at loggerheads with Perugia and Arezzo; in 1258 the **Aretines** destroyed Cortona, but the town soon revived under the patronage of Siena. It changed hands yet again at the start of the fifteenth century, when it was appropriated by the Kingdom of Naples and then sold off to the **Florentines**, who never let go.

## Arrival and information

Cortona can be reached easily from Florence, and even more easily from Arezzo – there are hourly LFI **buses**, as well as local **trains** that call at Camucia-Cortona station, from where a shuttle (roughly every 30min) takes ten minutes to run up to the old town. Florence–Rome trains (hourly) stop at Teróntola, 10km south, which is also served by a shuttle roughly every hour (25min to Cortona's Piazza Garibaldi). The centre is closed to all but essential traffic, so if you're driving you should use one of the free car parks on the periphery – they are all well signposted.

The **tourist office** at Via Nazionale 42 (May–Sept Mon–Sat 9am–1pm & 3–7pm, Sun 9am–1pm; Oct–April Mon–Sat 9am–1pm & 3–6pm; ⓣ0575.630.352, ⓦwww.cortonaweb.net) can provide leaflets and help out with accommodation.

## Accommodation

**Il Falconiere San Martino a Bocena ⓣ0575.612.679, ⓦwww.ilfalconiere.com.** Located 3km out of central Cortona on the SS71 towards Arezzo, this intimate four-star has nineteen beautifully presented rooms (some frescoed) and two swimming pools: one in the luscious garden, the other amid the hotel's vineyards and olive groves. The restaurant is justly celebrated, and like several other top-rank Tuscan hotel-restaurants, the *Falconiere* offers residential cookery courses. Doubles start at a little under €300 and go up to just under €600 for the best suite. ❻

**Italia Via Ghibellina 5 ⓣ0575.630.254, ⓦwww.planhotel.com.** A decent three-star occupying a renovated fifteenth-century house, with a panoramic breakfast terrace. It's not the most attractive hotel in Cortona, but the location – very near Piazza della Repubblica – makes the price more than reasonable. ❸

**Ostello San Marco Via G. Maffei 57 ⓣ0575.601.392, ⓦwww.cortonahostel.com.** Clean and spacious 80-bed HI hostel situated in the heart of the town in an old monastery, with fantastic views from the dormitories and friendly management. Dorm beds €14; doubles and family rooms available (€18 per person). Open mid-March to mid-Oct; reception open daily 7–10am & 3.30pm–midnight.

**Sabrina Via Roma 37 ⓣ0575.630.397, ⓔinfo@cortonastorica.com.** With just eight rooms, Cortona's other three-star is considerably smaller than its rival, the nearby *Italia,* and is somewhat cheaper as well. ❷

**San Luca Piazza Garibaldi 2 ⓣ0575.630.460, ⓦwww.sanlucacortona.com.** The four-star *San Luca* is somewhat functional, but many of its rooms have lovely views over the Valdichiana. Its prices are low for a four-star too. ❸

**San Michele Via Guelfa 15 ⓣ0575.604.348, ⓦwww.hotelsanmichele.net.** The most expensive and luxurious in-town choice, this handsome four-star has been converted from a rambling medieval town house. The rooms are a generous size, even if the decor is rather routine. ❹

**Villa Marsili Via Cesare Battisti 13 ⓣ0575.605.252, ⓦwww.villamarsili.net.** Situated a short distance down the slope from Piazza Garibaldi, this capacious four-star – occupying an eighteenth-century villa – looks unexceptional from the outside, but the rooms are nicely furnished with antiques (not suffocatingly so) and command a photogenic view of the valley. Prices are very good as well – even in high season it's sometimes possible to pick up a room for a little over €100, though you're likelier to pay in the region of €150–200. ❹

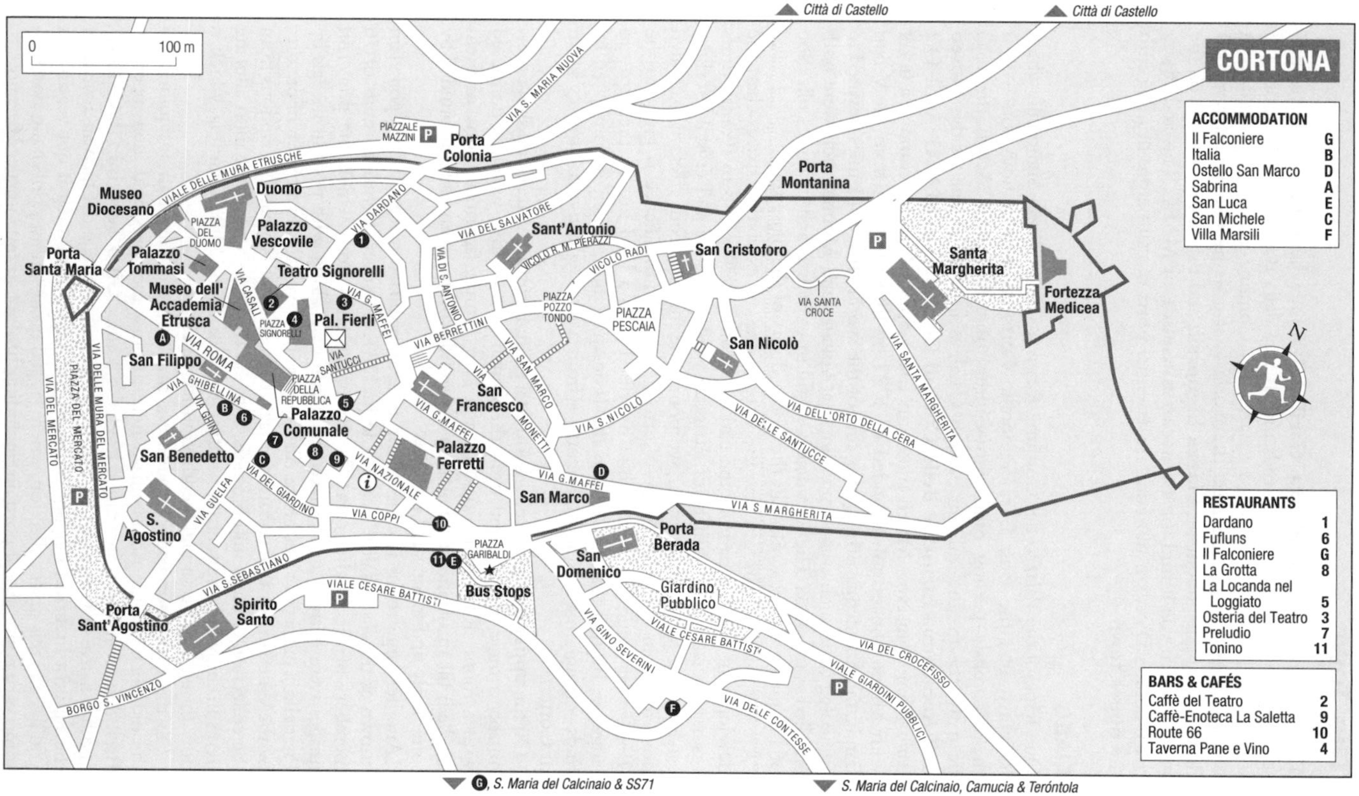

# CORTONA

**ACCOMMODATION**

| | |
|---|---|
| Il Falconiere | G |
| Italia | B |
| Ostello San Marco | D |
| Sabrina | A |
| San Luca | E |
| San Michele | C |
| Villa Marsili | F |

**RESTAURANTS**

| | |
|---|---|
| Dardano | 1 |
| Fufluns | 6 |
| Il Falconiere | G |
| La Grotta | 8 |
| La Locanda nel Loggiato | 5 |
| Osteria del Teatro | 3 |
| Preludio | 7 |
| Tonino | 11 |

**BARS & CAFÉS**

| | |
|---|---|
| Caffè del Teatro | 2 |
| Caffè-Enoteca La Saletta | 9 |
| Route 66 | 10 |
| Taverna Pane e Vino | 4 |

0 100 m

N

Città di Castello
Città di Castello
G, S. Maria del Calcinaio & SS71
S. Maria del Calcinaio, Camucia & Teróntola

Porta Colonia
Piazzale Mazzini
Porta Montanina
Museo Diocesano
Duomo
Piazza del Duomo
Palazzo Vescovile
Porta Santa Maria
Palazzo Tommasi
Museo dell' Accademia Etrusca
Teatro Signorelli
Piazza Signorelli
Pal. Fierli
Sant'Antonio
San Cristoforo
Santa Margherita
Fortezza Medicea
Piazza Pozzo Tondo
Piazza Pescaia
Via Santa Croce
San Nicolò
San Filippo
Piazza della Repubblica
Palazzo Comunale
San Francesco
San Benedetto
Palazzo Ferretti
San Marco
S. Agostino
Piazza Garibaldi
Bus Stops
Porta Berada
San Domenico
Giardino Pubblico
Porta Sant'Agostino
Spirito Santo
Via S. Maria Nuova
Viale delle Mura Etrusche
Via Dardano
Via del Salvatore
Vicolo R. M. Pierazzi
Vicolo Radi
Via Casali
Via G. Maffei
Via di S. Antonio
Via Berrettini
Via Santucci
Via Roma
Via Ghibellina
Via Ghini
Via San Marco
Via S. Nicolò
Via Monetti
Via Santa Margherita
Via dell'Orto della Cera
Via delle Santucce
Via S Margherita
Via Nazionale
Via del Giardino
Via Coppi
Via Guelfa
Via S. Sebastiano
Viale Cesare Battisti
Via Gino Severini
Via del Crocefisso
Viale Giardini Pubblici
Via delle Contesse
Via delle Mura del Mercato
Piazza del Mercato
Via del Mercato
Borgo S. Vincenzo

## The Town

The bus terminus is in **Piazza Garibaldi**, from where the only horizontal street in town, Via Nazionale, leads into Piazza della Repubblica. Here the tall staircase of the squat, castellated Palazzo del Comune is the grandstand from which the local *ragazzi* appraise the world as it goes by. The Saturday market flows through neighbouring **Piazza Signorelli** and Piazza del Duomo, on the first of which you'll find the **Etruscan museum**, or MAEC. This and Piazza del Duomo's Diocesan museum are essential ports of call before heading into the **upper town**.

### MAEC

One flank of the Palazzo del Comune forms a side of Piazza Signorelli, which is named after the artist Luca Signorelli, Cortona's most famous son – as is the decorously peeling nineteenth-century theatre-cinema. Across the road from the theatre, the hulking Palazzo Casali is now the home of the **Museo dell'Accademia Etrusca e della Città di Cortona** – or **MAEC** (April–Oct daily 10am–7pm; Nov–March Tues–Sun 10am–5pm; €7, or €10 combined ticket with Museo Diocesano). Founded in 1727 by three brothers from the Venuti family, the Accademia Etrusca was one of the world's first academies devoted to archeology, and such was its prestige that Voltaire and Montesquieu were both enrolled as members. The Accademia is still in existence, and its huge collection of antiquities and art works fills the upper floors of the museum.

On the **lowest floor** – where the state-of-the-art exhibition spaces chart the development of Cortona from the earliest recorded settlements to Roman times – some spectacular specimens of Etruscan gold, turquoise and crystal jewellery catch the eye, along with armour, weaponry and miscellaneous artefacts excavated from tombs in the valley below Cortona. Special prominence is given to the *Tabula Cortonensis*, a bronze plaque inscribed with a legal text in the Etruscan language. Beyond that, you're into the Roman section, which is dominated by finds – mainly mosaics and terracotta – from a large villa five kilometres south of Cortona.

On the **upper floors** there's a good deal more Etruscan material on show, most notably a huge bronze lamp from the fourth century BC, which is honoured with a room all to itself. Etruscan and later bronze figurines (none of them labelled) fill an avenue of cabinets in the middle of the main hall, surrounded by some fairly undistinguished pictures.

Another large room is centred on an extraordinary piece of frilly porcelain known as the *Tempio di Ginori*; made in 1737, it's covered with portraits of 76 members of the Medici clan. The bronze medals from which the porcelain images were derived are displayed in a wall case, along with portrait medals by Pisanello, a pioneer of this genre. Also on this floor you'll find a clutch of pictures by the Venetian artist Giambattista Piazzetta, a stack of Roman inscriptions from the collection of the Venuti brothers, and – at the end – one of the most alluring items in the whole museum: a painting on slate, of the Muse Polimnia, which is now thought to be an eighteenth-century fake.

On the **top floor** you can admire a small array of Egyptian antiquities and the old library of the Accademia, where the first members held their meetings. Back downstairs, on a mezzanine level, the painter **Gino Severini** (1883–1966), another native of Cortona, gets a room to himself at the end. Once an acolyte of the Futurist firebrand Filippo Marinetti, Severini was nothing if not versatile, as you'll see in this small collection, where jagged quasi-Cubist prints hang alongside some very conventional portraits, including his best-known image, *Maternity*.

## The Duomo and Museo Diocesano

Via Casali links Piazza Signorelli with Piazza del Duomo. Though rebuilt in the sixteenth century, the **Duomo** (daily 8.30am–12.30pm & 3–6.30pm; free) retains elements of its Romanesque precursor in its flaking facade; the interior is rather chilly and grey, but there's a Pietro da Cortona *Nativity* on the third altar on the left, and a possible Andrea del Sarto (an *Assumption*) to the left of the high altar.

The church that used to face the Duomo now forms part of the **Museo Diocesano** (same hours as MAEC; €5, or €10 combined ticket with MAEC), a tiny but high-quality collection of Renaissance art plus a fine Roman sarcophagus, carved with fighting centaurs. Predictably Luca Signorelli features strongly, though only two works – *Lamentation* (1502) and *The Communion of the Apostles* (1512) – are unequivocally his: seven others are attributed to him and his school.

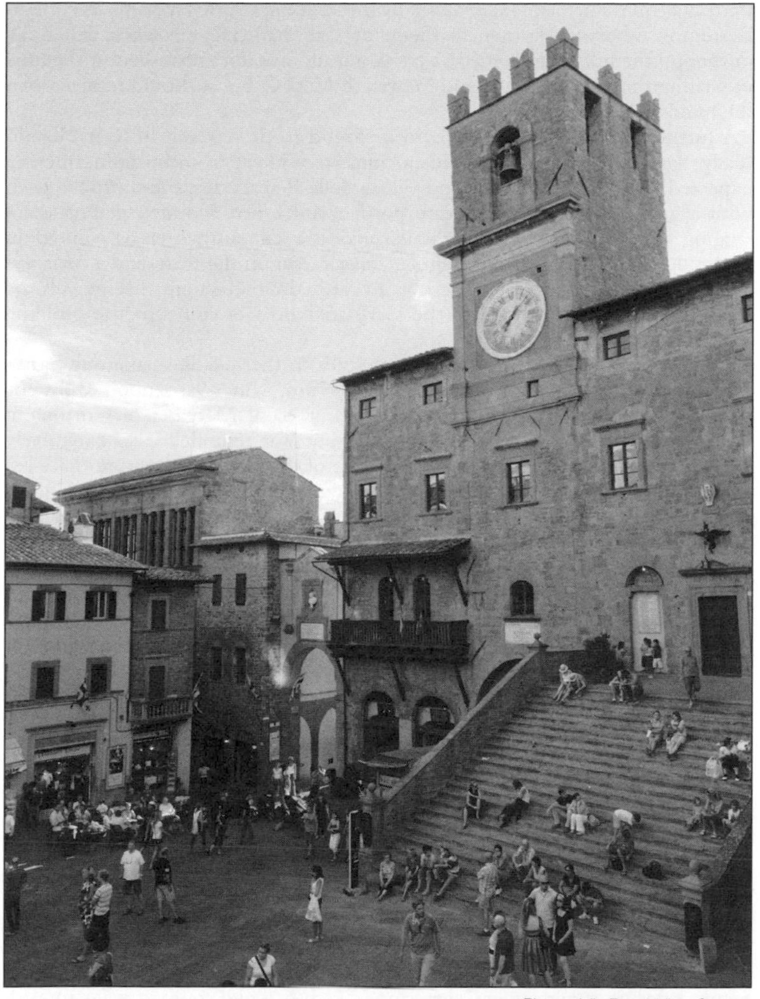

▲ Piazza della Repubblica, Cortona

Outstanding paintings from Sassetta, Bartolomeo della Gatta and Pietro Lorenzetti are also on show, but none of these measures up to Fra' Angelico, represented by a *Madonna, Child and Saints* and an exquisite *Annunciation*, painted while the artist was living at Cortona's monastery of San Domenico.

### The upper town

To explore the upper town take Via Santucci from Piazza della Repubblica and then clamber along Via Berrettini, at the near end of which stands the crusty and ancient church of **San Francesco** – designed by St Francis's disciple Brother Elias, this was the first Franciscan church to be built outside Assisi after the death of Francis himself. It's been under restoration for many years, but if you find it open you might see a Byzantine ivory reliquary for a piece of the True Cross on the high altar (behind which Brother Elias is buried), and on the third altar on the left an *Annunciation* by the man the street is named after, Pietro Berrettini, otherwise known as Pietro da Cortona. (He was born at no. 33, further up the hill.) This is Pietro's last work, and was left unfinished; at the time of writing the picture had been removed to MAEC, but it should return when the builders have finished.

A further work by Signorelli is to be found in the church of **San Nicolò** (daily 9am–noon & 3–7pm; closes 5pm in winter; €1 minimum offering expected), signposted just beyond Piazza della Pescaia. It's a frail little church with a gravel forecourt, a delicate portico and a fine wooden ceiling that's sagging with age. Signorelli's high altarpiece is a standard which he painted on both sides: a characteristically angular *Entombment* on the front and a *Madonna and Saints* on the back – revealed by a neat hydraulic system that swivels the picture away from the wall, as the sacristan who lets you into the building will demonstrate.

From Piazza della Pescaia, a steep path leads to the neo-Romanesque **Santa Margherita** (daily: summer 8am–noon & 3–7pm; winter 9am–noon & 3–6pm; free). Built to honour the town's patron saint, Saint Margaret of Cortona, it was begun in 1297, the year of her death, but was remodelled so extensively in the nineteenth century that the only part of the original structure that's left is the rose window of the facade. The daughter of a local farmer, Margaret seems to have been a spectacularly beautiful young woman, and to have led a wild life before becoming the servant and lover of a lord whose castle was near Montepulciano. When she was 27 years old he was murdered, and soon afterwards Margaret underwent a drastic conversion: she took vows as a Franciscan nun and devoted herself to helping the poor and sick of Cortona, for whom she founded a hospital that stood close to the site of the church. So intense was her relationship with the Almighty that the townspeople would pack into San Francesco to observe her delirious behaviour at Mass: "She became ashen pale, her pulse ceased, she froze, her throat was so affected by hoarseness that she could scarcely be understood when she returned to her senses," one witness recorded. Her tomb (1362), with marble angels lifting the lid of her sarcophagus, is now mounted on the wall to the left of the chancel; it's unoccupied, as her mummified body lies in a glass coffin at the high altar. The main altarpiece, Signorelli's *Lamentation*, has been removed to the Museo Diocesano, but in the chapel to the right of the chancel you can see a thirteenth-century Crucifix that is said to have spoken to Margaret on a number of occasions, when it was hanging in San Francesco.

The **Fortezza Medicea**, at the summit of the town, is sometimes used as an exhibition space in summer, and the area in front of it is good ground for a picnic, offering superb views over ruined Etruscan and Roman walls towards

Trasimeno. You could descend to Piazza Garibaldi by the stepped Via Crucis, where the Stations of the Cross are represented by mosaics by Severini.

### San Domenico and Santa Maria del Calcinaio

A last church in the centre of town to check out is **San Domenico** (daily 3–6pm; free), a half-minute's walk from Piazza Garibaldi. Completed in 1438, it has a fine high altarpiece by Lorenzo di Niccolò Gerini (*Coronation of the Virgin*), yet another Signorelli (*Madonna and Child with Saints*) and a dilapidated fresco by Fra' Angelico in the lunette above the main door, but it's hard to see behind its screen of protective glass.

Below the piazza, the middle distance is occupied by the perfectly proportioned though severely eroded Renaissance church of **Santa Maria del Calcinaio** (summer Mon–Sat 4–7pm & Sun 10am–12.30pm; winter Mon–Sat 3–5pm & Sun 10am–12.30pm; free). The masterpiece of Giorgio di Martini, it was begun in 1484 to enshrine a miraculous image of Mary that a lime burner (*calcinaio*) had unearthed at the tannery here (lime was used in the tanning process). Another Tuscan church of this vintage – Santa Maria delle Carceri in Prato – was built for similar reasons, but the sheer number of pilgrims who flocked to Cortona made it impossible for the architect to employ the fashionable central-plan design used in Prato. Hence this highly refined compromise: classical detailing applied to an old-fashioned and capacious cruciform church. Inside, the miraculous Madonna is still displayed on the high altar.

## Eating and drinking

For a town of its size, Cortona has an abundance of good **restaurants**. Nearly all the places to eat and drink are within a very short distance of Piazza della Repubblica.

### Restaurants

**Dardano Via Dardano 24 ⓣ0575.601.944.** An excellent, unpretentious, inexpensive and very popular trattoria – it's full to bursting most nights. Closed Wed.

**Fufluns Via Ghibellina 1–3.** If pizza's all you need, this spacious and bustling place is the first choice. Closed Tues.

**Il Falconiere San Martino a Bocena ⓣ0575.612.679, ⓦwww.ilfalconiere.com.** The Michelin-awarded restaurant of the *Falconiere* hotel uses ingredients that are produced on the hotel's own land. It's expensive (budget for around €70 per person) but worth every euro. Closed 3 weeks in Jan.

**La Grotta Piazzetta Baldelli 3 ⓣ0575.630.271.** Much like *Dardano*, *La Grotta* is a straight-down-the-line trattoria, albeit with a slightly higher percentage of tourists among the clientele. Closed Tues.

**La Locanda nel Loggiato Piazza Pescheria 3–4 ⓣ0575.630.575.** This place offers a small, high-quality and meat-centric menu, at around €35 a head; the wine list is equally classy, and the loggia, overlooking Piazza della Repubblica, is the nicest dining spot in the centre of town. Closed Wed.

**Osteria del Teatro Via Maffei 5 ⓣ0575.630.556, ⓦwww.osteria-del-teatro.it.** Occupying the whole lower floor of a rambling old mansion, this is a good-naturedly busy (sometimes frantic) place, featuring delicious home-made pastas on a meat-heavy menu; portions are generous and the prices more than fair – the bill should be around €35 per person. Closed Wed & mid-Nov to mid-Dec.

**Preludio Via Guelfa 11 ⓣ0575.630.104.** The food is invariably good and prices surprisingly moderate (around €30) in this smartly turned-out restaurant. Closed Mon, and lunchtime in winter.

**Tonino Piazza Garibaldi 1 ⓣ0575.630.500.** Good antipasti and a wonderful panoramic view from the terrace are the chief attractions of the dependable *Tonino*. Closed Mon evening, plus all Tues in winter.

## Bars and cafés

**Caffè del Teatro** On the terrace of the Teatro Signorelli. On summer evenings this is a favourite night-time hangout, with live music some weekends. Closed Mon.

**Caffè-Enoteca La Saletta Via Nazionale 26–28.** A glossy café-cum-wine shop, which also does simple meals.

**Route 66 Via Nazionale 78.** This self-styled "music bar" attracts the youngest crowd in town – the soundtrack is usually loud and it has occasional DJ nights. It does food too, but it's not the nosh that makes it popular. Open Tues–Sun until 3am.

**Taverna Pane e Vino Piazza Signorelli 27.** A good choice if you're after a quick lunch or a light evening meal: the menu offers various types of bruschetta, a wide selection of salamis and cheeses, plus a few more substantial dishes – and the wine list runs to some nine hundred different vintages. Closed Mon.

# Contexts

# Contexts

History....345

A directory of artists and architects....359

Books....371

# History

A comprehensive history of Tuscany in its medieval and Renaissance heyday would consist in large part of a mosaic of more or less independent histories, as each of the region's cities has a complex story to tell. In an overview such as this, fidelity to the entanglements of central Italy's past is impossible. Instead, within a broad account of the main trends in the evolution of Tuscany, we have concentrated on the city that emerged as the dominant force – Florence. The brief reviews of the other major towns – Siena, Pisa, Arezzo, Prato, Pistoia and so on – are supplemented by background given in the appropriate sections of the Guide. Similarly, crucial episodes in the history of Florence and its culture – for instance, the ascendancy of Savonarola – are covered in greater detail in the chapter on that city.

# Etruscans and Romans

The name of the province of Tuscany derives from the **Etruscans**, the most powerful civilization of pre-Roman Italy. There's no scholarly consensus on the origins of this people, with some experts insisting that they migrated into Italy from Anatolia at the start of the ninth century BC, and others maintaining that they were an indigenous tribe. All that's known for certain is that the Etruscans were spread thoughout central Italy from the eighth century BC, and that the centre of gravity of their domain was in the southern part of the modern province, roughly along a line drawn from Orbetello to Lago Trasimeno. Their principal settlements in Tuscany were Roselle, Vetulonia, Populonia, Volterra, Chiusi, Cortona, Arezzo and – most northerly of all – Fiesole.

It seems that the Etruscans absorbed elements of those cultures with whom they came into contact, thus their trade with Greek settlements produced some classically influenced art that can be seen at its best in Florence's archeological museum and in Cortona. The Etruscan language has still not been fully deciphered (a massive translation programme is under way in Perugia), so at the moment their wall paintings and terracotta funerary sculptures are the main source of information about them, and this is open to widely differing interpretations. Some people have inferred an almost neurotic fear of death from the evidence of their burial sites and monuments, while others – most notably D.H. Lawrence – have intuited an irrepressible and uncomplicated vitality.

There may have been an Etruscan settlement where Florence now stands, but it would have been subservient to their base in the hill-town of Fiesole. The substantial development of Tuscany's chief city began with the **Roman** colony of Florentia, established by Julius Caesar in 59 BC as a settlement for army veterans – by which time Romans had either subsumed or exterminated most Etruscan towns. Expansion of Florentia itself was rapid, with a steady traffic of trading vessels along the Arno providing the basis of accelerated growth in the second and third centuries AD.

This rise under the empire was paralleled by the growth of **Siena**, **Pisa** and **Lucca**, establishing an economic primacy in the north of Tuscany that has endured to the present. According to legend Siena was founded by the sons of Remus, supposedly fleeing their uncle Romulus, while the port at Pisa was developed by the Romans in the second century BC. Lucca was even more important, and it was here that Julius Caesar, Crassus and Pompey established their triumvirate in 56 BC.

## Barbarians and margraves

Under the comparative tranquillity of the Roman colonial regime, **Christianity** began to spread through the region. Lucca claims to have been the first Christian city in Tuscany – evangelized by a disciple of St Peter – though Pisa's church of San Pietro a Grado is said to have been founded by Peter himself. In Florence, the church of San Lorenzo and the martyr's shrine at San Miniato were both established in the fourth century.

This period of calm was shattered in the fifth century by the invasions of the **Goths** from the north, though the scale of the destruction in this first barbarian wave was nothing compared to the havoc of the following century. After the fall of Rome, the empire had split in two, with the western half ruled from Ravenna and the eastern from Constantinople (Byzantium). By the 490s Ravenna was occupied by the Ostrogoths, and forty years later the Byzantine Emperor Justinian launched a campaign to repossess the Italian peninsula.

The ensuing mayhem between the Byzantine armies of Belisarius and Narsus and the fast-moving Goths was probably the most destructive phase of central Italian history, with virtually all major settlements ravaged by one side or the other – and sometimes both. In 552 Florence fell to the hordes of the Gothic king **Totila**, whose depredations so weakened the province that less than twenty years later the **Lombards** were able to storm in, subjugating Florence to the duchy whose capital was in Pavia, though its dukes preferred to rule from Lucca.

By the end of the eighth century Charlemagne's **Franks** had taken control of much of Italy, with the administration overseen by imperial **margraves**, again based in Lucca. These proxy rulers developed into some of the most powerful figures in the Holy Roman Empire and were instrumental in spreading Christianity even further, founding numerous religious houses. Willa, widow of the margrave Uberto, established the Badìa in Florence in 978, the first monastic foundation in the centre of the city; her son Ugo, margrave in turn, is buried in the Badìa's church.

The hold of the central authority of the Holy Roman Empire was often tenuous, with feudal grievances making the region all but ungovernable, and it was under the imperial margraves that the notion of an autonomous Tuscan entity began to emerge. In 1027 the position of margrave was passed to the **Canossa** family, who took the title of the Counts of Tuscia, as Tuscany was then called. The most influential figure produced by this dynasty was **Matilda**, daughter of the first Canossa margrave. When her father died she was abducted by the German Emperor Henry III, and on her release and return to her home territory she began to take the side of the papacy in its protracted disputes with the empire. The culmination of her anti-imperialist policy came in 1077, when she obliged the Emperor Henry IV to wait in the snow outside the gates of Canossa before making obeisance to Pope Gregory VII. Later friction between the papacy, empire and Tuscan cities was assured when Matilda bequeathed all her lands to the pope, with the crucial exceptions of Florence, Siena and Lucca.

# Guelphs and Ghibellines

Though Lucca had been the titular base of the imperial margraves, Ugo and his successors had shown a degree of favouritism towards **Florence**, and over the next three hundred years Florence gained pre-eminence among the cities of Tuscany, becoming especially important as a religious centre. In 1078 Countess Matilda supervised the construction of new fortifications for Florence, and in the year of her death – 1115 – granted it the status of an independent city. The new *comune* of Florence was essentially governed by a council of one hundred men, the great majority drawn from the rising merchant class. In 1125 the city's increasing dominance of the region was confirmed when it crushed the rival city of Fiesole. Fifty years later, as the population boomed with the rise of the textile industry, new walls were built around what was then one of the largest cities in Europe.

Not that the other mercantile centres of Tuscany were completely eclipsed, as their magnificent heritage of medieval buildings makes plain. **Pisa** in the tenth and eleventh centuries had become one of the peninsula's wealthiest ports and its shipping lines played a vital part in bringing the cultural influences of France, Byzantium and the Muslim world into Italy. Twelfth-century **Siena**, though racked by conflicts between the bishops and the secular authorities and between the nobility and the merchant class, was booming thanks to its cloth industries and its exploitation of a local silver mine – the twin foundations of a financial empire that was to see the city rivalling the bankers of Venice and Florence on the international markets.

Throughout and beyond the thirteenth century Tuscany was torn by conflict between the **Ghibelline** faction and the **Guelphs**. The names of these two political alignments derive from Welf, the family name of Emperor Otto IV, and Waiblingen, the name of a castle owned by their implacable rivals, the Hohenstaufen. Though there's no clear documentation, it seems that the terms Guelph and Ghibelline entered the Italian vocabulary at the end of the twelfth century, when supporters of Otto IV battled for control of the central peninsula with the future Frederick II, nephew of Otto and grandson of the Hohenstaufen Emperor Barbarossa (1152–90). Within the first few years of Frederick II's reign (1212–50), the labels Guelph and Ghibelline had changed their meaning – the latter still referred to the allies of the Hohenstaufen, but the Guelph party was defined chiefly by its loyalty to the papacy, thus reviving the battle lines drawn up during the reign of Matilda.

To muddy the waters yet further, when Charles of Anjou conquered Naples in 1266, alliance with the anti-imperial French became another component of Guelphism, and a loose Guelph alliance soon stretched from Paris to Naples, substantially funded by the bankers of Tuscany.

Ghibelline and Guelph divisions approximately corresponded to a split between the feudal **nobility** and the rising **business classes**, but this is only the broadest of generalizations. By the beginning of the thirteenth century the major cities of Tuscany were becoming increasingly self-sufficient and inter-city strife was soon a commonplace of medieval life. In this climate, affiliations with the empire and the papacy were often struck on the basis that "my enemy's enemy is my friend", and allegiances changed at baffling speed: if, for instance, the Guelphs gained the ascendancy in a particular town, its neighbours might switch to the Ghibelline camp to maintain their rivalry. Nonetheless, certain patterns did emerge from the confusion: Florence and Lucca were generally Guelph strongholds, while Pisa, Arezzo, Prato, Pistoia and Siena tended to side with the empire.

As a final complicating factor, this was also the great age of **mercenary** armies, whose loyalties changed even quicker than those of the towns that paid for their services. Thus **Sir John Hawkwood** – whose White Company was the most fearsome band of hoodlums on the peninsula – is known today through the monument to him in Florence's Duomo, but early in his career was employed by Ghibelline Pisa to fight the Florentines. He was then taken on by Pope Gregory XI, whom he deserted on the grounds of underpayment, and in the end was granted a pension of 1200 florins a year by Florence, basically as a form of protection money. Even then he was often absent fighting for other cities whenever a fat purse was waved in his direction.

## Medieval Florence before the Medici

In this period of superpower manoeuvring and shifting economic structures, city governments in Tuscany were volatile. The administration of Siena, for example, was carried out by various combinations of councils and governors and in 1368 its constitution was redrawn no fewer than four times. However, Florence provides perhaps the best illustration of the turbulence of Tuscan politics in the late Middle Ages.

In 1207 the city's governing council was replaced by the **podestà**, an executive official who was traditionally a non-Florentine, in a semi-autocratic form of government that was common throughout the region. It was around this time, too, that the first **arti** (guilds) were formed to promote the interests of the traders and bankers, a constituency of ever-increasing power. Then in 1215 Florence was riven by a feud that was typical of the internecine violence of central Italy at this period. On Easter Sunday one **Buondelmonte de' Buondelmonti**, on his way to his wedding, was stabbed to death at the foot of the Ponte Vecchio by a member of the Amidei clan, in revenge for breaking his engagement to a young woman of that family. The prosecution of the murderers and their allies polarized the city into those who supported the *comune* – which regarded itself as the protector of the commercial city against imperial ambitions – and the followers of the Amidei, who seem to have politicized their personal grievances by aligning themselves against the *comune* and with the emperor.

These Ghibellines eventually enlisted the help of Emperor Frederick II to oust the Guelphs in 1248, but within two years they had been displaced by the Guelph-backed regime of the **Primo Popolo**, a quasi-democratic government drawn from the mercantile class. The *Primo Popolo* was in turn displaced in 1260, when the Florentine army marched on Siena to demand the surrender of some exiles who were hiding out in the city. Though greatly outnumbered, the Sienese army and its Ghibelline allies overwhelmed the aggressors at **Montaperti**, after which the Sienese were prevented from razing Florence only by the intervention of Farinata degli Uberti, head of the Ghibelline exiles.

By the 1280s the balance had again moved back in favour of Florence, where the Guelphs were back in control – after the intervention of Charles of Anjou – through the **Secondo Popolo**, a regime run by the *Arti Maggiori* (Great Guilds). It was this second bourgeois administration that definitively shifted the fulcrum of power in Florence towards its bankers, merchants and manufacturers – whereas in Siena, the second richest city in Tuscany, the feudal families retained a stranglehold for far longer. Agitation from the landed nobility of the countryside around Florence had been a constant fact of life until the *Secondo Popolo*, which in 1293 passed a programme of political reforms known as the *Ordinamenti della Giustizia*, excluding the nobility from government and investing power in the **Signoria**, a council drawn from the *Arti Maggiori*.

Strife between the virulently anti-imperial "Black" and more conciliatory "White" factions within the Guelph camp marked the start of the fourteenth century in Florence, with many of the Whites – Dante among them – being exiled in 1302. Worse disarray was to come. In 1325 the army of Lucca under **Castruccio Castracani** defeated the Florentines and was about to overwhelm the city when the death of their leader took the momentum out of the campaign. Then in 1339 the Bardi and Peruzzi banks – Florence's largest – both collapsed, mainly owing to the bad debts of Edward III of England. The ultimate catastrophe came in 1348, when the **Black Death** destroyed as many as half the city's population.

However, even though the epidemic hit Florence so badly that it was generally referred to throughout Europe as the Florentine Plague, its effects were equally devastating throughout the region, and did nothing to reverse the economic – and thus political – supremacy of the city. Florence had subsumed Pistoia in 1329 and gained Prato in the 1350s. In 1406 it took control of Pisa and thus gained a long-coveted sea port, and five years later Cortona became part of its territory. From this time on, despite the survival of Sienese independence into the sixteenth century, the history of Tuscany increasingly becomes the history of Florence.

# The early Medici

A crucial episode in the liberation of Florence from the influence of the papacy was the so-called **War of the Eight Saints** in 1375–78, which brought Florence into direct territorial conflict with Pope Gregory XI. This not only signalled the dissolution of the old Guelph alliance, but had immense repercussions for the internal politics of Florence. The increased taxation and other economic hardships of the war provoked an uprising of the industrial day-labourers, the **Ciompi**, on whom the wool and cloth factories depended. Their short-lived revolt resulted in the formation of three new guilds and direct representation for the workers for the first time. However, the prospect of increased proletarian presence in the machinery of state provoked a consolidation of the city's oligarchs and in 1382 an alliance of the city's Guelph party and the **Popolo Grasso** (the wealthiest merchants) took control of the *Signoria* away from the guilds, a situation that lasted for four decades.

Not all of Florence's most prosperous citizens aligned themselves with the *Popolo Grasso*, and the foremost of the well-off mavericks were the **Medici**, a family from the agricultural Mugello region whose fortune had been made by the banking prowess of Giovanni Bicci de' Medici. The political rise of his son, **Cosimo de' Medici**, was to some extent due to his family's sympathies with the *Popolo Minuto*, as the members of the disenfranchised lesser guilds were known. With the increase in public discontent at the autocratic rule of the *Signoria* – where the Albizzi clan were the dominant force – Cosimo came to be seen as the figurehead of the more democratically inclined sector of the upper class. In 1431 the authorities imprisoned him in the tower of the Palazzo Vecchio and two years later, as Florence became embroiled in a futile and domestically unpopular war against Lucca, they sent him into exile. He was away for only a year. In 1434, after a session of the *Parlamento* – a general council called in times of emergency – it was decided to invite him to return. Having secured the military support of the Sforza family of Milan, Cosimo became the pre-eminent figure in the city's political life, a position he maintained for more than three decades.

Cosimo il Vecchio – as he came to be known – rarely held office himself, preferring to exercise power through backstage manipulation and adroit investment.

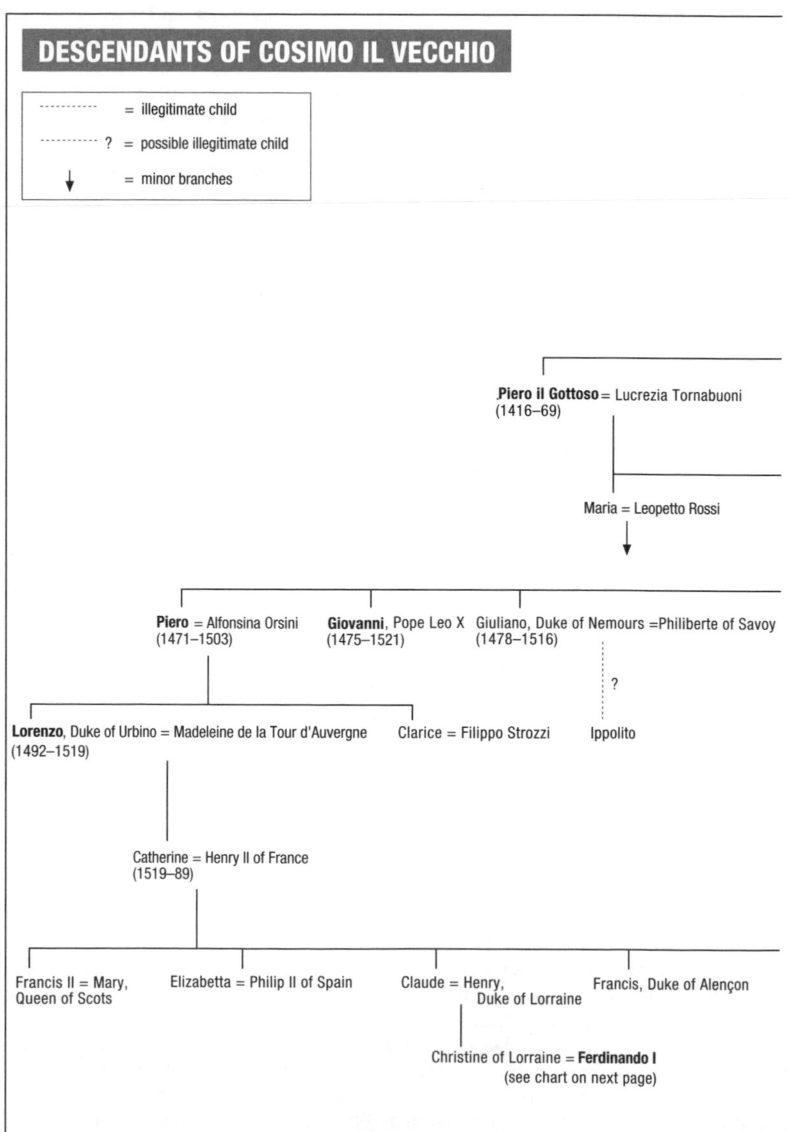

His extreme generosity to charities and religious foundations in Florence was no doubt motivated in part by genuine piety, but clearly did no harm as a public relations exercise – even if it didn't impress the contemporary who recorded that his munificence was due to the fact that "he knew his money had not been over-well acquired".

Dante, Boccaccio and Giotto in the first half of the fourteenth century had established the literary and artistic ascendancy of Florence, laying the foundations

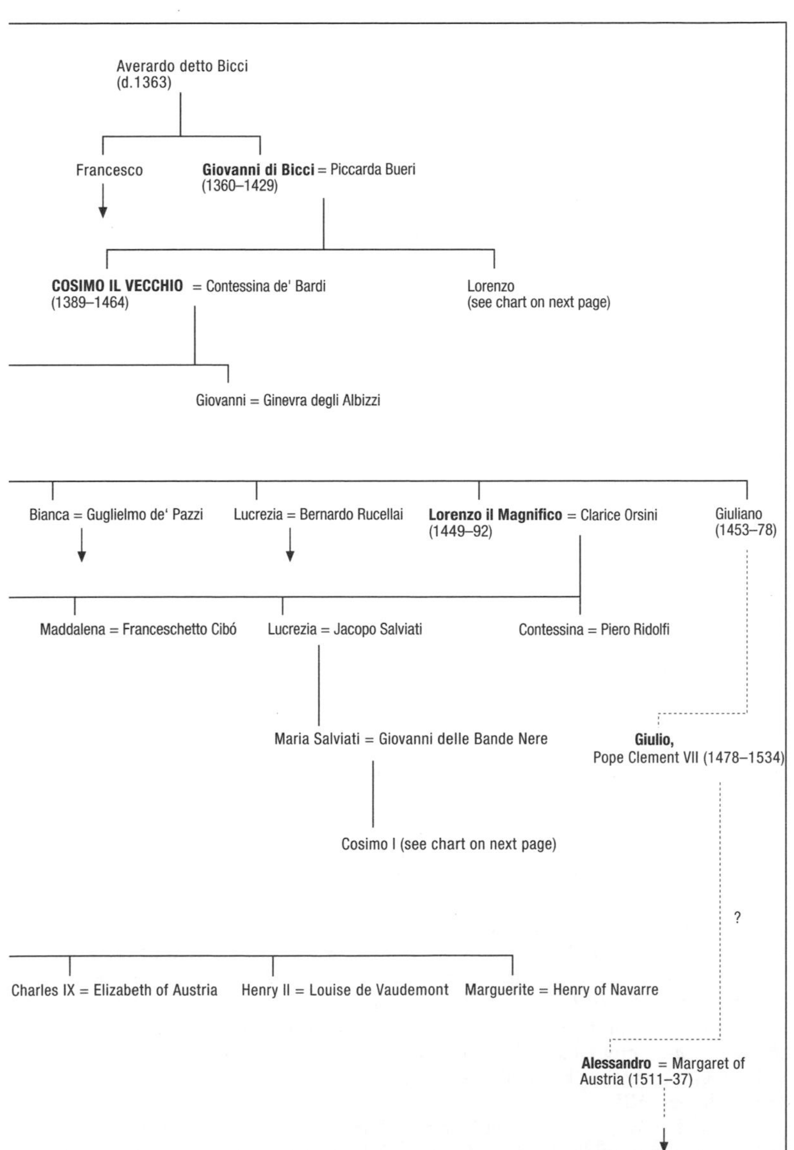

of Italian humanism with their emphasis on the importance of the vernacular and the dignity of humanity. Florence's reputation as the most innovative cultural centre in Europe was strengthened during the fifteenth century, to a large extent through Medici patronage. Cosimo commissioned work from Donatello, Michelozzo and a host of other Florentine artists, and took advantage of the 1439 Council of Florence – a conference of the Catholic and Eastern churches – to foster scholars who were familiar with the literatures of the ancient world. His grandson **Lorenzo il Magnifico** (who succeeded Piero il Gottoso, the Gouty) continued this literary patronage, promoting the study of the classics in the Platonic academy that used to meet at the Medici villas. Other Medici were to fund projects by Botticelli, Michelangelo, Pontormo – in fact, most of the seminal figures of the Florentine Renaissance.

Lorenzo il Magnifico's status as the *de facto* ruler of Florence was even more secure than that of Cosimo il Vecchio, but it did meet one stiff challenge. While many of Florence's financial dynasties were content to advise and support the Medici, others – notably the mighty Strozzi clan – were resentful of the power now wielded by their fellow businessmen. In 1478 one of these disgruntled families, the Pazzi, conspired with Pope Sixtus IV, who had been riled by Lorenzo's attempt to break the papal monopoly of alum mining. This **Pazzi Conspiracy** resulted in an assault on Lorenzo and his brother Giuliano during Mass in the Duomo; Lorenzo was badly injured and Giuliano murdered, an outcome that only increased the esteem in which Lorenzo was held. Now that the plot had failed, Pope Sixtus joined forces with the ferocious King Ferrante of Naples to launch a war on Florence, and excommunicated Lorenzo into the bargain. Taking his life in his hands, Lorenzo left Florence to persuade Ferrante to leave the alliance, a mission he somehow accomplished successfully, to the jubilation of the city.



## The Wars of Italy

Before Lorenzo's death in 1492 the Medici bank failed, and in 1494 Lorenzo's son Piero was obliged to flee following his surrender to the invading French army of Charles VIII. This invasion was the commencement of a bloody half-century dominated by the so-called **Wars of Italy**.

After the departure of Charles's troops, Florence for a while was virtually under the control of the inspirational monk **Girolamo Savonarola**, but his career was brief. He was executed as a heretic in 1498, after which the city continued to function as a more democratic republic than that of the Medici. In 1512, however, following Florence's defeat by the Spanish and papal armies, the Medici returned, in the person of the vicious **Giuliano, Duke of Nemours**.

Giuliano's successors – his equally unattractive nephew Lorenzo, the Duke of Urbino, and Giulio, illegitimate son of Lorenzo il Magnifico's brother – were in effect just the mouthpieces of Giovanni de' Medici (the Duke of Nemours' brother), who in 1519 became **Pope Leo X**. Similarly, when Giulio became **Pope Clement VII**, he was really the absentee ruler of Florence, where the family presence was maintained by the ghastly **Ippolito** (the illegitimate son of the Duke of Nemours) and **Alessandro** (acknowledged by the Duke of Urbino as his illegitimate son, but believed by most historians to have been the son of Pope Clement VII).



The Medici were again evicted from Florence in the wake of Charles V's pillage of Rome in 1527, Pope Clement's humiliation by the imperial army providing the spur to eject his deeply unpopular relatives. Three years later the pendulum swung the other way: after a siege by the combined papal and imperial forces, Florence capitulated and was obliged to receive Alessandro, who was proclaimed **Duke of Florence**, the first Medici to bear the title of ruler. Though the sadistic Alessandro lost no opportunity to exploit the immunity that came from his title, in the wider scheme of Italian politics he was a less powerful figure than his ancestors. Tuscany was becoming just one more piece in the vast jigsaw of the Habsburg Empire, a superpower far more interventionist than the medieval empire of Frederick II could ever have been.

## The later Medici

After the assassination of Alessandro in 1537, power passed to another **Cosimo**, not a direct heir but rather a descendant of Cosimo il Vecchio's brother. The emperor Charles V, now related to the Medici through the marriage of his daughter to Alessandro, gave his assent to the succession of this seemingly pliable young man – indeed, without Habsburg consent it would not have happened. Yet it turned out that Cosimo had the clear intention of maintaining Florence's role as the regional power-broker, and he proved immensely skilful at judging just how far he could push the city's autonomy without provoking the imperial policy-makers.

Having finally extinguished the subversive threat of the Strozzi faction at the battle of **Montemurlo**, Cosimo went on to buy the territory of Siena from the Habsburgs in 1557, giving Florence control of all of Tuscany with the solitary exception of Lucca. Two years later Florentine hegemony in Tuscany was confirmed in the Treaty of Cateau-Cambrésis, the final act in the Wars of Italy. Soon after, though, the new Habsburg Emperor, Philip II, installed a military outpost in the Orbetello area to keep Tuscany under scrutiny.

Imperial and papal approval of Cosimo's rule was sealed in 1570, when he was allowed to take the title **Cosimo I, Grand Duke of Tuscany**. In European terms Tuscany was a second-rank power, but by comparison with other states on the peninsula it was in a very comfortable position, and during Cosimo's reign there would have been little perception that Florence was drifting inexorably towards the margins of European politics. It was Cosimo who built the Uffizi, extended and overhauled the Palazzo Vecchio, installed the Medici in the Palazzo Pitti, had the magnificent Ponte Santa Trìnita constructed across the Arno and commissioned much of the public sculpture around the Piazza della Signoria.

Cosimo's descendants were to remain in power until 1737, and aspects of their rule continued the city's intellectual tradition: the Medici were among Galileo's strongest supporters, for example. Yet it was a story of almost continual if initially gentle economic decline, as bad harvests and recurrent epidemics worsened the gloom created by the shift of European trading patterns in favour of northern Europe. The half-century reign of **Ferdinando II** had scarcely begun when the market for Florence's woollen goods collapsed in the 1630s, and the city's banks simultaneously went into a terminal slump. The last two male Medici, the insanely pious **Cosimo III** and the drunken pederast **Gian Gastone** – who was seen in public only once, vomiting from the window of the state coach – were fitting symbols of the moribund Florentine state.

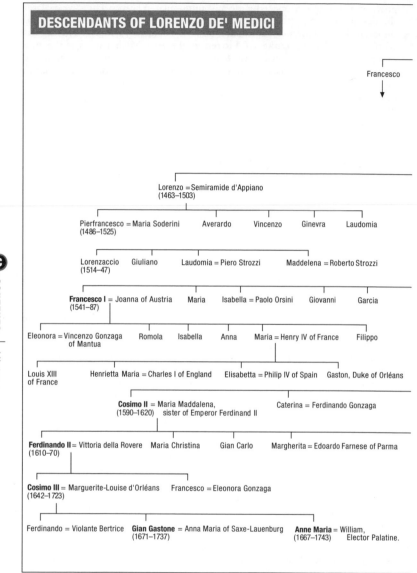

## DESCENDANTS OF LORENZO DE' MEDICI

Francesco

Lorenzo = Semiramide d'Appiano
(1463–1503)

Pierfrancesco = Maria Soderini
(1486–1525)

Averardo

Vincenzo

Ginevra

Laudomia

Lorenzaccio
(1514–47)

Giuliano

Laudomia = Piero Strozzi

Maddelena = Roberto Strozzi

**Francesco I** = Joanna of Austria
(1541–87)

Maria

Isabella = Paolo Orsini

Giovanni

Garcia

Eleonora = Vincenzo Gonzaga of Mantua

Romola

Isabella

Anna

Maria = Henry IV of France

Filippo

Louis XIII of France

Henrietta Maria = Charles I of England

Elisabetta = Philip IV of Spain

Gaston, Duke of Orléans

**Cosimo II** = Maria Maddalena, sister of Emperor Ferdinand II
(1590–1620)

Caterina = Ferdinando Gonzaga

**Ferdinando II** = Vittoria della Rovere
(1610–70)

Maria Christina

Gian Carlo

Margherita = Edoardo Farnese of Parma

**Cosimo III** = Marguerite-Louise d'Orléans
(1642–1723)

Francesco = Eleonora Gonzaga

Ferdinando = Violante Bertrice

**Gian Gastone** = Anna Maria of Saxe-Lauenburg
(1671–1737)

**Anne Maria** = William, Elector Palatine.
(1667–1743)

# To the present

Under the terms of a treaty signed by Gian Gastone's sister, Anna Maria de' Medici, Florence passed in 1737 to the **House of Lorraine**, cousins of the Austrian Habsburgs. The first Lorraine prince, the future Francis I of Austria, was a more

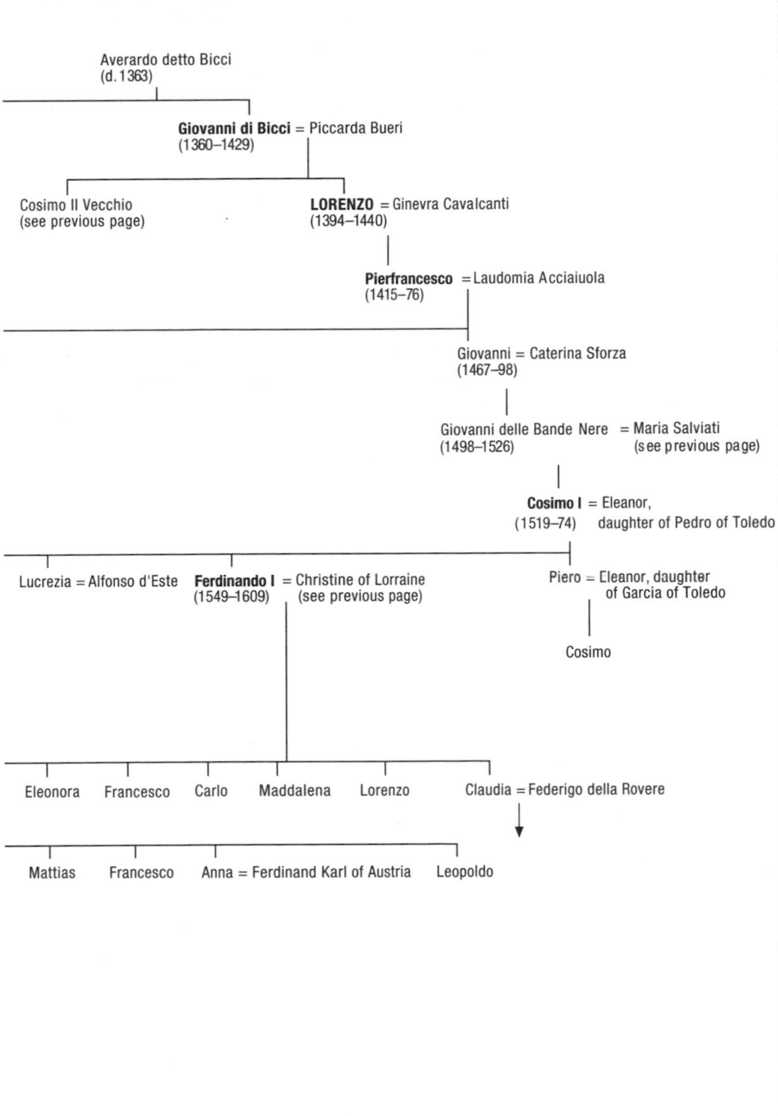


enlightened ruler than the last Medici had been and his successors presided over a placid and generally untroubled region, doing much to improve the condition of Tuscany's agricultural land and rationalize its production methods. Austrian rule lasted until the coming of the French in 1799, an interlude that ended with the fall of **Napoleon**, who had made his sister Elisa Baciocchi Grand Duchess of Tuscany.

After this, the Lorraine dynasty was brought back, remaining in residence until the last of the line, Leopold II, consented to his own deposition in 1859. Absorbed into the new **Kingdom of Italy** in the following year, Florence became the **capital** in 1865, a position it held until the beginning of 1871, when Rome – having at last become part of the otherwise united country – took over the role.

Italy's unpopular entry into World War I cost thousands of Tuscan lives, and the economic disruption that followed was exploited by the regime of Benito **Mussolini**. The corporate Fascist state of the 1920s did effect various improvements in the infrastructure of the region, but Mussolini's alliance with Hitler's Germany was to prove a calamity. In 1943, as the Allied landing at Monte Cassino was followed by a campaign to sweep the occupying German forces out of the peninsula, Tuscany became a battlefield between the Nazis and the **partisans**. The districts around Monte Amiata and the Val d'Órcia sheltered particularly strong partisan groups, and many of the province's hill-towns had their resistance cells, as numerous well-tended war memorials testify.

## What is the Renaissance?

In the middle of the sixteenth century Giorgio Vasari coined the term *Rinascenza* (rebirth) to designate the period that stretched from around 1300 (the lifetime of Giotto) to the time of Michelangelo. In the late nineteenth century the term "Renaissance" entered general usage, largely thanks to the writings of Jacob Burckhardt, whose book *The Civilization of the Renaissance in Italy* is perhaps the single most influential study of the subject. To historians of this period, the Renaissance was often seen as a singular and all-pervasive phenomenon, in which the rediscovery of ancient classical culture gave impetus to a regeneration of European civilization after the intellectual impoverishment of the Middle Ages. It was characterized by its focus on humanity, and the epicentre of this explosion of humanist art and scholarship was Florence.

While nobody doubts that many of the artists, writers and patrons of Renaissance Italy believed themselves to be participants in the creation of a new society, it's debatable that "Renaissance values" reached deeply into the lives of most ordinary people. For the general populace, life continued to be "medieval" long after their masters had taken to reading Plato. Not only was a peasant's existence as harsh as ever, but there can have been few more dangerous periods in Italian history than the so-called "High Renaissance". From 1494 to 1559 the peninsula was an almost continuous battleground for the major powers of Europe, and at the end of this period, with Habsburgs as the dominant force, most of the Italian city-states were reduced to the ranks of bit-players.

### The problem of beginnings

Locating the beginnings of the Italian Renaissance is a problematic business. **Giotto** (1267–1337) is often taken as a starting point, and when his paintings are compared to the art of the "Gothic" era, it does seem as if he introduced a new realism and drama to European art. His great contemporary **Dante** (1265–1321), who presents Giotto as an innovator in the *Divine Comedy*, appears modern in his use of vernacular Tuscan rather than Latin. On the other hand, the stern theology of Dante's masterpiece strikes us as belonging to a distinctly pre-modern world.

Dante's immediate successors, **Petrarch** (1304–74) and **Boccaccio** (1313–75) – both of them Tuscans – certainly feel more modern than he does. Petrarch's love poetry, his collecting of classical manuscripts and his appreciation of landscape for itself might be described as manifestations of a Renaissance spirit. Similarly, Boccaccio's *Decameron* has a claim to be the first example of modern prose fiction. And yet in the visual arts it can seem that in the century after Giotto painting didn't change enough to support the idea that his work initiated an unstoppable process. It wasn't until **Masaccio**'s frescoes in the Brancacci chapel, painted a hundred years after Giotto's in Santa Croce, that Italian art could be said to have taken its next leap forward.

Yet, as elsewhere in Italy, the loyalties of Tuscany were split, as is well illustrated by the case of Florence, an ideological centre for the resistance but also home to some of Italy's most ardent Nazi collaborators. Wartime Florence in fact produced one of the strangest paradoxes of the time: a Fascist sympathizer in charge of the British Institute and a German consul who did so much to protect suspected partisans that he was granted the freedom of the city after the war.

Although most of the major monuments of Tuscany survived the war – sometimes as a result of pacts between the two sides – there was inevitably widespread destruction. Grosseto, Pisa and Livorno were badly damaged by Allied bombing raids, while Florence was wrecked by the retreating German army, who bombed all the bridges except the Ponte Vecchio and blew up much of the medieval city near the banks of the Arno.

### The case of Florence

If it's impossible to say exactly where and when the Renaissance begins, there's no doubt that the high culture of Florence (and most of Italy) in 1500 was radically different from that of 1300. Furthermore, Florence in the fifteenth century nurtured more of these "avant garde" figures than any other city in Italy. But what were the circumstances that made Florence the pre-eminent centre of creativity?

A primary factor was the city's wealth. Buoyed by revenues from banking and manufacture, the Florentine upper classes had plenty of surplus cash with which to fund the accumulation of libraries and art collections. Competing against each other in displays of educated taste, clans such as the Strozzi, the Medici, the Rucellai and the Tornabuoni were furthering a Florentine self-image that can be traced back at least as far as Giovanni Villani (1275–1348), author of a twelve-volume history of the city (written in Tuscan), in which he wrote that Florence, "the daughter and offspring of Rome, is on the increase and destined to do great things".

Even before Villani, Florence had something of a humanist tradition. Dante's teacher, **Brunetto Latini** (c.1210–94), for instance, studied Aristotle and Cicero, wrote in the vernacular (both Italian and French) and with his *Livre du trésor* produced what might be called the first encyclopaedia. A century later, Florence's university invited Manuel Chrysoloras (c.1350–1415) to travel from Constantinople to teach Greek – the first time for seven hundred years that the language had been taught in Italy. Chrysoloras translated Plato and Homer, wrote about the monuments of Rome and Byzantium, and numbered among his pupils Leonardo Bruni – chancellor of the Florentine Republic, author of the *History of the Florentine People* and books on Dante, Petrarch and Boccaccio, translator of Plato and Aristotle, and the first scholar to define his work as *studia humanitatis*.

In 1439 the Council of Florence – convened to forge a reconciliation between the Roman and Eastern churches – brought a host of classical scholars to the city, some of whom remained in Florence, to be joined after 1453 by others who fled from Constantinople following its conquest by the Turks. These refugees further enriched an environment in which developed so many great artists and such prodigious philosopher scholars as Marsilio Ficino, Poliziano and Pico della Mirandola, all of whom were members of the Medici court.

But while Botticelli's *Birth of Venus* or Michelangelo's *David* unarguably embody something new, Renaissance philosophy was essentially an elaboration of the work of ancient thinkers – of Plato in particular. For all their learning, Ficino and the rest produced nothing to equal the originality of medieval philosophers such as Thomas Aquinas or Duns Scotus.

## Postwar Tuscany

Tuscany is a prosperous and conservative region that in the past has tended to elect right-of-centre members of parliament. On a local level, however, left-wing support is high, partly as a consequence of the Italian communist party's record in the war and subsequent work on land reform. The communists were effectively excluded from national government by the machinations of the now-defunct Christian Democrat party (which, like the old Socialist party, was undone by the corruption scandals of the early 1990s), but the newer left-leaning parties that have emerged over the past couple of decades have projected themselves as the grassroots opposition to the centralization and corruption of Roman politics. It's a strategy that has been particularly successful in Tuscany, which has clung onto an image of itself as a state within the state. Since the 1970s the town halls of the region have been governed predominantly by communist-led coalitions, forming the heartland of the so-called "red belt" of central Italy.

Despite migration from the land in the 1950s and 1960s, the **economy** of Tuscany has been adroitly managed. The labour-intensive vineyards, olive groves and farms continue to provide a dependable source of income, boosted by industrial development in the Arno valley and around Livorno and Piombino. Production of textiles, leather goods and jewellery has brought money into Prato, Florence and Arezzo, while wine has brought untold prosperity to previously moribund towns such as Montalcino and Montepulciano. But **tourism** plays an uncomfortably large and ever-increasing part in balancing the books of these and other historic centres. This is a mixed blessing, since sheer weight of numbers in places such as Florence, Siena and San Gimignano overburdens an already creaking infrastructure and – worse – undermines the charm and damages the historic and artistic treasures that attract visitors in the first place.

# A directory of artists and architects

**Alberti, Leon Battista** (1404–72). Born illegitimately to a Florentine exile, probably in Genoa, Alberti was educated in Padua and Bologna. One of the most complete personifications of the Renaissance ideal of universal genius, he was above all a writer and theorist: his *De Re Aedificatoria* (1452) was the first architectural treatise of the Renaissance, and he also wrote a tract on the art of painting, *Della Pittura*, dedicated to his friend Brunelleschi. His theory of harmonic proportions in musical and visual forms was first put into practice in the facade of Santa Maria Novella in Florence, while his archeological interest in classical architecture found expression in the same city's Palazzo Rucellai, his first independent project. Even more closely linked to his researches into the styles of antiquity is the miniature temple built for the Rucellai family in the church of San Pancrazio. His other buildings are in Mantua and Rimini.

**Ammannati, Bartolomeo** (1511–92). A Florentine sculptor-architect, much indebted to Michelangelo, Ammannati is best known for his additions and amendments to the Palazzo Pitti and for the graceful Ponte Santa Trìnita (though in all likelihood this was largely designed by Michelangelo). He created the fountain in the Piazza della Signoria, with some assistance from his pupil Giambologna, and the Bargello contains some of his pieces made for the Bóboli gardens.

**Andrea del Sarto** (1486–1530). The dominant artist in Florence at the time of Michelangelo and Raphael's ascendancy in Rome. He made his name with frescoes for two Florentine churches in the San Marco district – the Scalzo and Santissima Annunziata. For a period in the 1510s he was in France, and the received wisdom is that his talent did not develop after that. However, two of his other major works in Florence date from after his return – the *Last Supper* in San Salvi and the *Madonna del Sacco* in the cloister of the Annunziata. His major easel painting is the *Madonna of the Harpies* in the Uffizi.

**Arnolfo di Cambio** (c.1245–1302). Pupil of Nicola Pisano, with whom he worked on sculptural projects in Bologna, Siena and Perugia before going to Rome in 1277. The most important of his independent sculptures are the pieces in Florence's Museo dell'Opera del Duomo and the *Tomb of Cardinal de Braye* in San Domenico in Orvieto. The latter defined the format of wall tombs for the next century, showing the deceased lying on a coffin below the Madonna and Child, set within an elaborate architectural framework. However, Arnolfo is best known as the architect of Florence's Duomo and Palazzo Vecchio, and various fortifications in central Tuscany, including the fortress at Poppi.

**Beccafumi, Domenico** (1484/86–1551). The last great Sienese painter, Beccafumi was in Rome during the painting of the Sistine chapel ceiling and Raphael's *Stanze*. He returned to Siena in 1513, when his work showed tendencies that were to become prevalent in Mannerist art – contorted poses, strong lighting, vivid artificial colouration. His decorative skill is especially evident in his illusionist frescoes in the Palazzo Pubblico and the pavement of the Duomo.

**Benedetto da Maiano** (1442–97). Florentine sculptor, best known for his portrait busts in the Bargello and the pulpit in Santa Croce.

**Botticelli, Sandro** (c.1445–1510). Possibly a pupil of Filippo Lippi, Botticelli was certainly influenced by the Pollaiuolo brothers, whose paintings of the *Virtues* he completed. The mythological paintings for which he is celebrated – including the *Birth of Venus* and *Primavera* – are distinguished by their emphasis on line rather than mass, and by their complicated symbolic meaning, a reflection on his involvement with the Neoplatonist philosophers whom the Medici gathered about them. In the last decade of his life his devotional pictures became almost clumsily didactic – a result, perhaps, of his involvement with Savonarola and his followers.

**Bronzino, Agnolo** (1503–72). The adopted son of Pontormo, Bronzino became the court painter to Cosimo I. He frescoed parts of the Palazzo Vecchio for Eleonora di Toledo, but his reputation rests on his glacially elegant portraits.

**Brunelleschi, Filippo** (1377–1446). Trained as a sculptor and goldsmith, Brunelleschi abandoned this career after his failure in the competition for the Florence Baptistery doors. The main product of this period is his contribution to the St James altarpiece in Pistoia. He then devoted himself to the study of the building techniques of the classical era, travelling to Rome with Donatello in 1402. In 1417 he submitted his design for the dome of Florence's Duomo, and all his subsequent work was in that city – San Lorenzo, the Spedale degli Innocenti, Cappella Pazzi (Santa Croce) and Santo Spirito. Unlike the other great architect of this period, Alberti, his work is based on no theoretical premise, but rather on an empiricist's admiration for the buildings of Rome. And unlike Alberti, he oversaw every stage of construction, even devising machinery that would permit the raising of the innovative structures he had planned.

**Buonarroti, Michelangelo** (1475–1564). See box, pp.110–111.

**Castagno, Andrea** (c.1421–57). The early years of Castagno's life are mysterious, and the exact year of his birth is not known. Around 1440 he painted the portraits of some executed rebels in the Bargello, a job that earned him the nickname "Andrea of the Hanged Men". In 1442 he was working in Venice, but a couple of years later he was back in Florence, creating stained glass for the Duomo and frescoes for Sant'Apollonia. His taut, sinewy style is to a large extent derived from the sculpture of his contemporary, Donatello, an affinity that is especially clear in his frescoes for Santissima Annunziata. Other major works in Florence include the series of *Famous Men and Women* in the Uffizi and the portrait of *Niccolò da Tolentino* in the Duomo – his last piece.

**Cellini, Benvenuto** (1500–71). Cellini began his career in Rome, where he fought in the siege of the city by the imperial army in 1527. His sculpture is greatly influenced by Michelangelo, as is evident in his most famous large-scale piece, the *Perseus* in the Loggia della Signoria. His other masterpiece in Florence is the heroic *Bust of Cosimo I* in the Bargello. Cellini was an even more accomplished goldsmith and jeweller, creating some exquisite pieces for Francis I, by whom he was employed in the 1530s and 1540s. He also wrote a racy autobiography, a fascinating insight into the artistic world of sixteenth-century Italy and France.

**Cimabue** (c.1240–1302). Though celebrated by Dante as the foremost painter of the generation before

Giotto, very little is known about Cimabue – in fact, the only work that is unquestionably by him is the mosaic in Pisa's Duomo. He is generally given credit for the softening of the hieratic Byzantine style of religious art, a tendency carried further by his putative pupil, Giotto. Some works can be attributed to him with more confidence than others: the shortlist would include *The Madonna of St Francis* in the lower church at Assisi, the *Passion* cycle in the upper church, the *Maestà* in the Uffizi, and the crucifixes in Santa Croce (Florence) and San Domenico (Arezzo).

**Daddi, Bernardo** (c.1290–1349). A pupil of Giotto, Daddi combined the solidity of his master's style with the more decorative aspects of the Sienese style. His work can be seen in the Uffizi and Santa Croce in Florence.

**Desiderio da Settignano** (c.1428–64). Desiderio continued the low relief technique pioneered by Donatello in the panel for the Orsanmichele *St George*, and carved the tomb of Carlo Marsuppini in Santa Croce, Florence. He's better known for his exquisite busts of women and children, a good selection of which are on show in the Bargello.

**Donatello** (c.1386–1466). A pupil of Ghiberti, Donatello assisted in the casting of the first set of Florence Baptistery doors in 1403, then worked for Nanni di Banco on the Duomo. His early marble *David* (Bargello) is still Gothic in its form, but a new departure is evident in his heroic *St Mark* for Orsanmichele (1411) – possibly produced after a study of the sculpture of ancient Rome. Four years later he began the intense series of prophets for the Campanile, and at the same time produced the *St George* for Orsanmichele, the epitome of early Renaissance humanism, featuring a relief that is the very first application of rigorous perspective in Western art.

In the mid-1420s Donatello started a partnership with Michelozzo, with whom he created the tomb of Pope John XXIII in the Florence Baptistery. He went to Rome in 1431, possibly with Brunelleschi, and it was probably on his return that he made the classical bronze *David* (Bargello), one of the first nude statues of the Renaissance period. Also at this time he made the cantoria to be placed opposite the one already made by Luca della Robbia, the pulpit for Prato cathedral (with Michelozzo) and the decorations for the old sacristy in Florence's church of San Lorenzo – the parish church of his great patrons, the Medici.

After a period in Padua – where he created the first bronze equestrian statue since Roman times – he returned to Florence, where his last works show an extraordinary harshness and angularity. The main sculptures from this period are the *Judith and Holofernes* (Palazzo Vecchio), the *Magdalene* (Museo dell'Opera del Duomo) and the two bronze pulpits for San Lorenzo.

**Duccio di Buoninsegna** (c.1255–c.1318). Though occupying much the same pivotal position in the history of Sienese art as Giotto does in Florentine art, Duccio was a less revolutionary figure, refining the stately Byzantine tradition rather than subverting its conventions. One of his earliest works was ordered by Florence's church of Santa Maria Novella – the *Maestà* now in the Uffizi – but the bulk of his output is in his home city. Despite frequent ructions with the civic authorities, for refusing to do military service among other transgressions, in 1308 he received his most prestigious assignment, the painting of a *Maestà* for Siena's Duomo. The polyptych no longer exists in its original form, but most of the panels are now in Siena's Museo dell'Opera del Duomo.

**Fra' Angelico** (1387/1400–55). Born in Vicchio, Fra' Angelico joined the Dominican order in Fiesole and later entered their monasteries in Cortona and Foligno. His first authenticated painting dates from the mid-1420s, but the first one that can be definitely dated is a *Madonna* he produced for the linen guild of Florence in 1433. Three years later the Dominicans took over the San Marco monastery in Florence, and soon after he embarked on the series of frescoes and altarpieces now displayed in the museum there. In the mid-1440s he was called to Rome to work on the Vatican, after which he worked at Orvieto, served for three years as prior of the monastery in Fiesole, and returned to Rome around 1452, where he died. His altarpieces of the Madonna and Saints – a genre known as *sacre conversazione* – were extremely influential compositions.

**Fra' Bartolommeo** (c.1474–1517). Fra' Bartolommeo's earliest known work is the Raphael-influenced *Last Judgement* painted for the San Marco monastery in Florence in 1499. The following year he became a monk there, then in 1504 became head of the workshop, a post previously occupied by Fra' Angelico. In 1514 he was in Rome, but according to Vasari was discouraged by Raphael's fame. The works he later produced in Florence had an influence on High Renaissance art, with their repression of elaborate backgrounds and anecdotal detail, concentrating instead on expression and gesture.

**Francesco di Giorgio Martini** (1439–1501/2). Sienese painter, sculptor and architect, whose treatise on architectural theory was circulated widely in manuscript form; Leonardo had a copy. Employed for a long period by Federico da Montefeltro – also a patron of Piero della Francesca – he probably designed the loggia for the Palazzo Ducale in Urbino and the church of San Bernardino. The church of Santa Maria degli Angeli in Siena and the Palazzo Ducale in Gubbio might be by him; the one Tuscan building that was certainly designed by him is Santa Maria del Calcinaio in Cortona.

**Gaddi, Taddeo** (d.1366). According to tradition, Taddeo Gaddi worked with Giotto for 24 years, and throughout his life barely wavered from the precepts of his master's style. His first major independent work is the cycle for the Cappella Baroncelli in Santa Croce, Florence. Other works by him are in Florence's Uffizi, Accademia, Bargello and Museo Horne. **Agnolo Gaddi** (d.1396), Taddeo's son, continued his father's Giottesque style; his major projects were for Santa Croce in Florence and the Duomo of Prato.

**Gentile da Fabriano** (c.1370–1427). Chief exponent of the International Gothic style in Italy, Gentile da Fabriano came to Florence in 1422, when he painted the gorgeous *Adoration of the Magi*, now in the Uffizi. In 1425 he went on to Siena and Orvieto, where the intellectual climate was perhaps more conducive to an artist of his conservative temperament; he finished his career in Rome.

**Ghiberti, Lorenzo** (1378–1455). Trained as a goldsmith, painter and sculptor, Ghiberti concentrated on the last discipline almost exclusively after winning the competition to design the doors for Florence's Baptistery. His first set of doors are to a large extent derived from Andrea Pisano's earlier Gothic panels for the building, yet his workshop was a virtual academy for the seminal figures of the early Florentine Renaissance, Donatello and Uccello among them. The commission took around twenty years to complete, during which time he also worked on the Siena Baptistery and the church of Orsanmichele in Florence, where his *Baptist* and *St Matthew* show the influence of Classical statuary. This classicism reached its peak in the second set of doors for Florence's Baptistery (the *Gates of Paradise*) – taking the innovations of Donatello's low relief carving to a new pitch of perfection. The panels occupied much of the rest of his life but in his final years he wrote his *Commentarii*, the main source of information on fourteenth-century art in Florence and Siena, and the first autobiography by an artist.

**Ghirlandaio, Domenico** (1449–94). The most accomplished fresco artist of his generation, Ghirlandaio was the teacher of Michelangelo. After a short period working on the Sistine Chapel with Botticelli, he came back to Florence, where his cycles in Santa Trìnita and Santa Maria Novella provide some of the most absorbing documentary images of the time, being filled with contemporary portraits and vivid anecdotal details.

**Giambologna** (1529–1608). Born in northern France, Giambologna – Jean de Boulogne – arrived in Italy in the mid-1550s, becoming the most influential Florentine sculptor after Michelangelo's death. Having helped Ammannati on the fountain for the Piazza della Signoria, he went on to produce a succession of pieces that typify the Mannerist predilection for sculptures with multiple viewpoints, such as the *Rape of the Sabines* (Loggia della Signoria) and the *Mercury* (Bargello). His workshop also turned out scores of reduced bronze copies of his larger works; the Bargello has an extensive collection.

**Giotto di Bondone** (1266–1337). It was with Giotto's great fresco cycles that religious art shifted from being a straightforward act of devotion to the dramatic presentation of incident. His unerring eye for the significant gesture, his ability to encapsulate moments of extreme emotion and his technical command of figure modelling and spatial depth brought him early recognition as the greatest artist of his generation – and even as late as the sixteenth century artists were studying his frescoes for their solutions to certain compositional problems. Yet, as with Cimabue, the precise attribution of work is problematic. In all probability his first major cycle was the *Life of St Francis* in the upper church at Assisi, though the extent to which his assistants carried out his designs is still disputed. The Arena chapel in Padua is certainly by him, as are large parts of the Bardi and Peruzzi chapels in Santa Croce in Florence. Of his attributed panel paintings, the Uffizi *Maestà* is the only one universally accepted.

**Gozzoli, Benozzo** (1421–97). Though a pupil of Fra' Angelico, Gozzoli was one of the more worldly artists of the fifteenth century, with a fondness for pageantry that is seen to most impressive effect in the frescoes in Florence's Palazzo Medici-Riccardi. His celebrated cycle in Pisa's Camposanto was all but destroyed in World War II; his other surviving fresco cycles include the *Life of St Francis* in Montefalco and the *Life of St Augustine* in San Gimignano.

**Guido da Siena** (active mid-thirteenth century). Guido was the founder of the Sienese school of painters, but his life is one of the most problematic areas of Siena's art history. A signed painting by him in the Palazzo Pubblico is dated 1221, but some experts think the date may have been altered, and that the work is from the 1260s or 1270s – a period when other pictures associated with him are known to have been painted.

**Leonardo da Vinci** (1452–1519). Leonardo trained as a painter under Verrocchio, and it is said that his precocious talent caused his master to abandon painting in favour of sculpture. Drawings of landscapes and drapery have survived from the 1470s, but the first completed picture by him is the *Annunciation* in the Uffizi. The sketch of the *Adoration of the Magi*, also in the Uffizi, dates from 1481, at which time there was no precedent for its fusion of geometric form and dynamic action. Two years later he was in the employment of Lodovico Sforza of Milan, remaining there for sixteen years. During this second phase of his career he produced the *Lady with the Ermine* (now in Kraków), the fresco of the *Last Supper* and – probably – the two versions of *The Virgin of the Rocks*, the fullest demonstrations to date of his so-called *sfumato*, a blurring of tones from light to dark. Innumerable scientific studies and military projects engaged him at this time, and he also made a massive clay model for an equestrian statue of Francesco Sforza – never completed, like so many of his schemes. When the French took Milan in 1499 Leonardo returned to Florence, where he devoted much of his time to anatomical research. It was during this second Florentine period that he was commissioned to paint a fresco of the *Battle of Anghiari* in the main hall of the Palazzo Ducale, where his detested rival Michelangelo was also set to work. Only a fragment of the fresco was completed, and the innovative technique that Leonardo had employed resulted in its speedy disintegration. His cartoons for the *Madonna and Child with St Anne* (Louvre and National Gallery, London) also date from this period, as does the most famous of all his paintings, the Louvre's *Mona Lisa*, the portrait of the wife of a Florentine merchant. In 1506 he went back to Milan, thence to Rome and finally, in 1517, to France. Again, military and scientific work occupied much of this last period – the only painting to have survived is the *St John*, also in the Louvre.

**Lippi, Filippo** (c.1406–69). In 1421 Filippo Lippi was placed in the monastery of the Carmine in Florence, just at the time Masaccio was beginning work on the Cappella Brancacci there. His early works all bear the stamp of Masaccio, but by the 1530s he was becoming interested in the representation of movement and a more luxuriant surface detail. The frescoes in the cathedral at Prato, executed in the 1550s, show his highly personal, almost hedonistic vision, as do his panel paintings of wistful Madonnas in patrician interiors or soft landscapes – many of them commissioned by the Medici. His last work, the *Life of the Virgin* fresco cycle in Spoleto, was probably largely executed by assistants.

**Lippi, Fillippino** (1457/58–1504) Fillippino Lippi completed his father's work in Spoleto – aged about 12 – then travelled to Florence, where his first major commission was the completion of Masaccio's frescoes in Santa Maria del Carmine (c.1484). At around this time he also painted the *Vision of St Bernard* for the Badìa, which shows an affinity with Botticelli, with whom he is known to have worked. His later researches in Rome led him to develop a self-consciously antique style – seen at its most ambitious in Santa Maria Novella.

**Lorenzetti, Ambrogio** (active 1319–47). Though Sienese, Ambrogio spent part of the 1320s and 1330s in Florence, where he would have witnessed the decoration of Santa Croce by Giotto and his pupils. He's best known for the *Allegory of Good and Bad Government* in the

Palazzo Pubblico, which shows painting being used for a secular, didactic purpose for the first time. The Uffizi *Presentation of the Virgin* highlights the difference between Ambrogio's inventive complexity and the comparative simplicity of his brother's style (see below).

**Lorenzetti, Pietro** (active 1306–48). Brother of Ambrogio, Pietro Lorenzetti was possibly a pupil of Duccio's in Siena. His first authenticated work is the altarpiece in Arezzo's Pieve di Santa Maria (1320); others include frescoes in Assisi's lower church, in which the impact of Giotto is particularly noticeable, and the *Birth of the Virgin* in Siena's Museo dell'Opera del Duomo, one of the best demonstrations of his skill as a narrative painter. It's probable that both the Lorenzettis died during the Black Death.

**Lorenzo Monaco** (1372–1425). A Sienese artist, Lorenzo Monaco joined the Camaldolese monastery in Florence, for which he painted the *Coronation of the Virgin*, now in the Uffizi. This and his other earlier works are fairly conventional Sienese-style altarpieces, with two-dimensional figures on gold backgrounds. However, his late *Adoration of the Magi* (Uffizi), with its fastidious detailing and landscape backdrop, anticipates the arrival of Gentile da Fabriano and fully fledged International Gothic.

**Martini, Simone** (c.1284–1344). The most important Sienese painter, Simone Martini was a pupil of Duccio but equally influenced by Giovanni Pisano's sculpture and the carvings of French Gothic artists. He began his career by painting a fresco counterpart of Duccio's *Maestà* in the city's Palazzo Pubblico (1315). Soon after he was employed by Robert of Anjou, King of Naples, and there developed a sinuous, graceful and courtly style. In the late 1320s he was back in Siena, where he probably produced the portrait of Guidoriccio da Fogliano – though some experts doubt its authenticity. At some point he went to Assisi, where he painted a cycle of *The Life of St Martin* in the lower church. In 1333 he produced a sumptuous *Annunciation* for the Siena Duomo; now in the Uffizi, this is the quintessential fourteenth-century Sienese painting, with its immaculately crafted gold surfaces and emphasis on fluid outline and bright colouration. In 1340 Martini travelled to the papal court of Avignon, where he spent the rest of his life. It was at Avignon that he formed a friendship with Petrarch, for whom he illustrated a magnificent copy of Virgil's poetry.

**Masaccio** (1401–28). Born just outside Florence, Tommaso di ser Giovanni di Mone Cassai – universally known as Masaccio – entered the city's painters' guild in 1422. His first large commission was an altarpiece for the Carmelites of Pisa (the central panel is now in the National Gallery in London), which shows a massive grandeur at odds with the International Gothic style then being promulgated in Florence by Gentile da Fabriano. His masterpieces – the *Trinity* fresco in Santa Maria Novella and the fresco cycle in Santa Maria del Carmine – were produced in the last three years of his life, the latter being painted in collaboration with Masolino. With the architecture of Brunelleschi and the sculpture of Donatello, the Carmine frescoes are the most important achievements of the early Renaissance.

**Masolino da Panicale** (1383–1447). Masolino was employed in Ghiberti's workshop for the production of the first set of Baptistery doors, and the semi-Gothic early style of Ghiberti conditioned much of his subsequent work. His other great influence was the younger Masaccio, with whom he worked on the Brancacci chapel.

**Michelangelo** - see box, pp.110–111.

**Michelozzo di Bartolommeo** (1396–1472). Born in Florence, Michelozzo worked in Ghiberti's studio and collaborated with Donatello before turning exclusively to architecture. His main patrons were the Medici, for whom he altered the villa at Careggi and built the Palazzo Medici, which set a prototype for patrician mansions in the city. He later designed the Villa Medici at Fiesole for the family, and for Cosimo de' Medici he added the light and airy library to the monastery of San Marco. In the Alberti-influenced tribune for the church of Santissima Annunziata, Michelozzo produced the first centrally planned church design to be built in the Renaissance period.

**Mino da Fiesole** (1429–84). Florentine sculptor, perhaps a pupil of Desiderio da Settignano, Mino is known chiefly for his tombs and portrait busts; there are examples of the former in Fiesole's Duomo and the Badìa in Florence, and of the latter in the Bargello.

**Nanni di Banco** (c.1384–1421). A Florentine sculptor who began his career as an assistant to his father on the Florence Duomo, Nanni was a contemporary of Donatello, with whom he shared some early commissions: Donatello's first *David* was ordered at the same time as an *Isaiah* from Nanni. The finest works produced in his short life are his niche sculptures at Orsanmichele (especially the *Four Saints*) and the relief above the Duomo's Porta della Mandorla.

**Orcagna, Andrea** (c.1308–68). Architect-sculptor-painter, Orcagna was a dominant figure in the period following the death of Giotto, whose emphasis on spatial depth he rejected – as shown in his only authenticated panel painting, the Strozzi altarpiece in Santa Maria Novella. Damaged frescoes can be seen in Santa Croce and Santo Spirito, but Orcagna's principal work in Florence is the massive tabernacle in Orsanmichele. Orcagna's brothers Nardo and Jacopo di Cione were the most influential painters in Florence at the close of the fourteenth century; the frescoes in the Strozzi chapel are by Nardo.

**Perugino** (1445/50–1523). Born Pietro di Cristoforo Vannucci in Città della Pieve, Perugino was the greatest Umbrian artist. Possibly a pupil of Piero della Francesca, he later trained in Florence in the workshop of Andrea Verrocchio, studying alongside Leonardo da Vinci. By 1480 his reputation was such that he was invited to paint in the Sistine Chapel, filling the east wall with his distinctive gently melancholic figures; today only one of Perugino's original three panels remains. In 1500 he executed his greatest work in Umbria, a fresco cycle commissioned by the bankers' guild of Perugia for their Collegio di Cambio. This was probably the first time he was assisted by his pupil Raphael – and the moment his own career began to wane. Vasari claimed that he was "a man of little or no religion, who could never bring himself to believe in the immortality of the soul" and the production-line altarpieces that his workshop later turned out were often lacking in genuine passion. Yet he was still among the most influential of the Renaissance painters, the catalyst for Raphael and mentor for a host of Umbrian artists. In Tuscany he is best seen in the Uffizi and in the church of Santa Maria Maddalena dei Pazzi.

**Piero della Francesca** (1410/20–92). Piero was born in Borgo Sansepolcro, on the border of Tuscany and Umbria. In the late 1430s he was in Florence, working with Domenico Veneziano, and his later work shows the influence of such Florentine contemporaries as

Castagno and Uccello, as well as the impact of Masaccio's frescoes. The exact chronology of his career is contentious, but much of his working life was spent in his native town, for which he produced the *Madonna della Misericordia* and the *Resurrection*, both now in the local Museo Civico. In the 1450s he was in Arezzo, working on the fresco cycle in the church of San Francesco, the only frescoes in Tuscany that can bear comparison with the Masaccio cycle in Florence. He seems to have stopped painting completely in the early 1470s, perhaps to concentrate on his vastly influential treatises on perspective and geometry, but more likely because of failing eyesight.

**Piero di Cosimo** (c.1462–1521). One of the more enigmatic figures of the High Renaissance, Piero di Cosimo shared Leonardo's scholarly interest in the natural world, but turned his knowledge to the production of allusive mythological paintings. There are pictures by him in the Uffizi, Palazzo Pitti, Museo degli Innocenti and Museo Horne.

**Pietro da Cortona** (1596–1669). Painter-architect, born Pietro Berrettini, who with Bernini was the guiding force of Roman Baroque. The style was introduced to Florence by Pietro's ceiling frescoes in the Palazzo Pitti.

**Pinturicchio** (1454–1513). Born Bernardino di Betto in Perugia, Pinturicchio was taught by Perugino, with whom he collaborated on the painting of the Sistine Chapel. His rich palette earned him his nickname, as well as Vasari's condemnation for superficiality. Most of his work is in Rome but his last commission, one of his most ambitious projects, was his *Life of Pius II* for the Libreria Piccolomini in Siena.

**Pisano, Andrea** (c.1290–1348). Nothing is known of Andrea Pisano's life until 1330, when he was given the commission to make a new set of doors for the Florence Baptistery. He then succeeded Giotto as master mason of the Campanile; the set of reliefs he produced for it are the only other works definitely by him (now in the Museo dell'Opera del Duomo). In 1347 he became the supervisor of Orvieto's Duomo, a job later held by his sculptor son, Nino.

**Pisano, Nicola** (c.1220–84). Born somewhere in the southern Italian kingdom of the Emperor Frederick II, Nicola Pisano was the first great classicizing sculptor in pre-Renaissance Italy; the pulpit in Pisa's Baptistery (1260), his first masterpiece, shows clearly the influence of Roman figures. Five years later he produced the pulpit for the Duomo in Siena, with the assistance of his son Giovanni (c.1248–1314) and Arnolfo di Cambio. Father and son again worked together on the Fonte Gaia in Perugia, which was Nicola's last major project. Giovanni's more turbulent Gothic-influenced style is seen in two other pulpits, for San Andrea in Pistoia and for the Pisa Duomo. The Museo dell'Opera del Duomo in Siena has some fine large-scale figures by Giovanni, while its counterpart in Pisa contains a large collection of work by both the Pisani.

**Pollaiuolo, Antonio del** (c.1432–98) and **Piero del** (c.1441–96). Though their Florence workshop turned out engravings, jewellery and embroideries, the Pollaiuolo brothers were known mainly for their advances in oil-painting technique and for their anatomical researches, which bore fruit in paintings and small-scale bronze sculptures. The influences of Donatello and Castagno (Piero's teacher) are evident in their dramatic, often violent sculptural work, which is especially well represented in the Bargello. The Uffizi's collection of paintings suggests that Antonio was by far the more skilled artist.

**Pontormo, Jacopo** (1494–1556). Born near Empoli, Pontormo studied under Andrea del Sarto in Florence in the early 1510s. His friendship with Rosso Fiorentino was crucial in the evolution of the hyper-refined Mannerist aesthetic. His early independent works include the frescoes in the atrium of Santissima Annunziata in Florence, showing an edgy quality quite unlike that of his master, who also frescoed this part of the church. His masterpiece in Florence is the *Deposition* in Santa Felìcita (1525), unprecedented in its lurid colour scheme but showing some indebtedness to Michelangelo's figures. The major project of his later years, a fresco cycle in San Lorenzo, Florence, has been totally destroyed. Other pieces by him are to be seen in the Uffizi and at Carmignano and Sansepolcro.

**Quercia, Jacopo della** (1374–1438). A Sienese contemporary of Donatello and Ghiberti, della Quercia entered the competition for the Florence Baptistery doors which Ghiberti won in 1401. The first known work by him is the tomb of Ilaria del Carretto in Lucca's Duomo. His next major commission was a fountain for Siena's main square, a piece now reassembled in the loggia of the Palazzo Pubblico; before that was finished (1419) he had begun work on a set of reliefs for Siena's Baptistery, a project to which Ghiberti and Donatello also contributed. From 1425 he expended much of his energy on reliefs for San Petronio in Bologna – so much so, that the Sienese authorities ordered him to return some of the money he had been paid for the Baptistery job.

**Raphael** - see Sanzio, Raffaelo

**Robbia, Luca della** (1400–82). Luca della Robbia began as a sculptor in conventional materials, his earliest achievement being the marble *cantoria* (choir gallery) now in the Museo dell'Opera del Duomo in Florence, typifying the cheerful tone of most of his work. Thirty years later he made the sacristy doors for Florence's Duomo, but by then he had devised a technique for applying durable potter's glaze to clay sculpture and most of his energies were given to the art of glazed terracotta. His distinctive blue, white and yellow compositions are seen at their best in the Pazzi chapel in Santa Croce, the Bargello, and at Impruneta, just outside Florence. The best work of his nephew, Andrea della Robbia (1435–1525), who continued the lucrative terracotta business, is at the Spedale degli Innocenti in Florence and at the monastery of La Verna. Giovanni della Robbia (1469–1529), son of Andrea, is best known for the frieze of the Ceppo in Pistoia.

**Rossellino, Bernardo** (1409–64). An architect-sculptor, Rossellino worked with Alberti and carried out his plans for the Palazzo Rucellai in Florence. His major architectural commission was Pius II's new town of Pienza. As a sculptor he's best known for the monument to Leonardo Bruni in Santa Croce – a derivative of Donatello's tomb of John XXIII in the Baptistery. His brother and pupil Antonio (1427–79) produced the tomb of the Cardinal of Portugal in Florence's San Miniato al Monte, and a number of excellent portrait busts (in the Bargello).

**Rosso Fiorentino** (1494–1540). Like Pontormo, Rosso Fiorentino was a pupil of Andrea del Sarto, but went on to develop a far more aggressive, acidic style than his colleague and friend. His early *Deposition* in Volterra (1521) and the roughly contemporaneous *Moses Defending the Daughters of Jethro* (Uffizi) are typical of his extreme foreshortening and tense deployment of figures. After a period in Rome and Venice, he eventually went to

France, where with Primaticcio he developed the distinctive Mannerist art of the Fontainebleau school.

**Sangallo, Antonio da, the Elder** (1455–1534). A Florence-born architect, Antonio da Sangallo the Elder produced just one major building, but one of the most influential of his period – San Biagio in Montepulciano, based on Bramante's plan for St Peter's in Rome. His nephew, Antonio the Younger (1485–1546), was also born in Florence but did most of his work in Rome, where he began his career as assistant first to Bramante then to Peruzzi. He went on to design the Palazzo Farnese, the most spectacular Roman palace of its time. In Tuscany his most important building is the Fortezza da Basso in Florence.

**Sangallo, Giuliano da** (1445–1516). Sculptor, architect and military engineer, Giuliano was the brother of Antonio the Elder. A follower of Brunelleschi, he produced a number of buildings in and around Florence – the Villa Medici at Poggio a Caiano, Santa Maria delle Carceri in Prato (the first Renaissance church to have a Greek-cross plan) and the Palazzo Strozzi in Florence, the most ambitious palace of the century.

**Sanzio, Raffaelo (Raphael)** (1483–1520). With Leonardo and Michelangelo, Raphael forms the triumvirate whose works define the essence of the High Renaissance. Born in Urbino, he joined Perugino's workshop some time around 1494 and within five years was receiving commissions independently of his master. From 1505 to 1508 he was in Florence, where he absorbed the compositional and tonal innovations of Leonardo; many of the pictures he produced at that time are now in the Palazzo Pitti. From Florence he went to Rome, where Pope Julius II set him to work on the papal apartments (the Stanze). Michelangelo's Sistine ceiling was largely instrumental in modulating Raphael's style from its earlier lyrical grace into something more monumental, but all the works from this more rugged later period are in Rome.

**Signorelli, Luca** (1450–1523). Though a pupil of Piero della Francesca, Signorelli is more indebted to the muscular drama of the Pollaiuolo brothers and the gestural vocabulary developed by Donatello. In the early 1480s he was probably working on the Sistine Chapel with Perugino and Botticelli, but his most important commission came in 1499, when he was hired to complete the cycle begun by Fra' Angelico in Orvieto's Duomo. The emphasis on the nude figure in his *Last Judgement* was to affect Michelangelo greatly. Shortly after finishing this cycle he went to Rome but the competition from Raphael and Michelangelo drove him back to his native Cortona, where he set up a highly proficient workshop. Works are to be seen in Cortona, Arezzo, Monte Oliveto, Perugia, Sansepolcro, and in the Uffizi and Museo Horne in Florence.

**Sodoma, Il** (1477–1549). After training in Milan (where he became familiar with the work of Leonardo da Vinci) and Siena, Giovanni Antonio Bazzi was taken to Rome by the Sienese banker Agostino Chigi in 1508. Having failed to make much of an impact there (he began work on the papal apartments but was replaced by Raphael), he returned to Siena, where he married in 1510. Though Siena was his base for the rest of his life, his work took him to various Italian cities, notably Florence, Lucca, Pisa and Volterra; his major creation in Tuscany is the fresco cycle at the monastery of Monte Oliveto Maggiore, begun immediately before his sojourn in Rome. Vasari states that the nickname by which he's always known came about because he "loved small boys more than was decent", but it's possible that it was a joke of Bazzi's own devising – and it seems unlikely that he would have received as many church commissions as he did if his proclivities were as Vasari said.

**Spinello Aretino** (active 1370–1410). Probably born in Arezzo, Spinello studied in Florence, possibly under Agnolo Gaddi. He harks back to the monumental aspects of Giotto's style – thus paradoxically paving the way for the most radical painter of the next generation, Masaccio. His main works are in Florence's church of San Miniato al Monte, and Santa Caterina d'Antella, just to the south of the city.

**Uccello, Paolo** (1396–1475). After training in Ghiberti's workshop, Uccello went to Venice, where he worked on mosaics for the Basilica di San Marco. He returned to Florence in 1431 and five years later was contracted to paint the commemorative portrait of Sir John Hawkwood in the Duomo. This trompe l'oeil painting is the first evidence of his interest in the problems of perspective and foreshortening, a subject that was later to obsess him. After an interlude in Padua, he painted the frescoes for the cloister of Santa Maria Novella (c.1445), in which his systematic but non-naturalistic use of perspective is seen at its most extreme. In the following decade he painted the three-scene sequence *Battle of San Romano* (Louvre, London National Gallery and Uffizi) for the Medici – his most ambitious non-fresco paintings, and similarly notable for their strange use of foreshortening.

**Vasari, Giorgio** (1511–74). Born in Arezzo, Vasari trained with Luca Signorelli and Andrea del Sarto. He became the leading artistic impresario of his day, working for the papacy in Rome and for the Medici in Florence, where he supervised (and partly executed) the redecoration of the Palazzo Vecchio. His own house in Arezzo is perhaps the most impressive display of his limited pictorial talents. He also designed the Uffizi gallery and oversaw a number of other architectural projects, including the completion of the massive Madonna dell'Umiltà in Pistoia. He is now chiefly famous for his Tuscan-biased *Lives of the Most Excellent Painters, Sculptors and Architects*.

**Veneziano, Domenico** (1404–61). Despite the name, Domenico Veneziano was probably born in Florence, though his preoccupation with the way in which colour alters in different light conditions is more of a Venetian concern. From 1439 to 1445 he was working on a fresco cycle in Florence with Piero della Francesca, a work that has now perished. Only a dozen surviving works can be attributed to him with any degree of certainty and only two signed pieces by him are left – one of them is the central panel of the so-called *St Lucy Altar* in the Uffizi.

**Verrocchio, Andrea del** (c.1435–88). A Florentine painter, sculptor and goldsmith, Verrocchio was possibly a pupil of Donatello and certainly his successor as the city's leading sculptor. A highly accomplished if sometimes over-facile craftsman, he ran one of Florence's busiest workshops, whose employees included the young Leonardo da Vinci. In Florence his work can be seen in the Uffizi, Bargello, San Lorenzo, Santo Spirito, Orsanmichele and Museo dell'Opera del Duomo.

# Books

Most of the books recommended below are currently in print, and those that aren't shouldn't be too difficult to track down on websites such as Ⓦwww.abebooks.com or www.alibris.com. Titles that are currently out of print in both the US and UK are marked "o/p". The ⛹ symbol indicates titles that are especially recommended.

## Travel books and journals

**Charles Dickens** *Pictures from Italy.* The classic mid-nineteenth-century Grand Tour, recording the sights of Emilia, Tuscany, Rome and Naples in measured and incisive prose.

**Wolfgang Goethe** *Italian Journey.* Revealing for what it says about the tastes of the time – Roman antiquities taking precedence over the Renaissance. Penguin publishes a good translation.

**Edward Hutton Florence** *Country Walks About Florence; The Valley of the Arno; A Wayfarer in Unknown Tuscany; Siena and Southern Tuscany; Cities of Umbria; Assisi and Umbria Revisited; The Cosmati* (all o/p). A Tuscan resident from the 1930s to 1960s, Hutton was nothing if not prolific. Some of his prose adds a new shade to purple, but his books, between them, cover almost every inch of Tuscany and Umbria, and are packed with assiduous background on the art and history.

**Henry James** *Italian Hours.* Urbane travel pieces from the young James; perceptive about particular monuments and works of art, superb on the different atmospheres of the great Italian cities.

**Mary McCarthy** *The Stones of Florence.* Written in the mid-1960s, this is a mix of high-class reporting on the contemporary city and anecdotal detail on its history – one of the few accounts that doesn't read as if it's been written in a library.

**H.V. Morton** *A Traveller in Italy.* Morton's leisurely and amiable books were written in the 1930s and their nostalgic charm has a lot to do with their enduring popularity. But this title – recently reissued – is also packed with learned details and marvellously evocative descriptions.

## History and society

### Italy: general history

**Harry Hearder** *Italy: A Short History.* The best one-volume survey of the country from prehistory to the present.

**Giuliano Procacci** *History of the Italian People.* A comprehensive if dense history of the peninsula, charting the development of Italy as a nation state and giving a context for the story of Tuscany.

## The late medieval period

**Frances Stonor Saunders** *Hawkwood: Diabolical Englishman.* Fascinating study of the rapacious mercenary captain whose private army terrorized vast tracts of Italy in the late fourteeenth century, in the wake of the miseries of the Black Death. More than an excellent biography, this book is a vivid reconstruction of a hellish period of Italian history.

## The Renaissance: general history

**Jacob Burckhardt** *The Civilization of the Renaissance in Italy.* A pioneering nineteenth-century classic of Renaissance scholarship – the book that did more than any other to form our image of the period.

**Mary Hollingsworth** *Patronage in Renaissance Italy* (o/p). The first comprehensive English-language study of the relationship between artist and patron in fifteenth-century Italy's city-states. A salutary corrective to the mythology of self-inspired Renaissance genius.

**George Holmes** *Florence, Rome and the Origins of the Renaissance.* Magnificent – and costly – portrait of the world of Dante and Giotto, with especially compelling sections on the impact of St Francis and the role of the papacy in the political and cultural life of central Italy.

## Florence

**Gene A. Brucker** *Renaissance Florence.* Concentrating on the years 1380–1450, this brilliant study of Florence at its cultural zenith uses masses of archival material to fill in the social, economic and political background to its artistic achievements.

**J.R. Hale** *Florence and the Medici.* Scholarly yet lively, this covers the full span of the Medici story from the foundation of the family fortune to the calamitous eighteenth century. Vivid in its recreation of the various personalities involved, it also presents a fascinating picture of the evolution of the mechanics of power in the Florentine state.

**Christopher Hibbert** *The House of Medici: Its Rise and Fall.* More anecdotal than Hale's book, this is a gripping read, chock-full of heroic successes and squalid failures.

**Christopher Hibbert** *Florence: The Biography of a City.* Yet another excellent Hibbert production, packed with illuminating anecdotes and fascinating illustrations – unlike most books on the city, it's as interesting on the political history as on the artistic achievements, and doesn't grind to a standstill with the fall of the Medici.

**Michael Levey** *Florence: A Portrait.* An often illuminating analysis of the city's history, and its artistic history in particular, with snippets and details missed by other accounts.

**Luaro Martines** *April Blood: Florence and the Plot Against the Medici.* A thorough and engrossing account of the Pazzi conspiracy.

**Douglas Preston, with Mario Spezi** *The Monster of Florence.* Between 1974 and 1985 the area around Florence was terrorized by Italy's most notorious serial killer. The crimes were truly monstrous, and Preston describes them without prurience, but much of this gripping and horrifying book is devoted to the still unfinished hunt for the murderer – a tale of vainglorious and incompetent investigators, deranged conspiracy theorists and unbelievable "witnesses".

**Paul Strathern** *The Medici: God-fathers of the Renaissance*. Like Hibbert's book, this is a pacy and well-researched narrative of Florence's most famous family, but gives a little more space to the various luminaries (Michelangelo, Galileo etc) who were drawn into their orbit.

## Siena

**Edmund G. Gardner** *The Story of Siena*. Published in Dent's "Medieval Towns" series in the 1920s, this pocket encyclopedia contains lots of anecdote and historical detail you won't find elsewhere.

## Contemporary Italy

**Paul Ginsborg** *Italy and Its Discontents*. If you want to understand contemporary Italy's baffling mixture of dynamism and ideological sterility, this book – lucidly argued and formidably well informed – is an essential read. There is no better book on the subject.

**Tobias Jones** *The Dark Heart of Italy*. Written during a three-year period in Parma, and comprising essays dealing with aspects of modern Italian society, from the legal and political systems to the media and football. Bewildered and fascinated at every turn, Jones offers a clear-eyed corrective to the sentimentalizing claptrap perpetrated by so many English and American expats.

**Charles Richards** *The New Italians*. An affectionate and very well-informed survey of modern Italy, with plenty of vivid anecdotes that illustrate the tensions within a culture that is at once deeply traditional yet at the same time enthralled by the trappings of modernity.

# Art and architecture

**Michael Baxandall** *Painting and Experience in Fifteenth-Century Italy*. Invaluable analysis, concentrating on the way in which the art of the period would have been perceived at the time.

**Rona Goffen** *Renaissance Rivals*. Rona Goffen's masterly book is revelatory in its analysis of the complexity of the antagonisms involved in the production of high art in this period. Concentrating on the work of Michelangelo, Leonardo, Raphael and Titian, she illuminates a world in which painters, sculptors and architects were ceaselessly endeavouring to supersede their rivals and the exemplars of the ancient world.

**Richard Goy** *Florence: the City and Its Architecture*. Instead of writing a doggedly sequential history, Goy's book uses multiple perspectives to illuminate the architecture of Florence: the first section summarizes the city's development up to the unification of Italy; part two looks at the influence of the two chief "nuclei of power" – the Church and the State; part three analyses the fabric of the city according to building type (*palazzi*, churches, fortifications, etc); and the final section looks at the changes that Florence has undergone in the last century and a half. Encompassing everything from the Baptistery to the football stadium, and magnificently illustrated, this is a clear first choice.

**J.R. Hale** (ed.) *Concise Encyclopaedia of the Italian Renaissance* (o/p). Exemplary reference book, many of whose summaries are as informative as essays twice their length; covers individual artists, movements, cities, philosophical concepts, the lot.

**Frederick Hartt & David Wilkins** *History of Italian Renaissance Art*. If one book on this vast subject can be said to be indispensable, this is it. In view of its comprehensiveness and the range of its illustrations, it's a bargain.

**Michael Levey** *Early Renaissance* (o/p). Precise and fluently written account from a former director of the National Gallery, and well illustrated; probably the best introduction to the subject. Levey's *High Renaissance* continues the story in the same style.

**Peter Murray** *The Architecture of the Italian Renaissance*. Begins with Romanesque buildings and finishes with Palladio – useful both as a gazetteer of the main monuments and as a synopsis of the underlying concepts.

**John Shearman** *Mannerism* (o/p). The self-conscious art of sixteenth-century Mannerism is one of the most complex topics of Renaissance studies; Shearman's brief discussion analyses the main currents, and never succumbs to oversimplification or pedantry.

**Giorgio Vasari** *Lives of the Artists*. Penguin's two-volume abridgement is the fullest available translation of Vasari's classic (and highly tendentious) work on his predecessors and contemporaries. Includes essays on Giotto, Brunelleschi, Leonardo and Michelangelo. The first real work of art history, and still among the most revealing books on Italian Renaissance art.

## Individual artists

**James A. Ackerman** *The Architecture of Michelangelo*. A concise, scholarly and highly engaging survey, which will make you see Michelangelo's architecture with fresh eyes.

**Luciano Bellosi** *Duccio: The Maestà*. Published in 1999, this superb production aims to present "a very direct experience of Duccio di Buoninsegna's masterpiece", and it does just that, with page after page of the highest quality details from the greatest of all Sienese paintings.

**Ludwig Goldscheider** *Michelangelo: Paintings, Sculpture, Architecture*. Virtually all monochrome reproductions, but an extremely good pictorial survey of Michelangelo's output, covering everything except the drawings.

**Anthony Grafton** *Leon Battista Alberti*. A fascinating study of one of the central figures of the Renaissance, Grafton's book illuminates every aspect of Alberti's astonishingly versatile career, which encompassed not just the visual arts and architecture, but also music, law, science and literature.

**James Hall** *Michelangelo and the Reinvention of the Human Body*. A provocative and frequently brilliant study of Michelangelo, arguing for the essential modernity of Michelangelo's unprecedented emphasis on the male nude. On almost every page there's an insight that will make you look afresh.

**Anthony Hughes** *Michelangelo*. This was one of the first titles in Phaidon's "Art & Ideas" series, a project which aims to present well-illustrated overviews of the work of individual artists and art movements, written by scholars but in a style that's accessible to all. *Michelangelo* is a superb advertisement for the series, giving a clear narrative while delineating the social and cultural milieu, and explaining clearly the key issues of style, technique and intepretation.

**Ross King** *Brunelleschi's Dome*. The tale of one of the most remarkable feats of engineering in European history – the design and construction of the dome of Florence's cathedral. King is good on the social and intellectual atmosphere, and has a thriller-writer's sense of pace.

**Marilyn Aronberg Lavin** *Piero della Francesca*. Another title in Phaidon's "Art & Ideas" project, this is the best English-language introduction to this most elusive of major Renaissance artists. This overview is perfectly pitched for the general reader, and benefits from having been published after the restoration of the Arezzo cycle, so its illustrations are uniquely accurate.

**Charles Nicholl** *Leonardo: The Flights of the Mind*. Leonardo left more than seven thousand pages of manuscript notes, and Nicholl's dazzling biography is founded on an intensive study of these largely unpublished writings. The result is a book which is both a highly persuasive portrait of this elusive genius, and a compendious reconstruction of the milieu in which he worked.

**Jeffrey Ruda** *Fra Filippo Lippi*. Ruda's monograph is a fine achievement, combining a biographical study of the most wayward of early Renaissance masters with a consistently illuminating analysis of the paintings, which are reproduced in gorgeous large-format colour plates.

## Literature

**Dante Alighieri** *The Divine Comedy*. No work in any other language bears comparison with Dante's poetic exegesis of the moral scheme of God's creation: in late medieval Italy it was venerated both as a book of almost scriptural authority and as the ultimate refinement of the vernacular Tuscan language. There are numerous translations; John D. Sinclair's prose version (published in three volumes by Oxford University Press) has the huge advantage of presenting the original text opposite the English, and has exemplary notes. Newcomers to Dante will get a lot out of *Dante in English*, an excellent Penguin anthology of English-language translations from Dante and poetry influenced by Dante; it has an illuminating and thought-provoking hundred-page introduction.

**Ludovico Ariosto** *Orlando Furioso*. Barbara Reynolds has done a fine job in her two-volume verse translation of Italy's chivalric epic (published by Penguin), which is set in Charlemagne's Europe. Oxford University Press produces a good one-volume prose translation.

**Giovanni Boccaccio** *The Decameron*. Set in the plague-racked Florence of 1348, Boccaccio's assembly of one hundred short stories is a fascinating social record as well as a constantly diverting and often smutty comedy.

**Benvenuto Cellini** *Autobiography*. Shamelessly egocentric record of the travails and triumphs of the sculptor and goldsmith's career; one of the freshest literary productions of its time. There are two good translations – one from Penguin and one from Oxford University Press (under the title *My Life*).

**Niccolo Machiavelli** *The Prince*. A treatise on statecraft which actually did less to form the political thought of Italy than it did to form foreigners' perceptions of the country; yet there was far more to Machiavelli than the *Realpolitik* of *The Prince*, as is shown by the selection of writings included in Viking's superb anthology, *The Portable Machiavelli*.

**Petrarch (Francesco Petrarca)** *Selections from the Canzoniere*. Often described as the first modern poet, by virtue of his preoccupation with worldly fame and secular love, Petrarch wrote some of the Italian language's greatest lyrics. Oxford University Press's slim selection at least hints at what is lost in translation.

**Leonardo da Vinci** *Notebooks*. This Oxford University Press selection gives you a fascinating miscellany of speculation and observation from the universal genius of Renaissance Italy; essential to any understanding of the man.

# Language

# Language

Pronunciation.......379

Italian words and phrases.......379

Italian menu reader.......383

# Italian

The ability to speak English confers prestige in Italy, and there's often no shortage of people willing to show off their knowledge, particularly in the main cities and resorts. However, in more remote areas you may find no one speaks English at all.

## Pronunciation

Wherever you are, it's a good idea to master at least a little Italian, a task made easier by the fact that your halting efforts will often be rewarded by smiles and genuine surprise. In any case, it's one of the easiest European languages to learn, especially if you already have a smattering of French or Spanish, both of which are extremely similar grammatically.

Easiest of all is the **pronunciation**, since every word is spoken exactly as it's written, and usually enunciated with exaggerated, open-mouthed clarity. The only difficulties you're likely to encounter are the few **consonants** that are different from English:

**c** before e or i is pronounced as in **ch**urch, while **ch** before the same vowel is hard, as in **c**at.

**sci** or **sce** are pronouced as in **sh**eet and **sh**elter respectively. The same goes with **g** – soft before e or i, as in **g**eranium; hard when followed by h, as in **g**arlic.

**gn** has the ni sound of our o**ni**on.

**gl** in Italian is softened to something like li in English, as in stal**li**on.

**h** is not aspirated, as in **h**onour.

When **speaking** to strangers, the third person is the polite form (ie *Lei* instead of *Tu* for "you"); using the second person is a mark of disrespect or stupidity. It's also worth remembering that Italians don't use "please" and "thank you" half as much as we do: it's all implied in the tone, though if you're in any doubt, err on the polite side.

All Italian words are **stressed** on the penultimate syllable unless an **accent** (´ or `) denotes otherwise, although accents are often left out in practice. Note that the ending -ia or -ie counts as two syllables, hence trattoria is stressed on the i. Generally, in the text we've put accents in whenever it isn't immediately obvious how a word should be pronounced – though you shouldn't assume that this is how you'll see the words written in Italian. For example, in *Maríttima*, the accent is on the first i, but on Italian maps it's often written Marittima.

## Italian words and phrases

### Numbers

| | | | |
|---|---|---|---|
| 1 | uno | 4 | quattro |
| 2 | due | 5 | cinque |
| 3 | tre | 6 | sei |

| | | | |
|---|---|---|---|
| 7 | sette | 30 | trenta |
| 8 | otto | 40 | quaranta |
| 9 | nove | 50 | cinquanta |
| 10 | dieci | 60 | sessanta |
| 11 | úndici | 70 | settanta |
| 12 | dódici | 80 | ottanta |
| 13 | trédici | 90 | novanta |
| 14 | quattórdici | 100 | cento |
| 15 | quíndici | 101 | centuno |
| 16 | sédici | 110 | centodieci |
| 17 | diciassette | 200 | duecento |
| 18 | diciotto | 500 | cinquecento |
| 19 | diciannove | 1000 | mille |
| 20 | venti | 5000 | cinquemila |
| 21 | ventuno | 10,000 | diecimila |
| 22 | ventidue | 50,000 | cinquanta mila |

## Basics

| | |
|---|---|
| **Good morning** | Buongiorno |
| **Good afternoon/ evening** | Buona sera |
| **Good night** | Buona notte |
| **Hello/goodbye (informal)** | Ciao |
| **Goodbye (formal)** | Arrivederci |
| **Yes** | Sì |
| **No** | No |
| **Please** | Per favore |
| **Thank you (very much)** | Grázie (molte/ grazie mille) |
| **You're welcome** | Prego |
| **Alright/that's OK** | Va bene |
| **How are you? (informal/formal)** | Come stai/sta? |
| **I'm fine** | Bene |
| **Do you speak English?** | Parla inglese? |
| **I don't understand** | Non ho capito |
| **I don't know** | Non lo so |
| **Excuse me** | Mi scusi/Prego |
| **Excuse me (in a crowd)** | Permesso |
| **Sorry** | Mi dispiace |
| **I'm here on holiday** | Sono qui in vacanza |
| **I'm English/Scottish/ Welsh/Irish** | Sono inglese/scozzese/ gallese/irlandese |
| **I live in …** | Abito a … |

| | |
|---|---|
| **Today** | Oggi |
| **Tomorrow** | Domani |
| **Day after tomorrow** | Dopodomani |
| **Yesterday** | Ieri |
| **Now** | Adesso |
| **Later** | Più tardi |
| **Wait a minute!** | Aspetta! |
| **In the morning** | di mattina |
| **In the afternoon** | nel pomeriggio |
| **In the evening** | di sera |
| **Here (there)** | Qui/La |
| **Good/bad** | Buono/Cattivo |
| **Big/small** | Grande/Píccolo |
| **Cheap/expensive** | Económico/Caro |
| **Early/late** | Presto/Ritardo |
| **Hot/cold** | Caldo/Freddo |
| **Near/far** | Vicino/Lontano |
| **Quickly/slowly** | Velocemente/ Lentamente |
| **Slowly/quietly** | Piano |
| **With/without** | Con/Senza |
| **More/less** | Più/Meno |
| **Enough, no more** | Basta |
| **Mr …** | Signor … |
| **Mrs …** | Signora … |
| **Miss …** | Signorina … |

(il Signor, la Signora, la Signorina **when speaking about someone else**)

## Driving

| | |
|---|---|
| Go straight ahead | Sempre diritto |
| Turn to the right/left | Gira a destra/sinistra |
| Parking | Parcheggio |
| No parking | Divieto di sosta/ Sosta vietata |
| One-way street | Senso único |
| No entry | Senso vietato |
| Slow down | Rallentare |
| Road closed/up | Strada chiusa/guasta |
| No through road | Vietato il transito |
| No overtaking | Vietato il sorpasso |
| Crossroads | Incrocio |
| Speed limit | Limite di Velocità |

## Some signs

| | |
|---|---|
| Entrance/exit | Entrata/Uscita |
| Free entrance | Ingresso líbero |
| Gentlemen/ladies | Signori/Signore |
| WC | Bagno |
| Vacant/engaged | Libero/Occupato |
| Open/closed | Aperto/Chiuso |
| Arrivals/departures | Arrivi/Partenze |
| Closed for restoration | Chiuso per restauro |
| Closed for holidays | Chiuso per ferie |
| Pull/push | Tirare/Spingere |
| Out of order | Guasto |
| Drinking water | Acqua potabile |
| To let | Affítasi |
| Platform | Binario |
| Cash desk | Cassa |
| Go/walk | Avanti |
| Stop/halt | Alt |
| Customs | Dogana |
| Do not touch | Non toccare |
| Danger | Perícolo |
| Beware | Attenzione |
| First aid | Pronto soccorso |
| Ring the bell | Suonare il campanello |
| No smoking | Vietato fumare |

## Accommodation

| | |
|---|---|
| Hotel | Albergo |
| Is there a hotel nearby? | C'è un albergo qui vicino? |
| Do you have a room … | Ha una camera … |
| for one/two /three people | per una/due /tre person(a/e) |
| for one/two/three nights | per una/due/tre nott(e/i) |
| for one/two weeks | per una/due settiman(a/e) |
| with a double bed | con un letto matrimoniale |
| with a shower/bath | con una doccia/ una vasca |
| with a balcony hot/ cold water | con una terrazza acqua calda/freddo |
| How much is it? | Quanto costa? |
| It's expensive | È caro |
| Is breakfast included? | È compresa la prima colazione? |
| Do you have anything cheaper? | Ha niente che costa di meno? |
| Full/half board | Pensione completa/ mezza pensione |
| Can I see the room? | Posso vedere la camera? |
| I'll take it | La prendo |
| I'd like to book a room | Vorrei prenotare una camera |
| I have a booking | Ho una prenotazione |
| Can we camp here? | Possiamo fare il campeggio qui? |
| Is there a campsite nearby? | C'è un camping qui vicino |
| Tent | Tenda |
| Cabin | Cabina |
| Youth hostel | Ostello per la gioventù |
| Single room | una camera singola |
| Double room | una camera doppia |
| Room with twin beds | una camera a due letti |
| Room with private bathroom | una camera con bagno |

| | |
|---|---|
| **Do you have rooms free?** | avete camere libere |
| **I have a reservation** | ho una prenotazione |
| **Could I see another room?** | potrei guardare un'altra camera? |
| **Porte** | il facchino |
| **Lift** | ascensore |
| **Key** | la chiave |

## Questions and directions

| | |
|---|---|
| **Where? (where is/are)** | Dove? (Dov'è/ Dove sono) |
| **When?** | Quando? |
| **What? (what is it?)** | Cosa? (Cos'è?) |
| **How much/many?** | Quanto/Quanti? |
| **Why?** | Perchè? |
| **It is/there is (is it/is there ...?)** | È/C'è (È/C'è ...?) |
| **What time is it?** | Che ora è/Che ore |
| **How do I get to ...?** | Come arrivo a ...? |
| **How far is it to ...?** | Quant'è lontano a ...? |
| **Can you give me a lift to ...?** | Mi può dare un passaggio a ...? |
| **Can you tell me when to get off?** | Mi può dire di scendere alla fermata giusta? |
| **What time does it open?** | A che ora apre? |
| **What time does it close?** | A che ora chiude? |
| **How much does it cost (... do they cost?)** | Quanto costa? (Quanto costano?) |
| **What's it called in Italian?** | Come si chiama in italiano? |

## Travelling

| | |
|---|---|
| **Aeroplane** | Aeroplano |
| **Port** | Porto |
| **Bicycle** | Bicicletta |
| **Ferry** | Traghetto |
| **Railway station** | Stazione ferroviaria |
| **Bus** | Autobus/pullman |
| **Hitchhiking** | Autostop |
| **Ship** | Nave |
| **Bus station** | Autostazione |
| **Hydrofoil** | Aliscafo |
| **Taxi** | Taxi |
| **Car** | Macchina |
| **On foot** | A piedi |
| **Train** | Treno |
| **A ticket to ...** | Un biglietto a ... |
| **One-way/return** | Solo andata/ andata e ritorno |
| **Can I book a seat?** | Posso prenotare un posto? |
| **What time does it leave?** | A che ora parte? |
| **When is the next bus/train/ferry to ...?** | Quando parte il prossimo pullman/ treno/traghetto per ...? |
| **Do I have to change?** | Devo cambiare? |
| **Where does it leave from?** | Da dove parte? |
| **What platform does it leave from?** | Da quale binario parte? |
| **How many kilometres is it?** | Quanti chilometri sono? |
| **How long does it take?** | Quanto ci vuole? |
| **What number bus is it to ...?** | Que número di autobus per ...? |
| **Where's the road to ...?** | Dov'è la strada a ...? |
| **Next stop please** | La prossima fermata, per favore |

# Italian menu reader

## Meals and courses

| | |
|---|---|
| la colazione | breakfast |
| pranzo | lunch |
| cena | evening meal |
| antipasti | starters |
| primi | first courses |
| zuppe/minestre | soups |
| secondi | main courses |
| contorni | vegetables |
| dolci | desserts |
| menù degustazione | tasting menu |

## General terms

| | |
|---|---|
| il cameriere | waiter |
| il menù/la lista | menu |
| la lista dei vini | wine list |
| un coltello | knife |
| una forchetta | fork |
| un cucchiaio | spoon |
| senza carne | without meat |
| coperto | cover charge |
| servizio | service charge |
| aceto | vinegar |
| aglio | garlic |
| biscotti | biscuits |
| burro | butter |
| caramelle | sweets |
| cioccolato | chocolate |
| focaccia | oven-baked snack |
| frittata | omelette |
| grissini | breadsticks |
| maionese | mayonnaise |
| marmellata | jam (jelly) |
| olio | oil |
| olive | olives |
| pane | bread |
| pane integrale | wholemeal bread |
| panino | bread roll/sandwich |
| panna | cream |
| patatine | crisps (potato chips) |
| patatine fritte | chips (french fries) |
| pepe | pepper |
| pizzetta | small cheese and tomato pizza |
| riso | rice |
| sale | salt |
| uova | eggs |
| zucchero | sugar |

## Cooking terms

| | |
|---|---|
| affumicato | smoked |
| arrosto | roast |
| ben cotto | well done |
| bollito/lesso | boiled |
| brasata | cooked in wine |
| cotto | cooked (not raw) |
| crudo | raw |
| al dente | firm (not overcooked) |
| aí ferri | grilled without oil |
| fritto | fried |
| grattuggiato | grated |
| alla griglia | grilled |
| al Marsala | cooked with Marsala wine |
| Milanese | fried in egg and breadcrumbs |
| pizzaiola | cooked with tomato sauce |
| al puntino | medium (steak) |
| ripieno | stuffed |
| al sangue | rare (steak) |
| allo spiedo | on the spit |
| surgelato | frozen |
| umido | steamed/stewed |

## Pizzas

**calzone** folded pizza with cheese, ham and tomato

**capricciosa** literally "capricious"; topped with whatever they've got in the kitchen, usually including baby artichoke, ham and egg

**cardinale** ham and olives

**frutta di mare** seafood; usually mussels, prawns and clams

**funghi** mushrooms; the tinned sliced variety, unless it specifies fresh (**funghi freschi**)

**margherita** cheese and tomato

**marinara** tomato, anchovy and olive oil

**napo/napoletana** tomato

**quattro formaggi** "four cheeses", usually including mozzarella, fontina and gruyère

**quattro stagioni** "four seasons"; the toppings split into four separate sections, usually including ham, green pepper, onion, egg etc

## Antipasti

**antipasto misto** mixed cold meats and cheese

**caponata** mixed aubergine, olives, tomatoes

**caprese** tomato and mozzarella salad

**crostini** mixed canapés

**crostini di milza** minced spleen on pieces of toast

**donzele/donzelline** fried dough balls

**fettuna/bruschetta** garlic toast with olive oil

**finocchiona** pork sausage flavoured with fennel

**insalata di mare** seafood salad

**insalata di riso** rice salad

**insalata russa** Russian salad (diced vegetables in mayonnaise)

**melanzane in parmigiana** aubergine in tomato and Parmesan cheese

**peperonata** green and red peppers stewed in olive oil

**pinzimonio** raw seasonal vegetable in olive oil, with salt and pepper

**pomodori ripieni** stuffed tomatoes

**prosciutto** ham

**prosciutto di cinghiale** cured wild boar ham

**salame toscano** pork sausage with pepper and cubes of fat

**salsicce** pork or wild boar sausage

## Primi

### Soups

**acquacotta** onion soup served with toast and poached egg

**brodo** clear broth

**carabaccia** onion soup

**garmugia** soup made with fava beans, peas, artichokes, asparagus and bacon

**minestra di farro** wheat and bean soup

**minestrina** any light soup

| | |
|---|---|
| **minestrone** | thick vegetable soup |
| **minestrone alla fiorentina** | haricot bean soup with red cabbage, tomatoes, onions and herbs |
| **pappa al pomodoro** | tomato soup thickened with bread |
| **pasta fagioli** | pasta soup with beans |
| **pastini in brodo** | pasta pieces in clear broth |
| **ribollita** | winter vegetable soup, based on beans and thickened with bread |
| **stracciatella** | broth with egg |
| **zuppa di fagioli** | bean soup |

### Pasta

| | |
|---|---|
| **cannelloni** | large tubes of pasta, stuffed |
| **farfalle** | literally "butterfly"-shaped pasta |
| **fettuccine** | narrow pasta ribbons |
| **gnocchi** | small potato and dough dumplings |
| **gnocchi di ricotta** | dumplings filled with ricotta and spinach |
| **maccheroni** | tubular spaghetti |
| **pappardelle** | wide, short noodles, often served with hare sauce (**con lepre**) |
| **pasta al forno** | pasta baked with minced meat, eggs, tomato and cheese |
| **pasta alla carrettiera** | pasta with tomato, garlic, pepper, parsley and chilli |
| **penne** | smaller pieces of rigatoni |
| **penne strasciate** | quill-shaped pasta in meat sauce |
| **rigatoni** | large, grooved tubular pasta |
| **risotto** | cooked rice dish, with sauce |
| **risotto nero** | rice cooked with cuttlefish (in its own ink) |
| **spaghettini** | thin spaghetti |
| **tagliatelle** | pasta ribbons (another word for **fettuccine**) |
| **tortellini** | small rings of pasta stuffed with meat or cheese |
| **vermicelli** | "little worms" (very thin spaghetti) |

### Pasta sauce (salsa)

| | |
|---|---|
| **arrabbiata** | spicy tomato sauce with chillies |
| **bolognese** | tomato and meat |
| **burro** | butter |
| **carbonara** | cream, ham and beaten egg |
| **funghi** | mushrooms |
| **matriciana** | tomato and cubed pork |
| **panna** | cream |
| **parmigiano** | Parmesan cheese |
| **peperoncino** | olive oil, garlic and fresh chillies |
| **pesto** | green basil and garlic sauce |
| **pomodoro** | tomato sauce |
| **ragù** | meat sauce |
| **vongole** | clam and tomato sauce |

## Secondi

### Meat (carne)

| | |
|---|---|
| **agnello** | lamb |
| **bistecca** | steak |
| **cervello** | brain |
| **cinghiale** | wild boar |
| **coniglio** | rabbit |
| **costolette** | chops |
| **cotolette** | cutlets |
| **fagiaon** | pheasant |
| **faraona** | guinea fowl |
| **fegatini** | chicken livers |
| **fegato** | liver |
| **involtini** | meat slices, rolled and stuffed |
| **lepre** | hare |

| | |
|---|---|
| **lingua** | tongue |
| **maiale** | pork |
| **manzo** | beef |
| **mortadella** | salami-type cured meat |
| **osso buco** | shin of veal |
| **pernice** | partridge |
| **pancetta** | bacon |
| **pollo** | chicken |
| **polpette** | meatballs |
| **rognoni** | kidneys |
| **salsiccia** | sausage |
| **saltimbocca** | veal with ham |
| **spezzatino** | stew |
| **tacchino** | turkey |
| **trippa** | tripe |
| **vitello** | veal |

## Fish (pesce) and shellfish (crostacei)

| | |
|---|---|
| **acciughe** | anchovies |
| **anguilla** | eel |
| **aragosta** | lobster |
| **baccalà** | dried salted cod |
| **calamari** | squid |
| **céfalo** | mullet |
| **cozze** | mussels |
| **dentice** | dentex |
| **gamberetti** | shrimps |
| **gámberi** | prawns |
| **granchio** | crab |
| **merluzzo** | cod |
| **ostriche** | oysters |
| **pescespada** | swordfish |
| **polpo** | octopus |
| **sarde** | sardines |
| **sgombro** | mackerel |
| **sogliola** | sole |
| **tonno** | tuna |
| **triglie** | red mullet |
| **trota** | trout |
| **vóngole** | clams |

## Tuscan specialities

| | |
|---|---|
| **arista** | roast pork loin with garlic and rosemary |
| **asparagi alla fiorentina** | asparagus with butter, fried egg and cheese |
| **baccalà alla livornese** | salt cod with garlic, tomatoes and parsley |
| **bistecca alla fiorentina** | thick grilled T-bone steak |
| **cibreo** | chicken liver and egg stew |
| **cieche alla pisana** | small eels cooked with sage and tomatoes, served with Parmesan |
| **lombatina** | veal chop |
| **peposo** | peppered beef stew |
| **pollo alla diavola/ al mattone** | chicken flattened with a brick, grilled with herbs |
| **scottiglia** | stew of veal, game and poultry, cooked with white wine and tomatoes |
| **spiedini di maiale** | skewered spiced cubes of pork loin and liver, with bread and bay leaves |
| **tonno con fagioli** | tuna with white beans and raw onion |
| **trigile alla livornese** | red mullet cooked with tomatoes, garlic and parsley |
| **trippa alla fiorentina** | tripe in tomato sauce, served with Parmesan |

# Vegetables (contorni) and salad (insalata)

| | |
|---|---|
| **asparagi** | asparagus |
| **basílico** | basil |
| **capperi** | capers |
| **carciofi** | artichokes |
| **carciofini** | artichoke hearts |
| **carotte** | carrots |
| **cavolfiori** | cauliflower |
| **cávolo** | cabbage |
| **cetriolo** | cucumber |
| **cipolla** | onion |
| **fagioli all'olio** | white beans served with olive oil |

| | |
|---|---|
| **fagioli all'uccelletto** | white beans cooked with tomatoes, garlic and sage |
| **fagiolini** | green beans |
| **finocchio** | fennel |
| **frittata di carciofi** | fried artichoke flan |
| **funghi** | mushrooms |
| **insalata mista** | mixed salad |
| **insalata verde** | green salad |
| **melanzane** | aubergine |
| **orígano** | oregano |
| **patate** | potatoes |
| **peperoni** | peppers |
| **piselli** | peas |
| **pomodori** | tomatoes |
| **radicchio** | chicory |
| **spinaci** | spinach |
| **zucchini** | courgettes |

## Sweets (dolci), fruit (frutta), cheese (formaggi) and nuts (noce)

| | |
|---|---|
| **amaretti** | macaroons |
| **ananas** | pineapple |
| **anguria/coccómero** | watermelon |
| **arance** | oranges |
| **banane** | bananas |
| **brigidini** | anise wafer biscuits |
| **buccellato** | anise raisin cake |
| **cacchi** | persimmons |
| **cantucci/cantuccini** | small almond biscuits, served with Vinsanto wine |
| **castagnaccio** | unleavened chestnut-flour cake containing raisins, walnuts and rosemary |
| **cenci** | fried dough dusted with powdered sugar |
| **ciliégie** | cherries |
| **fichi** | figs |
| **fichi d'India** | prickly pears |
| **fontina** | Northern Italian cooking cheese |
| **fragole** | strawberries |
| **frittelle di riso** | rice fritters |
| **gelato** | ice cream |
| **gorgonzola** | a soft blue cheese |
| **limone** | lemon |
| **macedonia** | fruit salad |
| **mandorle** | almonds |
| **mele** | apples |
| **melone** | melon |
| **meringa** | frozen meringue with whipped cream and chocolate |
| **mozzarella** | bland soft white cheese used on pizzas |
| **necci** | chestnut-flour crêpes |
| **nespole** | medlars |
| **panforte** | hard fruit, nut and spice cake |
| **parmigiano** | Parmesan cheese |
| **pecorino** | strong hard sheep's cheese |
| **pere** | pears |
| **pesche** | peaches |
| **pignoli** | pine nuts |
| **provolone** | strong hard cheese |
| **ricciarelli** | marzipan almond biscuits |
| **ricotta** | soft white sheep's cheese |
| **schiacciata alla fiorentina** | orange-flavoured cake covered with powdered sugar, eaten at carnival time |
| **schiacciata con l'uva** | grape- and sugar-covered bread dessert |
| **torta** | cake, tart |
| **uva** | grapes |
| **zabaglione** | dessert made with eggs, sugar and Marsala wine |
| **zuccotto** | sponge cake filled with chocolate and whipped cream |
| **zuppa inglese** | trifle |

## Drinking essentials

| | |
|---|---|
| aperitivo | pre-dinner drink |
| digestivo | after-dinner drink |
| vino rosso | red wine |
| vino bianco | white wine |
| vino rosato | rosé wine |
| spumante | sparkling wine |
| secco | dry |
| dolce | sweet |
| birra | beer |
| litro | litre |
| mezzo | half-litre |
| quarto | quarter-litre |
| Salute! | Cheers! (toast) |
| acqua minerale | mineral water |
| aranciata | orangeade |
| bicchiere | glass |
| bottiglia | bottle |
| caffè | coffee |
| cioccolata calda | hot chocolate |
| frappé | milkshake made with ice cream |
| frullato | milkshake |
| ghiaccio | ice |
| granita | iced drink with coffee or fruit |
| latte | milk |
| limonate | lemonade |
| selz | soda water |
| spremuta | fresh fruit juice |
| succo di frutta | concentrated fruit juice with sugar |
| tazza | cup |
| tè | tea |
| tonico | tonic water |

# Travel store

# Small print and Index

## A Rough Guide to Rough Guides

Published in 1982, the first Rough Guide – to Greece – was a student scheme that became a publishing phenomenon. Mark Ellingham, a recent graduate in English from Bristol University, had been travelling in Greece the previous summer and couldn't find the right guidebook. With a small group of friends he wrote his own guide, combining a highly contemporary, journalistic style with a thoroughly practical approach to travellers' needs.

The immediate success of the book spawned a series that rapidly covered dozens of destinations. And, in addition to impecunious backpackers, Rough Guides soon acquired a much broader and older readership that relished the guides' wit and inquisitiveness as much as their enthusiastic, critical approach and value-for-money ethos.

These days, Rough Guides include recommendations from shoestring to luxury and cover more than 200 destinations around the globe, including almost every country in the Americas and Europe, more than half of Africa and most of Asia and Australasia. Our ever-growing team of authors and photographers is spread all over the world, particularly in Europe, the USA and Australia.

In the early 1990s, Rough Guides branched out of travel, with the publication of Rough Guides to World Music, Classical Music and the Internet. All three have become benchmark titles in their fields, spearheading the publication of a wide range of books under the Rough Guide name.

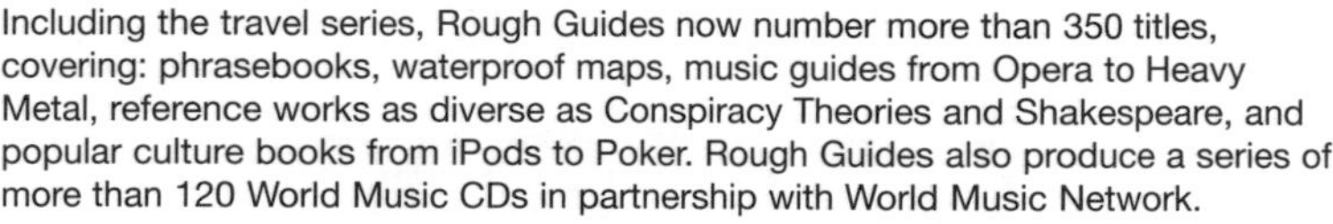

Including the travel series, Rough Guides now number more than 350 titles, covering: phrasebooks, waterproof maps, music guides from Opera to Heavy Metal, reference works as diverse as Conspiracy Theories and Shakespeare, and popular culture books from iPods to Poker. Rough Guides also produce a series of more than 120 World Music CDs in partnership with World Music Network.

Visit www.roughguides.com to see our latest publications.

Rough Guide travel images are available for commercial licensing at www.roughguidespictures.com

## Rough Guide credits

**Text editor**: James Rice
**Layout**: Nikhil Agarwal
**Cartography**: Jai Prakash Mishra/Karobi Gogoi
**Picture editor**: Nicole Newman
**Production**: Rebecca Short
**Proofreader**: Karen Parker
**Cover design**: Chloë Roberts
**Photographers**: Roger d'Olivere Mapp, Chris Hutty, Michelle Grant
**Editorial**: **London** Ruth Blackmore, Andy Turner, Keith Drew, Edward Aves, Alice Park, Lucy White, Jo Kirby, James Smart, Natasha Foges, Róisín Cameron, Emma Traynor, Emma Gibbs, Kathryn Lane, Christina Valhouli, Monica Woods, Alison Roberts, Mani Ramaswamy, Joe Staines, Peter Buckley, Matthew Milton, Tracy Hopkins, Ruth Tidball; **New York** Andrew Rosenberg, Steven Horak, AnneLise Sorensen, Ella Steim, Anna Owens, Sean Mahoney, Paula Neudorf; **Delhi** Madhavi Singh, Karen D'Souza, Lubna Shaheen
**Design & Pictures**: **London** Scott Stickland, Dan May, Diana Jarvis, Mark Thomas, Sarah Cummins, Emily Taylor; **Delhi** Umesh Aggarwal, Ajay Verma, Jessica Subramanian, Ankur Guha, Pradeep Thapliyal, Sachin Tanwar, Anita Singh
**Production**: Vicky Baldwin
**Cartography**: **London** Maxine Repath, Ed Wright, Katie Lloyd-Jones; **Delhi** Rajesh Chhibber, Ashutosh Bharti, Rajesh Mishra, Animesh Pathak, Jasbir Sandhu, Alakananda Bhattacharya, Swati Handoo, Deshpal Dabas
**Online**: **London** George Atwell, Faye Hellon, Jeanette Angell, Fergus Day, Justine Bright, Clare Bryson, Áine Fearon, Adrian Low, Ezgi Celebi, Amber Bloomfield; **Delhi** Amit Verma, Rahul Kumar, Narender Kumar, Ravi Yadav, Debojit Borah, Rakesh Kumar, Ganesh Sharma, Shisir Basumatari
**Marketing & Publicity**: **London** Liz Statham, Niki Hanmer, Louise Maher, Jess Carter, Vanessa Godden, Vivienne Watton, Anna Paynton, Rachel Sprackett, Libby Jellie, Holly Dudley; **New York** Geoff Colquitt, Nancy Lambert, Katy Ball; **Delhi** Ragini Govind
**Manager India**: Punita Singh
**Reference Director**: Andrew Lockett
**Operations Manager**: Helen Phillips
**PA to Publishing Director**: Nicola Henderson
**Publishing Director**: Martin Dunford
**Commercial Manager**: Gino Magnotta
**Managing Director**: John Duhigg

ROUGH GUIDES

## Publishing information

This first edition published March 2009 by
**Rough Guides Ltd**,
80 Strand, London WC2R 0RL
345 Hudson St, 4th Floor,
New York, NY 10014, USA
14 Local Shopping Centre, Panchsheel Park,
New Delhi 110017, India
**Distributed by the Penguin Group**
Penguin Books Ltd,
80 Strand, London WC2R 0RL
Penguin Group (USA)
375 Hudson Street, NY 10014, USA
Penguin Group (Australia)
250 Camberwell Road, Camberwell,
Victoria 3124, Australia
Penguin Group (Canada)
195 Harry Walker Parkway N, Newmarket, ON,
L3Y 7B3 Canada
Penguin Group (NZ)
67 Apollo Drive, Mairangi Bay, Auckland 1310,
New Zealand

Cover concept by Peter Dyer.

Typeset in Bembo and Helvetica to an original design by Henry Iles.

Printed and bound in China



400pp includes index

A catalogue record for this book is available from the British Library.

ISBN: 978-1-84836-030-3

The publishers and authors have done their best to ensure the accuracy and currency of all the information in **The Rough Guide to Florence and the best of Tuscany**, however, they can accept no responsibility for any loss, injury, or inconvenience sustained by any traveller as a result of information or advice contained in the guide.

1 3 5 7 9 8 6 4 2

## Help us update

We've gone to a lot of effort to ensure that the first edition of **The Rough Guide to Florence and the best of Tuscany** is accurate and up to date. However, things change – places get "discovered", opening hours are notoriously fickle, restaurants and rooms raise prices or lower standards. If you feel we've got it wrong or left something out, we'd like to know, and if you can remember the address, the price, the hours, the phone number, so much the better.

Please send your comments with the subject line "**Rough Guide Florence and the best of Tuscany Update**" to Ⓔ mail@roughguides.com. We'll credit all contributions and send a copy of the next edition (or any other Rough Guide if you prefer) for the very best emails.

Have your questions answered and tell others about your trip at Ⓦ community.roughguides.com

## Acknowledgements

**Tim Jepson**: Thanks to Duncan and Amanda Baird, Marella Caracciolo, Michael Sheridan and Yasmin Sethna.

## Readers' letters and emails

Thanks to all the readers who have taken the time to write in with comments and suggestions (and apologies if we've omitted or misspelt anyone's name):

Even though this is a first edition, we'd still like to thank those readers who took the time to write or email with comments for the *Rough Guide to Florence & Siena*. Thanks to: Richard Daugherty, Stephen Kerr, Kamin Mohammadi, Linda Shrier and Niall Teskey.

## Photo credits

All photos © Rough Guides except the following:

**Things not to miss**
**05** The Birth of Venus, Botticelli © The Bridgeman Art Library

**Florence as capital of Italy colour section**
Michelangelo's David, Piazza della Signoria © Ripani Massimo/SIME-4Corners Images
Aerial view of Piazza Beccaria © Atlantide Phototravel/Corbis
Porta San Gallo, Piazza della Liberta © The Photolibrary Wales/Alamy

**Tuscan food and wine colour section**
Feast at Palio, Siena © drr.net
Vineyards and cypresses near Montalcino © Berndt Fischer/photolibrary

**Black and whites**
**p.128** Piazza dell Santissima Annunziata, Florence © The Photolibrary Wales/Alamy

# Index

Map entries are in colour.


A

**Accademia** .......... 119–120
**accommodation in Florence** ............ 169–182
Central Florence....170–171
Outer Florence..... 176–177
accommodation in Italy ........................ 24–26
addresses in Florence .... 42
*agriturismo* ...................... 25
airlines ............................ 21
airports for Florence ....... 41
Amerigo Vespucci airport ........................... 41
apartment rental ............. 25
Appartamenti Reali ....... 149
**AREZZO** ............... 327–334
Arezzo ............................. 328
accommodation ............... 329
Casa Vasari ...................... 333
Casa-Museo Ivan Bruschi .......................... 332
Duomo ............................. 332
festivals ........................... 333
Museo Archeologico ........ 333
Museo d'Arte Medioevale e Moderna .................... 333
Pieve di Santa Maria ........ 331
restaurants ....................... 334
San Domenico ................. 332
San Francesco ................. 330
Santa Maria delle Grazie.... 334
**artists & architects, directory of** ....... 359–370

B

B&B in Florence.... 179–181
B&B in Italy ...................... 26
Badìa a Coltibuono ....... 256
Badìa Fiorentina ............. 80
banks in Florence ......... 210
**Baptistery** ................ 53–57
Baptistery, east doors ... 56
**Bargello** ................... 83–86
bars in Florence.... 190–195
Biblioteca Medicea-Laurenziana ............... 112
bike rental in Florence ... 210
**Bóboli Gardens** ..... 150–152
Bologna airport ............... 42
**books** .................. 371–376
**Brancacci Chapel** ........................... 155–156
Brolio ............................ 256
bus station, Florence ...... 42
buses in Florence .... 43, 210
buses in Italy .................. 23

C

**cafés in Florence** ........................... 190–193
Calcio Storico ............... 200
**Campanile** ..................... 53
camping in Italy .............. 26
Campo di Marte ........... 144
campsites in Florence ... 182
**Cappella Brancacci** ........................... 155–156
Cappella Brancacci ..... 155
Cappella dei Pazzi ........ 139
Cappella di San Sepolcro ...................... 97
Cappella Rucellai ............ 97
**Cappelle Medicee** ........................... 113–115
car parks, Florence ......... 42
car rental in Florence .... 210
Casa Buonarroti ........... 141
Casa di Dante ................. 82
Casa Guidi .................... 152
Cascine ......................... 105
Casentino ..................... 335
Castelli di Meleto .......... 256
Castellina in Chianti ...... 254
Castello di Brolio .......... 256
Cenacolo di Fuligno ..... 117
Cenacolo di Sant'Apollonia ........... 126
**Chianti** ................ 250–256
Chianti .......................... 251
children, travelling with ...... 33
Chiostro dello Scalzo .... 126
cinema in Florence ....... 203
classical music in Florence ...................... 202
**clubs in Florence** ........................... 197–199
Collezione Contini Bonacossi ................. 150
consulates ...................... 35
consulates in Florence ................................ 210
Corridoio Vasariano ........ 77
**CORTONA** ........... 335–342
Cortona ........................... 337
accommodation ............... 336
bars & cafés ..................... 342
Duomo ............................. 339
Fortezza Medicea ............ 340
MAEC ............................... 338
Museo Diocesano ............ 339
restaurants ....................... 341
San Domenico ................. 341
San Francesco ................. 340
San Niccolò ...................... 340
Santa Margherita.............. 340
Santa Maria del Calcinaio ........................ 341
crime in Italy ................... 34
currency .......................... 37
cycling & motorcycling in Italy .......................... 23

D

dance in Florence ......... 202
disabled travellers .......... 38
doctors in Florence ...... 210
doctors in Italy ................ 36
drinking in Italy ......... 28–30
driving in Italy ................. 22
**Duomo** ..................... 47–52
Duomo ........................... 48

E

electricity ........................ 35
embassies ....................... 35
emergency phone numbers ....................... 34

F

festivals in Florence ........................... 200–201
festivals in Italy ......... 31–33
**Fiesole** ................. 164–166
Fiesole ........................... 165
Firenze Musei ................. 43
flights ....................... 19–20
Florence (east) .............. 134
Florence (north) ... 108–109

Florence (west) ........ 90–91
food ............27 & 383–388; see also *Tuscan food and wine* colour section
football.......................... 143
Forte di Belvedere ........ 162
Fortezza da Basso ....... 118

G

Gaiole ........................... 256
Galileo Galilei airport ...... 42
Galleria d'Arte Moderna .................... 149
**Galleria degli Uffizi** .... 71–77
Galleria del Costume .... 150
**Galleria dell'Accademia** ........................... 119–120
Galleria Palatina ........... 148
gay & lesbian travellers....35
gelaterie in Florence ..... 195
Giardino Bardini ............ 158
**Giardino di Bóboli** ........................... 150–152
Greve ........................... 251

H

**history of Tuscany** ........................... 345–358
hospital in Florence ...... 210
hostels in Florence ....... 181
hostels in Italy ................ 26
**hotels in Florence** ............................. 169–179
hotels in Italy .................. 24

I

ice-cream in Florence ... 195
insurance ........................ 36
internet access in Florence ..................... 210
internet access in Italy ... 37
Iris Garden .................... 158
Italian language (words and phrases) ...... 379–388

L

laundry in Florence ....... 210
Laurentian Library ......... 112
left luggage in Florence ..................... 210
live music in Florence ............. 199–201
Loggia dei Rucellai ......... 97
Loggia del Bigallo ........... 60
Loggia del Pesce .......... 142
Loggia della Signoria ...... 65
lost property in Florence ..................... 210
**LUCCA** ................ 239–249
- Lucca ........................240–241
- accommodation ............... 242
- Casa di Puccini ................ 243
- city walls .......................... 247
- Duomo di San Martino ..... 244
- Museo della Cattedrale .... 245
- Museo Nazionale di Villa Guinigi .................. 248
- Orto Botanico .................. 248
- Piazza Anfiteatro ............. 247
- Pinacoteca Nazionale ...... 243
- restaurants & bars ............ 248
- San Cristoforo ................. 246
- San Frediano .................... 246
- San Giovanni e Reparata ...................................... 246
- San Michele in Foro ......... 243
- San Pietro Somaldi .......... 247
- Santa Maria Forisportam ................. 246
- Torre delle Ore ................. 246
- Torre Guinigi .................... 248
- Via Fillungo ...................... 246

M

Maggio Musicale .......... 202
markets in Florence ...... 205
**Medici Chapels** .....113–115
Mercato Centrale ... 117, 205
Mercato delle Pulci .................. 142, 205
Mercato di Sant'Ambrogio ............................ 142, 205
Mercato Nuovo .............. 88
**MONTALCINO** ..... 297–304
- Montalcino ....................... 300
- accommodation ............... 299
- Duomo ............................. 303
- Fonte Castellane .............. 304
- Museo di Montalcino ....... 301
- restaurants & bars ........... 304
- Rocca ............................... 301
- San Francesco ................. 304
- Sant'Agostino .................. 303
- Santa Maria della Croce .... 303
- Santuario della Madonna del Soccorso ............... 303
Monte Oliveto Maggiore ................... 298
Montefioralle ................ 253
**MONTEPULCIANO** ........................... 309–315
- Montepulciano ................. 310
- accommodation ............... 311
- Casa di Poliziano ............. 312
- Colonna del Marzocco ..... 312
- Corso ............................... 312
- Duomo ............................. 313
- Gesù ................................ 312
- Loggia del Mercato .......... 312
- Museo Civico ................... 313
- Palazzo Avignonesi .......... 312
- Palazzo Bucelli ................. 312
- Palazzo Cantucci ............. 313
- Palazzo Cervini ................ 312
- Palazzo Cocconi .............. 312
- Palazzo Comunale ........... 313
- Palazzo Nobili-Tarugi ....... 313
- Porta al Prato ................... 311
- restaurants ....................... 314
- San Biagio ........................ 314
- San Francesco ................. 313
- Sant'Agnese ..................... 311
- Sant'Agostino ................... 312
- Santa Lucia ...................... 313
- Santa Maria dei Servi ....... 313
Monterchi ..................... 335
Museo Archeologico .... 131
Museo Bardini .............. 157
Museo degli Argenti ..... 149
Museo del Bigallo ........... 60
**Museo dell'Opera del Duomo** .................. 57–59
Museo dell'Opera di Santa Croce ............... 140
**Museo della Casa Fiorentina Antica** ............................... 89–92
Museo delle Carrozze .................... 150
Museo delle Porcellane ................. 150
Museo di Firenze com'era ........................ 60
**Museo di San Marco** ................ 121–125
Museo di San Marco .................122, 123
Museo di Santa Maria Novella ....................... 102
Museo di Storia della Scienza ........................ 86
Museo Horne ................ 140
Museo Marino Marini ..... 97
Museo Nazionale Alinari Fotografia .................. 103
**Museo Nazionale del Bargello** .......... 83–86
Museo Stibbert ............. 127
music in Florence .... 199–202

# N


Neptune Fountain........... 63
newspapers.................... 30


# O


Ognissanti .................... 104
Oltrarno................ 146–147
opening hours ................ 37
**Orsanmichele**.......... 78–80
Orsanmichele................. 78
Ospedale degli
Innocenti.................... 128


# P


**Palazzo Davanzati**....89–92
**Palazzo Medici-Riccardi**
........................... 115–117
**Palazzo Pitti** ........ 148–152
Palazzo Rucellai ............. 96
Palazzo Strozzi ............... 96
**Palazzo Vecchio**...... 67–71
Palazzo Vecchio ......67, 70
Panzano........................ 253
parking in Florence......... 42
Pazzi Chapel................. 139
Perétola airport............... 41
pharmacies in
Florence..................... 210
pharmacies in Italy ......... 36
phones in Italy ................ 38
Piazza del Duomo ......... 46
**Piazza della**
**Signoria** ................ 62–66
Piazza della Signoria..... 63
Piazza Santa Croce...... 133
Piazza Santa Maria
Novella......................... 97
Piazza Santa Trìnita........ 92
Piazza Santissima
Annunziata................. 127
Piazzale Michelangelo
.................................... 158
**PIENZA** ................ 304–309
Pienza ............................. 306
accommodation ............... 305
Duomo ............................ 306
Museo Diocesano ............ 308
Palazzo Piccolomini......... 307
Piazza Pio II .................... 306
Pieve di Corsignano......... 309
restaurants ....................... 309
San Francesco ................. 309
**PISA** ..................... 227–239
Pisa .................................. 228
accommodation .............. 229
Arsenale Mediceo ............ 237
Baptistery ........................ 233
Borgo Stretto ................... 236
Campo dei Miracoli...230–235
Camposanto ................... 233
Cappella di Sant'Agata.... 238
Duomo .....................231–233
Fortezza Vecchia............. 237
Gioco del Ponte .............. 238
Leaning Tower.................. 231
Logge di Banchi............... 237
Museo dell'Opera del
Duomo ......................... 234
Museo delle Sinopie ........ 235
Museo Nazionale di
San Matteo .................. 236
Muso Nazionale di
Palazzo Reale .............. 237
Orto Botanico.................. 237
Palazzo dei Cavalieri........ 236
Palazzo dell'Orologio ....... 236
Palazzo Scotti ................. 237
Palazzo Toscanelli ............ 236
Piazza dei Cavalieri .......... 236
Ponte di Mezzo ................ 236
Porta Lucca...................... 236
restaurants ...................... 238
San Francesco ................. 236
San Frediano.................... 237
San Michele ..................... 236
San Nicola........................ 237
San Paolo a Ripa d'Arno..... 238
San Sepolcro ................... 237
San Zeno......................... 236
Santa Caterina ................. 236
Santa Maria della Spina..... 237
Santo Stefano .................. 236
Torre Guelfa..................... 237
Torre Pendente................. 231
**PISTOIA** .............. 219–226
Pistoia ............................. 220
Abbazia di San Bartolomeo
in Pantano .................... 224
accommodation ............... 219
Baptistery ........................ 223
Cappella del Tau .............. 221
Duomo ............................ 222
Fattoria di Celle............... 225
festivals ........................... 222
Madonna dell'Umiltà........ 221
Museo Civico ................... 223
Museo del Ricamo........... 223
Museo di San Zeno.......... 223
Museo Marino Marini ....... 221
Museo Rospigliosi............ 223
Nuovo Museo
Diocesano..................... 223
Ospedale del Ceppo........ 224
Palazzo Comunale ........... 223
Palazzo del Podestà ........ 223
Palazzo Fabroni ............... 224
Piazza del Duomo............ 222
restaurants ...................... 226
San Domenico ................. 220
San Francesco al Prato ... 225
San Giovanni Fuorcivitas
...................................... 221
San Paolo........................ 221
Sant'Andrea .................... 224
**Pitti Palace** .......... 148–152
police in Italy .................. 34
police in Florence ......... 210
Ponte Santa Trìnita ......... 92
**Ponte Vecchio**............ 145
Poppi ........................... 335
Porta San Miniato......... 158
Porta San Niccolò ........ 158
post offices in
Florence..................... 210
postal services in Italy.... 37
**PRATO** ................. 213–218
Prato................................ 215
accommodation ............... 214
Cassero ........................... 214
Castello dell'Imperatore..... 214
Duomo ............................ 216
Museo Civico ................... 216
Museo del Tessuto........... 214
Museo dell'Opera
del Duomo .................... 218
Museo di Pittura
Murale ........................... 218
Palazzo Datini .................. 216
restaurants ....................... 218
San Francesco ................. 215
Santa Maria delle
Carceri .......................... 215
public holidays ............... 38


# R


Radda in Chianti........... 254
radio in Italy.................... 31
*residenze* in
Florence............ 179–181
**restaurants in**
**Florence**........... 183–190
restaurants in Italy .......... 27


# S


**SAN GIMIGNANO**
........................... 317–321
San Gimignano ................ 318
accommodation ............... 317
Collegiata ........................ 319
Galleria d'Arte
Contemporaneo............ 321
Museo Archeologico........ 321
Museo Civico ................... 320
Piazza del Cisterno .......... 319
Piazza del Duomo............ 319
Pinacoteca ....................... 320
restaurants ....................... 321
Rocca............................... 321

San Lorenzo in Ponte ...... 320
Sant'Agostino.................. 321
San Leonardo in Arcetri ........................ 162
**San Lorenzo** ........ 106–115
San Lorenzo................. 112
San Marco church ........ 125
San Martino del Vescovo ........................ 82
**San Miniato al Monte**................ 159–162
San Miniato al Monte ... 159
San Niccolò sopr'Arno.................. 158
San Salvi........................ 144
Sansepolcro ................. 335
Sant'Ambrogio church........................ 142
Sant'Ambrogio market........................ 142
Sant'Antimo.................. 302
**Santa Croce** ........ 134–140
Santa Croce................. 136
Santa Felìcita................ 146
Santa Lucia dei Magnoli...................... 157
Santa Margherita de' Cerchi .......................... 82
**Santa Maria del Carmine** ........... 154–156
**Santa Maria del Fiore**...................... 47–52
Santa Maria Maddalena dei Pazzi .................... 142
**Santa Maria Novella**................ 98–102
Santa Maria Novella ................98, 100
Santa Maria Novella station.......................... 42
Santa Reparata .............. 50
**Santa Trìnita** ............ 94–96
Santa Trìnita.................... 93
**Santissima Annunziata** ....... 129–131
Santissima Annunziata................ 130
Santo Spirito......... 153–154
Scalzo........................... 126
Science Museum............ 86
scooter rental in Florence..................... 210
Scoppio del Carro ........ 200
self-catering in Italy........ 25
shopping in Florence............ 204–209
**SIENA**.................. 257–296
Museo Civico .................. 269
San Martino and Città ...................... 266–267
Terzo di Camollia ............. 289
The Duomo ....................... 274
accommodation ........ 262–264
Archivio di Stato.............. 283
Baptistery........................ 277
bars ................................ 295
bus station ...................... 262
Campo ...................... 265–268
car rental ......................... 296
Casa e Santuario di Santa Caterina.............. 290
contrade........................... 258
Duomo ...................... 273–277
festivals ........................... 295
Fonte Branda ................... 290
Fonte Nuova .................... 291
Fonte Ovile....................... 291
Forte di Santa Barbara .... 291
hospital............................ 296
internet access................. 296
left luggage ...................... 296
Lizza, La........................... 291
Loggia del Papa............... 283
Loggia di Mercanzia......... 283
market ............................. 296
Monte dei Paschi di Siena............................ 290
Museo Civico ........... 268–272
Museo dell'Opera del Duomo ......................... 282
Museo Diocesano ............ 292
Oratorio di San Bernardino .................... 292
Osservanza ...................... 292
Palazzo Chigi-Saracini ..... 285
Palazzo Piccolomini (delle Papesse) ............. 286
Palazzo Piccolomini......... 283
Palazzo Pubblico ...... 268–272
Palio ................................. 261
Pinacoteca Nazionale ...... 286
Porta Camollia ................. 291
Porta Romana.................. 285
restaurants ............... 293–295
San Bartolomeo .............. 291
San Domenico ................. 288
San Francesco ................. 292
San Martino...................... 284
San Niccolò al Carmine ... 287
San Rocco ....................... 291
San Sebastiano................ 288
Sant'Agostino................... 287
Santa Caterina ................. 290
Santa Maria dei Servi....... 284
Santa Maria della Scala..................... 278–282
Santa Maria delle Nevi.............................. 291
Santuccio ......................... 285
taxis.................................. 296
Torre del Mangia .............. 272
Specola, La .................. 152
Spedale degli Innocenti.................... 128
Stadio Artemio Franchi....................... 144
Stadio Comunale.......... 144
Synagogue .................. 142

# T

taxis .............................. 44
theatre in Florence........ 202
Torre della Castagna ...... 82
train station, Florence..... 42
trains from UK ................ 21
trains in Italy .................. 22
Tramvia .......................... 43
travel agents in Britain ..... 21
TV in Italy........................ 31

# U

**Uffizi** ......................... 71–77

# V

Vasari Corridor................ 77
Verna, La ...................... 335
Via de' Tornabuoni.......... 96
Villa Bardini................... 158
villa rental ....................... 25
Vinci ............................. 225
Volpaia.......................... 255
**VOLTERRA**........... 322–326
Volterra...................... 324–325
accommodation ............... 323
Arco Etrusco .................... 324
Balze ................................ 326
Baptistery......................... 324
Duomo ............................. 324
Museo d'Arte Sacra......... 324
Museo dell'Alabastro ....... 325
Museo Etrusco Guarnacci ..................... 325
Palazzo Pretorio............... 324
Palazzo Viti....................... 325
Piazza dei Priori ............... 324
Pinacoteca e Museo Civico ............................ 325
restaurants ....................... 326
Rocca................................ 324
Roman theatre ................. 325
San Francesco ................. 326
San Giusto ....................... 326
Torre Buomparenti ........... 324

# W

wine bars in Florence............ 193–195

# Map symbols

maps are listed in the full index using coloured text

| | | | |
|---|---|---|---|
| | Chapter boundary | | Point of interest |
| | Province boundary | | Tourist office |
| | Motorway | | Post office |
| | Major road | | Bus stop |
| | Minor road | | Parking |
| | Pedestrianized street | | Hospital |
| | Unpaved road | | Tower |
| | Steps | | Campsite |
| | Railway line | | Synagogue |
| | Path | | Church |
| | Wall | | Building |
| | River | | Stadium |
| | Gate | | Park |
| | Mountain peak | | Cemetery |

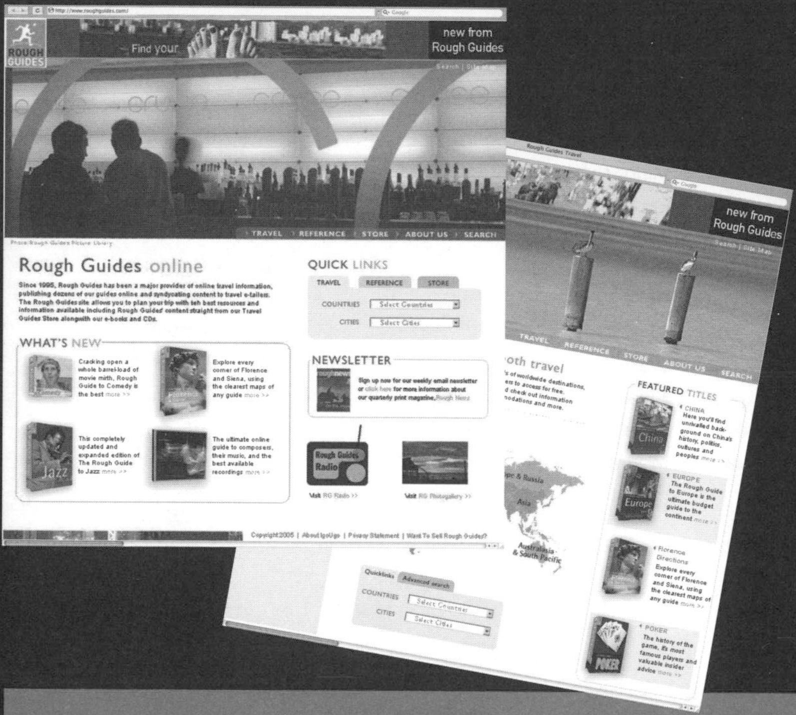

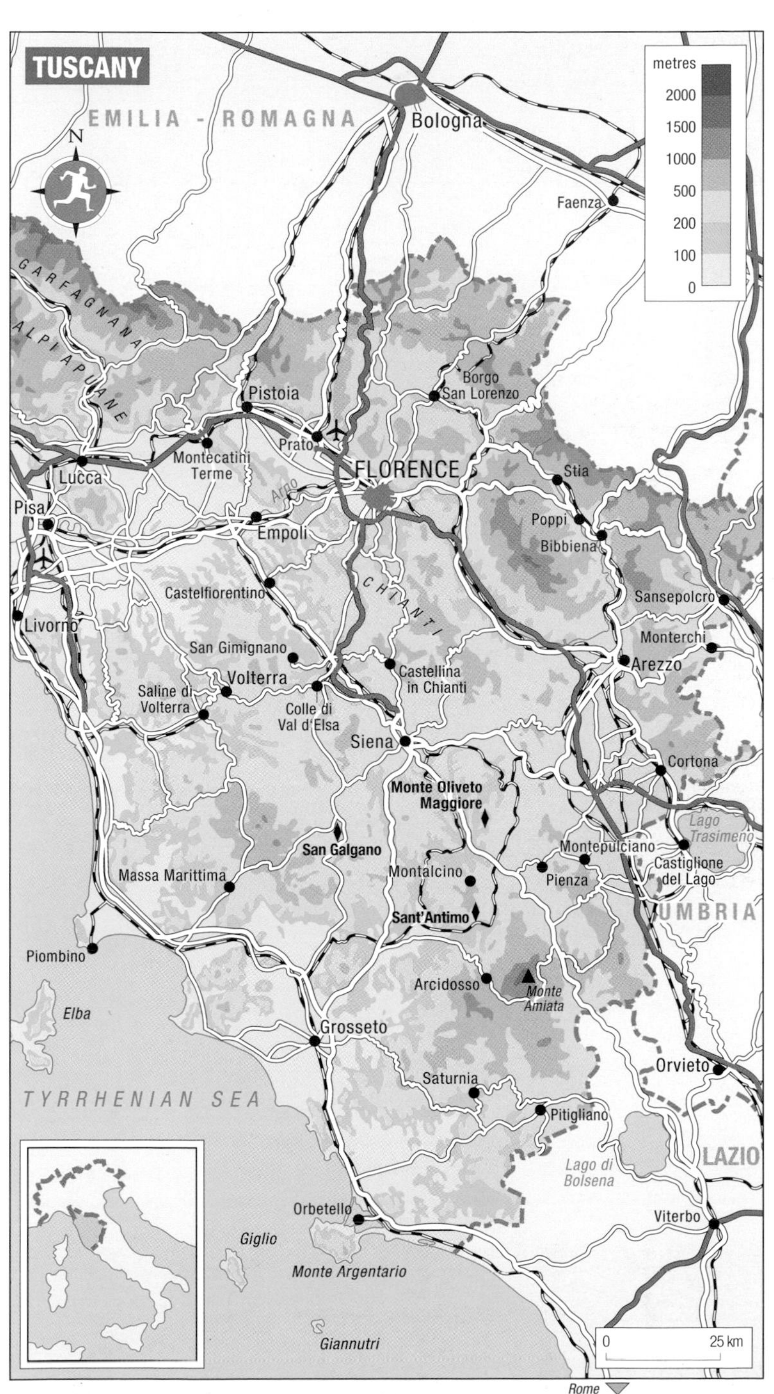
TUSCANY
metres
2000
1500
1000
500
200
100
0
N
EMILIA - ROMAGNA
Bologna
Faenza
GARFAGNANA
ALPI APUANE
Borgo San Lorenzo
Pistoia
Prato
Montecatini Terme
Lucca
FLORENCE
Stia
Arno
Pisa
Empoli
Poppi
Bibbiena
Castelfiorentino
CHIANTI
Sansepolcro
Livorno
Monterchi
San Gimignano
Arezzo
Castellina in Chianti
Volterra
Saline di Volterra
Colle di Val d'Elsa
Siena
Cortona
Monte Oliveto Maggiore
Lago Trasimeno
San Galgano
Montepulciano
Castiglione del Lago
Montalcino
Pienza
Massa Marittima
Sant'Antimo
UMBRIA
Piombino
Arcidosso
Monte Amiata
Elba
Grosseto
Orvieto
Saturnia
TYRRHENIAN SEA
Pitigliano
LAZIO
Lago di Bolsena
Orbetello
Viterbo
Giglio
Monte Argentario
Giannutri
0
25 km
Rome

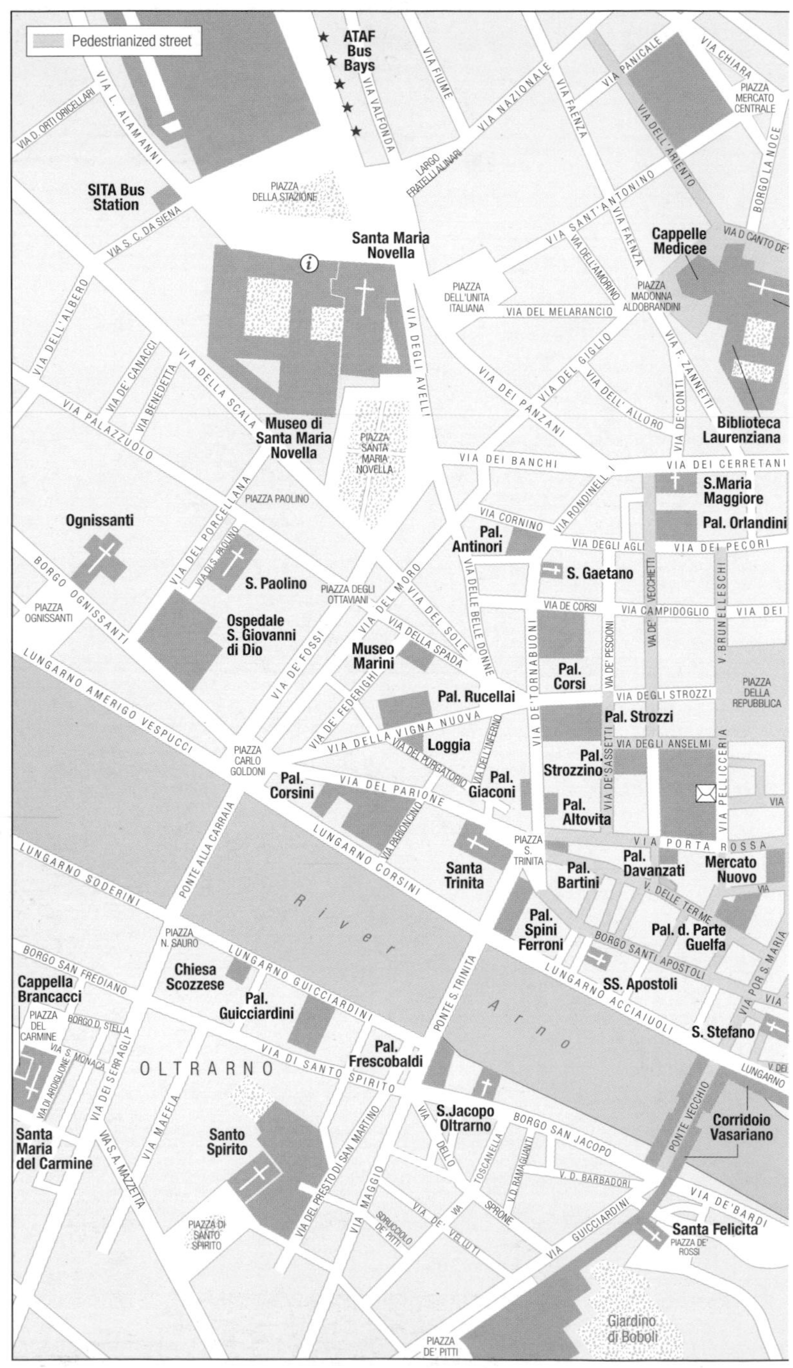

Pedestrianized street
ATAF Bus Bays
SITA Bus Station
PIAZZA DELLA STAZIONE
Santa Maria Novella
Museo di Santa Maria Novella
PIAZZA SANTA MARIA NOVELLA
PIAZZA DELL'UNITA ITALIANA
Cappelle Medicee
PIAZZA MADONNA ALDOBRANDINI
PIAZZA MERCATO CENTRALE
Biblioteca Laurenziana
S.Maria Maggiore
Pal. Orlandini
Ognissanti
PIAZZA OGNISSANTI
S. Paolino
PIAZZA PAOLINO
Ospedale S. Giovanni di Dio
PIAZZA DEGLI OTTAVIANI
Museo Marini
Pal. Antinori
S. Gaetano
Pal. Corsi
Pal. Rucellai
Pal. Strozzi
PIAZZA DELLA REPUBBLICA
Loggia
Pal. Strozzino
Pal. Giaconi
Pal. Altovita
Pal. Corsini
PIAZZA CARLO GOLDONI
Santa Trinita
PIAZZA S. TRINITA
Pal. Bartini
Pal. Davanzati
Mercato Nuovo
Pal. Spini Ferroni
Pal. d. Parte Guelfa
SS. Apostoli
S. Stefano
River Arno
PIAZZA N. SAURO
Chiesa Scozzese
Pal. Guicciardini
Cappella Brancacci
PIAZZA DEL CARMINE
OLTRARNO
Pal. Frescobaldi
S.Jacopo Oltrarno
Corridoio Vasariano
Santo Spirito
PIAZZA DI SANTO SPIRITO
Santa Maria del Carmine
Santa Felicita
PIAZZA DE' ROSSI
Giardino di Boboli
PIAZZA DE' PITTI
VIA D. ORTI ORICELLARI
VIA L. ALAMANNI
VIA S. C. DA SIENA
VIA VALFONDA
VIA FIUME
VIA NAZIONALE
LARGO FRATELLI ALINARI
VIA FAENZA
VIA PANICALE
VIA CHIARA
VIA DELL'ARIENTO
BORGO LA NOCE
VIA SANT'ANTONINO
VIA DELL'AMORINO
VIA D. CANTO DE'
VIA DEL MELARANCIO
VIA DEGLI AVELLI
VIA DELL'ALBERO
VIA DE' CANACCI
VIA BENEDETTA
VIA DELLA SCALA
VIA PALAZZUOLO
VIA DEI PANZANI
VIA DEL GIGLIO
VIA DELL'ALLORO
VIA DE' CONTI
VIA F. ZANNETTI
VIA DEI BANCHI
VIA DEI CERRETANI
VIA DEL PORCELLANA
VIA D.S. PAOLINO
BORGO OGNISSANTI
VIA CORNINO
VIA RONDINELLI
VIA DEGLI AGLI
VIA DEI PECORI
VIA DEL MORO
VIA DEL SOLE
VIA DELLE BELLE DONNE
VIA DE' VECCHIETTI
VIA BRUNELLESCHI
VIA DE CORSI
VIA CAMPIDOGLIO
VIA DEI
VIA DE' FOSSI
VIA DELLA SPADA
VIA DE' TORNABUONI
VIA DE' PESCIONI
LUNGARNO AMERIGO VESPUCCI
VIA DE' FEDERIGHI
VIA DEGLI STROZZI
VIA DELLA VIGNA NUOVA
VIA DEL PURGATORIO
VIA DELL'INFERNO
VIA DE' SASSETTI
VIA DEGLI ANSELMI
VIA PELLICCERIA
VIA DEL PARIONE
VIA PARIONCINO
VIA PORTA ROSSA
LUNGARNO CORSINI
LUNGARNO SODERINI
PONTE ALLA CARRAIA
V. DELLE TERME
BORGO SANTI APOSTOLI
VIA POR S. MARIA
LUNGARNO ACCIAIUOLI
BORGO SAN FREDIANO
LUNGARNO GUICCIARDINI
BORGO D. STELLA
VIA S. MONACA
VIA DEI SERRAGLI
VIA DI ARDIGLIONE
PONTE S. TRINITA
VIA DI SANTO SPIRITO
LUNGARNO
PONTE VECCHIO
VIA MAFFIA
VIA S. A. MAZZETTA
VIA DEL PRESTO DI SAN MARTINO
VIA MAGGIO
VIA DELLO
BORGO SAN JACOPO
TOSCANELLA
V. D. RAMAGLIANTI
V. D. BARBADORI
VIA DE' BARDI
SDRUCCIOLO DE' PITTI
VIA DE' VELLUTI
VIA SPRONE
VIA GUICCIARDINI

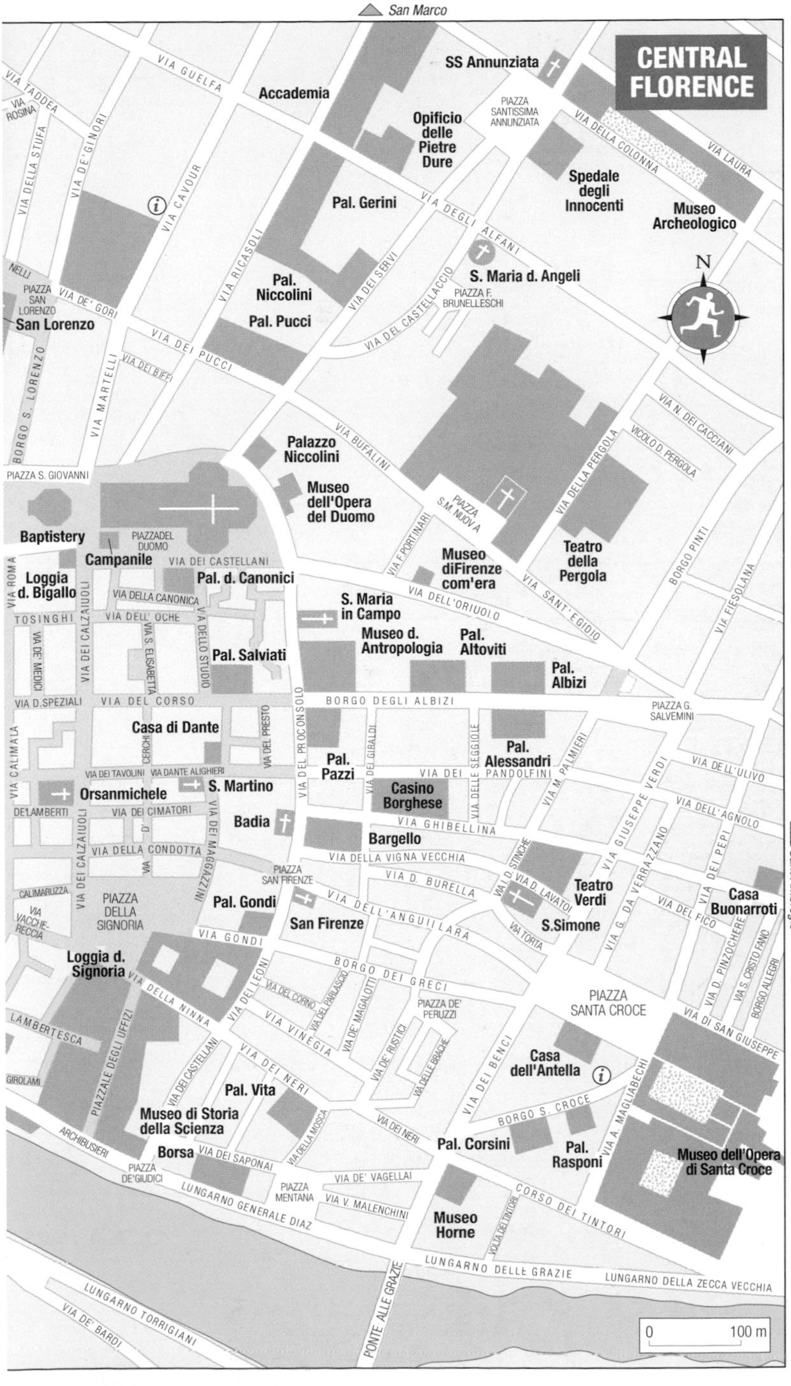

# CENTRAL FLORENCE

San Marco

Sant'Ambrogio

N

0 100 m

SS Annunziata
Accademia
Opificio delle Pietre Dure
PIAZZA SANTISSIMA ANNUNZIATA
Spedale degli Innocenti
Museo Archeologico
Pal. Gerini
S. Maria d. Angeli
PIAZZA F. BRUNELLESCHI
Pal. Niccolini
Pal. Pucci
PIAZZA SAN LORENZO
San Lorenzo
Palazzo Niccolini
Museo dell'Opera del Duomo
PIAZZA S.M. NUOVA
Teatro della Pergola
Museo diFirenze com'era
PIAZZA S. GIOVANNI
Baptistery
PIAZZADEL DUOMO
Campanile
Loggia d. Bigallo
Pal. d. Canonici
S. Maria in Campo
Museo d. Antropologia
Pal. Altoviti
Pal. Salviati
Pal. Albizi
PIAZZA G. SALVEMINI
Casa di Dante
Pal. Pazzi
Pal. Alessandri
Casino Borghese
Orsanmichele
S. Martino
Badia
Bargello
PIAZZA SAN FIRENZE
Teatro Verdi
Casa Buonarroti
PIAZZA DELLA SIGNORIA
Pal. Gondi
San Firenze
S.Simone
Loggia d. Signoria
PIAZZA DE' PERUZZI
PIAZZA SANTA CROCE
Casa dell'Antella
Pal. Vita
Museo di Storia della Scienza
Borsa
PIAZZA DE'GIUDICI
PIAZZA MENTANA
Pal. Corsini
Pal. Rasponi
Museo dell'Opera di Santa Croce
Museo Horne

VIA GUELFA
VIA TADDEA
VIA ROSINA
VIA DELLA STUFA
VIA DE' GINORI
VIA CAVOUR
VIA RICASOLI
VIA DEGLI ALFANI
VIA DELLA COLONNA
VIA LAURA
VIA DEI SERVI
VIA DEL CASTELLACCIO
NELLI
VIA DE' GORI
VIA DEI PUCCI
VIA DEI BIFFI
VIA MARTELLI
BORGO S. LORENZO
VIA BUFALINI
VIA N. DEI CACCIANI
VICOLO D. PERGOLA
VIA DELLA PERGOLA
BORGO PINTI
VIA FIESOLANA
VIA F. PORTINARI
VIA SANT'EGIDIO
VIA DELL'ORIUOLO
VIA DEI CASTELLANI
VIA ROMA
VIA DELLA CANONICA
TOSINGHI
VIA DELL' OCHE
VIA DE' MEDICI
VIA DEI CALZAIUOLI
VIA S. ELISABETTA
VIA DELLO STUDIO
VIA D.SPEZIALI
VIA DEL CORSO
BORGO DEGLI ALBIZI
VIA DEL PROCONSOLO
VIA DEI GIRALDI
VIA DELLE SEGGIOLE
VIA M. PALMIERI
VIA GIUSEPPE VERDI
VIA DELL'ULIVO
VIA CALIMALA
VIA CERCHI
VIA DEL PRESTO
VIA DEI TAVOLINI
VIA DANTE ALIGHIERI
VIA DEI PANDOLFINI
VIA DELL'AGNOLO
DE'LAMBERTI
VIA DEI CIMATORI
VIA D'
VIA DEI MAGGAZZINI
VIA GHIBELLINA
VIA DELLA CONDOTTA
VIA DELLA VIGNA VECCHIA
VIA D. STINCHE
VIA D. LAVATOI
VIA G. DA VERRAZZANO
VIA DEI PEPI
CALIMARUZZA
VIA VACCHE-RECCIA
VIA D. BURELLA
VIA DELL'ANGUILLARA
VIA DEL FICO
VIA TORTA
VIA GONDI
BORGO DEI GRECI
VIA D. PINZOCHERE
VIA S. CRISTOFANO
BORGO ALLEGRI
VIA DELLA NINNA
VIA DEI LEONI
VIA DEL CORNO
VIA DEL PARLASCIO
VIA DE' MAGALOTTI
LAMBERTESCA
VIA VINEGIA
VIA DE' RUSTICI
VIA DELLE BRACHE
VIA DEI BENCI
VIA DI SAN GIUSEPPE
VIA A. MAGLIABECHI
GIROLAMI
PIAZZALE DEGLI UFFIZI
VIA DEI CASTELLANI
VIA DEI NERI
BORGO S. CROCE
ARCHIBUSIERI
VIA DELLA MOSCA
VIA DEI SAPONAI
VIA DE' VAGELLAI
VIA V. MALENCHINI
VOLTA DEI TINTORI
CORSO DEI TINTORI
LUNGARNO GENERALE DIAZ
LUNGARNO DELLE GRAZIE
LUNGARNO DELLA ZECCA VECCHIA
LUNGARNO TORRIGIANI
VIA DE' BARDI
PONTE ALLE GRAZIE

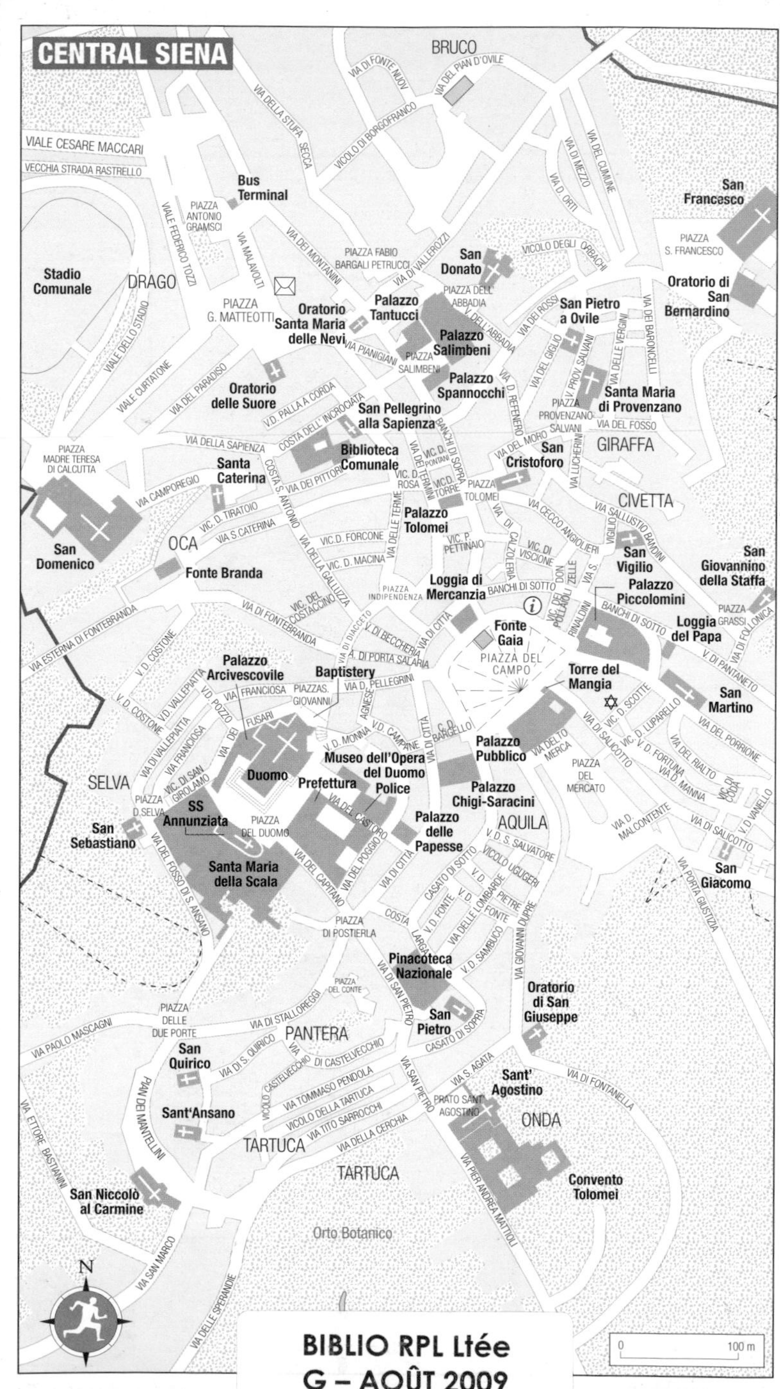
CENTRAL SIENA
BRUCO
Bus Terminal
Stadio Comunale
DRAGO
San Francesco
San Donato
Palazzo Tantucci
Palazzo Salimbeni
Palazzo Spannocchi
Oratorio Santa Maria delle Nevi
Oratorio di San Bernardino
San Pietro a Ovile
Santa Maria di Provenzano
Oratorio delle Suore
San Pellegrino alla Sapienza
Biblioteca Comunale
Santa Caterina
San Cristoforo
GIRAFFA
CIVETTA
Palazzo Tolomei
San Domenico
OCA
Fonte Branda
Loggia di Mercanzia
San Vigilio
Palazzo Piccolomini
San Giovannino della Staffa
Loggia del Papa
Fonte Gaia
PIAZZA DEL CAMPO
Torre del Mangia
Palazzo Arcivescovile
Baptistery
San Martino
Duomo
Museo dell'Opera del Duomo
Prefettura
Police
Palazzo Pubblico
Palazzo Chigi-Saracini
SELVA
SS Annunziata
San Sebastiano
Palazzo delle Papesse
AQUILA
Santa Maria della Scala
San Giacomo
Pinacoteca Nazionale
Oratorio di San Giuseppe
San Pietro
PANTERA
San Quirico
Sant' Agostino
Sant'Ansano
ONDA
TARTUCA
Convento Tolomei
San Niccolò al Carmine
Orto Botanico
N
0
100 m